T0214142

Lecture Notes in Computer Science   11852

More information about this series at http://www.springer.com/series/7408

Yamine Ait-Ameur · Shengchao Qin (Eds.)

Formal Methods and Software Engineering

21st International Conference
on Formal Engineering Methods, ICFEM 2019
Shenzhen, China, November 5–9, 2019
Proceedings

 Springer

Editors
Yamine Ait-Ameur 🄳
IRIT/INPT - ENSEEIHT
Toulouse, France

Shengchao Qin 🄳
Teesside University
Middlesbrough, UK

ISSN 0302-9743   ISSN 1611-3349   (electronic)
Lecture Notes in Computer Science
ISBN 978-3-030-32408-7   ISBN 978-3-030-32409-4   (eBook)
https://doi.org/10.1007/978-3-030-32409-4

LNCS Sublibrary: SL2 – Programming and Software Engineering

This Springer imprint is published by the registered company Springer Nature Switzerland AG
The registered company address is: Gewerbestrasse 11, 6330 Cham, Switzerland

Preface

The International Conference on Formal Engineering Methods (ICFEM) gathers researchers and practitioners interested in the recent progress in the use and development of formal engineering methods for software and system design. It records the latest development in formal engineering methods.

The 21st edition of ICFEM took place in Shenzhen, China during November 5–9, 2019. ICFEM 2019 received 94 submissions covering theory and applications of formal engineering methods together with case studies. Each paper was reviewed by at least three reviewers and the Program Committee accepted 28 long papers leading to an attractive scientific program.

ICFEM 2019 was marked by the presence of four keynote speakers. The first two talks dealt with machine learning techniques. Yang Liu from Nanyang Technological University, Singapore gave a talk entitled "Secure Deep Learning Engineering: a Road towards Quality Assurance of Intelligent Systems." The second talk, entitled "Probabilistic Programming for Bayesian Machine Learning," was given by Luke Ong from Oxford University, United Kingdom. Zhendong Su, from the Swiss Federal Institute of Technology Zurich, Switzerland, gave a talk entitled "Specification-less Semantic Bug Detection" addressing rigorous software bug detection. Finally, with his talk entitled "Taming Delays in Cyber-Physical Systems," Naijun Zhan from the state key laboratory of Computer Science of the Chinese Academy of Sciences, China addressed formal engineering of Cyber-Physical Systems. The four talks covered current hot research topics. In addition to the mentioned obtained results, these talks revealed many research directions.

After the success of the doctoral symposium of the previous edition, ICFEM 2019 decided to host it again. The doctoral symposium Program Committee chaired by Yi Li from Nanyang Technological University, Singapore and Xin Peng from Fudan University, China accepted eight doctoral papers to be included in the ICFEM 2019 proceedings.

ICFEM 2019 would not have been successful without the deep investment and involvement of the Program Committee members and the external reviewers who contributed by reviewing (with more than 260 reviews) and selecting the best contributions. This event would not exist if authors and contributors did not submit their proposals. We address our thanks to every person, reviewer, author, Program Committee member, and Organization Committee member involved in the success of ICFEM 2019.

The EasyChair system was set up for the management of ICFEM 2019, supporting submission, review, and volume preparation processes. It proved to be a powerful framework.

ICFEM 2019 had three affiliated workshops: the 9th International Workshop on SOFL+MSVL for Reliability and Security (SOFL+MSVL 2019), the 7th International Workshop on Formal Techniques for Safety-Critical Systems (FTSCS 2019), and the first International Workshop on Artificial Intelligence and Formal Methods (AI&FM 2019). These workshops brought in additional participants to the ICFEM week and helped make it an interesting and successful event. We thank all the workshop organizers and authors for their hard work.

ICFEM 2019 was hosted and sponsored by Shenzhen University, China. The local Organization Committee offered all the facilities to run the conference in a lovely and friendly atmosphere. Many thanks to all the local organizers.

Lastly, we wish to express our special thanks to the general co-chairs Jifeng He and Zhong Ming, and to the Steering Committee members in particular Shaoying Liu and Jin Song Dong for their valuable support.

November 2019   Yamine Ait-Ameur
                                                            Shengchao Qin

Organization

Program Committee

Bernhard K. Aichernig	TU Graz, Austria
Yamine Ait Ameur	IRIT/INPT-ENSEEIHT, France
Étienne André	Université Paris 13, LIPN, CNRS, UMR 7030, France
Christian Attiogbe	University of Nantes, France
Guangdong Bai	Griffith University, Australia
Christel Baier	TU Dresden, Germany
Richard Banach	The University of Manchester, UK
Luis Barbosa	University of Minho, Portugal
Michael Butler	University of Southampton, UK
Franck Cassez	Macquarie University, Australia
Ana Cavalcanti	University of York, UK
Yuting Chen	Shanghai Jiao Tong University, China
Zhenbang Chen	National University of Defense Technology, China
Wei-Ngan Chin	National University of Singapore, Singapore
Sylvain Conchon	Université Paris-Sud, France
Florin Craciun	Babes-Bolyai University Cluj, Romania
Frank De Boer	CWI, The Netherlands
Yuxin Deng	East China Normal University, China
Jin Song Dong	National University of Singapore, Singapore
Zhenhua Duan	Institute of Computing Theory and Technology, China
Marc Frappier	Université de Sherbrooke, Canada
Stefania Gnesi	ISTI-CNR, Italy
Lindsay Groves	Victoria University of Wellington, New Zealand
Ichiro Hasuo	National Institute of Informatics, Japan
Xudong He	Florida International University, USA
Fuyuki Ishikawa	National Institute of Informatics, Japan
Jie-Hong Roland Jiang	National Taiwan University, Taiwan
Fabrice Kordon	LIP6/Sorbonne Université, CNRS, France
Mark Lawford	McMaster University, Canada
Michael Leuschel	University of Düsseldorf, Germany
Xuandong Li	Nanjing University, China
Yi Li	Nanyang Technological University, Singapore
Yuan-Fang Li	Monash University, Australia
Shaoying Liu	Hosei University, Japan
Shuang Liu	Singapore Institute of Technology, Singapore
Yang Liu	Nanyang Technological University, Singapore
Zhiming Liu	Southwest University, China
Brendan Mahony	Defence Science and Technology Group, Australia

Jim McCarthy	Defence Science and Technology Group, Australia
Dominique Mery	Université de Lorraine, Loria, France
Stephan Merz	Inria Nancy, France
Mohammadreza Mousavi	University of Leicester, UK
Cesar Munoz	NASA, USA
Shin Nakajima	National Institute of Informatics, Japan
Jun Pang	University of Luxembourg, Luxembourg
Yu Pei	The Hong Kong Polytechnic University, SAR China
Xin Peng	Fudan University, China
Geguang Pu	East China Normal University, China
Shengchao Qin	Teesside University, UK
Silvio Ranise	FBK-Irst, Italy
Elvinia Riccobene	University of Milan, Italy
Adrian Riesco	Universidad Complutense de Madrid, Spain
Klaus-Dieter Schewe	Zhejiang University, China
Jing Sun	The University of Auckland, New Zealand
Jun Sun	Singapore Management University, Singapore
Meng Sun	Peking University, China
Cong Tian	Xidian University, China
Elena Troubitsyna	KTH Royal Institute of Technology, Sweden
Jaco van de Pol	Aarhus University, Denmark
Hai H. Wang	University of Aston, UK
Virginie Wiels	ONERA/DTIM, France
Zhiwu Xu	Shenzhen University, China
Naijun Zhan	Chinese Academy of Sciences, China
Jian Zhang	Chinese Academy of Sciences, China
Huibiao Zhu	East China Normal University, China
Peter Ölveczky	University of Oslo, Norway

Additional Reviewers

An, Jie
Araujo, Hugo
Basile, Davide
Borde, Etienne
Bournat, Marjorie
Braghin, Chiara
Bu, Lei
Cai, Chenghao
Cheng, Zheng
Chien, Po-Chun
Chondamrongkul, Nacha
Ciancia, Vincenzo
Ciobanu, Gabriel

Dima, Cătălin
Dong, Yunwei
Dong, Zhijiang
Du, Dehui
Feliu Gabaldon, Marco Antonio
Ferrarotti, Flavio
Gazda, Maciej
González, Senén
Guan, Ji
H. Pham, Long
He, Chunhui
He, Mengda
Hiep, Hans Dieter

Laarman, Alfons
Li, Jiaying
Liyun, Dai
Ma, Feifei
Masci, Paolo
Miao, Weikai
Monin, Jean-Francois
Omitola, Tope
Safey El Din, Mohab
Shi, Ling
Song, Yahui
Sun, Weidi
Tang, Enyi
Vandin, Andrea

Vistbakka, Inna
Waga, Masaki
Wang, Fan
Wang, Qing
Wang, Shuling
Yu, Nengkun
Zhan, Bohua
Zhang, Yuanrui
Zhang, Yueling
Zhao, Hengjun
Zhao, Liang
Zhao, Yongxin
Zuo, Zhiqiang

Abstracts of Invited Talks

Probabilistic Programming for Bayesian Machine Learning

Luke Ong

University of Oxford
Luke.Ong@cs.ox.ac.uk

Abstract. Probabilistic programming is a general-purpose means of expressing probabilistic models as computer programs, and automatically performing Bayesian inference such as posterior probability and marginalisation. By providing implementations of these generic inference algorithms, probabilistic programming systems enable data scientists and domain experts to focus on what they can do best, i.e., utilising their domain knowledge to design good models; the task of constructing efficient inference engines can be left to researchers with expertise in statistical machine learning and programming languages. By promoting the separation between model construction and inference procedures, probabilistic programming can democratise access to Bayesian machine learning, with potentially huge benefits to AI and scientific modelling. Because of their generality, probabilistic programming poses interesting and challenging research problems for (both pragmatic and semantic aspects of) programming languages, Bayesian statistics, and machine learning.

In this talk I will introduce probabilistic programming for Bayesian machine learning as a general concept, and explain a number of research directions unique to probabilistic programming.

Specification-Less Semantic Bug Detection

Zhendong Su

Swiss Federal Institute of Technology – ETHZ, Zurich, Switzerland
zhendong.su@inf.ethz.ch

Abstract. The lack of specifications has been the most difficult practical and technical obstacle to software reliability. Without detailed application-specific properties, one cannot utilize formal verification and is confined to detecting generic bugs such as program crashes and memory safety violations, rather than deeper semantic bugs. Breaking this paradoxical impasse is very difficult, and impossible in general. This talk shows how to mitigate it via effective techniques for constructing tests with expected results, thus tackling both test and oracle generation. It illustrates this view with recent successful attacks on difficult testing and analysis problems from diverse domains, ranging from compilers, database engines, to deep learning systems. The talk discusses

1. the high-level principles and core techniques,
2. their significant practical successes—hundreds and thousands of confirmed/ fixed bugs in the most widely-used software, and
3. future opportunities and challenges.

Taming Delays in Cyber-Physical Systems

Naijun Zhan

State Key Lab. of Comput. Sci., Institute of Software, CAS
znj@ios.ac.cn

Extended Abstract

Historical motivation (predating digital control):

> *"Despite [...] very satisfactory state of affairs as far as [ordinary] differential equations are concerned, we are nevertheless forced to turn to the study of more complex equations. Detailed studies of the real world impel us, albeit reluctantly, to take account of the fact that the rate of change of physical systems depends not only on their present state, but also on their past history."*

[Richard Bellman and Kenneth L. Cooke, 1963, see [1]]

Conventional embedded systems have over the past two decades vividly evolved into an open, interconnected form that integrates capabilities of computing, communication and control, thereby triggering yet another round of global revolution of the information technology. This form, now known as cyber-physical systems (CPS), has witnessed an increasing number of safety-critical systems particularly in major scientific projects vital to people's livelihood. Prominent examples include automotive electronics, health care, nuclear reactors, high-speed trains, aircrafts, spacecrafts, etc., in which a malfunction of any software or hardware component would potentially lead to catastrophic consequences. Meanwhile with the rapid development of feedback control, sensor techniques and computer control, time delays have become an essential feature underlying both the continuous evolution of physical plants and the discrete transition of computer programs, which may well annihilate the stability/safety certificate and control performance of embedded systems. Traditional engineering methods, e.g., testing and simulations, are nevertheless argued insufficient for the zero-tolerance of failures incurred in time-delayed systems in a safety-critical context. Therefore, how to rigorously verify and design reliable safety-critical embedded systems involving delays tends to be a grand challenge in computer science and the control community.

In contrast to delay-free systems, time-delayed systems yield substantially higher theoretical complexity thus rendering the underlying design and verification tasks exceedingly harder, e.g., unlike Ordinary Differential Equations (ODEs) being

This work is partly funded by NSFC under grant No. 61625206 and 61732001.

Markovian process, Delay Differential Equations (DDEs) turn out to be non-Markovian, heavily depending on their execution histories, and consequently any solution to a DDE is an infinite dimensional functional, rather than a point in the n-dimensional Hilbert space like ODE's. The major problems that we faced include the formal verification and controller synthesis of time-delayed, networked hybrid systems.

Though time delays have been extensively studied in the literature of mathematics and control theory from a qualitative perspective, automatic verification and synthesis methods addressing feedback delays in hybrid discrete-continuous systems are still in their infancy. In this extended abstract, we summarize our recent efforts towards the above issues, including

- Firstly, we will discuss how to synthesize controllers for time-delayed discrete systems, based on the work in [3]. The basic idea is to reduce the controller synthesis problem to a two-player delay safety game, further to a two-player delay-free safety game with memory. Based on the reduction, an efficient incremental synthesis algorithm is presented. According to the work in [4], we further discuss generalized settings of controller synthesis where messages may arrive out of order or even get lost, and show –on top of the incremental synthesis– the equivalence of qualitative controllability over these settings.
- Then, we discuss bounded reachability analysis of DDEs, mainly focusing on two approaches: the first one is to extend the technique of *simulation* plus *sensitivity analysis* for ODEs [6] to DDEs [2]; the other is to extend the set-boundary reachability analysis methods for ODEs [8] to DDEs [7].
- Finally, we discuss unbounded verification of DDEs, mainly focusing on the following two approaches: the first one is to deal with DDEs of the form

$$\frac{d}{dt}x(t) = f(x(t - \delta))$$

by exploiting *interval Taylor models* and *stability analysis*. The basic idea can be sketched as follows:

1. predefine a parametric interval polynomial containing all possible solutions of the DDE on the given segment,
2. derive an operator between the paramenters of the solution on the previous segment and the ones on the next segment, forming a time-invariant discrete dynamical system,
3. exploit the stability analysis of the resulted time-invariant dynamical system, thus reducing the safety verification and stability analysis to bounded cases.

The detail can be found in [9]; the other approach is to deal with the general DDEs of the form

$$\frac{d}{dt}x(t) = f(x(t), x(t - \delta_1), \ldots, x(t - \delta_n))$$

by using *linearisation* and *spectral analysis*. The reader can refer to [5] for the detail. The basic idea can be sketched as follows:

1. linearise a non-linear DDE,
2. exploit spectral analysis to obtain the stability of the linear part,
3. reduce unbounded verification and analysis to bounded case.

Finally, we will also discuss trends and challenges in the formal verification and synthesis of time-delayed systems.

Acknowledgements. First of all, I thank Mingshuai Chen and Bai Xue for their useful comments on the early version of the manuscript which improve the presentation so much.

I would like to take this opportunity to thank all collaborators involved in this research, including Martin Fränzle, Bai Xue, Liang Zou, Mingshuai Chen, Peter Nazier Mosaad, Yangjia Li, Shenghua Feng, etc.

References

1. Bellman, R., Cooke, K.L.: Differential-difference equations. Technical report R-374-PR, The RAND Corporation, Santa Monica, California, January 1963
2. Chen, M., Fränzle, M., Li, Y., Mosaad, P.N., Zhan, N.: Validated simulation-based verification of delayed differential dynamics. In: Fitzgerald, J., Heitmeyer, C., Gnesi, S., Philippou, A. (eds.) FM 2016. LNCS, vol. 9995, pp 137–154. Springer, Cham (2016). https://doi.org/10.1007/978-3-319-48989-6_9
3. Chen, M., Fränzle, M., Li, Y., Mosaad, P.N., Zhan, N.: What's to come is still unsure - synthesizing controllers resilient to delayed interaction. In: Lahiri, S., Wang, C. (eds.) ATVA 2018. LNCS, vol. 11138, pp. 56–74. Springer, Cham (2018).https://doi.org/10.1007/978-3-319-48989-6_9
4. Chen, M., Fränzle, M., Li, Y., Mosaad, P.N., Zhan, N.: Indecision and delays are the parents of failure: taming them algorithmically by synthesizing delay-resilient control. Acta Informatica (2019). Under minor revision
5. Feng, S., Chen, M., Zhan, N., Fränzle, M., Xue, B.: Taming delays in dynamical systems: unbounded verification of delay differential equations. In: Dillig, I., Tasiran, S. (eds.) CAV 2019. LNCS, vol. 11561, pp. 650–669. Springer, Cham (2019). https://doi.org/10.1007/978-3-030-25540-4_37
6. Nahhal, T., Dang, T.: Test coverage for continuous and hybrid systems. In: Damm, W., Hermanns, H. (eds.) CAV 2007. LNCS, vol. 449–462. Springer, Heidelberg (2007). https://doi.org/10.1007/978-3-540-73368-3_47
7. Xue, B., Mosaad, P.N., Fränzle, M., Chen, M., Li, Y., Zhan, N.: Safe over- and under-approximation of reachable sets for delay differential equations. In: Abate, A., Geeraerts, G. (eds.) FORMATS 2017. LNCS, vol. 10419, pp. 281–299. Springer, Cham (2017). https://doi.org/10.1007/978-3-319-65765-3_16
8. Xue, B., She, Z., Easwaran, A.: Under-approximating backward reachable sets by polytopes. In: Chaudhuri, S., Farzan, A. (eds.) CAV 2016. LNCS, vol. 9779, pp. 457–476. Springer, Cham (2016). https://doi.org/10.1007/978-3-319-41528-4_25
9. Zou, L., Fränzle, M., Zhan, N., Mosaad, P.N.: Automatic verification of stability and safety for delay differential equations. In: Kroening, D., Păsăreanu, C. (eds.) CAV 2015. LNCS, vol. 9207, pp. 338–355. Springer, Cham (2015). https://doi.org/10.1007/978-3-319-21668-3_20

Secure Deep Learning Engineering: A Road Towards Quality Assurance of Intelligent Systems

Yang Liu

Nanyang Technological University, Singapore, Singapore
yangliu@ntu.edu.sg

Abstract. Over the past decades, deep learning (DL) systems have achieved tremendous success and gained great popularity in various applications, such as intelligent machines, image processing, speech processing, and medical diagnostics. Deep neural networks are the key driving force behind its recent success, but still seem to be a magic black box lacking interpretability and understanding. This brings up many open safety and security issues with enormous and urgent demands on rigorous methodologies and engineering practice for quality enhancement. A plethora of studies have shown that state-of-the-art DL systems suffer from defects and vulnerabilities that can lead to severe loss and tragedies, especially when applied to real-world safety-critical applications.

In this paper, we perform a large-scale study and construct a paper repository of 223 relevant works to the quality assurance, security, and interpretation of deep learning. Based on this, we, from a software quality assurance perspective, pinpoint challenges and future opportunities to facilitate drawing the attention of the software engineering community towards addressing the pressing industrial demand of secure intelligent systems.

Contents

Doctoral Symposium Papers

Invited Talk

Secure Deep Learning Engineering: A Road Towards Quality Assurance of Intelligent Systems

Yang Liu[1], Lei Ma[2(✉)], and Jianjun Zhao[2(✉)]

[1] Nanyang Technological University, Singapore, Singapore
yangliu@ntu.edu.sg
[2] Kyushu University, Fukuoka, Japan
{malei,zhao}@ait.kyushu-u.ac.jp

Abstract. Over the past decades, deep learning (DL) systems have achieved tremendous success and gained great popularity in various applications, such as intelligent machines, image processing, speech processing, and medical diagnostics. Deep neural networks are the key driving force behind its recent success, but still seem to be a magic black box lacking interpretability and understanding. This brings up many open safety and security issues with enormous and urgent demands on rigorous methodologies and engineering practice for quality enhancement. A plethora of studies have shown that state-of-the-art DL systems suffer from defects and vulnerabilities that can lead to severe loss and tragedies, especially when applied to real-world safety-critical applications.

In this paper, we perform a large-scale study and construct a paper repository of 223 relevant works to the quality assurance, security, and interpretation of deep learning. Based on this, we, from a software quality assurance perspective, pinpoint challenges and future opportunities to facilitate drawing the attention of the software engineering community towards addressing the pressing industrial demand of secure intelligent systems.

Keywords: Artificial intelligence · Deep learning · Software engineering · Security · Quality assurance · Reliability · Deep learning engineering

1 Introduction

In company with massive data explosion and powerful computational hardware enhancement, deep learning (DL) has recently achieved substantial strides in cutting-edge intelligent applications, ranging from virtual assistant (e.g., Alex, Siri), art design [18], autonomous vehicles [13,19], to medical diagnoses [1,3] – tasks that until a few years ago could be done only by humans. DL has become the innovation driving force of many next generation's technologies. We have been witnessing on the increasing trend of industry stakeholders' continuous

Y. Ait-Ameur and S. Qin (Eds.): ICFEM 2019, LNCS 11852, pp. 3–15, 2019.
https://doi.org/10.1007/978-3-030-32409-4_1

investment on DL based intelligent system [5–8,40], penetrating almost every application domain, revolutionizing industry manufacturing as well as reshaping our daily life.

However, current DL system development still lacks systematic engineering guidance, quality assurance standards, as well as mature toolchain support. The *magic box*, such as DL training procedure and logic encoding (as high dimensional weight matrices and complex neural network structures), further poses challenges to interpret and understand behaviors of derived DL systems [4,16,26]. The latent software quality and security issues of current DL systems, already started emerging out as the major vendors, rush in pushing products with higher intelligence (e.g., Google/Uber car accident [21,41], Alexa and Siri could be manipulated with hidden command [39]. A DL image classifier with high test accuracy is easily fooled by a single-pixel perturbation [2]). Deploying such cocooned DL systems to the real-world environment without quality and security assurance leaves high risks, where newly evolved cyber- and adversarial-attacks are inevitable.

To bridge the pressing industry demand and future research directions, this paper first performs a large-scale empirical study on the most-recent curated 223 relevant works on deep learning engineering from a software quality assurance perspective. Based on this, we perform a quantitative and qualitative analysis to identify the common issues that the current research community most dedicated to. With an in-depth investigation on current works, and our in-company DL development experience obtained, we find that the development of secure and high quality deep learning systems requires enormous engineering effort, while most AI communities focus on the theoretical or algorithmic perspective of deep learning. Indeed, the development of modern complex deep learning systematic solutions could be a challenge for an individual research community alone. We propose the *Secure Deep Learning Engineering* (SDLE) development process specialized for DL software, which we believe is an interdisciplinary future direction (e.g., AI, SE, security) towards constructing DL applications, in a systematic method from theoretical foundations, software & system engineering, to security guarantees. We further discuss current challenges and opportunities in SDLE from a software quality assurance perspective.

To the best of our knowledge, our work is the first study to vision SDLE, from the quality assurance perspective, accompanied by a state-of-the-art literature curation. We hope this work facilitates drawing the attention of the software engineering community on necessity and demands of quality assurance for SDLE, which altogether lays down the foundations and conquers technical barriers towards constructing robust and high-quality DL systems. The repository is available at: https://sdle2018.github.io/.

2   Research Methodology

This section summarizes our concerned research questions, and discusses the detail of paper collection procedure for further analysis.

2.1   Research Questions

This paper mainly focuses on following research questions.

- **RQ-1:** What are mostly studied research topics and the common challenges relevant to quality assurance of deep learning?
- **RQ-2:** What is secure deep learning engineering and its future direction in perspective of quality assurance?

From the RQ-1, we intend to identify the mostly concerned topics in the research community and their common challenges, while RQ-2 concerns the key activities in SDLE life cycle, based on which we discuss our vision and future opportunities.

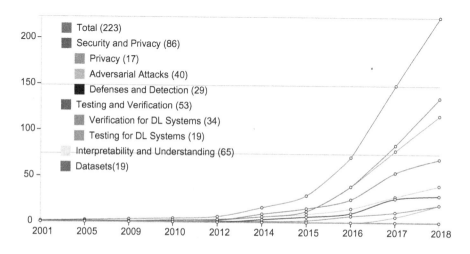

Fig. 1. The accumulative number of selected publications over Years

2.2   Data Collection Methodology

Extensive research contributions are made on deep learning over the past decades, we adopt the following procedure to select works most relevant to the theme of this work.

- We first collect papers from conferences listed on the *Computer Science Rankings* within the scope of AI & machine learning, software engineering, and security.[1] To automate the paper collection procedure, we develop a Python-based crawler to extract paper information of each listed conference since the year 2000 and filter with keywords.

---

[1] http://csrankings.org/#/index?all.

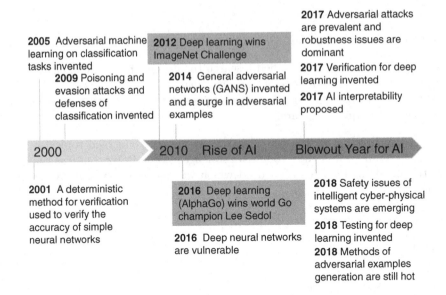

Fig. 2. Milestones of deep learning engineering relevant to security and software quality.

- To further reduce the search space for relevant topics, we use keywords (e.g., deep learning, AI, security, testing, verification, quality, robustness) to filter the collected papers.
- Even though, scraping all the listed conferences may still be insufficient, we therefore crawl outwards – extract all the related work for each keyword-filtered paper and crawl one level down of these papers.
- This finally results in 223 papers and we manually confirmed and labeled each paper to form a final categorized list of literature.

Paper Category and Labeling. To categorize the selected papers, we perform paper clustering by taking into account the title, abstract, and listed keywords. Based on further discussion of all authors (from both academia and industry with AI, SE, and security background), we eventually identify four main paper categories, and seven fine-grained categories in total (see Fig. 1). In the next step, each paper is manually labelled into a target category for further analysis.

The Dataset and the Trend. Figure 1 shows the general trends of publication on secure deep learning research area, where the publication number (i.e., both total paper as well as in each category) dramatically increases over years. Such booming trend becomes even more obvious accompanied with the milestones of DLs (e.g., DL won ImageNet Challenge in 2012, AlphaGo defeated human championship in 2016), which is highlighted in Fig. 2. For the four main categories, we find the most publications are relevant to Security and Privacy (SP, 86 papers), followed by Interpretability and Understanding (IU, 65), Testing and Verification (TV, 53), and Datasets (17).

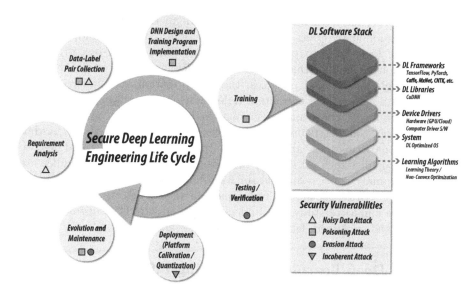

Fig. 3. Secure deep learning engineering life cycle

The SP category with the highest paper publication number is not surprising. Since Goodfellow et al. [20] posted the security issues of DLs, it attracted both the AI and security communities to escalate and burst a research competition on defending and attacking techniques. Even though, it still lacks a complete understanding of why current DL systems are still vulnerable against adversarial attacks. This draws the attention of researchers on interpreting and understanding how DL works, which would be important for both application and construction of robust DLs. As the recent emerging investment blowout in DL applications to safety-critical scenarios (e.g., autonomous driving, medical diagnose), its software quality has become a big concern, where researchers find that the different programming paradigm of DL makes existing testing and verification techniques unable to directly handle DLs [25,30,35]. Therefore, we have observed that many recent works are proposing novel testing and verification techniques for DLs, from testing criteria, test generation techniques, test data quality evaluation, to static analysis. Meanwhile, the dataset benchmarks of different DL application domains emerge to grow as well [15,24,37,42], in order to facilitate the study of solving domain-specific problems by DLs (e.g., image classification, 3D object recognition, autonomous driving, skin disease classification).

Common Issues. In contrast to traditional software of which the decision logic is mostly programmed by human developers, deep learning adopts a data-driven programming paradigm. Specifically, a DL developer's major effort is to prepare the training data (including knowledge to resolve a task) and neural network architecture, after which the decision logic is automatically obtained through the training procedure. On one hand, this paradigm reduces the burden of a developer who manually crafts the decision logic. On the other hand, for a DL developer, the logic training procedure is almost like a magic-box driven by an optimization technique. Due to the decision logic of DL is encoded into a DNN with high dimensional matrices, the interpretation and understanding, training procedure, as well as the obtained decision logic are all very difficult [28], which could be a root cause and a common challenge among all categories. For example, without completely understanding the decision logic of DL, it is hard to know in what particular case an adversarial attack could penetrate, and how we could defend against such attacks. In the case of testing, extensive studies are performed on analysis of traditional software bugs, their relations to software development activities, as well as techniques for defect detection. However, a comprehensive empirical study and understanding on why DL bugs occur still could not be well explained, let alone the root case analysis.

3   Secure Deep Learning Engineering Life Cycle

Due to the fundamental different programming paradigms of deep learning and traditional software, the secure deep learning engineering practice and techniques are largely different with traditional software engineering, although the major life cycle phases could still be shared.

> We define *Secure Deep Learning Engineering (SDLE) as an engineering discipline of deep learning software production, through a systematic application of knowledge, methodology, practice on deep learning, software engineering and security, to requirement analysis, design, implementation, testing, deployment, and maintenance of deep learning software.*

Figure 3 shows the key life cycle phases of SDLE. In the rest of this section, we first describe each of the key development phases, their uniqueness and difference compared with traditional practices in software engineering, and then we discuss the security issues in current SDLE. In the next section, we explain the quality assurance necessity in SDLE life cycle, and highlight the challenges and opportunities.

Requirement Analysis. Requirement analysis investigates the needs, determines, and creates detailed functional documents for the DL products. DL-based software decision logic is learned from the training data and generalized to the testing data. Therefore, the requirement is usually measured in terms of an expected prediction performance, which is often a statistics-based requirement with uncertainty, as opposed to the rule-based one in traditional SE.

Data-Label Pair Collection. After the requirements of the DL software become available, a DL developer (potentially with domain experts for supervision and labeling) tries to collect representative data that incorporate the knowledge on a specific target task. For traditional software, a human developer needs to understand the specific task, figures out a set of algorithmic operations to solve the task, and programs such operations in the form of source code for execution. On the other hand, one of the most important sources of DL software is training data. The DL software automatically distills the computational solutions of a specific task under a designed neural network architecture.

DNN Design and Training Program Implementation. When the training data become available, a DL developer designs the DNN architecture, taking into account of requirement, data complexity, as well as the problem domain. For example, when addressing a general-purpose image processing task, convolutional layer components are often included in the DNN model design, while recurrent layers are often used to process tasks that has sequential inputs (e.g., natural language processing, speech recognition). To concretely implement the desired DNN architecture, a DL developer often leverages an existing DL framework to encode the designed DNN into a training program. Furthermore, the runtime training behaviors are also needed to be specified through the APIs provided by the DL framework (e.g., training epochs, learning rate, GPU/CPU configurations).

Runtime Training. After the DL programming ingredients (i.e., training data and training program) are ready. The runtime training procedure starts and systematically evolves the decision logic learning towards effectively resolving (e.g., classification, numerical prediction, synthesis & generation) a target task. The training procedure and training program adjustment might go back-and-forth several rounds until a satisfying performance is achieved. Although the training program itself is often written as traditional software (e.g., in `Python`, `Java`, `C++`), the obtained DL software is often encoded as a DNN model, consisting of the DNN architecture and weight matrices. The training process plays a central role in the DL software learning, to distill knowledge and solution from the sources. It involves quite a lot of software and system engineering effort to realize the learning theory to DL software (see Fig. 3) over years.

Testing & Verification. When the DNN model completes training with its decision logic determined, it goes through the systematic evaluation of its generality and quality through testing (or verification). Note that the testing activity in the AI community mainly considers whether the obtained DL model generalizes to the prepared test dataset, to obtain high test accuracy. On the other hand, the testing activity (or verification) in SDLE considers a more general evaluation scope, such as generality, robustness, defect detection, as well as other nonfunctional requirement (e.g., efficiency). The early weakness detection of the DL software provides valuable feedback to a DL developer for solution enhancement [47].

Deployment. A DL software passed the testing phase reaches a certain level of quality standard, and is ready to be deployed to a target platform. However, due to the platform diversity, DL framework supportability, and computation limitations of a target device, the DL software often needs to go through the platform calibration (e.g., compression, quantization, DL framework migration) procedure for deployment on a target platform. For example, once a DL software is trained and obtained on the `Tensorflow` framework, it needs to be successfully transformed to its counterpart of `TensorflowLite` (resp. `CoreML`) framework to `Android` (resp. `iOS`) platform. It still needs to go through on-device testing after deployment [22]. The testing during deployment not only considers the potentially incorrect behaviors that could be triggered at runtime, but also considers the behavior differences before and after deployment. In particular, whether a deployed version is an intended version for runtime execution. Due to the difference in platform, deep learning framework as well as hardware resources before and after deployment, systematically testing and providing feedback on the behavior changes of a deployed deep learning software would assist a DL developer to further enhance its quality.

Evolution and Maintenance. After a DL product is deployed, it might experience the procedure of modification for bug correction, performance and feature enhancements, or other attributes. The major effort in evolution and maintenance phases relies on the manual revision on design, source code, documentation, or other software artifacts. On the other hand, DL software focuses more on comprehensive data collection, DL model continuous learning (e.g., re-fitting, retro-fitting, fine-tuning, and re-engineering). For example, it is not uncommon that the new data are continuously collected that contain more domain-specific information of a particular task. A DL developer often considers how to incorporate the knowledge of such data into a target DL system to further enhance a DL software. During such a phase, a DL product would experience evolution, to update the feature, fix bugs, enhance robustness, etc. However, such a procedure are mostly driven by training data, which guides the direction of a DL produce enhancement. Furthermore, special engineering methods to better manage the version variants of a DL product (e.g., DL training program, models), as well as the data, would also be necessary, which to a large extent differs to those in the traditional software evolution and maintenance.

Security Issues in DL. The current practice of security in deep learning has fallen into the trap that many other domains have experienced. Almost every month new attacks are identified [9,12,14,20,32,33,46] followed by new countermeasures [34,45] which are subsequently broken [12,23], and so on ad-infinitum. There is a broad and pressing need for a frontier-level effort on trustworthiness and security in DL to break this cycle of attacks and defenses. We have a unique opportunity at this time—before deep learning is widely deployed in critical systems—to develop the theory and practice needed for robust learning algorithms that provide rigorous and meaningful guarantees. If we rethink the SDLE life cycle (see Fig. 3), security vulnerabilities can happen in almost every step. For instance, for the training related steps such as *Requirement Analysis, Data-Label Pair Collection* and *DNN design and training*, poisoning attacks can easily happen via manipulating training data. In the testing related steps, such as *testing & verification*and *deployment*, evasion attacks can take place by perturbing the testing data slightly (e.g. adversarial examples). In addition, when deploying the DL software to different platforms or with different implementation frameworks, there will always be opportunities for adversaries to generate attacks from one to the other.

We believe many of these security issues are highly intertwined the quality of current DL software, lacking systematic quality assurance solutions over the entire SDLE process which is largely missed in research works as described in the next section.

4   Towards Future Quality Assurance of SDLE

Over the past decades, software quality assurance discipline [36, 38] has been well-established for traditional software, with many experiences and practices widely applied in the software industry. However, the fundamentally different programming paradigm and decision logic representation of DL software make existing quality assurance techniques unable to be directly applied, forcing us to renovate the entire quality assurance procedure for SDLE. In this section, we pose our vision and challenges on quality assurance in SDLE to guide future research.

From the very beginning of SDLE, we need to rethink how to accurately define, specify, and document the of DL software requirement, especially for the functional requirements. This leaves us a question of whether we should follow a statistical-based approach, a rule-based approach, or their combination, which has not been well investigated yet.

The data play a key role in shaping the learning process and DL decision logic. However, most current research treats the data (e.g., training data) as high quality for granted, without a systematic quality control, inspection, and evaluation process. As poisoning attacks show, many incorrect behaviors and security issues could be introduced with the maliciously tweaked training data. How to select a suitable size while representative data would be an important question. In addition, data supervision and labeling process are also labor-intensive and error-prone. For example, ImageNet dataset contains more than one million general-purpose images. We also need to provide assistance and quality control for the data management (e.g., labeling, versioning, de-noising) procedure.

It becomes even more challenging, when it comes to the implementation of the training program and framework. Most state-of-the-art DL frameworks are implemented as traditional software on top of the DL software stack. Even the learning theory is perfect, it still has a big gap to transfer such ideally designed DL models to a DL application encoded on top of the DL framework. One big challenge is how to ensure the software stack (e.g., hardware drivers, DL library, DL framework) correctly implements the learning algorithm.

Another challenge is to provide useful interactive support to debug and visualize the training process. Most current DL training procedure only shows training loss (accuracy), validation loss (accuracy), which is mostly a black box to a DL developer. When the training procedure goes beyond expectation, the root-cause analysis becomes extremely difficult, which may come from the DL architecture issue, training program implementation issue, or the hardware configuration issue. Hence, the software engineering community needs to consider providing the novel debugging, runtime monitoring, and profiling support for the training procedure, which is involved with non-determinism and runtime properties hard to specify.

The large input space has already been a challenge for testing and verifying traditional software. Such a challenge is further escalated for DL software, due to its high dimensional input space and the internal latent space. Even though, traditional software testing has already explored many testing criteria as the goal to guide testing. How to design suitable testing criteria to capture the testing confidence still remains unclear. Even with some preliminary progress on testing criteria designed for DLs [27,29,30,35], there are many more testing issues needed to be addressed, such as how to effectively generate tests [17,29,43, 44], how to measure the test data quality [31], and how to test DL robustness and vulnerabilities [10,11]. More in-depth empirical studies that uncover the unique issues (e.g., [48]) of SDLE are also necessary to provide insight and guidance to build deep learning systems with better quality and reliability.

Further DL challenge comes up with current deployment process: (1) target device computation limitations, and (2) DL framework compatibility across platforms and frameworks. The DL software is mostly developed and trained on the cloud or PCs with powerful GPU support. When it needs to be deployed on a mobile device or edge-computing device with limited computation power, the DL software must be optimized or quantized for computation/energy efficiency, which could introduce defects or behavior differences. How to ensure the quality and detect the potential issues during this process is an important problem. In addition, the current DL frameworks might not always be supported by different platforms. For example, the TensorFlow is not directly supported by Android or iOS, and how to make DL software cross-platform compatible would be an important direction.

Last but not least, the quality assurance concerns in DL software evolution and maintenance are mostly focused on avoiding introducing defects during change, which might rely on regression testing. However, how to effectively evolve the DL software and how to engineer the artifacts (e.g., data, training program, DL model) of a DL product during evolution still remains unknown, which we leave as an open question for further study.

5   Conclusion

Considering deep learning is likely to be one of the most transformative technologies in the 21st century, it appears essential that we begin to think about how to design fully-fledged deep learning systems under a well-tested development discipline. This paper defines the secure deep learning engineering and discusses the current challenges, opportunities, and puts forward open questions from the quality assurance perspective, accompanied by a paper repository. We hope our work can inspire future studies towards constructing robust, reliable and safe DL software with high quality.

Acknowledgments. We thank Felix Juefei-Xu, Xiaofei Xie, Minhui Xue, Qiang Hu, Xiaoning Du, Yi Li, Sen Chen, Bo Li, Jianxiong Yin, Simon See for their contribution to initiate the early work of this paper. We also acknowledge the support of NVIDIA AI Tech Center (NVAITC) to our research, which largely shapes the direction of this work. This research was supported (in part) by the National Research Foundation, Prime Ministers Office, Singapore under its National Cybersecurity R&D Program (Award No. NRF2018NCR-NCR005-0001), National Satellite of Excellence in Trustworthy Software System (Award No. NRF2018NCR-NSOE003-0001) administered by the National Cybersecurity R&D Directorate; JSPS KAKENHI Grant NO.19H04086, NO. 18H04097, and Qdai-jump Research Program NO. 01277.

References

1. BBC: Google's DeepMind to peek at NHS eye scans for disease analysis (2016). https://www.bbc.com/news/technology-36713308
2. BBC: AI image recognition fooled by single pixel change (2018). https://www.bbc.com/news/technology-41845878
3. BBC: Artificial intelligence 'did not miss a single urgent case' (2018). https://www.bbc.com/news/health-44924948
4. BBC: Can we trust AI if we don't know how it works? (2018). https://www.bbc.com/news/business-44466213
5. BBC: General Motors and Fiat Chrysler unveil self-driving deals (2018). https://www.bbc.com/news/business-44325629
6. BBC: Google cars self-drive to Walmart supermarket in trial (2018). https://www.bbc.com/news/technology-44957251
7. BBC: Honda to invest $2.8bn in GM's self-driving car unit (2018). https://www.bbc.com/news/business-45728169
8. BBC: Jaguar self-drive car revealed in New York (2018). https://www.bbc.com/news/technology-43557798
9. Biggio, B., et al.: Evasion attacks against machine learning at test time. In: Blockeel, H., Kersting, K., Nijssen, S., Železný, F. (eds.) ECML PKDD 2013. LNCS (LNAI), vol. 8190, pp. 387–402. Springer, Heidelberg (2013). https://doi.org/10.1007/978-3-642-40994-3_25
10. Breier, J., Hou, X., Jap, D., Ma, L., Bhasin, S., Liu, Y.: DeepLaser: practical fault attack on deep neural networks. ArXiv e-prints
11. Breier, J., Hou, X., Jap, D., Ma, L., Bhasin, S., Liu, Y.: Practical fault attack on deep neural networks. In: Proceedings of the 2018 ACM SIGSAC Conference on Computer and Communications Security, CCS 2018 (2018)
12. Carlini, N., Wagner, D.: Towards evaluating the robustness of neural networks. In: IEEE Symposium on Security and Privacy (SP), pp. 39–57 (2017)
13. Chen, C., Seff, A., Kornhauser, A., Xiao, J.: Deepdriving: learning affordance for direct perception in autonomous driving. In: 2015 IEEE International Conference on Computer Vision (ICCV), pp. 2722–2730, December 2015. https://doi.org/10.1109/ICCV.2015.312
14. Chen, P.Y., Sharma, Y., Zhang, H., Yi, J., Hsieh, C.J.: Ead: elastic-net attacks to deep neural networks via adversarial examples. arXiv preprint arXiv:1709.04114 (2017)
15. Chen, Y., et al.: Lidar-video driving dataset: Learning driving policies effectively. In: The IEEE Conference on Computer Vision and Pattern Recognition (CVPR), June 2018

16. Doshi-Velez, F., Kim, B.: Towards a rigorous science of interpretable machine learning. ArXiv e-prints
17. Du, X., Xie, X., Li, Y., Ma, L., Liu, Y., Zhao, J.: Deepstellar: model-based quantitative analysis of stateful deep learning systems. In: Proceedings of the 2019 27th ACM Joint Meeting on European Software Engineering Conference and Symposium on the Foundations of Software Engineering, pp. 477–487. ESEC/FSE 2019 (2019)
18. Elgammal, A.M., Liu, B., Elhoseiny, M., Mazzone, M.: CAN: creative adversarial networks, generating "art" by learning about styles and deviating from style norms. CoRR abs/1706.07068 (2017). http://arxiv.org/abs/1706.07068
19. Eliot, L.B.: Advances in AI and Autonomous Vehicles: Cybernetic Self-Driving Cars Practical Advances in Artificial Intelligence (AI) and Machine Learning, 1st edn. LBE Press Publishing (2017)
20. Goodfellow, I.J., Shlens, J., Szegedy, C.: Explaining and harnessing adversarial examples. In: ICLR (2015)
21. Google Accident: A Google self-driving car caused a crash for the first time (2016). https://www.theverge.com/2016/2/29/11134344/google-self-driving-car-crash-report
22. Guo, Q., et al.: An empirical study towards characterizing deep learning development and deployment across different frameworks and platforms. In: Proceedings of the 34rd ACM/IEEE International Conference on Automated Software Engineering, ASE 2019 (2019)
23. He, W., Wei, J., Chen, X., Carlini, N., Song, D.: Adversarial example defenses: ensembles of weak defenses are not strong. arXiv preprint arXiv:1706.04701 (2017)
24. Huang, X., Wang, P., Cheng, X., Zhou, D., Geng, Q., Yang, R.: The ApolloScape open dataset for autonomous driving and its application. ArXiv e-prints
25. Huang, X., Kwiatkowska, M., Wang, S., Wu, M.: Safety verification of deep neural networks. In: Majumdar, R., Kunčak, V. (eds.) CAV 2017. LNCS, vol. 10426, pp. 3–29. Springer, Cham (2017). https://doi.org/10.1007/978-3-319-63387-9_1
26. Kim, B., et al.: Interpretability beyond feature attribution: quantitative testing with concept activation vectors (TCAV). ArXiv e-prints
27. Kim, J., Feldt, R., Yoo, S.: Guiding deep learning system testing using surprise adequacy arXiv:1808.08444 (2018)
28. Lipton, Z.C.: The mythos of model interpretability. CoRR abs/1606.03490 (2016). http://arxiv.org/abs/1606.03490
29. Ma, L., et al.: DeepCT: tomographic combinatorial testing for deep learning systems. In: 2019 IEEE 26th International Conference on Software Analysis, Evolution and Reengineering (SANER), pp. 614–618, February 2019
30. Ma, L., et al.: DeepGauge: multi-granularity testing criteria for deep learning systems. In: Proceedings of the 33rd ACM/IEEE International Conference on Automated Software Engineering, ASE 2018, pp. 120–131 (2018)
31. Ma, L., et al.: DeepMutation: mutation testing of deep learning systems. In: The 29th IEEE International Symposium on Software Reliability Engineering (ISSRE) (2018)
32. Moosavi-Dezfooli, S.M., Fawzi, A., Frossard, P.: DeepFool: a simple and accurate method to fool deep neural networks. arXiv preprint arXiv:1511.04599 (2015)
33. Papernot, N., McDaniel, P., Jha, S., Fredrikson, M., Celik, Z.B., Swami, A.: The limitations of deep learning in adversarial settings. In: 2016 IEEE European Symposium on Security and Privacy (EuroS&P), pp. 372–387. IEEE (2016)

34. Papernot, N., McDaniel, P.D., Wu, X., Jha, S., Swami, A.: Distillation as a defense to adversarial perturbations against deep neural networks. In: IEEE Symposium on Security and Privacy, SP 2016, pp. 582–597 (2016)
35. Pei, K., Cao, Y., Yang, J., Jana, S.: DeepXplore: automated whitebox testing of deep learning systems. In: Proceedings of the 26th Symposium on Operating Systems Principles, pp. 1–18 (2017)
36. Pressman, R.: Software Engineering: A Practitioner's Approach, 7th edn. McGraw-Hill Inc., New York (2010)
37. Ramanishka, V., Chen, Y.T., Misu, T., Saenko, K.: Toward driving scene understanding: a dataset for learning driver behavior and causal reasoning. In: The IEEE Conference on Computer Vision and Pattern Recognition (CVPR), June 2018
38. Ruparelia, N.B.: Software development lifecycle models. SIGSOFT Softw. Eng. Notes **35**(3), 8–13 (2010). https://doi.org/10.1145/1764810.1764814
39. The New York Times: Alexa and Siri Can Hear This Hidden Command. You Can't (2018). https://www.nytimes.com/2018/05/10/technology/alexa-siri-hidden-command-audio-attacks.html
40. The New York Times: Toyota, SoftBank Setting Up Mobility Services Joint Venture (2018). https://www.nytimes.com/aponline/2018/10/04/world/asia/ap-as-japan-toyota-softbank.html
41. Uber Accident: After Fatal Uber Crash, a Self-Driving Start-Up Moves Forward (2018). https://www.nytimes.com/2018/05/07/technology/uber-crash-autonomous-driveai.html
42. Xiang, Y., et al.: ObjectNet3D: a large scale database for 3D object recognition. In: Leibe, B., Matas, J., Sebe, N., Welling, M. (eds.) ECCV 2016. LNCS, vol. 9912, pp. 160–176. Springer, Cham (2016). https://doi.org/10.1007/978-3-319-46484-8_10
43. Xie, X., et al.: DeepHunter: a coverage-guided fuzz testing framework for deep neural networks. In: Proceedings of the 28th ACM SIGSOFT International Symposium on Software Testing and Analysis, ISSTA 2019, pp. 146–157 (2019)
44. Xie, X., Ma, L., Wang, H., Li, Y., Liu, Y., Li, X.: DiffChaser: detecting disagreements for deep neural networks. In: Proceedings of the 28th International Joint Conference on Artificial Intelligence (2019)
45. Xu, W., Evans, D., Qi, Y.: Feature squeezing: Detecting adversarial examples in deep neural networks. arXiv preprint arXiv:1704.01155 (2017)
46. Xu, W., Qi, Y., Evans, D.: Automatically evading classifiers. In: Proceedings of the 2016 Network and Distributed Systems Symposium (2016)
47. Zhang, J.M., Harman, M., Ma, L., Liu, Y.: Machine learning testing: survey, landscapes and horizons. arXiv e-prints, June 2019
48. Zhang, T., Gao, C., Ma, L., Lyu, M.R., Kim, M.: An empirical study of common challenges in developing deep learning applications. In: The 30th IEEE International Symposium on Software Reliability Engineering (ISSRE) (2019)

Regular Papers

Using DimSpec for Bounded
and Unbounded Software Model Checking

Marko Kleine Büning, Tomáš Balyo, and Carsten Sinz[✉]

Karlsruhe Institute of Technology (KIT), Karlsruhe, Germany
{marko.kleinebuening,tomas.balyo,carsten.sinz}@kit.edu

Abstract. This paper describes a unified approach for both bounded
and unbounded software model checking to find errors in programs written in the programming language C. It is based on a propositional logic
intermediate representation, called DimSpec, that has been successfully
applied in SAT-based automated planning. Using DimSpec formulas
allows us to exploit the advantages of incremental SAT solving and provides an alternative approach to using the universal incremental SAT
API IPASIR or native solver APIs. The DimSpec formula can be used
for bounded model checking (via incremental SAT solving) as well as
unbounded model checking (using a backend that implements an IC3-
style algorithm). We also present an implementation of our approach,
called LLUMC, which encodes the presence of certain errors in a C program into a DimSpec formula. We evaluate our approach on benchmark
problems from the Software Verification Competition (SV-COMP) and
compare it with other tools to demonstrate runtime and functionality
advantages compared to state-of-the-art solvers.

1 Introduction

A DimSpec formula [30] consists of four CNF formulas $\mathcal{I}, \mathcal{U}, \mathcal{T}$ and $\mathcal{G}$ which
specify a transition system. The formula $\mathcal{I}$ describes the initial state, $\mathcal{G}$ the goal
state, $\mathcal{U}$ describes the constraints that must hold in each individual step of the
process and finally $\mathcal{T}$ describes the relation of each pair of neighboring steps.
DimSpec has been very successfully used for SAT-based automated planning
[16]. In this paper we demonstrate that the DimSpec format is also very useful
for software verification.

Software has become an important part of almost all modern technical
devices, such as cars, airplanes, household appliances, therapy machines, and
many more. The cars of tomorrow will drive on their own, controlled by software. As shown by serious accidents like the rocket crash of Ariane flight 501 [24],
the massive overdoses of radiation generated by the therapy machine Therac-25
[25] or the car crash of the Toyota Camry in 2005 [22], software is never perfect
and almost inevitably contains errors and bugs. While testing of software can,

---

This work was partially supported by Baden-Württemberg Stiftung within project
HIVES.

Y. Ait-Ameur and S. Qin (Eds.): ICFEM 2019, LNCS 11852, pp. 19–35, 2019.
https://doi.org/10.1007/978-3-030-32409-4_2

in practice, only cover a limited number of program executions, software verification can guarantee a much higher coverage while producing proofs for the existence or absence of errors. Many software verification approaches have been developed, for instance symbolic execution [19], (bounded) model checking [9], or abstraction and interpolation [1]. In bounded model checking, function calls are inlined and loops unrolled a finite number of times. This unrolling reduces the complexity of the problem to a computationally feasible level, though it limits coverage and thus precision of the approach.

We developed an approach that is suitable for both bounded and unbounded model checking. To this end, we produce a SAT encoding of a transition system that is general enough to be solved with different solver back-ends, based on, e.g., incremental SAT or on an invariant checking algorithm. We focus on sequential programs written in C, and use the low-level code representation of the compiler framework LLVM as an intermediate language. Based on this representation, we derived an encoding of the program verification task into a DimSpec formula. We first encode the program into four SMT formulas and, subsequently, generate the SAT-level representation in the desired DimSpec format. The resulting formula is then solved by either an incremental SAT solver that unrolls the transition system to find a path to an error state, or an invariant checking algorithm that refines an over-approximation.

Our verification system uses Clang and LLVM version 3.7.1 to compile C-code into LLVM Intermediate Representation. Then our new tool LLUMC (Low-Level Unbounded Model Checker) translates the LLVM-IR representation of the program P to be verified to a DimSpec formula with error states that are reachable iff P contains a corresponding error. To solve the generated formulas we either use the incremental SAT solver IncPlan [16] or the invariant checking algorithm implemented in the solver MinireachIC3 [30]. LLUMC was inspired by the bounded model checker LLBMC [28] but runs independently. Our evaluation is based on the Software Verification Competition (SV-COMP) and shows the correctness and feasibility of our approach. LLUMC is available online at [21].

2   The DimSpec Format

We assume the reader to be familiar with propositional logic, first-order-logic and the Boolean satisfiability problem (SAT), and use definitions and notations standard in SAT. In this section, for completeness, we introduce incremental SAT-solving and describe the theory of bit-vectors in the context of SMT-solving.

Incremental SAT-Solving. Incremental SAT-solving is an approach to solve several related SAT-problems efficiently. In the *assumption based interface* [14], two methods are used to describe a related problem relative to a base problem: add(C) and solve(A), where C is a clause and A a set of literals called assumptions. Clauses can be added with the add method and their conjunction, together with previously added clauses, can then be solved under the condition that all literals in A are true by solve(A). To enable simulating the removal of a clause C between invocations of `solve(A)`, a clause $C' = C \cup a$ is passed to the solver instead of C, with a (called an *activation literal*) being an otherwise unused literal. C is then effectively taken into account iff $\neg a$ is present in A.

DimSpec Formulas. A DimSpec formula [31] represents a transition system with a finite number of states $t_0, t_1, \ldots, t_k$, where each state is a full truth assignment on n Boolean variables $x_1, \ldots, x_n$. It consists of four CNF formulas: $\mathcal{I}, \mathcal{U}, \mathcal{G}$ and $\mathcal{T}$, where $\mathcal{I}$ encodes the set of initial states, $\mathcal{G}$ describes the set of goal states (that in our case indicate occurrence of a program error). Formula $\mathcal{U}$ encodes global constraints that have to hold in each state, and finally the transition clauses $\mathcal{T}$ are satisfied by each pair of consecutive states t_i, t_{i+1}. The clause sets $\mathcal{I}, \mathcal{U}$, and $\mathcal{G}$ contain variables $x_1, \ldots, x_n$, and $\mathcal{T}$ contains $x_1, \ldots, x_{2n}$, where $x_1, \ldots, x_n$ encodes the current and $x_{n+1}, \ldots, x_{2n}$ the next state. Testing whether the goal state is reachable from the initial state within k steps is equivalent to checking whether the following formula F_k is satisfiable.

$$F_k = \mathcal{I}(0) \wedge \left(\bigwedge_{i=0}^{k-1} (\mathcal{U}(i) \wedge \mathcal{T}(i, i+1)) \right) \wedge \mathcal{U}(k) \wedge \mathcal{G}(k),$$

where $\mathcal{I}(i)$, $\mathcal{G}(i)$, $\mathcal{U}(i)$ and $\mathcal{T}(i, i+1)$ denote the respective formulas without index, where each variable x_j is replaced by $x_{j+i \cdot n}$.

DimSpec formulas have been successfully employed in SAT-based automated planning [16,30], but they represent a generic approach to utilize incremental SAT solving for reachability analysis of transition systems. DimSpec solvers can be developed independently of their usage and also be parallelized, which brings benefit to all DimSpec applications.

Incremental SAT Solving for DimSpec. The straightforward way to solve a DimSpec formula is to unroll the transition relation step by step, constructing and solving the resulting formula F_i at each step, until a satisfiable formula is observed. An efficient way to implement this is to use an incremental SAT solver with the assumption-based interface via the following steps:

$$\begin{aligned}
\text{step}(0): \quad & \texttt{add}(\mathcal{I}(0) \wedge (a_0 \vee \mathcal{G}(0)) \wedge \mathcal{U}(0)) \\
& \texttt{solve}(\{\neg a_0\}) \\
\text{step}(k): \quad & \texttt{add}(\mathcal{T}(k-1, k) \wedge (a_k \vee \mathcal{G}(k)) \wedge \mathcal{U}(k)) \\
& \texttt{solve}(\{\neg a_k\}).
\end{aligned}$$

This algorithm, in practice, only terminates in reasonable time if the goal state is reachable from the initial state. Otherwise it searches "endlessly", i.e. up to a bound of 2^n in the worst case. A more sophisticated approach that can detect unreachability is described next.

IC3 Algorithm. A different approach to solve a DimSpec formula is described in [12] and implemented, among others, in the tool IC3 (Incremental Construction of Inductive Clauses for Indubitable Correctness). Given a transition system S and a safety property P, the algorithm can prove that P is *S-invariant*, meaning that, regarding S, property P is true in all reachable states, or produce a counterexample. IC3 incrementally refines a sequence of formulas $F_0', F_1', \dots, F_k'$ that describe over-approximations of the set of states reachable in at most k steps. It can extend the formula sequence in major steps that increase k by one. In minor steps the algorithm refines the approximations F_i' with $0 \le i \le k$ by conjoining clauses to the F_i'. Given a finite transition system S and a safety property P, the IC3 algorithm terminates and returns true, iff P is true in all reachable states of S [12]. The IC3 algorithm was implemented and adjusted[1] to the DimSpec format in the tool MinireachIC3 by Suda [30].

Comparison to Other SAT Formats. An alternative approach to DimSpec for utilizing the benefits of incremental SAT solving is the IPASIR interface introduced for the 2015 International SAT Race [4]. In contrast to DimSpec, which is a file format, IPASIR is a collection of C/C++ function prototypes, i.e., an application program interface (API). Numerous state-of-the-art SAT solvers implement the IPASIR interface, which makes it very easy and convenient to develop applications using incremental SAT solving without committing to any particular SAT solver.

The advantages of IPASIR over DimSpec are more flexibility (the clauses for the next incremental SAT call can be constructed dynamically based on previous results), more functionality (IPASIR provides much more control over the SAT solver and allows the user to extract more information from the SAT solving process, such as learned clauses or failed assumptions). On the other hand, DimSpec is much easier to use since it does not require any programming and it can be used to express unreachability of transition systems, which is impossible with IPASIR. Furthermore, any SAT solver supporting IPASIR be can used in the IncPlan application [16], which renders it into a DimSpec solver. In summary, DimSpec is a purely declarative approach while IPASIR is procedural.

Another declarative format related to DimSpec is AIGER [10] with safety invariants. AIGER is the format for representing and-inverter graphs, which represent a structural implementation of the logical functionality of a circuit or network. DimSpec and AIGER-safety are mutually translatable[2].

3   Encoding for Software Model Checking

We give a short introduction into the Satisfiability Modulo Theories (SMT) and the LLVM Framework, which are necessary to understand the encoding.

---

[1] The clause sets $\mathcal{I}, \mathcal{U}, \mathcal{T}$ represent the transition system S, and $\mathcal{G}$ represents the negation of the invariant property P.

[2] We omit the description of these translations due to space limitations.

Afterwards, we will describe a DimSpec encoding for the software model checking approach in more detail to show the feasibility and advantages of encoding problems into the DimSpec format.

Satisfiability Modulo Theories (SMT). Due to quantifiers and infinite domains, first-order-logic is generally undecidable but there are numerous decidable sub-theories. As is for example described in [11], the problem of solving those subsets or theories is called satisfiability modulo theories or SMT. These theories can be seen as restrictions on possible models of first-order-logic formulas [27]. For our encoding, we will only use the theory of bit-vectors. SMT was standardized by the SMT-LIB initiative [5]. We will use the same notations, especially when referring to SMT functions defined in the different theories. Such an SMT-LIB function could for example be bvadd(b_1, b_2), describing the addition of two bit-vectors b_1 and b_2. A more complex function is called `if-then-else` (ite) and is defined by:

$$\forall c \in BV_1, x, y, z \in BV_i \, (x = \text{ite}(c, y, z) \Leftrightarrow c \wedge x = y \vee \neg c \wedge x = z). \quad (1)$$

We refer to the *theory of fixed-size bit-vectors* defined by the SMT-LIB standard in [5]. The theory of bit-vectors models finite bit-vectors BV_n of length n and operations on these vectors in first-order-logic. The set of function symbols contains standard operations on bit-vectors such as addition or concatenation.

LLVM Representation. LLVM is an open source compiler framework that consists of a "collection of modular and reusable compiler and tool-chain technologies" [26]. It supports compilation for a wide range of languages and is known for its research friendliness and good documentation. To work directly on C-code is very complex and it is extremely cumbersome to support all language features. Thus, we use the intermediate language of LLVM, which allows for a much simpler characterization of the semantics of statements and provides a number of optimizations and simplifications suitable for our approach. We describe the constructs of LLVM bottom up. The smallest executable unit is called an *instruction*. An instruction is an atomic unit of execution that performs a single operation. A basic block is a linear sequence of program instructions having one entry point and one exit point. It may have multiple predecessors and successors and may also be its own successor. The last instruction of every basic block is called *terminator*. Every basic block is part of a *function*. A function (n, B, e) is a tuple of a name n, a sequence of basic blocks $B = (b_0, b_1, ..., b_m)$, and an entry block $e \in B$. Hereinafter, we will denote the main function of a program with f_{main}. A module $m = (F_m, G_m)$ is a pair of a set of functions F_m (including f_{main}) and a set of global variables G_m.

To optimize our encoding, we run some predefined optimization passes from LLVM and LLBMC on the generated LLVM-module. Among other things, these optimizations handle uninitialized local variables in C-code, promote memory references to register references (as far as possible) and inline all functions into one main function. These optimizations are described in more detail in [20]. The resulting LLVM-module is then used as input for our encoding.

3.1 Idea and Error Definition

A bug or error in a software program is a well-known notion, but there exists no universal definition. A general concept is that a program has an error, if it does not act according to its specification. For this paper we concentrate on notions standardized in the SV-COMP competitions. Thus, we consider calls to assume and assert and support both standard ANSI-C and notions used in benchmarks of the competition. We state that a program acts according to its specification if the assert statements are true if all assume conditions are met. If an assume condition is not met, the further run of the program is not specified and thus no errors can occur.

Definition 1 (Program Error in LLUMC). *Let P be a program. Then there exists an error in P, if all calls to assume that are prior to an assert statement are true and a call to assert with a parameter value of false is invoked.*

Of course, there are other errors that can happen during a program execution like irregular bit-shifting, non-termination, or integer and buffer overflows.[3]

To verify a C program P with respect to Definition 1, we first translate P to LLVM-IR (i.e. an LLVM-module) using the Clang compiler. After inlining all function calls, we can concentrate on just the main function. Every basic block together with its variable assignment can be seen as a *state*. We then add a special *error state* and try to find a path from the entry state, defined by the entry block of the main function, to the error state.

3.2 State Space

Transitions from one state to a next state will always represent transitions from one basic block to the next with respect to its current variable assignment. Often this kind of encoding is called *small block encoding* [7]. According to the theory of bit-vectors, we define every state variable as a bit-vector of length n. The number of bit-vectors in the state, including the bit-vectors representing the current and previous basic block, define the number of SMT variables that are needed to encode the state. The number of bits in total, i.e. the sum of the length of all bit-vectors encoding a state, equals the number of CNF variables needed.

In our approach, we ignore memory accesses by over-approximating them (i.e. each memory read results in a non-deterministic value). Accesses to stack variables, which in most cases can be put into virtual registers by LLVM, are handled precisely, though, and are sufficient in many cases.[4] First of all, every state has to save the current basic block. Hereinafter, $|B|$ denotes the number of

---

[3] In our tool LLUMC, we have additionally implemented checks for integer overflows. These are not part of our experimental evaluation, though.

[4] Integrating a full memory model into our approach is part of future work.

basic blocks of the main function after inlining. For our encoding we need two additional blocks. The *ok* block represents a safe state from which no more errors can occur. This block is reached when the program terminates or when an assume condition is not met. The second block is called *error* and is our goal state, representing that an error occurred. With the function $enc(bb) : BasicBlock \rightarrow \mathbb{N}$ we injectively map every basic block to a natural number. If there are $|B|$ basic blocks in *main*, the required length of the bit-vector encoding a state's basic block is $\lceil \log_2(|B| + 2) \rceil$. We call the SMT-variable encoding the current basic block *curr*. In LLVM, the value of a register can depend on the previous basic block (more specifically, this is the case for `phi` instructions) and must thus also be encoded, resulting in another bit-vector of length $\lceil \log_2(|B| + 2) \rceil$, called *pred*. Furthermore, we need to save the current variable assignment. We do not need the assignment of all variables, but should focus on those that will be accessed later on and cannot be eliminated through optimization. Those variables can be classified by two properties. We call the set of those variables V, consisting of

1. variables that are used in more than one basic block and
2. variables that are read before written in a basic block that is part of a loop.

The length of the variables depends on their type. The standard integer type (int) in C has a width of 32 bits on many architectures, long has 64, and Boolean values have a width of 1. There are other types, but their lengths are always specified by LLVM and thus can easily be extracted.

Definition 2 (State). *The state space is the Cartesian product over the set V^* of all state variables and the two state-encoding basic-block variables: $V^* = \{curr, \; pred\} \cup V$. Every variable v of the state space has a fixed bit-length ℓ_v. For a specific step k, the state* state(k) *is the assignment of concrete bit-vector values to every variable.*

3.3 Encoding to DimSpec Format

Our goal is to encode an LLVM-module as defined at the beginning of this section into DimSpec format. Therefore, we must define the four CNF formulas $\{\mathcal{I}, \mathcal{G}, \mathcal{U}, \mathcal{T}\}$ in such a way that if there exists a transition from $\mathcal{I}$ to $\mathcal{G}$ defined by $\mathcal{T}$ and restricted by $\mathcal{U}$ then there exists an error in the given program code.[5]

The initial formula $\mathcal{I}$ can be created by encoding the entry block of the LLVM-module. The encoding has to represent the state that we are currently at the first basic block and that there were no prior actions. We declare the entry block itself as the predecessor to exclude any prior actions. The entry block and thus the initial formula is independent from any transition. The rest of the variable assignment is arbitrary at this point and can be left undeclared. The encoding of the goal formula $\mathcal{G}$ can be defined accordingly.

---

[5] A detailed example of the encoding, starting with C-code, over the LLVM representation to the SMT encoding, can be found online at https://baldur.iti.kit.edu/icfem2019/Appendix.pdf.

Definition 3 (Encoding of the Initial and Goal Formula). *Let* entry *be the name of the first block and let* error *be the name of the error block, then the initial formula* $\mathcal{I}(k)$ *and the goal formula* $\mathcal{G}(k)$ *for the LLVM-module and for* $k \in \mathbb{N}$ *are defined as:*

$$\mathcal{I}(k) = \quad curr = \text{enc}(entry) \ \wedge \ pred = \text{enc}(entry),$$
$$\mathcal{G}(k) = \quad curr = \text{enc}(error).$$

The universal formula consists of constraints that have to be true in all states. In our case, that are boundaries for the variables $curr$ and $pred$. In the previous section, the number of bits needed to encode the current and previous basic block were defined as $\lceil \log_2(|B|+2) \rceil$. In most cases $|B|+2$ is not a power of two and thus bigger numbers can be represented. These numbers must be excluded at all times in the universal formula $\mathcal{U}$.

Definition 4 (Encoding of the Universal Formula). *Let* $|B|$ *be the number of basic blocks in the LLVM-module, then the universal formula* $\mathcal{U}(k)$ *for* $k \in \mathbb{N}$ *is defined as:*

$$\mathcal{U}(k) = \quad curr \leq (|B|+2) \ \wedge \ pred \leq (|B|+2) \, .$$

At last, we have to define the transition formula. It represents the transition between state k and state $k+1$. It is important to notice that the transition formula has twice as much variables as the other formulas. To distinguish between the variables in time-point k and $k+1$ every variable v of our state space is called v' at time-point $k+1$. Otherwise, every transition formula would be evaluated to false and thus no transition step could ever be taken. In general, the encoding of one transition has the form:

$$state(k) \Rightarrow state(k+1). \tag{2}$$

We call $state(k)$ antecedent and $state(k+1)$ consequent. For each $state(k)$ that is reachable from our initial state, a transition must be defined. An undefined transition leads to an undefined $state(k+1)$ with arbitrary values. Thus, if there is a reachable, undefined transition all goal states can be reached. For the same reason, we determine that for each $state(k)$ the transition must be explicit. Variables that are not important for the transition should not be declared in the antecedent but should be specified in the consequent to avoid undefined values. We will use the auxiliary function

$$same(bb) : \text{Basic Block} \rightarrow \text{SMT-formula}$$

to encode that variables which are not modified in a basic block maintain their current value. The function $same(bb)$ returns the conjunction of all $var = var'$, for all variables in our state space, that have not been modified in the transition of our basic block bb.

To encode the transition between steps, we take a closer look at the current basic block, further denoted as bb and customize Eq. 2 for different branching possibilities. We divide basic blocks into three groups and distinguish them by means of their terminator. The three different types of terminator instructions are called unconditional branching, conditional branching and return.

Unconditional Branching (br %bb2): Branches to the basic block with the label $bb2$ and creates a transition from the current basic block to $bb2$. If the current basic block has no other instructions, only the change of basic block and the saving of the predecessor have to be encoded. Furthermore, we have to state that no variables have changed during this transition:

$$curr = enc(bb) \Rightarrow curr' = enc(bb2) \wedge pred' = enc(bb) \wedge same(bb). \qquad (3)$$

This encoding is rarely complete, because it does not regard all other instructions in the basic block bb. Let rl_{bb} be the ordered list of instructions from bottom to top in bb. Then we iterate over rl_{bb} and regard all instructions $inst$ that are part of our state variables $inst \in V$ and are not the terminator instruction. The instruction is then recursively encoded according to its type and its operands. When an instruction like `%tmp3 = add i32 10 %tmp2` is encoded by the method `visitInst(%tmp3)`, the algorithm checks the operands first. When regarding the value `%tmp2`, the algorithm checks whether it is a variable that is part of our state or a value calculated by an instruction, which the algorithm has to then encode recursively. The stop criterion is always the occurrence of a state variable, a constant or a call to assert, assume or error. The encoding then creates SMT formulas dependent on the operands. Assuming `%tmp2` is a variable from our state space, the encoding for the add instruction would result in `tmp3' = add(10, tmp2)`. This generated SMT formula is then conjuncted with the consequent of Eq. 3. The algorithm continues by iterating further through the list rl_{bb} until there are no instructions left.

Conditional Branching (br %cond, %bb1, %bb2): Creates a transition to $bb1$ with the condition $cond = 1$ and a transition to $bb2$ with the condition $cond = 0$. Every conditional branch has a branching condition represented as a variable ($cond$). We can extract that condition by visiting and encoding the variable representing the branching condition. In LLVM this branching condition is represented as a Boolean value that is assigned by the so called *icmp-instruction*. This instruction returns a Boolean value based on the comparison of two values and it supports equality, unsigned and signed comparison. The icmp-instruction is then encoded recursively by visiting its two operands with the same visiting approach as described for the unconditional branching. The result could for example be the SMT encoding of the mathematical condition $tmp2 > 10$. Based on it, the algorithm creates two separate transitions.

$$curr = enc(bb) \wedge visitInst(cond) \Rightarrow$$
$$curr' = enc(bb1) \wedge pred' = enc(bb) \wedge same(bb).$$
$$curr = enc(bb) \wedge \neg(visitInst(cond)) \Rightarrow$$
$$curr' = enc(bb2) \wedge pred' = enc(bb) \wedge same(bb).$$

Furthermore, the list rl_{bb} is traversed as described previously resulting in a final encoding of the current basic block.

Return Value (*ret val*): The value *val* can be an arbitrary integer and represents the return value of the program as usual. This terminator creates a transition to *ok*. In an extended and already implemented version, another check is inserted verifying that the result value of a correct program is 0 and if this does not hold a transition to *error* is created.

After encoding branching possibilities, we will look at the calls to assume, assert, error. During the instruction iteration of a basic block, we regard these instructions differently because they lead to a split of our transitions.

Method Calls (Error, Assume, Assert): If the *error*-method, which is used to specify program errors in C-code, is called inside a basic block, we do not have to regard any other instructions and thus delete all other transitions from this basic block. We produce a single transition:

$$curr = enc(bb) \Rightarrow curr' = enc(error) \wedge same(\emptyset).$$

The other three possibilities lead to a split of our transitions similar to the conditional branching. A call of *assume(var)* divides the set of current transitions for our basic block. The condition is *var* = 0 and leads to a transition to the *ok* state with $s' = enc(ok)$. The call to *assert(var)* is similar only with the transition to $s' = enc(error)$ if *var* = 0 holds true. In both cases, the encoding continues normally with the next instruction if the conditions are not met.

All components of the transition formula have now been discussed. To obtain the complete transition formula the algorithm has to iterate over all basic blocks of the main function. Depending on their terminator instruction, every basic block has to be encoded according to the definitions above. To predict which transition is taken in which step would be equal to solving the whole formula. Thus, the transition formula is time independent and the transition possibilities for all time steps are part of the formula.

Definition 5 (Encoding of the Transition Formula). *Let BB be the set of all basic blocks of f_{main} and let $encode(b)$ with $b \in BB$ be the encoding as shown above, then the transition formula $\mathcal{T}(k, k+1)$ for $k \in \mathbb{N}$ is defined by:*

$$\mathcal{T}(k, k+1) = \bigwedge_{b \in BB} encode(b). \tag{4}$$

Claim. There exists an error as defined by Definition 1 in program p iff

1. p is transformed into an LLVM-module ℓ as described in Sect. 3 and
2. there exists a transition path in ℓ from the initial state to the goal state while the universal formula holds in all states.

Proof Idea: We forego on a formal proof, because it would require a structural induction over huge sets of C-Code and the LLVM-language. Instead, we present short arguments and references for our claim.

(1): Using LLVM as a representation for C-code is widely accepted and used in research and industry. We assume that the transformation from C-code into a LLVM-module does not remove or add any errors based on the high number of research papers [1,3,6] and tools like LLBMC [27] and SeaHorn [17].

(2): The error node has two types of incoming edges: from an assert statement and an edge from the error node itself. We disregard the edge that points to itself and are left with the option that match the property defined in Definition 1. If the encoding of the variables is, as we claim, correct and our state space is closed under $\mathcal{T}$ and $\mathcal{U}$, we can assume that the a transition path from the initial state to the error state complies with an error in the LLVM-module.

From SMT to SAT Formula. The encoding of the LLVM-module gives us four SMT formulas. Currently, there are no SMT solver that support the Dim-Spec format and thus these formulas have to be translated into four CNFs in DimSpec format. The most widespread approach to transform SMT to CNF formulas is called *bit-blasting*. We have taken one approach implemented in STP [15] and the ABC-library [18] and modified these algorithms to correspond to some technical requirements of the DimSpec format. Finally, a CNF in the DimSpec format is created that can be used as input for a number of SAT solvers.

4   Solving the Formula: Bounded vs. Unbounded Model Checking

The general idea of bounded model checking (BMC) is to encode paths of a transition system up to a certain bound. For software, the bound is maintained by unrolling loops and inlining function calls at most k times. The number k is called the *bound* and is the reason for the decidability of bounded model checking but also for its limitations. After the unrolling and encoding of the program, a formula that represents the negation of a desired property is added, and the formula is solved with an SMT or SAT-solver. If the solver finds a model for the formula, the approach has found an error and the model can be used as a counterexample. The loop-bound can be increased step by step until a fixed bound k is reached. The question to which bound the loops should be unrolled is complex and further discussed for example by Biere et al. [9].

As mentioned earlier, our encoding to the DimSpec format leads to a unified encoding for both bounded and unbounded model checking. Whether our approach can be categorized as a bounded or unbounded model checking technique depends on the kind of solver that is used to solve the generated formula.

A first approach is solving the formula with an incremental SAT-solver as described in Sect. 2. We argue that the approach using an incremental SAT-solver has to be categorized as bounded, because the problem is unrolled during solving time and the verification is limited by the number of unrolling steps that can be performed under time and memory restrictions. However, compared with state-of-the-art bounded model checkers, there is a crucial difference in how our verification approach is bounded. Bounded model checkers require a fixed bound early during their analysis to generate the corresponding problem instance, which cannot be directly reused for other bound settings. For our approach the encoding itself is independent of any unrolling. Only during solving of the instance the loop is unrolled leading to the bound that is perceptible through the time and memory limit which allows us to unroll only a finite number of times.

When solving the generated formula with an invariant checking algorithm as e.g. the in Sect. 2 described IC3-algorithm, the approach becomes unbounded. The whole path to the error label is computed using abstractions which are iteratively refined until either the error path is concrete and no further refinement is possible or a repetition is detected, from which the absence of errors can be deduced. Thus, our approach is truly unbounded, but of course limited by time and memory constraints when solving difficult problems. In summary, our unified encoding can be used for both unbounded and bounded model checking.

5   Experimental Results

The LLUMC-approach is implemented as a tool chain. The input file, a C source file, is compiled with Clang (version 3.7.1) and then optimized with LLVM and LLBMC passes. This optimized LLVM module serves as input for the program LLUMC, which performs the encoding as described above. We modified the tool STP to translate SMT formulas to DimSpec problems. The final renaming and aggregation is implemented directly in LLUMC.

We combined the two different approaches described in Sect. 4 to solve the generated DimSpec/CNF formulas. The tool IncPlan [16] was developed at KIT and implements the incremental SAT-solving interface described in Sect. 3. It can be used with every SAT-solver that accepts the Re-entrant Incremental Satisfiability Application Program Interface (IPASIR). We have evaluated IncPlan with a number of SAT-solvers including Minisat [29], abcdSat [13], Glucose [2] and Picosat [8]. While Glucose and Minisat produced good results for some benchmarks, the IncPlan implementation for these solvers exhibited segmentation-fault errors for some of the benchmark instances. Thus, we focused on the usage of abcdSat and PicoSat. We only show the results of running IncPlan with abcd-Sat as the backend solver since exchanging abcdSat with PicoSAT resulted in negligible performance differences. For the incremental SAT-solving performed with IncPlan and abcdSat, we are only able to find errors in programs but cannot prove their absence. The reason is the design of the incremental solver IncPlan. It regards the encoding as a path to the error label that has to be found and if there is no such path, the program does not terminate. To also be able to prove the nonexistence of errors an analysis for repetition in the state space has to be performed, which is part of future research.

Secondly, the IC3 algorithm was implemented and adjusted to the DimSpec format in the tool MinireachIC3 [30]. The safety property P expresses that the error state should not be reachable, and thus P is given by $\neg G$, G being the goal formula of the DimSpec encoding. Thus, we are not only able to prove the existence of errors but also their absence.

We ran both tools in parallel and took the results of the tool that terminated first. As both tools are sound, this approach guaranteed the correct result while circumventing disadvantages of each single approach, like the inability to prove the absence of errors through the tool IncPlan. Thus, we are able to take full advantage of the usability of the encoding for different solving techniques.

5.1 Benchmarks

We evaluated our approach using benchmarks from the Software Verification Competition [6]. The SV-COMP is an annual competition for academic software verification tools, with the aim to compare software verifiers. While we did not submit our tool to the competition, the collected benchmarks serve as an excellent evaluation basis for every verifier. All benchmarks are available at [32] and we regarded the sub-folder c with programs written in the language C.

The benchmark problem sets are organized by topics. From these benchmarks, we selected all problems compatible with our current LLUMC implementation and thus obtained a total of over 200 problems as a benchmark set. We excluded some benchmarks that included memory accesses or floating point arithmetic. Furthermore, we excluded recursive and concurrent tasks due to the inlining in our approach and thus leaving us with 95 incorrect and 107 correct programs. The benchmarks vary between 14 and 1500 lines of code (LoC).

The evaluation was performed on a system with 64 CPUs with 2.3 GHz and 126 GB working memory. We set a time limit of 600s (wall-clock time) per benchmark problem. We decided to measure the wall-clock-time for the whole LLUMC tool-chain. Due to using GNU parallel [33], we were able to run benchmarks in parallel, but decided to use only 8 CPUs to limit run-time noise arising e.g. due to processes sharing CPU caches. Our approach works sequentially, and parallelism is only achieved by running several benchmarks at once. The DimSpec format supports parallelism on the SAT level, the advantages remain to be evaluated thoroughly in future research.

5.2 Evaluation

We compared our approach to the bounded model checking approach which is implemented for example in the tools CBMC (C Bounded Model Checker) [23] and LLBMC (Low Level Bounded Model Checker) [28]. Both tools, CBMC and LLBMC, are powerful state-of-the-art verification tools, which also earned a number of gold, silver and bronze medals in the SV-COMP competitions.

We created scripts similar to the respective SV-COMP submissions from recent years, but handled some configurations differently. Benchmarking with bounded model checkers requires choosing a suitable loop unroll bound B, resulting in a trade off between precision (increases with B) and speed (decreases with B). For the competition both solvers used specific bounds that were determined through "educated guesses" [23]. Furthermore, in the competition, if a loop-bound was reached and the solver failed to produce an answer, an educated guess was made for the result. In our evaluation, we used the loop unroll bounds

10, 100 and 1000 (in that order), aborting the solving process as soon as a verification result was achieved. When reaching a time or memory limit, we classified the problem instance as *unknown*. The scripts, benchmark sets and detailed results are available at [21].

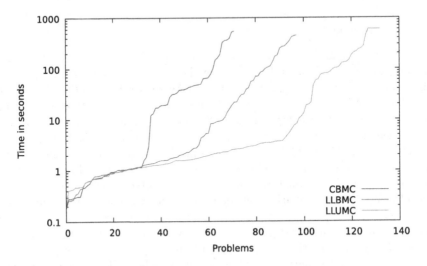

Fig. 1. Comparison of LLUMC with CBMC and LLBMC. The x-axis represents the number of problems the solvers were able to solve and the y-axis the time they needed.

The results of our evaluation are shown in Fig. 1 and indicate both functionality and runtime advantages on the chosen benchmarks[6]. To explain the advantage of our approach and the encoding over the state-of-the-art for bounded model checking, we have to look at the solving approaches individually.

The advantage of the incremental solving with abcdSAT over bounded model checking approaches is caused by our new approach of encoding the verification problem and thereby the bound. With bounded model checking, programs are unrolled to a fixed bound in an early phase of the analysis and the SAT encoding is specifically created for this one bound. This fixed bound is mostly given by the user and when not sufficient enough the verification has to be reattempted for the new bound. With our approach, an unbounded low-level encoding is used, with the unrolling bound being iteratively increased by the incremental backend solver, which is able to reuse facts learned with lower bounds.

The chosen benchmark-set from the SV-COMP includes a large number of problems with unbounded loops and loops with large bounds. While the basic bounded model checking approach cannot handle unbounded loops, the abstraction refinement of MinireachIC3 is able to abstract the state space and prove the absence of errors better then state-of-the-art tools. The number of benchmark

---

[6] Detailed figures about the single solving approaches can be found online at https://baldur.iti.kit.edu/icfem2019/Appendix.pdf.

problems solved still indicates that proving the absence of errors for programs with large loops is still a difficult task, but the approach using MinireachIC3 leads to a significant improvement.

This experimental evaluation illustrates the feasibility and potential of our approach. We show that our flexible encoding supports a variety of different approaches for solving the generated CNF in DimSpec format. In total, our algorithm is competitive with existing bounded model checkers and can even outperform them on some instances, especially ones with large loop bounds or unbounded loops.

6   Conclusion and Future Work

In this paper we presented the DimSpec format for specifying properties of transition systems on the SAT level. It has already been successfully employed in SAT-based automated planning in the past, and we showed that it can also be advantageous to handle software verification problems. Our new DimSpec-based encoding tool LLUMC can be used to express software verification problems independently from loop-bounds, and thus can be used for both bounded and unbounded model checking. Basing our encoding on DimSpec enables us to leverage powerful DimSpec solvers for software verification.

In future work the performance of the LLUMC approach could be improved by enlarging the incremental steps of the solver. A first evaluation shows that merging basic blocks in LLVM leads to performance improvements, indicating that a large block encoding could be advantageous. Furthermore, adding a full memory model to the LLUMC approach will enable us to support a wider range of C language constructs.

References

1. Albarghouthi, A., Li, Y., Gurfinkel, A., Chechik, M.: UFO: a framework for abstraction- and interpolation-based software verification. In: Madhusudan, P., Seshia, S.A. (eds.) CAV 2012. LNCS, vol. 7358, pp. 672–678. Springer, Heidelberg (2012). https://doi.org/10.1007/978-3-642-31424-7_48
2. Audemard, G., Simon, L.: Glucose in the SAT 2014 competition. SAT Compet. **2014**, 31 (2014)
3. Babić, D., Hu, A.J.: Structural abstraction of software verification conditions. In: Damm, W., Hermanns, H. (eds.) CAV 2007. LNCS, vol. 4590, pp. 366–378. Springer, Heidelberg (2007). https://doi.org/10.1007/978-3-540-73368-3_41
4. Balyo, T., Biere, A., Iser, M., Sinz, C.: SAT race 2015. Artif. Intell. **241**, 45–65 (2016)
5. Barrett, C., Stump, A., Tinelli, C., et al.: The SMT-lib standard: version 2.0. In: Proceedings of the 8th International Workshop on SMT, vol. 13, p. 14 (2010)
6. Beyer, D.: Second competition on software verification. In: Piterman, N., Smolka, S.A. (eds.) TACAS 2013. LNCS, vol. 7795, pp. 594–609. Springer, Heidelberg (2013). https://doi.org/10.1007/978-3-642-36742-7_43

34   M. Kleine Büning et al.

7. Beyer, D., Cimatti, A., Griggio, A., Keremoglu, M.E., Sebastiani, R.: Software model checking via large-block encoding. In: FMCAD, pp. 25–32. IEEE (2009)

8. Biere, A.: PicoSAT essentials. J. Satisf. Boolean Model. Comput. **4**, 75–97 (2008)

9. Biere, A., Cimatti, A., Clarke, E.M., Strichman, O., Zhu, Y.: Bounded model checking. Adv. Comput. **58**, 117–148 (2003)

10. Biere, A., Heljanko, K., Wieringa, S.: AIGER 1.9 and beyond. Technical report, Johannes Kepler University, FMV Reports Series, Institute for Formal Models and Verification, Johannes Kepler University, Altenbergerstr. 69, 4040 Linz, Austria (2011)

11. Biere, A., Heule, M., van Maaren, H.: Handbook of Satisfiability, vol. 185. IOS press, Amsterdam (2009)

12. Bradley, A.R.: SAT-based model checking without unrolling. In: Jhala, R., Schmidt, D. (eds.) VMCAI 2011. LNCS, vol. 6538, pp. 70–87. Springer, Heidelberg (2011). https://doi.org/10.1007/978-3-642-18275-4_7

13. Chen, J.: MiniSAT BCD and abcdSAT: solvers based on blocked clause decomposition. SAT RACE (2015)

14. Eén, N., Sörensson, N.: An extensible SAT-solver. In: Giunchiglia, E., Tacchella, A. (eds.) SAT 2003. LNCS, vol. 2919, pp. 502–518. Springer, Heidelberg (2004). https://doi.org/10.1007/978-3-540-24605-3_37

15. Ganesh, V., Dill, D.L.: A decision procedure for bit-vectors and arrays. In: Damm, W., Hermanns, H. (eds.) CAV 2007. LNCS, vol. 4590, pp. 519–531. Springer, Heidelberg (2007). https://doi.org/10.1007/978-3-540-73368-3_52

16. Gocht, S., Balyo, T.: Accelerating SAT based planning with incremental SAT solving. In: International Conference on Automated Planning and Scheduling (2017)

17. Gurfinkel, A., Kahsai, T., Navas, J.A.: SeaHorn: a framework for verifying C programs (competition contribution). In: Baier, C., Tinelli, C. (eds.) TACAS 2015. LNCS, vol. 9035, pp. 447–450. Springer, Heidelberg (2015). https://doi.org/10.1007/978-3-662-46681-0_41

18. Jha, S., Limaye, R., Seshia, S.A.: Beaver: engineering an efficient SMT solver for bit-vector arithmetic. In: Bouajjani, A., Maler, O. (eds.) CAV 2009. LNCS, vol. 5643, pp. 668–674. Springer, Heidelberg (2009). https://doi.org/10.1007/978-3-642-02658-4_53

19. Khurshid, S., PǍsǍreanu, C.S., Visser, W.: Generalized symbolic execution for model checking and testing. In: Garavel, H., Hatcliff, J. (eds.) TACAS 2003. LNCS, vol. 2619, pp. 553–568. Springer, Heidelberg (2003). https://doi.org/10.1007/3-540-36577-X_40

20. Kleine Büning, M.: Unbounded Software Model Checking with Incremental SAT-Solving. Master Thesis at the Karlsruhe Institute for Technology (2017)

21. Kleine Büning, M.: LLUMC (Low Level Unbounded Model Checker (2019). https://github.com/MarkoKleineBuening/LLUMC-Publications

22. Koopman, P.: A case study of Toyota unintended acceleration and software safety. Carnegie Mellon University Presentation, September 2014

23. Kroening, D., Tautschnig, M.: CBMC – C bounded model checker. In: Ábrahám, E., Havelund, K. (eds.) TACAS 2014. LNCS, vol. 8413, pp. 389–391. Springer, Heidelberg (2014). https://doi.org/10.1007/978-3-642-54862-8_26

24. Le Lann, G.: An analysis of the Ariane 5 flight 501 failure-a system engineering perspective. In: Proceedings of the International Conference and Workshop on Engineering of Computer-Based Systems, 1997, pp. 339–346 (1997)

25. Leveson, N.G., Turner, C.S.: An investigation of the Therac-25 accidents. Computer **26**(7), 18–41 (1993)

26. The LLVM Compiler Infrastructure. http://llvm.org/. Accessed Nov 2018
27. Merz, F.: Theory and Implementation of Software Bounded Model Checking. Ph.D. thesis, Dissertation, Karlsruher Institut für Technologie (KIT) (2016)
28. Merz, F., Falke, S., Sinz, C.: LLBMC: Bounded model checking of C and C++ programs using a compiler IR. Verified Software: Theories, Tools, Experiments (2012)
29. Sorensson, N., Een, N.: An Extensible SAT-solver. In: 6th International Conference of the Theory and Applications of Satisfiability Testing, SAT 2003, Santa Margherita Ligure, Italy, 5–8 May 2003, pp. 502–518 (2003)
30. Suda, M.: Property directed reachability for automated planning. J. Artif. Intell. Res. (JAIR) **50**, 265–319 (2014)
31. Suda, M.: Dimspec, a format for specifying symbolic transition systems (2016). http://forsyte.at/dimspec
32. SV-Benchmarks. https://github.com/sosy-lab/sv-benchmarks/. Accessed 01 Nov 2018
33. Tange, O., et al.: Gnu parallel-the command-line power tool. USENIX Mag. **36**(1), 42–47 (2011)

SMTBCF: Efficient Backbone Computing for SMT Formulas

Yueling Zhang$^{(\boxtimes)}$, Geguang Pu$^{(\boxtimes)}$, and Min Zhang$^{(\boxtimes)}$

East China Normal University, Shanghai 200062, China
ylzhang.ecnu@gmail.com,{ggpu,mzhang}@sei.ecnu.edu.cn

Abstract. SMT (Satisfiable Module Theory) formulas have been widely used in practical applications. In some of the applications, including finding program bugs, plainly solving an SMT formula is sufficient. For other applications, besides solving the SMT formula, backbone variables of the SMT formulas are also needed in order to tackle the practical problems including finding invariant of certain properties in program analysis. This paper proposed a new approach **SMTBCF** to compute backbone variables for SMT formulas in order to accelerate the computing of backbone variables in SMT formulas and increase the efficiency of SMT formulas in practical applications. **SMTBCF** is the first algorithm that uses the backbone predicates to find part of the backbone variables in the SMT formulas. **SMTBCF** is also the first algorithm that uses the constants in the relating predicates of a backbone variable to quickly find the Unsatisfiable Evaluation of the backbone variable. In this way, **SMTBCF** is able to find backbone variables of SMT formulas, reduce the number of SMT solving in SMT backbone computing, and increase the efficiency of backbone variables in SMT formulas.

Keywords: Backbone · SMT · Verification

1 Introduction

During the years, SAT formulas and its applications have been widely used in computer science areas. Biere et al. [1] use SAT formulas to prove the correctness of properties in the systems. By encoding hardware states into SAT formulas, the BMC (Bounded Model Checking) method is able to prove the correctness of some properties within the given bounded steps. Bradley [2] also encodes hardware states into SAT formulas and uses it to check the safety properties of the system, without unrolling the states, IC3 is able to prove the correctness of some properties in all the possible states with the help of reachability analysis.

There are backbone variables in SAT formulas that are always assigned to true in every solution of the formula. Both BMC and IC3 will benefit from backbone computing of SAT formulas since the SAT solving in them are incremental, finding backbone variables in an earlier SAT solving will accelerate the efficiency of the following SAT solving. The identification of backbone improves the performance of random SAT solvers [3,4,6], Lin-Kernighan local search algorithms for

© Springer Nature Switzerland AG 2019
Y. Ait-Ameur and S. Qin (Eds.): ICFEM 2019, LNCS 11852, pp. 36–51, 2019.
https://doi.org/10.1007/978-3-030-32409-4_3

Travel Salesman Problem [5] and the post-silicon fault localization in integrated circuits [7,8]. It also improves the performance of chip verification [9], graph coloring problems [11], and the artificial intelligence strategies generation [10]. Therefore, computing backbone variables is useful in practice for SAT applications. Based on the impacts of backbone variables with SAT formulas, it is convincing that backbone variables are also going to be helpful in SMT formulas and applications.

Combined with specific background theories (logics) and propositional logic, SMT formulas are able to express more complicate applications. For example, Abdulla et al. [12] use SMT formulas and SMT solvers to check the security of web applications, Barnett et al. [13] use SMT formulas and SMT solvers to verify the correctness of programs, and Cadar et al. [14] use SMT formulas and SMT solvers in symbolic execution to automatically generate testing cases for programs. Katz et al. [15] use SMT formulas and SMT solvers (customized) to find adversarial examples of Deep Neural Network and verify the robustness of Deep Neural Network.

There are also backbone variables in SMT formulas, for a backbone variable x of a given SMT formula F, there must exist at least one assignment s of x, such that F is not satisfiable if x is assigned to s. Similar to SAT backbone variables, SMT backbone variables are also able to accelerate the following SMT solving, explain the reasons why a certain property holds or does not hold in an SMT formula, which is helpful in practice.

For instance, in Linear Optimization applications, given an encoded SMT formula F and an object variable o, SMT solving is able to solve the maximum value of o with the given constraints, but we are not able to find which variables of F are important to keep o greater than the threshold t. By adding the constraint $v(o) > t$ to the original SMT formula F to build F', and computing the backbone variables of F', important factors that keep the value of o greater than t are recognized, the backbone variables of F' are exactly the important factors. In program testing and verification, the reasons that cause certain errors are able to found by backbone variables. In Deep Neural Network Robustness verification, the reasons that cause adversarial examples are able to found by backbone variables.

In this paper, an SMT formula F is first converted to a corresponding SAT formula F_b, if F_b is not satisfiable, then F is not satisfiable and no backbone variable is in F. If F_b is satisfiable and there are backbone variables in F_b, then the corresponding predicates p in F are the backbone predicates. For a backbone predicate p in F, the SMT variable $x \in p$ is a backbone variable of F if x is the only variable in p. If there is no backbone variable in F_b, then SMTBCF selects a variable x in F based on a certain sorting and checks if x is a backbone variable. If there exists an assignment s of x such that when x is assigned to s, F is unsatisfiable, then x is a backbone variable. After finding a backbone variable, SMTBCF computes the Largest Satisfiable Evaluation Range R_F^x for every backbone variable x. There does not exist an assignment s' of x such that $s' \notin R_F^x$ and F is satisfiable when the value of x is s'.

There are 3 main contributions in this paper:

(1) A systematic framework from the view of Evaluation (Range) to define and describe the backbone variable of SMT formulas has been proposed.
(2) An efficient algorithm to find the backbone variables of SMT formulas has been proposed.
(3) An efficient algorithm to compute the Largest Satisfiable Evaluation Range of a given backbone variable x for an SMT formula has been proposed.

2   Preliminaries

A SAT (Satisfiability) formula F consists of SAT clauses, a SAT clause c consists of SAT variables, a SAT variable x is a Boolean variable, a literal l is either a SAT variable x of its negation $\neg x$, $x = \neg\neg x$.

For a given SAT formula F, $C(F)$ represents the set of clauses that are in F, for a clause c if $c \in C(F)$, then $c \in F$. For a given SAT clause c, $X(c)$ represents the set of variables that are in c, for a variable x if $x \in X(c)$, then $x \in c$. For a given SAT clause c, $L(c)$ represents the set of literals that are in c, for a literal l if $l \in L(c)$, then $l \in c$. For a given SAT formula F, $X(F)$ represents the set of literals that are in F, for a variable x if $x \in X(F)$, the $x \in F$. For a given SAT formula F, $L(F)$ represents the set of literals that are in F, for a literal l if $x \in L(F)$, the $l \in F$.

A SAT formula F is the conjunction of every clause in $C(F)$, i.e., $F = \bigwedge, c \in C(F)$. A SAT clause c is the disjunction of every literal in $L(c)$, i.e., $F = \bigvee, l \in X(c)$.

Example 1 (SAT Formula). $F = (a \vee b) \wedge (a \vee \neg b)$ is a SAT formula, the clauses in F are $a \vee b$ and $a \vee \neg b$, the variables in F are a and b, the literals in F are a, b and $\neg b$. The variables in $a \vee \neg b$ are a and b and the literals in $a \vee \neg b$ are a and $\neg b$.

Similar to SAT formula, an SMT (satisfiable modulo theory) formula consists of SMT constraints c, an SMT constraints consists of SMT predicates p, an SMT predicate consists of SMT variables x. an SMT variable is a variable in the background modulo theory of the SMT formula. In this paper, we focus on LIA (Linear Integer Arithmetic) Theory, such that an SMT variable is an Integer variable. A predicate is a sub-formula consisted of SMT variable and LIA computing symbols (operators), including equals to (=), greater than >, less than <, addition (+)... A formula is a conjunction of constraints, the conjunction/disjunction of predicates is a constraint.

$X(F)$ is the set of SMT variables in a given formula F, if $x \in X(F)$ then x is an SMT variable of F, denoted as $x \in F$. $X(c)$ is the set of SMT variables in a given constraint c, if $x \in X(c)$ then x is an SMT variable of c, denoted as $x \in c$. $X(p)$ is the set of SMT variables in a given predicate p, if $x \in X(p)$ then x is an SMT variable of c, denoted as $x \in p$. $P(F)$ is the set of SMT predicates in a given formula F, if $p \in P(F)$ then p is an SMT predicate of F, denoted as $p \in F$. $C(F)$ is the set of SMT constraints in a given formula F, if $c \in C(F)$ then c is an SMT constraint of F, denoted as $c \in F$.

Example 2 (SMT Formula). $F = ((x > 0) \lor (x + y > 0)) \land (y = 2)$ is an SMT formula. The set of SMT constraints in F are $(x > 0) \lor (x + y > 0)$ and $y = 2$, the SMT predicates in $(x > 0) \lor (x + y > 0)$ are $x > 0$ and $x + y > 0$, the SMT variable in $x > 0$ is x, and the SMT variables in $x + y > 0$ are x and y. $x > 0$ is an SMT predicate of F and $x + y > 0$ is also an SMT predicate of F.

Definition 1 (SAT Assignment). *A SAT assignment a is a function that maps each variable $x \in F$ to either true or false, i.e., $a : x \to \{0, 1\}$ for every $x \in F$. An assignment (value) of a variable x is the value of x has been assigned in the given assignment, i.e., an assignment (value) of x is $a(x)$, a is the given assignment.*

Given an assignment a, the value of F is either *true* of *false*, if the value of F is *true*, then a is a model of F, denoted as $a \models F$. If F a satisfiable formula, there must exist a model $v \models F$, if F is an unsatisfiable formula, then for every assignment a of F, $a \not\models F$.

Definition 2 (SMT Assignment). *In SMT formulas with LIA as background theory, an SMT assignment a is a function that maps each variable $x \in F$ to Integers, i.e., $a : x \to I$, for every $x \in F$, where I is the set of all Integers. an SMT assignment also assigns every predicate $p \in F$ to either true or false, i.e., $a : p \to \{0, 1\}$ for every $p \in F$. An assignment (value) of a variable x is the value of x has been assigned in the given assignment, i.e., an assignment (value) of x is $a(x)$, a is the given assignment.*

An SMT assignment a is called a model of F if the value of F under the assignment of a is *true*, i.e., $a \models F$.

For every SMT formula F, there is a *corresponding SAT formula F_b* of F. The set of variables $X(F_b)$ is the same size as the set of predicates in $P(F)$, i.e., for every $p \in F$, there exists a SAT variable $x_b \in F_b$, and for every such (p, x) in F and F_b, there exists an SMT assignment a and a SAT assignment a_b such that $a(p) = a(x_b)$.

Suppose F_b is a corresponding formula of an SMT formula F, F is unsatisfiable if F_b is unsatisfiable, but F might still be unsatisfiable even if F_b is satisfiable, because F needs to satisfy the constraints from the background theory additionally.

Definition 3 (Predicate Valid Evaluation). *For an SMT formula F and a predicate $p \in F$, the Valid Evaluation of $x \in p$ is an assignment x such that there exists an assignment a, where $a(p) = true$ and $a(x) = s$.*

A Valid Range of an SMT variable x in a predicate p is the set of all the Valid Evaluation of $x \in p$. For simplicity, if there is only one SMT variable x in a predicate p, this paper assumes that the Valid Range of $x \in p$ is a subset of the Range of all the parameters in the background Modulo Theory, otherwise the predicate p is removed since is trivial.

Definition 4 (SAT Backbone Variable). *For a SAT formula F, x is a backbone variable of F, if for every model $v \models F$, $v(x) = 0$ for all the time or $v(x) = 1$ for all the time. $v(x)$ is always assigned to 1 in all the models of F, if x is called a backbone literal of F, otherwise $\neg x$ is called a backbone literal of F.*

If a SAT variable x is not a backbone variable of F, then x is a non-backbone variable of F, indicating that there exists at least two models v_1, v_2 of F such that $v_1(x) = 0$ and $v_2(x) = 1$.

Definition 5 (Satisfiable Evaluation of x). *For an SMT formula F, an SMT variable $x \in F$, and an assignment s_F^x of x, s_F^x is called a satisfiable Evaluation of x, if there exists a model $v \models F$ such that $v(x) = s_F^x$.*

For a constraint $c \in F$, s_c^x is a satisfiable Evaluation of x to c if there exists a model $v \models c$ such that $v(x) = s_c^x$.

Definition 6 (Unsatisfiable Evaluation of x). *For an SMT formula F, an SMT variable $x \in F$, and an assignment $s_F^{\hat{x}}$ of x, $s_F^{\hat{x}}$ is called the Unsatisfiable Evaluation of x, if for every assignment a of F such that $a(x) = s_F^{\hat{x}}$, a is not the model of F.*

For a constraint $c \in F$, $s_c^{\hat{x}}$ is a Unsatisfiable Evaluation of x to c if there does not exist a model $v \models c$ such that $v(x) = s_c^{\hat{x}}$.

Similarly, for a non-backbone SAT variable x, there does not exist an Unsatisfiable Evaluation of x, for a backbone SAT variable x, the Unsatisfiable Evaluation of x is 0 (*false*).

Definition 7 (Satisfiable Evaluation Range of x). *For an SMT formula F, an SMT variable $x \in F$, and a evaluation range r_F^x for x, r_F^x is a satisfiable Evaluation Range of x, if for every $s \in r_F^x$, s is a satisfiable Evaluation of x.*

For a constraint $c \in F$, r_c^x is the Satisfiable Evaluation Range of x to c if $\forall s \in r_c^x$, s is a satisfiable Evaluation of x to c.

For a range r' if r' is a continuous sub-range of the Satisfiable Evaluation Range of x, then r' is called a continuous Satisfiable Evaluation Sub-Range of x.

Definition 8 (Unsatisfiable Evaluation Range of x). *For an SMT formula F, an SMT variable $x \in F$, and a evaluation range $r_F^{\hat{x}}$ for x, $r_F^{\hat{x}}$ is a Unsatisfiable Evaluation Range of x, if for every $s \in r_F^{\hat{x}}$, s is a Unsatisfiable Evaluation of x.*

For an SMT formula F and an SMT variable $x \in F$, the intersection of r_F^x and $r_F^{\hat{x}}$ is empyt, because a value s can not be both a satisfiable Evaluation of x and an Unsatisfiable Evaluation of x at the same time.

For a constraint $c \in F$, $r_F^{\hat{x}}$ is the Unsatisfiable Evaluation Range of x to c if $\forall s \in r_F^{\hat{x}}$, s is a Unsatisfiable Evaluation of x to c.

For a range r' if r' is a continuous sub-range of the Unsatisfiable Evaluation Range of x, then r' is called a continuous Unsatisfiable Evaluation Sub-Range of x.

Definition 9 (SMT Backbone Predicate). *For an SMT formula F, p is a backbone predicate of F, if for every model $v \models F$, $v(p) = 1$.*

Definition 10 (SMT Backbone Variable). *For an SMT formula F, x is a backbone variable of F, if there exists at least exist an assignment s of x, when the value of x is s, F is not satisfiable.*

Lemma 1. *Given an SMT formula F, a backbone variable x of F, there must exist an Unsatisfiable Evaluation of x.*

For every backbone variable x of an SMT formula F, the Largest Satisfiable Evaluation Range of x is denoted as R_F^x, there does not exist a satisfiable Evaluation s of x such that $s \notin R_F^x$. For every continuous Satisfiable Evaluation Sub-Range of r_F^x of x, $r_F^x \subseteq R_F^x$. The Largest Satisfiable Evaluation Range R_F^x of x is the intersection of the Largest Satisfiable Evaluation Range R_c^x of x to every clause c, i.e., $R_F^x = \bigcap r_c^x, c \in F$.

For every backbone variable x of an SMT formula F, the Least Unsatisfiable Evaluation Range of x is denoted as $\hat{R}_F^x$, there does not exist a satisfiable Evaluation s of x such that $s \in \hat{R}_F^x$. For every continuous Unsatisfiable Evaluation Sub-Range of $r_F^{\hat{x}}$ of x, $r_F^{\hat{x}} \subseteq \hat{R}_F^x$. The Least Unsatisfiable Evaluation Range $\hat{R}_F^x$ of x is the union of the Least Unsatisfiable Evaluation Range $\hat{R}_c^x$ of x to every clause c, i.e., $\hat{R}_F^x = \bigcup r_c^{\hat{x}}, c \in F$.

Notice that an Unsatisfiable Evaluation $\hat{s}$ of x can not be computed by simply solve the SMT formula $\neg F$. For example, for the formula $x + y > 0$, $x = 1$ and $y = -2$ is a model of $\neg F$, but $x = 1$ and $y = 2$ is also a model of F. Since the computing of backbone variables only focus on a single variable x, it is easy for both F and $\neg F$ are satisfiable with the same assignment of x. Therefore, the quantifier SMT solving have to be used without consider the structure of the SMT formula, in this case, the quantifier SMT formula is $\exists \hat{s} \forall v, s.t.v(x) = \hat{s}, v \models \neg F$. Actually, neither x nor y is a backbone variable of F.

3 Systematic Framework for Backbone Variables of SMT Formulas

A systematic framework to define and describe the properties of backbone variables of SMT formulas form the range interval view is proposed in this section. Given an SMT formula F, and a variable x, if x is a backbone variable of F, then there exists at least an Unsatisfiable Evaluation of x, otherwise, there does not exist an Unsatisfiable Evaluation of x.

If x is not a backbone variable of F, the only way to know is using quantifier SMT solving. If x is a backbone variable of F, then the Largest Satisfiable Evaluation Range of x is a piece-wise interval, separating by the Unsatisfiable Evaluations. Therefore, by using the constants in the constraints c such that $x \in c$, an Unsatisfiable Evaluation $\hat{s}$ could be guessed, and the backbone checking of x could be finished without quantifier SMT solving. Since quantifier SMT solving is extremely time consuming, by reducing quantifier SMT solving, efficiency has been improved.

Figure 1 shows the Largest Satisfiable Evaluation Range of x in the formula $F = (x \leq -2 \wedge x \geq -4) \vee (x \leq 4 \wedge x \geq 2) \wedge (x + y > 0)$, as observed from Fig. 1, the Largest Satisfiable Evaluation Range of x in F are piece-wise intervals. Actually, in SMT formulas that use Linear Integer Arithmetic as background Modulo Theory, the evaluation range of an SMT variable x are always piece-wise intervals. To compute the Largest Satisfiable Evaluation Range R_F^x of x, only Unsatisfiable Evaluation Ranges $\hat{R}_F^x$ of x is needed, since the complementing set of R_F^x is $\hat{R}_F^x$.

Fig. 1. Largest Satisfiable Evaluation Range of x for a given formula F

A continuous Unsatisfiable Evaluation Range $\hat{r}$ is able to be computed with an Unsatisfiable Evaluation $\hat{s} \in \hat{r}$. Therefore, by using the constants in each constraint c such that $x \in c$, Unsatisfiable Evaluations are computed and Unsatisfiable Evaluation Ranges are computed correspondingly. After finding all Unsatisfiable Evaluation Ranges from the constant in constraints, only one quantifier SMT solving is needed to check there is no other Unsatisfiable Evaluation.

For a SAT formula, if x is a backbone variable of F, then either *true* or *false* is an Unsatisfiable Evaluation of x, and applications of SAT formulas are able to accelerate the computing efficiency by avoiding the Unsatisfiable Evaluation. For an SMT formula, if x is a backbone variable of F, there must exists at least an Unsatisfiable Evaluation of x, and there must exist at least one Unsatisfiable Evaluation Range of x. In order to accelerate SMT applications by avoiding the Unsatisfiable Evaluation Range of x, we need to compute the Largest Satisfiable Evaluation Range of x, i.e., R_F^x. Figure 2 shows the overall working flow of SMTBCF finding backbone variables in an SMT formulas and computing the corresponding Largest Satisfiable Evaluation Ranges.

For a given SMT formula F, SMTBCF first computes the corresponding SAT formula F_b of F. If F_b is not satisfiable, SMTBCF terminates since F is not satisfiable, otherwise, SMTBCF computes the backbone variables of F_b. For every backbone variable x_b in F_b, there exists a corresponding backbone predicate p in F, if there is only one single SMT variable x in F, then x is a backbone variable of F, and x is in the set of $BX(F, 0)$.

The set of backbone variables of F is $BX(F)$, and SMTBCF gradually finds all variables in $BX(F)$. For the rest of variables $X(F) \setminus BX(F, 0)$ in F, SMTBCF assigns a certain weight to each variable and sorts them in a descending order based on their weights. For a variable x, if x appears multiple times in a constraint $c \in F$, then the weight of x is 3, if x appears in a constraint c with some other known backbone variables x', the weight of x is 2, for the rest of the variables, the weight of them are 1. With the computing of SMTBCF , the weights of variables may change. SMTBCF then start to check if a variable x is a backbone variable or not, starting with the variables that have the greatest weights. Notice that with more and more backbone variables found by SMT-BCF , the variables that are originally weighted as 1 may increase their weights to 2 as they may appear in the same constraints with some newly found backbone variables. During the checking, SMTBCF uses the constants in the related constraints of x to find an Unsatisfiable Evaluation s quickly.

4   Design and Implementation of **SMTBCF**

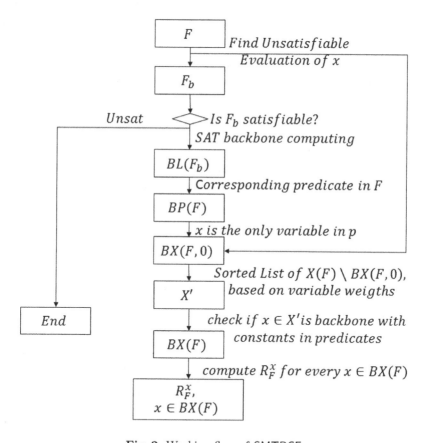

Fig. 2. Working flow of SMTBCF

After finding all backbone variables in F, SMTBCF then computes the Largest Satisfiable Evaluation Range R_F^x of x using the constants in each related constraints and the quantifier SMT solving. For a backbone variable x, SMTBCF uses the constants in constraints that x appears and the known Largest Satisfiable

Range of backbone variables that appears in the same constraint c to find the Unsatisfiable Evaluation Ranges of x, the Unsatisfiable Evaluation Ranges of x found this way (without quantifier SMT solving) are in the set of $\neg R$. After finding all ranges in $\neg R$, SMTBCF uses only one quantifier SMT solving to check if all Unsatisfiable Evaluation Ranges of x are found.

4.1   Find Backbone Variables Using Backbone Predicates

To find backbone predicates of a given SMT formula F, the corresponding SAT formula F_b of F need to built. For every $p \in F$, there exists a SAT variable x_b in F_b, the same conjunctions and disjunctions operate on every p are also operate on every x_b. For example, for an SMT formula $F = ((x > 2) \vee (x < 4)) \wedge (y > 3) \wedge (x + y > 0)$, there are 4 predicates in F, including $x > 2$, $x < 4$, $y > 3$, $x + y > 0$, then there are 4 SAT variables in F_b, and x_b^1 denotes $x > 2$, x_b^2 denotes $x < 4$, x_b^3 denotes $y > 3$ and x_b^4 denotes $x + y > 0$. The corresponding SAT formula F_b of F is $F_b = (x_b^1 \vee x_b^2) \wedge x_b^3 \wedge x_b^4$. After building F_b, this paper uses on-the-shelf tool to compute backbone variables of F_b, including minibones in [16], and DUCIBone in [17]

Theorem 1. *Given an SMT formula F and an SMT predicate $p \in F$, if p is a backbone predicate of F, and x is the only SMT variable in p, then x is a backbone variable of F.*

Proof. For an SMT formula F and a backbone predicate $p \in F$, then for every model $v \models F$, $v(p) = 1$. And if x is the only SMT variable in p, then the Valid Range of $x \in p$ is a subset of the background modulo theory. The there must exist an Unsatisfiable Evaluation s of x such that s is in the range of the background modulo theory, but s is not in the Valid Range of $x \in p$. Therefore, x is a backbone variable of F.

4.2   Intuition of Weighting Variables in SMT Formulas

Although SMTBCF is able to find backbone variables using backbone predicates, but there are still backbone variables that can't be found using backbone predicates. For example, given a formula $F = (x > 3) \vee (x < 1)$, x is a backbone variable of F since when $x = 2$, F is not satisfiable, but in the corresponding SAT formula $F_b = x_b^1 \vee x_b^2$, neither x_b^1 nor x_b^2 is a backbone variable of F_b. This is because that the constraints with the background modulo theory is the reason that making the SMT variable x as a backbone variable, and the constraints related with the background modulo theory can not be transferred into the SAT formula F_b. Therefore, there is no backbone variable in F_b.

To deal with the constraints lost in the transferring, SMTBCF checks each variable $x \in F$ to determine if x is a backbone variable or not.

For the variables in $X(F) \setminus BX(F, 0)$, SMTBCF assigns weights to the variables and sorts the weights in a descending order to generate an ordered list of $X(F) \setminus BX(F, 0)$, which is X_s. For a variable x in X_s, if x appears multiple times in a constraint $c \in F$, then the weight of x is 3. If x is in the same constraint $c \in F$ with a known backbone variable x', then the weight of x is 2. Otherwise, the weight of x is 1. With more and more backbone variables in $BX(F)$ known by SMTBCF , the weight of a variable may change to 2 (for the variables that has the weight of 1 only).

Observation 1. *Given an SMT formula F and a constraint $c \in F$, if a variable x appears multiple times in c then x is more likely to be a backbone variable.*

There are two kinds of reason for a variable to become a backbone variable in an SMT formula, propositional logical reasons and modulo theory logical reasons. In this paper, the modulo theory used is Linear Integer Arithmetic Theory, for a constraint $c \in F$, if a variable x appears for multiple times, then there is a chance for x to become a backbone variable because of the modulo theory logical reasons.

Observation 2. *Given an SMT formula F and a constraint $c \in F$, if there is another known backbone variable $x' \in c$, then x is more likely to be a backbone variable.*

For an SMT formula F and a constraint $c \in F$, if c already has a known backbone variable x', then if x' is the only variable in a predicate $p \in c$, the value of p could be *false* in all the models of F, which may force another predicate p to be assigned to *true* in all the models of F. Therefore, the variable $x \in p$ may become a backbone variable because of the constraint c.

Based on the two observations, the paper weights different variables differently. The different weighting could be considered as heuristic strategies.

After weighting all the variables in $X(F) \setminus BX(F, 0)$, SMTBCF sorts all the weighted variables in an descending order based on their weights. The sorted list of the variables is X_s. SMTBCF then decide the variable in X_s to be a backbone variable or not one by one. Algorithm 1 shows the procedure used in SMTBCF to decide whether a variable x is a backbone variable or not. At Line 2, Algorithm 1 starts a loop for every constraint $c \in F$ that has the current variable x, at Line 3, Algorithm 1 starts a loop for every predicate $p \in c$ that has the current variable x. At Line 4, Algorithm 1 gathers all constants appears in p. For each constant c in p, Algorithm 1 checks the satisfiability of F when x is assigned to c at Line 6. If F is unsatisfiable with the current configuration (c), then c is an Unsatisfiable Evaluation of x, and x is a backbone variable of F. Otherwise, at Line 11, Algorithm 1 finds the constants in the Largest Satisfiable Evaluation Ranges of all known backbone variables in p. At Line 12, Algorithm 1 then combines the constants C found in p, the constants R found in the range r of known backbone variables in p, and the arithmetic symbols in p together, and generates a set of new constants. The new constants are generated as follows: Suppose the constant in p is c, a constant in the range of a known backbone variable in p is r, and one of the symbol is $\circ$, the constants are $c \circ r$, $c \circ (r + 1)$, and $c \circ (r - 1)$. If there are k constants in the ranges of known backbone variables and there are m symbols in p, the number of new constants generated by the combination are $3 * k * m$.

For each new constant generated from Line 12, Algorithm 1 checks the satisfiability of F when x is assigned to a value $const'$ in the new constants at Line 14.

If F is satisfiable when x is assigned to $const'$, then Algorithm 1 uses quantifier SMT solving at Line 19 to confirm that there is no Unsatisfiable Evaluation of x and x is a non-backbone variable. Otherwise, x is a backbone variable.

If x is a backbone variable, x is added to $BX(F)$ and the Largest Satisfiable Evaluation Range of x is computed immediately. If x is a non-backbone variable, x is added to $NBX(F)$.

An example is given for Algorithm 1, for a given formula $F = (x > 3) \wedge (x + y < 5)$, Algorithm 1 first finds all constants in F, which are 3 and 0. For the constant 3, $SMT(F, x, 3)$ is not satisfiable, therefore, x is a backbone variable and the valid range of x is $(3, \infty)$. For the constant 4, $SMT(F, x, 4)$ is satisfiable and $SMT(F, y, 4)$ is also satisfiable, the combine strategy is triggered in Algorithm 1. The symbols (operators) of the combines are $+$ and $-$, and the new constants returned by the $Combine(Const, R, symbols)$ are -1, 1, and 7, and $SMT(F, y, 7)$ is not satisfiable, therefore, y is also a backbone variable and the valid range of y is $(-\infty, 1)$. Algorithm 1 has now successfully proved that both x and y are backbone variables.

4.3   Compute Largest Satisfiable Ranges of Backbone Variables

After finding a backbone variable x, SMTBCF immediately computes the Largest Satisfiable Evaluation Range of x. Since the Largest Satisfiable Evaluation Range of known backbone variables are useful in the backbone checking of related variables, i.e., variables that appear in the same constraint with x.

Algorithm 2 shows the procedure to compute the Largest Satisfiable Evaluation Range of a backbone variable x. At Line 2, the Largest Satisfiable Evaluation Range of x is initialized as the Valid of Range of Parameters in the Background Theory, in ILA Theory, the valid range is $\mathbf{Z}$. At Line 5, Algorithm 2 finds all constants appears in the current predicate p, such that $x \in p$, and at Line 6, Algorithm 2 finds all constants appears in the Largest Satisfiable Evaluation Range of known backbone variables that also appears in the predicate, if there is no known backbone variables in the predicate, then E is an empty set.

Algorithm 2 then combines the set of C, E, and the symbols in p together to generate a set of new constants $Const'$, with the same strategy used in Algorithm 1. Then Algorithm 2 starts a loop to check the satisfiability of F when x is assigned to every new constant in $Const'$, if F is not satisfiable when x is assigned to current $const'$, it means $const'$ is an Unsatisfiable Evaluation of x. Algorithm 2 uses upper boundary SMT solving to find the least Satisfiable Evaluation $ub(const')$ of x such that $ub(const') > const'$ (at Line 11), and uses lower boundary SMT solving to find the largest Satisfiable Evaluation $lb(const')$ of x such that $const' > lb(const')$ (at Line 12). Then $(lb(const'), ub(const'))$ is a continuous Unsatisfiable Evaluation Range of x, and is excluded from R_F^x at Line 13.

Algorithm 1. Decide a Variable x to Be a Backbone Variable

---

1 **Procedure** CHECK($F, x, BX(F)$)
2   **foreach** $c, s.t. x \in c$ **do**
3   **foreach** $p \in c$ **do**
4              $Const := Constant(p)$;
5   **foreach** $const \in C$ **do**
6                  $ret := SMT(F, x, const)$;
7   **if** $!ret$ **then**
8                      $BX(F) := BX(F) \cup \{x\}$;
9                      $compute Range(x)$;
10   **return** $true$;
11             $R := Range(p)$;
12             $Const' := Combine(Const, R, symbols)$;
13   **foreach** $const' \in Const'$ **do**
14                 $ret := SMT(F, x, const')$;
15   **if** $!ret$ **then**
16                     $BX(F) := BX(F) \cup \{x\}$;
17                     $compute Range(x)$;
18   **return** $true$;
19     $ret := SMT(F, x, q)$;
20   **if** $!ret$ **then**
21         $BX(F) := BX(F) \cup \{x\}$;
22         $compute Range(x)$;
23   **return** $true$;
24     $NBX(F) := NBX(F) \cup \{x\}$;
25   **return** $false$;

Algorithm 2 then checks if there still exists an Unsatisfiable Evaluation u in the current R_F^x at Line 14, if there does not exist such an Unsatisfiable Evaluation, then R_F^x is the Largest Satisfiable Evaluation Range of x. Otherwise, Algorithm 2 uses the Unsatisfiable Evaluation u to compute another continuous Unsatisfiable Evaluation Range of x, updated R_F^x by excluding the new Unsatisfiable Evaluation Range and check if there still exists an Unsatisfiable Evaluation u again (from Line 19 to Line 22). A detailed example of how Algorithm 2 works is given in Sect. 5.1 with Table 2.

5 Efficiency Analysis

5.1 Demo Analysis

Given a formula $F = (x \leq 7 \vee (x \geq 11 \wedge x \leq 13) \vee (x \leq 16 \wedge x \geq 20)) \wedge (x + y \leq 0)$, the computing procedure of $BBopt$ is shown in Table 1 and the computing procedure of SMTBCF is shown in Table 2.

In Table 1, there are 11 steps needs to be executed to compute the backbone variables and the Largest Satisfiable Evaluation Range of backbone variables

---

Algorithm 2. Compute the Largest Satisfiable Evaluation Range of a Backbone x

---

1 **Procedure** RANGE(F, x)
2      $R_F^x := \mathbf{Z}$;
3   **foreach** $c, s.tx \in c$ **do**
4   **foreach** $p \in c$ **do**
5                $Const := Constant(p)$;
6                $E := Evaluation(p)$;
7                $Const' := Combine(Const, E, symbols)$;
8   **foreach** $const' \in Const$; **do**
9                     $ret := SMT(F, x, const')$;
10   **if** $!ret$ **then**
11                         $ub(const') := SMT(F, x, const', u)$;
12                         $lb(const') := SMT(F, x, const', l)$;
13                         $R_F^x := R_F^x \setminus (lb(const'), ub(const'))$;
14      $(ret, u) := SMT(F, x, R_F^x)$;
15   **if** ret **then**
16   **return** R_F^x;
17   **else**
18   **while** $!ret$ **do**
19                $U := U \cup \{u\}$;
20                $ub := SMT(F, x, u)$;
21                $lb := SMT(F, x, l)$;
22                $R_F^x := R_F^x \setminus (lb, ub)$;
23                $(ret, u) := SMT(F, x, R_F^x)$;
24   **return** R_F^x;

---

in F. The second and third columns show the Satisfiable Evaluation or Unsatisfiable Evaluation found by the current SMT solving, the forth and fifth columns indicate the current SMT solving is a Boundary SMT Solving or a Quantifier SMT Solving. In total, there are 6 Quantifier SMT Solving and 5 Boundary SMT solving executed.

In Table 2, there are only 10 times of Plain SMT Solving and 1 time of Quantifier SMT Solving are executed with the help of constants in the predicates. A Plain SMT Solving is to check if the given SMT formula is satisfiable with the given assignments to the variable x. The computing of a Plain SMT Solving is relatively faster than the computing of a Boundary SMT Solving or a computing of Quantifier SMT Solving. The efficient of SMTBCF is improved by using more Plain SMT solving and less Boundary or Quantifier SMT Solving.

5.2   General Analysis

Comparing to the existing tool BBopt [18], SMTBCF has three advantages that improves the efficiency. Firstly, SMTBCF uses the corresponding SAT formula F_b of an SMT formula F, by computing the backbone variables of F_b, SMTBCF is

Table 1. Backbone variables computing procedure of F using $BBopt$

Step	Satisfiable Evaluation	Unsatisfiable Evaluation	B-Solving	Q-Solving
1		21		✓
2	Continuous satisfiable range		$x > 21$	✓
3		14	$x < 21$	✓
4	16		$x > 14$	
5	Continuous satisfiable range		$16 < x < 21$	✓
6	13		$x < 14$	
7		8	$x < 13$	✓
8	11		$x > 8$	
9	Continuous satisfiable range		$11 < x < 13$	
10		7	$x < 8$	
11	Continuous satisfiable range		$x < 7$	✓

Table 2. Backbone variables computing procedure of F using SMTBCF

Step	Unsatisfiable Evaluation	P-Solving	B-Solving	Q-Solving
1	$8, 10, 14, 15, 21$			
2	$(7, 11), (13, 16), (20, +\infty)$	10		
3	Continuous satisfiable range			✓

able to find backbone predicates in F and find backbone variables in F directly from the backbone predicates, without using additional SMT solving.

Secondly, SMTBCF uses the constants in the predicates to find an Unsatisfiable Evaluation of x with a normal SMT solving, instead of a quantifier SMT solving. Thanks to the efficiency advantage of the normal SMT solving compared to the quantifier efficiency, SMTBCF improves the general efficiency of SMT backbone computing.

Thirdly, in computing the Largest Satisfiable Evaluation Range of backbone variables, SMTBCF is still able to use the information of the constants in the predicates and the ranges of other backbone variables. With the help of these constants, SMTBCF is able to enumerate large number of continuous Unsatisfiable Range of x using upper and lower boundaries SMT solving, which is also more efficient than the quantifier SMT solving used in other approaches.

6 Conclusion and Discussion

This paper proposed a new method to compute backbone variables of SMT formulas, using the backbone predicates of SMT formulas computed from the corresponding SAT formula, constants in the predicates of the SMT formula, and constants in the ranges of known backbone variables. SMTBCF is the first technique that uses backbone predicates and formula constants to compute the backbone variables of SMT formulas efficiently.

SMTBCF is designed for the Linear Integer Arithmetic (LIA) theory of SMT, which is widely used in program analysis and verification industrial, for other Arithmetic with continuous range for parameter values, SMTBCF is able to adapt with them.

Acknowledgements. Yueling Zhang is partially supported by the NSFC Projects (Nos. 61572197 and 61632005). Geguang Pu was partially supported by NSFC grant (No. 61572197). Min Zhang is partially supported by the NSFC Project (No. 61672012).

References

1. Biere, A.: Bounded model checking. Adv. Comput. **58**(11), 117–148 (2003)
2. Bradley, A.R.: Understanding IC3. In: Cimatti, A., Sebastiani, R. (eds.) SAT 2012. LNCS, vol. 7317, pp. 1–14. Springer, Heidelberg (2012). https://doi.org/10.1007/978-3-642-31612-8_1
3. Selman, B.: Local search strategies for satisfiability testing. Cliques Color. Satisf. Second DIMACS Implement. Chall. **26**, 521–532 (1993)
4. Zhang, W.: Backbone guided local search for maximum satisfiability. In: IJCAI 2013, pp: 1179–1186 (2003)
5. Zhang, W.: A novel local search algorithm for the traveling salesman problem that exploits backbones. In: IJCAI 2015, pp. 343–350 (2015)
6. Montanari, A.: Solving constraint satisfaction problems through belief propagation-guided decimation. arXiv preprint arXiv:0709.1667 (2007)
7. Zhu, C.S.: SAT-based techniques for determining backbones for post-silicon fault localization. In: IEEE International High Level Design Validation and Test Workshop (2011)
8. Zhu, C.S.: Post-silicon fault localization using maximum satisfiability and backbones. In: FMCAD 2011 (2011)
9. Velev, M.N.: Formal verification of VLIW microprocessors with speculative execution. In: Emerson, E.A., Sistla, A.P. (eds.) CAV 2000. LNCS, vol. 1855, pp. 296–311. Springer, Heidelberg (2000). https://doi.org/10.1007/10722167_24
10. Berg, J.: Cost-optimal constrained correlation clustering via weighted partial Maximum Satisfiability. Artif. Intell. **244**, 110–142 (2017)
11. Culberson, J.: Frozen development in graph coloring. Theor. Comput. Sci. **265**(1), 227–264 (2001)
12. Abdulla, P.A., et al.: Norn: an SMT solver for string constraints. In: Kroening, D., Păsăreanu, C.S. (eds.) CAV 2015. LNCS, vol. 9206, pp. 462–469. Springer, Cham (2015). https://doi.org/10.1007/978-3-319-21690-4_29
13. Barnett, M., Chang, B.-Y.E., DeLine, R., Jacobs, B., Leino, K.R.M.: Boogie: a modular reusable verifier for object-oriented programs. In: de Boer, F.S., Bonsangue, M.M., Graf, S., de Roever, W.-P. (eds.) FMCO 2005. LNCS, vol. 4111, pp. 364–387. Springer, Heidelberg (2006). https://doi.org/10.1007/11804192_17
14. Cadar, C.: KLEE: unassisted and automatic generation of high-coverage tests for complex systems programs. In: OSDI, pp. 209–224 (2008)

15. Katz, G., Barrett, C., Dill, D.L., Julian, K., Kochenderfer, M.J.: Reluplex: an efficient SMT solver for verifying deep neural networks. In: Majumdar, R., Kunčak, V. (eds.) CAV 2017. LNCS, vol. 10426, pp. 97–117. Springer, Cham (2017). https://doi.org/10.1007/978-3-319-63387-9_5
16. Janota, M.: Algorithms for computing backbones of propositional formulae. AI Commun. **28**(2), 161–177 (2015)
17. Zhang, Y.: Optimizing backbone filtering. In: TASE 2017, pp. 1–8. IEEE (2017)
18. Previti, A.: On Computing Generalized Backbones. In: ICTAI 2017, pp. 1050–1056. IEEE (2017)

Automatic Verification for Node-Based Visual Script Notation Using Model Checking

Isamu Hasegawa[1(✉)] and Tomoyuki Yokogawa[2(✉)]

[1] SQUARE ENIX CO., LTD., Tokyo, Japan
haseisam@square-enix.com
[2] Okayama Prefectural University, Okayama, Japan
t-yokoga@cse.oka-pu.ac.jp

Abstract. Visual script languages with a node-based interface have commonly been used in the video game industry. We examined the bug database obtained in the development of FINAL FANTASY XV (FFXV), and noticed that several types of bugs were caused by simple mis-descriptions of visual scripts and could therefore be mechanically detected.

We propose a method for the automatic verification of visual scripts in order to improve productivity of video game development. Our method can automatically detect those bugs by using symbolic model checking. We show a translation algorithm which can automatically convert a visual script to an input model for NuSMV that is an implementation of symbolic model checking.

For a preliminary evaluation, we applied our method to visual scripts used in the production for FFXV. The evaluation results demonstrate that our method can detect bugs of scripts and works well in a reasonable time.

Keywords: Formal methods · Symbolic model checking · Visual script · Game development

1 Introduction

In the recent video game industry, game designers write game logic using script languages. Since most of game designers are not familiar with writing programs, the use of visual script languages allow designers to perform such scripting operation, and thus help improve the productivity of game logic development. In particular, visual script languages with a node-based interface are widely used in game development.

However, it is hard to maintain game logic written in visual script languages because they can quickly become large and complicated during the course of production, and thus become hard to verify or modify, and very prone to human error.

© Springer Nature Switzerland AG 2019
Y. Ait-Ameur and S. Qin (Eds.): ICFEM 2019, LNCS 11852, pp. 52–68, 2019.
https://doi.org/10.1007/978-3-030-32409-4_4

We examined the bug database obtained in the development of FINAL FAN-TASY XV (FFXV) [7], and noticed that several types of bugs were caused indeed by simple mis-descriptions of visual scripts. A system that can automatically detect such mis-descriptions would had been a great help to our production.

Since most visual script implementations could be treated as a kind of state machine [8], and model checking is a well-researched technique to automatically verify finite state machines [5], we propose in this paper a method for automatic verification of visual script notations with symbolic model checking [3] for efficient game production. Our main contributions are the following. (1) To apply symbolic model checking to verify visual scripts, we provide a translation algorithm from a visual script description to an input model for NuSMV [5], that is an implementation of symbolic model checking. (2) We show a preliminary evaluation of our method by applying it to visual scripts which are produced in the development of FFXV, and demonstrate that most of the verification tasks are completed in a realistic amount of time.

The rest of this paper is organized as follows. We first introduce prerequisite topics and show a motivating example in Sect. 2. Section 3 explains the proposed method. Section 4 provides the translation algorithm from a visual script to an input model which can be accepted to NuSMV. Section 5 explains how to write node semantics. We show the results of our preliminary evaluation in Sect. 6 and conclude our work in Sect. 7.

2   Background

2.1   Model Checking

Model checking is an automatic technique for verifying correctness properties of a finite-state system [6]. The verification procedure is performed by an exhaustive search over the state space. Since the size of the state space exponentially increases with the number of system components, it is difficult to apply model checking to large-scale systems. Symbolic model checking can efficiently handle large-scale systems by replacing explicit state representation with boolean formula.

NuSMV [5] is one of the most successful implementations of symbolic model checking. The model verified by NuSMV is written by a specific input language (called SMV language). The properties to be checked is expressed by temporal logic LTL (Linear Temporal Logic) [14] and CTL (Computational Tree Logic) [1].

```
MODULE main
VAR
  sw : {on, off};
ASSIGN
  init(sw) := {on, off};
  next(sw) := case
    sw = on : off;
    TRUE : sw;
  esac;
CTLSPEC AG (AF sw = on)
```

Fig. 1. An example model described in SMV language

Figure 1 is an example of an input model to NuSMV. The input model described by SMV language is composed of variable declaration part (described by VAR) and transition relation definition part (described by ASSIGN). The property is expressed as a LTL formula (described by LTLSPEC) or a CTL formula (described by CTLSPEC).

This example has one variable sw which may have one of the two values on and off. In its initial state, either on or off is assigned to sw non-deterministically. In the case that sw is on, sw becomes off in the next state, or sw does not change its value. Thus the sequence of the value of sw can be either on, off, off ... (when the initial value is on) or off, off ... (when the initial value is off). The CTL formula in this example has two CTL operators **AG** and **AF**. **AG** represents "in Any path" and "Globally," and **AF** represents "in Any path" and "in the Future." This formula expresses the following property: the system always satisfies that sw necessarily becomes on. When the model is inputted to NuSMV, NuSMV returns FALSE for this property because there is a path where sw continues to be off. Figure 2 shows the result and the counterexample generated by NuSMV. The counterexample shows the path where sw continues to be off.

```
-- specification AG (AF sw = on)  is false
-- as demonstrated by the following
   execution sequence
Trace Description: CTL Counterexample
Trace Type: Counterexample
-> State: 1.1 <-
sw = on
-- Loop starts here
-> State: 1.2 <-
sw = off
-> State: 1.3 <-
```

Fig. 2. A counterexample generated by NuSMV

2.2 Motivating Example

Many game development environments have their own visual scripting system such as Blueprint in Unreal Engine [9,12,18]. Although there are slight differences among each visual scripting systems, their syntax and semantics are basically the same. In this paper, readers can assume Blueprint [18] as the visual scripting system since its syntax and semantics are very similar to our in-house visual scripting system.

In the development with node-based visual script languages, logic is described as a *node graph* which is composed of *nodes* and *edges*. Nodes express values, variables, arithmetic operators, or control statements of the visual script, which correspond to statements in text-based script languages such as if/while-statements, assignments, and so on. Since the purpose of visual scripts is to control game components such as sound, visual effect, and so on, many nodes express invocations of APIs of those components. For example, "Play SE" node notifies sound component of the game system to start playing sound effect, "Fade Out" node notifies screen effect component to start fade-out effect[1]. Edges connect nodes through input and output *ports*, and express data and control flows.

Figure 3 shows an example of visual script. Note that we omitted data flow edges in Fig. 3 such as the condition value inputted to If node. This is because our method does not address the detection of bugs caused by an illegal data flow. This example has the following behavior:

- When the Movie Clip node receives an input signal through the Start port, it starts playing the movie clip, and sends output signal through the Finished port when it finishes playing. If the movie clip is skipped by a game player, it sends output signal through the Skipped port instead of the Finished port.
- The Set Event Mode node modifies the global flag variable "event mode". When it receives the input signal through the Enable or Disable port, the event mode flag becomes true or false respectively. This example includes two Set Event Mode nodes, and both of them modify the same variable instance since the "event mode" variable is not a variable in the script but a variable in the external game system.
- The If node is used for conditional branch like if-statement in text-based languages. Its condition value is inputted through data flow port. As stated above, we omit such ports.
- The global flag variable "event mode" must be true during playing the movie clip, and must be false otherwise in order to change some game state during playing movie such as disabling gamepad, etc.

Note that Movie Clip node has its own state transition, and sends output Finished or Skipped independently from the original control flow. It means that there can be multiple activated nodes and multiple activated control signals in a graph. It is one of the significant differences of visual script languages from Statecharts and a reason that we can not directly apply prior research to visual script languages.

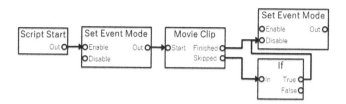

Fig. 3. An example of node-based visual script (including a typical bug)

This example contains a bug that actually often occurred during the development of FFXV. It appears that the False port of the If node has no connection.

---

[1] "fade out" is a gradual transition from the game screen to blank image, used in movies, games, etc.

Therefore, if Movie Clip branches to Skipped and then If branches to False, the event mode flag is not changed and remains to be true. It causes incorrect behavior since the event mode flag is true after playing the movie.

There were a wide variety of similar bugs during the development of FFXV, e.g. "BGM is not changed correctly in some cases.", "Enemy characters never respawn in a specific condition.", and so on. Moreover, since many game logic scripts are written by game designers who are not familiar with writing programs, scripts often become large and complicated. Therefore, it is tough to find those bugs by visual inspection, even though these are caused by trivial misdescriptions such as missing one node, or missing one edge, and so on. Our goal is to detect those large amounts of trivial but hard-to-find bugs automatically and exhaustively. Since our products already have a lot of massive scripts, we should cover not only newly written scripts but also those existing scripts.

2.3   Related Work

Video games essentially have a large number of combinations of internal states and external stimuli. This makes it difficult to detect problems which come out under specific conditions by testing. Model checking has been applied to video game developments since it can solve such problems by exhaustive verification. Moreno-Ger et al. [13] proposed a method for verifying game scripts created in ⟨e-Adventure⟩ platform using NuSMV. Radomski et al. [15] showed a framework in which video game logics are modeled by State Chart XML (SCXML) formalism and their properties can be checked by the SPIN model checker. Rezin et al. [16] developed a method to model a multi-player game design as a Kripke structure and to verify it by NuSMV. These studies show that applying model checking to video game development is very promising and application to game logic described by node-based visual scripts is also expected.

There have been a number of studies that have applied model checking to verification of node-based state transition system designs. Statecharts and its variants, such as UML state machine [17] and RSML (Requirements State Machine Language) [11], are one of the most popular notations for describing state transition systems in a node-based manner. Chan et al. [4] provided a translation from RSML notation to a model described by SMV language. This translation procedure encodes components of the inputted RSML by SMV variables and expresses changes of the components as transition relation. Zhao et al. [19] studied representation of Statecharts step-semantics as a Kripke structure, which is a graph-based state transition representation, and carried out verification using SMV model-checker. Jussila et al. [10] presented a representation of a subset of UML state machines as Promela which is an input language of SPIN model-checker.

In the semantics of Statecharts and its variants, their nodes represent states and only simple actions (enter/exit or do action in the case of UML state machine) can be assigned to each node. While in the visual script notations that we focus, each node expresses some game logic computation which can be performed individually and can have a particular semantics. Thus it is difficult

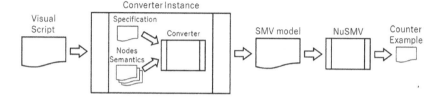

Fig. 4. System overview

to directly apply the existing procedures to the verification of such a visual script notation. In this paper, we propose a method to translate from visual scripts to models by SMV language.

3 Approach

3.1 System Overview

Figure 4 shows the system overview of the visual script verification environment with NuSMV. This environment carries out verification by converting a visual script into an SMV model. First, the system generates a converter instance from specifications to be checked and the corresponding node semantics. Then the visual script is converted into an SMV model by using the converter instance. NuSMV can verify whether the inputted visual script satisfies the specifications or not. When the specifications are not satisfied, NuSMV outputs counterexamples.

In this section, we explain the overview of the SMV models that our method generates from visual scripts (Sect. 3.2), specifications to be checked (Sect. 3.3), and how to detect bugs using counterexamples (Sect. 3.4).

3.2 Model Overview

We first show the overview of SMV model generated by the proposed method with an example. Figure 5 is an SMV model converted from the visual script shown in Fig. 3.

SMV Variables. We prepare four types of SMV variables to describe the behavior of a visual script.

– *Input* and *output variables* represent activated ports of each node in visual script. Since only one input/output port can be activated at the same time in most cases[2], we declare just one input/output variable for one node even if the node has two or more input/output ports. E.g. SetEventMode2In and

---

[2] There are a few exceptions such as a node that can accept 2 inputs simultaneously, we address them in Sect. 4.2.

```
MODULE main
VAR
  ScriptStart1Out   : {none, Out};
  SetEventMode2In   : {none, Enable, Disable};              -- (1)
  SetEventMode2Out  : {none, Out};                          -- (1)
  MovieClip3In      : {none, Start};
  MovieClip3Out     : {none, Finished, Skipped};
  MovieClip3State   : {Stopped, Playing, Finished, Skipped}; -- (2)
  SetEventMode4In   : {none, Enable, Disable};
  SetEventMode4Out  : {none, Out};
  If5In             : {none, In};
  If5Out            : {none, True, False};
  EventMode         : {true, false};                        -- (3)
FAIRNESS MovieClip3State = Stopped;                          -- (4)
ASSIGN
  init(ScriptStart1Out) := Out;
  next(ScriptStart1Out) := none;
  init(SetEventMode2In) := none;
  next(SetEventMode2In) := case
    ScriptStart1Out = Out : Enable;                          -- (5)
    TRUE                  : none;
  esac;
  init(SetEventMode2Out) := none;                            -- (6)
  next(SetEventMode2Out) := case                             -- (6)
    SetEventMode2In = Enable | SetEventMode2In = Disable : Out;  -- (6)
    TRUE                                          : none;   -- (6)
  esac;
  init(MovieClip3In) := none;
  next(MovieClip3In) := case
    SetEventMode2Out = Out : Start;
    TRUE                   : none;
  esac;
  init(MovieClip3Out) := none;
  next(MovieClip3Out) := case
    MovieClip3State = Finished : Finished;                   -- (7)
    MovieClip3State = Skipped  : Skipped;                    -- (7)
    TRUE                       : none;
  esac;
  init(MovieClip3State) := Stopped;                          -- (8)
  next(MovieClip3State) := case
    MovieClip3In = Start      : Playing;                     -- (9)
    MovieClip3State = Playing : {Playing, Finished, Skipped}; -- (10)
    TRUE                      : Stopped;                     -- (11)
  esac;
  init(SetEventMode4In) := none;                             -- (12)
  next(SetEventMode4In) := case
    MovieClip3Out = Finished : Disable;                      -- (13)
    If5Out = True            : Disable;                      -- (13)
    TRUE                     : none;                         -- (14)
  esac;
  init(SetEventMode4Out) := none;                            -- (15)
  next(SetEventMode4Out) := case                             -- (15)
    SetEventMode4In = Enable | SetEventMode4In = Disable : Out; -- (15)
    TRUE                                          : none;   -- (15)
  esac;
  init(If5In) := none;
  next(If5In) := case
    MovieClip3Out = Skipped : In;
    TRUE                    : none;
  esac;
  init(If5Out) := none;
  next(If5Out) := case
    If5In = In : {True, False};                              -- (16)
    TRUE       : none;
  esac;
  init(EventMode) := false;
  next(EventMode) := case
    SetEventMode2In = Enable | SetEventMode4In = Enable   : true;  -- (17)
    SetEventMode2In = Disable | SetEventMode4In = Disable : false; -- (18)
    TRUE                      : EventMode;
  esac;

CTLSPEC AG(EventMode = true -> AF(EventMode = false))       -- (19)
```

Fig. 5. Converted SMV model

`SetEventMode2Out` (Fig. 5 (1)) are the *input* and *output* variable for the left-most Set Event Mode node in Fig. 3. The value domains of *input/output* variables are the names of ports and special value `none` which represents that no port is activated. E.g. since Set Event Mode node has 2 input ports `Enable` and `Disable`, the value domain of `SetEventMode2In` is `none`, `Enable`, and `Disable`. When the value of `SetEventMode2In` is `Enable`, it means that the input port `Enable` is active in the leftmost Set Event Mode node.

- *Script variables* represent variables used in visual scripts and states of external components that the visual scripts interact with. E.g. the global flag "event mode" stated in Sect. 2.2 is a flag variable of the external game system that the visual scripts interact with, and is declared as a *script variable* `EventMode` (Fig. 5 (3)). The specification often specifies the correct behavior of those variables.
- *State variables* represent the internal state of each node whose semantics has state transition. E.g. `MovieClip3State` is the state variable for Movie Clip node (Fig. 5 (2)).

Control Flow. An edge in visual scripts express a portion of control flow that is defined as a set of output port O and input port I, where I is activated iff O is activated. Therefore, we can describe an edge as a value definition of an input variable according to values of output variables in SMV models. E.g. the value of `SetEventMode2In` becomes `Enable` when the value of `ScriptStart1Out` is `Out` (Fig. 5 (5)). It describes that Out port of Script Start node is connected to Enable port of the leftmost Set Event Mode node.

Thus the value transitions of *input* and *output* variables express the control flow in visual scripts. For example, assuming that the control flow of Sect. 2.2 is: `ScriptStart:Out` → `SetEventMode:Enable` → `SetEventMode:Out` → `MovieClip:Start` → `MovieClip:Skipped` → `If:In` → `If:False` , and Fig. 6 shows the value transitions in this case.

Node Semantics. Value definition of *output variables*, *script variables* and *state variables* are specified by semantics of each node. E.g. the node semantics of Set Event Mode is: "when it receives input signal Enable or Disable, it edits the global flag EventMode respectively, and immediately output signal through Out port". This node semantics corresponds to the definition of the variables `SetEventMode2Out` and `EventMode` (Fig. 5 (6), (17)).

3.3 Specification

A specification in this system consists of a specification formula, and the list of *script variable(s)* used in the formula. For example, if we want to detect the bugs stated in Sect. 2.2, the specification can be described as CTL formula Fig. 5 (19), and the *script variable* Fig. 5 (3). We can expect to verify those kinds of bugs with symbolic model checking by modeling the visual scripts in SMV language.

```
-> State: 1.1 <-                    MovieClip3In = Start
   ScriptStart1Out = Out         -> State: 1.5 <-
   SetEventMode2In = none           MovieClip3In = none
   ...                              MovieClip3State = Playing
   MovieClip3State = Stopped      -> State: 1.6 <-
   EventMode = false                MovieClip3State = Skipped
-> State: 1.2 <-                 -> State: 1.7 <-
   ScriptStart1Out = none           MovieClip3Out = Skipped
   SetEventMode2In = Enable          MovieClip3State = Stopped
-> State: 1.3 <-                 -> State: 1.8 <-
   SetEventMode2In = none           MovieClip3Out = none
   SetEventMode2Out = Out           If5In = In
   EventMode = true              -> State: 1.9 <-
-> State: 1.4 <-                    If5In = none
   SetEventMode2Out = none          If5Out = False
```

Fig. 6. Value transition of the example control flow

In our system, users need to write a specification and corresponding node semantics manually. However, users need to write them just once, and after that users can verify scripts automatically. Therefore, we don't think it is a big problem.

3.4   Bug Detection Using Counterexample

As we stated in Sect. 3.2, a control flow of a node graph correspond to value transitions of input and output variables. If the property given by CTLSPEC is violated, NuSMV generates a counterexample which indicates the witness of property violation. Since the counterexample can be obtained as the form of the value transitions of SMV variables, we can identify the control flow which causes the violation from the counterexample. For example, executing the model in Fig. 5 by NuSMV outputs a value transition shown in Fig. 6. It means that the control flow through Skipped port of Movie Clip node and False port of If node causes violation of the specification. Thus we can detect a bug stated in Sect. 2.2.

3.5   Scope and Limitations

Soundness. Strictly speaking, the behavior of our model is not exactly the same as the actual behavior of target visual scripts especially from the viewpoint of signal propagation delay. This is because our model needs one state transition to propagate a signal, even though a visual script implementation usually has no delay. For example, in the case of the following 2 signal propagations in Fig. 3, the former is faster than the latter in our model, though both of them are the same in visual script implementation. This difference might cause false positive and false negative results of the verification.

- Movie Clip:Finished → Set Event Mode:Disable
- Movie Clip:Skipped → If:True → Set Event Mode:Disable

External Components. We also only focus on behaviors of scripts which are independent of external components. This is because such behaviors of external components are not documented completely and thus it is difficult to model those behaviors. Even if it is difficult to model such behaviors completely, we can partially capture them by assuming that those components behave non-deterministically. For example, the behavior of Movie Clip node in Fig. 3 depends on the external components such as "movie player" and "game player input", and we abstract those behavior as non-deterministic state transition (Fig. 5 (10)). However, since this assumption allows the model to have non-existent behaviors, it may cause false positive and negative.

State Explosion. When the SMV model becomes too large, it is impossible to fully avoid state explosion problem. We address this topic in Sect. 6.

Scope. We might be able to avoid the above limitations by more strict modeling. However, since strict modeling can enlarge the model size and causes state explosion easily, we decided to accept these risks. In fact, we currently target the detection of obvious mis-descriptions of visual scripts as stated in Sect. 2.2 and the risk is not a practical problem so far considering the result of our preliminary evaluation.

4 Translation Algorithm

4.1 Translation Overview

The procedure that converts a visual script to a corresponding SMV model is shown below with the example of the conversion from the visual script Fig. 3 to the SMV model Fig. 5. Note that we can implement this conversion as a fully automatic process. However we need to describe specifications and node semantics manually. We explain those issues in Sect. 5.

1. Regarding the **VAR** section in SMV models, process the following steps for each node in the visual script:
   (a) Declare an *input* and an *output* variable for the node. Their value domains are **none** and the name of the ports of the node. E.g. Set Event Mode node in Fig. 3 has 2 input ports Enable and Disable and 1 output port Out, so the *input* and *output* variables are like Fig. 5 (1).
   (b) If the semantics of the node has state transition, declare a *state* variable for the node. E.g. Fig. 5 (2) is a *state* variable for the Movie Clip node.
2. Add declaration of *script* variable(s) to **VAR** section according to the specification, e.g. Fig. 5 (3).
3. Add **FAIRNESS** constraints for each *state variables*, e.g. Fig. 5 (4) (see also: Sect. 4.3).
4. Regarding **ASSIGN** section in SMV models, process the following steps for each node in the visual script:

(a) Convert each input edges of the node to the definition of the *input* variable, e.g. Fig. 5 (5) (see also: Sect. 4.2).

(b) Define the *output* variable and the *state* variable by applying the node semantics, e.g. Fig. 5 (7)–(11) (see also: Sect. 4.4).

5. Add the value transition rules for the *script* variable, e.g. Fig. 5 (17)–(18).
6. Insert SPEC in SMV models from the specification (Fig. 5 (19)).

4.2   Convert Control Flow Edges

In our SMV model, edges in visual scripts are described as definitions of *input variables* as we stated in Sect. 3.2 Control Flow. Consequently, we can convert edges with the following steps:

1. Define the initial value of the *input variable* as none, e.g. Fig. 5 (12).
2. For each input edge to an input port of the node (from Port1 of Node1 to Port2 of the node), add a rule: Node1Out = Port1 : Port2, e.g. Fig. 5 (13).
3. Add the default rule that describes the case of no input signal, e.g. Fig. 5 (14).

Thus, we can define all the *input variable* according to graph structure of visual scripts automatically.

Handling Simultaneous Inputs. As we stated in the Sect. 2.2, more than one node in visual scripts can work in parallel. It means that a node might receive multiple input signals simultaneously. Since only one value can be assigned to an input variable in our model, other input signals are ignored in such case. It might cause an incorrect behavior if some nodes are assumed to handle multiple input signals simultaneously (fortunately these are very rare though).

To avoid this problem, we can declare two input variables for the node whose semantics require to handle two input signals in parallel.

4.3   FAIRNESS Constraints

Some node semantics has the nondeterministic assignment for their *state variables* like MovieClip3State. This model accepts that it continues to have the value Playing infinitely in the context of NuSMV. However, this model is not reasonable, and is expected to finish in a short time. To avoid such a problem, we introduce a fairness constraint which restricts the verification scope to only "fair" state transition. Since our model intends that all nodes eventually return to the initial state, we mechanically add fairness constraints for *state variables* like Fig. 5 (4). By adding this constraint, the behavior where the node never returns to the initial state is not considered in verification by NuSMV.

4.4   Apply Node Semantics

Node semantics are given as templates of definition of *output, state* (if the node has state transition) and *script variables*, e.g. Fig. 7. Note that these definitions only depend on the variables of the node itself, so we can define node semantics independent from graph structure. When our conversion algorithm add definitions of *output* and *state variables* for a node, it selects the appropriate templates for the node and applies them according to the context like the variable names for the node. E.g. there are 2 Set Event Mode nodes, so our conversion algorithm applies the templates (Fig. 7) to SetEventMode2Out and SetEventMode4Out (Fig. 5 (6), (15)). However, writing those node semantics as templates is a manual process. We address this issue in Sect. 5.

```
@SetEventMode:define:output_variable
   init(<output_variable>) := none;
   next(<output_variable>) := case
      <input_variable> = Enable | <input_variable> = Disable  : Out;
      TRUE : none;
   esac;
@SetEventMode:rule:EventMode
      <input_variable> = Enable | <input_variable> = Enable  : true;
```

Fig. 7. An example of node semantics

5   Writing Node Semantics

As we stated in Sect. 4.4, node semantics are described as templates of *output, state* and *script variables* definitions. We show how to describe those definitions in this section.

Writing the semantics for every kind of nodes sounds very hard. However, we can classify most of nodes into five types empirically (Sect. 6). Since these semantics are very similar in each class, we can describe node semantics for those classified nodes with a small human cost.

5.1   Output Variables

In our model, value of an output variable describes when and how the node sends output signals. The definition of an output variable is described according to the semantics of the node. E.g. Set Event Mode nodes output signal immediately when they receive input, so the value of SetEventMode2Out is changed to Out when its input variable SetEventMode2In has the value except none (Fig. 5 (6)). On the other hand, a Movie Clip node output signal after it finishes playing movie, so the value of MovieClip3Out is not changed immediately (Fig. 5 (7)).

Nondeterministical Branch. In the case of If node in Fig. 3, it branches True or False according to the condition value. A typical approach to model this branch is to decide the output signal non-deterministically since we do not consider data flow and external behavior which affects the condition value. As shown in Fig. 5 (16), the next value of If5Out is assigned to True or False non-deterministically. Thus, NuSMV verifies the both branch of True and False exhaustively.

5.2 State Transition

Some nodes have state transition semantics where the node differently behaves for the same stimuli depending on its internal state. To model such a node, we introduce the *state* variable that represents the internal state of the node.

In the case of Movie Clip node in Fig. 3, it starts playing the movie clip when it receives an input signal, and then outputs Skipped if the game player skips playing the movie, otherwise it outputs Finished when it finishes playing the movie. With this behavior in mind, we can define the following four states for the state variable MovieClip3State:

- Stopped: the node is in the initial state.
- Playing: the node receives input and playing the movie clip.
- Finished: playing movie has finished, and the node sends output through Finished.
- Skipped: a game player has skipped playing the movie, and the node sends output through Skipped.

With these states, we can model the semantics of the Movie Clip node with the following steps:

1. The initial state is Stopped (Fig. 5 (8)).
2. When the node receives the input signal through Start, the state is changed to Playing (Fig. 5 (9)).
3. When the state is Playing, the next state is either Playing, Finished, or Skipped non-deterministically. This description represents the behavior of waiting for completion of the movie playback (Fig. 5 (10)).
4. When the state becomes Finished or Skipped, the node outputs signal through Finished or Skipped respectively (Fig. 5 (7)), and the state is back to Stopped (Fig. 5 (11)).

5.3 Script Variables

Script variables represent variables used in visual scripts and states of external components that visual scripts interact. By defining *Script variables* and describing the conditions for those variables, we can verify those conditions with NuSMV. Note that we need not to define all the variables in visual scripts, but minimum variables that we want to verify in the specification.

Table 1. Preliminary evaluation of our method

#	# of nodes	# of vars	conv. time[s]	eval. time[s]	detected?
#1	156	356	5.434	192.786	False
#2	94	214	3.878	3.330	False
#3	37	84	1.746	0.056	False
#4	49	119	2.301	0.111	False
#5	177	414	6.625	36.675	True
#6	73	162	2.768	0.173	False
#7	162	408	9.187	98.102	True
#8	430	980	13.286	-	-

Env.: Intel(R) Core(TM) i7-3770 CPU @ 3.40 GHz/32 GB/Windows 7 (64 bit)/NuSMV 2.6.0

Figure 5 contains a *script variable* EventMode that expresses the global flag variable "event mode" in the game system. The value of EventMode is defined according to the input of Set Event Mode nodes (Fig. 5 (17)). The specification for the script variable can be described in CTLSPEC description, we can check the specification stated in Sect. 2.2 with NuSMV.

6 Preliminary Evaluation

For a preliminary evaluation, we implemented a prototype and applied it to the visual scripts that are randomly selected from the scripts used in the production for FFXV. However, we arbitrarily selected a very large script only as #8 so that we can identify the limitation on the script size of our method. Table 1 shows the results of the evaluation. The column descriptions are the following:

- # of nodes: The number of visual script nodes in the target script.
- # of vars: The number of SMV variables in the generated SMV model.
- conv. time: Conversion time from the visual script to the SMV model. We tried 5 times for each script and adopted a median value of those trial.
- eval. time: Execution time of NuSMV for the model. We tried 5 times for each script and adopted a median value of those trial.
- detected?: Whether NuSMV detected a problem in the script or not.

Node Semantics. We prepared an encoding by SMV language for each node in the scripts. As stated in Sect. 5, we can straightforwardly prepare an encoding for nodes with simplified semantics. The eight scripts shown in Table 1 have 164 kinds of nodes, and they are classified as follows:

1. single output: 98 kinds of nodes.
2. multi-outputs with conditions (non-deterministic choice): 7 kinds of nodes.
3. multi-outputs with state-transition: 14 kinds of nodes.

4. multi-outputs with conditions (non-deterministic choice) and state-transition: 12 kinds of nodes.
5. entry point: 3 kinds of nodes.
6. node with custom semantics: 30 kinds of nodes.

30 kinds of nodes have custom semantics and we manually prepared encodings for them. However, we can mechanically translate the 134 kinds of nodes (82%) which are classified to (1) to (5) into the SMV model. This result demonstrates that our translation method has enough availability in practical use.

Results. Regarding precision, our method found counterexamples on two scripts during the preliminary evaluation. We confirmed with the game designers that the counterexamples are not false positives.[3] This result demonstrates that our method can detect the specific types of bugs that we are focusing on.

Regarding recall, we also checked these scripts by visual inspection. As long as our inspection, there was no false negative.

Limitation. It appeared that our algorithm cannot handle very large scripts, since the verification of #8 had not finished within 3 h. Improving our algorithm to handle those large scripts is future work.

7   Summary and Future Work

We described an automatic verification method for node-based visual script notation for efficient game production. Our method automatically converts visual script implementation to the input model for NuSMV. We confirmed through a preliminary evaluation that our method can detect the specific types of bugs that we are focusing on in realistic time on most of the visual scripts used in the production for FFXV.

A next step for extending this work would be compositional verification [2]. It appears that there are some very large scripts used in the production for FFXV, that our method cannot handle. If we can split the model and verify those sub-models separately, we can reduce the exponential order of the verification and expect that those verifications can be handled in a reasonable time. Also, if we can verify more than one script together, we can track the control flow across the scripts and can expect to reduce false positives/negatives. Compositional verification might make it possible to verify multiple models too. Another next step would be the automated generation of node semantics. Currently, we need to write node semantics manually. If we can extract semantics from node implementation, we can increase the range of automation of our method.

---

[3] According to the game designers, those scripts are used only in the trial version, so they will not fix the bugs though.

Acknowledgment. We wish to thank the collaborative researchers for helpful discussions. We also wish to thank the FINAL FANTASY XV development team for supporting our research. UNREAL ENGINE is a trademark or registered trademark of Epic Games, Inc. Windows is a trademark or registered trademark of Microsoft Corporation. All other trademarks are the property of their respective owners.

References

1. Ben-Ari, M., Pnueli, A., Manna, Z.: The temporal logic of branching time. Acta Informatica **20**(3), 207–226 (1983)
2. Berezin, S., Campos, S., Clarke, E.M.: Compositional reasoning in model checking. In: de Roever, W.-P., Langmaack, H., Pnueli, A. (eds.) COMPOS 1997. LNCS, vol. 1536, pp. 81–102. Springer, Heidelberg (1998). https://doi.org/10.1007/3-540-49213-5_4
3. Burch, J.R., Clarke, E.M., McMillan, K.L., Dill, D.L., Hawng, L.J.: Symbolic model checking: 10^{20} states and beyond. Inf. Comput. **98**(2), 142–170 (1992)
4. Chan, W., et al.: Model checking large software specifications. IEEE Trans. Softw. Eng. **24**(7), 498–520 (1998)
5. Cimatti, A., Clarke, E., Giunchiglia, F., Roveri, M.: NuSMV: a new symbolic model verifier. In: Halbwachs, N., Peled, D. (eds.) CAV 1999. LNCS, vol. 1633, pp. 495–499. Springer, Heidelberg (1999). https://doi.org/10.1007/3-540-48683-6_44
6. Clarke, E.M., Grumberg, O., Peled, D.: Model Checking. MIT Press, Cambridge (1999)
7. FINAL FANTASY XV. http://www.jp.square-enix.com/ff15/
8. Harel, D.: Statecharts: a visual formalism for complex systems. Sci. Comput. Program. **8**(3), 231–274 (1987)
9. Hasegawa, I., Nozoe, R., Ono, T., Koyama, M., Ishida, T.: Visual effects of final fantasy XV: concept, environment and implementation. In: ACM SIGGRAPH 2016 Talks, SIGGRAPH 2016, pp. 23:1–23:2. ACM, New York (2016)
10. Jussila, T., et al.: Model checking dynamic and hierarchical UML state machines. In: Proceedings of the 3rd International Workshop on Model Development, Validation and Verification (MoDeVa 2006), pp. 94–110 (2006)
11. Leveson, N.G., Heimdahl, M.P.E., Hildreth, H., Reese, J.D.: Requirements specification for process-control systems. IEEE Trans. Softw. Eng. **20**(9), 684–707 (1994)
12. Lumberyard Script Canvas. https://docs.aws.amazon.com/lumberyard/latest/userguide/script-canvas-intro.html
13. Moreno-Ger, P., Fuentes-Fernández, R., Sierra-Rodríguez, J.L., Fernández-Manjón, B.: Model-checking for adventure videogames. Inf. Softw. Technol. **51**(3), 564–580 (2009)
14. Pnueli, A.: A temporal logic of concurrent programs. Theor. Comput. Sci. **13**, 45–60 (1981)
15. Radomski, S., Neubacher, T.: Formal verification of selected game-logic specifications. In: Proceedings of the 2nd EICS Workshop on Engineering Interactive Computer Systems with SCXML, pp. 30–34 (2015)
16. Rezin, R., Afanasyev, I., Mazzara, M., Rivera, V.: Model checking in multiplayer games development. In: 2018 IEEE 32nd International Conference on Advanced Information Networking and Applications (AINA), pp. 826–833 (2018)
17. Rumbaugh, J., Jacobson, I., Booch, G.: The Unified Modeling Language Reference Manual, 2nd edn. Pearson Higher Education, London (2004)

18. Unreal Engine 4 Blueprints. https://docs.unrealengine.com/en-US/Engine/Blueprints/
19. Zhao, Q., Krogh, B.H.: Formal verification of statecharts using finite-state model checkers. IEEE Trans. Control. Syst. Technol. **14**(5), 943–950 (2006)

A Reo Model of Software Defined Networks

Hui Feng[1][✉], Farhad Arbab[1,2], and Marcello Bonsangue[1,2]

[1] LIACS, Leiden University, Leiden, The Netherlands
[2] CWI, Amsterdam, The Netherlands
{h.feng,f.arbab,m.m.bonsangue}@liacs.leidenuniv.nl

Abstract. Reo is a compositional coordination language for component connectors with a formal semantics based on automata. In this paper, we propose a formal model of software defined networks (SDNs) based on Reo where declarative constructs comprising of basic Reo primitives compose to specify descriptive models of both data and control planes of SDNs. We first describe the model of an SDN switch which can be compactly represented as a single state constraint automaton with a memory storing its flow table. A full network can then be compositionally constructed by composing the switches with basic communication channels. The reactive and proactive behaviour of the controllers in the control plane of an SDN can also be modelled by Reo connectors, which can compose the connectors representing data plane. The resulting model is suitable for testing, simulation, visualization, verification, and ultimately compilation into SDN switch code using the standard tools already available for Reo.

Keywords: Formal model · Software defined networks · Reo · Constraint automata · Component composition · Coordination

1 Introduction

Since the concept of software defined network (SDN) was introduced in 2006 [9] it has become increasingly popular in both academia and industry as a new architecture for operating and managing computer networks via the OpenFlow protocol [19]. In traditional networks, the control plane (where the packet forwarding strategy is set up) is tightly coupled with the data plane (where the actual packet forwarding happens) and distributed in a multitude of hardware devices. Because no entity has a global view of the network, and the size and complexity of today's networks are very large, it has become extremely complicated to program network-wide decisions for end-to-end policies and to verify their compliance with global objectives.

Different from traditional network, SDN offers a network architecture that decouples data from its routing control, and places network intelligence and

This research is supported by China Scholarship Council.

Y. Ait-Ameur and S. Qin (Eds.): ICFEM 2019, LNCS 11852, pp. 69–85, 2019.
https://doi.org/10.1007/978-3-030-32409-4_5

states in a logically centralized routing control entity, the so called controllers. Controllers operate independently from network switches which contain programmable forwarding tables that are set up and managed by the controllers. Since controllers can be programmed, SDN enables the application of formal methods to prove the correctness of computer networks. In the recent years several formal models of SDN (e.g. [2,15,16]) have been proposed in order to test or check that a network behave correctly.

In this paper we present a formal model of SDN based on Reo [3], a graphical language for compositional construction of interaction protocols, manifested as connectors. A connector consist of several typed channel and nodes, arranged in a graph of edges and vertices. Every edge in this graph represents a channel of a specific type and every vertex represents a node. The type of a channel determines its data-flow behaviour. Nodes regulate data-flow by non-deterministically selecting data items available through their incoming channel ends and replicating them through their outgoing channel ends. Nodes with both incoming and outgoing channel ends are called mixed nodes. Nodes with no incoming channel end are called source nodes, and those with no outgoing channel end are called sink nodes. Source and sink nodes collectively comprise the boundary nodes of a connector, forming the interface that regulates its communication with the environment. Every connector can be described by functional constraints that relate the timing and the contents of the data-flows at its interface [7]. Reo was originally introduced as a coordination language. Since its introduction, however, Reo has become a domain-specific language for compositional specification of protocols based on an interaction-centric model of concurrency [4,14].

Using Reo we regard components in an SDN as constraints imposed on the interactions of parties engaged in the processing of network packets. Starting with a small set of simple constraints, we obtain a declarative descriptions of switches in the data plane as well as controllers in the control plane. Composition of these components is supported through other simpler connectors which give a global description of the topology of the network.

The formal semantics of Reo is based on automata [7] and as such it supports formal analysis, testing and verification as well as distributed automatic code generation [14]. For a more compact representation and for enabling constraints depending on stored data we consider basic channels with memory, and as such we present a variation of the original semantics of Reo to support constraints on stored and to be stored data. The result is a compact finite state model for SDN particularly suited for formal verification using techniques as in [17]. While we are only considering functional modelling in this paper, extensions for capturing the notions of time, quality of service, resources, as well as probabilistic behaviour can be captured by similar extension of the underlying Reo model [6].

In order to scale up to handle large networks, our resulting SDN model is compositional in the sense that the meaning of the entire computer network is obtained by composing that of the individual models of the switches, network topology, and controllers. The resulting model is independent from the possibly infinite sequences of packets traversing the network.

Recent interest in the application of formal methods to software defined networks started with VeriCon [8], an interactive verification system based on first order logic to model admissible network topologies and network invariants. Similar to our model is a finite state machine model of SDN introduced in [25]. In this work model checking is possible via a translation to binary decision diagrams, under a similar assumption to ours: controllers are described as finite state machines. Another relevant work on automated verification is [22]. Our approach however is based on a declarative descriptions of controllers, switches, and network topology as a Reo circuits, whose automatic composition yields a finite automaton.

Different from our declarative approach, [1] proposes an actor-based modelling to verify concurrent features of SDN via the ABS toolsuite. The use of automata in our work instead of actors make it easier to specify real time and other quantitative properties of SDN. We do not explore this direction in this paper, leaving it for future work. Variation of regular expressions have been very successful in modelling network programming languages [2,21,23]. In particular NetKAT offers a sound and complete algebraic reasoning systems with an interesting coalgebraic decision procedure. However NetKAT models only a stateless snapshot of the data plane traversed by a single packet. It does not support update of flow tables nor routing of multiple packets. TLA+ [18] has also been used to model the behaviour of SDN but in a very restrictive manner, allowing only a single switch [16]. Formal models are used not only to verify properties of an SDN such as consistency of flow tables, violation of safety policies, or forwarding loops, but also for finding flaws in security protocols using CSP and the model checker PAT [24].

This paper proceed as follows. In Sect. 2 we give a brief introduction to the main concepts of software defined networks, while in Sect. 3 we introduce Reo and give a new automata based semantics using memory cells for storing data. This model is used in Sect. 4 where we present a Reo circuit for the data plane and the control plane of an SDN. We conclude with an example showing the semantic difference between two controllers.

2   A Primer on Software Defined Networks

Network management includes many different tasks that, traditionally, have been realized through manufacturer-specific low-level languages for the configuration of hardware network devices, e.g., switches and routers. The primary function of a network management task is to ensure transport of packets, and entails two planes: the control plane for making routing decisions and the data plane concerned with packet forwarding. In traditional networks, the control plane is coupled with the data plane on each hardware device. As such the control plane is highly distributed, with no global view of the network, making it impossible to program network-wide decisions and verify their compliance with global specifications.

SDN offers a network architecture that simplifies the design and deployment of network management tasks: the control plane is a logically centralized controller that gathers information from the data plane and provides a global view to applications running on top of the controller. These applications make packet routing decisions based on the global view and distribute the decisions to the data plane via the controller using the OpenFlow protocol [19].

Each switch in the data plane consists of a number of ports where packets are received or forwarded. Further, each switch is connected to at least one controller, from which it may receive or to which it may send messages. The basic messages forwarded from switch to switch are packets. A packet consists of a finite set of fields, grouped in header information and pure data, as the two packets in the example below show, where the header of each packet contains the information about the `tcp` and `ethernet` destination address of the packet:

| tcp_dst:22, eth_dst:11 | data: d1 | | tcp_dst:23, eth_dst:11 | data: d2 |

Forwarding of packets is implemented in each switch through a flow table, a memory store consisting of an ordered set of pairs (b, a). Here b is a Boolean condition on the packet fields (the so called matching criteria) and a is the corresponding action to be executed on the matching packet. The order of the matching-action pairs gives a priority on the application of the matching condition. There are basically three types of actions: *forwarding* a packet to one or more ports of the switch, *dropping* a packet, and *updating* a field of a packet with some value. For example, the leftmost packet above matches the first rule of table below and it is forwarded to the output ports 3 and 4. The rightmost packet however matches only the last rule and it is forwarded to port 1 after its field `tcp_dst` is updated to 22.

Matching condition	Action
`tcp_dst:22`	`Forward[3, 4]`
`tcp_dst:23, eth_dst:12`	`drop`
`true`	`tcp_dst := 22; Forward[1]`

Controllers and switches communicate through messages. A `PktIn` message is a packet sent from a switch to a controller, typically to be processed there or to trigger an update of the flow tables. A `PktOut` message sent from the controller to a switch consists of a packet together with a flow table action to be executed by the switch. This way a packet need not pass through the flow table but is, for example, immediately forwarded to other switches.

The flow table of a switch is updated by `FlowMod` messages, another type of message from a controller to a switch. Each `FlowMod` message consists of a `ModType` t (`Add`, `Remove`, `Modify`), a matching condition b and an action a. If t = Add then the pair (b, a) is added on top of the table (higher priority), while if t = `Modify` then the first pair in the flow table (b', a') with b implying b' is substituted with the pair (b, a). In remaining case when with $t = \texttt{Remove}$ the first pair in the flow table (b', a') with b implying b' is removed from the table. In this case the action a does not play any role and therefore can be considered empty. Those three types of messages plus dedicated packets to communicate data allow controllers to gather information about the network and manage it.

3   Reo and Constraint Automata

Reo is a coordination language for compositional construction of component connectors [3]. The emphasis in Reo is on connectors, their behaviour and composition out of simple channels. Reo can also be used to define an interaction protocol as a connector, a graph-like structure that enables (a)synchronous data flow along its edges. Each edge is called a channel and it specifies constraints on the flows of data at its ends. A channel end is either a source end through which the channel accepts data, or a sink end through which the channel offers data. Multiple channel ends coincident at a vertex of the connector together form a node. Nodes have predefined 'merge-replicate' behaviour: a node repeatedly accepts a datum from one of its coincident sink ends, chosen non-deterministically, and offers that datum through all of its coincident source ends.

3.1   Constraint Automata

Constraint automata are a formalism to describe the "behaviour" of Reo channels and their composition as connectors [7]. Constraint automata can be thought of as conceptual generalizations of finite state automata where data constraints influence applicable state transitions.

We assume a finite set $\mathbb{D}$ of data ranged over by d, a finite set $\mathbb{P}$ of ports ranged over by p, q (note that ports in Reo are distinct from ports in SDN switches), and a finite set $\mathbb{M}$ of memory cells ranged over by m. Further, let $\mathcal{F}$ be a set of function symbols and $\mathcal{P}$ a set of predicate symbols. Each predicate symbol and each function symbol comes with an arity, the number of arguments it expects. A term is defined as follows:

$$t ::= d \mid p \mid m \mid m^{\bullet} \mid f(t, ..., t)$$

Terms are used in constraints defined by the following predicate formulas:

$$\phi ::= \top \mid p = t \mid m = t \mid m^{\bullet} = t \mid P(t, ..., t) \mid \phi \wedge \phi \mid \neg \phi$$

The constraint $p = t$ denotes the equality between the value passing through the port p, and the value obtained by evaluating the term t; $m = t$ is the equality between the value stored in the memory m before evaluating the constraint and the value denoted by t; $m^{\bullet} = t$ is equality between the value stored in the memory m immediately after the evaluation of the constraint and the value denoted by t. The others are just the usual constraints.

In order to define the satisfaction of constraints, we assume the existence of a function $\hat{f} : \mathbb{D}^n \to \mathbb{D}$ for each $f \in \mathcal{F}$ of arity n, and a subset $\hat{P} \subseteq \mathbb{D}^m$ for each predicate symbol $P \in \mathcal{P}$ of arity m. For fixed sets of input ports I, output ports O and hidden ports H, the evaluation of constraint is defined by using the function $\alpha : I \cup O \cup M \to \mathbb{D}_\perp$, and an environment $\eta : H \to \mathbb{D}_\perp$ assigning values to hidden ports. α is used for the visible components of a Reo connector. Here $\alpha(A)$ represents the value passing though the port A unless $\alpha(A) = \perp$ that denotes the absence of flow of data though port A. Similarly $\alpha(m)$ denotes the value stored in the memory cell m.

We denote by At the set of all atoms α. Note that $m^\bullet$ is not a part of an atom, because it refer to the value of m after the evaluation of a transition. Therefore we need pairs of atoms, one for the current values stored in memory cells, and another for storing the side effect of evaluation, i.e., the value of a memory cell after the evaluation. Evaluations of guards is defined inductively as follow:

$$
\begin{array}{llll}
\alpha_1\alpha_2 & \models_\eta & \top & \\
\alpha_1\alpha_2 & \models_\eta & p = t & \text{iff} \quad \alpha_1(p) = [\![t]\!]^\eta_{\alpha_1\alpha_2} \\
\alpha_1\alpha_2 & \models_\eta & m = t & \text{iff} \quad \alpha_1(m) = [\![t]\!]^\eta_{\alpha_1\alpha_2} \\
\alpha_1\alpha_2 & \models_\eta & m^\bullet = t & \text{iff} \quad \alpha_2(m) = [\![t]\!]^\eta_{\alpha_1\alpha_2} \\
\alpha_1\alpha_2 & \models_\eta & P(t_1,...,t_n) & \text{iff} \quad \langle [\![t_1]\!]^\eta_{\alpha_1\alpha_2}, ..., [\![t_n]\!]^\eta_{\alpha_1\alpha_2} \rangle \in \hat{P} \\
\alpha_1\alpha_2 & \models_\eta & \phi_1 \wedge \phi_2 & \text{iff} \quad \alpha_1\alpha_2 \models_\eta \phi_1 \text{ and } \alpha_1\alpha_2 \models_\eta \phi_2 \\
\alpha_1\alpha_2 & \models_\eta & \neg\phi & \text{iff} \quad \alpha_1\alpha_2 \not\models_\eta \phi
\end{array}
$$

Finally, we define the evaluation of a guard without hidden ports as follows:

$$\alpha_1\alpha_2 \models \phi \text{ if and only if there is } \eta \text{ such that } \alpha_1\alpha_2 \models_\eta \phi.$$

Here $[\![t]\!]^\eta_{\alpha_1\alpha_2}$ denotes the value of the term t and is defined inductively by:

$$
\begin{aligned}
[\![d]\!]^\eta_{\alpha_1\alpha_2} &= d \\
[\![p]\!]^\eta_{\alpha_1\alpha_2} &= \begin{cases} \alpha_1(p) \text{ , if } p \in I \cup O \\ \eta(p) \quad \text{ , if } p \in H \end{cases} \\
[\![m]\!]^\eta_{\alpha_1\alpha_2} &= \alpha_1(m) \\
[\![m^\bullet]\!]^\eta_{\alpha_1\alpha_2} &= \alpha_2(m) \\
[\![f(t_1,...,t_n)]\!]^\eta_{\alpha_1\alpha_2} &= \hat{P}([\![t_1]\!]^\eta_{\alpha_1\alpha_2},...,[\![t_n]\!]^\eta_{\alpha_1\alpha_2})
\end{aligned}
$$

We are now ready for the definition of constraint automata with memory cells describing operationally the behaviour of a Reo connector.

Definition 1. *A constraint automaton is a tuple* $(Q, I, O, H, M, \longrightarrow, q_0)$ *where* Q *is a finite set of states with* $q_0 \in Q$ *the initial state,* $I, O, H \subseteq \mathbb{P}$ *are sets of ports known by the automaton,* $M \subseteq \mathbb{M}$ *is the set of memory cells, and* $\longrightarrow$ *is a transition relation with* $q \xrightarrow{N,\phi} q'$ *denoting a transition from q to q' synchronizing a set of ports* $N \subseteq I \cup O \cup H$ *under the data constraint ϕ. We assume that the ports appearing in ϕ are a subset of N and the memory cells occurring in ϕ are a subset of M.*

An *execution* of a constraint automaton is described by means of infinite strings [12] in At^ω. An infinite string $\alpha \cdot w$ is an execution from the state q, denoted by $\alpha \cdot w \in E(q)$ if and only if there is a transition $q \xrightarrow{N,\phi} q'$ such that the following three conditions hold:

1. $\forall p \in I \cup O, p \notin N$ iff $\alpha(p) = \perp$;
2. $w = \alpha' \cdot w'$ and $\alpha\alpha' \models \phi$;
3. $w \in E(q')$

By the above definition a constraint of a transition $q \xrightarrow{N,\phi} q'$ is evaluated in an execution $\alpha \cdot w$ starting from q with respect to its first two atoms. Furthermore, only the ports in N fire, meaning that a value passes through them as recorded by α, and the rest of the string w is an execution of the target state q'.

Consider the following constraint automaton:

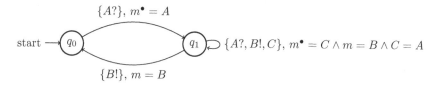

Here "?" and "!" are syntactic means for indicating which ports belong to I and O, respectively. The unmarked ports belong to H. An example of an execution of the above automaton starting from q_0 is the infinite string:

$$[A = 1, B = \perp, m = 22] \cdot [A = 3, B = 1, m = 1] \cdot [A = 5, B = 3, m = 3] \cdot$$
$$[A = \perp, B = 5, m = 5] \cdot [A = 7, B = \perp, m = 33] \cdot \ldots$$

Note that the value of the memory of the second element of the string is equal to the value at port A of the first element, and the value of port B of the second element. Similarly for the value of A in the second element and the value of B and the memory m in the third element.

The above automaton has the same executions from the initial state as the following automaton without hidden ports.

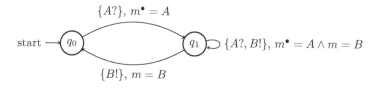

While in general it is not always possible to remove all hidden ports without modifying the set of executions, for simplicity and when there is no problem, in the sequel we will simplify a constraint automaton by removing hidden ports obtaining an automaton with the same structure (states and transitions) and the same executions from its initial state.

The language of a constraint automaton consists of the projection with respect to the ports of all executions starting from the initial state. A language represents the behaviour of the automaton as visible from the environment. Therefore, only input and output ports are visible, but not hidden ports or memory cells. For example, the language accepted by the above two constraint automata is the same and it includes the following infinite string:

$$[A = 1, B = \bot] \cdot [A = 3, B = 1] \cdot [A = 5, B = 3] \cdot [A = \bot, B = 5] \cdot \ldots .$$

3.2 Basic Channels and More Complex Connectors

Next, we briefly introduce the constraint automata and the their graphical representation for all basic Reo channels [3,17] we use in this paper.

The *synchronous channel* accepts data from its input port A, and it passes them synchronously to its output port B.

$\{A?, B!\},$
$A = B$

The *synchronous drain* has two input ports A and B, from which it accepts any data, but only when the two ports can be synchronized. The data received as input is not important, only the ports' synchronization matters.

$\{A?, B?\}$

The *non-deterministic merger* receives data from either A or B and sends them to the sink node C synchronously. If data is available from both A and B at the same time, one of them is chosen non-deterministically.

$\{A?, C!\},$
$C = A$

$\{B?, C!\},$
$C = B$

The *replicator* receives data from A and replicates them to both sink nodes B and C.

$\{A?, B!, C!\},$
$B = A \wedge$
$C = A$

The *FIFO1* channel receives data from the input port A if the internal buffer m is empty. The data is stored in the buffer, which can only contain at most one data item. When m is full its content flows to the output port B and it becomes empty. The behavior of a similar channel with dot inside is represented by the automaton with the other state as the starting state.

$\{A?\}, \quad A = m^{\bullet}$

$\{B!\}, \quad B = m$

The *transformer* channel applies a user-defined function f to a data item consumed from its source end A, and synchronously offers $f(A)$ through its channel end B.

$\{A?, B!\},$
$B = f(A)$

The pattern of *filter* channel $P \subseteq Data$ specifies the type of data items that can be transmitted through the channel. Any value $d \in P$ is accepted through its source end if its sink end can simultaneously dispense d; all data items $d \notin P$ are always accepted through the source end but are immediately lost.

$$\{A?, B!\},$$
$$B = A \wedge P(A)$$

$$\{A?\}, \neg P(A)$$

The *PairMerger* accepts two data items d_1 and d_2 through the source ends A and B, merges them and synchronously offers the pair $\langle d_1, d_2 \rangle$ through its sink end C.

$$\{A?, B?, C!\},$$
$$C = \langle A, B \rangle$$

The *variable* can accept a data item d through source end A, update its memory τ, synchronously offer the data stored in τ through sink end B if B fires; also it can directly synchronously offer τ through B if B fires but A doesn't fire, τ remains in the buffer.

$$\{A?, B!\}, \tau = B \wedge$$
$$\tau^{\bullet} = A$$

$$\{A?\}, \tau^{\bullet} = A$$

$$\{B!\}, \tau = B \wedge$$
$$\tau^{\bullet} = \tau$$

Note that the PairMerger uses a binary function symbol $\langle -, - \rangle$ interpreted as the usual pairing. In all automata in the table, we assume that the ports known by each automaton are those used in the channels.

A Reo circuit is built out of some basic channels via the join operation which is performed by joining common ports of the channels. On the automata level, the join operation is realized by the following product construction.

Definition 2. *The product of the two constraint automata* $A_1 = (Q_1, I_1, O_1, H_1, M_1, \longrightarrow_1, q_1)$ *and* $A_2 = (Q_2, I_2, O_2, H_2, M_2, \longrightarrow_2, q_2)$ *with disjoint sets of states* Q_1 *and* Q_2, *and disjoint sets of memory cells* M_1 *and* M_2 *is:*

$$A_1 \bowtie A_2 = (Q, I, O, H, M_1 \cup M_2, \longrightarrow, \langle q_1, q_2 \rangle)$$

where $Q = Q_1 \times Q_2$, $I = (I_1 - O_2) \cup (I_2 - O_1)$, $O = (O_1 - I_2) \cup (O_2 - I_1)$, $H = (I_1 \cap O_2) \cup (I_2 \cap O_1) \cup H_1 \cup H_2$, *and* $\longrightarrow$ *is defined by the following rules:*

$$\frac{q_1 \xrightarrow{N_1, \phi_1}_1 q_1' \text{ and } q_2 \xrightarrow{N_2, \phi_2}_2 q_2' \text{ and } Prt_1 \cap N_2 = Prt_2 \cap N_1}{\langle q_1, q_2 \rangle \xrightarrow{N_1 \cup N_2, \phi_1 \wedge \phi_2} \langle q_1', q_2' \rangle}$$

Here $Prt_1 = I_1 \cup O_1 \cup H_1$, *and* $Prt_2 = I_2 \cup O_2 \cup H_2$.

Figure 1 shows an example of composition of a non-deterministic merger (on the left) on ports $\{A?, B?, C!\}$ with a synchronous channel (second automata from the left) acting on port $\{C?, D!\}$. The result is a new automaton with C as hidden port (third automaton from the left), which however is language equivalent to the automaton of a non-deterministic merger (the rightmost one) on ports $\{A?, B?, D!\}$.

Note that the port C is a hidden port in the resulting automaton because it is an output port of one channel and input of the other. It is not hard to see that the join operation is associative and commutative.

As another example, in Fig. 2 we introduce the circuit of a three-port sequencer and its corresponding constraint automaton [11]. This three-port-sequencer regulates the flow of data from ports A, B and C, in a sequential order. Similar sequencers can be defined for any number of ports.

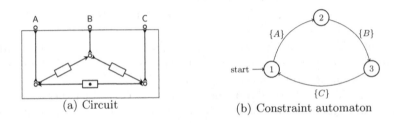

Fig. 1. The example of automata conjunction

A   B   C

(a) Circuit   (b) Constraint automaton

Fig. 2. A three-port sequencer

4   A Reo Model of Software Defined Networks

In this section, we present an SDN model based on the Reo language. First, we describe the switches of the data plane as Reo circuits, and we translate it into its corresponding constraint automaton. Afterwards, we describe two examples of controllers managing a simple network with two switches. The goal is to send packets from one host to another. We conclude by combining the automata of these two layers with a network topology.

4.1   Data Plane

The basic data type we use is that of a packet. We see a packet as a record $\pi : Fields \rightarrow Data$ assigning fields from a finite set of $Fields$ to data in $Data$. We denote a packet by $\pi = [f_0 = d_0, f_1 = d_1, ..., f_n = d_n]$, and use the notation $\pi.f$ to denote the value of the field f of the packet π. The set $Fields$ is assumed to include a field IPt for storing the identity of the input port of the switch where the packet is received, OPt for the output port of the switch where the packet is forwarded.

Figure 3 introduces the Reo circuit representing a switch with an interface consisting of input ports $\{P_0, P_1, ..., P_n\}$ and output ports $\{Q_0, Q_1, ..., Q_m\}$. Here both n and m are greater than or equal to 0 so that a switch has always at least two ports: P_0 and Q_0. Port P_0 is used to receive messages from the controller supervising the switch, whereas port Q_0 is meant for sending packets to the controller. All other ports are connected to other switches or open to the environment for communication with hosts. The input ports receive packets, and the output ports send packets.

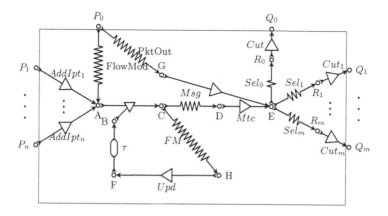

Fig. 3. Reo circuit of one switch

We can describe the behaviour of the circuit representing a switch by means of three scenarios.

1. The first one is when a packet π is received from a host or another switch. In this case the input port is P_i for some $1 \leq i \leq n$, The transformer `AddIpt_i` of the channel connected to P_i assign $\pi.IPt$ to i and outputs to A a triple $(FlowMsg, \pi, \emptyset)$. The first component of the triple is the tag $FlowMsg$ indicating that π is an ordinary network packet with no side effect on the flow table. The last component is the subset of output ports of the switch where the packet needs to be forwarded.

The above triple is paired with the current flow table stored in τ and received by the filters FM and Msg. These filters check the first component of the triple. In our case only the filter Msg will succeed, and will pass the triple $(FlowMsg, \pi, \emptyset)$ together with the table τ to the transformer Mtc via node D. This transformer matches the packet π against the table τ, executes the corresponding field assignment modifying π into a new packet π' and outputs the pair (π', F) to node E. Here the set F contains all output ports where the packet π' needs to be forwarded, according to the action of the matching pair in the flow table τ.

The filters Sel_i regulate the forwarding by outputting the pair (π', F) to node R_i if $i \in F$. Note that the same pair may be duplicated to many nodes, and in case $F = \emptyset$ it will be dropped. Also, If $0 \in F$ then the packet is forwarded to the controller. From the node R_i the transformer Cut_i receiving as input the pair (π', F) will output the packet π', removing the information about the forwarding ports.

2. The second situation is when a $PktOut$ message from the controller is received at the input port P_0. A $PktOut$ message is a triple $\langle FlowMsg, \pi, F \rangle$ consisting of a tag $FlowMsg$ as in the previous case, a packet pi and a set of output ports F where π needs to be forwarded. Only the filter $PktOut$ lets this triple flow to the node G, where a transformer receives it, removes the tag, and outputs the pair (π, F) to node E. The selection and forwarding of π to each port in F is as before.

3. The third and last situation is when a $FlowMod$ message from the controller is received at the input port P_0. Also in this case it consist of a triple $\langle t, B, A \rangle$, but unlike the previous cases, this message is meant to update the table stored in τ. More specifically, B is a Boolean condition on $Fields$ matching the pair of τ to be updated, and A is the action for field updating and packet forwarding. The tag t can be either add, $remove$ or $modify$ to add (B, A) on top of table τ, remove the first pair (b, a) of τ with b implying B, or to modify the first pair (b, a) of τ with b implying B into the new pair (b, A). Note that in the case of $t = remove$, the action A does not play any role.

Of the two filters with input at P_0 only the filter $FlowMod$ will succeed, so the triple $\langle t, B, A \rangle$ can be paired with the current flow table τ and reach node C. Here the filter Msg will fail but FM will succeed, passing all $\langle t, B, A \rangle$ and τ to the transformer Upd. This transformer will update the table τ as described in the triple $\langle t, B, A \rangle$, and will output a new table τ'. The latter is stored as the new current table by the variable channel with input node F.

While the Reo circuit of a switch may look complicated, its actual constraint automaton is rather simple. It consists of only one state (because all channels used have one single state) and three types of transitions (see Fig. 4).

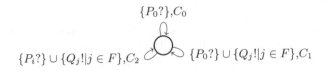

$\{P_0?\},C_0$

$\{P_i?\} \cup \{Q_j! | j \in F\},C_2$ $\{P_0?\} \cup \{Q_j! | j \in F\},C_1$

Fig. 4. Constraint automaton of a switch

The conditions C_0, C_1 and C_2 are:

1. C_0: $P_0 = \langle t, B, A \rangle \wedge t \neq Msg \wedge \tau^\bullet = Upd(\langle \tau, P_0 \rangle)$;
2. C_1: $P_0 = \langle Msg, \pi, F \rangle \wedge \bigwedge_{j \in F} Q_j = \pi$;
3. C_2: $Mtc(\langle \tau, \langle Msg, \pi[i/Ipt], \emptyset \rangle \rangle) = \langle \pi', F \rangle \wedge \tau^\bullet = \tau \wedge \bigwedge_{j \in F} Q_j = \pi'$.

Condition C_0 specifies when a *FlowMod* message is received by a switch so that the flow table is updated. Transitions labelled by condition C_1 or C_2 are dependent on the subset of output ports F received as input from P_0 or assigned after a matching action. This means that there is a concrete transition for each possible subset of the output ports, but only one will eventually be chosen. Condition C_1 concerns *FlowMsg* messages received by a controller, while condition C_2 defines the handling of a packet received from a host or another switch.

If we assume that in a switch the number of input ports is n, and that the number of output ports is m, then the resulting constraint automata will have one state and $1 + 2^m + (n-1) * 2^m$ transitions.

Each switch in the data plane can be considered as a Reo connector interacting with others only via its input and output ports, while all other nodes and memory cells of the components are hidden. For example, while too large to depict here, the constraint automaton of the data plane composed of two simple switches connected by a synchronous channel as described in Fig. 5 consists of one state, two memory cells (one for each switch flow table) and 26 transitions, which can be generated using automated tools [5].

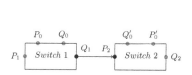

Fig. 5. Data plane

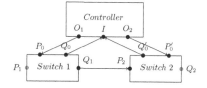

Fig. 6. A simple example

4.2 Control Plane and the Whole SDN Model

The SDN control plane contains a set of controllers. Each controller behaves as a reactive system, responding to `PktIn` messages received from switches by sending either `PktOut` or `FlowMod` messages. We assume controllers to be specified as Reo circuits, and thus with a behaviour described by means of constraint automata. Input ports and output ports represent the connection of a controller with the switches under its control. Figure 6 shows a simple example of a controller with two switches. A controller need not know the operational details of any of the switches that it controls (e.g., their automata); its concern consists of deciding *when* to update the flow table of a switch, and *what* modification constitutes that update. For instance, it may decide to modify the flow table of a switch in reaction to the switch receiving (and escalating) a packet for which it has no matching condition.

For example, the controller described in Fig. 7 guarantees a flow of messages from the host connected to port P_1 to the host connected to port Q_2. It updates the flow table of a switch every time a new packet is received that does not match any condition of the table. In the second controller shows in Fig. 8, we see a similar specification of a controller flowing a packet from P_1 to Q_2, but each time it updates switches apart.

We combine constraint automata of controllers and switches together to get a complete model of an SDN. Because the rate of forwarding by a switch is different from the rate of processing by a controller, we put a **Queue** channel between output ports of each switch and input ports of the controller (like channels $\{Q_0, I\}$ and $\{Q'_0, I\}$ in Fig. 6), a synchronous channel between input ports of each switch and output ports of the controller (like channels $\{O_1, P_0\}$ and $\{O_2, P'_0\}$). Here are the description of Queue.

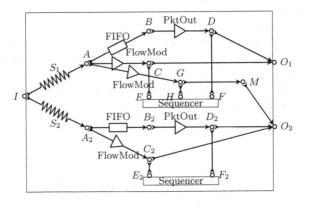

Fig. 7. Reo circuit of controller 1

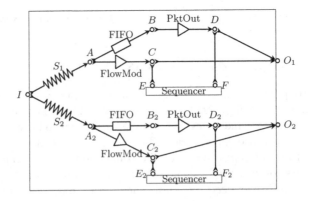

Fig. 8. Reo circuit of controller 2

The *Queue* channel behaves as a FIFO1, but it has an unbounded internal buffer. As such, data can always be received from the input port A and stored in the buffer. If the buffer is non empty then the first element received by A flows from the buffer to the output port B.

$$\{A\}, q^\bullet = A \cdot q$$

$$\{B\}, q = q^\bullet \cdot B$$

While the two models guarantee packets to flow from one host to another, they have different semantics and therefore they are language distinguishable. The two cases have different behaviours because in the first case when the controller receive a `PktIn` message, it sends a `FlowMod` message to switch one and another `FlowMod` to switch two, so that the packet π can pass the two switches directly. But in the second case, every time the controller receives a `PktIn` message, it just sends a `FlowMod` message to the current switch, so π can only pass the current switch.

5   Conclusion

In this paper we presented a Reo model of SDN, based on a novel semantics for constraint automata with memory, recently studied in [13]. The difference is in a neater treatment of the values in the memory before and after the execution of a transition. The model is stateful, and allows concurrency at the level of controllers but also at the level of the packets. The model can immediately be used for verification of quantitative and qualitative properties of SDN, such as consistency of flow tables, violation of safety policies, or forwarding loops. In the future, we plan to verify these properties by using tools like ReoLive [10], or mCRL2 [17], which are part of the Reo framework [20] and can directly generate executable code for the switches. Another line of research easily supported by our model is the development of simulation and visualization tools for packets flowing into the network.

References

1. Albert, E., Gómez-Zamalloa, M., Rubio, A., Sammartino, M., Silva, A.: SDN-actors: modeling and verification of SDN programs. In: Havelund, K., Peleska, J., Roscoe, B., de Vink, E. (eds.) FM 2018. LNCS, vol. 10951, pp. 550–567. Springer, Cham (2018). https://doi.org/10.1007/978-3-319-95582-7_33
2. Anderson, C.J., et al.: NetKAT: semantic foundations for networks. ACM Sigplan Not. **49**(1), 113–126 (2014)
3. Arbab, F.: Reo: a channel-based coordination model for component composition. Math. Struct. Comput. Sci. **14**(3), 329–366 (2004)
4. Arbab, F.: Proper protocol. In: Ábrahám, E., Bonsangue, M., Johnsen, E.B. (eds.) Theory and Practice of Formal Methods. LNCS, vol. 9660, pp. 65–87. Springer, Cham (2016). https://doi.org/10.1007/978-3-319-30734-3_7

5. Arbab, F., Koehler, C., Maraikar, Z., Moon, Y.J., Proença, J.: Modeling, testing and executing Reo connectors with the eclipse coordination tools. Presented at the 5th International Workshop on Formal Aspects of Component Systems (2008)

6. Arbab, F., Meng, S., Moon, Y.J., Kwiatkowska, M., Qu, H.: Reo2MC: a tool chain for performance analysis of coordination models. In: van Vliet, H., Issarny, V. (eds.) Proceedings of the of the 7th Joint Meeting of the European Software Engineering Conference and the ACM SIGSOFT Symposium on the Foundations of Software Engineering, pp. 287–288. ACM (2009)

7. Baier, C., Sirjani, M., Arbab, F., Rutten, J.: Modeling component connectors in Reo by constraint automata. Sci. Comput. Program. **61**(2), 75–113 (2006)

8. Ball, T., et al.: Vericon: towards verifying controller programs in software-defined networks. SIGPLAN Not. **49**(6), 282–293 (2014)

9. Casado, M., et al.: SANE: a protection architecture for enterprise networks. In: Keromytis, A.D. (ed.) USENIX Security Symposium, p. 50. USENIX Association (2006)

10. Cruz, R., Proença, J.: ReoLive: analysing connectors in your browser. In: Mazzara, M., Ober, I., Salaün, G. (eds.) STAF 2018. LNCS, vol. 11176, pp. 336–350. Springer, Cham (2018). https://doi.org/10.1007/978-3-030-04771-9_25

11. Ghassemi, F., Tasharofi, S., Sirjani, M.: Automated mapping of Reo circuits to constraint automata. Electron. Notes Theor. Comput. Sci. **159**, 99–115 (2006)

12. Izadi, M., Bonsangue, M.M.: Recasting constraint automata into Büchi automata. In: Fitzgerald, J.S., Haxthausen, A.E., Yenigun, H. (eds.) ICTAC 2008. LNCS, vol. 5160, pp. 156–170. Springer, Heidelberg (2008). https://doi.org/10.1007/978-3-540-85762-4_11

13. Jongmans, S.S., Kappé, T., Arbab, F.: Constraint automata with memory cells and their composition. Sci. Comput. Program. **146**, 50–86 (2017)

14. Jongmans, S.S.T.Q.: Automata-theoretic protocol programming. Ph.D. thesis, Leiden University (2016)

15. Kang, M., et al.: Formal modeling and verification of SDN-openflow. In: 6th International Conference on Software Testing, Verification and Validation, pp. 481–482. IEEE (2013)

16. Kim, Y.M., Kang, M., Choi, J.Y.: Formal specification and verification of firewall using TLA+. In: Daimi, K., Arabnia, H.R. (eds.) Proceedings of the International Conference on Security and Management (SAM), pp. 247–251 (2017)

17. Kokash, N., Krause, C., de Vink, E.P.: Data-aware design and verification of service compositions with Reo and mCRL2. In: Shin, S.Y., Ossowski, S., Schumacher, M., Palakal, M.J., Hung, C. (eds.) Proceedings of the 2010 ACM Symposium on Applied Computing, pp. 2406–2413. ACM (2010)

18. Lamport, L.: Specifying Systems, The TLA+ Language and Tools for Hardware and Software Engineers. Addison-Wesley (2002)

19. McKeown, N., et al.: Openflow: enabling innovation in campus networks. Comput. Commun. Rev. **38**(2), 69–74 (2008)

20. Proença, J., Clarke, D., De Vink, E., Arbab, F.: Dreams: a framework for distributed synchronous coordination. In: Ossowski, S., Lecca, P. (eds.) Proceedings of the 27th Annual ACM Symposium on Applied Computing, pp. 1510–1515. ACM (2012)

21. Reitblatt, M., Canini, M., Guha, A., Foster, N.: FatTire: declarative fault tolerance for software-defined networks. In: Foster, N., Sherwood, R. (eds.) Proceedings of the 2nd ACM SIGCOMM Workshop on Hot topics in Software Defined Networking, pp. 109–114. ACM (2013)

22. Schnepf, N., Badonnel, R., Lahmadi, A., Merz, S.: Automated verification of security chains in software-defined networks with synaptic. In: 2017 IEEE Conference on Network Softwarization (NetSoft), pp. 1–9. IEEE (2017)
23. Soulé, R., et al.: Merlin: a language for provisioning network resources. In: Seneviratne, A., Diot, C., Kurose, J., Chaintreau, A., Rizzo, L. (eds.) Proceedings of the 10th ACM International Conference on Emerging Networking Experiments and Technologies, pp. 213–226. ACM (2014)
24. Xiang, S., Zhu, H., Xiao, L., Xie, W.: Modeling and verifying TopoGuard in OpenFlow-based software defined networks. In: Pang, J., Zhang, C., He, J., Weng, J. (eds.) 2018 International Symposium on Theoretical Aspects of Software Engineering (TASE), pp. 84–91. IEEE Computer Society (2018)
25. Zakharov, V.A., Smelyansky, R.L., Chemeritsky, E.V.: A formal model and verification problems for software defined networks. Autom. Control. Comput. Sci. **48**(7), 398–406 (2014)

Design of Point-and-Click User Interfaces for Proof Assistants

Bohua Zhan[1(✉)], Zhenyan Ji[2(✉)], Wenfan Zhou[2], Chaozhu Xiang[2], Jie Hou[2], and Wenhui Sun[2]

[1] State Key Laboratory of Computer Science, Institute of Software, Chinese Academy of Sciences, Beijing, China
bzhan@ios.ac.cn
[2] Beijing Jiaotong University, Beijing, China
{zhyji,zhouwenfan,czxiang,houjie,whsun1}@bjtu.edu.cn

Abstract. In interactive theorem proving, human users interact with proof assistants to construct and verify formal proofs. The most popular proof assistants today all have user interfaces that are largely text-based. This leads to a steep learning curve for new users of these tools. In this paper, we propose a framework for designing user interfaces for proof assistants based on pointing and clicking. While a main goal of the design is ease of learning for new users, we intend for the design to be suitable for real verification tasks. The design is also extensible, allowing custom proof methods and search functionality to be added in a convenient way. We implement our ideas in a web interface, with backend provided by holpy, a new system for interactive theorem proving implemented in Python. The resulting user interface is tested on theorems in logic, sets, functions, Peano arithmetic, and lists, demonstrating its applicability in a wide range of areas.

Keywords: Proof assistants · User interface · Tactics

1 Introduction

Interactive theorem proving aims to construct and verify formal proofs via interaction between the computer and the human user. In recent years, it has seen several major accomplishments, including formal verification of the seL4 microkernel [13], verification of a realistic C compiler [14], and formal proofs of the Feit-Thompson theorem [11] and Kepler's conjecture [10]. These works show that interactive theorem proving can be applied to very complex mathematical theorems and computer systems. However, verification projects still take considerable human effort. Work on the seL4 project, the Feit-Thompson theorem, and Kepler's conjecture each have an estimated cost of over 20 person years. In addition, the proof assistants used – HOL Light [12], Coq [4], and Isabelle [15], are generally considered to have a steep learning curve for new users, making it difficult and time consuming to form and train new teams. These factors can be

© Springer Nature Switzerland AG 2019
Y. Ait-Ameur and S. Qin (Eds.): ICFEM 2019, LNCS 11852, pp. 86–103, 2019.
https://doi.org/10.1007/978-3-030-32409-4_6

seen as a major obstacle to more widespread application of interactive theorem proving. Hence, how to design proof assistants to make it more accessible to users is an important problem for this field.

The most popular proof assistants today have user interfaces that are largely text-based. The main form of interaction consists of the user editing a text file containing the proof, either as a sequence of tactics or (as in Isabelle/Isar [17]) written in a structured proof language. During editing, the user interface displays the state of the proof at the current location of the proof text. To use the proof assistant, the user needs to be familiar with names of the major tactics, as well as some of the commonly used theorems. The Isabelle/Isar language makes the resulting proof text more readable. However, it requires the user to further understand the use of a number of keywords for structuring the proof.

Naturally, we may ask whether it is realistic to have user interfaces for proof assistants that is based on pointing and clicking. In an ideal setting, most of the interaction with the user interface should consist of choosing which facts to consider, and which actions to take through clicks of the mouse. The user interface performs the selected actions, and offers suggestions for future actions. Only occasionally will the user need to enter text using the keyboard, and even then only mathematical expressions rather than names of tactics or theorems.

While there have been attempts to build point-and-click user interfaces in the past, they have not gained widespread adoption for general-purpose theorem proving. Potential problems with existing designs include limited search functionality – the user still need to find names of theorems to use, and limited extensibility – there is usually a fixed set of proof methods, with no easy way to grow them for new application domains. This limits the use of user interfaces to simple examples, or to the special domains for which they are designed.

In this paper, we propose a new framework for designing user interfaces for proof assistants that is based on pointing and clicking. In this design, the user interacts with the interface mainly in three ways. First, at each step of the proof, the user chooses which goal to consider and which facts in the proof to use. Second, the user chooses an action from the list of actions suggested by the computer. The suggestion process may involve (but is not limited to) matching the chosen facts and goal with existing theorems. Third, the user annotates each proved theorem, to tell the computer which directions for applying the theorem are the most common, and should be considered during the suggestion process in future proofs. We give a general definition of *proof methods*. Any function satisfying this general definition can be added as a method in the user interface. This makes the design extensible: new proof methods reflecting domain-specific knowledge can be added in a convenient way.

We implement our design in a web interface[1]. The backend for the interface is provided by holpy, a new system for interactive theorem proving implemented in Python [18]. There are several aspects in holpy's design that are different from systems such as Isabelle and Coq, including a format for explicit representation of proofs and theories based on JSON [8]. The format for theory files is not designed

---

[1] Code available at https://gitee.com/bhzhan/holpy.

for direct editing by the user. This means any user interface must interpret the theory files for display in a more readable form, and reflect user changes back to the file. While this makes user interfaces more difficult to implement at first, it has the long-term advantage of allowing more flexibility in its design. The current work can be viewed as a first attempt to implement a user interface for holpy, justifying its choice of the theory format.

We now give an outline for the rest of this paper. In Sect. 2, we give an overview of the holpy system, focusing on those aspects of design that are different from the major proof assistants, and which are relevant to the current work. In Sect. 3, we describe the design of the user interface on an abstract level, then present the concrete implementation in Sect. 4, and give some statistics from tests on theorems from various domains. In Sect. 5, we present the proof of the Knaster-Tarski fixed point theorem as a detailed example. Finally, we conclude in Sect. 6 with a discussion of future work.

Related Work. There have been a few early attempts to build point-and-click user interfaces for proof assistants. The work of Bertot et al. in [5], and extended in [6], introduced the idea of "Proof by Pointing". In this framework, the user can trigger deduction rules in logic by pointing to specific parts of the goal formula. The latter work also studied how to implement script management (including undoing and redoing steps), and textual explanation of proofs. Another line of work by Abrial et al. [2] developed a user interface for Atelier B to perform formal proofs in set theory. The work by Breitner in [7] constructed a visual theorem proving interface based on connecting blocks, albeit also limited to proofs in logic.

In the area of program and system verification, several tools have user interfaces that allow proofs to be conducted by pointing-and-clicking. These include KeY [3] and KeYmaera/KeYmaera X [9,16]. These tools allow users to choose subgoals and select which actions to take from a menu. There is some similarity in the mode of interaction between our work and these systems. However, our focus is on general-purpose theorem proving in higher-order logic, rather than for specific program logics.

2 Overview of holpy

In this section, we give an overview of the holpy system, focusing on aspects that are different from systems such as Isabelle and Coq, and which are relevant to the current work. More details on the design of holpy can be found in [18].

holpy is a new system for interactive theorem proving implemented in Python. Its logical foundation is higher-order logic, similar to existing proof assistants such as Isabelle/HOL [15], HOL Light [12], and HOL4 [1]. On the other hand, holpy makes major changes to how proofs and theories are represented. In particular, it exports explicit proofs, with abbreviations by macros so they can be stored and checked by third-party tools without running into the usual scalability problems. For representing theories, holpy chooses a JSON-based format.

This format is not designed for direct human editing, but is convenient to read and write by computer programs. Finally, holpy provides an API in Python for implementing proof automation (as well as other tools). A major goal of holpy's design is to show that with export of explicit proofs, the type and memory safety issues of Python does not pose any problems for the soundness of proof-checking.

In the remainder of this section, we discuss various aspects of holpy in more detail, in particular the concepts of macros, proof representation, and tactics as it relates to holpy.

2.1 Proof Rules and Macros

Proofs in holpy are conducted in natural deduction style. The basic objects are sequents with a number of antecedents and a single consequent. A sequent with antecedent $A_1, \ldots, A_n$ and consequent C is written in the usual notation as $A_1, \ldots, A_n \vdash C$.

The logical foundation fixes a set of *primitive deduction rules*, with each rule taking a number of input sequents and possibly additional arguments, and outputs a sequent (or raises an exception). Examples of primitive deduction rules include introduction and elimination rules for implication and forall quantification, congruence properties of equality, substitution of type and term variables, and so on.

Proof rules can be considered as a generalization of primitive deduction rules. They are intended to represent a number of more basic steps of proof. In general, a proof rule takes as input the current theory environment (list of existing constants, theorems, etc.), a list of input sequents, and possibly additional arguments, and outputs a single sequent (or raises an exception). Each proof rule defines a precise signature for its additional arguments.

Primitive deduction rules form one class of proof rules. Another fundamental proof rule is `theorem`, which takes no input sequents and a theorem name as additional argument. If there exists a theorem with that name in the current theory environment, it outputs that theorem as a sequent. Otherwise, it raises an exception.

The other proof rules are called *macros*. They represent multiple steps of proof as a single step. In addition to the function returning the output sequent directly, each macro may also specify an expansion function which, given the same inputs, returns the invocations of proof rules used to obtain the output sequent (or raises an exception). The expanded proof can be used during proof checking, so the implementation of the macro need not be trusted. The use of macros means any portion of proof that can be algorithmically generated can be stored as a single step, so large proofs can be stored for proof-checking by third-party tools, without encountering the usual scalability issues. Some examples of common macros will be given in the following sections.

2.2 Format for Proofs

Proofs in holpy are exported into a linear form. A linear proof consists of an ordered list of *proof items*. Each proof item consists of an identifier, the name of a proof rule, additional arguments for the proof rule, and a list of identifiers of earlier proof items, representing the input sequents. A linear proof can be checked (within a theory environment) by reading the proof items in order, computing the sequent for each proof item by invoking the corresponding proof rule. The result of a linear proof is the sequent corresponding to the last proof item.

How to represent identifiers is largely conventional. We choose to represent each identifier as a tuple of natural numbers, written in dot-separated form (e.g. 0.2.1). This allows us to express sub-proofs. For example, steps in the main trunk of the proof have identifiers 0, 1, 2, etc. Proving the sequent in the proof item with identifier 1 may take place outside the main trunk, with steps having identifiers 1.0, 1.1, 1.2, and so on. In practice, we use sub-proofs when introducing variables and assumptions, as will be seen in the examples in the next subsection.

Internally for proof automation, holpy works with another form of proof representation: as directed acyclic graphs located in memory. Each vertex of the graph is a proof item, where the input sequents are referenced directly (so identifiers are not needed). There is a standard algorithm for converting proof terms to linear proofs. Hence, the general idea for proof automation in holpy is to first construct proof terms, then convert them to linear proofs for storage and viewing by the user.

2.3 Examples of Proofs

We give two simple examples of proofs for illustration. First, consider the proposition $A \wedge B \longrightarrow B \wedge A$. The linear proof is as follows:

0. $A \wedge B \vdash A \wedge B$ **by** assume $A \wedge B$
1. $A \wedge B \vdash A$ **by** apply_theorem conjD1 **from** 0
2. $A \wedge B \vdash B$ **by** apply_theorem conjD2 **from** 0
3. $A \wedge B \vdash B \wedge A$ **by** apply_theorem conjI **from** 2, 1
4. $\vdash A \wedge B \rightarrow B \wedge A$ **by** implies_intr **from** 3.

Each line in the above text represents a proof item. It starts with the identifier of the proof item. The part before **by** is the computed sequent. The part after **by** specifies the proof rule, the additional arguments, and identifiers of the input sequents. The proof rules `assume` and `implies_intr` are primitive deduction rules. The proof rule `apply_theorem` is the macro for applying a single theorem. It can be expanded into `theorem` rule for obtaining the theorem with the given name, `subst_type` (resp. `substitution`) for substituting the type (resp. term) variables, and `implies_elim` for discharging the assumptions.

As another example, consider the proof by induction of $n + 0 = n$ in Peano arithmetic.

0. $\vdash 0 + 0 = 0$ **by** rewrite_goal plus_def_1, $\langle goal \rangle$
1.0. $\vdash$ _VAR n **by** variable n :: nat
1.1. $n + 0 = n \vdash n + 0 = n$ **by** assume $n + 0 = n$
1.2. $n + 0 = n \vdash$ Suc $(n + 0) =$ Suc n **by** rewrite_goal_with_prev $\langle goal \rangle$ **from** 1.1
1.3. $n + 0 = n \vdash$ Suc $n + 0 =$ Suc n **by** rewrite_goal plus_def_2, $\langle goal \rangle$ **from** 1.2
  1. $\vdash \forall n.\ n + 0 = n \longrightarrow$ Suc $n + 0 =$ Suc n **by** intros **from** 1.0, 1.1, 1.3
  2. $\vdash n + 0 = n$ **by** apply_theorem_for nat_induct, $\{P\colon \lambda n.\ n + 0 = n,\ x\colon n\}$
    from 0, 1.

Here $\langle goal \rangle$ is an abbreviation for the goal statement, the trivial rule `variable` designate new variables, and macro `intros` introduces variables and assumptions (expanding into `forall_intr` and `implies_intr`). The macro `rewrite_goal` as well as `rewrite_goal_with_prev` are for rewriting (using a theorem and using a previous fact). Items 1.1 to 1.3 should be read in the backward direction: the goal from applying induction is Suc $n + 0 =$ Suc n. Rewriting using `plus_def_2` (inductive definition of $+$) changes it to Suc $(n + 0) =$ Suc n, which is resolved by rewriting using the inductive hypothesis.

This format for displaying linear proofs is still not easy to read. We choose to use this format in this and the next section in order to show the workings of tactics and methods more clearly. An improved format will be introduced in Sect. 4.

2.4 Format for Theories

In holpy, as in other proof assistants such as Isabelle and Coq, mathematical knowledge is organized as a collection of *theories*. Each theory imports a list of other theories, and may define new types, constants, and theorems. Proof of theorems are also contained in theories. The format for theories in holpy is based on JSON, hence holpy theory files have extension `.json`.

The main part of the theory file consists of a list of items, where each item represent a new type, constant, theorem, and so on. Each item is a dictionary consisting of both required and optional data for the item. For example, a theorem item may contain the proof of the theorem. It may also contain theorem attributes: a list of strings indicating (among others) how the theorem is usually used in proofs (the name is taken from a similar notion in Isabelle). For example, the attribute `backward` means the theorem is usually applied in the backward direction. This information is used during the search for suggested actions, in order to limit the number of suggestions (see Sect. 3.4).

Storing theories as a JSON file, rather than as a text file to be edited directly, makes the initial implementation of a user interfaces more difficult. However, it also creates more flexibility when designing the user interface. In particular, not all information in the JSON file has to be displayed. Some information can be hidden depending on the context. Another advantage is that it is easier to develop other tools to analyze theories – for example, to profile the performance of proof automation or the search functionality. In particular, we make use of this to produce the test results shown in Table 1.

2.5 Tactics

The notion of *tactics* in holpy is analogous, but not exactly the same, to tactics in Isabelle and Coq. In holpy, a tactic is a function taking as input a sequent to be proved, a list of input sequents, and possibly additional arguments (with fixed signature for each tactic), and returns a proof whose output is the target sequent (or raises an exception). The resulting proof may refer to input sequents, and it may also contain *holes*: sequents whose proof is left for later, indicated by the **sorry** proof rule. Intuitively, a tactic converts the current goal (the sequent to be proved) to a list of subgoals (those proof items with rule **sorry**), possibly making use of other known facts (the input sequents).

We give two examples for illustration. First, consider the introduction tactic, which takes a goal in the forall-implies form, and introduces the variables and assumptions in a sub-proof. It takes as additional arguments the names of the new variables (and no input sequents). For example, given the goal

$$\vdash \forall n.\ n + 0 = n \longrightarrow \mathrm{Suc}\ n + 0 = \mathrm{Suc}\ n,$$

and name n for the new variable, the tactic returns the proof

0.0. $\vdash$ _VAR n **by** variable n :: nat
0.1. $n + 0 = n \vdash n + 0 = n$ **by** assume $n + 0 = n$
0.2. $n + 0 = n \vdash \mathrm{Suc}\ n + 0 = \mathrm{Suc}\ n$ **by** sorry
0. $\vdash \forall n.\ n + 0 = n \longrightarrow \mathrm{Suc}\ n + 0 = \mathrm{Suc}\ n$ **by** intros **from** 0.0, 0.1, 0.2.

As a second example, consider the tactic for applying a theorem in the backward direction. Given the goal $A \wedge B \vdash B \wedge A$, a theorem name `conjI`, and no input sequents, the tactic produces the following proof:

0. $A \wedge B \vdash B$ **by** sorry
1. $A \wedge B \vdash A$ **by** sorry
2. $A \wedge B \vdash B \wedge A$ **by** apply_theorem conjI **from** 0, 1.

Note how the *macro* `apply_theorem` is used in the last step of the proof generated by the *tactic* for applying a theorem. If $A \wedge B \vdash B$ is given as an input sequent, the resulting proof has only one **sorry**, and the invocation of `apply_theorem` refers to that input sequent.

3 Design of the User Interface

In this section, we describe the overall design of the user interface on an abstract level, leaving the concrete implementation to the next section.

The basic principle of the design is as follows: we primarily allow user interaction with the interface in the following three ways:

1. During the proof, choose the current goal to consider and a list of facts available in the proof to use.
2. After choosing the current goal and a list of facts, choose an action to perform from the list of suggestions or from the menu, entering additional arguments for the action if necessary.
3. After a theorem is proved, annotate the theorem with how it should be used in future proofs (for example, direction of rule application or rewriting).

A key component of the user interface is the search functionality. Depending on the user annotations, the system searches in the list of existing theorems to see which ones are applicable to the current goal and selected facts, and display the results among the list of suggestions.

3.1   Methods

The central concept in this design is that of *methods*. Our definition of methods has some similarities to that in Isabelle, but there are also some important differences.

In our framework, the proof state is simply a linear proof with gaps. These gaps can be considered as the remaining goals. A method defines a transformation on the proof state. More precisely, it is a function taking the following input arguments, and either returns a new proof state or raises an exception:

- The current proof state.
- One selected goal in the proof state.
- A list of selected facts in the proof state (which must occur before the goal).
- Some additional arguments, with signature fixed by the method.

Unlike macros and tactics, the additional arguments for methods are always strings indexed by a set of keys (as determined by the method). Each method is responsible for parsing the input strings to the right kinds of objects (e.g. types and terms).

The above definition of methods is quite general. A method can literally make any change to the proof state. In practice, most methods fall into one of two common forms, corresponding to backward and forward reasoning. We now describe these two kinds of methods in more detail.

3.2   Backward Reasoning

Methods for backward reasoning take the selected goal, and attempt to replace it by a number of simpler goals. Such methods can be constructed directly from tactics. Given a tactic, the corresponding method performs the following actions:

1. Lookup the selected goal and facts in the proof state, to obtain the sequent to be proved and the list of input sequents.
2. Parse the input strings to the right kinds of objects (e.g. types and terms).

3. Apply the tactic on these inputs (and the theory environment of the proof), yielding a proof (possibly with holes) of the goal.
4. *Splice the proof into the proof state.* This involves modifying the proof item for the goal so it is no longer a `sorry`, and possibly inserting proof items before the goal.

The last splicing process is easy to understand intuitively, but can be quite tricky to implement. Inserting proof items in the middle of a proof involves changing the identifiers in the output of the tactic, and also in the part of the proof state after the goal (if we wish to keep the identifiers in order). It also needs to link up references to input sequents in the output of the tactic. We give two examples for illustration.

Introduction. Consider the proof of $n + 0 = n$ by induction. After applying induction, we have the following proof state:

0. $\vdash 0 + 0 = 0$ **by** sorry
1. $\vdash \forall n.\ n + 0 = n \longrightarrow \text{Suc } n + 0 = \text{Suc } n$ **by** sorry
2. $\vdash n + 0 = n$ **by** apply_theorem_for nat_induct, $\{P: \lambda n.\ n + 0 = n,\ x: n\}$ **from** 0, 1.

We invoke the method corresponding to the introduction tactic, with item 1 as the goal, and **n** as the additional argument for the name of the new variable. The result is:

0. $\vdash 0 + 0 = 0$ **by** sorry
1.0. $\vdash \_\text{VAR}\, n$ **by** variable n :: nat
1.1. $n + 0 = n \vdash n + 0 = n$ **by** assume $n + 0 = n$
1.2. $n + 0 = n \vdash \text{Suc } n + 0 = \text{Suc } n$ **by** sorry
  1. $\vdash \forall n.\ n + 0 = n \longrightarrow \text{Suc } n + 0 = \text{Suc } n$ **by** intros **from** 1.0, 1.1, 1.2
  2. $\vdash n + 0 = n$ **by** apply_theorem_for nat_induct, $\{P: \lambda n.\ n + 0 = n,\ x: n\}$ **from** 0, 1.

Note the output of the tactic (shown in Sect. 2.5) is modified to start with identifier 1, and spliced into the proof state.

Applying a Theorem. For this example, consider again the proof of $A \wedge B \longrightarrow B \wedge A$. Suppose we are at the following intermediate stage of the proof:

0. $A \wedge B \vdash A \wedge B$ **by** assume $A \wedge B$
1. $A \wedge B \vdash B$ **by** apply_theorem conjD2 **from** 0
2. $A \wedge B \vdash B \wedge A$ **by** sorry
3. $\vdash A \wedge B \rightarrow B \wedge A$ **by** implies_intr **from** 2.

Invoking the method corresponding to backward application of a theorem, with item 2 as the selected goal, item 1 as (the only) selected fact, and `conjI` as the name of the theorem, the result is:

0. $A \wedge B \vdash A \wedge B$ **by** assume $A \wedge B$
1. $A \wedge B \vdash B$ **by** apply_theorem conjD2 **from** 0
2. $A \wedge B \vdash A$ **by** sorry
3. $A \wedge B \vdash B \wedge A$ **by** apply_theorem conjI **from** 1, 2
4. $\vdash A \wedge B \rightarrow B \wedge A$ **by** implies_intr **from** 3.

Note items 2 and 3 in the original proof state are automatically re-numbered, along with their references.

3.3   Forward Reasoning

Methods for forward reasoning considers only the selected facts. It can be created directly from a macro: the selected facts become the input sequents to the macro, and the input strings are parsed to the arguments for the macro. The output of the macro is added as a new proof item directly in front of the selected goal.

For example, given the following initial proof state:

0. $A \wedge B \vdash A \wedge B$ **by** assume $A \wedge B$
1. $A \wedge B \vdash B \wedge A$ **by** sorry
2. $\vdash A \wedge B \rightarrow B \wedge A$ **by** implies_intr **from** 1.

We invoke the method corresponding to the macro `apply_theorem`, with item 1 as goal, item 0 as fact, and `conjD2` for the theorem name. The resulting proof state is as follows.

0. $A \wedge B \vdash A \wedge B$ **by** assume $A \wedge B$
1. $A \wedge B \vdash B$ **by** apply_theorem conjD2 **from** 0
2. $A \wedge B \vdash B \wedge A$ **by** sorry
3. $\vdash A \wedge B \rightarrow B \wedge A$ **by** implies_intr **from** 2.

Again, note the re-numbering of proof items 1 and 2 and their references after adding a new proof item before 1.

3.4   Search for Suggestions

In addition to the function transforming the proof state, each method also provides a search function. The search function takes as input the current proof state, the selected goal, and the list of selected facts, and outputs a list of suggested invocations of the method. Each suggested invocation provides input strings for some (but not necessarily all) of the required arguments.

For example, the method applying a single theorem in the forward (resp. backward) direction has search function that iterates through theorems having the `forward` (resp. `backward`) attribute. For each theorem, it matches the selected facts and goal with the assumptions and conclusion of the theorem, and returns a suggestion whenever the match succeeds. Likewise, the method for rewriting a fact (resp. goal) using a theorem has search function matching the left side of each theorem having the `rewrite` attribute with subterms of the selected fact (resp. goal).

The search function for methods is an important part of the system. The output of all search functions are combined to form the list of suggestions to the user. For methods applying a theorem in the forward/backward direction or for rewriting, this means the user does not need to lookup the name of the theorem, but the system will find it automatically based on the selected goal and facts. For methods requiring no input arguments (for example, automation that attempts to directly resolve the goal), the search function tests whether the method can be applied.

3.5   Summary

We now summarize the three notions of macros, tactics, and methods. All of them can be defined by the user, through which the system can be extended with domain-specific functionality. All three take as side inputs the current theory environment and additional arguments (where the signature is specified by individual functions). They are distinguished by their main input and output. We summarize these below.

- Macros take a list of sequents and return a new sequent. They may also return a proof of the new sequent when desired. They are mainly used to abbreviate a proof.
- Tactics take a sequent and return a proof (possibly with holes) of the sequent. A common pattern is to use a macro in the last step of the output proof.
- Methods take a proof state with selected goal and facts and apply a transformation to the proof state, and may provide a search functionality. Common patterns include applying a tactic at some goal, or applying a macro to obtain a new sequent just before the goal. They form the direct link to the user interface.

4   Implementation

We implemented the above design in a web interface. The main reason for building a user interface from scratch (as well as using the new holpy system as backend) is to allow full flexibility in its design. In principle, the core ideas can be applied to other proof assistants, perhaps with additional work on creating another layer of proof representation in these systems.

Besides functionality for constructing a proof, the user interface handles display and editing of theory files. In particular, it allows the user to manage the list of theories, and the list of items in a theory. The user may also specify attributes for theorems in the edit area. Hence, it provides all of the necessary functionality for interactive theorem proving based on holpy.

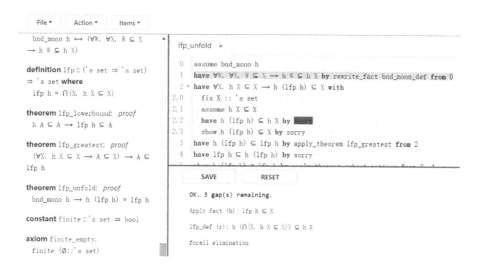

Fig. 1. Screenshot showing an intermediate stage in the proof of `lfp_unfold`.

Figure 1 shows a screenshot of the user interface. At the top, there is a menu of commands for file management, actions during a proof, and managing the list of items in a theory. The left panel displays the content of the current theory (it can also be changed to display the list of theories, or show more information about the current state of the proof). On the right side, the top panel displays the current state of the proof. The user selects goal and facts in the proof by clicking on the corresponding lines. The selected goal and facts are colored in red and yellow, respectively. After each change of selection, the user interface queries the backend for a list of suggestions of method applications, and displays them in the bottom panel, together with their expected effects. The user performs one of the suggested actions by clicking on the corresponding line. If the suggestion does not provide all of the required arguments, the user is prompted to enter the missing arguments.

Occasionally, the user will want to invoke a method not among the suggestions. Two common methods that are not searched are **cases** and **cut**. Both take a string which is parsed into a term A of boolean type. The **cases** method reduces the selected goal C into two goals $A \longrightarrow C$ and $\neg A \longrightarrow C$. The **cut** method inserts A as a new goal right before the current goal. When A is proved, it can be used in the proof of the original goal. The user can select invocation of these (and other) methods from the menu, and then enter the required arguments.

When displaying the proof, the user interface converts the proof to a more readable form compared to that used in Sects. 2 and 3. The basic transforms applied include the following. Examples will be given in Sect. 5.

- Use **fix** and **assume** for `variable` and `assume` rules.
- Hide antecedents of sequents (which can be inferred from previous **assumes**).

- Change invocations of `intros` to **with** blocks.
- Add **show** for the last sequent of a block, and **have** for other intermediate sequents.
- Indentation according to **with** blocks.

We applied our tool to a selection of theorems about logic, sets, functions, Peano arithmetic, and lists. The results are given in Table 1. In the table, $\#S$ is the total number of steps to prove the theorem, $\#Y$ is the number of steps that are among the suggestions, and $\#N$ is the number of steps that must

Table 1. Statistics on the test suite.

Name	Proposition	$\#S$	$\#Y$	$\#N$
double_neg	$\neg\neg A \longleftrightarrow A$	9	8	1
disj_conv_imp	$\neg A \vee B \longleftrightarrow A \longrightarrow B$	12	11	1
ex_conj_distrib	$(\exists x.\ A\ x \wedge B\ x) \longrightarrow (\exists x.\ A\ x) \wedge (\exists x.\ B\ x)$	6	6	0
all_conj_distrib	$(\forall x.\ A\ x \wedge B\ x) \longrightarrow (\forall x.\ A\ x) \wedge (\forall x.\ B\ x)$	7	7	0
conj_disj_distribL1	$A \wedge (B \vee C) \longleftrightarrow A \wedge B \vee A \wedge C$	23	23	0
pierce	$((A \longrightarrow B) \longrightarrow A) \longrightarrow A$	5	4	1
drinker	$\exists x.\ P\ x \longrightarrow (\forall x.\ P\ x)$	11	8	3
subset_antisym	$A \subseteq B \longrightarrow B \subseteq A \longrightarrow A = B$	7	7	0
subset_trans	$A \subseteq B \longrightarrow B \subseteq C \longrightarrow A \subseteq C$	4	4	0
cantor	$\exists S.\ \forall x.\ \neg f\ x = S$	13	12	1
Inter_subset	$A \in S \longrightarrow \bigcap S \subseteq A$	4	4	0
subset_Inter	$(\forall C.\ C \in S \longrightarrow A \subseteq C) \longrightarrow A \subseteq \bigcap S$	6	6	0
Union_union	$\bigcup(A \cup B) = \bigcup A \cup \bigcup B$	43	43	0
lfp_lowerbound	$h\ A \subseteq A \longrightarrow \text{lfp}\ h \subseteq A$	3	3	0
lfp_greatest	$(\forall X.\ h\ X \subseteq X \longrightarrow A \subseteq X) \longrightarrow A \subseteq \text{lfp}\ h$	5	5	0
lfp_unfold	$\text{bnd\_mono}\ h \longrightarrow h\ (\text{lfp}\ h) = \text{lfp}\ h$	10	9	1
fun_upd_triv	$(f)(a := f\ a) = f$	8	7	1
fun_upd_upd	$(f)(a := b, a := c) = (f)(a := c)$	9	8	1
fun_upd_twist	$\neg c = a \longrightarrow (f)(a := b, c := d) = (f)(c := d, a := b)$	19	17	2
comp_fun_assoc	$(f \circ g) \circ h = f \circ g \circ h$	4	4	0
injective_comp_fun	injective $f \longrightarrow$ injective $g \longrightarrow$ injective$(g \circ f)$	5	5	0
surjective_comp_fun	surjective $f \longrightarrow$ surjective $g \longrightarrow$ surjective$(g \circ f)$	11	9	2
add_comm	$x + y = y + x$	7	6	1
add_assoc	$x + y + z = x + (y + z)$	6	6	0
distrib_l	$x * (y + z) = x * y + x * z$	7	7	0
mult_assoc	$x * y * z = x * (y * z)$	7	6	1
mult_comm	$x * y = y * x$	7	6	1
less_eq_trans	$k \leq m \longrightarrow m \leq n \longrightarrow k \leq n$	9	9	0
append_right_neutral	$xs\ @\ [] = xs$	5	5	0
append_assoc	$(xs\ @\ ys)\ @\ zs = xs\ @\ ys\ @\ zs$	6	6	0
length_append	length $(xs\ @\ ys) = $ length $xs + $ length ys	9	9	0
rev_append	rev $(xs\ @\ ys) = $ rev $ys\ @\ $ rev xs	9	8	1
rev_rev	rev $($ rev $xs) = xs$	12	12	0
rev_length	length $($ rev $xs) = $ length xs	10	10	0
Total: 34 theorems		318	300	18

be invoked from the menu. The results show that the current user interface is already applicable to a wide range of areas, allowing proofs of basic results to be conducted largely by choosing from the suggestions.

5   Case Study: Knaster-Tarski Theorem

In this section, we use the proof of the Knaster-Tarski fixed point theorem to demonstrate how user interaction works in practice for a nontrivial result. Roughly speaking, the theorem states that any bounded monotone function has a (smallest) fixpoint. We state and prove a basic version of the theorem using our user interface.

The definition of bounded monotone functions is given as follows (here h is of type $'a\ set \Rightarrow\ 'a\ set$, and we assume the bound on h is given by the type $'a$).

$$\text{bnd\_mono } h \longleftrightarrow (\forall W.\ \forall X.\ W \subseteq X \longrightarrow h\,W \subseteq h\,X)$$

Given a bounded monotone function, its least fixed point is constructed using the following definition:

$$\text{lfp } h = \bigcap \{X.\ h\,X \subseteq X\}$$

Two properties of lfp h follow immediately from the definition. The first says that lfp h is contained in any set A satisfying $h\,A \subseteq A$. The second says that in order to show any set A is a subset of lfp h, it suffices to show A is a subset of any X satisfying $h\,X \subseteq X$. These properties are stated in higher-order logic as follows.

$$\text{lfp\_lowerbound} : h\,A \subseteq A \longrightarrow \text{lfp } h \subseteq A$$
$$\text{lfp\_greatest} : (\forall X.\ h\,X \subseteq X \longrightarrow A \subseteq X) \longrightarrow A \subseteq \text{lfp } h$$

The main theorem states that lfp h is in fact a fixed point of h:

$$\text{lfp\_unfold} : \text{bnd\_mono } h \longrightarrow h\,(\text{lfp } h) = \text{lfp } h$$

We now show how to prove this theorem using our user interface. The initial state of the proof is:

0 **assume** bnd_mono h
1 **show** $h\,(\text{lfp } h) = \text{lfp } h$ **by** sorry.

First, select item 0 as a fact, and apply the suggestion to rewrite the fact using theorem **bnd_mono_def**. Next, select item 1 (now item 2) as the goal (without selecting any facts), and use the suggestion to apply **subset_antisym**, to reduce the goal to two subset relations. The resulting state after these two operations is:

0 **assume** bnd_mono h

1 **have** $\forall W.\ \forall X.\ W \subseteq X \longrightarrow h\,W \subseteq h\,X$ **by** rewrite_fact bnd_mono_def **from** 0

2 **have** $h\,(\text{lfp}\,h) \subseteq \text{lfp}\,h$ **by** sorry

3 **have** $\text{lfp}\,h \subseteq h\,(\text{lfp}\,h)$ **by** sorry

4 **show** $h\,(\text{lfp}\,h) = \text{lfp}\,h$ **by** apply_theorem subset_antisym **from** 2, 3.

Next, select item 2 and follow the suggestion to apply `lfp_greatest`. This results in a forall goal. Select the goal and using the introduction method, entering X for the name of the new variable, we get the following proof state:

0 **assume** bnd_mono h

1 **have** $\forall W.\ \forall X.\ W \subseteq X \longrightarrow h\,W \subseteq h\,X$ **by** rewrite_fact bnd_mono_def **from** 0

2 **have** $\forall X.\ h\,X \subseteq X \longrightarrow h\,(\text{lfp}\,h) \subseteq X$ **with**

2.0   **fix** X $::'a$ set

2.1   **assume** $h\,X \subseteq X$

2.2   **show** $h\,(\text{lfp}\,h) \subseteq X$ **by** sorry

3 **have** $h\,(\text{lfp}\,h) \subseteq \text{lfp}\,h$ **by** apply_theorem lfp_greatest **from** 2

4 **have** $\text{lfp}\,h \subseteq h\,(\text{lfp}\,h)$ **by** sorry

5 **show** $h\,(\text{lfp}\,h) = \text{lfp}\,h$ **by** apply_theorem subset_antisym **from** 3, 4.

Next, we perform the only manual step in this proof, inserting an intermediate goal $h\,(\text{lfp}\,h) \subseteq h\,X$ before $h\,(\text{lfp}\,h) \subseteq X$ (choose "Insert goal" from the menu with item 2.2 selected as goal). The resulting proof state is (now showing only the block for proof of item 2):

2 **have** $\forall X.\ h\,X \subseteq X \longrightarrow h\,(\text{lfp}\,h) \subseteq X$ **with**

2.0   **fix** X $::'a$ set

2.1   **assume** $h\,X \subseteq X$

2.2   **have** $h\,(\text{lfp}\,h) \subseteq h\,X$ **by** sorry

2.3   **show** $h\,(\text{lfp}\,h) \subseteq X$ **by** sorry.

Next, select goal 2.2 and fact 1, and follow the suggestion to apply fact 1 to goal 2.2, resulting in a new goal $\text{lfp}\,h \subseteq X$:

2 **have** $\forall X.\ h\,X \subseteq X \longrightarrow h\,(\text{lfp}\,h) \subseteq X$ **with**

2.0   **fix** X $::'a$ set

2.1   **assume** $h\,X \subseteq X$

2.2   **have** $\text{lfp}\,h \subseteq X$ **by** sorry

2.3   **have** $h\,(\text{lfp}\,h) \subseteq h\,X$ **by** apply_fact_for lfp h, X **from** 1, 2.2

2.4   **show** $h\,(\text{lfp}\,h) \subseteq X$ **by** sorry.

Select item 2.2, the user interface suggests using the theorem `lfp_lowerbound`, reducing the goal to $h\,X \subseteq X$, which is already available as a fact. This proves 2.2. Next, select goal 2.4 and fact 2.3, the user interface suggests use of the theorem `subset_trans`, again reducing the goal to $h\,X \subseteq X$. Performing these two steps finishes the proof of item 2. The resulting proof state is:

2 **have** $\forall X.\, h\,X \subseteq X \longrightarrow h\,(\mathrm{lfp}\,h) \subseteq X$ **with**
2.0   **fix** $X ::'a$ set
2.1   **assume** $h\,X \subseteq X$
2.2   **have** $\mathrm{lfp}\,h \subseteq X$ **by** apply_theorem_for lfp_lowerbound, ... **from** 2.1
2.3   **have** $h\,(\mathrm{lfp}\,h) \subseteq h\,X$ **by** apply_fact_for lfp h, X **from** 1, 2.2
2.4   **show** $h\,(\mathrm{lfp}\,h) \subseteq X$ **by** apply_theorem subset_trans **from** 2.3, 2.1.

Two more steps are needed to finish the overall proof: reducing goal 4 to showing $h\,(h\,(\mathrm{lfp}\,h)) \subseteq h\,(\mathrm{lfp}\,h)$ using `lfp_lowerbound`, then using item 1 and 3 to resolve the goal. The user interaction is similar to before. The final state of the proof is:

0 **assume** bnd_mono h
1 **have** $\forall W.\, \forall X.\, W \subseteq X \longrightarrow h\,W \subseteq h\,X$ **by** rewrite_fact bnd_mono_def **from** 0
2 **have** $\forall X.\, h\,X \subseteq X \longrightarrow h\,(\mathrm{lfp}\,h) \subseteq X$ **with**
2.0   **fix** $X ::'a$ set
2.1   **assume** $h\,X \subseteq X$
2.2   **have** $\mathrm{lfp}\,h \subseteq X$ **by** apply_theorem_for lfp_lowerbound, ... **from** 2.1
2.3   **have** $h\,(\mathrm{lfp}\,h) \subseteq h\,X$ **by** apply_fact_for lfp h, X **from** 1, 2.2
2.4   **show** $h\,(\mathrm{lfp}\,h) \subseteq X$ **by** apply_theorem subset_trans **from** 2.3, 2.1
3 **have** $h\,(\mathrm{lfp}\,h) \subseteq \mathrm{lfp}\,h$ **by** apply_theorem lfp_greatest **from** 2
4 **have** $h\,(h\,(\mathrm{lfp}\,h)) \subseteq h\,(\mathrm{lfp}\,h)$ **by** apply_fact_for ... **from** 1, 3
5 **have** $\mathrm{lfp}\,h \subseteq h\,(\mathrm{lfp}\,h)$ **by** apply_theorem_for lfp_lowerbound, ... **from** 4
6 **show** $h\,(\mathrm{lfp}\,h) = \mathrm{lfp}\,h$ **by** apply_theorem subset_antisym **from** 3, 5.

As we can see, the resulting proof is quite readable, similar to a proof written in Isabelle/Isar. All intermediate conclusions are shown, as well as the name of each theorem and proof rule used. However, the entire proof is constructed using just a few clicks, occasionally entering names of variables, instantiations (when it cannot be derived by matching), and intermediate goals.

6 Conclusion

In this paper, we presented a framework for designing point-and-click user interfaces in interactive theorem proving. While a major goal of the design is ease of learning for newcomers to this field, we also intend to produce a fully functional system, able to be used for general purpose theorem proving. We implemented a prototype user interface based on this framework, and tested it on theorems about logic, sets, functions, Peano arithmetic, and lists, showing that these theorems can be proved largely by clicking on suggestions, and occasionally entering additional information.

We intend the current work to be the beginning of a long-term project to build a proof assistant that is both easy to use and scalable to large formalizations. Immediate next steps include extending the prover to make it work smoothly over a larger variety of domains. In addition, we envision two major improvements to the user interface. First, we currently lack strong proof automation in the system. This can be seen in the examples above, where the resulting proof consists of low-level theorem applications. Proof assistants such as Isabelle benefit from powerful tactics (such as `auto` and `blast`), as well as calls to external provers via Sledgehammer. In the future, we intend to incorporate both powerful internal automation, as well as connection to external provers. They fit nicely into the current framework as follows: the user selects the goal and a number of facts to use, and the system invokes proof automation in the background to check whether the goal can be solved using the selected facts. In this way, we intend to allow proofs that are a mix of high-level and low-level steps, where the user can choose the granularity of the argument.

Second, we currently make no attempt to order the list of suggestions of method applications. This does not pose a problem so far, since the test examples are still in the beginning stages of mathematical development, so there are few options at each step. As we move to formalizing deeper mathematical theories, it is expected that the number of options at each step will increase, even as we try to control it with theorem annotations and allowing the user to select which facts in the proof to use. One potentially promising approach is to use machine learning models for ordering the suggestions.

Acknowledgements. We would like to thank the referees for their helpful comments. This work is supported by the CAS Pioneer Hundred Talents Program under grant No. Y9RC585036.

References

1. The HOL 4 system. http://hol.sourceforge.net/
2. Abrial, J.-R., Cansell, D.: Click'n prove: interactive proofs within set theory. In: Basin, D., Wolff, B. (eds.) TPHOLs 2003. LNCS, vol. 2758, pp. 1–24. Springer, Heidelberg (2003). https://doi.org/10.1007/10930755_1
3. Ahrendt, W., Beckert, B., Bubel, R., Hähnle, R., Schmitt, P.H., Ulbrich, M. (eds.): Deductive Software Verification - The KeY Book - From Theory to Practice. LNCS, vol. 10001. Springer, Cham (2016). https://doi.org/10.1007/978-3-319-49812-6
4. Bertot, Y., Castéran, P.: Interactive Theorem Proving and Program Development - Coq'Art: The Calculus of Inductive Constructions. Texts in Theoretical Computer Science An EATCS Series. Springer, Heidelberg (2004). https://doi.org/10.1007/978-3-662-07964-5
5. Bertot, Y., Kahn, G., Théry, L.: Proof by pointing. In: Hagiya, M., Mitchell, J.C. (eds.) TACS 1994. LNCS, vol. 789, pp. 141–160. Springer, Heidelberg (1994). https://doi.org/10.1007/3-540-57887-0_94
6. Bertot, Y., Théry, L.: A generic approach to building user interfaces for theorem provers. J. Symb. Comput. **25**(2), 161–194 (1998)
7. Breitner, J.: Visual theorem proving with the incredible proof machine. In: Blanchette, J.C., Merz, S. (eds.) ITP 2016. LNCS, vol. 9807, pp. 123–139. Springer, Cham (2016). https://doi.org/10.1007/978-3-319-43144-4_8
8. The JSON data interchange syntax, December 2017. http://ecma-international.org/publications/files/ECMA-ST/ECMA-404.pdf

9. Fulton, N., Mitsch, S., Quesel, J., Völp, M., Platzer, A.: KeYmaera X: an axiomatic tactical theorem prover for hybrid systems. In: Automated Deduction - CADE-25 - 25th International Conference on Automated Deduction, Berlin, Germany, 1–7 August 2015, Proceedings, pp. 527–538 (2015)

10. Gonthier, G., et al.: A machine-checked proof of the odd order theorem. In: Blazy, S., Paulin-Mohring, C., Pichardie, D. (eds.) ITP 2013. LNCS, vol. 7998, pp. 163–179. Springer, Heidelberg (2013). https://doi.org/10.1007/978-3-642-39634-2_14

11. Hales, T., et al.: A formal proof of the Kepler conjecture. Forum Math. Pi 5, e2 (2017)

12. Harrison, J.: HOL light: an overview. In: Berghofer, S., Nipkow, T., Urban, C., Wenzel, M. (eds.) TPHOLs 2009. LNCS, vol. 5674, pp. 60–66. Springer, Heidelberg (2009). https://doi.org/10.1007/978-3-642-03359-9_4

13. Klein, G., et al.: Comprehensive formal verification of an OS microkernel. ACM Trans. Comput. Syst. 32(1), 2:1–2:70 (2014)

14. Leroy, X.: Formal verification of a realistic compiler. Commun. ACM 52(7), 107–115 (2009)

15. Nipkow, T., Paulson, L.C., Wenzel, M.: Isabelle/HOL - A Proof Assistant for Higher-Order Logic. Lecture Notes in Computer Science, vol. 2283. Springer, Heidelberg (2002). https://doi.org/10.1007/3-540-45949-9

16. Platzer, A., Quesel, J.-D.: KeYmaera: a hybrid theorem prover for hybrid systems (system description). In: Armando, A., Baumgartner, P., Dowek, G. (eds.) IJCAR 2008. LNCS (LNAI), vol. 5195, pp. 171–178. Springer, Heidelberg (2008). https://doi.org/10.1007/978-3-540-71070-7_15

17. Wenzel, M.: Isar — a generic interpretative approach to readable formal proof documents. In: Bertot, Y., Dowek, G., Théry, L., Hirschowitz, A., Paulin, C. (eds.) TPHOLs 1999. LNCS, vol. 1690, pp. 167–183. Springer, Heidelberg (1999). https://doi.org/10.1007/3-540-48256-3_12

18. Zhan, B.: holpy: Interactive Theorem Proving in Python. arXiv e-prints arXiv:1905.05970, May 2019

SqlSol: An accurate SQL Query Synthesizer

Lin Cheng[✉]

Western Michigan University, Kalamazoo, USA
lin.cheng@wmich.edu

Abstract. SQL is the programming language for communicating with relational databases, but writing SQL queries is challenging for many end users due to lack of programming knowledge. In this paper, we present an efficient and accurate algorithm that helps users to synthesize SQL queries from IO examples, which is the first algorithm to encode SQL synthesis problem into constraint-solving problem. We propose an axiom that encodes the semantics of a SQL query into logic constraints, and decompose the SQL synthesis problem into two parts: problem-encoding and constraint-solving. For the problem-encoding part, we use a SQL template that is same as prior work and parameterize it, then based on this axiom, we encode the parameters into logic constraints. For the constraint-solving part, we use the off-the-shelf modern SMT solvers. Our algorithm supports multiple IO examples, therefore users can add more examples to refine the solution until a correct one is found. We implemented a tool, SqlSol, and evaluated it on 171 benchmarks. The results showed that it efficiently solved 68% of the benchmarks in 3 s in average. For those SqlSol cannot solve, SqlSol terminated in 4 s in average.

Keywords: SQL · SMT solver · Program synthesis · Program by example

1 Introduction

Relational database is one of the most important data management infrastructure in the modern era of data technology. Structured query language (SQL) is the language that is used to manipulate relational databases. According to TIOBE index [4], SQL is one of the top 10 ranked programming languages, the best-ranked database query language in the year of 2018. However, writing SQL queries is difficult because of the high expressiveness of the language structs. Searching on Stack Overflow with the keyword SQL, we got over 30000 pages of results, each of which contains 15 questions. That is, more than 450K questions about writing SQL queries asked.

Programming By Example (PBE) has attracted research interests as a technique to help end-user programming computers by demonstrating concrete examples [8,9,11,12]. Observing users usually provide input-output (IO) tables as

© Springer Nature Switzerland AG 2019
Y. Ait-Ameur and S. Qin (Eds.): ICFEM 2019, LNCS 11852, pp. 104–120, 2019.
https://doi.org/10.1007/978-3-030-32409-4_7

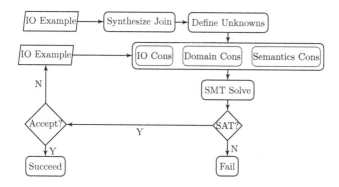

Fig. 1. The architecture of SqlSol

examples when raising questions, researchers have proposed different algorithms to synthesize SQL queries by examples [15,16].

The state-of-the-art SQL synthesizers, SQLSynthesizer [16] and Scythe [15], use hand-crafted search algorithms to automatically generate SQL queries from input-output examples. SQLSynthesizer uses a parameterized SQL template, which is showed by a survey that it supports the mostly wide used SQL features, and uses a decision tree to decide the parameters, and uses an online database to validate the result. Scythe enlarges the supported SQL subset by allowing nested queries, and uses abstract SQL query to prune the search space, and manually implements SQL semantics to validate the result. Both SQLSynthesizer and Scythe support one IO example and use heuristics to rank solutions because there may be many SQL queries that satisfy the IO example.

Instead of manually creating search algorithms, we propose an axiom which encodes the semantics of a SQL query and a new algorithm that encodes the SQL synthesis problem into logic constraints and uses the off-the-shelf satisfiability modulo theory (SMT) solvers to solve for the solution. Nowadays, SMT solvers, Z3 [7] and CVC4 [5] et al., have become the corner stones of modern computer science. The rich features of modern SMT solvers allow us to express complicate datatypes, like `table`. For example, in this paper, we encode `table` as a datatype of `Array(String Int Cell)`, Where `Cell` is a datatype which can hold `int`, `float`, `string` or `null` values of a table cell.

Our algorithm enjoys the following benefits brought by the logic constraints based approach. First, it inherits the theoretic properties from the formal methods. That is, because the logic constraints are sound and complete, if the algorithm of SMT solver is sound and complete, the whole algorithm is sound and complete. Second, our algorithm enjoys performance improvement, because the implementations of modern SMT solvers focus on performance and are battle-hardened, [3]. Third, it is made easy for our approach to support multiple IO examples, because our algorithm decomposes the SQL synthesis problem into two parts: logic encoding and logic solving. Actually, we only need to conjuncture the logic constraints for all IO examples. Therefore, instead of heuristically ranking

```
Select t2.student,t2.avg_score
 From
 (Select t4.student, t4.level, t4.avg_score,
         t5.student As student1,
         t5.level As level1, t5.course, t5.score
  From ((Select
            t3.student, t3.level, Avg(t3.score) As avg_score
         From
           (Select *
              From
               input_table_0
              Where input_table_0.score > 59.0) As t3
         Group By
           t3.student, t3.level) As t4 Join
       (Select *
          From
           input_table_0
          Where input_table_0.score = 59.0) As t5)) As t2
 Where t2.level = t2.level1;
```

Fig. 2. Solution generated by Scythe. It has 3 levels of nested queries and 4 sub-queries.

solution to match an IO example, our algorithm is able to synthesize the *correct* SQL query, i.e., capture the user intent. For example, in our motivating example in Sect. 2, our algorithm generates the SQL query that matches the specification in natural words exactly. However, the state-of-the-art tool, Scythe, generates the solution, Fig. 2, which is more complicate and semantically different because its predicate is `score > 59` instead of `average(score) > 59`.

Figure 1 is the overall flow of our tool, SqlSol. It starts with one IO example provided by the user, and synthesizes the JOIN conditions. Then, it determines the number and types of the unknowns in a parameterized SQL query, and encodes IO constrains, domain constraints, and semantics constraints. Then, it sends all constraints to an SMT solver to check for satisfiability. If the solver returns unsatisfiable, it declares failure. If the solver returns satisfiable, it fetches the model generated by the solver and compiles a SQL query and asks the user to decide whether to accept or not. If yes, the algorithm returns; Otherwise, the algorithm asks the user to add new IO examples to refine the solution until a solution is accepted or failure declared. Note that our algorithm joins input tables same way and supports same SQL subset as SQLSynthesizer.

We evaluated SqlSol on two benchmark sets used by previous work, SQL-Synthesizer and Scythe [15,16]. Under a reasonable setting, on SQLSynthesizer benchmark set, SqlSol solved more problems than both SQLSynthesizer and Scythe. On Scythe benchmark set, although SqlSol solved less problems than Scythe because the supported SQL subset is smaller, SqlSol is faster for both solved and unsolved problems. Specially, for unsolved problems, SqlSol terminates in seconds, while Scythe only terminates after time out of 120 s. We evaluated the scalability of SqlSol and Scythe on another 25 hand-written benchmarks, and the result showed that SqlSol is 2X to 10X faster than Scythe. Our evaluation also showed that supporting multiple IO examples not only help user to find the *correct* SQL query, but also can speedup the algorithm.

```
SELECT student.name AS name, average(grade.score) AS average
FROM student
JOIN grade
ON student.id = grade.s_id
WHERE student.level = 'senior'
GROUP BY student.name
HAVING average(grade.score) > 59.
```

Fig. 3. Hand-written solution for the motivating example

We have the following contributions:

- We propose an axiom to model the SQL semantics for SQL synthesis. We propose an innovative algorithm which encodes SQL synthesis problem into logic constraints, then solve it with modern SMT solvers.
- Our algorithm supports multiple examples and iteratively refines the solution space to find a solution accepted by the user, in addition to a solution satisfying one IO example.
- We implemented an end-to-end synthesis tool, SqlSol, and evaluated the results experimentally.

The rest of the paper is organized as follows: In Sect. 2, we use a motivating example to demonstrate our algorithm step by step. In Sect. 3, we introduce our SQL subset. In Sect. 4, we present our technique in details. In Sect. 5, we evaluate our algorithm and compare to the state-of-the-art SQL synthesizing tools.

2   Motivating Example

In this section, we use an example to demonstrate our algorithm. Consider the following SQL writing problem, which is taken from a classic database management textbook [13] and modified for the purpose of illustration.

Find the name and average score of each senior student whose average score is greater than 59.

Figure 3 is our hand-written solution of the problem. The SQL query first joins two tables on the columns student.id and grade.student_id. Then, it selects all senior students using the condition in the WHERE clause. Next, it computes the average score for each student and selects those rows where the average scores are greater than 59 using the condition in the HAVING clause. Finally, it projects the selected columns to the columns name and average of the output table.

Figure 4 is an IO example we manually wrote for the input of the synthesis algorithm. It includes two input tables, Student and Grade, and one output table, Output. The column s_id of table Grade is a *foreign key* of the column id of table Student. The goal of the SQL synthesizer is to automatically generate a SQL query which satisfies the IO example. Ideally, it returns the exact solution, Fig. 3, instead of other solutions like Fig. 2.

Student		
id	name	level
1	stu1	senior
2	stu2	senior
3	stu3	senior
4	stu4	junior
5	stu5	junior
6	stu6	senior
7	stu7	senior

Grade		
s_id	course	score
1	Math	70
1	English	80
2	Math	59
3	English	40
4	Math	70
5	English	85
6	English	60
7	Computer	90

Output	
name	average
stu1	75
stu6	60
stu7	90

Fig. 4. Input-output tables for motivation example

Input				
id	name	level	course	score
1	stu1	senior	Math	70
1	stu1	senior	English	80
2	stu2	senior	Math	59
3	stu3	senior	English	40
4	stu4	junior	Math	70
5	stu5	junior	English	85
6	stu6	senior	English	60
7	stu7	senior	Computer	90

Output	
name	average
stu1	75
stu6	60
stu7	90

Fig. 5. Input-output tables after join in motivation example

Our tool, SqlSol, joins the two input tables on the foreign key relation, and creates a parameterized SQL query, Fig. 6. Then, it encodes constraints for the IO example, the domain of the unknowns, and the semantics of the SQL query, and then it sends the constraints to a SMT solver, Z3 we used, to check satisfiability. After the SMT solver returns satisfiable, it fetches the models of the unknowns from the solver and compiles a SQL query, Fig. 3. The user accepts the solution, and the algorithm terminates.

2.1   Join Conditions

For the purpose of simplifying the synthesis algorithm, without loss of information, we join the input tables using two heuristic rules same as SQLSynthesizer. The first rule is to match the column names and types; the second rule is to compare the constants in the columns. Figure 5 shows the IO example after the input tables are joined. The join condition is `student.id = grade.s_id`, which is a foreign key constraint of the schema of the two input tables.

2.2   Parameterized SQL Query

We create a parameterized SQL query, Fig. 6, for the motivating example. A parameterized SQL query is a SQL query skeleton that has unknowns regarding to the IO table schema and constants et al. The unknowns can be represented by uninterpreted variables when encoded into logic constraints.

In Fig. 6, there are two unknowns, $??^1_s$ and $??^2_s$, for there are two columns in table Output. The tuple $(??_{wpop}, ??_{wpc}, ??_{wpv})$ is the predicate in the WHERE

```
SELECT   ??¹ₛ AS name , ??²ₛ AS average FROM input
WHERE (??_wpop ??_wpc ??_wpv) GROUP BY ??_gc HAVING (??_hpop ??_hpc ??_hpv)
```

Fig. 6. Parameterized SQL query for motivation example

clause, and the unknowns stand for the logic comparator, column name in table `Input` and a constant. The tuple $(??_{hpop}, ??_{hpc}, ??_{hpv})$ is the predicate in the `HAVING` clause, and the unknowns stand for the logic comparator, column name of the aggregation column and a constant. We set the upper bound of length of the predicates in both `WHERE` and `HAVING` clause to be 1. Note that the constant $??_{hpv}$ is a constant in the aggregation column, and has to be computed before it can be used.

2.3   Auxiliary Columns

We add an auxiliary aggregation column, to encode the SQL query with an aggregation column. An aggregation column depends on three variables: the aggregation function $??_{af}$, the aggregation column $??_{ac}$, and the group column $??_{gc}$, which are all unknowns in our synthesis algorithm. The aggregation column can be computed with the unknowns in the SMT language, as presented in details in Sect. 4.4.

2.4   Logic Constraints for SQL Synthesis Problem

The logic constraints for SQL synthesis problem fall into three categories: `IO constraints`, `domain constrains`, and `semantics constraints`. IO constraints encode the IO examples into logic constraints. However, because there is no `Table` data structure and no polymorphism support in SMT language, we define an innovative `Table` and `Cell` data structure, to effectively implement the constraints of IO examples in SMT language.

Domain constraints are the domains of the unknowns. In Fig. 6, the unknowns $??^1_s$ and $??^2_s$ in the `SELECT` clause are column names or aggregation column names of table `input`. The unknown $??_{af}$ is an aggregation function. The unknowns $??_{ac}, ??_{wpc}, ??_{hpc}$ are column names. The unknowns $??_{wpop}$ and $??_{hpop}$ are logic comparators. The unknowns $??_{wpv}$ and $??_{hpv}$ are constants in the columns of $??_{wpc}$ and $??_{hpc}$.

Let `input.cols` be the column names of table `input`, `input.acols` be the aggregation column names `acol`, `afs` be the set of aggregation functions, `ops` be the set of logic comparators. We have

$$input.cols = \{id, name, level, course, score\}$$
$$input.acols = \{acol\}$$
$$afs = \{count, sum, avg, min, max\}$$
$$ops = \{=, >, <, \neq, \leq, \geq\}$$

The domain constraints for the unknowns are

$$??^1_s, ??^2_s \in input.cols \cup input.acols$$
$$??_{af} \in afs$$
$$??_{ac}, ??_{wpc}, ??_{gc} \in input.cols$$
$$??_{hpc} \in input.acols$$
$$??_{wpop}, ??_{hpop} \in ops$$
$$??_{wpv} \in input.??_{wpc}$$
$$??_{hpv} \in input.??_{hpc}$$

The semantics constraints encode the semantics of a SQL query with respect to the IO example. For each row r in the table input, the SQL query first checks the predicates in the WHERE and HAVING clause. If they are both true, the columns of the row in the SELECT clause will form a row s in the table output. Otherwise the row will be skipped. In the other direction, for a row s in the table output, there exists a row in the table input that satisfies the predicates in the WHERE and HAVING clause. The semantic constraints for the parameterized SQL query are

$$\forall 1 \leq r \leq 8, \ (??_{wpop} \ ??_{wpc} \ ??_{wpv}) \wedge (??_{hpop} \ ??_{hpc} \ ??_{hpv}))$$
$$\implies \exists 1 \leq s \leq 3, \ (input(??_{c1}, r) = output(name, s))$$
$$\wedge \ (input(??_{c2}, r) = output(average, s))$$
$$\forall 1 \leq s \leq 3 \implies$$
$$\exists 1 \leq r \leq 8, \ (??_{wpop} \ ??_{wpc} \ ??_{wpv}) \wedge (??_{hpop} \ ??_{hpc} \ ??_{hpv}))$$
$$(input(??_{c1}, r) = output(name, s))$$
$$(input(??_{c1}, r) = output(name, s))$$

2.5   Solve

We sent the constraints above to an SMT solver, Z3, to check for satisfiability, and the solver returned satisfiable. Then, we fetched the model from the solver and substituted the unknowns in the abstract query with the model, and a concrete SQL query was generated. We manually checked and accepted the solution, since it is exactly the one that solves the question of this motivating example. Then the algorithm terminated. The computation took less than 1 s.

3   SQL Subset Syntax

Figure 7 shows the syntax of the standard SQL subset supported by our tool SqlSol, which is similar to the state-of-the-art tool, SQLSynthesizer [16]. This subset is designed to support the most widely used SQL features according to a survey by Zhang et al. [16].

$\langle query \rangle ::= \langle sfw \rangle \mid \langle sfwgh \rangle$
$\langle sfw \rangle \quad ::= \text{SELECT } \langle expr \rangle^+ \text{ FROM } \langle table \rangle^+ \text{ WHERE } \langle wp \rangle^+$
$\langle sfwgh \rangle ::= \text{SELECT } \langle expr \rangle^+ \text{ FROM } \langle table \rangle^+ \text{ WHERE } \langle wp \rangle^+ \text{ GROUP BY } \langle col \rangle^+$
$\qquad\qquad \text{HAVING } \langle hp \rangle^+$
$\langle table \rangle ::= \text{atom}$
$\langle col \rangle \quad ::= \langle table \rangle.\text{atom}$
$\langle af \rangle \quad ::= \text{COUNT} \mid \text{SUM} \mid \text{AVG} \mid \text{MIN} \mid \text{MAX}$
$\langle acol \rangle ::= (\langle af \rangle \, \langle col \rangle)$
$\langle op \rangle \quad ::= \, = \mid > \mid < \mid \neq \mid \geq \mid \leq$
$\langle expr \rangle ::= \langle col \rangle \mid \langle acol \rangle$
$\langle wp \rangle \quad ::= \langle wp \rangle \wedge \langle wp \rangle \mid \langle wp \rangle \vee \langle wp \rangle \mid \neg \langle wp \rangle \mid (\langle op \rangle \, \langle col \rangle \, \text{atom}) \mid \text{true} \mid \text{false}$
$\langle hp \rangle \quad ::= \langle hp \rangle \wedge \langle hp \rangle \mid \langle hp \rangle \vee \langle hp \rangle \mid \neg \langle hp \rangle \mid (\langle op \rangle \, \langle acol \rangle \, \text{atom}) \mid \text{true} \mid \text{false}$

Fig. 7. Syntax of the supported SQL subset in SqlSol: atom is a table name, or column name, or a cell value.

While mostly same, there are two differences between SqlSol and SQLSynthesizer. One difference is that the logic constraints in SqlSol cannot support DISTINCT and ORDER BY. That is because SqlSol models tables as sets, which is common in formal methods. For example, relational algebra is defined based on sets [1]; previous work, [14], models tables as sets. Fortunately, because both DISTINCT and ORDER BY are of arity 0, synthesis of them only needs to compare rows of the result table and the output table in the IO example, therefore can be done in a post-process step.

Another difference is that, in addition to the three logic comparators $=, >, <$ supported by SQLSynthesizer, SqlSol also supports $\neq, \geq, \leq$.

4 Technique

In this section, we present the technique details of our algorithm.

4.1 Overview

Algorithm 1 is the high-level algorithm of SqlSol. Line 2 joins all input tables into one input table. Line 3 declares all unknowns in the parameterized SQL query as uninterpreted functions in SMT language. Line 4–6 add the domain constraints for all unknowns. Line 7–22 are the iteration process that adds one new example each time. For every example, line 8–9 encode it with our new Table datatype in SMT language; line 10 encodes the semantics of parameterized SQL query into constraints with respect to the input-output tables. In line 10–22, we send all constraints to the SMT solver to check for satisfiability. If the solver returns satisfiable, we fetch the model and compile a concrete SQL query, which satisfies the IO examples. Then, instead of stopping here, we let the user decide whether to accept the query or not: if yes, the algorithm returns with success; otherwise, the user can add a new IO example, and the loop continues. If the solver returns unsatisfiable, the algorithm declares failure.

Algorithm 1. SqlSol SQL Synthesizer

1: Let (I_1, O_1) be the Input Output example, $X = \emptyset$ be the set of unknowns, $B = \emptyset$ be the set of constraints, S be the SMT solver
2: $\tilde{I} = join(I_1)$, $O = O_1$
3: $X = makeUnknowns(\tilde{I}, O)$
4: **for** $x \in X$ **do**
5:     $B.add(encodeDomain(\tilde{I}, O, x))$
6: **end for**
7: **while** True **do**
8:     $B.add(encodeTable(\tilde{I}))$
9:     $B.add(encodeTable(O))$
10:     $B.add(encodeSemantics(\tilde{I}, O, X))$
11:     **if** $S.solve(B) == SAT$ **then**
12:         $m = S.model()$
13:         **if** $m.accepted()$ **then**
14:             **return**   // solution
15:         **else**
16:             $(I, O) = addExample()$
17:             $\tilde{I} = join(I)$
18:             **continue**
19:         **end if**
20:     **else**
21:         **return**   // no solution
22:     **end if**
23: **end while**

4.2 New SMT Datatype for Table Encoding and IO Constraints

Satisfiability modulo theories (SMT) solve decision problems using background theories expressed in logic constraints. Though modern SMT solvers have theories of various data structures such as List, Array, Bit Vector, they do not have theories for Table. Veanes et al., [14], proposed a theory which uses a list of tuples to model Table. The unknowns in this theory are table cells, therefore the theory is able to synthesize input tables given a SQL query. However, because our algorithm synthesizes a SQL query given IO examples and the unknowns are elements in the SQL query, we can not simply use the theory.

We use a new Table SMT datatype to model input-output tables. The table datatype is a customized 2-dimension Array. Because we handle different types of table cells, including Int, Float, String, and Null, but SMT language does not support polymorphism, we work around by using the datatype feature of the latest SMT-lib standard [6]. We define a new datatype Cell and define the Table datatype as Array(String Int Cell), where the elements are the column name, row index, and cell value of the table, respectively.

With our new Table datatype, we can efficiently encode the IO constrains of the input-output tables in SMT language. The IO constraints of each table is the union of the constraints of all table cells. An example use of the table datatype is (assert (= (select table col 1) (String John))), which asserts that the cell value of table at column col and row 1 equals to John of String type.

4.3   Parameterize SQL Query and Domain Constraints

A parameterized SQL Query is a SQL query that has unknowns in the SELECT, WHERE, GROUP BY, HAVING clauses. In this section, we define the unknowns and their domain constraints.

Parameterize SELECT Clause. The unknowns in the SELECT clause define the original or aggregated column names in the **input** table that are projected to the **output** table. The number of unknowns in the SELECT clause equal to the number of columns in the output table. Each unknown is of **String** type. The domain of the unknowns is the set of original and aggregated column names.

Let *input.cols* and *input.acols* be the set of original and aggregated column names of table *input*. Let *noc* be the number of columns of table *output*. Let $??^i_s$ be the $i - th$ unknown in the SELECT clause. The domain constraints of an unknown in the SELECT clause is the union of *input.cols* and *input.acols*.

$$??^i_s \in input.cols \cup input.acols, \ i = 1, \cdots, noc \tag{1}$$

Parameterize WHERE Clause. The predicate in the WHERE clause is a boolean expression which decides whether a row in the table **input** will be selected to the table **output**. The boolean expression is comparison patterns connected by logic conjunctive connector $\wedge$ or logic disjunctive connector $\vee$. A comparison pattern is a basic pattern or logic constant **true** or **false**.

Let nwp be the upper bound of the number of basic comparison patterns. Let $??^i_{wpop}$ be the unknowns for logic comparators of Enumeration type, $??^i_{wpc}$ be the unknowns for column names of String type, $??^i_{wpv}$ be the unknowns for values of the columns of Cell type, $??^i_{wpm}$ be unknowns of Boolean type, $??^i_{wpb}$ be unknowns of Enumeration type $\{\wedge, \vee\}$.

A basic comparison pattern is of form $bcp = (??_{wpop} \ ??_{wpc} \ ??_{wpv})$, whose semantics is executing the comparator $??_{wpop}$ with operands $??_{wpc}$ and $??_{wpv}$. A comparison pattern is defined as $cp = (??_m \ bcp)$, whose semantics is when $??^i_m$ is *true*, it evaluates to *true*, otherwise bcp. The predicate wp is defined in such a way that it covers basic predicates of length from 0 to nwp. The definition of wp is $wp = wp^{nwp}$, where wp^i is defined recursively:

$$wp^i = \begin{cases} true & i = 0 \\ cp^1 & i = 1 \\ (??^i_{wpb} \ cp^i \ wp^{i-1}) & i = 2, \cdots, nwp \end{cases} \tag{2}$$

Let ops be the set of logic comparators, $input.??^i_{wpc}$ be the cell values of column $??^i_{wpc}$, cs be the set of logic connectors $\{\wedge, \vee\}$. The domain constraints in the WHERE clause are

$$??^i_{wpop} \in ops$$
$$??^i_{wpc} \in input.cols$$
$$??^i_{wpv} \in input.??^i_{wpc}, i = 1, \cdots, nwp \tag{3}$$
$$??^j_{wpb} \in cs, j = 2, \cdots, nwp$$

Parameterize GROUP BY Clause. The unknowns in the GROUP BY clause define the columns by which the output table is grouped. In addition to original columns of the input table, we added special columns to the input table to support special groups. Particularly, we added two special group-by columns: ucol and scol. The column ucol has values that are all unique. Grouping by ucol means every row is one group. Therefore, queries with GROUP BY clause generalize to queries without GROUP BY clause. The column scol has values that are all equal. Grouping by scol means all rows is one group.

Let ng be the upper bound of the number of group-by columns, $input.cols$ and $input.hcols$ be the original columns and added group-by columns. Let $??_{gc}^i$ be the unknown in the GROUP BY clause. The domain constraints for the GROUP BY clause are

$$??_{gc}^i \in input.cols \cup \{input.hcols\}, \ i = 1, \cdots, ng \tag{4}$$

Parameterize HAVING Clause. The predicate in the HAVING clause is the same as the predicate in the WHERE clause except that it only applies to the aggregation column, i.e., input.acols, while the predicate in the WHERE clause only applies to the original column, i.e., input.cols.

Let nhp be the upper bound of the number of basic comparison pattern. Let $??_{hpop}^i$ be the unknowns for logic comparators of Enumeration type, $??_{hpc}^i$ be the unknowns for column names of String type, $??_{hpv}^i$ be the unknowns for values of the columns of Cell type, $??_{hpm}^i$ be unknowns of Boolean type, $??_{hpb}^i$ be unknowns of Enumeration type $\{\wedge, \vee\}$.

Let a basic comparison pattern be $bcp = (??_{hpop} \ ??_{hpc} \ ??_{hpv})$, a comparison pattern be $cp = (??_m \ bcp)$. The definition of predicate hp is $hp = hp^{nhp}$, where hp^i is defined recursively:

$$hp^i = \begin{cases} true & i = 0 \\ cp^1 & i = 1 \\ (??_{hpb}^i \ cp^i \ hp^{i-1}) & i = 2, \cdots, nhp \end{cases} \tag{5}$$

The domain constraints in the HAVING clause are

$$\begin{aligned} ??_{hpop}^i &\in ops \\ ??_{hpc}^i &\in input.cols \\ ??_{hpv}^i &\in input.??_{hpc}^i, i = 1, \cdots, nhp \\ ??_{hpb}^j &\in cs, j = 2, \cdots, nhp \end{aligned} \tag{6}$$

4.4   Compute Aggregation Columns

Aggregation columns are computed before semantics constraints are encoded. Unlike explicit search algorithms enumerate all combinations of group-by columns and aggregation columns, our algorithm computes the aggregation columns only once with the unknowns defined before.

Let r be a row index, n be the number of rows, *ite* be the `if-then-else` struct, *wp* be the predicate in the `WHERE` clause, *col* be the columns in the `GROUP BY` clause, $col(r)$ be the cell value of column *col* at row r.

Compute Aggregation COUNT. Let *count* be the aggregation column for aggregation function `COUNT`. The formula to compute `count` is

$$count(r) = \sum_{1 \leq i \leq n} ite(wp(r) \wedge (col(i) = col(r)), 1, 0) \tag{7}$$

Compute Aggregation SUM. Let *acol* be the column to apply the aggregation function `SUM` on, *sum* be the aggregation column for aggregation function `SUM`. The formula to compute *sum* is

$$sum(r) = \sum_{1 \leq i \leq n} ite(wp(r) \wedge (col(i) = col(r)), acol(r), 0) \tag{8}$$

The aggregation column `AVERAGE` is computed as the division of `SUM` and `COUNT`.

Compute Aggregation MAX. Let *acol* be the column to apply the aggregation function `MAX` on, *max* be the aggregation column for aggregation function `MAX`. The formula to compute the aggregation column *max* is recursive:

$$max(r) = ite((wp(r) \wedge (acol(r) > max(r-1)),$$
$$acol(r), max(r-1)) \tag{9}$$

Compute Aggregation MIN. Let *acol* be the column to apply the aggregation function `MIN` on, *min* be the aggregation column for aggregation function `MIN`. The formula to compute the aggregation column *min* is recursive:

$$min(r) = ite((wp(r) \wedge (acol(r) > min(r-1)),$$
$$acol(r), min(r-1)) \tag{10}$$

4.5   Encode Semantics Constraints

In this section, we introduce the axiom that models the semantics of SQL queries in logic language. On one hand, the axiom considers the direction from input to output. For each row in the table **input**, if it satisfies the predicate *wp* in the `WHERE` clause and the predicate *hp* in the `HAVING` clause, it should be selected into table **output**, i.e., there exists a row in the table **output** that contains the selected columns. On the other hand, the axiom considers the direction from output to input. For each row in the table **output**, there exists a row in the table **input** which satisfies the predicate *wp* and *hp* and the selected column equals to the column in the output row.

Table 1. Statistics of numbers of solved (unsolved) benchmarks, percentage, time usage, average time usage on SQLSynthesizer and Scythe benchmark set. Columns marked by sqlsyn, scythe, sqlsol1, sqlsol2, and sqlsol3 are the results of the algorithms SQLSynthesizer, Scythe, SqlSol with the number of predicates in the WHERE clause, wp, set to 1, 2, and 3. Timeout for Scythe is 120 s.

		SqlSynthesizer					Scythe			
		sqlsyn	scythe	sqlsol1	sqlsol2	sqlsol3	scythe	sqlsol1	sqlsol2	sqlsol3
Solved	Count	20	20	17	22	25	150	93	112	116
	%	71	71	61	79	89	88	54	65	68
	Time	176	254	48	170	239	983	103	265	396
	Average	9	13	3	8	10	7	1	2	3
Unsolved	Count	8	8	11	6	3	21	78	59	55
	%	29	29	39	21	11	12	46	35	32
	Time	24	960	77	65	123	2520	233	221	266
	Average	3	120	7	11	41	120	3	4	5
Total	Time	200	1214	125	235	362	3503	336	487	662
	Average	7	43	4	8	13	20	2	3	4

Let nrow be the number of rows of a table, let wp be the predicates in the WHERE clause, let hp be the predicates in the HAVING clause, let PC be set of the selected columns. The axiom for the semantics of the SQL query is:

$$\forall r \in input.nrow, wp(r) \wedge hp(r) \implies$$
$$\exists s \in output.nrow, \forall c \in PC, input(c,r) = output(c,s)$$
$$\forall s \in output.nrow \implies \tag{11}$$
$$\exists r \in input.now, \forall c \in PC, wp(r) \wedge hp(r)$$
$$\wedge input(c,r) = output(c,s)$$

5   Evaluation

We implemented our algorithm, SqlSol, in Java. We use Z3, [7], as the backend SMT solver. In this section, We present our evaluation of SqlSol.

We set the upper bound of GROUP BY columns be 1, the upper bound of aggregation column be 1, The upper bound of basic predicates in the WHERE clause be 1, 2, or 3. the upper bound of basic predicates in the HAVING clause be 1. The evaluation was conducted on a quad-core Intel Core i7 3.3 GHz CPU with 8 GB memory.

5.1   Experiments on SQLSynthesizer and Scythe benchmarks

We evaluated SqlSol on two open-source benchmark sets: SQLSynthesizer benchmark set and Scythe benchmark set. The benchmarks were downloaded from the site [2] of the open-source project Scythe. All benchmarks in both benchmark sets have one IO example. The SQLSynthesizer benchmark set contains 28 benchmarks, including 23 benchmarks collected from the classic database textbook [13], and 5 ones collected from forums. The average number of table cells of an IO example in SQLSynthesizer benchmark set is 57. The Scythe benchmark set has three folders: dev-set, top-rated, recent-posts. We combined all the benchmarks in the three folders, and removed some empty files. The final benchmark set has 143 benchmarks. The average number of table cells in one benchmark in the final set is 29. We downloaded Scythe from its github page [2]. However, we could not obtain an effectively working software of SQLSynthesizer, so the data of SQLSynthesizer was from its paper [16].

Table 1 shows the result of evaluation. On the SQLSynthesizer benchmark set, SqlSol solved up to 5, 18%, more problems than SQLSynthesizer and Scythe, while the average time usage is comparable to SQLSynthesizer, but smaller than Scythe. On the Scythe benchmark set, for the solved benchmarks SqlSol is over 2X faster than Scythe; for the unsolved case, SqlSol is 44X faster than Scythe. Overall, SqlSol is over 8X times faster than Scythe.

Note that on Scythe benchmark set, the number of problems solved by SqlSol is less than by Scythe. We manually checked the unsolved problems, and found that all are not in our SQL subset, mostly are nested queries. We leave nested queries support for future work.

5.2 Scalability Comparison of SqlSol and Scythe

We created 25 benchmarks, each of which is an IO example to solve the problem in the motivating example in Sect. 2. The number of rows in the input tables in the benchmarks increases from 5 to 30, and each row contains 5 constants. Constants are unique except those in the first 5 rows. The output tables in all benchmarks are the same, containing 3 rows.

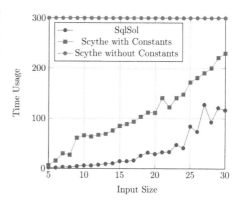

We tested Scythe with two settings. One is Scythe with all constraints provided: constants `senior`, 59, and the aggregation function `average`. The other is Scythe with no

Fig. 8. Time usage with increasing number of rows in input table.

constraints provided. The timeout is set to be 300 s. In SqlSol, the `wp` is set to be 2.

Figure 8 plots the result. The x-axis is the number of rows in the input table, and the y-axis is the time usage. We can see that Scythe without constants cannot solve any problem before timeout. SqlSol performs better than Scythe at every input size and the speedup is between 2X to 10X.

Single Input

id	name
1	Rose
2	John
3	Mary
2	Bob

Fig. 9. Single input

Multi Input: 1

1	John
2	Bob

Multi Input: 2

1	Bob
2	John

Fig. 10. Multi inputs

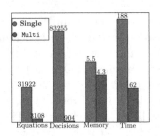

Fig. 11. Statistics comparison

5.3   Benefits from Multiple IO Examples Support

Given an IO example, there are many SQL queries that satisfy them, but only one is the user intention. In this section, we first evaluate how many IO examples are needed to find the user intention. We picked 6 benchmarks, whose solutions fall into our SQL subset, from the SQLSynthesizer benchmark set and manually wrote solution for them. The numbers of IO examples that SqlSol took to synthesize the solution are: 5, 4, 1, 1, 1, 1.

Another benefit from multiple IO examples support is that multiple examples contain less constants than single example, therefore can speed up the algorithm. For example, consider the synthesis problem: SELECT id, name FROM input where id = 2. Figure 9 is the input table of one IO example, and Fig. 10 is two IO examples derived from Fig. 9. Although the output of SqlSol are the same, but the number of constants in Figs. 9 and 10 are different: 7 in single input, 4 in multiple inputs. We ran SqlSol with the two cases and fetched the statistics data from Z3 solver. The result, Fig. 11, shows that in the number of added equations, the number of decisions, the memory used (in MB), the time used (in mini-seconds), multiple IO examples require less and perform better.

6   Related Work

Program Synthesis is the task that automatically generates programs that satisfy some high-level specifications. Our synthesis algorithm belongs to SMT-solver aided program synthesis, is particularly inspired by [10]. In [10], Gulwani etc. parameterized sequential programs by making the line numbers of a program symbolic variables, and encoded the syntax and semantics of a sequential program into logic constraints. Their algorithm lets the user refine the solution by providing more examples. Our algorithm differs from [10] in that it is the first to encode the syntax and semantics of SQL queries for inductive SQL query synthesis, to our knowledge.

SQL Query Synthesis. Paper [15,16] use search algorithms to synthesize SQL queries from IO examples. Our work differs from those in that we delegate the searching algorithm to modern SMT solvers, so we can focus on a sound and complete logic encoding of the SQL semantics and at the same time enjoys the performance of state-of-the-art SMT solvers. Paper [14] proposes axiom system for SQL semantics to synthesize input tables from SQL queries. Our work solves the reverse problem that synthesizes SQL queries from input-output examples.

7   Conclusion

We present an algorithm, SqlSol, which encodes the semantics of a SQL query into logic constraints, and leverages SMT solvers to synthesize SQL queries from IO examples. The evaluation shows that SqlSol outperforms the state-of-the-art tools, SQLSynthesizer and Scythe. Furthermore, by supporting multiple examples, SqlSol is able to find the user-intended solution and improve the speed at the same time.

References

1. Relatioal algebra. https://en.wikipedia.org/wiki/Relational_algebra
2. Scythe. https://github.com/Mestway/Scythe
3. SMT-COMP. https://smt-comp.github.io
4. TIOBE. https://www.tiobe.com/tiobe-index/
5. Barrett, C., et al.: CVC4. In: Gopalakrishnan, G., Qadeer, S. (eds.) CAV 2011. LNCS, vol. 6806, pp. 171–177. Springer, Heidelberg (2011). https://doi.org/10.1007/978-3-642-22110-1_14
6. Barrett, C., Fontaine, P., Tinelli, C.: The SMT-LIB Standard: Version 2.6. Technical report, Department of Computer Science, The University of Iowa (2017). www.SMT-LIB.org
7. de Moura, L., Bjørner, N.: Z3: an efficient SMT solver. In: Ramakrishnan, C.R., Rehof, J. (eds.) TACAS 2008. LNCS, vol. 4963, pp. 337–340. Springer, Heidelberg (2008). https://doi.org/10.1007/978-3-540-78800-3_24
8. Feng, Y., Martins, R., Van Geffen, J., Dillig, I., Chaudhuri, S.: Component-based synthesis of table consolidation and transformation tasks from examples. ACM SIGPLAN Not. **52**(6), 422–436 (2017)
9. Gulwani, S.: Dimensions in program synthesis. In: Proceedings of the 12th International ACM SIGPLAN Symposium on Principles and Practice of Declarative Programming, pp. 13–24. ACM (2010)
10. Gulwani, S., Jha, S., Tiwari, A., Venkatesan, R.: Synthesis of loop-free programs. ACM SIGPLAN Not. **46**(6), 62–73 (2011)
11. Halbert, D.C.: Programming by example. Ph.D. thesis, University of California, Berkeley (1984)
12. Lieberman, H.: Programming by example. Commun. ACM **43**(3), 72 (2000)
13. Ramakrishnan, R., Gehrke, J.: Database Management Systems, 3rd edn. McGraw-Hill Inc., New York (2003)
14. Veanes, M., Tillmann, N., de Halleux, J.: Qex: symbolic SQL query explorer. In: Clarke, E.M., Voronkov, A. (eds.) LPAR 2010. LNCS (LNAI), vol. 6355, pp. 425–446. Springer, Heidelberg (2010). https://doi.org/10.1007/978-3-642-17511-4_24

15. Wang, C., Cheung, A., Bodik, R.: Synthesizing highly expressive sql queries from input-output examples. In: Proceedings of the 38th ACM SIGPLAN Conference on Programming Language Design and Implementation, pp. 452–466. ACM (2017)
16. Zhang, S., Sun, Y.: Automatically synthesizing SQL queries from input-output examples. In: 2013 IEEE/ACM 28th International Conference on Automated Software Engineering (ASE), pp. 224–234. IEEE (2013)

Towards Verifying Ethereum Smart Contracts at Intermediate Language Level

Ximeng Li[1,3(✉)], Zhiping Shi[1(✉)], Qianying Zhang[2], Guohui Wang[2],
Yong Guan[3,4], and Ning Han[1]

[1] Beijing Key Laboratory of Electronic System Reliability and Prognostics,
Capital Normal University, Beijing, China
{lixm,shizp,2181002006}@cnu.edu.cn

[2] Beijing Engineering Research Center of High Reliable Embedded System,
Capital Normal University, Beijing, China
{qyzhang,ghwang}@cnu.edu.cn

[3] Beijing Advanced Innovation Center for Imaging Theory and Technology,
Capital Normal University, Beijing, China
guanyong@cnu.edu.cn

[4] International Science and Technology Cooperation Base of Electronic System
Reliability and Mathematical Interdisciplinary,
Capital Normal University, Beijing, China

Abstract. Smart contracts have exhibited great potential in a spectrum of applications, ranging from digital currency to online gaming. Yet smart contracts are known to be prone to errors and vulnerable to attacks. The validation of smart contracts before their deployment is an indispensable step for their correctness and security, and the highest level of guarantee can be provided using formal verification. The level of difficulty, reliability, etc., of the formal verification of a smart contract is deeply affected by the programming language in which the contract is implemented. In this paper, we discuss the benefits of verifying smart contracts at the level of intermediate languages, in comparison with machine-level languages and user-level languages. We augment the existing formalization of Yul – the intermediate language of Ethereum, realize an ERC20 token contract in this language, and verify the guarantees of all the functions provided by this contract. All this development has been performed in the proof assistant Isabelle/HOL. It demonstrates the feasibility and some of the most important advantages of mechanized verification for smart contracts at the intermediate-language level, such as a balance between the intuitiveness of the verification target and the ability to validate lower-level mechanisms like the function dispatcher.

1 Introduction

The blockchain technology [29] has raised a significant amount of attention both from the technological community specifically and from the society at large. A blockchain is a digital ledger consisting of blocks of records, which are linked together through hash values. Copies of the same ledger are maintained at a great

© Springer Nature Switzerland AG 2019
Y. Ait-Ameur and S. Qin (Eds.): ICFEM 2019, LNCS 11852, pp. 121–137, 2019.
https://doi.org/10.1007/978-3-030-32409-4_8

number of network nodes. The ledger is append-only, with a consensus mechanism guaranteeing a unified view of newly appended blocks. This design enables distributed consensus over data, while providing guarantees such as tamper-resistance, denial-resistance, and backward-traceability.

The blockchain hosts not only plain data but also executable programs. The programs executed over the blockchain are often called smart contracts (as was conceptualized in [25]). Typically, they prescribe the actions performed (e.g., money transfer between accounts) under a number of predefined conditions. Owing to the guarantees provided by the underlying blockchain, distributed consensus is obtained over the outcome of the execution of smart contracts. Smart contracts have found application in numerous areas, such as financing, supply-chain management, smart manufacturing, health information management, etc.

While adding much to the versatility and power of the blockchain, smart contracts can be prone to errors, and vulnerable to security attacks – just like ordinary computer programs. Since they often deal with monetary concerns, the misbehaviors of smart contracts could directly cause harm to the economic rights of the participants. The fact that smart contracts are often written in an unconventional language (e.g., Solidity), and run on unconventional infrastructure, invites further possibilities of attack. One of the most notorious attacks on smart contracts is the DAO attack, which caused $\sim\$60M$ to be lost (e.g., [11]) by the legitimate participants of the DAO contract [6].

To minimize the chances of errors and attacks, smart contracts must be thoroughly validated before being deployed. Formal verification provides the highest level of correctness and security guarantees in the validation of IT systems, smart contracts included. When formally verifying a smart contract, the abstraction level of the contract is a critical factor to be considered. This abstraction level is determined by the language in which the contract is to be realized. For Ethereum smart contracts, verification has been attempted both for high-level languages such as Solidity (e.g., [30]), and low-level languages such as EVM (Ethereum Virtual Machine) bytecode (e.g., [19]). In general, the use of a high-level language adds to the intuitiveness and manageability of the verification, while the use of a low-level language minimizes the trust base of the verification. Neither approach tends to enjoy the most important benefits of both.

In this paper, we explore the middle ground – the verification of smart contracts in an intermediate language (IL). This helps strike a balance between the intuitiveness of the verification, and the ability to reduce the needed trust base, in ensuring the safety and security of smart contracts. Based on formal semantics, we conduct a substantial case study for IL-level verification of smart contracts. The verification is performed in a proof assistant (Isabelle/HOL), adding to the confidence level on the results obtained. Our main technical contributions are:

- revised formalization of the Yul language (the IL of Ethereum), including the formalization of function lookup due to observed mismatch between the specification of Yul in English and its existing formalization (Sect. 3),
- realization of an ERC20 token contract [2] in Isabelle/HOL, in the formalized Yul language (Sect. 4), and

```
contract Token {
    mapping(address⇒uint256) public balances;
    ...
    function balanceOf(address _owner) public view returns(uint256) {
        return balances[_owner];
    }
    ...
}
```

Fig. 1. The token contract with Balance-retrieval Functionality in solidity

– mechanized proofs of the guarantees provided by each function in the contract – in the form of pre/post-conditions for the body of each function, and for the external call invoking each function (Sect. 5).

Our development totals ~10k lines of code in Isabelle/HOL, of which ~500 lines correspond to the realization of the token contract, ~4k lines correspond to the specification and proof for the function definitions in this contract, and the rest correspond to the specification and proof for the calls to these functions.

2   Verifying Smart Contracts at the IL Level

In this section, we discuss the comparative benefits of formally verifying smart contracts at the intermediate-language level. We use Solidity [4], EVM byte-code [28], and Yul [8] as representative examples for smart contract languages at the high level, the low level, and the intermediate level, respectively.

Verifying Contracts in Solidity. Solidity is the official programming language of Ethereum. It offers contracts, balances, transfers, etc., as programming abstractions. A contract allowing for the retrieval of the balances of all the participants in some token could be implemented as in Fig. 1. In this figure, the contract is represented by the *contract* construct of Solidity, the balances are maintained in a *mapping* (from the address of each owner of the token to the current balance of the owner), and the operation retrieving the balance of a specific owner is implemented as a *function*.

As a structured, user-level language for smart contracts, Solidity allows for intuitive representation of the business logic of each contract. This facilitates the development of a specification in a formal verification (e.g., preconditions, post-conditions, loop invariants, etc.). On the other hand, as a high-level language, the features of Solidity are relatively complicated (with static and dynamic arrays, mappings, inheritable contracts, access modifiers, imports, etc.). Furthermore, the language is partly in its maturing process, and, hence, the evolvement of its features is relatively fast. These two facts pose great challenges to the development and stabilization of a formal semantics for Solidity, and the implementation of a verification system on top of the semantics.

```
function balanceOf(owner) -> bal {
    bal := sload(accountToStorageOffset(owner))
}
```

Fig. 2. The Balance-retrieving function of token contract in Yul

Verifying Contracts in EVM Bytecode. EVM bytecode is the language of the execution engine of Ethereum – the Ethereum Virtual Machine (EVM). Implementing the contract of Fig. 1 in EVM bytecode requires the implementation of e.g., a function dispatcher that directs each call to the contract to a specific function using the JUMPI instruction, the computation of the storage location of a specific owner's balance using arithmetic and stack-operating instructions, the retrieval of the balance of the specified owner using the SLOAD instruction, etc.

As a machine-level language, EVM bytecode does not permit a verification engineer to clearly see the business logic of the smart contract to be verified. This could lead to difficulties in developing the specification for the verification, and in coming up with the necessary auxiliary information to guide the verification. On the other hand, EVM bytecode is much less involved and more stable in terms of language features, than a user-level language such as Solidity. This facilitates the development and stabilization of a formal semantics. Furthermore, verifying the bytecode excludes the possibilities for errors introduced by the compiler, adding to the level of confidence on the verification result.

Verifying Contracts in Yul. Yul is the intermediate language of Ethereum, it enables structured programming with constructs for contracts, functions, conditional branches, and loops. At the same time, it supports the direct programming of low-level mechanisms such as the dispatcher of calls to specific contract functions, and the direct obtainment of the return data from calls.

An implementation of the balance-retrieval function in Fig. 1 in the Yul language is shown in Fig. 2. The computation of the storage address for the owner's balance is performed using the auxiliary function *accountToStorageOffset*, the implementation of which is elided from the figure.

The aforementioned characteristics of Yul indicate that it would not be difficult to comprehend the business logic of a smart contract while making a formal specification for the code of the contract (as is the case for a high-level language such as Solidity). At the same time, Yul supports functionalities that are occasionally necessary in the implementation of smart contracts, but are not directly offered by a high-level language (e.g., retrieval of resulting data of contract calls). Furthermore, the function dispatcher and other low-level mechanisms explicitly contained in a contract implemented in Yul can be directly examined in a formal verification, excluding the chances for the introduction of errors into these mechanisms by a compiler. Finally, the feature set of Yul is succinct and stable in comparison to that of Solidity, which reduces the difficulty level of formalization.

3   The Formalization of Yul

The formalization of the Yul language in Isabelle/HOL serves as the (only) basis of our verification of the ERC20 token contract. A preliminary formalization of Yul (previously called Julia) has been performed by Hirai [3] in the Lem tool [22]. From Lem, we generate definitions of the syntax and (big-step) semantics of Yul in Isabelle/HOL, and we revise the formalization for use as a basis of our work. In this section, we first briefly introduce the basics of Isabelle/HOL, and then describe the formalization of Yul by Hirai and our revision of it.

3.1   The Basics of Isabelle/HOL

Isabelle/HOL is an environment that provides the ability to reason formally in Higher Order Logic inside the Isabelle framework [27]. System verification using Isabelle/HOL reduces the verification problem to the construction of a formal proof. The modeling of the system is often performed by functional programming, and the proofs are often constructed by applying predefined tactics, or using the declarative-style language Isar.

For simple definitions, the keyword *definition* is used. In case the definition involves pattern matching or recursion, the keyword *function* or *fun* is needed. In lemmas and theorems, all the hypotheses can be listed between a pair of semantic brackets $[\![\ldots]\!]$ and separated with semicolons.

The notation $[]$ represents an empty list, and $e\#l$ represents the list that results from prepending the element e to the list l. The term *Map.empty* represents an empty map (the map that takes each key to *None*), $mp[k \mapsto v]$

> **datatype** *expression* =
>   *FunctionCall id0 "expression list"*
> | *Identifier id0*
> | *Literal "literal_kind" "type_name"*

Fig. 3. The existing formalization of Yul expressions

> **datatype** *statement* =
>   *Block "statement list"*
> | *FunctionDefinition id0 "(id0 × type_name) list"*
>   *"(id0 × type_name) list" statement*
> | *VariableDeclaration "(id0 × type_name) list" expression*
> | *Assignment "id0 list" expression*
> | *If expression statement*
> | *ForLoop expression statement statement*
> | *Expression expression*
>   ...   ...

Fig. 4. The existing formalization of Yul statements

represents the map that results from updating the map mp by mapping k to $Some(v)$, and $mp_1 \mathbin{+\!\!+} mp_2$ represents the map that results from updating the map mp_1 according to the map mp_2, i.e., for each key k, if mp_2 takes k to $Some(v)$, then $mp_1 \mathbin{+\!\!+} mp_2$ takes k to $Some(v)$; otherwise $mp_1 \mathbin{+\!\!+} mp_2$ takes k to $(mp_1 \ k)$. For a record rcd with field fd, $(fd \ rcd)$ represents the value of fd in rcd, and $rcd(\!| fd := v |\!)$ represents the record rcd with the field fd updated to the value v.

3.2   The Original, and Revised, Formalization of Yul

The two main syntactical categories of Yul are expressions and statements. Their formalizations are shown in Figs. 3 and 4, respectively. In both figures, $id0$ is the type for the identifiers of variables and functions. There are two types of function calls – the call to a function in the current contract (internal calls), and the call to a different contract (external calls). Both are supported by the type $FunctionCall \ id0$ "$expression \ list$" in Fig. 3: if a function defined in the current scope is associated with the function identifier, then an internal call is performed, while if the builtin function $Call$ is associated with the function identifier, an external call is performed. Since a function may have a list of return values (in addition to a list of parameters), the type constructor $FunctionDefinition$ in Fig. 4 has two lists as arguments. Although Fig. 4 is non-exhaustive in the statements of Yul, the full definition of $statement$ is not much more involved than what is shown. It can be seen that the language has a succinct syntax.

> **fun** $func\_map$ :: "$statement \Rightarrow ((id0, value0) \ Map.map)$" **where**
> "$func\_map \ (Block \ []) = Map.empty$"
> | "$func\_map \ (Block \ (stmt \ \# \ stmts)) =$
> $(func\_map \ stmt \mathbin{+\!\!+} func\_map \ (Block \ stmts))$"
> | "$func\_map \ (FunctionDefinition \ f \ params \ rets \ stmt) =$
> $(Map.empty)(f \mapsto FunctionV \ f \ params \ rets \ stmt)$"
> | "$func\_map \ \_ = (Map.empty)$"

Fig. 5. The definition of $func\_map$

A *global state* g of a contract contains the address of the currently executing contract $address \ g$, the currently executing contract $current \ g$, the memory of the execution engine $memory \ g$, the active number of bytes in the memory $memory\_size \ g$, the value transfered with the call invoking the execution of the current contract $tmoney \ g$, the input data of this call $calldata \ g$, the current log content $logs \ g$, the function from account addresses (modeled by integers) to the corresponding accounts $accounts \ g$, and other components relevant to the execution of contracts. A *local state* l is a map from identifiers (of type $id0$) to values of type $value0$. For each account at address $addr$ (a 160-bit address), i.e., $acc = accounts \ g \ addr$, $storage \ acc$ represents the storage of the account, *balance acc* represents the balance of the account, and *code acc* represents the code of the account. A contract is an account with non-empty code.

The existing formalization of Yul also contains the big-step semantics for expressions and statements, defined using two *evaluation functions*. The function *eval_expression* takes a global state, a local state, an expression, and a natural number as arguments, and returns the final result of evaluating the expression. Here, the natural number is a counter introduced only to facilitate a termination proof for the well-definedness of *eval_expression* in Isabelle/HOL. The function *eval_statement* takes a global state, a local state, a statement and a natural number (serving also as a counter for proving termination), and returns the result of executing the statement. The two functions are mutually recursive since a statement may have in it a function call (an expression), and an expression may be the invocation of a function whose body is a statement.

In the original formalization [3], the functions that can be internally called in the current scope are maintained by associating each such function to its identifier in the local state, after processing the function definition. However, this only allows for calling functions whose definitions are syntactically located before the calls. Nonetheless, as mandated in the informal specification of Yul [8]

"Functions can be referenced already before their declaration (if they are visible)."

To rectify this mismatch between the official documentation of Yul, and its existing formalization, we define the function *func_map* to build a map *fctx* for all the functions defined in a statement (see Fig. 5). We augment the parameter list of the functions *eval_statement* and *eval_expression* to contain this map, thereby recording which functions are defined in the current scope, both before and after the point where a function is called. With this revision, the terms

$$eval\_expression \ g \ l \ fctx \ expr \ n$$
$$eval\_statement \ g \ l \ fctx \ stmt \ n$$

represent the evaluation of expressions and execution of statements, respectively, with knowledge of the available functions in the current scope. We inductively prove that the result of evaluation a statement or an expression does not depend on the value of the counter n, as long as n is sufficiently large for the evaluation function to be fully unrolled.

Our revision of the formalization of Yul also contains the addition of a number of definitions for the evaluation of builtin functions, such as subtraction, multiplication, division, the function retrieving the value transfered with the current call, the function returning the address of the caller account, etc. Most of these additions to the original formalization are used in our realization of the token contract in the formal Yul language.

4   Realizing the Token Contract in Yul

A token contract keeps track of the total supply of a token, its current distribution among its owners, and its flow between its owners. The ERC20 standard for token contracts mandates a number of interfaces to be provided, such as querying the total supply of the token and the current balances of the owners, and transferring a specified amount of tokens to a specified user [2].

We realize a version of ERC20 token contract in the formalized Yul language in Isabelle/HOL. However, in the presentation of this section, we refrain from using the Isabelle syntax due to its verbosity.

4.1 The Storage Layout of the Contract

The storage of an Ethereum smart contract is arranged in slots that are addressed by 256-bit integers. We model the storage layout of the token contract as follows, where *keccak* is the keccak-256 hash function, and $uint256(n)$ is the bit string of length 256 for the unsigned integer n.

- The owner of the contract is stored at slot 0.
- The total supply of the token is stored at slot 1.
- The balance of the account at address *addr* is stored at slot

$$keccak(uint256(addr).uint256(2))$$

- The allowance for token transfer from the account at address $addr_1$ by the account at address $addr_2$ is stored at slot

$$keccak(uint256(addr_2).keccak(uint256(addr_1).uint256(3)))$$

In the above, the use of the keccak function to obtain the storage locations of the balances and allowance mimics how the storage is allocated by a compiler of the Solidity language. It utilizes the fact that the population of data in the storage space is sparse, and properties of a secure hash function such as collision avoidance, to avoid the mapping of different data to the same storage slot.

Table 1. The functions provided by the token contract to its users

total_supply_func	Query the total supply of the token
balance_of_func	Query the balance of a specific owner of the token
allowance_func	Query the amount of tokens an owner allows a spender to spend
transfer_func	Transfer a specified amount of tokens to a specified user
transfer_from_func	Transfer a specified amount of tokens from a specified user to a specified second user
approve_func	Approve transfer of a specified amount of tokens by a spender

4.2 The Code Layout of the Contract

The code layout of the token contract is shown in Fig. 6. The code is organized as a *Block* (cf. Fig. 4) consisting of the functions in the user interface, the utility functions that support the implementation of the contract, and the dispatcher statement that directs each contract call to the specific function invoked. There are altogether 19 functions. The functions in the user interface and their description are given in Table 1. Below, we selectively elaborate on the dispatcher statement and the interface function *transfer_func*.

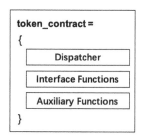

Fig. 6. The code layout of the token contract

```
if  gt(callvalue(), 0) { revert(0, 0) }
switch  selector_func()
case  0x10991a86 /* "balance_of_func(address)" */ {
   return_uint_func(balance_of_func(decode_as_address_func(0)))
}
. . .
case  0xb513186f /* "transfer_func(address, uint256)" */ {
   transfer_func(decode_as_address_func(0), decode_as_uint_func(1))
}
default  { revert(0, 0) }
```

Fig. 7. The dispatcher statement

The Dispatcher. A call to the token contract essentially triggers the execution of the dispatcher statement. The code of the dispatcher statement is given in Fig. 7. It is first checked that no money is transfered to the contract using the condition that the value of the call should not be greater than zero. The value of the call as an unsigned integer is retrieved using the builtin function *callvalue*. Then, the function to which a call should be directed is obtained using the function *selector_func* and the switch statement. The function *selector_func* (also included in the implementation) computes the first 4 bytes of the input data to the call – these 4 bytes represent the keccak-256 hash of the signature of the function to be invoked. The subsequent chunks of the input data (of 32 bytes each) contain the arguments to be passed to the specific function invoked. The i-th argument is retrieved using *decode_as_uint_func(i)* or *decode_as_address_func(i)*. In addition to decoding an argument from the input data (or call data), the latter also checks that the decoded argument is in the form of an account address (of 160 bits). The function *return_uint_func* signals the exit of the currently executing contract, with the result placed at bit 0 in the memory of the execution engine. In case the caller attempts to send ether to the contract, or the invoked function is not found, the state is reverted using the builtin function *revert*.

```
function transfer_func(to, amount) {
    deduct_from_balance_func(caller(), amount)
    add_to_balance_func(to, amount)
    log(1, caller(), to, amount)
}
```

Fig. 8. The function `transfer_func`

The Function transfer_func. The code of the function *transfer_func* (the functionality of which is informally explained in Table 1) is given in Fig. 8. In the function body, the function *deduct_from_balance_func* is first invoked to deduce the specified amount of tokens from the caller account. The function *add_to_balance_func* is then invoked to add the same amount of tokens to the destination account of the transfer. Finally, the transfer event is logged with topic 1, together with the caller of *transfer_func*, the destination of the transfer, and the amount of transfered tokens as parameters.

In Fig. 8, *log* is a builtin function [8]. On the other hand, *deduct_from_balance_func* and *add_to_balance_func* are part of the contract implementation. The latter function makes use of a function for safe addition (*safe_add_func*) to avoid overflow when increasing the balance of the destination account.

The Readability of Yul Code. It is demonstrated by Figs. 7 and 8 that smart contract code in Yul has a greater level of readability than low-level instructions. This benefits the intuitiveness level of formal verification.

5   Verification of the Token Contract

We prove the guarantees of calling *each function of the token contract* in the ERC20 interface (c.f., Table 1) in Isabelle/HOL. To this end, we first establish the guarantees of all the utility functions that are used to implement the interface functions. Below, we *selectively* present our results.

5.1   The Guarantees of the Utility Functions

Below, we present the theoretical result about the guarantees of the utility function for safe addition. This function is used by the function *add_to_balance_func* that increases the balance of a specified account by a specified amount (cf. Fig. 8).

lemma *safe_add_body_correct:*   1
"⟦ $n > 4$;
   $\forall fid.\ builtin\_ctx\ fid \neq None$
          $\longrightarrow\ (context0\ g\ {+}{+}\ fctx)\ fid = builtin\_ctx\ fid;$ 4
   $l\ a\_id = Some\ (IntV\ a);\ l\ b\_id = Some\ (IntV\ b);$
   $is\_uint256\ a;\ is\_uint256\ b$
⟧ $\Longrightarrow$ 7
  $(a + b < two256\ \wedge$
   $eval\_statement\ g\ l\ fctx\ (body\_of\ safe\_add\_func)\ n$
   $=\ Normal\ (g,\ \ l(r\_id{:=}Some\ (IntV\ (a{+}b))),\ RegularMode)$ 10
   $\vee$
   $a + b \geq two256\ \wedge$
   $eval\_statement\ g\ l\ fctx\ (body\_of\ safe\_add\_func)\ n$ 13
   $=\ Exit\ (RevertExit\ g\ 0\ 0)$
  $)$ "

In the above, the identifiers *a_id* and *b_id* are the parameters of the function *safe_add_func*. The lemma *safe_add_body_correct* asserts that if *a_id* and *b_id* have values a and b, respectively, that are 256-bit unsigned integers, then evaluating the body of *safe_add_func* yields $a + b$ (that is stored in the return variable *r_id*) if $a + b$ does not exceed $2^{256} - 1$, and an exception reverting the state otherwise. The condition $n > 4$ is imposed only because when fully evaluating the body of *safe_add_func* in the semantics, the counter n decreases 5 times. The evaluation would result in an error for any $n \leq 4$. The condition at lines 3 and 4, on the other hand, requires that each identifier of a builtin function should indeed be mapped to the right builtin function by *context0 g ++ fctx*. Here, *builtin_ctx* is a pre-defined mapping from each identifier of a builtin function to the builtin function, and *context0 g* is the map for all the globally available identifiers.

The proof of the lemma *safe_add_body_correct* is by case analysis on the truth of $a + b < two256$, and by simplification using the semantics of Yul. We omit the discussion of the statement/proof of the lemmas for the other utility functions.

Remark 1. The guarantees for the functions of the token contract (e.g., *safe_add_func*) correspond to the notion of *total correctness* [10] – it is stated that under specific conditions the execution terminates, resulting in global and local states that satisfy specific conditions.

5.2   The Guarantees of Calls to the Token Contract

We first introduce a series of definitions that are used to formulate the theoretical results about the calls to the contract. The term *"keccak_base_key base key"* is defined to give the keccak-256 hash value of the list of 64 bytes where the first 32 bytes are those of the value *key* and the next 32 bytes are those of the value *base*. The term *"memory_values m addr sz"* is defined to give the list of bytes (each as an integer) in the memory m starting at the address *addr* and ending at the address $addr + sz - 1$. The term *"sel_val cd val"* is defined to say that the signature hash of the function to which the current call is dispatched is *val*. The term *"uint_arg_idx cd idx val"* is defined to say that the *idx*-th argument value in the input data cd of the call is the unsigned integer val. The term "$addr\_arg\_idx\ cd\ idx\ val$" is defined to require that in addition to $uint\_arg\_idx\ cd\ idx\ val$, the idx-th argument has the form of an account address. For the account acc, storage offsets o_1 and o_2, balances b_1 and b_2, and the amount a of tokens, "$upd\_bal\ acc\ o_1\ o_2\ b_1\ b_2\ a$" is written for $acc(\!|storage :=$ $(storage\ acc)(o_1 := IntV(b_1 - a), o_2 := IntV(b_2 + a))|\!)$.

$n > k;\ \ length\ args = 7;\ \ length\ gs = 8;\ \ length\ ls = 8;$
$argvs\ =\ [IntV\ gas,\ IntV\ addr,\ IntV\ val,$ 2
        $IntV\ offt_{\mathrm{in}},\ IntV\ sz_{\mathrm{in}},\ IntV\ offt_{\mathrm{out}},\ IntV\ sz_{\mathrm{out}}];$
$\forall i.\ \ i \geq 0\ \wedge\ i < 7 \longrightarrow$
    $eval\_expression\ (gs!i)\ (ls!i)\ fctx\ (args!i)\ n$ 5
    $=\ Normal\ (gs!(i+1),\ ls!(i+1),\ (argvs!i));$
$g'\ =\ gs!7;\ \ l'\ =\ ls!7;$
$(context0\ g'\ +\!\!+\ fctx)\ b\_call\_id = Some\ (GBuiltinV\ Call);$ 8
$\forall fid.\ \ context0\ g'\ fid = builtin\_ctx\ fid$

Fig. 9. The list $assms$ of assumptions

A number of conditions are shared as assumptions by multiple theoretical results about calls to contracts. We write

$$assms\ args\ argvs\ gas\ addr\ val\ offt_{\mathrm{in}}\ sz_{\mathrm{in}}\ offt_{\mathrm{out}}\ sz_{\mathrm{out}}\ gs\ ls\ g'\ l'\ fctx\ n\ k$$

for the list of assumptions shown in Fig. 9. Here, $args$ is a list of 7 argument expressions for a contract call, $argvs$ is a list of 7 argument values for the same call, $addr$ is an account address, val is an amount of money, $offt_{\mathrm{in}}$ and $offt_{\mathrm{out}}$ are two memory offsets, sz_{in} and sz_{out} are two counts of memory bytes, gs is a list of global states, ls is a list of local states, and n and k are two natural numbers. The condition spanning lines 2 and 3 says that the list $argvs$ is obtained by wrapping the series of integer values provided using the type constructor $IntV$. The condition spanning lines 4–6 says that the evaluation of the i-th argument expression yields the i-th argument value, turning the global and local states to the next ones in the respective lists gs and ls. The condition at line 8 says that after evaluating all the arguments (thereby reaching the global state g'), the identifier for the builtin function $Call$ is still properly mapped to $Call$ according to g' and the local function context $fctx'$. The condition at line 9 says that the global state g' properly maintains the mapping for the builtin functions.

Below, we present the theorem about the guarantees of each call to the token contract that invokes the function $transfer\_func$ (cf. Table 1), when the source account (the caller) has a sufficient amount of tokens to transfer, and the transfer does not lead to an overflow of the balance at the destination.

theorem $normal\_call\_transfer$:

"⟦ $assms\ args\ argvs\ gas\ addr\ 0\ offt_{in}\ sz_{in}\ offt_{out}\ sz_{out}\ gs\ ls\ g'\ l'\ fctx\ n\ 17$;

    $current\ g'\ =\ accounts\ g'\ (address\ g')$;   3

    $balance\ ((accounts\ g')\ (address\ g'))\ \geq\ 0$;

    $code\ ((accounts\ g')\ addr)\ =\ Some\ token\_contract$;

    $cd_0\ =\ memory\_values\ (memory\ g')\ offt_{in}\ (nat\ |sz_{in}|)$;   6

    $valid\_mem\ (list\_to\_map\ cd_0)\ 4\ 64$;

    $sel\_val\ cd_0\ 0xb513186f$; $addr\_arg\_idx\ cd_0\ 0\ to_0$; $uint\_arg\_idx\ cd_0\ 1\ a_0$;

    $o_1\ =\ keccak\_base\_key\ 2\ (address\ g')$; $o_2\ =\ keccak\_base\_key\ 2\ to_0$;   9

    $storage\ (accounts\ g'\ addr)\ o_1\ =\ IntV\ b_1$;

    $((storage\ (accounts\ g'\ addr))\ (o_1\ :=\ IntV\ (b_1-a_0)))\ o_2\ =\ IntV\ b_2$;

    $is\_uint256\ a_0$; $is\_uint256\ b_2$; $b_1\ \geq\ a_0$; $b_2+a_0\ <\ two256$ 12

⟧ $\Longrightarrow$

$eval\_expression\ (gs!0)\ (ls!0)\ fctx\ (FunctionCall\ b\_call\_id\ args)\ (n_0+1)$

$=\ Normal\ ($ 15

    $g'(\!|memory\_size\ :=\ max\ (max\,(memory\_size\ g')\ (offt_{in}+sz_{in}))\ (offt_{out}+sz_{out})$,

        $current\ :=\ if\ address\ g'=addr\ then\ upd\_bal(current\ g',o_1,o_2,b_1,b_2,a_0)$

                                  $else\ current\ g'$,   18

     $accounts\ :=\ (accounts\ g')(addr:=upd\_bal(accounts\ g'\ addr,o_1,o_2,b_1,b_2,a_0))$

     $logs\ :=\ ListV\ (memory\_values$

                            $(mem\_upd_4\ (memory\ g')\ 1\ (address\ g')\ to_0\ a_0)$ 21

                            $0\ 128)\ \#\ logs\ g'\ |\!)$,

    $context0\ g'\ ++\ fctx\_erc20$, $TrueV)$"

In the theorem statement, the condition at line 3 says that *address* g' is indeed the address of the currently executing account in g'. The condition at line 5 requires that the code being called is that of the token contract (c.f. Fig. 6). The condition at line 6 says that the input data to the call (as obtained from the global state g' reached after the evaluation of the arguments) is cd_0. The condition at line 7 says that the input data to the call contains valid data after four initial bytes, for 64 bytes in a row – the argument values are contained in these bytes. The conditions at line 8 say that the signature hash for the function to be executed is the one for *transfer_func*, and the 0-th and 1-th arguments in the input data of the call are to_0 (the address of the destination account of the transfer) and a_0 (the amount of tokens to be transfered), respectively. The conditions at line 9 say that the storage offsets for the balances of the source and destination accounts of the transfer are o_1 and o_2, respectively. The conditions at line 10 and line 11 say that these two balances are b_1 and b_2, respectively. The latter condition is stated with consideration of the fact that if the destination account is the same as the source account, then the balance of the destination account decreases when the tokens have been sent but not received. The updated global state described in lines 16–22 reflects the change in the account balances due to the transfer, and the recording of the transfer in the log.

    The proof of theorem *normal_call_transfer* is conducted using lemmas that connect the result of calling the token contract to the result of evaluating the function *transfer_func*. These latter lemmas are in turn based on lemmas about the guarantees of the utility functions (e.g., for safe addition, as shown in Sect. 5.1). Transformations are performed such that the resulting global state is described directly wrt. g' that is reached after evaluating the arguments for the call. Hence, for side-effectless argument expressions, it is also directly in terms of the initial global state $gs\,!\,0$. The case where the source account does not have a sufficient amount of tokens to be transfered, or the transfer leads to an overflow of the balance at the destination, is covered by a separate theorem.

As a corollary, we have formally shown that a token transfer preserves the total amount of tokens, provided that there is no collision of the keccak-256 hash values of the addresses for all the accounts that own the token.

Remark 2. As is demonstrated in the theorem *normal_call_transfer*, the guarantees for the calls to the contract functions are formulated to precisely reflect all changes in the global and local states. This provides a solid basis for establishing further safety and security properties in a broad range (e.g., [15]).

Finally, if the caller of the contract attempts to send money to the contract, then the call is terminated with the effects on the states reverted.

theorem *call_with_money:*
"$\llbracket val_0 > 0$;
  assms args argvs gas addr val_0 $offt_{in}$ sz_{in} $offt_{out}$ sz_{out} gs ls g' l' fctx n $\rrbracket$
$\rrbracket \Longrightarrow$
eval_expression $(gs\,!\,0)$ $(ls\,!\,0)$ fctx $(FunctionCall\ b\_call\_id\ args)$ $(n_0 + 1)$
  $= Normal\ (g\,'\langle memory\_size := max\ (max\ (memory\_size\ g')(offt_{in} + sz_{in}))$
$(offt_{out} + sz_{out})\ \rangle,$
        l', FalseV)"

Note that the potential increase in the number of active memory bytes is not canceled, which is consistent with the semantics described in [17,28].

In the verification of the token contract in Isabelle/HOL, the contract code in Yul has been sufficiently comprehensible for it to be used as the reference for specifying the initial pre/post-conditions. These pre/post-conditions are further revised in the proving process – the formal proof helps make all the assumptions and effects associated with an invocation of the token contract explicit. Furthermore, since the dispatching logic of calls to specific functions is an integral part of the token contract at the IL-level, the dispatcher is naturally covered by the verification. This provides added confidence that the dispatcher does not contain errors that could have otherwise been introduced by a compiler.

6   Related Work

Verification of Smart Contracts by Theorem Proving. The strongly negative impact of errors and flaws of smart contracts motivated their verification by theorem proving. In [19], the EVM is formalized in Lem [22], and a few safety properties of simple contracts are proven in Isabelle/HOL based on formal definitions generated in this proof assistant. In [9], a program logic is defined to syntactically reason about properties of EVM bytecode. This development is based on the formalization of [19]. In [18], a semantics of EVM bytecode is defined in the K-framework, which provides the basis for program analysis and theorem proving [23] for Ethereum smart contracts. In [17], a small-step semantics of EVM bytecode is defined (with partial mechanization in the F* language), and a few security properties are defined on the basis of this semantics for the verification of Ethereum smart contracts. In [5], a library of formal proofs is developed for Ethereum smart contracts in the Coq proof assistant, based on a demand-driven formalization of a Solidity-like language. In [30], a type system and a big-step semantics are defined (in Coq) for Lolisa – a Solidity-like programming language developed by the authors. In [14], an approach to verifying Hyperledger Fabric chaincode (in Java) in the KeY prover is proposed. The main idea is to extend KeY to handle the major API methods that are provided by the Hyperledger blockchain and used for writing the chaincode.

The developments mentioned above formalize smart contracts and prove their properties at either the user-language level or the machine-language level. In [24], an intermediate language, Scilla, is defined in Coq, for the analysis and verification of smart contracts. Unlike our development that leverages the existing intermediate language in the ecosystem of Ethereum, Scilla is a new language for which the translation from high-level languages like Solidity, and into low-level languages like EVM bytecode is yet to be defined.

Validation of Smart Contracts in General. Numerous developments have been carried out to validate smart contracts by non-theorem-proving means. For space reasons, the following discussion is non-exhaustive on these developments.

In [13], the role of refinement in verifying and preserving the correctness of smart contract designs (e.g., in the Event-B formalism) is discussed. In [20], the problem of verifying smart contracts is addressed by generating and solving horn clauses. In [16], a static analysis is proposed for Ethereum smart contracts, and the analysis comes with a soundness proof. In [12], the SPIN tool is leveraged to model check smart contracts. In [26], the target properties of a smart contract is expressed as patterns, and the verification/falsification of properties is performed by finding the corresponding patterns. In [21], a method of finding bugs in smart contracts via symbolic execution is proposed. In addition, hybrid approaches to the verification of smart contracts are proposed and used in the VaaS framework [7] and the CertiK project [1].

7 Conclusion

Formal verification can be applied to provide the highest level of correctness and security guarantee for smart contracts. The language used to realize the smart contract affects multiple aspects of the verification. Specifically, the use of an intermediate language (IL) ensures a relatively low level of complexity in formalizing the language itself (owing to the succinctness of the language features), a relatively high level of intuitiveness of the verification (owing to the existence of structured programming constructs), and a relatively high level of confidence on the verification result (owing to the partially reduced trust base).

To demonstrate some of these benefits, we present a concrete formal verification of an Ethereum smart contract at the IL-level, in a proof assistant. The smart contract is an ERC20 token contract, which we realize in the Yul language, the formalization of which we revise to rectify its observed deviation from its informal specification. We prove the guarantees of calls to all the interface functions of the token contract in Isabelle/HOL. The development totals ∼10k lines of code (excl. code generated from Lem). In the verification, we take advantage of the good level of comprehensibility of Yul to devise the initial pre/post-conditions for the contract functions. These pre/post-conditions are then revised in the proving process, such that all the assumptions and effects for the contract functions are precisely identified. The complexity of the formal proof is partially reduced by the simplicity of Yul and its formal semantics relative to a high-level language. The overall approach applies easily to other Ethereum contracts.

Potential directions for future work include support for easier smart contract proofs for Yul via proof automation and program logics, as well as refinement verification of Yul contracts to preserve guarantees down to the lowest level.

Acknowledgments. This work was supported by the National Key R&D Plan (2017YFB1301100), National Natural Science Foundation of China (61876111, 61572331, 61602325), Capacity Building for Sci-Tech Innovation – Fundamental Scientific Research Funds (025185305000), and the Youth Innovative Research Team of Capital Normal University. We thank the anonymous reviewers for their valuable comments that helped with the improvement of this paper.

References

1. CertiK. https://certik.org/
2. ERC20 standard. https://theethereum.wiki/w/index.php/ERC20_Token_Standard
3. Eth-isabelle. https://github.com/pirapira/eth-isabelle
4. Solidity (v0.5.8). https://solidity.readthedocs.io/en/v0.5.8/
5. Token libraries with proofs. https://github.com/sec-bit/tokenlibs-with-proofs
6. Understanding the DAO attack. http://www.coindesk.com/understanding-dao-hack-journalists/
7. VaaS. https://sso.beosin.com/#/?vaas
8. Yul. https://solidity.readthedocs.io/en/v0.5.8/yul.html
9. Amani, S., Bégel, M., Bortin, M., Staples, M.: Towards verifying Ethereum smart contract bytecode in Isabelle/HOL. In: 7th ACM SIGPLAN International Conference on Certified Programs and Proofs (CPP), pp. 66–77 (2018)
10. Apt, K.R.: Ten years of Hoare's logic: a survey - part 1. ACM Trans. Program. Lang. Syst. **3**(4), 431–483 (1981)
11. Atzei, N., Bartoletti, M., Cimoli, T.: A survey of attacks on Ethereum smart contracts (SoK). In: 6th International Conference on Principles of Security and Trust (POST), pp. 164–186 (2017)
12. Bai, X., Cheng, Z., Duan, Z., Hu, K.: Formal modeling and verification of smart contracts. In: 7th International Conference on Software and Computer Applications (ICSCA), pp. 322–326 (2018)
13. Banach, R.: Verification-led smart contracts. In: Proceedings of 3rd Workshop on Trusted Smart Contracts (2019)

14. Beckert, B., Herda, M., Kirsten, M., Schiffl, J.: Formal specification and verification of Hyperledger Fabric chaincode. In: Third Symposium on Distributed Ledger Technology (SDLT) (2018)
15. Clarkson, M.R., Schneider, F.B.: Hyperproperties. J. Comput. Secur. **18**(6), 1157–1210 (2010)
16. Grishchenko, I., Maffei, M., Schneidewind, C.: Foundations and tools for the static analysis of Ethereum smart contracts. In: Chockler, H., Weissenbacher, G. (eds.) CAV 2018. LNCS, vol. 10981, pp. 51–78. Springer, Cham (2018). https://doi.org/10.1007/978-3-319-96145-3_4
17. Grishchenko, I., Maffei, M., Schneidewind, C.: A semantic framework for the security analysis of Ethereum smart contracts. In: Bauer, L., Küsters, R. (eds.) POST 2018. LNCS, vol. 10804, pp. 243–269. Springer, Cham (2018). https://doi.org/10.1007/978-3-319-89722-6_10
18. Hildenbrandt, E., et al.: KEVM: a complete formal semantics of the Ethereum virtual machine. In: 31st IEEE Computer Security Foundations Symposium (CSF), pp. 204–217 (2018)
19. Hirai, Y.: Defining the Ethereum virtual machine for interactive theorem provers. In: Brenner, M., et al. (eds.) FC 2017. LNCS, vol. 10323, pp. 520–535. Springer, Cham (2017). https://doi.org/10.1007/978-3-319-70278-0_33
20. Kalra, S., Goel, S., Dhawan, M., Sharma, S.: ZEUS: analyzing safety of smart contracts. In: 25th Network and Distr. System Security Symposium (NDSS) (2018)
21. Luu, L., Chu, D., Olickel, H., Saxena, P., Hobor, A.: Making smart contracts smarter. In: ACM SIGSAC Conference on Computer and Communications Security (CCS), pp. 254–269 (2016)
22. Owens, S., Böhm, P., Nardelli, F. Z., Sewell, P.: Lem: a lightweight tool for heavyweight semantics. In: van Eekelen, M., Geuvers, H., Schmaltz, J., Wiedijk, F. (eds.) ITP 2011. LNCS, vol. 6898, pp. 363–369. Springer, Heidelberg (2011). https://doi.org/10.1007/978-3-642-22863-6_27
23. Park, D., Zhang, Y., Saxena, M., Daian, P., Rosu, G.: A formal verification tool for Ethereum VM bytecode. In: ACM Joint Meeting on European Software Engineering Conference and Symposium on the Foundations of Software Engineering, ESEC/SIGSOFT (FSE), pp. 912–915 (2018)
24. Sergey, I., Kumar, A., Hobor, A.: Scilla: a smart contract intermediate-level language. CoRR, abs/1801.00687 (2018)
25. Szabo, N.: Smart contracts (1994). http://www.fon.hum.uva.nl/rob/Courses/InformationInSpeech/CDROM/Literature/LOTwinterschool2006/szabo.best.vwh.net/smart.contracts.html
26. Tsankov, P., Dan, A.M., Drachsler-Cohen, D., Gervais, A., Bünzli, F., Vechev, M.T.: Securify: practical security analysis of smart contracts. In: ACM SIGSAC Conference on Computer and Communications Security (CCS), pp. 67–82 (2018)
27. Wenzel, M., Paulson, L.C., Nipkow, T.: The Isabelle framework. In: Mohamed, O.A., Muñoz, C., Tahar, S. (eds.) TPHOLs 2008. LNCS, vol. 5170, pp. 33–38. Springer, Heidelberg (2008). https://doi.org/10.1007/978-3-540-71067-7_7
28. Wood, G.: Ethereum: a secure decentralised generlised transaction ledger. https://gavwood.com/paper.pdf
29. Yaga, D., Mell, P., Roby, N., Scarfone, K.: Blockchain technology overview. Technical report, NISTIR 8202 (2018)
30. Yang, Z., Lei, H.: Lolisa: formal syntax and semantics for a subset of the solidity programming language. CoRR, abs/1803.09885 (2018)

Simulations for Multi-Agent Systems
with Imperfect Information

Patrick Gardy[(⊠)] and Yuxin Deng

Shanghai Key Laboratory of Trustworthy Computing,
East China Normal University, Shanghai, China
{gardy.patrick,yxdeng}@sei.ecnu.edu.cn

Abstract. Equivalence-checking and simulations are well-known methods used to reduce the size of a system in order to verify it more efficiently. While Alur et al. proposed a notion of simulation sound and complete for ATL as early as 1998, there have been very few works on equivalence-checking performed on extensions of ATL* with probabilities, imperfect information, counters etc. In the case of multi-agent systems (MASs) with imperfect information, the lack of sound and complete algorithm mostly follows from the undecidability of ATL model-checking. However, while ATL is undecidable overall, there exist sub-classes of MASs for which ATL becomes decidable. In this paper, we propose a notion of simulation sound for ATL/ATL* on any MASs and complete on naive MASs. Using our simulations we design an equivalence-checking algorithm sound and complete for MASs with public actions.

1 Introduction

With the rise of multi-agent systems (MASs), the software verification community has tried to extend methods useful for the verification of closed systems to multi-agent systems. The usual model represents each agent's local control through a transition graph with the edges labeled by the actions of all agents involved in the system. This way the agents may influence the state of one another, but each has its own separate control-graph. The overall system is then built as the product of all the agents' local systems. In many practical cases, some agents have only a partial view of the overall system and may not know the control-graph or the exact state of other agents. This can either follow from a faulty communication or be a design choice, either for security or cost purposes. To model this imperfect information, some partial observation relations are attached to each agent.

Many formalisms have been proposed in order to specify expected behaviors of MASs. Among the most famous ones we cite ω-regular conditions [1] and ATL, ATL* [2,13,15], the go-to adaptation of CTL, CTL* to multi-agent systems. Initially defined on MASs with perfect information, these formalisms were quickly adapted and studied in the context of imperfect information (for example in [11,14] for ATL*).

Supported by the National Natural Science Foundation of China (61672229, 61832015).

Y. Ait-Ameur and S. Qin (Eds.): ICFEM 2019, LNCS 11852, pp. 138–153, 2019.
https://doi.org/10.1007/978-3-030-32409-4_9

A Need for Equivalence-Checking. Simpler formalisms like Buchi conditions and ATL enjoy a polynomial model-checking for perfect information, making them target choices for practical applications. The situation is however drastically different in the presence of imperfect information. Thereby ATL goes from polynomial to exponential time model-checking (Δ_2^P to be precise) for positional strategies while it is outright undecidable for perfect recall strategies. The algorithm for positional strategies scales poorly and methods of minimizing the models are necessary to improve the practical uses. In this line of work, a proven concept consists in finding smaller and smaller models of the system and proving at each step that the new model despite its reduced size satisfies the same properties as the bigger one. Such method makes heavy use of an equivalence-check subroutine between two models. There are many ways to perform an equivalence-check: simulations [9,12], trace-equivalence [3], testing [17], etc. This idea was put in application in [5]. In their paper, Belardinelli et al. proposed a notion of simulation sound for ATL and discussed different modelizations of the three-ballot voting protocol (3BVP). ATL was shown to be a logic of choice to model security properties of voting protocols [4,23]. The authors of [5] proposed three models of the 3BVP and showed that each model can simulate the others. We can then check ATL security properties on the smallest model, gaining a considerable amount of time and space.

Contributions. We propose a notion of simulation for games with imperfect information by extending the one of [5]. This simulation is sound for ATL/ATL*, works with both positional and perfect recall strategies, and (with a minor change in the definition) works for both the objective and subjective semantics. Our notion, unlike the one in [5], does not require perfect replication of the partial observation but instead focuses on similarity of results. To be more precise, for four states q, s, q', s' with q, q' similar, s, s' similar and $s' \sim_C q'$, we do not require the states q, s to have the same observation C. This makes our notion of simulation coarser than the only other existing one.

Due to the undecidability of ATL with perfect recall strategies and imperfect information, our notion is not proven to be complete[1]. We however prove completeness on *naive games*, a subclass of MASs with imperfect information. A naive game is one where by design the imperfect information is "state based" in the sense that no history can augment the information of an agent. The concept is illustrated later in Fig. 4. Using our result on naive games, we develop an equivalence-checking algorithm for MASs with public actions, which is both sound and complete. The proof proceeds by restructuring public-actions MASs into naive MASs equivalent on all ATL formulas. To perform equivalence checking, both public-actions MASs are transformed into naive games which are then checked using our notion of simulation.

Related Works. ATL was proven undecidable in perfect recall strategies and Δ_2^P with positional strategies [11,14]. To regain decidability for perfect recall

---

[1] Continuing the tradition in multi-agent systems with the exception of the initial paper on alternating refinement relations [3].

strategies, there are two possibilities. The first option is to restrict the MASs to public actions [6]. A MAS has public actions whenever any agent can see the actions played by all other agents. In such case, ATL* model-checking is 2-EXPTIME. The second option is to use hierarchical observations (and other derivative options) for which ATL/ATL* model-checking is Non-Elementary. A MAS has hierarchical observation whenever there is an order on the agents such that an agent A dominated by another agent B has a strictly less complicated partial observation relation than B.

In a slightly more distant fashion, we mention the work of Berthon et al. [7] on strategy logic with imperfect information and also the work of Laroussinie et al. [16] on ATL with strategy contexts and partial observations (both logics extend ATL*). Each paper proposes small fragments on which the model-checking is decidable in the presence of partial observations.

There are two main related works on equivalence-checking. The first is by Alur et al. [3] on alternating refinement relations with two main contributions: alternating simulations (sound and complete for ATL/ATL*) and alternating trace containment (sound and complete for LTL). The second [5] proposes a simulation sound for ATL* in the presence of imperfect information with an application to model the 3BVP. The protocol is a voting process that does not rely on cryptographic methods for its security [25]. Interestingly, some practical problems and security failures were quickly detected in the 3BVP following its presentation [22]. In [5], the authors proposed different modelizations possible for the protocol as MASs with imperfect information. They discussed the size of each modelization before showing all the models to be equivalent. In a more distant fashion we also cite [26] which proposes a concept of simulation sound for ATL on probabilistic MASs.

Outline. In Sect. 2, we introduce games with imperfect information (used to represent MASs) and ATL*. Section 3 covers the notion of simulation with its soundness relative to ATL* for games with imperfect information. Section 4 discusses the completeness of our notion for the subclass of naive games. In Sect. 5, we present an algorithm to perform equivalence checking on games with public actions based on the work done in previous sections. Finally, we conclude in Sect. 6.

2   Games, Imperfect Information and ATL*

Games with Imperfect Information

For the rest of the paper, fix AP a finite set of atomic propositions. A multi-agent system is usually represented in the following way: each agent has its own control-graph whose edges are labeled by tuples of actions (one per agent), the overall system is then represented by a product of all local control-graphs of the agents. To model this product, we use the notion of concurrent game structures. This is the method used in the open-source tool MCMAS [18,24] and the ISPL language it uses.

Definition 1. *A concurrent game structure with imperfect information (CGS for short) is a tuple* $\mathcal{G} := (S, \mathsf{Agt}, \mathsf{Act}, \mathsf{Label}, \Delta, \{\sim_P\}_{P \in \mathsf{Agt}})$ *where S is a nonempty set of states;* $\mathsf{Agt} = \{P_1, ..., P_n\}$ *is a nonempty finite set of agents;* Act *is a nonempty finite set of actions;* $\mathsf{Label} : S \to 2^{AP}$ *is a labeling function;* $\Delta : S \times \mathsf{JAct} \to S$ *is a transition function with* $\mathsf{JAct} := \prod_{i \in \mathsf{Agt}} \mathsf{Act}$ *the set of joint actions (where the ith component represents the choice of the agent P_i); and for each $P \in \mathsf{Agt}$, $\sim_P \in S \times S$ is an equivalence relation marking the partial observation of agent P.*

A CGS is said to have *perfect information* when $\sim_P = \{(s, s) \mid s \in S\}$ for each $P \in \mathsf{Agt}$. A *path* (or *outcome*) $\rho = s_0 s_1 \ldots$ in a CGS $\mathcal{G}$ is a (finite or infinite) sequence of states such that for every $j \geq 0$, $s_{j+1} = \Delta(s_j, \bar{a}_j)$ for some joint action $\bar{a}_j \in \mathsf{JAct}$. We let $\mathsf{Path}_\mathcal{G}$ denote the set of paths in $\mathcal{G}$. When clear from context, we will drop the game from the notation. We write $|\rho| \in \mathbb{N} \cup \{\infty\}$ for the length of ρ, $\mathsf{last}(\rho)$ for the last state of ρ (when it is finite), and $\mathsf{Prefix}(\rho)$ for the set of all prefixes of ρ. Finally, we write $\rho_{<i+1}$ for the prefix of length i of ρ. Given two paths ρ and ρ', and an agent P we write $\rho \sim_P \rho'$ if for all index i, $\rho(i) \sim_P \rho'(i)$. We then call a set of agents with common knowledges the set of agents A such that $\rho \sim_P \rho'$ iff $P \in A$.

A function $\delta : S^+ \to \mathsf{Act}$ is called a *strategy* (with perfect recall and no randomness). We denote by $\mathsf{Strat}_\mathcal{G}$ the set of strategies. We say that a strategy δ conforms to the partial observation of a player P if for any two paths ρ and π of the same length such that $\rho(i) \sim_P \pi(i)$ for any i, we have $\delta(\pi) = \delta(\rho)$. Consider a state s, a coalition of agents $\mathbf{C} \subseteq \mathsf{Agt}$ and a set of strategies $\overline{\delta_\mathbf{C}} = (\delta_P)_{P \in \mathbf{C}}$ for players in $\mathbf{C}$. A path ρ is compatible with $\overline{\delta_\mathbf{C}}$ and s when $\rho(1) = s$ and for all $0 < i < |\rho|$ there exists a joint action $\bar{a}$ such that $\bar{a}(P) = \delta_P(\rho_{<i})$ for each agent P in $\mathbf{C}$ and $\rho(i+1) = \Delta(\mathsf{last}(\rho_{\leq i}), \bar{a})$. There are two ways to define outcomes in games with imperfect information: *objective* and *subjective*. The objective outcome $\mathsf{Out}_{obj}(\overline{\delta_\mathbf{C}}, s)$ is the set of all paths compatible with $\overline{\delta_\mathbf{C}}$ starting from s, thus it differentiates the initial state from similar states. The subjective semantics makes no such distinction, $\mathsf{Out}_{sub}(\overline{\delta_\mathbf{C}}, s) = \bigcup_{s' \sim_{PS}, P \in \mathbf{C}} \mathsf{Out}_{obj}(\overline{\delta_\mathbf{C}}, s')$. In order to analyze outcomes, we need the last concept: *traces*. A trace of a path is the projection of the path onto the set of atomic propositions AP.

ATL* on Games with Imperfect Information

ATL^* is a well-known and widely used logic introduced in [2] for games with perfect information as an extension of the logic CTL^* for closed systems. It extends relatively simply to games with imperfect information, only using a little semantic change on the quantification operator. ATL^* is defined with respect to a set of agents Agt and a set of atomic propositions AP by the following grammar (note that as usual we do not allow the universal quantifier when dealing with simulations):

$$\mathsf{ATL}^* \ni \phi \; := \; \ll\!\mathbf{C}\!\gg \varphi \mid \phi \wedge \phi \mid \phi \vee \phi$$
$$\varphi \; := \; \mathbf{p} \mid \neg \mathbf{p} \mid \mathbf{X}\varphi \mid \varphi \mathbf{U} \varphi \mid \varphi \wedge \varphi \mid \varphi \vee \varphi \mid \phi$$

where $\mathbf{p}$ is an atomic proposition and $\mathbf{C}$ is a subset of $\mathtt{Agt}$.

The ϕ-type formulas are *state formulas* and are evaluated on a state s of a CGS $\mathcal{G}$. The semantic interpretation of boolean operators is as usual. We recall that there are two semantics to define outcomes, subjective and objective. This gives rise to two semantics for the quantification, with the first being the objective definition and the second being the subjective definition:

$$\mathcal{G}, s \models_{obj} \ll\!\mathbf{C}\!\gg \varphi \quad \text{iff} \quad \begin{cases} \exists \overline{\delta} = \{\delta_P\}_{P \in \mathbf{C}} \in \mathtt{Strat} \text{ s.t. } \forall P \in \mathbf{C}, \ \delta_P \text{ conforms to the} \\ \text{information of } P \text{ and } \forall \rho \in \mathtt{Out}_{obj}(\overline{\delta}, s) \text{ it holds } \mathcal{G}, \rho, 1 \models \varphi \end{cases}$$

$$\mathcal{G}, s \models_{sub} \ll\!\mathbf{C}\!\gg \varphi \quad \text{iff} \quad \begin{cases} \exists \overline{\delta} = \{\delta_P\}_{P \in \mathbf{C}} \in \mathtt{Strat} \text{ s.t. } \forall P \in \mathbf{C}, \ \delta_P \text{ conforms to the} \\ \text{information of } P \text{ and } \forall \rho \in \mathtt{Out}_{sub}(\overline{\delta}, s) \text{ it holds } \mathcal{G}, \rho, 1 \models \varphi \end{cases}$$

The φ-type formulas are called *path-formulas* and are evaluated with respect to a path within the CGS. The semantics of the boolean operators and the atomic propositions is standard. The other operators follow the semantics below.

$$\begin{aligned} \mathcal{G}, \rho, i \models \mathbf{X}\,\varphi \quad &\text{iff} \quad \mathcal{G}, \rho, i+1 \models \varphi \\ \mathcal{G}, \rho, i \models \varphi_1 \, \mathbf{U}\, \varphi_2 \quad &\text{iff} \quad \exists j > i. \ \mathcal{G}, \rho, j \models \varphi_2 \text{ and } \forall i < k < j. \ \mathcal{G}, \rho, k \models \varphi_1 \\ \mathcal{G}, \rho, i \models \phi \quad &\text{iff} \quad \mathcal{G}, \rho(i) \models \phi \end{aligned}$$

We call ATL the fragment of ATL* obeying the syntax

$$\text{ATL} \ni \phi \quad := \quad \ll\!\mathbf{C}\!\gg \varphi \mid \ll\!\mathbf{C}\!\gg \mathbf{X}\,\varphi \mid \ \mid \ll\!\mathbf{C}\!\gg \varphi\,\mathbf{U}\,\varphi$$
$$\varphi \quad := \quad \mathbf{p} \mid \neg\mathbf{p} \mid \varphi \wedge \varphi \mid \varphi \vee \varphi \mid \phi$$

3 Simulation in Games with Imperfect Information

In [5] the authors propose a notion of equivalence sound for ATL that works for both the subjective and the objective semantics. This notion is however rather restrictive. We develop our own notion, which shares some similarities with the one of [5], yet is more general. The simulation we propose is also sound for ATL*, works on both subjective and objective semantics. Besides those properties already present in [5], our simulations do not require a perfect replication of the partial information. By "replication of partial information", we mean the following. Consider three states q, s', q' with q, q' similar and $s' \sim_P q'$, there is no need for the existence of a state s with $s \sim_P q$ and s, q similar. Finally our notion is complete on a small class of games: *naive games*, and from this completeness one can deduce an equivalence-checking algorithm for games with public actions.

For the rest of the paper, we consider two games $\mathcal{G}, \mathcal{G}'$ that build upon the same atomic propositions and upon the same set $\mathtt{Agt}$ of agents. Simulation – or equivalence-checking in general – in multi-agent systems is parameterized by a coalition of agents (made of all agents to be existentially quantified in the formulas we are interested in). Therefore we also fix a coalition $\mathbf{C} \subseteq \mathtt{Agt}$ as a parameter. We first describe the simulation and soundness for the objective semantics. The case for the subjective semantics is similar and will be discussed in the end. The main idea behind our algorithm is to keep track of all imperfect information scenarios possible through a tracker. We represent the tracker, written Λ, as a relation on $S \times S \times 2^{\mathtt{Agt}} \times S' \times S' \times 2^{\mathtt{Agt}}$.

Definition 2. *A simulation of $\mathcal{G}$ by $\mathcal{G}'$ for $\mathbf{C}$ is a relation $\mathcal{R} \subseteq S \times S'$ such that there is another relation $\Lambda \subseteq S \times S \times 2^{\mathtt{Agt}} \times S' \times S' \times 2^{\mathtt{Agt}}$ where*

1. *for each $(q, q') \in \mathcal{R}$, $\mathtt{Label}(q) = \mathtt{Label}(q')$.*
2. *for any (q, q') in $\mathcal{R}$, we have $(q, q, \mathbf{C}, q', q', \mathbf{C}) \in \Lambda$*
3. *– for each $(q, q') \in \mathcal{R}$, there is a function $\mathcal{T}_{q,q'} : \mathtt{JAct}_{\mathcal{G}}^{\mathbf{C}} \mapsto \mathtt{JAct}_{\mathcal{G}'}^{\mathbf{C}}$*
   – for each $(q, q') \in \mathcal{R}$ and each $\bar{a} \in \mathtt{JAct}_{\mathcal{G}}^{\mathbf{C}}$ there exists a function
   $\mathcal{U}_{q,q'}^{\bar{a}} : \mathtt{JAct}_{\mathcal{G}'}^{\mathtt{Agt} \setminus \mathbf{C}} \mapsto \mathtt{JAct}_{\mathcal{G}}^{\mathtt{Agt} \setminus \mathbf{C}}$
   such that the following two properties hold:
   (a) *consider any $(q_1, q_2, A, q_1', q_2', B) \in \Lambda$, any two joint actions $\bar{a}, \bar{b} \in \mathtt{JAct}_{\mathcal{G}}^{\mathbf{C}}$ such that $\bar{a}(A) = \bar{b}(A)$, and any two joint actions $\bar{c}'$ and $\bar{d}' \in \mathtt{JAct}_{\mathcal{G}'}^{\mathtt{Agt} \setminus \mathbf{C}}$. Write k_1 for the successor of q_1 by $\bar{a} \cdot \mathcal{U}_{q_1,q_1'}^{\bar{a}}(\bar{c}')$, k_2 for the successor of q_2 by $\bar{b} \cdot \mathcal{U}_{q_2,q_2'}^{\bar{b}}(\bar{d}')$, k_1' for the successor of q_1' by $\mathcal{T}_{q_1,q_1'}(\bar{a}) \cdot \bar{c}'$, k_2' for the successor of q_2' by $\mathcal{T}_{q_2,q_2'}(\bar{b}) \cdot \bar{d}'$, C the set of agent with information common to k_1, k_2; and D the set of agents with information common to k_1', k_2'. Then $(k_1, k_2, E, k_1', k_2', F) \in \Lambda$ where $E = A \cap C$ and $F = B \cap D$.*
   (b) *for each $(q, q') \in \mathcal{R}$, each joint action $\bar{a} \in \mathtt{JAct}_{\mathcal{G}}^{\mathbf{C}}$, there is a joint action $\bar{c}' \in \mathtt{JAct}_{\mathcal{G}'}^{\mathtt{Agt} \setminus \mathbf{C}}$ such that the pair consisting of a successor of q by $\bar{a} \cdot \mathcal{U}_{q,q'}^{\bar{a}}(\bar{c}')$ and a successor of q' by $\mathcal{T}_{q,q'}(\bar{a}) \cdot \bar{c}'$ is in $\mathcal{R}$.*
4. *for each $(q_1, q_2, A, q_1', q_2', B) \in \Lambda$*

$$\forall \bar{a}, \bar{b} \in \mathtt{JAct}_{\mathcal{G}}^{\mathbf{C}}. \quad [\bar{a}(A) = \bar{b}(A)] \implies [\mathcal{T}_{q_1,q_1'}(\bar{a})(B) = \mathcal{T}_{q_2,q_2'}(\bar{b})(B)] \quad (1)$$

The above definition of simulations may look complicated but is in fact relatively similar to the one of ATL* with the addition of the syntactic sugar to manage the tracker Λ. Indeed, Points 1 and 3.b are similar to the requirements of the simulations for ATL with perfect information [3]. Points 2 and 3.a are there to build the tracker properly. Intuitively, the tracker can be built based on $\mathcal{R}$ by a fix-point algorithm using Point 2 for initialization and Point 3.a as recurrence relation. Point 4 enforces the simulation to make coherent choices for the scenarios in the tracker. Note that if the tracker is larger than the one of the definition above, but the property in Point 4 still holds for the larger tracker, then the soundness for ATL will also hold. Note also that, while it may not look obvious, this kind of simulations is closed by union. The tracker for the union of two simulations is simply the union of the trackers from each simulation.

We provide a small example for the games on Fig. 1. There exists a simulation of domain (where we omit the last states for clarity)

$$\mathcal{R} := \{(A, A'), (B, B'), (B, C'), (C, B'), (C, C')\}$$

and where the tracker is made of

$$\Lambda := \begin{cases} (A, A, \{P_i\}_{i\leq 3}, A', A', \{P_i\}_{i\leq 3}) \\ (B, C, \{P_1\}, B', C', \{P_2\}) \\ (C, B, \{P_1\}, B', C', \{P_2\}) \\ (C, B, \{P_1\}, C', B', \{P_2\}) \\ (B, C, \{P_1\}, C', B', \{P_2\}) \end{cases}$$

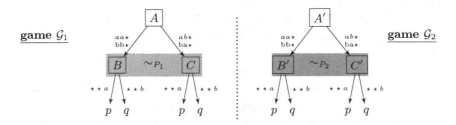

Fig. 1. Two games bisimilar, each with 3 agents. The bisimilarity is relatively trivial as only the third player is active on the B, C, B' and C' states.

Remark 1. Using a naive approach, finding if there exists a simulation takes an exponential time.

Strategic Characterization. To establish the soundness of simulations for ATL*, we restate simulations as relations between strategies. We need a few notations first. An *existential profile* $\overline{\delta}$ is a set of strategies $(\delta_{P_1}, \ldots, \delta_{P_n})$, one per agents in $\mathbf{C}$. Universal profiles are defined similarly as sets of strategies from the agents in $\mathtt{Agt}\backslash\mathbf{C}$. We write $\mathtt{Profile}^*_\star$ with $* \in \{\mathbf{C}, \mathtt{Agt}\backslash\mathbf{C}\}$ and $\star \in \{\mathcal{G}, \mathcal{G}'\}$ for the set of $*$-profiles in the $\star$-game. A *strategic characterization* is a set $\{\mathcal{S}^{\mathbf{C}}_{q,q'}, \mathcal{S}^{\mathtt{Agt}\backslash\mathbf{C}}_{q,q'}\}_{q,q'\in Z}$ of functions on some domain $Z \subseteq S \times S'$ where the functions are of the form $\mathcal{S}^{\mathbf{C}}_{q,q'} : \mathtt{Profile}^{\mathbf{C}}_{\mathcal{G}'} \mapsto \mathtt{Profile}^{\mathbf{C}}_{\mathcal{G}}$ and $\mathcal{S}^{\mathtt{Agt}\backslash\mathbf{C}}_{q,q'} : \mathtt{Profile}^{\mathtt{Agt}\backslash\mathbf{C}}_{\mathcal{G}'} \mapsto \mathtt{Profile}^{\mathtt{Agt}\backslash\mathbf{C}}_{\mathcal{G}}$ that obey two features:

Feat.1 for all q, q', any two profiles $\overline{\delta}, \overline{\gamma'}$, and any two states s, s' belonging to the objective outcomes of $\overline{\delta}$ and $\mathcal{S}^{\mathtt{Agt}\backslash\mathbf{C}}_{q,q'}(\overline{\gamma'})$ and of $\mathcal{S}^{\mathbf{C}}_{q,q'}(\overline{\delta})$ and $\overline{\gamma'}$, the pair (s, s') belongs to the domain Z of the strategic profile.

Feat.2 for any pair of states q, q', any two profiles $\overline{\delta}, \overline{\gamma'}$, the objective outcomes of $\overline{\delta}$ and $\mathcal{S}^{\mathtt{Agt}\backslash\mathbf{C}}_{q,q'}(\overline{\gamma'})$ and of $\mathcal{S}^{\mathbf{C}}_{q,q'}(\overline{\delta})$ and $\overline{\gamma'}$ have the same traces starting from q and q', respectively.

Simulations can be linked to strategic characterizations via Theorem 1 below.

Theorem 1. *If there exists a simulation $\mathcal{R}$ of $\mathcal{G}$ by $\mathcal{G}'$, then there is a strategic characterization defined on $\mathcal{R}$.*

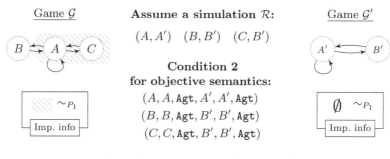

For subjective semantics, we add

$$(A, C, \{P_1\}, A', A', \mathsf{Agt}) \qquad (A, C, \{P_1\}, B', B', \mathsf{Agt})$$
$$(C, A, \{P_1\}, A', A', \mathsf{Agt}) \qquad (C, A, \{P_1\}, B', B', \mathsf{Agt})$$

Fig. 2. Illustration of Point 2 of simulation for the subjective semantic.

Simulation Soundness for ATL

Theorem 2. *Let $\mathcal{R}$ be a simulation of $\mathcal{G}$ by $\mathcal{G}'$. For any $(q, q') \in \mathcal{R}$ and any $\Phi \in \mathsf{ATL}^*$, if $q \models \Phi$ then $q' \models \Phi$ (for the objective semantics).*

Proof. Assume there is a simulation $\mathcal{R}$ of $\mathcal{G}$ by $\mathcal{G}'$. The proof is by induction on the nesting of quantifier operators. Consider the case where Φ has no nested quantification. If Φ holds on $\mathcal{G}$, then there is an existential winning strategy profile $\bar{\delta}$. Using Theorem 1, we obtain a strategy $\mathcal{S}^{\exists}(\bar{\delta})$. Then $\mathcal{S}^{\exists}(\bar{\delta})$ is a winning strategy in $\mathcal{G}'$ for the temporal property of Φ. Indeed, if there was a universal strategy $\overline{\gamma'}$ falsifying Φ against $\mathcal{S}^{\exists}(\bar{\delta})$, we could use $\mathcal{S}^{\forall}(\overline{\gamma'})$ to get a strategy falsifying the temporal property of Φ against $\bar{\delta}$, which would contradict the hypothesis that $\bar{\delta}$ is winning for Φ. The case where Φ has nested quantifications is similar, only using the induction hypothesis to check the sub-formulas. $\square$

Simulation in the Subjective Semantics. The notion of simulation in the subjective semantics is similar with the exception of the requirement on the tracker Λ (the second point of the definition). In the objective semantic, Point 2 provides an initialization of the tracker for the different possible starting states while Point 3.a provides a recurrence condition. Subjective semantics do not make a difference between a starting state q in $\mathcal{G}$ and a state h indistinguishable from q for some agent P. Thus a strategy δ for P must be conform to $q \sim_P h$. Something similar occurs in $\mathcal{G}'$. The tracker in a simulation between $\mathcal{G}$ and $\mathcal{G}'$ must handle this potential scenario, hence we adapt the tracker initialization (Point 2).

2. for any (q, q') in $\mathcal{R}$, any $h \in \bigcup_{P \in \mathbf{C}} \{h \mid q \sim_P h\}$, $h' \in \bigcup_{P \in \mathbf{C}} \{h' \mid q' \sim_P h'\}$, the following holds

$$(q, h, A, q', h', B) \in \Lambda \text{ where } \begin{cases} A = \{P \in \mathsf{Agt} \mid q \sim_P h\} \\ B = \{P \in \mathsf{Agt} \mid q' \sim_P h'\} \end{cases}$$

The proof of soundness is similar, using a definition of strategic characterization with subjective outcomes (in both features). The change in definition is illustrated in Fig. 2. In the figure, we can see two games (on the left and on the right) with the imperfect information described just below (in $\mathcal{G}$, the information is for player P between A and C; in $\mathcal{G}'$ there is no imperfect information). For the relation $\mathcal{R}$, we describe the initialization of the tracker for both the objective and subjective semantics in the central part of the figure.

Remark 2. In the subjective semantics, it may be necessary to have some degree of imperfect information replication in order to establishing a simulation (some knowledge operators of epistemic logics can be expressed by subjective ATL). This is however covered through the definition: the tracker will enforce a minimum replication required.

Comparison to the Existing Notion of Simulation. Our notion is more general than the one of [5] as it needs not to reproduce similar observations. This way the game on the right of Fig. 3, defined over a single (existential) agent P, is not similar for [5] to the game on the left since there is no state similar to h' in both the possibilities and the observation: r lacks the similar observation while s lacks the successor with similar label. Trivially, the games satisfy the same for-

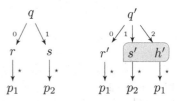

Fig. 3. Two games similar with common observation in color. (Color figure online)

mulas with existential quantification over the single agent P. The two games are also similar for our notion. Indeed, we can build a relation $\mathcal{R}$ with (q, q'), (r, r'), (s, s') and (r, h'). The Λ relation follows trivially with $(*, *, P, *', *', P)$ for $(*, *') \in \mathcal{R}$ and $(r, s, \emptyset, h', s', P)$. Take $\mathcal{T}$ as the identity function plus $\mathcal{T}_{h',h}(2) \mapsto 0$. With this choice, the fourth condition is trivially satisfied.

4 Naive Games and Completeness

As ATL with perfect recall is undecidable [21], it is very unlikely that there exists a notion of simulation provably sound and complete for ATL. There exist some model restrictions which make the ATL model-checking decidable: hierarchical observations and the many derivatives (hierarchical information, dynamic hierarchies) [8, 21], public actions [6]. The search for completeness relative to these fragments is not a vain quest, unlike the general case. In this section we identify a small subclass of games, *naive games*, for which our concept of simulation is complete. This concept will also prove itself crucial to develop an equivalence-checking algorithm in games with public actions in the next section. A game is naive when the imperfect information is state-based, meaning that two states can or cannot be distinguished by the same agents regardless of the histories; a formal definition is given below and an illustration in Fig. 4. From the definition, any game with a tree-shape structure is de-facto naive (see Fig. 3 for example). This approach (restriction) on imperfect information is also used in the MCMAS tool [18].

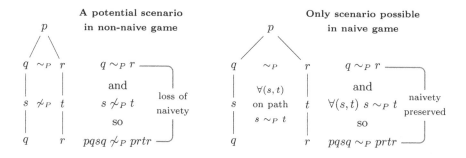

Fig. 4. History influence on partial observation in both non-naive and naive games.

Definition 3. *A* naive game *is a game in which for any two finite paths ρ_A, ρ_B,*

$$\{P \in \text{Agt} \mid \rho_A \sim_P \rho_B\} = \{P \in \text{Agt} \mid last(\rho_A) \sim_P last(\rho_B)\}$$

Note that the left-to-right inclusion is always true in CGS, naive games guarantee that the converse inclusion (right-to-left) also holds. Naive games are interesting for simulations because they have a very simplified tracker. The inputs are all of shape (h, k, A, h', k', B) where $A = \{P \in \text{Agt} \mid h \sim_P k\}$ and $B = \{P \in \text{Agt} \mid h' \sim_P k'\}$ whereas general inputs for non-naive games can also be of shape (h, k, C, h', k', D) with $C \subsetneq A$ and $D \subsetneq B$. They are incomparable with both games with public actions and games with hierarchical observations. On them, ATL model-checking is decidable.

Theorem 3. ATL *and* ATL* *model-checking are decidable on naive games with imperfect information.*

Proof (Sketch). The result is relatively trivial so we only provide a sketch of the proof. Transform the temporal objective into a parity automaton $\mathcal{A}$ and cross it with the CGS. Let $\mathcal{G}_{\mathcal{A}}$ be the result. We get a parity game with imperfect information for which the property of naive games still applies. On $\mathcal{G}_{\mathcal{A}}$, optimal strategies can be chosen positional even if we allow perfect recall strategies. This is because the imperfect information is fixed and will not evolve with the choices made previously by either player. We can then simply enumerate the positional strategies conform to imperfect information in $\mathcal{G}_{\mathcal{A}}$ and see if some works. □

Proving the completeness of our simulation on non-naive games seems an herculean task. It requires to build a formula which can fully encode all scenarios possible from an initial state. Such formula would require to not only handle the atomic propositions seen along the way but also the potential changes in imperfect information with other paths. With naive games, there are no changes in the imperfect information. This brings us back to a situation close to games with perfect information for which there exist sound and complete notions of alternating simulations [3]. Using similar ideas to the ones used to prove the completeness of alternating simulations for ATL, we prove that our simulations are complete for naive games.

Theorem 4. *Fix two naive games $\mathcal{G}$ and $\mathcal{G}'$. Let $\mathcal{R}$ be the set*

$$\mathcal{R} := \{(q, q') \mid q \in S, \ q' \in S' \text{ s.t } \forall \phi \in ATL \ [q \models \phi \Rightarrow q' \models \phi]\}$$

then $\mathcal{R}$ is the domain of a simulation.

5   Equivalence Checking in Games with Public Actions

Games with public actions are games on which agents have perfect visibility of the other agents actions. On them, ATL enjoys a decidable model-checking [6]. Using the completeness of our simulations for naive games, we develop a sound and complete algorithm to check simulations on public action games.

Definition 4. *A game $\mathcal{G}$ has public actions when*

$$\left.\begin{array}{l} \forall P \in \mathsf{Agt} \\ \forall q, q' \in \mathcal{G} \\ \forall \overline{a}, \overline{a'} \in \mathsf{Act}^{\mathsf{Agt}} \end{array}\right\} \quad [\overline{a} \neq \overline{a'} \text{ and } q \sim_P q' \ \Rightarrow \ \delta(q, \overline{a}) \not\sim_P \delta(q', \overline{a'})]$$

From the definition, any two histories of equal length are distinguishable as long as they start in the same initial state. So, in the objective semantics, games with public actions are equivalent to games with perfect information. Games with public actions are only interesting in that semantics if multiple starting states are considered. In the setting of this paper, it corresponds to using subjective semantics. In such cases, games with public actions are strictly more expressive than perfect information games. For the rest of this section we fix a game $\mathcal{G}$ with public actions and a coalition C of agents.

Lemma 1. (Consequence of Remark 2 in [6]). *Consider a strategy profile $\overline{\delta_C}$ for the coalition C, a starting state q, and a finite path ρ compatible with $\overline{\delta_C}$ starting in q. Then ρ has at most $|\{q' \mid q' \sim_P q, P \in C\}|$ outcomes indistinguishable from ρ in $\mathsf{Out}_{sub}(\overline{\delta_C}, q)$.*

Intuitively, there is only a finite number of paths indistinguishable from the "objective" path. Each of theses paths can be identified by its starting state (within $\{q' \mid q' \sim_P q, P \in C\}$) and the sequence of actions played (common to all these paths).

   So, as there are only a finite number of paths indistinguishable, we can track them easily within the state space. By doing so, we can go from public action games to naive games; this is what the lemma below does. In it we call an ATL formula principal when it has no closed sub-formula.

Theorem 5. *For each public action game $\mathcal{G}$, there exists a naive game $\mathcal{H}$ such that $\mathcal{G}$ and $\mathcal{H}$ satisfy exactly the same ATL principal formulas existentially quantifying over the coalition C of agents.*

Construction of the Naive Game

$\mathcal{H}$ is a version of $\mathcal{G}$ which records all possible paths indistinguishable from the current one for each agent. Each indistinguishable path will be summarized by the starting and finishing states. Each state q in $\mathcal{G}$ is augmented with a function $f : \mathtt{Agt} \mapsto 2^{G \times G}$, making the state space of $\mathcal{H}$ equal to $G \times (2^{G \times G})^{\mathtt{Agt}}$. Intuitively, if a path ends in a state q augmented by f_q with $(r, s) \in f_q(P)$, then it means there is a path indistinguishable from the current one starting in r and ending in s.

Remark 3. The construction can be seen as building an information set of a tree automaton for games with perfect information [10,19,20].

Formally, the state space of $\mathcal{H}$ is $G \times (2^{G \times G})^{\mathtt{Agt}}$. For each joint action $\bar{a}$ for $\mathtt{Agt}$, we create an edge from (q, f) to (q', f') when

- $q \xrightarrow{\bar{a}} q'$ in $\mathcal{G}$
- $f'(P) := \{(r, s') \mid \exists (r, s) \in f(P) \text{ and } s' \sim_P q' \text{ and } s \xrightarrow{\bar{a}} s'\}$ for every agent P.

The imperfect information is created inductively. Initially, it follows from $q \sim_P q'$ in $\mathcal{G}$ that

$$(q, f : P \mapsto \{(r, r) \mid r \sim_P q\})) \sim_P (q', f' : P \mapsto \{(r', r') \mid r' \sim_P q'\}) \text{ in } \mathcal{H}, \quad (2)$$

then inductively,

$$\left. \begin{array}{l} (q, f) \sim_P (q', f') \\ (q', f') \xrightarrow{\bar{a}} (r', g') \end{array} \quad \begin{array}{l} (q, f) \xrightarrow{\bar{a}} (r, g) \\ r \sim_P r' \text{ in } \mathcal{G} \end{array} \right\} \quad \Rightarrow \quad (r, g) \sim_P (r', g') \quad (3)$$

The induction trivially reaches a fixed point and terminates. The initial relation is reflexive (inherited from the relation on $\mathcal{G}$), symmetric (by definition) and transitive (inherited from the relation on $\mathcal{G}$ and the definition). At each step of the induction, these three properties are preserved. Indeed reflexivity is trivially preserved. The definition of (3) is symmetric, so the relation is also symmetric. Finally, the transitivity is preserved through the use of similar joint actions, as in lines 2 and 3 in (3). The relation thus defined is indeed an equivalence relation on states of $\mathcal{H}$ and therefore an imperfect information relation.

The set of initial states we consider in $\mathcal{H}$ is $\{(q, f) \mid f : P \mapsto \{(r, r) \mid r \sim_P q\}\}$. By definition of the imperfect information in $\mathcal{H}$:

$$\forall (q, f), (q', f') \in \mathcal{H}. \ \forall P \in \mathtt{Agt}. \quad \left[(q, f) \sim_P (q', f') \text{ in } \mathcal{H} \Rightarrow q \sim_P q' \text{ in } \mathcal{G} \right] \quad (4)$$

The idea is partially illustrated in Fig. 5, with the public-actions game on the left and the naive game on the right. The functions f and g are described at the top.

Correctness of the Construction

Notations: In the following we write a state $(q, \star)$ of $\mathcal{H}$ for a pair of shape (q, f) for some function f, and write a state of $\mathcal{H}$ $(\star, f)$ for a pair (q, f) for some state q of $\mathcal{G}$. This allows us to ease the reading.

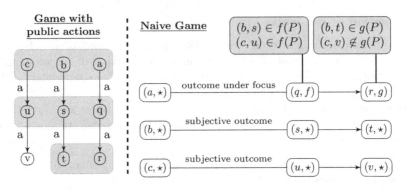

Fig. 5. Construction (with a single agent P). The imperfect information on the public action game is represented by colored areas. (Color figure online)

Lemma 2. *The following holds for any two paths ρ, ρ' and any agent P. Write $\rho'(1) := (q', \star)$, $\rho(|\rho|) := (\star, g)$ and $\rho'(|\rho|) := (s', \star)$. Then*

I if $\rho \sim_P \rho'$ then $(q', s') \in g(P)$.
II if $\rho \not\sim_P \rho'$ then $(q', s') \notin g(P)$.

Lemma 3. *Let P be any agent, (r, f) and (t, g) be any two states such that $(r, f) \sim_P (t, g)$. There are two paths ρ_C and ρ_D of shapes $\rho_C : (u, \star) \mapsto^* (r, f)$ and $\rho_D := (v, \star) \mapsto^* (t, g)$ such that $(v, t) \in f(P)$ and $(u, r) \in g(P)$.*

Lemma 4. $\mathcal{H}$ *is a naive game.*

Proof. Toward a contradiction, suppose the game is not naive. Then there must be two finite paths ρ_A, ρ_B and an agent $P \in \mathtt{Agt}$ such that $\rho_A \not\sim_P \rho_B$ but $last(\rho_A) \sim_P last(\rho_B)$. Write $\mathtt{last}(\rho_A) = (r, f)$ and $\mathtt{last}(\rho_B) = (t, g)$. Since $(r, f) \sim_P (t, g)$, by Lemma 3, there are two paths ρ_C and ρ_D of the shapes $\rho_C : (u, \star) \mapsto^* (r, f)$ and $\rho_D := (v, \star) \mapsto^* (t, g)$ such that $(v, t) \in f(P)$ and $(u, r) \in g(P)$. By Lemma 2, since $(v, t) \in f(P)$, we have $\rho_A \sim_P \rho_D$. Then by Lemma 2 once again, since $last(\rho_D) = (t, g)$, we have $(first(\rho_A), r) \in g$. Applying one last time Lemma 2, since $(first(\rho_A), r) \in g$ and $last(\rho_B) = (t, g)$ we get $\rho_A \sim_P \rho_B$, which is a contradiction. $\square$

Lemma 5. *A principal formula $\phi \in ATL$ existentially quantifying $\mathbf{C}$ holds from state q in $\mathcal{G}$ if and only if ϕ holds from (q, f) in $\mathcal{H}$ with $f : P \mapsto \{(r, r) \mid r \sim_P q\}$.*

Proof. For this we simply show an equivalence between paths in $\mathcal{G}$ and paths in $\mathcal{H}$ (from the starting states), in which a state q in $\mathcal{G}$ is always linked to a state of shape $(q, \star)$ in $\mathcal{H}$. We proceed by induction on the length of the paths. First note that for a state q in $\mathcal{G}$ there is a single initial state (q, f) in $\mathcal{H}$. We can therefore establish an equivalence between starting states. For the induction case, consider a path ρ in $\mathcal{H}$ and π in $\mathcal{H}$ and write $last(\rho) = (q, f)$ and $\mathtt{last}(\pi) = q$. For each joint-action $\bar{a}$ there is a single q' such that $q \xrightarrow{\bar{a}} q'$ in $\mathcal{G}$, and a single (q', f') such that $(q, f) \xrightarrow{\bar{a}} (q', f')$. We can therefore extend the correspondence one more step. And with the induction step sorted out, we can conclude the existence of a one-to-one correspondence between paths in both $\mathcal{G}$ and $\mathcal{H}$. Through a simple induction, we obtain that two paths (from the starting state) are indistinguishable in $\mathcal{H}$ if and only if their counterparts in $\mathcal{G}$ are indistinguishable. From the path correspondence, it is trivial to establish a correspondence between conform strategies, and to establish an equivalence between the formulas that can be satisfied (as long as we start from the appropriate starting state in $\mathcal{H}$). □

Theorem 5 then follows from the construction and Lemmas 4 and 5.

Sound and Complete Checking of Public-Actions Games

By combining Theorems 4 and 5, we can obtain a sound and complete way for ATL principal formulas to check simulation on public-action games. The process is presented in Algorithm 1. The correctness of the algorithm is ensured by the following lemma whose proof is in annex:

Lemma 6. *In Algorithm 1, define $\mathcal{R}_\mathcal{H}$ as the largest simulation of $\mathcal{H}'$ by $\mathcal{H}$. Then*

$$\{(q, q') \mid \forall \phi \text{ principal in ATL } [q \models \phi \Rightarrow q' \models \phi]\}$$

$$= \left\{(q, q') \mid \exists \ f_{ini}, f'_{ini} \text{ s.t } \begin{cases} (q, f_{ini}) \text{ is an initial state of } \mathcal{H} \\ (q', f'_{ini}) \text{ is an initial state of } \mathcal{H}' \\ ((q, f_{ini}), (q', f'_{ini})) \in \mathcal{R}_\mathcal{H} \end{cases} \right\}$$

Algorithm 1 does not work for non-principal ATL formulas. Indeed, two elements in the simulation relation $\mathcal{R}$ may not be starting states of $\mathcal{H}$, and therefore the correctness which only applies from starting states may not hold. The lemma below tells us precisely when our algorithm extends to non-principal formulas.

Lemma 7. *In Algorithm 1, if $\mathcal{R}$ satisfies*

$$\forall ((r, f), (s, g)) \in \mathcal{R} \qquad \exists f_{ini}, g_{ini} \text{ such that } \begin{cases} ((r, f_{ini}), (s, g_{ini})) \in \mathcal{R} \\ (r, f_{ini}) \text{ is an initial state in } \mathcal{H} \\ (s, g_{ini}) \text{ is an initial state in } \mathcal{H} \end{cases}$$

then

$$\{(q, q') \mid \forall \phi \text{ (principal or not) in ATL } [q \models \phi \Rightarrow q' \models \phi]\}$$

$$= \left\{(q, q') \mid \exists \ f_{ini}, f'_{ini} \text{ s.t } \begin{cases} (q, f_{ini}) \text{ is an initial state} \\ (q', f'_{ini}) \text{ is an initial state} \\ ((q, f_{ini}), (q', f'_{ini})) \in \mathcal{R}_\mathcal{H} \end{cases} \right\}$$

The proof follows from the definition of the condition and Theorem 5. With the lemma above, we can develop an algorithm for non-principal formulas simply by requiring step 3 to find the maximal simulation relation $\mathcal{R}$ which satisfies the condition of the lemma above.

Algorithm 1. Check for principal formulas in public-action games.

INPUT: Two games $\mathcal{G}$ and $\mathcal{G}'$ and two initial states q, q' respectively in $\mathcal{G}$ and $\mathcal{G}'$.
OUTPUT: Does $\mathcal{G}$ and $\mathcal{G}'$ satisfy the same principal formulas from q and q'.

1: $\mathcal{H} \rightarrow$ naive game satisfying the same ATL formulas as $\mathcal{G}$ through Theorem 5
2: $\mathcal{H}' \rightarrow$ naive game satisfying the same ATL formulas as $\mathcal{G}'$ through Theorem 5
3: Find the maximal simulation relation $\mathcal{R}$ of $\mathcal{H}$ by $\mathcal{H}'$
4: **if** $\exists f_{ini}, f'_{ini}$ such that $((q, f_{ini}), (q', f'_{ini})) \in \mathcal{R}$ **then**
5:     return $True$
6: **else**
7:     return $False$
8: **end if**

---

6   Concluding Remarks

We have proposed a notion of simulation sound for ATL on multi-agent systems in general and complete on naive systems where the information is state-based. Using the completeness of our concept of simulation for naive games, we have designed a simulation-checking algorithm for public-action games. A remaining interrogation is whether there is an equivalence-checking algorithm that is both sound and complete for ATL on hierarchical information systems.

References

1. de Alfaro, L., Henzinger, T.A.: Concurrent omega-regular games. In: Proceedings of LICS 2000 (2000)
2. Alur, R., Henzinger, T.A., Kupferman, O.: Alternating-time temporal logic. In: de Roever, W.-P., Langmaack, H., Pnueli, A. (eds.) COMPOS 1997. LNCS, vol. 1536, pp. 23–60. Springer, Heidelberg (1998). https://doi.org/10.1007/3-540-49213-5_2
3. Alur, R., Henzinger, T.A., Kupferman, O., Vardi, M.Y.: Alternating refinement relations. In: Sangiorgi, D., de Simone, R. (eds.) CONCUR 1998. LNCS, vol. 1466, pp. 163–178. Springer, Heidelberg (1998). https://doi.org/10.1007/BFb0055622
4. Baskar, A., Ramanujam, R., Suresh, S.P.: Knowledge-based modelling of voting protocols. In: Proceedings of TARK 2007 (2007)
5. Belardinelli, F., Condurache, R., Dima, C., Jamroga, W., Jones, A.V.: Bisimulations for verifying strategic abilities with an application to ThreeBallot. In: Proceedings of AAMAS 2017 (2017)
6. Belardinelli, F., Lomuscio, A., Murano, A., Rubin, S.: Verification of multi-agent systems with imperfect information and public actions. In: Proceedings AAMAS 2017. International Foundation for Autonomous Agents and Multiagent Systems (2017)
7. Berthon, R., Maubert, B., Murano, A., Rubin, S., Vardi, M.Y.: Strategy logic with imperfect information. In: Proceedings of LICS 2017, pp. 1–12 (2017)
8. Berwanger, D., Mathew, A.B., van den Bogaard, M.: Hierarchical information and the synthesis of distributed strategies. Acta Informatica 55, 669–701 (2018)
9. Blackburn, P., Rijke, M.D., Venema, Y.: Modal Logic. Cambridge Tracts in Theoretical Computer Science. Cambridge University Press, Cambridge (2001)

10. Chatterjee, K., Doyen, L.: The complexity of partial-observation parity games. In: Fermüller, C.G., Voronkov, A. (eds.) LPAR 2010. LNCS, vol. 6397, pp. 1–14. Springer, Heidelberg (2010). https://doi.org/10.1007/978-3-642-16242-8_1
11. Dima, C., Tiplea, F.L.: Model-checking ATL under imperfect information and perfect recall semantics is undecidable. CoRR (2011)
12. Goltz, U., Kuiper, R., Penczek, W.: Propositional temporal logics and equivalences. In: Cleaveland, W.R. (ed.) CONCUR 1992. LNCS, vol. 630, pp. 222–236. Springer, Heidelberg (1992). https://doi.org/10.1007/BFb0084794
13. Goranko, V., van Drimmelen, G.: Complete axiomatization and decidability of alternating-time temporal logic. Theor. Comput. Sci. **353**, 93–117 (2006)
14. Jamroga, W., Dix, J.: Model checking abilities under incomplete information is indeed delta2-complete. In: Proceedings of EUMAS 2006 (2006)
15. Laroussinie, F., Markey, N., Oreiby, G.: On the expressiveness and complexity of ATL. In: Seidl, H. (ed.) FoSSaCS 2007. LNCS, vol. 4423, pp. 243–257. Springer, Heidelberg (2007). https://doi.org/10.1007/978-3-540-71389-0_18
16. Laroussinie, F., Markey, N., Sangnier, A.: ATLsc with partial observation. In: Proceedings of GandALF 2015 (2015)
17. Larsen, K.G., Skou, A.: Bisimulation through probabilistic testing. Inf. Comput. **94**, 1–28 (1991)
18. Lomuscio, A., Qu, H., Raimondi, F.: MCMAS: an open-source model checker for the verification of multi-agent systems. Int. J. Softw. Tools Technol. Transf. **19**, 9–30 (2017)
19. van der Meyden, R., Vardi, M.Y.: Synthesis from knowledge-based specifications. In: Sangiorgi, D., de Simone, R. (eds.) CONCUR 1998. LNCS, vol. 1466, pp. 34–49. Springer, Heidelberg (1998). https://doi.org/10.1007/BFb0055614
20. van der Meyden, R., Wilke, T.: Synthesis of distributed systems from knowledge-based specifications. In: Abadi, M., de Alfaro, L. (eds.) CONCUR 2005. LNCS, vol. 3653, pp. 562–576. Springer, Heidelberg (2005). https://doi.org/10.1007/11539452_42
21. Peterson, G.L., Reif, J.H.: Multiple-person alternation. In: Proceedings of FOCS 1979 (1979)
22. Strauss, C.: A critical review of the triple ballot voting system, part2: cracking the triple ballot encryption (2006)
23. Tabatabaei, M., Jamroga, W., Ryan, P.Y.: Expressing receipt freeness and coercion-resistance in logics of strategic ability preliminary attempt. In: Proceedings of PrAISe 2016 (2016)
24. VAS-Group. In: Imperial college of London. https://vas.doc.ic.ac.uk/software/mcmas/
25. Wikipedia: Three ballot voting system. https://en.wikipedia.org/wiki/threeballot
26. Zhang, C., Pang, J.: On probabilistic alternating simulations. In: Calude, C.S., Sassone, V. (eds.) TCS 2010. IAICT, vol. 323, pp. 71–85. Springer, Heidelberg (2010). https://doi.org/10.1007/978-3-642-15240-5_6

On the Generation of Equational Dynamic Logics for Weighted Imperative Programs

Leandro Gomes[1][⊠], Alexandre Madeira[1,2], Manisha Jain[2], and Luis S. Barbosa[1,3]

[1] HASLab INESC TEC - Univ. Minho, Braga, Portugal
leandro.r.gomes@inesctec.pt
[2] CIDMA - Univ. Aveiro, Aveiro, Portugal
[3] QuantaLab, INL, Braga, Portugal

Abstract. Dynamic logic is a powerful framework for reasoning about imperative programs. This paper extends previous work [9] on the systematic generation of dynamic logics from the propositional to the equational case, to capture 'full-fledged' imperative programs. The generation process is parametric on a structure specifying a notion of 'weight' assigned to programs. The paper introduces also a notion of bisimilarity on models of the generated logics, which is shown to entail modal equivalence with respect to the latter.

1 Introduction

The development of dynamic logic [3] along the past twenty years went hand-in-hand with the evolution of its object, i.e. *the very notion of a program.* The result was the emergence of a plethora of dynamic logics tailored to specific programming paradigms. This ranges from the well-known classical case [2] to less conventional examples for which e.g. programs are compositions of actions in UML state machines [6] or event/actions regular expressions [4]. Other rephrasing of what should count for a program in each specific context, lead to different variants of dynamic logics: Examples include probabilistic [7], fuzzy, concurrent [10], quantum [1] and continuous [11] computations, and combinations thereof.

Reference [9] initiated a research agenda on the systematic development of propositional, multi-valued dynamic logics parametric on an algebraic structure, actually an action lattice, which defines both the computational paradigm

This work was founded by the ERDF—European Regional Development Fund through the Operational Programme for Competitiveness and Internationalisation - COMPETE 2020 Programme and by National Funds through the Portuguese funding agency, FCT - Fundação para a Ciência e a Tecnologia, within project POCI-01-0145-FEDER-030947. The second author is supported in the scope of the framework contract foreseen in the numbers 4, 5 and 6 of the article 23, of the Decree-Law 57/2016, of August 29, changed by Portuguese Law 57/2017, of July 19 and by UID/MAT/04106/2019 at CIDMA.

© Springer Nature Switzerland AG 2019
Y. Ait-Ameur and S. Qin (Eds.): ICFEM 2019, LNCS 11852, pp. 154–169, 2019.
https://doi.org/10.1007/978-3-030-32409-4_10

where programs live, and the truth space where assertions take value. This paper extends this agenda to a new level, taking computational states as valuations of variables over a given domain, and programs as their modifiers. The idea is to capture typical imperative programs and their interpretation over different notions of 'weighted' computation—the very notion of *weight* being brought to scene as a parameter, encoded in the action lattice, for the generation of the corresponding dynamic logic. Depending on each action lattice chosen, such weights will be interpreted as e.g. vagueness degree associated to the effectiveness of a particular computation, or a measure of the resources consumed in it, or even the associated cost or execution time.

Note that in all approaches discussed in the literature, even when some form of structured computation is considered, validity of assertions is always stated in classical terms. The approach proposed here goes a step further in the sense that validity of structured computation (e.g. fuzzy, costed, timed) is discussed in a logic capturing itself the corresponding notion of behaviour.

Differently from our previous work [9], 'fully-fledged' programs are considered here. This means that assignment of values from a data space to a variable is taken as the elementary construction, programs being defined over an equational signature of program variables, predicate and function symbols. Thus, in the sequel, programs are expressions generated by the following grammar:

$$\pi ::= x := t \mid \pi; \pi \mid \textbf{ if } c \textbf{ then } \pi \textbf{ else } \pi \textbf{ fi } \mid \textbf{ while } c \textbf{ do } \pi \textbf{ od} \quad (1)$$

where t denote terms with variables from a set X.

Bisimulation is defined parametrically on an action lattice, over the resulting computational models. Finally, bisimilarity is shown to entail modal equivalence for the corresponding dynamic logic.

The remaining of this paper is organised as follows. After a brief background overview in Sect. 2, to recap the definition of an action lattice and some of its fundamental properties, Sect. 3 extends the method proposed in [9] to incorporate 'fully-fledged' imperative programs, i.e. program variables and assignments. All constructions are illustrated in detail for three paradigmatic parameters: classical Boolean lattices, Gödel algebras to capture vagueness in computation, and the tropical semiring to reason about resource consumption. Bisimilarity and an invariance result is discussed, as a second contribution of the paper, in Sect. 4. Finally, Sect. 5 concludes, and enumerates topics for future work.

2   Action Lattices

As explained in the Introduction, the construction of multi-valued, equational, dynamic logics is parametric on an action lattice which induces both the computational model for programs and the truth space for logics. This section recalls the relevant definition and properties [9].

Definition 1. *An action lattice is a tuple*

$$\mathbf{A} = (A, +, ;, \mathbf{0}, \mathbf{1}, ^{*}, \rightarrow, \cdot)$$

*where A is a set, **0** and **1** constants, and $+, ;, \rightarrow$ and $\cdot$ binary operations and* *
a unary operation in A satisfying the axioms in Fig. 1, where the relation $\leq$ is
induced by $+$: $a \leq b$ *iff* $a + b = b$.

$$a + (b + c) = (a + b) + c \tag{2}$$
$$a + b = b + a \tag{3}$$
$$a + a = a \tag{4}$$
$$a + 0 = 0 + a = a \tag{5}$$
$$a; (b; c) = (a; b); c \tag{6}$$
$$a; 1 = 1; a = a \tag{7}$$
$$a; (b + c) = (a; b) + (a; c) \tag{8}$$
$$(a + b); c = (a; c) + (b; c) \tag{9}$$
$$a; 0 = 0; a = 0 \tag{10}$$

$$1 + a + (a^*; a^*) \leq a^* \tag{11}$$
$$a; x \leq x \Rightarrow a^*; x \leq x \tag{12}$$
$$x; a \leq x \Rightarrow x; a^* \leq x \tag{13}$$
$$a; x \leq b \Leftrightarrow x \leq a \rightarrow b \tag{14}$$
$$a \cdot (b \cdot c) = (a \cdot b) \cdot c \tag{15}$$
$$a \cdot b = b \cdot a \tag{16}$$
$$a \cdot a = a \tag{17}$$
$$a + (a \cdot b) = a \tag{18}$$
$$a \cdot (a + b) = a \tag{19}$$

Fig. 1. A possible axiomatisation of action lattices.

An action lattice **A** is *complete* when every subset of its carrier A has both supremum and infimum with respect to $\leq$. The greatest and least elements are denoted in the sequel by $\top$ and $\bot$, respectively. Note that in any action lattice $\bot = 0$, since for any $a \in A$, $a + 0 = a$, i.e. $0 \leq a$. Consider a non-empty set I. We say that **A** is *linear* if it satisfies, for any set $\{a_i | i \in I\}$, the property

$$\sum_{i \in I} a_i = a_j, \text{ for some } j \in I \tag{20}$$

Since operators $+$, ; and $\cdot$ are associative, they admit a n-ary iterated version, represented by $\sum$, $\prod$ and $\bigwedge$, respectively. Note that the structure $(A, +, ;, \mathbf{0}, \mathbf{1},^*)$ axiomatised by (2)–(13) forms a Kleene algebra. The following handy properties are easily proved [9]:

$$x \leq y \Rightarrow x; a \leq y; a \tag{21}$$
$$a \leq b \,\&\, c \leq d \Rightarrow a + c \leq b + d \tag{22}$$

The generation of dynamic logics illustrated in the following sections will be parametric on the class of complete action lattices. Actually, completeness is required to guarantee the existence of infinite sums. The following are examples of complete action lattices, with which the proposed constructions will be illustrated along the paper.

Example 1. The first example is the Boolean lattice

$$\mathbf{2} = (\{\top, \bot\}, \vee, \wedge, \bot, \top,^*, \rightarrow, \wedge)$$

with the standard interpretation of Boolean connectives. Operator * maps each element of $\{\top, \bot\}$ to $\top$, and $\rightarrow$ corresponds to logical implication.

Example 2. Gödel algebras are the locally finite variety of Heyting algebras. Formally,

$$\mathbf{G} = ([0,1], max, min, 0_\mathbf{G}, 1,^*, \rightarrow, min)$$

where

$$x \rightarrow y = \begin{cases} 1, & \text{if } x \leq y \\ y, & \text{if } y < x \end{cases}$$

Example 3. Finally, the $(min, +)$ Kleene algebra [8], known as the *tropical semiring*, can be extended to an action lattice through the introduction of residuation $\rightarrow$:

$$\mathbf{R} = (\mathbb{R}_0^+ \cup \{+\infty\}, min, +_\mathbf{R}, +\infty, 0_\mathbf{R},^*, \rightarrow, min)$$

where, for any $x, y \in \mathbb{R}_0^+ \cup \{+\infty\}$, $x^* = 0_\mathbf{R}$ and $x \rightarrow y = max\{y - x, 0\}$, with $\mathbb{R}_0^+ = \{x \in \mathbb{R} \mid x \geq 0\}$.

3   Generation of Equational, Dynamic Logics

Each complete action lattice $\mathbf{A}$ induces a multi-valued, equational dynamic logic $\Gamma(\mathbf{A})$ to reason, as explained above, about 'full-fledged' imperative programs with weighted computations interpreted over $\mathbf{A}$. Such programs are generated as indicated in (1).

Example 4. This toy program over a set of variables $\{x, y\}$ and the real numbers as data space will be used for illustration purposes in the sequel.

$$x := 2; x := x + y; (\text{ if } x \leq 3 \text{ then } x := x + 1 \text{ else } y := y \times 2)$$

Note that its execution can be represented by the following transition system, where the conditional statement is encoded as a sum of alternatives guarded by a test.

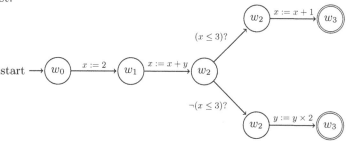

Let us start by carefully fixing the syntactic support for the generated logics. Programs are defined over a data signature $\Sigma = (F, P)$, where F and P denote sets of function and predicate symbols, respectively. As usual, let notation $T_\Sigma(X)$ stand for the set of Σ-terms with variables in X, and represent by $T_\Sigma^F(X)$ (respectively, $T_\Sigma^P(X)$) its restriction to functional (respectively, predicate) terms. Thus,

$$\text{Prg}_0(\Sigma, X) = \{x := t \mid x \in X \text{ and } t \in T_\Sigma(X)\}$$

defines the set of *atomic* programs for the pair (Σ, X), from which an arbitrary (composed) program is generated as an expression described by the following rule

$$\pi ::= \pi_0 \mid \phi? \mid \pi; \pi \mid \pi + \pi \mid \pi^*$$

with $\pi_0 \in \mathrm{Prg}_0(\Sigma, X)$, and $\phi?$ standing for a suitable notion of *test*. The latter, however, needs to be handled with some care: indeed the meaning of a test depends on the logic $\Gamma(\mathbf{A})$, and therefore on $\mathbf{A}$ itself, as we will discuss below on defining its semantics in terms of the satisfaction relation for $\Gamma(\mathbf{A})$. For the moment, it is enough to notice that choice $(+)$, iteration $(^*)$ and tests $(\phi?)$ encode the usual 'syntactic sugar' constructs for conditionals and loops as considered in rule (1). The set of composed programs for (Σ, X) is denoted by $\mathrm{Prg}(\Sigma, X)$.

Once a language for programs is fixed, the set of formulas for $\Gamma(\mathbf{A})$ introduces, as expected, the universal and existential modalities over programs. Formally,

Definition 2. *A* signature *for* $\Gamma(\mathbf{A})$ *is a tuple*

$$\Delta = (\Sigma, \Pi)$$

where Σ is a data signature and $\Pi \subseteq \mathrm{Prg}_0(\Sigma, X)$ is a set of variable assignments. The set of formulas *for* Δ, *denoted by* $\mathrm{Fm}^{\Gamma(\mathbf{A})}(\Delta)$, *are the ones generated by the rule*

$$\varphi ::= \top \mid \bot \mid p \mid \varphi \vee \varphi \mid \varphi \wedge \varphi \mid \varphi \rightarrow \varphi \mid \langle \pi \rangle \varphi \mid [\pi] \varphi$$

for $p \in T_{\Sigma}^P(X)$ and π is a program in $\mathrm{Prg}(\Sigma, X)$ that only uses atomic programs in Π.

Note that we sometimes make use of $\neg \varphi$ as an abbreviation for $\varphi \rightarrow \bot$, as in Example 4.

We can now turn to semantics. For each $\mathbf{A}$, models are defined over state spaces whose elements are graded valuations of variables, i.e. functions $w : X \times \mathbb{R} \rightarrow A$, where A is the carrier of action lattice $\mathbf{A}$. We denote the set of all states by $A^{X \times \mathbb{R}}$.

Definition 3 (Models). *Let $\Delta = (\Sigma, \Pi)$ be a signature and X a set of variables. A $\Gamma(\mathbf{A})$-model for Δ is a structure*

$$M = (W, E)$$

where

- $W \subseteq A^{X \times \mathbb{R}}$ *is a set of states;*
- $E : \Pi \times (W \times W) \rightarrow A$ *is a program grading function.*

The set of $\Gamma(\mathbf{A})$-models for Δ is denoted by $\mathrm{Mod}^{\Gamma(\mathbf{A})}(\Delta)$.

Intuitively the value of $E(\pi, (w_0, w_1))$ represents the graded execution of program π from state w_0 to w_1, i.e. the weight associated to corresponding transition. For instance, in Example 4, taking $\mathbf{A}$ as a Gödel algebra (Example 2), the expression $E(x := 2, (w_0, w_1)) = 0.6$ would mean that the system allows the execution of the assignment $x := 3$ from state w_0 to w_1 with 0.6 as a degree of certainty. Note that these values are attributed in the model. The interpretation of functional terms and predicates becomes as detailed in the following definitions.

Definition 4 (Interpretation of functional terms). *Let $\Delta = (\Sigma, \Pi)$ be a signature and $M \in \mathrm{Mod}^{\Gamma(\mathbf{A})}(\Delta)$. The interpretation of a functional term $t \in T_\Sigma^F(X)$ in M, for each $w \in W$, is given by the map*

$$[\![t]\!]_w : T_\Sigma^F(X) \to A^{\mathbb{R}}$$

defined recursively as follows:

- $[\![x]\!]_w(r) = w(x, r)$
- $[\![c]\!]_w(r) = \begin{cases} 1 & \text{if } r = c \\ 0 & \text{otherwise} \end{cases}$
- $[\![f(t_1, \ldots, t_n)]\!]_w(r) = \sum_{i \in I} \{ \prod_{j=1}^n [\![t_j]\!]_w(r_j^i) \mid f(r_1^i, \ldots, r_n^i) = r \}$, *where I is the cardinality of the set of all possible solutions of $f(r_1^i, \ldots, r_n^i) = r$ in $\mathbb{R}$, with each f of arity n being interpreted as a function on real numbers $\mathbb{R}^n \to \mathbb{R}$ (e.g. $+$, $\times$, ^{2}, $\sqrt{}$, ...).*

where $x \in X$ and c is the syntactic representation of the constant $c \in \mathbb{R}$.

Example 4 may also help in illustrating this issue. Consider a model $M = (W, E)$, $w_0, w_1, w_2 \in W$, $X = \{x, y\}$, and the complete action lattice $G = ([0, 1], max, min, 0, 1, ^*, \to, min)$ of Example 2. Take $[\![x]\!]_{w_0}(1) = w_0(x, 1) = 0.5$, $[\![x]\!]_{w_0}(2) = w_0(x, 2) = 0.2$, $[\![y]\!]_{w_0}(1) = w_0(y, 1) = 0.1$, $[\![y]\!]_{w_0}(2) = w_0(y, 2) = 0.4$ and 0 otherwise for state w_0. The interpretation of the term 2 in w_0 is given by $[\![2]\!]_{w_0}(2) = 1$ and 0 otherwise. The interpretation of the term $x + y$ in w_0 is given by:

$$[\![x + y]\!]_{w_0}(2) = [\![x]\!]_{w_0}(1); [\![y]\!]_{w_0}(1) = min\{0.5, 0.1\} = 0.1$$
$$[\![x + y]\!]_{w_0}(3) = [\![x]\!]_{w_0}(1); [\![y]\!]_{w_0}(2) + [\![x]\!]_{w_0}(2); [\![y]\!]_{w_0}(1)$$
$$= w_0(x, 1); w_0(y, 2) + w_0(x, 2); w_0(y, 1)$$
$$= max\{min\{0.5; 0.4\}\}, min\{0.2; 0.1\}\} = 0.4$$
$$[\![x + y]\!]_{w_0}(4) = [\![x]\!]_{w_0}(2); [\![y]\!]_{w_0}(2) = min\{0.2, 0.4\} = 0.2$$

and 0 otherwise.

Definition 5 (Interpretation of predicates). *Let Δ be a signature and $M \in \mathrm{Mod}^{\Gamma(\mathbf{A})}(\Delta)$. The interpretations of a predicate $p \in T_\Sigma^P(X)$ in M is given by the map*

$$[\![p]\!]_w : T_\Sigma^P(X) \to A$$

defined by

$$[\![p(t_1,\ldots,t_n)]\!]_w = \sum_{i\in I}\{\prod_{j=1}^{n}[\![t_j]\!]_w(r_j^i) \mid p(r_1^i,\ldots,r_n^i) \text{ is true}\}$$

where I is the cardinality of the set of all possible values $(r_1^i,\ldots,r_n^i) \in \mathbb{R}^n$ satisfying $p(r_1^i,\ldots,r_n^i)$, with each p of arity n being interpreted as a function over terms $T_\Sigma^F(X)$ like boolean predicate symbols (e.g. $\leq$, $=$, ...).

Again this can be illustrated by computing the truth degree of predicate $x \leq 3$ in state w_2, of Example 4. $[\![x \leq 3]\!](w_2) = [\![x]\!]_{w_2}(3); [\![3]\!]_{w_2}(3)$:

G: $min\{0.3,1\} = 0.3$. The value 0.3 means that the predicate is true with a certainty 0.3.

R: $1.2 +_R 3.7 = 4.9$. This interpretation corresponds to the energy consumed by evaluating the predicate.

Definition 6 (Interpretation of atomic programs). *The interpretation of atomic programs in a $\Gamma(\mathbf{A})$-model $M \in \mathrm{Mod}^{\Gamma(\mathbf{A})}(\Delta)$ is a map*

$$[\![\_]\!]_0 \colon \Pi \to A^{W \times W}$$

mapping each $x := t \in \Pi$ into function

$$[\![x := t]\!]_0(w, w') = \begin{cases} E(x := t, (w, w')) & \text{if } (w, w') \in (\!|x := t|\!) \\ 0 & \text{otherwise} \end{cases}$$

where $(\!|x := t|\!)$ is the standard relational semantics of a program assignment, typically given by:

$$(w, w') \in (\!|x := t|\!) \Leftrightarrow \begin{cases} w'(y, r) = w(y, r) & \text{if } y \neq x \\ w'(x, r) = [\![t]\!]_w(r) & \text{otherwise} \end{cases}$$

This is made concrete by interpretation in each of the three distinct models of computation considered in the paper, as captured in the action lattices of Examples 1, 2 and 3, respectively.

2: The degree of certainty of execution is bivalente: either $\top$ or $\bot$, coinciding with the classical setting where an action simply may or may not execute.
G: Assume $[\![x := 2]\!]_0(w_0, w_1) = E(x := 2, (w_0, w_1)) = 0.8$, $[\![x := x + y]\!]_0(w_1, w_2) = E(x := x + y, (w_1, w_2)) = 0.4$, $[\![x := x + 1]\!]_0(w_2, w_3) = E(x := x+1, (w_2, w_3)) = 0.7$ and $[\![y := y \times 2]\!]_0(w_2, w_3) = E(y := y \times 2, (w_2, w_3)) = 0.9$. Such values are regarded as degrees of certainty, or, in a complementary reading, vagueness, associated to the execution of actions $x := 2$, $x := x + y$, $x := x + 1$ and $y := y \times 2$, respectively.

As a consequence of executing these assignments, the weights of the variables are updated accordingly in the next state. That is the case of x in state w_1, by assuming the value $w_1(x, 1) = [\![2]\!]_{w_0}(2) = 1$, and 0 otherwise, according to Definition 6. The weights of y are maintained, since the assignment $x := 2$ does not modify the value of y. The situation may be interpreted as follows: from a state where property $x = 1$ has a truth degree of 0.5 and $x = 2$ has a truth degree of 0.2, the execution of action $x := 2$ with a certainty value of 0.8, whenever occurs, leads to a state where $x = 2$ is true (i.e. has 1 as its truth degree). The weights of the variable x in w_2 are updated as follows:

$$w_2(x, 3) = [\![x + y]\!]_{w_1}(3) = [\![x]\!]_{w_1}(2); [\![y]\!]_{w_1}(1) = min\{1, 0.1\} = 0.1$$
$$w_2(x, 4) = [\![x + y]\!]_{w_1}(4) = [\![x]\!]_{w_1}(2); [\![y]\!]_{w_1}(2) = min\{1, 0.4\} = 0.4$$

R: Consider, for example, $E(x := 2, (w_0, w_1)) = 8$, $E(x := x + y, (w_1, w_2)) = 4$, $E(x := x + 1, (w_2, w_3)) = 7$ and $E(y := y \times 2, (w_2, w_3)) = 9$. These values can be regarded as resources (e.g. energy) consumed by executing the associated actions. Analogously to the previous case, the weights associated to y are kept.

Finally, to interpret an arbitrary program in $Prg(\Sigma, X)$ one proceeds in two steps. First, the semantics of composed program constructs is given directly in terms of operations on A-valued binary relations $A^{W \times W}$: union, composition, and Kleene closure. To interpret such operators, we define the following algebra:

Definition 7. *Let* $\mathbf{A} = (A, +, ;, 0, 1, *, \rightarrow, \cdot)$ *be an action lattice and* W *be a finite set of states. The algebra of* program grading functions *is the structure*

$$\mathbf{E} = (Z(E), \cup, \circ, \varnothing, \chi, *)$$

where:

- $Z(E)$ *is the universe of all the program grading functions*
- $(E(\pi_1) \cup E(\pi_2))(w, w') = E(\pi_1, (w, w')) + E(\pi_2, (w, w'))$
- $(E(\pi_1) \circ E(\pi_2))(w, w') = \sum_{w'' \in W} E(\pi_1, (w, w'')); E(\pi_2, (w'', w'))$
- $\varnothing(w, w') = 0$
- $\chi(w, w') = \begin{cases} 1, & \text{if } w = w' \\ 0, & \text{otherwise} \end{cases}$
- $(E(\pi))^*(w, w') = \sum_{i \geq 0} (E(\pi))^i(w, w') = (E(\pi))^0(w, w') + (E(\pi))^1(w, w') + (E(\pi))^2(w, w') + \dots$

with $E(\pi_1), E(\pi_2) \in Z(E)$.

Note that operator $*$ can be defined as an infinite sum due to the completeness of the action lattice.

Definition 8. *Let* $M \in \mathrm{Mod}^{\Gamma(\mathbf{A})}(\Delta)$ *be a model of* $\Gamma(\mathbf{A})$. *The interpretation of a program* $\pi \in \mathrm{Prg}(\Sigma, X)$ *is a map*

$$[\![-]\!] \colon \mathrm{Prg}(\Sigma, X) \to A^{W \times W}$$

recursively defined by

- $[\![\pi_0]\!] = [\![\pi_0]\!]_0$, *for each* $\pi_0 \in \mathrm{Prg}_0(\Delta)$
- $[\![\pi; \pi]\!] = [\![\pi]\!] \circ [\![\pi']\!]$
- $[\![\pi + \pi]\!] = [\![\pi]\!] \cup [\![\pi']\!]$
- $[\![\pi^*]\!] = [\![\pi]\!]^*$.

where, for $r \in A^{W \times W}$, $r^*(w, w') = \sum_{k \geq 0} r^k(w, w')$.

Again Example 4 can be called to illustrate choice and sequential composition by interpreting fragments $(x := 2); (x := x + y)$ and $(x := x + 1) + (y := y \times 2)$. The first one yields,

$$
\begin{aligned}
[\![x := 2; x := x + y]\!](w_0, w_2) &= ([\![x := 2]\!]_0 \circ [\![x := x + y]\!]_0)(w_0, w_2) \\
&= [\![x := 2]\!]_0(w_0, w_1); [\![x := x + y]\!]_0(w_1, w_2) \\
&= E(x := 2, (w_0, w_1)); E(x := x + y, (w_1, w_2))
\end{aligned}
$$

which can be instantiated within the three usual lattices we have been considering:

2: Under this interpretation programs either fail or succeed. In the absence of failure execution proceeds sequentially; otherwise, if one (or both) fails (takes 'weight' $\bot$), so does the composite.

G: In this case a degree of confidence, or certainty, is associated to the composition based on the corresponding degree for the atomic components. This is computed as a minimum. For example, if $E(x := 2, (w_0, w_1)) = 0.8$ and $E(x := x+y, (w_1, w_2)) = 0.4$ the overall confidence degree for the composition becomes $min\{0.8, 0.4\} = 0.4$.

R: Computations have a cost, under this interpretation, for example the amount of energy dissipated. Thus, $E(x := 2, (w_0, w_1)); E(x := x + y, (w_1, w_2)) = 8 +_{\mathbf{R}} 4 = 12$ represents the sum of the energy consumed by both atomic programs $x := 2$ and $x := x + y$.

The interpretation of $(x := x + 1) + (y := y \times 2)$, on the other hand, is given by

$$
\begin{aligned}
[\![(x := x + 1) + (y := y \times 2)]\!](w_2, w_3) &= ([\![x := x + 1]\!]_0 \cup [\![y := y \times 2]\!]_0)(w_2, w_3) \\
&= [\![x := x + 1]\!]_0(w_2, w_3) + [\![y := y \times 2]\!]_0(w_2, w_3) \\
&= E(x := x + 1, (w_2, w_3)) + E(y := y \times 2, (w_2, w_3))
\end{aligned}
$$

Again,

2: In this case choice is exactly nondeterministic choice: either one of $x :=$ $x + 1$ or $y := y \times 2$ will be executed.

G: This interpretation yields the maximum certainty degree of executing the composition, e.g. $E(x := x + 1, (w_2, w_3)) + E(y := y \times 2, (w_2, w_3)) = max\{0.7, 0.9\} = 0.9$.

R: In this action lattice, operator $+$ picks the minimum value. This corresponds to choose the path that consumes less energy, e.g. $E(x := x + 1, (w_2, w_3)) + E(y := y \times 2, (w_2, w_3)) = min\{0.7, 0.9\} = 0.7$.

Note that nothing prevents the state space W from being infinite, because of completeness enforced upon **A**. However, one may only compute explicitly a truth value associated with a program execution when W is finite.

The second element to care about when computing the semantics is the interpretation of tests. Our goal is to introduce a notion of a test in an arbitrary dynamic logic generated by a parameter **A**. As mentioned above, tests are written as φ?, for $\varphi \in \mathrm{Fm}^{\Gamma(\mathbf{A})}(\Delta)$. Their semantics resort, therefore, to the satisfaction relation for $\mathrm{Fm}^{\Gamma(\mathbf{A})}(\Delta)$, which is defined as follows:

Definition 9. *Given a complete action lattice* **A** *over a carrier A, the graded satisfaction relation for a model $M \in \mathrm{Mod}^{\Gamma(\mathbf{A})}(\Delta)$, consists of a function*

$$\models_{\Gamma(\mathbf{A})} : W \times \mathrm{Fm}^{\Gamma(\mathbf{A})}(\Delta) \to A$$

recursively defined by

- $(w \models_{\Gamma(\mathbf{A})} \top) = \top$
- $(w \models_{\Gamma(\mathbf{A})} \bot) = \bot$
- $(w \models_{\Gamma(\mathbf{A})} p) = [\![p]\!]_w$, *for any $p \in T_\Sigma^P(X)$*
- $(w \models_{\Gamma(\mathbf{A})} \varphi \wedge \varphi') = (w \models_{\Gamma(\mathbf{A})} \varphi) \cdot (w \models_{\Gamma(\mathbf{A})} \varphi')$
- $(w \models_{\Gamma(\mathbf{A})} \varphi \vee \varphi') = (w \models_{\Gamma(\mathbf{A})} \varphi) + (w \models_{\Gamma(\mathbf{A})} \varphi')$
- $(w \models_{\Gamma(\mathbf{A})} \varphi \to \varphi') = (w \models_{\Gamma(\mathbf{A})} \varphi) \to (w \models_{\Gamma(\mathbf{A})} \varphi')$
- $(w \models_{\Gamma(\mathbf{A})} \langle \pi \rangle \varphi) = \sum_{w' \in W} ([\![\pi]\!](w, w'); (w' \models_{\Gamma(\mathbf{A})} \varphi))$
- $(w \models_{\Gamma(\mathbf{A})} [\pi] \varphi) = \bigwedge_{w' \in W} ([\![\pi]\!](w, w') \to (w' \models_{\Gamma(\mathbf{A})} \varphi))$

The interpretation of tests in the classical, Boolean case is given by co-reflexive relations $R_{\varphi?} = \{(w, w) | w \models \varphi\}$. In the generic setting of the present work this generalises to

$$[\![\varphi?]\!](w, w') = \begin{cases} (w \models_{\Gamma(\mathbf{A})} \varphi) & \text{if } w = w' \\ \bot & \text{otherwise} \end{cases}$$

Let us revisit Example 4 to interpret the conditional statement

$$\textbf{if } x \leq 3 \textbf{ then } x := x + 1 \textbf{ else } y := y \times 2$$

translated to $((x \leq 3?); x := x + 1) + ((((x \leq 3) \to \bot)?); y := y \times 2)$. Using the value computed for predicate $x \leq 3$, this leads to

$$[\![((x \leq 3)?; x := x + 1) + (((x \leq 3) \to \bot)?; y := y \times 2)]\!](w_2, w_3)$$
$$= [\![(x \leq 3)?; x := x + 1]\!](w_2, w_3) + [\![((x \leq 3) \to \bot)?; y := y \times 2]\!](w_2, w_3)$$
$$= [\![(x \leq 3)?]\!](w_2, w_2); [\![x := x + 1]\!]_0(w_2, w_3) + [\![((x \leq 3) \to \bot)?]\!](w_2, w_2); [\![y := y \times 2]\!]_0(w_2, w_3)$$
$$= (w_2 \models x \leq 3); E(x := x + 1, (w_2, w_3)) + (w_2 \models (x \leq 3) \to 0); E(y := y \times 2, (w_2, w_3))$$
$$= (w_2 \models x \leq 3); E(x := x + 1, (w_2, w_3)) + ((w_2 \models x \leq 3) \to (w \models 0)); E(y := y \times 2, (w_2, w_3))$$

which can be, once again, instantiated for the three action lattices under consideration, yielding

2: $(\top \wedge \top) \vee ((\top \to \bot) \wedge \top) = \top$. This interpretation coincides, as expected, with the standard **if-then-else** statement. In this case, only program $x := x + 1$ is executed, since $y = y \times 2$ is guarded by the test $((x \leq 3) \to \bot)?$ which has the value $\bot$ at state w_2.
G: $max\{min\{0.3, 0.7\}, min\{0.3 \to 0, 0.9\}\} = 0.3$, which expresses the weighted choice of executing $x := x + 1$.
R: $min\{3 + 7, 0 + 9\} = 9$. In this situation, contrary to what happens in the previous cases, the assignment $y := y \times 2$ is executed. The value 9 stands for the energy consumed by the machine when executing such an assignment.

4   Bisimulation

The characterisation of relations that identify states with equivalent behaviours is crucial to support a set of development practices, including reuse, refinement and minimization of programs and models. On the logic view, these relations usually enjoy a modal invariance property, i.e. they preserve the satisfaction of formulas. We introduce in this section a parametric notion of bisimulation, and we prove its modal invariant for any $\Gamma(\mathbf{A})$. The bisimulation generalises the notion recently introduced by the authors in [5] in the context of fuzzy modal logic.

Definition 10 (Π-Bisimulation). *Let $\Delta = (\Sigma, \Pi)$ be a signature, X a set of variables, and $M = (W, E)$ and $M' = (W', E')$ two $\Gamma(\mathbf{A})$-models, for any linear action lattice $\mathbf{A}$.*

A Π-bisimulation from M to M' is a non empty relation $B \subseteq W \times W'$ such that whenever $w \, B \, w'$, the following conditions hold:

(Atoms) *for any $x \in X$, $r \in R$, $[\![x]\!]_w(r) = [\![x]\!]_{w'}(r)$*
     and, for any $p \in T_\Sigma^P(X)$, $[\![p]\!]_w = [\![p]\!]_{w'}$
(Fzig) *for any $u \in W$ and $\pi \in \Pi$, $[\![\pi]\!]_0(w, u) \leq \sum_{u' \in B[\{u\}]} [\![\pi]\!]_0(w', u')$*
(Fzag) *for any $u' \in W'$ and $\pi \in \Pi$, $[\![\pi]\!]_0(w', u') \leq \sum_{u \in B^{-1}[\{u'\}]} [\![\pi]\!]_0(w, u)$*

We write $w \sim w'$ whenever, there is a bisimulation B such that $(w, w') \in B$.

Next result establishes the well-known *word bisimulation result* on this generic graded settings. This result reduces the invariance property of formulas involving composed programs in $\mathrm{Prg}(\Sigma, X)$ to the one involving just the set of atomic programs Π. In other words, it reduces the modal invariance problem of a generated dynamic logic to the modal invariance of the underlying multi-valued logic.

Proposition 1. *Let* $\mathbf{A}$ *be a linear action lattice and* (Σ, X) *a data signature. Then, any* Π-*bisimulation over* $\Gamma(\mathbf{A})$-*models is a* $\mathrm{Prg}(\Sigma, X)$-*bisimulation.*

Proof. The proof is done by induction over the programs structure. Let $B \subseteq W \times W'$ be a bisimulation and $w \in W, w' \in W'$ such that $(w, w') \in B$.

The result for atomic programs is given by hypothesis. Let us prove the **(Fzig)** condition for programs $\pi; \pi'$. By induction hypothesis, let us assume that **(Fzig)** of B for π and π'. Hence, for any $v \in W$

$$[\![\pi]\!](w, v) \leq \sum_{v' \in B(v)} [\![\pi]\!](w', v') \tag{23}$$

holds. By (20) we have also that, for any $v \in W$ there is a $v'_v \in B(v)$ such that $\sum_{v' \in B(v)} [\![\pi]\!](w', v') = [\![\pi]\!](w', v'_v)$. Moreover, since $(v, v'_v) \in B$, we have by **(Fzig)** of B for π' that

$$[\![\pi']\!](v, u) \leq \sum_{u' \in B(u)} [\![\pi']\!](v'_v, u') \tag{24}$$

By (21) in (23) we get, for any $v \in W$,

$$[\![\pi]\!](w, v); [\![\pi']\!](v, u) \leq [\![\pi]\!](w', v'_v); \sum_{u' \in B(u)} [\![\pi']\!](v'_v, u') \tag{25}$$

and by (22),

$$\sum_{v \in W} [\![\pi]\!](w, v); [\![\pi']\!](v, u) \leq \sum_{v'_v \in W'} [\![\pi]\!](w', v'_v); \sum_{u' \in B(u)} [\![\pi']\!](v'_v, u') \tag{26}$$

Moreover, since $\{v'_v : v \in W\} \subseteq \{v' : v' \in W'\}$, and by (8), (2) and (3), we have that

$$\sum_{v'_v \in W'} [\![\pi]\!](w', v'_v); \sum_{u' \in B(u)} [\![\pi']\!](v'_v, u') \leq \sum_{u' \in B(u)} \left(\sum_{v' \in W'} ([\![\pi]\!](w', v'); [\![\pi']\!](v', u')) \right) \tag{27}$$

By (26) and (27), we achieve $[\![\pi; \pi']\!](w, u) \leq \sum_{u' \in B(u)} [\![\pi; \pi']\!](w', u')$. The prove of **(Fzag)** condition is analogous.

For programs $\pi + \pi'$, we observe that

$$
\begin{aligned}
&[\![\pi + \pi']\!](w, u) \\
=\ & \{ \text{ interpretation of programs} \} \\
&[\![\pi]\!](w, u) + [\![\pi']\!](w, u) \\
\leq\ & \{ \textbf{(Fzig)} \text{ and } (22) \}
\end{aligned}
\quad
\begin{aligned}
&\sum_{u' \in B(u)} [\![\pi]\!](w', u') + \sum_{u' \in B(u)} [\![\pi']\!](w', u') \\
=\ & \{ \text{ definition of } + \} \\
&\sum_{u' \in B(u)} [\![\pi + \pi']\!](w', u')
\end{aligned}
$$

Finally, for programs π^* we observe that by definition of *

$$[\![\pi^*]\!](w,u) = \sum_{k \geq 0} [\![\pi]\!]^k(w,u) = [\![\pi]\!]^0(w,u) + [\![\pi]\!](w,u) + [\![\pi]\!]^2(w,u) + \ldots$$

But for each k, $[\![\pi]\!]^k(w,u) \leq \sum_{u \in B(u)} [\![\pi]\!]^k(w',u')$ by Fzig.
Hence,

$$
\begin{array}{ll}
\sum_{k \geq 0} [\![\pi]\!]^k(w,u) & \\
\leq \quad \{(22)\} & \sum_{u' \in B(u)} \left(\sum_{k \geq 0} [\![\pi]\!]^k(w',u') \right) \\
\sum_{k \geq 0} \left(\sum_{u' \in B(u)} [\![\pi]\!]^k(w',u') \right) = \quad \{ \text{ definition of } * \} \\
= \quad \{ (\} & \sum_{u' \in B(u)} [\![\pi^*]\!](w',u') \\
2)and(3) &
\end{array}
$$

$\square$

Now we are in conditions to prove the modal invariance for $\Gamma(\mathbf{A})$ with $\mathbf{A}$ linear.

Theorem 1 (Modal invariance). *Let $\Delta = (\Sigma, X)$ be a signature, $\mathbf{A}$ a linear action lattice, and $M = (W, E)$ and $M' = (W', E')$ two $\Gamma(\mathbf{A})$-models for Δ. Then, for any $w \in W$, $w' \in W'$ such that $w \sim w'$ and for all formulas $\varphi \in \mathrm{Fm}^{\Gamma(\mathbf{A})}(\Delta)$,*

$$(M, w \models \varphi) = (M', w' \models \varphi)$$

Proof. We prove this result by induction on the structure of formulas.
For the invariance of the formula $\top$, note that $(M, w \models \top) = \top = (M', w' \models \top)$ and similarly for the formula $\bot$.
Invariance of $p \in T_\Sigma^P(X)$ is a direct consequence of **(Atoms)**,

$$(M, w \models p) = [\![p]\!]_w = [\![p]\!]_{w'} = (M', w' \models p).$$

For the invariance of formulas $\varphi \wedge \psi$, we observe that

$$(M, w \models \varphi \wedge \psi) = (M, w \models \varphi) \cdot (M, w \models \psi) =^{I.H.}$$

$$(M', w' \models \varphi) \cdot (M', w' \models \psi) = (M', w' \models \varphi \wedge \psi)$$

and the proof for the invariance of formulas $\varphi \vee \psi$ and $\varphi \to \psi$ can be proved similarly.

Now it just remains to prove sentences $\langle \pi \rangle \varphi$ and $[\pi]\varphi$. Since $\mathbf{A}$ is linear, we have by Proposition 1 that, it is enough to prove the invariance for formulas involving atomic programs $\pi_0 \in \mathrm{Prg}_0(\Sigma, X)$. For the invariance of formulas $\langle \pi_0 \rangle \varphi$, we observe that By **(Fzig)** condition we have

$$\forall u \in W, [\![\pi_0]\!]_0(w,u) \leq \sum_{u' \in E[\{u\}]} [\![\pi_0]\!]_0(w',u') = [\![\pi_0]\!]_0(w',u'_u) \text{ for some } u'_u \in W'$$

$$\tag{28}$$

Since for every $u \in W, u'_u \in E[\{u\}]$, we have $u \, E \, u'_u$. By I. H., we have $(M, u \models \varphi) = (M', u'_u \models \varphi)$ and, by (28),

$$\forall u \in W, [\![\pi_0]\!]_0(w, u) \cdot (M, u \models \varphi) \leq [\![\pi_0]\!]_0(w', u'_u) \cdot (M, u'_u \models \varphi) \qquad (29)$$

and, in particular,

$$\sum_{u \in W} ([\![\pi_0]\!]_0(w, u) \cdot (M, u \models \varphi)) \leq \sum_{u'_u : u \in W} ([\![\pi_0]\!]_0(w', u'_u) \cdot (M, u'_u \models \varphi)) \qquad (30)$$

Since $\{u'_u : u \in W\} \subseteq \{u' : u' \in W'\}$ we have $\sum\{u'_u : u \in W\} \leq \sum\{u' : u' \in W'\}$ and by 30

$$\sum_{u \in W} ([\![\pi_0]\!]_0(w, u) \cdot (M, u \models \varphi)) \leq \sum_{u' \in W'} ([\![\pi_0]\!]_0(w', u') \cdot (M, u' \models \varphi)) \qquad (31)$$

i.e.$(M, w \models \langle \pi_0 \rangle \varphi) \leq (M', w' \models \langle \pi_0 \rangle \varphi)$. Similarly we can prove $(M, w \models \langle \pi_0 \rangle \varphi) \geq (M', w' \models \langle \pi_0 \rangle \varphi)$ by using **(Fzag)** condition.

For the invariance of formulas $[\pi_0]\varphi$, with $\pi_0 \in \Pi$, since $w \, E \, w'$ we have by **(Fzig)**

$$\forall u \in W, [\![\pi_0]\!]_0(w, u) \leq \sum_{u' \in \ E[\{u\}]} [\![\pi_0]\!]_0(w', u') = [\![\pi_0]\!]_0(w', u'_u) \text{ for some } u'_u \in W'$$
$$\qquad (32)$$

Since for every $u \in W, u'_u \in E[\{u\}]$, we have $u \in W, u \, E \, u'_u$. Hence, by I.H.

$$(M, u \models \varphi) = (M', u'_u \models \varphi) \qquad (33)$$

It follows from the definition of I that $x_0 \leq x_1$ implies $I(x_0, y) \geq I(x_1, y)$. Then, from (32) and (33) we have

$$\forall u \in W, I([\![\pi_0]\!]_0(w, u), (M, u \models \varphi)) \geq I([\![\pi_0]\!]_0(w', u'_u), (M', u'_u \models \varphi))$$

and, in particular

$$\prod_{u \in W} (I([\![\pi_0]\!]_0(w, u), (M, u \models \varphi))) \geq \prod_{u'_u : u \in W} (I([\![\pi_0]\!]_0(w', u'_u), (M', u'_u \models \varphi)))$$
$$\qquad (34)$$

Since $\{u'_u : u \in W\} \subseteq \{u' : u' \in W'\}$, we have $\prod\{u'_u : u \in W\} \geq \prod\{u' : u' \in W'\}$ and hence

$$\prod_{u \in W} (I([\![\pi_0]\!]_0(w, u), (M, u \models \varphi))) \geq \prod_{u' \in W'} (I([\![\pi_0]\!]_0(w', u'), (M', u' \models \varphi))) \qquad (35)$$

Therefore $(M, w \models [\pi_0]\varphi) \geq (M', w' \models [\pi_0]\varphi)$. The proof for $(M, w \models [\pi_0]\varphi) \leq (M', w' \models [\pi_0]\varphi)$ is analogous. $\qquad \square$

We now provide an illustration for the introduced notion of bisimulation.

Example 5. Consider the $\Gamma(\mathbf{G})$-models $M = (W, V, E)$, with $W = \{w_1, w_2, w_3, w_4\}$ and $M' = (W', V', E')$, with $W' = \{w'_1, w'_2, w'_3, w'_4\}$, and the programs $\Pi = \{x := x + 1, x := 3\}$, with $E(x := x + 1, (w_1, w_2)) = 0.9$, $E(x := 3, (w_1, w_3)) = 0.8$, $E(x := 3, (w_1, w_4)) = 0.7$, $E(x := x + 1, (w'_1, w'_2)) = 0.9$, $E(x := 3, (w'_1, w'_3)) = 0.8$, $E(x := x + 1, (w'_1, w'_4)) = 0.6$.

To show that the relation $B = \{(w_1, w'_1), (w_2, w'_2), (w_2, w'_4), (w_3, w'_3), (w_4, w'_3)\}$ is a bisimulation from M to M', the **(Fzig)** and **(Fzag)** conditions of Definition 10 need to be satisfied. To exemplify, only the calculations for the case $w_1 \sim w'_1$ are provided, since the other pairs can be verified analogously (Fig.2).

(Fzig):

$$[x := x + 1]_0(w_1, w_2) \leq max\{[x := x + 1]_0(w'_1, w'_2), [x := x + 1]_0(w'_1, w'_4)\}$$
$$\Leftrightarrow 0.9 \leq max\{0.9, 0.6\} \Leftrightarrow 0.9 \leq 0.9$$
$$[x := 3]_0(w_1, w_3) \leq [x := 3]_0(w'_1, w'_3) \Leftrightarrow 0.8 \leq 0.8$$
$$[x := 3]_0(w_1, w_4) \leq [x := 3]_0(w'_1, w'_3) \Leftrightarrow 0.7 \leq 0.8$$

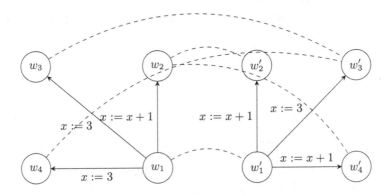

Fig. 2. Two bisimilar $\Gamma(\mathbf{G}) - models$

(Fzag):

$$[x := x + 1]_0(w'_1, w'_2) \leq [x := x + 1]_0(w_1, w_2) = 0.9$$
$$[x := x + 1]_0(w'_1, w'_4) \leq [x := x + 1]_0(w_1, w_2) = 0.9$$
$$[x := 3]_0(w'_1, w'_3) \leq max\{[x := 3]_0(w_1, w_3), [x := 3]_0(w_1, w_4)$$
$$\Leftrightarrow 0.8 \leq max\{0.8, 0.7\} \Leftrightarrow 0.8 \leq 0.8$$

5   Conclusions and Future Work

This paper extended the process of systematic generation of multi-valued dynamic logics from the original propositional case [9], to 'fully-fledged' programs, which incorporate variables and assignments. As before, the method is parametric on an action lattice which supports both a computational model in which programs are defined, and a truth space, suitable to handle different aspects of the application domain. Both states, specified by assignments of real values to variables, and transitions between them have an associated 'weight', i.e. a value taken from the carrier of a action lattice. As detailed in the examples discussed, the notion of 'weight' as formalised in an action lattice, is the real parameter of this process. Actually, they can capture quite a range of effects: from the degree of vagueness of an execution, to the cost of resources. The notion of bisimulation presented in Sect. 4 generalises previous work done by the authors [5], in the sense that a generic action lattice is considered as a parameter of the generated logics. A prominent application of dynamic logic lies in the field of formal verification of programs, as a simplification of the deductive apparatus of Hoare logic. In such formalism, the correctness of a program is proved by stating the validity of an Hoare triple $\varphi\{\pi\}\psi$. As it is well known, the validity of the dynamic logic formula $w \models \varphi \rightarrow [\pi]\psi$, is an abstraction of such proof. In this sense, the multi-valued nature of the logics generated in this paper may present a proper formalism to state program correctness in a multi-valued setting as well: the "degree of correctness" of a program may be computed as the value, in the parameter $\mathbf{A}$, of the above dynamic logic formula. Motivated by this example, it is our intention to include a calculi for such logics as part of our research agenda.

References

1. Baltag, A., Smets, S.: The dynamic turn in quantum logic. Synthese **186**(3), 753–773 (2012). https://doi.org/10.1007/s11229-011-9915-7
2. Fischer, M.J., Ladner, R.E.: Propositional dynamic logic of regular programs. J. Comput. Syst. Sci. **18**(2), 194–211 (1979). https://doi.org/10.1016/0022-0000(79)90046-1
3. Harel, D., Kozen, D., Tiuryn, J.: Dynamic Logic. MIT Press, Cambridge (2000)
4. Hennicker, R., Madeira, A., Knapp, A.: A hybrid dynamic logic for event/data-based systems. In: Hähnle, R., van der Aalst, W. (eds.) FASE 2019. LNCS, vol. 11424, pp. 79–97. Springer, Cham (2019). https://doi.org/10.1007/978-3-030-16722-6_5
5. Jain, M., Madeira, A., Martins, M.A.: A fuzzy modal logic for fuzzy transition systems. Electr. Notes Theor. Comput. Sci. (in print)
6. Knapp, A., Mossakowski, T., Roggenbach, M., Glauer, M.: An institution for simple UML state machines. In: Egyed, A., Schaefer, I. (eds.) FASE 2015. LNCS, vol. 9033, pp. 3–18. Springer, Heidelberg (2015). https://doi.org/10.1007/978-3-662-46675-9_1
7. Kozen, D.: A probabilistic PDL. J. Comput. Syst. Sci. **30**(2), 162–178 (1985). https://doi.org/10.1016/0022-0000(85)90012-1
8. Kozen, D.: The Design and Analysis of Algorithms. Springer, New York (1992). https://doi.org/10.1007/978-1-4612-4400-4
9. Madeira, A., Neves, R., Martins, M.A.: An exercise on the generation of many-valued dynamic logics. J. Log. Algebr. Methods Program. **1**, 1–29 (2016). https://doi.org/10.1016/j.jlamp.2016.03.004
10. Peleg, D.: Concurrent dynamic logic. J. ACM **34**(2), 450–479 (1987). https://doi.org/10.1145/23005.23008
11. Platzer, A.: Logical Analysis of Hybrid Systems - Proving Theorems for Complex Dynamics. Springer, Heidelberg (2010). https://doi.org/10.1007/978-3-642-14509-4

A Security Calculus for Wireless Networks of Named Data Networking

Yuan Fei[1]([✉]), Huibiao Zhu[2]([✉]), Haiying Sun[2], and Jiaqi Yin[2]

[1] College of Information, Mechanical and Electrical Engineering,
Shanghai Normal University, Shanghai, China
`yuanfei@shnu.edu.cn`
[2] Shanghai Key Laboratory of Trustworthy Computing,
East China Normal University, Shanghai, China
`hbzhu@sei.ecnu.edu.cn`

Abstract. Named Data Networking (NDN) is an architecture of Information-Centric Networking (ICN). The application of NDN on wireless networks is an important area. In this paper, we propose a Security Calculus for Wireless Networks of Named Data Networking (SCWN). Security feature is implemented by using different channel symbols to describe wireless network node. The feature of NDN is introduced by using particular sets to express the environment. We introduce the syntax and the operational semantics of SCWN calculus. By a rewriting logic-based language Maude, we support the automatic implementation of our SCWN calculus, which enhances its practicability. Finally, we apply SCWN calculus to LFBL protocol with its automatic implementation. It indicates that SCWN calculus is useful to describe realistic cases.

Keywords: NDN · Calculus of wireless networks · Maude

1 Introduction

Named Data Networking (NDN) [13] is an architecture of Information-Centric Networking (ICN). ICN aims to offer solutions to problems existing in TCP/IP Internet. Nowadays users pay more attention to named content rather than its location. Though TCP/IP Internet has shown great resilience over the years, it cannot support the newly evolving content distribution model successfully. One of the promising candidates of ICN is NDN, which supports multicast of data and adopts the publish/subscribe model. The data producers mean publishers and the data consumers represent subscribers in NDN. When data consumer needs data, it sends out an *Interest* packet with a required name of the data; according to the name, routers forward the packet over the network; and a *Data* packet is returned to the consumer when a data produced by the data producer is matched. As wireless network has a wide range of applications in daily life, there are several applications of NDN concept applied to wireless network. Meisel et al. [8]

© Springer Nature Switzerland AG 2019
Y. Ait-Ameur and S. Qin (Eds.): ICFEM 2019, LNCS 11852, pp. 170–185, 2019.
https://doi.org/10.1007/978-3-030-32409-4_11

adapted NDN to Ad Hoc Network to improve the efficiency and effectiveness of it. Li et al. [7] introduced hybrid wireless networks with FIB-based Named Data Networking, in which a novel FIB named MaFIB is proposed. In order to carry the signaling part of NDN, Bazzi et al. [2] proposed the use of cellular networks and wireless communications of the content distribution.

To the best of our knowledge, no process calculus is proposed for NDN in the field of wireless network applications currently. However, there are already a lot of process calculus for general wireless networks. The calculus CBS# [11] is proposed by Hanz and Hankin, which is extended from CBS [12]. It introduces local storage components, and adds the source of the information to describe some key security attributes. The calculus CMN [10] presented a bisimulation to prove some properties of the network. The calculus CMAN [4] is a broadcast calculus proposed by Godskesen that supports wireless network dynamic change topologies. It captures the mobility and the local broadcast mechanism of nodes.

The application of NDN on wireless networks becomes important. In this paper, we propose a calculus called SCWN (Security Calculus for Wireless Networks of Named Data Networking). Wireless network is described at both process level and network level. Our calculus will implement a special forwarding mechanism and a data caching mechanism for NDN. It is supported by particular sets to express the environment. The security feature is introduced by using different channel symbols to describe wireless network node. Furthermore, we give the predefined label transfer semantic of SCWN. It has detailed the internal behavior of the system and the interaction between the system and the environment. Using a rewriting logic-based language Maude [3], we support automatic implementation of our SCWN calculus, which is also applied to LFBL protocol. It illustrates SCWN calculus can be applied into real-world scenes.

The remainder of this paper is organized as follows. Section 2 introduces the SCWN syntax and its operational semantics. Section 3 gives the automatic implementation of SCWN calculus by a rewriting logic-based language Maude. Section 4 applies SCWN calculus to LFBL protocol. Section 5 concludes the paper and discusses the future work.

2   The SCWN Calculus

In this section, we present our SCWN calculus by introducing its syntax and the operational semantics.

2.1   The Syntax of SCWN

The syntax of process is used to characterize the actions of wireless nodes. Here we describe the detail cases of process P.

- *nil* means the process terminates.
- $send\langle k, v \rangle.P$ is a ready sending process, indicating that the current process is ready to broadcast a message. The message is denoted by a pair $\langle k, v \rangle$, where k

Table 1. SCWN syntax

Processes	$P ::= \textbf{nil}$	(termination)
	$\mid send\langle k, v\rangle.P$	(pre-output)
	$\mid \langle k, v\rangle.P$	(output)
	$\mid receive(k, v)^n.P$	(input)
	$\mid \lfloor receive(x, y)^n.send\langle x, y\rangle\rfloor.P$	(forward)
Networks	$N ::= n[P]_s^c$	(ordinary wireless node)
	$\mid n[P]_s^{\nu c}$	(protected wireless node)
	$\mid N\|N$	(parallel combination)

represents the type of message and v represents the content of message. When the ready action is completed, the process becomes the form of $\langle k, v\rangle.P$. It gives information to environment for forwarding mechanism.

- $\langle k, v\rangle.P$ is a sending process that indicates the current process is broadcasting a message. When the sending is completed, the process changes to P. The environment will be changed according to the forwarding mechanism.
- $receive(x, y)^n.P$ is a receiving process. It illustrates that the process of wireless node n is receiving a message from other processes. If there is a node sending acceptable messages around node n, the process evolves to P. The variable x and y in process P will be replaced with the values in the received message.
- $\lfloor receive(x, y)^n.send\langle x, y\rangle\rfloor.P$ is a receiving-forwarding process. It only appears on the node bearing the forwarding task. If it receives a message from neighbor nodes, the process decides whether to forward or discard the message according to its type. If the message is forwarded, the process evolves to $send\langle x, y\rangle.P$, in which variable x and y are replaced by the values in the message. If the message is discarded, the process changes to P.

The syntax of network expresses the basic information of each wireless node. Meanwhile, it illustrates how they communicate with each other. Explanations of network N are given here.

- $n[P]_s^c$ represents a normal wireless node in a wireless network, where n represents name of the current node, c means the name of the channel and s is a node set containing the nodes in the communication range of the current node. Channels are classified into normal channels and protected channels.
- $n[P]_s^{\nu c}$ shows a protected wireless node in a wireless network. Except using symbol ν to denote the protected channel, the rest of the symbols are the same as $n[P]_s^c$. The protected channel can only communicate with other protected channels, which indicates the security feature.
- $N\|N$ indicates that wireless nodes can be combined with each other to form a wireless network.

2.2   Particular Set

In order to formalise the operational semantics, we need to define some particular sets in advance.

– *Normal sending record set:* Normal sending record set is to record the relevant information of nodes using normal channels to send a message. It is represented by T_f. The element in the set is in the form (n, s, c), indicating that node n is sending a message to node set s via the normal channel c.
– *Protected sending record set:* Protected sending record set is to record the relevant information of nodes using protected channels to send a message. It is represented by T_t. The element in the set is in the form (n, s, c), indicating that node n is sending a message to node set s via the protected channel c.
– *Neighbor normal sending record set:* It records the message being sent around a node using a normal channel.

$$T_f|_{n,c} =_{df} \{ (n', s', c') \mid (n', s', c') \in T_f \wedge n \in s' \wedge c' = c \}$$

The element in set $T_f|_{n,c}$ is the message being sent around node n using normal channel c. That is, once a node around node n uses normal channel c to send a message, the message will be added into set $T_f|_{n,c}$.
– *Neighbor protected sending record set:* It records the message being sent around a node using a protected channel.

$$T_t|_{n,c} =_{df} \{ (n', s', c') \mid (n', s', c') \in T_t \wedge n \in s' \wedge c' = c \}$$

The element in set $T_t|_{n,c}$ is the message being sent around node n using protected channel c. In other words, when a node around node n sends a message by protected channel c, the message will be put into set $T_t|_{n,c}$.
– *Message record set:* It supports PIT (Pending Interest Table) and CS (Content Store) in NDN, denoted by C. The element in the set is in the form (n, I, v) or (n, D, v), which represents node n has received *Interest* package or *Data* package carrying value v.

2.3   Operational Semantics

In this subsection, we introduce the operational semantics of our SCWN calculus at process level and network level respectively.

Process Level of Label Transition Semantics. The transition rule of a process is $P \xrightarrow{\alpha} P'$, in which the definition of α is given as below.

$$\alpha :=! \mid !k.v \mid ?k.v$$

! represents a ready sending event. $!k.v$ means a sending event. $?k.v$ indicates a receiving event.

It should be noted here that once the process sends, receives and forwards message C, the corresponding (n, I, v) or (n, D, v) is added to the message record set according to the specific situation. In addition, once (n, D, v) is added into C, the corresponding (n, I, v) will be deleted. It simulates the forwarding mechanism of NDN.

Table 2 represents the label transition semantics at process level, where IP stands for the set of processes whose form are as $\lfloor receive(x, y)^n.send\langle x, y\rangle\rfloor.P$ and $receive(x, y)^n.P$.

Rule (PS-RECI1, PS-RECI2 and PS-RECI3) are for the processes running on forwarding nodes when they receives an $Interest$ packet. For example, the rule (PS-RECI1) represents the situation that a receiving-forwarding process receives an $Interest$ packet received before, then the message is discarded.

Rule (PS-RECD1 and PS-RECD2) describe the situation that the processes run on forwarding nodes when they receive a $Data$ packet. For example, the rule (PS-RECD1) denotes that a receiving-forwarding process receives a $Data$ packet received before, then the message is discarded.

Table 2. Process level of label transition semantics

(PS-PSEND) $send\langle k, v\rangle.P \xrightarrow{!} \langle k, v\rangle.P$	**(PS-SEND)** $\langle k, v\rangle.P \xrightarrow{!k.v} P$

(PS-REC) $\dfrac{(n, k, v) \notin C}{receive(x, y)^n.P \xrightarrow{?k.v} P\{k/x, v/y\}}$

(PS-RECI1) $\dfrac{(n, I, v) \in C}{\lfloor receive(x, y)^n.send\langle x, y\rangle\rfloor.P \xrightarrow{?I.v} P}$

(PS-RECI2) $\dfrac{(n, I, v) \notin C \wedge (n, D, v) \notin C}{\lfloor receive(x, y)^n.send\langle x, y\rangle\rfloor.P \xrightarrow{?I.v} send\langle I, v\rangle.P}$

(PS-RECI3) $\dfrac{(n, I, v) \notin C \wedge (n, D, v) \in C}{\lfloor receive(x, y)^n.send\langle x, y\rangle\rfloor.P \xrightarrow{?I.v} send\langle D, v\rangle.P}$

(PS-RECD1) $\dfrac{(n, I, v) \notin C}{\lfloor receive(x, y)^n.send\langle x, y\rangle\rfloor.P \xrightarrow{?D.v} P}$

(PS-RECD2) $\dfrac{(n, I, v) \in C \wedge (n, D, v) \notin C}{\lfloor receive(x, y)^n.send\langle x, y\rangle\rfloor.P \xrightarrow{?D.v} send\langle D, v\rangle.P}$

(PS-NOIN) $\dfrac{\alpha \in \{?k.v\} \quad P \notin IP}{P \xrightarrow{\alpha} P}$

Network Level of Label Transition Semantics. The transition rule of network level is $T_t, T_f, C \triangleright N \xrightarrow{\mu} N'$. It gives normal sending record set T_t, protected sending record set T_f and message record set C. T_t, T_f, C indicate the environment of network N is running in to support the transition. Network N changes to network N' when event μ happens. The event μ is defined as below.

$$\mu := c(\theta)!k.v \mid c(\theta)?k.v \mid \tau$$

where, θ can be true or false. When normal channel c in network N is used, then θ is false. When protected channel c in network N is used, then θ is true. $c(\theta)!k.v$ is a broadcast sending event. It means a node in network N is using channel c to broadcast a message with type p and value v. $c(\theta)?k.v$ is a receiving event.

It describes nodes in network N are using channel c to receive a message with type k and value v. In addition, τ means an internal event.

Table 3 lists the label transition semantics at the network level. For example, the rule (NS-SEND1) describes a wireless network node with name n and node set s, uses normal channel c to send a message with type p and value v, and the process inside changes from P to P'. The rules (NS-COM1 and NS-COM2) are applied to the parallel composition between networks. They describe message communications between nodes. Meanwhile, they characterize how a broadcast sending event generated from one network affects a broadcast receiving event in another network in parallel.

Table 3. Network level of label transition semantics

(NS-SEND1)
$$\frac{P \xrightarrow{!k.v} P'}{T_t, T_f, C \triangleright n[P]_s^c \xrightarrow{c(false)!k.v} n[P']_s^c}$$

(NS-SEND2)
$$\frac{P \xrightarrow{!k.v} P'}{T_t, T_f, C \triangleright n[P]_s^{vc} \xrightarrow{c(true)!k.v} n[P']_s^{vc}}$$

(NS-REC1)
$$\frac{P \xrightarrow{?k.v} P' \quad \exists m \in T_f|_{n,c}, \; n \in \pi_2(m)}{T_t, T_f, C \triangleright n[P]_s^c \xrightarrow{c(false)?k.v} n[P']_s^c}$$

(NS-REC2)
$$\frac{P \xrightarrow{?k.v} P' \quad \exists m \in T_f|_{n,c}, \; n \in \pi_2(m)}{T_t, T_f, C \triangleright n[P]_s^{vc} \xrightarrow{c(true)?k.v} n[P']_s^{vc}}$$

(NS-REC3)
$$\frac{c \neq c'}{T_t, T_f, C \triangleright n[P]_s^c \xrightarrow{c'(false)?k.v} n[P]_s^c}$$

(NS-REC4)
$$\frac{c \neq c'}{T_t, T_f, C \triangleright n[P]_s^{vc} \xrightarrow{c'(true)?k.v} n[P]_s^{vc}}$$

(NS-REC5)
$$\frac{\forall m \in T_t|_{n,c}, \; n \notin \pi_2(m)}{T_t, T_f, C \triangleright n[P]_s^c \xrightarrow{c(false)?k.v} n[P]_s^c}$$

(NS-REC6)
$$\frac{\forall m \in T_t|_{n,c}, \; n \notin \pi_2(m)}{T_t, T_f, C \triangleright n[P]_s^{vc} \xrightarrow{c(true)?k.v} n[P]_s^{vc}}$$

(NS-COM1)
$$\frac{T_t, T_f, C_1 \triangleright N_1 \xrightarrow{c(\theta)?k.v} N_1' \quad T_t, T_f, C_2 \triangleright N_2 \xrightarrow{c(\theta)!k.v} N_2'}{T_t, T_f, C_1 \cup C_2 \triangleright N_1 || N_2 \xrightarrow{c(\theta)!k.v} N_1' || N_2'}$$

(NS-COM2)
$$\frac{T_t, T_f, C_1 \triangleright N_1 \xrightarrow{c(\theta)!k.v} N_1' \quad T_t, T_f, C_2 \triangleright N_2 \xrightarrow{c(\theta)?k.v} N_2'}{T_t, T_f, C_1 \cup C_2 \triangleright N_1 || N_2 \xrightarrow{c(\theta)!k.v} N_1' || N_2'}$$

(NS-COM3)
$$\frac{T_t, T_f, C_1 \triangleright N_1 \xrightarrow{c(\theta)?k.v} N_1' \quad T_t, T_f, C_2 \triangleright N_2 \xrightarrow{c(\theta)?k.v} N_2'}{T_t, T_f, C_1 \cup C_2 \triangleright N_1 || N_2 \xrightarrow{c(\theta)?k.v} N_1' || N_2'}$$

(NS-COM4)
$$\frac{T_t, T_f, C_1 \triangleright N_1 \xrightarrow{\tau} N_1'}{T_t, T_f, C_1 \cup C_2 \triangleright N_1 || N_2 \xrightarrow{\tau} N_1' || N_2}$$
(NS-NULL) $T_t, T_f, C \triangleright 0 \xrightarrow{c(\theta)?k.v} 0$

(NS-PSEND1)
$$\frac{P \xrightarrow{!} P'}{T_t, T_f, C \triangleright n[P]_s^c \xrightarrow{\tau} n[P']_s^c}$$
(NS-PSEND2)
$$\frac{P \xrightarrow{!} P'}{T_t, T_f, C \triangleright n[P]_s^{vc} \xrightarrow{\tau} n[P']_s^{vc}}$$

Example 1. Consider a network with four nodes. Node n_1 is the source node to send *Interest* package. Node n_2 and node n_3 are forwarders. Node n_4 is the target node to receive *Interest* package. The network topology is given in Fig. 1. We assume that node n_1 has node n_2 and node n_3 in its transmission range, and node n_2 has node n_4 in its transmission range. Meanwhile, node n_3 and node n_4 have no node in their transmission ranges. Mathematically, $s_1 = \{n_2, n_3\}$, $s_2 = \{n_4\}$, $s_3 = \emptyset$ and $s_4 = \emptyset$. In the following two cases of forwarding *Interest* package, the network topology of nodes are the same but with the different channel types.

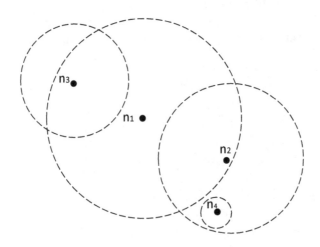

Fig. 1. Network topology

(a) Four nodes are using the protected channel c:

$$N =_{df} n_1[send\langle I, v\rangle.\mathbf{0}]_{s_1}^{\nu c} \;||\; n_2[\lfloor receive(x_1, y_1)^{n_2}.send\langle x_1, y_1\rangle\rfloor.\mathbf{0}]_{s_2}^{\nu c}$$
$$||\; n_3[\lfloor receive(x_2, y_2)^{n_3}.send\langle x_2, y_2\rangle\rfloor.\mathbf{0}]_{s_3}^{\nu c}||\; n_4[receive(x_3, y_3)^{n_4}.P]_{s_4}^{\nu c}$$

The migration path is described as below.
Step 1:

$$\emptyset, \emptyset, \emptyset \rhd N \xrightarrow{\tau} n_1[\langle I, v\rangle.\mathbf{0}]_{s_1}^{\nu c} \;||\; n_2[receive(x_1, y_1)^{n_2}.send\langle x_1, y_1\rangle.\mathbf{0}]_{s_2}^{\nu c}$$
$$||\; n_3[\lfloor receive(x_2, y_2)^{n_3}.send\langle x_2, y_2\rangle\rfloor.\mathbf{0}]_{s_3}^{\nu c}$$
$$||\; n_4[receive(x_3, y_3)^{n_4}.P]_{s_4}^{\nu c} \stackrel{def}{=} N_1$$

Step 2:

$$\{(n_1, \{n_2, n_3\}, c)\}, \emptyset, \emptyset \rhd N_1 \xrightarrow{c(true)!I.v} n_1[\mathbf{0}]_{s_1}^{\nu c} \;||\; n_2[send\langle I, v\rangle.\mathbf{0}]_{s_2}^{\nu c}$$
$$||\; n_3[send\langle I, v\rangle.\mathbf{0}]_{s_3}^{\nu c} \;||\; n_4[receive(x_3, y_3)^{n_4}.P]_{s_4}^{\nu c} \stackrel{def}{=} N_2$$

Step 3:

$$\emptyset, \emptyset, \{(n_1, I, v), (n_2, I, v), (n_3, I, v)\} \triangleright N_2 \xrightarrow{\tau \cdot \tau} n_1[\mathbf{0}]^{\nu c}_{s_1} \parallel n_2[\langle I, v\rangle.\mathbf{0}]^{\nu c}_{s_2} \parallel n_3[\langle I, v\rangle.\mathbf{0}]^{c}_{s_3}$$
$$\parallel n_4[receive(x_3, y_3)^{n_4}.P]^{\nu c}_{s_4} \stackrel{def}{=} N_3$$

Step 4:

$$\{(n_3, \emptyset, c)\}, \emptyset, \{(n_1, I, v), (n_2, I, v), (n_3, I, v)\} \triangleright N_3 \xrightarrow{c(true)!I.v} n_1[\mathbf{0}]^{\nu c}_{s_1} \parallel n_2[\langle I, v\rangle.\mathbf{0}]^{\nu c}_{s_2}$$
$$\parallel n_3[\mathbf{0}]^{\nu c}_{s_3} \parallel n_4[receive(x_3, y_3)^{n_4}.P]^{\nu c}_{s_4} \stackrel{def}{=} N_4$$

Step 5:

$$\{(n_2, \{n_4\}, c)\}, \emptyset, \{(n_1, I, v), (n_2, I, v), (n_3, I, v)\} \triangleright N_4 \xrightarrow{c(true)!I.v} n_1[\mathbf{0}]^{\nu c}_{s_1} \parallel n_2[\mathbf{0}]^{\nu c}_{s_2} \parallel n_3[\mathbf{0}]^{c}_{s_3}$$
$$\parallel n_4[P\{I/x_3, v/y_3\}]^{\nu c}_{s_4}$$

(b) Node n_3 uses the normal channel c and other three nodes use the protected channel c:

$$M =_{df} n_1[send\langle I, v\rangle.\mathbf{0}]^{\nu c}_{s_1} \parallel n_2[\lfloor receive(x_1, y_1)^{n_2}.send\langle x_1, y_1\rangle\rfloor.\mathbf{0}]^{\nu c}_{s_2}$$
$$\parallel n_3[\lfloor receive(x_2, y_2)^{n_3}.send\langle x_2, y_2\rangle\rfloor.\mathbf{0}]^{c}_{s_3} \parallel n_4[receive(x_3, y_3)^{n_4}.P]^{\nu c}_{s_4}$$

The migration path is depicted as below.

Step 1:

$$\emptyset, \emptyset, \emptyset \triangleright M \xrightarrow{\tau} n_1[\langle I, v\rangle.\mathbf{0}]^{\nu c}_{s_1} \parallel n_2[receive(x_1, y_1)^{n_2}.send\langle x_1, y_1\rangle.\mathbf{0}]^{\nu c}_{s_2}$$
$$\parallel n_3[\lfloor receive(x_2, y_2)^{n_3}.send\langle x_2, y_2\rangle\rfloor.\mathbf{0}]^{c}_{s_3}$$
$$\parallel n_4[receive(x_3, y_3)^{n_4}.P]^{\nu c}_{s_4} \stackrel{def}{=} M_1$$

Step 2:

$$\{(n_1, \{n_2, n_3\}, c)\}, \emptyset, \emptyset \triangleright M_1 \xrightarrow{c(true)!I.v} n_1[\mathbf{0}]^{\nu c}_{s_1} \parallel n_2[send\langle I, v\rangle.\mathbf{0}]^{\nu c}_{s_2}$$
$$\parallel n_3[\lfloor receive(x_2, y_2)^{n_3}.send\langle x_2, y_2\rangle\rfloor.\mathbf{0}]^{c}_{s_3}$$
$$\parallel n_4[receive(x_3, y_3)^{n_4}.P]^{\nu c}_{s_4} \stackrel{def}{=} M_2$$

Step 3:

$$\emptyset, \emptyset, \{(n_1, I, v), (n_2, I, v)\} \triangleright M_2 \xrightarrow{\tau} n_1[\mathbf{0}]^{\nu c}_{s_1} \parallel n_2[\langle I, v\rangle.\mathbf{0}]^{\nu c}_{s_2}$$
$$\parallel n_3[\lfloor receive(x_2, y_2)^{n_3}.send\langle x_2, y_2\rangle\rfloor.\mathbf{0}]^{c}_{s_3}$$
$$\parallel n_4[receive(x_3, y_3)^{n_4}.P]^{\nu c}_{s_4} \stackrel{def}{=} M_3$$

Step 4:

$$\{(n_2, \{n_4\}, c)\}, \emptyset, \{(n_1, I, v), (n_2, I, v)\} \triangleright M_3 \xrightarrow{c(true)!I.v} n_1[\mathbf{0}]^{\nu c}_{s_1} \parallel n_2[\mathbf{0}]^{\nu c}_{s_2}$$
$$\parallel n_3[\lfloor receive(x_2, y_2)^{n_3}.send\langle x_2, y_2\rangle\rfloor.\mathbf{0}]^{c}_{s_3}$$
$$\parallel n_4[P\{I/x_3, v/y_3\}]^{\nu c}_{s_4}$$

After applying our operational semantics, we can see that node n_1 successfully transmits message to node n_4 in both case (a) and case (b). The only difference is that in case (a) the message is transmitted to both node n_2 and node n_3. However, in case (b), the message is only transmitted to node n_2 not to node n_3. The reason is that node n_2 can not communicate with other nodes, for they own different channel types.

3   Automatic Implementation of SCWN

In this section, we give the automatic implementation of SCWN using a rewriting logic-based language Maude. We list several operations and objects to support the preparation of formalization of SCWN. Meanwhile, we also introduce the definition of variables, the declaration of the set of messages and the feature of multimessages. Then, the syntax and the semantics rules of SCWN calculus in Sect. 2 are formalized.

3.1   Preparation of Formalization of SCWN

In order to give the automatic implementation of SCWN, we need some preparation definitions. Using the object-oriented module in Maude, our definition of wireless node can be supported. With the predefined module QID, Oid stands for object identifier. Message, Type, Value, Process and Variable represent message, type, value, process and variable respectively. OidSet and MSet mean the set of Oid and the set of Message respectively. SChannel and NChannel are subsorts for Channel. SChannel is the protected channel. NChannel represents the normal channel. Type and Value are subsorts for Variable. We put Type and Value together to be recognized as Message.

```
1  protecting QID .
2  subsort Qid < Oid .
3  sorts OidSet Message MSet Type Value Process Variable Channel SChannel
         NChannel .
4  subsort Oid < OidSet .
5  subsort Message < MSet .
6  subsorts SChannel NChannel < Channel .
7  subsorts Type Value < Variable .
8  op __ : Type Value -> Message .
```

The definition of messages is also important to depict our SCWN calculus by Maude. It is declared as below.

```
1  msg Msg.value_type_channel_from_to_ :
2      Value Type Channel Oid Oid -> Msg .
```

where (msg v type t channel c from A to B) indicates a message with value v type t using channel c sent from A to B.

We first give the variable declarations.

```
1  vars A B : Oid . vars N N' : OidSet .
2  vars M1 M2 : Message . var MS : MSet .
3  vars P P' : Process . vars V1 V2 : Variable .
4  var CH : Channel . var SC : SChannel .
5  var NC : NChannel . var T : Type . var VA : Value .
```

In order to simulate the broadcasting mechanism of SCWN, we introduce the feature of "multimessages". A message

```
1 (Multimsg.value v type t channel c from A to N)
```

can be defined as denoting the construct below, in which set N represents the union of set B1, B2, ..., Bn.

```
1 (Msg.value v type t channel c from A to B1)
2 (Msg.value v type t channel c from A to B2)
3 ...
4 (Msg.value v type t channel c from A to Bn)
```

The feature of "multimessages" can be formalized in Maude concisely.

```
1 eq Multimsg.value VA type T channel CH from A to (B N) =
2   (Msg.value VA type T channel CH from A to B)
3   (Multimsg.value VA type T channel CH from A to (N - B)) .
4 eq Multimsg.value VA type T channel CH from A to nil = none .
```

In order to deal with the relationship between object and object set, we introduce the definition of the object set as well as the set operations.

```
1 op nil : -> OidSet .
2 op __ : OidSet OidSet -> OidSet [assoc comm id: nil] .
3 op in : Oid OidSet -> Bool .
4 op _-_ : OidSet Oid -> OidSet .
5 eq A A = A .
6 eq in(A, B N) = A == B or in(A,N) .
7 eq in(A,nil) = false .
8 eq (A N) - A = N - A .
9 ceq N - A = N if not in(A,N) .
```

To handle the storage mechanism of node, we also define the message set and its set operations. As it is almost the same with object set, the detail is omitted.

3.2   Formalization of the Syntax

In order to describe the processes and networks in Table 1, the following operators are declared. They are inspired by the syntax of SCWN. We first give the operators for the process parts.

```
1 op send(_,_) : Type Value -> Process .
2 op <_,_> : Type Value -> Process .
3 op receive(_,_) : Variable Variable -> Process .
4 op [receive(_,_)#send(_,_)] : Variable Variable Variable Variable ->
     Process .
5 op _{_/_,_/_} : Process Type Variable Value Variable -> Process .
```

The operator send(_,_) is defined to describe the pre-output action. The operator <_,_> describes the output action. The operator receive(_,_) describes the input action. The operator [receive(_,_)#send(_,_)] illustrates the forward action. In addition, the operator _{_/_,_/_} depicts the renaming of the process.

The class Node is declared to describe wireless network node.

```
1 class Node | snbs : OidSet, rnbs : OidSet, pro : Process,
2 mset : MSet, ch : Channel .
```

where snbs denotes the set of nodes that can receive message sent by the node, rnbs is the set of nodes that the node can receive message from, pro represents the process running on the node, mset is the set of message including type and value, ch means the channel of the node.

3.3 Formalization of the Semantics Rules

We formalize the operational semantics in Table 3 by rewrite rules in Maude. Due to space limitations, we only take several typical rewrite rules of the protected node as examples. The rewrite rule RECI1-S, RECI2-S and RECI3-S specify the protected node with the forward action to be done when receiving *Interest* packet.

```
1  crl [RECI1-S] :
2  (Msg.value VA type T channel SC from A to B)
3  < B : Node | snbs : N, rnbs : A N', pro : [receive(V1, V2)#send(V1, V2)] .
       P, ms : MS, ch : SC >
4  => < B : Node | snbs : N, rnbs : A N', pro : P, ms : MS, ch : SC >
5  if in((T VA),MS) == true /\ T == Interest .
```

The rewrite rule RECI1-S is for the case that the protected node receives *Interest* packet which belongs to the set of messages. The packet will be discarded.

```
1  crl [RECI2-S] :
2  (Msg.value VA type T channel SC from A to B)
3  < B : Node | snbs : N, rnbs : A N', pro : [receive(V1, V2)#send(V1, V2)] .
       P, ms : MS, ch : SC >
4  => < B : Node | snbs : N, rnbs : A N', pro : send(T, VA) . P, ms : MS, ch
       : SC >
5  if in((Interest VA),MS) == false /\ in((Data VA),MS) == false /\ T ==
       Interest .
```

```
1  crl [RECI3-S] :
2  (Msg.value VA type T channel SC from A to B)
3  < B : Node | snbs : N, rnbs : A N', pro : [receive(V1, V2)#send(V1, V2)] .
       P, ms : MS, ch : SC >
4  => < B : Node | snbs : N, rnbs : A N', pro : send(Data, VA) . P, ms : MS,
       ch : SC >
5  if  in((Interest VA),MS) == false /\ in((Data VA),MS) == true  /\ T ==
       Interest .
```

The rewrite rule RECI2-S and RECI3-S are for the situation that the protected node receives *Interest* packet which has not been received before. For the rewrite rule RECI2-S, if the corresponding *Data* packet is missing, the node performs the output action with *Interest* packet. For the rewrite rule RECI3-S, if its corresponding *Data* packet has been received, the node performs the output action with *Data* packet.

The rewrite rule RECD1-S and RECD2-S mean the protected node with the forward action when receiving *Data* packet.

```
1  crl [RECD1-S] :
2  (Msg.value VA type T channel SC from A to B)
3  < B : Node | snbs : N, rnbs : A N', pro : [receive(V1, V2)#send(V1, V2)] .
       P, ms : MS, ch : SC >
4  => < B : Node | snbs : N, rnbs : A N', pro : P, ms : MS, ch : SC >
5  if T == Data /\ in((Interest VA),MS) == false .
```

```
1  crl [RECD2-S] :
2  (Msg.value VA type T channel SC from A to B)
3  < B : Node | snbs : N, rnbs : A N', pro : [receive(V1, V2)#send(V1, V2)] .
       P, ms : MS, ch : SC >
4  => < B : Node | snbs : N, rnbs : A N', pro : send(Data, VA) . P, ms : MS -
       (Interest VA), ch : SC >
5  if in((T VA),MS) == false /\ T == Data /\ in((Interest VA),MS) == true .
```

For the rule RECD1-S, if the corresponding *Interest* packet has not been received before, the *Data* packet is discarded. For the rule RECD2-S, if the corresponding *Interest* packet has been received, the node performs the output action with *Data* packet and removes the *Interest* packet.

4   Applying SCWN Calculus to LFBL Protocol

In this section, we apply our SCWN calculus to LFBL protocol, which is a forwarding protocol for NDN wireless networks. Then the two cases in Example 1 are also implemented in Maude with LFBL protocol. According to the features of LFBL protocol, we update the Maude implementation of SCWN calculus to describe the data phase.

4.1   LFBL Protocol

Meisel et al. [9] proposed Listen First, Broadcast Later (LFBL). It is a forwarding protocol for NDN wireless networks. It uses a data-centric approach and therefore supports the applications in NDN. In LFBL protocol, each communication at runtime is divided into two phases: a request phase and a data phase.

The request phase is similar to the route request phase of the traditional on-demand routing protocols. Assuming that the requester has no prior knowledge, it will broadcast *Interest* packet over the network by flooding. *Interest* package carries the name of the requested data, and responds to the request if the receiving node has data with the corresponding name. The data phase begins when the response arrives at the requester. In the data phase, the responder returns *Data* packet corresponding to *Interest* packet by using special forwarding, so that the requester will eventually receive the required data.

Here we focus on this special forwarding. Each node will calculate the distance before forwarding after receiving *Data* packet from the neighbor node. If it is closer to the target node than the neighbor node, it is an eligible forwarder and continues to forward. If the neighbor node is closer to the target node, it is not an eligible forwarder and discards the packet.

4.2   Application of SCWN Calculus to the Request Phase

First, we apply the SCWN calculus to the request phase of LFBL protocol, according to the two cases in Example 1. test1 implements case (a) by Maude. It describes a network with four nodes using protected channels. Node n_1 is the source node to send *Interest* package. Node n_2 and node n_3 are forwarders. Node n_4 is the target node to receive *Interest* package.

```
1  eq test1 =
2  < n1 : Node | snbs : n2 n3, rnbs : nil, pro : send(Interest, va) . p, ms :
       nil, ch : sc >
3  < n2 : Node | snbs : n4, rnbs : n1, pro : [receive(v1, v2)#send(v1, v2)] .
       p, ms : nil, ch : sc >
4  < n3 : Node | snbs : nil, rnbs : n1, pro : [receive(v1, v2)#send(v1, v2)]
       . p, ms : nil, ch : sc >
5  < n4 : Node | snbs : nil, rnbs : n2, pro : receive(v1, v2) . p, ms : nil,
       ch : sc > .
```

Figure 2 illustrates the result of running `test1` in Maude. First of all, node n_1 is sending a message to node n_2 and node n_3. Then node n_2 and node n_3 receive the message. Node n_2 forwards the message to node n_4. Finally, node n_4 receives the message. The message is in `ms` of the four nodes.

```
Maude> (rew test1 .)
          SCWN
  test1
      Configuration
  < n1 : Node | ch : sc,ms : Interest va,pro : p,rnbs : nil,snbs : n2 n3 > < n2 :
Node | ch : sc,ms : Interest va,pro :
    p,rnbs : n1,snbs : n4 > < n3 : Node | ch : sc,ms : Interest va,pro : p,rnbs :
n1,snbs : nil > < n4 : Node | ch :
    sc,ms : Interest va,pro :(p{Interest / v1,va / v2}),rnbs : n2,snbs : nil >
```

Fig. 2. The result of running `test1` in Maude

Case (b) is implemented by `test2`. The only difference between case (a) and case (b) is node n_3 uses the normal channel. This is also described by `test2`.

```
1  eq test2 =
2  < n1 : Node | snbs : n2 n3, rnbs : nil, pro : send(Interest, va) . p, ms :
       nil, ch : sc >
3  < n2 : Node | snbs : n4, rnbs : n1, pro : [receive(v1, v2)#send(v1, v2)] .
       p, ms : nil, ch : sc >
4  < n3 : Node | snbs : nil, rnbs : n1, pro : [receive(v1, v2)#send(v1, v2)]
       . p, ms : nil, ch : nc >
5  < n4 : Node | snbs : nil, rnbs : n2, pro : receive(v1, v2) . p, ms : nil,
       ch : sc > .
```

Figure 3 shows the result of running `test2` in Maude. First, node n_1 is sending message to node n_2 and node n_3. Only node n_2 receives the message. The message is forwarded by node n_2, which is then received by node n_4. The message only appears in `ms` of the three nodes.

```
Maude> (rew test2 .)
          SCWN
  test2
      Configuration
  < n1 : Node | ch : sc,ms : Interest va,pro : p,rnbs : nil,snbs : n2 n3 > < n2 :
Node | ch : sc,ms : Interest va,pro :
    p,rnbs : n1,snbs : n4 > < n3 : Node | ch : nc,ms : nil,pro :([receive(v1,v2)#s
end(v1,v2)]. p),rnbs : n1,snbs : nil
    > < n4 : Node | ch : sc,ms : Interest va,pro :(p{Interest / v1,va / v2}),rnbs
: n2,snbs : nil >
```

Fig. 3. The result of running `test2` in Maude

Figures 2 and 3 show that automatic implementation of SCWN calculus is done successfully, and the results of the running `test1` and `test2` are consistent with the results by manual deduction in Example 1. It embodies that our SCWN calculus can be applied to realistic cases, which not only implements the special mechanism of NDN, but also supports the security feature.

4.3 Application of SCWN Calculus to the Data Phase

In order to describe the data phase of LFBL protocol, we update the definition of the node by adding an argument to describe the distance between the current node to the target node.

```
1  class NodeN | snbs : OidSet, rnbs : OidSet, pro : Process, ms : MSet, ch :
      Channel, d : Nat .
```

We add new operators for the process parts to support the special forwarding. Compared with the operators defined previously, the new operators add new arguments to describe the node and the distance between the node itself and the target node.

```
1  op send(_,_,_(_)) : Type Value Oid Nat -> Process .
2  op <_,_,_(_)> : Type Value Oid Nat -> Process .
3  op receive(_,_,_(_)) : Variable Variable Oid Nat -> Process .
4  op [receive(_,_,_(_))#send(_,_,_(_))] : Variable Variable Oid Nat Type
      Value Oid Nat -> Process .
```

We also update the rewrite rules of the new type of node. Because of the space constraints, we only give severl rules. The rule N-DIS-S indicates that if the node A is not closer to the target node C compared with its neighbour node B, the message is not forwarded.

```
1  crl [N-DIS-S] :
2  (Msg.value VA type T channel SC from A(DI1) to B end C(DI2))
3  < B : NodeN | snbs : N, rnbs : A N', pro : [receive(V1, V2, V3(V4))#send(
      V1, V2, V3(V4))] . P, ms : MS, ch : SC, d : DI >
4  => < B : NodeN | snbs : N, rnbs : A N', pro : P, ms : MS, ch : SC , d : DI
      >
5  if DI1 <= DI .
```

The rule N-RECD1-S is almost the same as the rule RECD1-S. As the related *Interest* packet is not in the set of messages, the node discards *Data* packet.

```
1  crl [N-RECD1-S] :
2  (Msg.value VA type T channel SC from A(DI1) to B end C(DI2))
3  < B : NodeN | snbs : N, rnbs : A N', pro : [receive(V1, V2, V3(V4))#send(
      V1, V2, V3(V4))] . P, ms : MS, ch : SC, d : DI >
4  => < B : NodeN | snbs : N, rnbs : A N', pro : P, ms : MS, ch : SC, d : DI
      >
5  if T == Data /\ in((Interest VA),MS) == false .
```

The rule N-RECD2-S is similar with the rule RECD2-S. The only difference is that the judgment of the distance is added.

```
1  crl [N-RECD2-S] :
2  (Msg.value VA type T channel SC from A(DI1) to B end C(DI2))
3  < B : NodeN | snbs : N, rnbs : A N', pro : [receive(V1, V2, V3(V4))#send(
      V1, V2, V3(V4))] . P, ms : MS, ch : SC, d : DI >
4  => < B : NodeN | snbs : N, rnbs : A N', pro : send(Data, VA, C(DI2)) . P,
      ms : MS - (Interest VA), ch : SC, d : DI >
5  if in((T VA),MS) == false /\ T == Data /\ in((Interest VA),MS) == true /\
      DI1 > DI .
```

Then we can describe the data phase with the update of SCWN calculus.

```
1  eq test3 =
2  < n1 : NodeN | snbs : n2 n3, rnbs : nil, pro : send(Data, va, n4(0)) . p,
      ms : nil, ch : sc, d : 20 >
3  < n2 : NodeN | snbs : n4, rnbs : n1, pro : [receive(v1, v2, v3(v4))#send(
      v1, v2, v3(v4))] . p, ms : Interest va, ch : sc, d : 10 >
```

```
4  < n3 : NodeN | snbs : nil, rnbs : n1, pro : [receive(v1, v2, v3(v4))#send(
       v1, v2, v3(v4))] . p, ms : Interest va, ch : sc, d : 30 >
5  < n4 : NodeN | snbs : nil, rnbs : n2, pro : receive(v1, v2, v3(v4)) . p,
       ms : nil, ch : sc, d : 0 > .
```

test3 also focuses on the network topology in Example 1, considering that the data phase is transmitting *Data* packet and the distance feature is added. Distance variable d for each node is introduced to give the distance from the destination node n4 to the node itself.

```
Maude> (rew test3 .)
        SCWN
  test3
    Configuration
  < n1 : NodeN | ch : sc,d : 20,ms : Data va,pro : p,rnbs : nil,snbs : n2 n3 > <
    n2 : NodeN | ch : sc,d : 10,ms : Data va,pro : p,rnbs : n1,snbs : n4 > < n3 :
    NodeN | ch : sc,d : 30,ms : Interest va,pro : p,rnbs : n1,snbs : nil > < n4 :
    NodeN | ch : sc,d : 0,ms : Data va,pro :(p{Data / v1,va / v2}),rnbs : n2,snbs
    : nil >
```

Fig. 4. The result of running test3 in Maude

Figure 4 shows the result of running test3 in Maude. First, node n_1 is sending message to node n_2 and node n_3. Only node n_2 receives the message. Node n_3 discards the message, because it is farther to node n_4 than node n_1. Node n_2 forwards the message to node n_4. Finally, node n_4 receives the message. This indicates that updated SCWN calculus can describe the request phase of the LFBL protocol. It illustrates that our SCWN calculus is extensible to more realistic cases.

5 Conclusion

In this paper, we introduced a process algebra called SCWN calculus. It characterizes special forwarding mechanism and data caching mechanism of NDN. The feature of NDN is implemented by introducing particular sets. Security feature is implemented using different channel symbols. We presented the automatic implementation of SCWN calculus to make it convenient and useful. Then SCWN calculus is applied to the LFBL protocol and several cases are implemented. It illustrates that our SCWN calculus is extensible to real-world scenes.

In the future, we plan to do the verification for NDN based on our SCWN calculus. It is a challenge to design a set of verification rules [1,6] for our SCWN calculus. Meanwhile, it is also interesting to study the denotational semantics and algebraic semantics for our SCWN calculus based on the UTP approaches [5].

Acknowledgement. This work was partly supported by National Natural Science Foundation of China (Grant No. 61872145), National Key Research and Development Program of China (Grant No. 2018YFB2101300), Shanghai Collaborative Innovation Center of Trustworthy Software for Internet of Things (Grant No. ZF1213) and the Fundamental Research Funds for the Central Universities of China.

References

1. Apt, K.R., de Boer, F.S., Olderog, E.: Verification of Sequential and Concurrent Programs. Texts in Computer Science. Springer, London (2009). https://doi.org/10.1007/978-1-84882-745-5
2. Bazzi, A., Masini, B.M., Zanella, A., Castro, C.D., Raffaelli, C., Andrisano, O.: Cellular aided vehicular named data networking. In: ICCVE 2014, pp. 747–752 (2014)
3. Clavel, M., et al.: All About Maude - A High-Performance Logical Framework: How to Specify, Program and Verify Systems in Rewriting Logic. LNCS, vol. 4350. Springer, Heidelberg (2007). https://doi.org/10.1007/978-3-540-71999-1
4. Godskesen, J.C.: A calculus for mobile ad hoc networks. In: Murphy, A.L., Vitek, J. (eds.) COORDINATION 2007. LNCS, vol. 4467, pp. 132–150. Springer, Heidelberg (2007). https://doi.org/10.1007/978-3-540-72794-1_8
5. He, J., Hoare, C.A.R.: Unifying theories of programming. In: RelMiCS 1998, pp. 97–99 (1998)
6. Hoare, C.A.R.: An axiomatic basis for computer programming. Commun. ACM **12**(10), 576–580 (1969)
7. Li, Z., Liu, K., Liu, D., Shi, H., Chen, Y.: Hybrid wireless networks with fib-based named data networking. EURASIP J. Wirel. Commun. Netw. **2017**, 54 (2017)
8. Meisel, M., Pappas, V., Zhang, L.: Ad hoc networking via named data. In: Proceedings of the Fifth ACM International Workshop on Mobility in the Evolving Internet Architecture, pp. 3–8 (2010)
9. Meisel, M., Pappas, V., Zhang, L.: Listen first, broadcast later: topology-agnostic forwarding under high dynamics. Technical report, Los Angeles, CA, USA (2010)
10. Merro, M.: An observational theory for mobile ad hoc networks (full version). Inf. Comput. **207**(2), 194–208 (2009)
11. Nanz, S., Hankin, C.: Formal security analysis for ad-hoc networks. Electr. Notes Theor. Comput. Sci. **142**, 195–213 (2006)
12. Prasad, K.V.S.: A calculus of broadcasting systems. Sci. Comput. Program. **25**(2–3), 285–327 (1995)
13. Zhang, L., et al.: Named data networking (NDN) project. Technical report NDN-0001, PARC (2010)

Automatic Modularization of Large Programs for Bounded Model Checking

Marko Kleine Büning and Carsten Sinz[✉]

Karlsruhe Institute of Technology (KIT), Karlsruhe, Germany
{marko.kleinebuening,carsten.sinz}@kit.edu

Abstract. The verification of real-world applications is a continuous challenge which yielded numerous different methods and approaches. However, scalability of precise analysis methods on large programs is still limited. We thus propose a formal definition of modules that allows a partitioning of the program into smaller code fragments suitable for verification by bounded model checking. We consider programs written in C/C++ and use LLVM as an intermediate representation. A formal trace semantics for LLVM program runs is defined that also takes modularization into account. Using different abstractions and a selection of fragments of a program for each module, we describe four different modularization approaches. We define desirable properties of modularizations, and show how a bounded model checking approach can be adapted for modularization. Two modularization approaches are implemented within the tool QPR-Verify, which is based on the bounded model checker LLBMC. We evaluate our approach on a medium-sized embedded system software encompassing approximately 160 KLoC.

1 Introduction

The increasing number of safety and security critical systems yields the need for software verification for real-world applications. Studies about the cost of software errors like [20] show the necessity of precise and thorough verification and are backed up by catastrophic experiences in past and present like the rocket crash of Ariane flight 501 [16] or the car crash of the Toyota Camry in 2005 [15]. Software verification approaches are making continuous progress, but at the same time the size of the systems embedded in aircrafts, cars, or mobile phones grow even faster. Modern cars are currently at around 100 MLoC and are estimated to go up to a total of 300 MLoC in the next years. Even current audio control software in a car can have several millions LoC and is thereby hardly verifiable by most if not all approaches.

For bounded model checking, a program under verification has to be encoded into a logical formula. Even when ignoring time constraints, the memory requirements to encode millions of lines of code is not attainable by state-of-the-art systems. A well-known approach to increase scalability of software verification is to partition the program into smaller modules that can then be solved individually. Such modularization typically requires formalization of interfaces and

© Springer Nature Switzerland AG 2019
Y. Ait-Ameur and S. Qin (Eds.): ICFEM 2019, LNCS 11852, pp. 186–202, 2019.
https://doi.org/10.1007/978-3-030-32409-4_12

dependencies between modules. Under the headline of *compositional verification* or *assume-guarantee reasoning* several approaches for modular verification have been proposed in the past [5,9,12]. This work, however, generally does not cover the aspect of how to generate modules; instead it relies on manual approaches for partitioning. There exist frameworks that automate part of the modularization task, e.g., by creating necessary preconditions automatically through an incremental learning algorithm [6], or by deducting modules from program design [8]. However, these approaches do not provide a framework for fully automatic verification of large systems. The same applies to modular interactive approaches like [3,18], where the user has to manually write interface specifications. The number of lines of specification that has to be written for one line of source code varies depending on approach and application. Typical factors range between 2 for specialized [19], 5 for SMT-based [11] or up to 20 for interactive theorem prover approaches [14], which is not feasible for large code bases.

To automatically verify large projects, an automatic modularization is needed. We first introduce definitions of program semantics and modules to then describe automatic modularization approaches based on abstractions. Then we define a general model for program modularization, followed by four concrete modularization techniques in the context of bounded model checking. We then define mandatory and desirable properties of an automatic modularization procedure for software verification, and report on the implementation and evaluation of a global and two modular approaches using a state-of-the art bounded model checker on a real-world application of approx. 160 KLoC.

2   Theoretical Foundations

In the following, we introduce the LLVM intermediate representation (IR) and its instruction set. We define a program trace semantics for LLVM IR and thereupon modularization of programs in LLVM IR for software verification.

2.1   Programs in LLVM Intermediate Representation

LLVM is a compiler framework that also provides an intermediate representation (IR) for programs written in C, C++, and other high-level languages, e.g. Rust. LLVM's IR is an abstract, RISC-like assembler language for a register machine with an unbounded number of registers. IR programs are always kept in static single assignment (SSA) form, meaning that each register is assigned exactly once. A program in LLVM-IR consists of type definitions, global variable declarations, and the program itself, which is represented as a set of functions, each consisting of a graph of basic blocks. Each basic block in turn is a list of instructions, where the instruction set, as of interest in this paper, can broadly be split into four types (see also Table 1):

- Memory-related instructions such as `load`, `store`, stack allocation (`alloca`) and address calculation via base pointer and offsets (`getelptr`)[1];

---

[1] For brevity, we use `getelptr` instead of LLVM's name `getelementptr`.

- Three-address-code (TAC) instructions working on registers or constants, mainly for arithmetical and logical operations.
- Bit-level conversion instructions like extensions, truncations, and type casts.
- Control-flow related instructions for conditional and unconditional branching, the phi instruction (which is typical for SSA form) to conditionally select a value, as well as function-call and return (ret) instructions.

All (conditional and unconditional) branch instructions are only allowed as the last instruction of a basic block. The branch instructions induce a basic block graph (a.k.a. control-flow graph), in which edges are annotated with the condition under which the transition between two basic blocks is taken.

Table 1. LLVM IR instructions

MEMORY OPERATIONS:

$p = \texttt{alloca } t$	allocate stack memory for type t
$q = \texttt{getelptr } p, o_1, \ldots, o_n$	address calc. (base pointer, offsets)
$x = \texttt{load } p$	load from memory address p
$\texttt{store } x, p$	store x at address p

ARITHMETICAL / LOGICAL OPERATIONS:

$z = x \texttt{ <op> } y$	where $\texttt{<op>} \in \{+, -, *, \ldots, \|, \&\&, \ldots\}$
$c = x \texttt{ <op> } y$	where $\texttt{<op>} \in \{<, =, >, \leq, \ldots\}$

CONVERSION OPERATIONS:

$y = \texttt{sext/zext } x \texttt{ to } t$	sign/zero extend x to width of type t
$y = \texttt{trunc } x \texttt{ to } t$	truncate x to width of type t
$y = \texttt{ptrtoint } p \texttt{ to } t_i$	convert a ptr. value p to integer type t_i
$p = \texttt{inttoptr } x \texttt{ to } t_p$	convert an int. value x to pointer type t_p

CONTROL FLOW:

$\texttt{br } bb$	unconditional branch to basic block bb
$\texttt{br } c, bb_1, bb_2$	conditionally branch to bb_1 or bb_2
$\texttt{call } f(x_1, \ldots, x_n)$	call (void) func. f with par. $x_1, \ldots$
$y = \texttt{call } f(x_1, \ldots, x_n)$	call func. f returning y
$\texttt{ret } y \ / \ \texttt{ret void}$	return value y / nothing
$y = \texttt{phi } [x_1, bb_1], \ldots, [x_n, bb_n]$	conditional selection of value x_i

VERIFICATION EXTENSIONS:

$\texttt{assert } c$	assert that condition c is true
$x = \texttt{nondet } t$	set x to a non-determ. value of type t

For the exposition of our approach, we have extended the IR language by two verification-related instructions (in the implementation these are modeled as intrinsic functions instead of instructions), one for checking assertions and another one to set a variable to a non-deterministic value.

2.2   Program Semantics of LLVM

We define the semantics of an LLVM IR program as a set of program traces. A trace T is a (possibly infinite) sequence of program states $T = (s_0, s_1, \ldots, s_n, \ldots)$, and the trace semantics of a program encompasses all traces the program can take. We denote the set of all such traces by $\mathcal{T}_P$. The set S of states is defined as $S = (Var \rightarrow Val) \times (Adr \rightarrow Val) \times Loc^*$. A state $s = (v, m, l)$

is thus a triple consisting of a variable-value-map v, a representation m of the memory content (including stack variables generated by LLVM's `alloca`), and a representation l for a program location, which is a sequence of triples $t = (f, b, i)$ encoding the call stack. Each triple consists of a function f, a basic block b and an instruction number i, consecutively numbering the instructions within basic block b, starting from 0. The first element in sequence l is the stack top, which we also denote by l_{top}, or $l_{top}(s)$, if we want to denote the topmost frame in the location stack of state s.

We assume that $Var = GVar \cup LVar$ is the set of program variables, split into local and global variables; $LVar = Loc^* \times Name$ characterizes a local variable consisting of a call stack and a name; $GVar = Name$ denotes a global variable (which, in LLVM, is always a pointer variable); $Val = Int \cup Adr$ is the set of variable values, consisting of integer variables and pointer variables[2]. To simplify access to both local and global variables by name n in a given call stack l, we define a variable's stack-related name n^l by n if $n \in GVar$ and by (l, n) if $n \in LVar$.

Each trace has to start in an initial state $s_0 \in I$, and the effects of LLVM operations is defined via transition relations $\tau : S \to \mathbb{P}(S)$. We define transition relations for instructions and functions. As the transition relation may be non-deterministic, each state can have multiple successors (next-states).

For an instruction I and a state $s_i = (v, m, l)$ we have, e.g.,

$$\tau_{x=\text{load } p}(v, m, l) = \{(v[x^l \leftarrow m(v(p^l))], m, next(l))\}$$

$$\tau_{\text{store } x, p}(v, m, l) = \{(v, m[v(p^l) \leftarrow v(x^l)], next(l))\}$$

$$\tau_{z=x \text{ <op> } y}(v, m, l) = \{v[z^l \leftarrow v(x^l) \text{ <op> } v(y^l)], m, next(l))\}$$

$$\tau_{\text{br } c, bb_1, bb_2}(v, m, (f, b, i) : ls) = \begin{cases} \{(v, m, (f, bb_1, 0) : ls)\} & \text{if } v(c^l) \neq 0 \\ \{(v, m, (f, bb_2, 0) : ls)\} & \text{if } v(c^l) = 0 \end{cases}$$

$$\tau_{y=\text{call } g(x_1, \ldots, x_n)}(v, m, l) = \{(v', m, l^*) \mid v' \in V\}$$
$$\text{where } l^* = ((g, bb_{\text{Entry}}, 0) : l),$$
$$v^* = v[p_1^{l^*} \leftarrow v(x_1^l)] \cdots [p_n^{l^*} \leftarrow v(x_n^l)],$$
$$V = \{v^* \text{ updated with local variables set to}$$
$$\text{arbitrary values in the topmost stack frame}\},$$
$$\text{and } p_i \text{ are the actual parameters of the called function } g$$

$$\tau_{\text{ret } y}(v, m, t : ls) = \{(v[ret(y) \leftarrow v(y^{(t:ls)})], m, next(ls))\}$$
$$\text{where } ret(y) = \text{ the return var. in the call instr. at loc. } t$$

$$\tau_{x=\text{nondet } t}(v, m, l) = \{(v[x \leftarrow i], m, next(l)) \mid i \in Val\}$$

---

[2] For simplicity, we assume that integer and pointer variables have the same bit-width, and that all program variables are of type integer. We also identify pointer values with integers, such that $Val = Adr$. A more refined model would differentiate between different data types stored in memory (including floating-point). In practice, a byte-oriented memory model is often used [17].

Here, $f[x \leftarrow y]$ stands for updating the function f at location x to a new value y; $next : Loc^* \rightarrow Loc^* : ((f, b, i) : ls) \mapsto ((f, b, i + 1) : ls)$ computes the next location within the top-most basic block of the call stack (":" shall denote the list constructor) for a non-terminator instruction.

We define the set of initial states I by

$$I = \{(v, m, l) \mid v(g) = \text{address of global variable } g \text{ for all globals}$$
$$v(x^l) = \text{arbitrary value for local variable } x$$
$$m : \text{any function } Adr \rightarrow Val, \text{ respecting initializers for globals}$$
$$l = (\texttt{main}, bb_{\texttt{Entry}}, 0)\}$$

A trace T for an LLVM program P is then defined as a sequence $s_0, s_1, \ldots$ of states with $s_0 \in I$ and $s_{i+1} \in \tau_I(s_i)$, where I is the instruction at $l_{\text{top}}(s_i)$, i.e. the program location of the top-most stack frame. The semantics of program P is the set of all such traces.

In our modularization approach, we also want to define traces that start at the entry of a particular function up to the execution of the last instruction in this function. We thus define trace sets $\mathcal{T}_f$ for functions f in a program P:

$$\mathcal{T}_f = \{(s_i, \ldots, s_j) \mid (s_0, \ldots, s_n, \ldots) \in \mathcal{T}_P \text{ and}$$
$$s_i = (v, m, (f, bb_{\texttt{Entry}}, 0) : l) \text{ and } s_j = (v', m', (f, bb_{\texttt{ret}}, k_{\texttt{ret}}) : l)$$
$$j > i \text{ is the smallest index such that } (f, bb_{\texttt{ret}}, k_{\texttt{ret}})$$
$$\text{is the location of a } \texttt{ret} \text{ instruction}$$
$$\text{for some } v, v', m, m', l, bb_{\texttt{ret}} \text{ and } k_{\texttt{ret}}\}$$

2.3   Modularization

There are several possible views on what a module in a program is. We thus want to give, in a first step, a very general definition of a module. In a later step, we will identify desirable properties of a modularization and refine our definition accordingly.

Definition 1 (Program). *A (LLVM) program $P = (\mathcal{F}, \mathcal{G})$ is a tupel of a non-empty set of functions $\mathcal{F} = \{f_1, ..., f_n\}$ ($n \geq 1$) and a set $\mathcal{G} = \{g_1, ..., g_m\}$ ($m \geq 0$) of global variables that may be referenced in the functions f_i.*

We do not demand that there is unique entry point in the program (a `main` function) nor that the program is "closed" in the sense that all functions called in $\mathcal{F}$ are contained in $\mathcal{F}$. A module is then just a subset of the functions and global variables in a program.

Definition 2 (Module). *Given a program $P = (\mathcal{F}, \mathcal{G})$ and sets $\mathcal{F}', \mathcal{G}'$ with $\emptyset \subset \mathcal{F}' \subseteq \mathcal{F}$ and $\mathcal{G}' \subseteq \mathcal{G}$, $M_P = (\mathcal{F}', \mathcal{G}')$ is a module for program P.*

Note that a module is itself a program according to our definition. We assume that program properties to be verified are included in the program in the form of **assert** instructions. Thus, a module "inherits" the assertions (which we will also call *checks* in the following) from the program that it is a part of via assertions present in $\mathcal{F}'$. In some decompositions we do not require that all checks are inherited from the original program. Instead we sometimes will allow that we only inherit checks for a subset of the functions $\mathcal{F}'$.

3   Decomposition of Programs

We will introduce four modularization approaches which partition a program P into a set of modules $M_P^1, \ldots, M_P^n$ such that a bounded model checker can derive results about program P by verifying each M_P individually. Dropping parts of the program in a module of course loses information. In our modularization approaches we do not require to add specifications about missing parts of the program. Instead, we want to make sure that a module represents an over-approximation (i.e. abstraction) of the original program.

3.1   Abstractions

Abstractions are an important technique to simplify verification tasks. Most often abstractions are over-approximations of variable values (such as in abstract interpretation [7]). The abstractions that we are interested in are different and of a "structural" kind. We abstract function calls and replace them by over-approximations of the function behavior, or we ignore the calling context of a function in a larger program. In applying these structural abstractions, we distinguish between abstracting the program "bottom up", where we abstract away called functions, and "top down", where we abstract away the calling context. We will now describe our four abstraction approaches in detail.

Havoc Called Functions. The first approach abstracts away calls to functions outside of the chosen module M_P. At first, assume that M_P only contains one function f and all global variables that are either read or written in f: $M_P = (\{f\}, \mathcal{G}')$. We only keep checks (assertions) in function f, and abstract away all functions calls in f. When abstracting a function call without any further knowledge, an over-approximation of its behavior has to be assumed. Next to the return value (if existent), memory content (including global variables) can be altered by the called function, and thus have to be assumed to be arbitrary. Therefore, to abstract away a function call in the context of LLVM means to set the return value and the memory content to a nondeterministic value (**nondet**). Referencing the trace semantics of a program, the abstraction updates all transition relations $\tau_{y=\text{call } f^*(\ldots)}$ where f^* is not part of the function set of M_P. The transition relation for such a call to f^* is replaced by the following:

$$\tau_{y=\text{call } f^*(x_1,\ldots,x_n)}(v, m, l)$$
$$= \{(v[y^l \leftarrow i], m', next(l)) \mid i \in Val, m' \in (Adr \rightarrow Val)\}$$

I.e., the variable that takes the value returned by f^* can be an arbitrary value and the memory in the follow-up state can be an arbitrary function $Adr \rightarrow Val$.

The updated transition relation τ allows a higher number of possible runs and is thus a clear over-approximation of the program semantics. Therefore, updating τ guarantees soundness of the approach. The cost of such an over approximation is the possibility of false positives – error reports where there actually is no error.

In the havoc-approach, we do not abstract away function call contexts. Therefore, the approach includes any function with a (transitive) call to function f into the module M_P, together with accessed global variables. Thus the module contains the main function, which is used as an entry point for analysis. A coarse slicing algorithm can improve the creation of M_P by removing function calls that are not needed to verify the checks in f and to thus minimize the module size.

Figure 1 shows the modularization of a simple program with four functions with the use of the described abstraction. The green arrows represent the entry point for verification. The triangles represent the checks that are verified and the boxes represent the modules M_P. The dotted boxes are parts of the program that are likely to be removed by a coarse slicing algorithm dependent on the implementation.

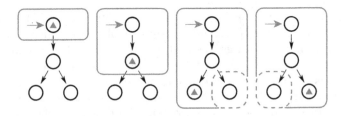

Fig. 1. Modularization into four independent modules based on abstraction of called functions. The entry point for every module (indicated by a green arrow) is the *main* function and the abstraction of called functions starts depending on the location of the assertions (indicated by a green triangle). (Color figure online)

We see that verifying a module created in this way encompasses fewer functions and thus increases scalability compared to a global analysis. For functions deep in the call graph the module size can still be too large. The abstraction can of course lead to false positives. In particular when checking for memory properties, the complete havoc of the heap at each call to a function outside of the module can lead to false error reports. Therefore, the goal of our next approach is to reduce the number of false positives.

Use Postconditions of Abstracted Functions. As a refinement of the first abstraction, we can create postconditions of called functions and replace the call of a function outside a module with the function's postcondition. While general postconditions might be used, we focus here on memory-related postconditions that result from an automatic analysis of memory locations that are written in functions abstracted away. The modularization itself stays the same as in the earlier approach, only the abstraction is refined.

As a first refinement step, we analyze memory accesses in the called function f^* with the aim of reducing memory locations we have to set to `nondet`. A rather simple analysis over the LLVM IR gives us all accesses of pointer and global variables in f^* and further called functions. After gaining all relevant memory changes, we have to obtain points-to information so that we can havoc only those memory locations written to by possible executions of f^*. This points-to information can be gained through a scalable and flow-sensitive alias analysis like e.g. described in [10]. The alias analysis has to be scalable to be run on large programs without negating the scalability benefit. Furthermore, a flow-sensitive approach takes the program flow into account and ignores the later-on called functions providing the necessary level of precision for our postconditions.

We denote the set of memory locations that have to be abstracted by $AbsM$. We then update the transition relation for a call instruction to a function f^* outside of the module $\tau_{y=\texttt{call}\,f^*(\dots)}$ to

$$\tau_{y=\texttt{call}\,f^*(x_1,\dots,x_n)}(v, m, l) = \{(v[y^l \leftarrow i], m', next(l))$$
$$| \; i \in Val, m'(a) = j \text{ with } j \in Val, \text{ if } a \in AbsM,$$
$$\text{and } m'(a) = m(a) \text{ for all } a \notin AbsM\}$$

Again, it is clear that the update of τ leads to more traces of P and is thus an over-approximation guaranteeing soundness.

The generation of such postconditions is feasible in reasonable time and mostly depends on the scalability of the alias analysis used. An adjusted alias analysis optimized specially for this use case is part of current work. Such created postcondition refines the abstraction of called functions but can further be improved by the more detailed calculation of values and the potential return value. Through symbolic execution one can extract formulas representing the values generated by the function. Such automatic and exact generation of postconditions is currently not feasible for large verification tasks. Still one can improve the postconditions through value ranges that are possible and thus further narrow the search space of the bounded model checking approach and excluding false positives. Such efficient generation is for example possible by the use abstract interpretation approaches.

Start Analysis at Entry of a Particular Function. The first approaches abstracted the program bottom up by regarding function calls. The next two approaches address the problem by abstracting the caller of module M_P. We again start with the assumption that the function set of M_P consists of one function f and the global variable set G' is created accordingly. We again insert checks only into f. In contrast to the earlier approaches, we do not abstract the transition relation τ of instructions, but the initial states I of the analysis. Thus we abstract the call context and the input parameters of f. We thereby do not have to include all functions of the call graph prior to f and can thus modularize the problem. The abstraction of the initial states I' for f is done by setting

$$I' = \{(v, m, l) \mid$$

$\qquad v(g) =$ address of global variable g for all globals

$\qquad v(x^l) =$ arbitrary value for local variable x for all local vars.

$\qquad v(p_k^l) =$ arbitrary value for parameter k of function f

$\qquad m :$ any function $Adr \to Val$

$\qquad l = (f, bb_{\texttt{Entry}}, 0)\}$

and considering function f as the start of the program. Note that we do not initialize global variables here, as their values may have changed before entering function f.

The new set of initial states is a superset of possible states that would be calculated during a normal program execution. Thus, the abstraction is again an over-approximation guaranteeing the soundness of the approach. For M_P to be verifiable, the approach has to include all called functions in M_P because no abstraction is defined and the transition relation τ needs the exact function semantics. The approach iteratively adds called functions while also adding all global variables that are needed. It thereby creates the final M_P. The modularization is demonstrated on the same abstract program in Fig. 2. The notations are equal to the figure above.

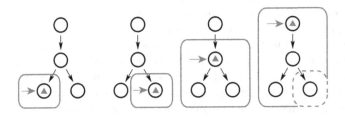

Fig. 2. Modularization into four independent modules based on abstraction of call environment. The entry point for every module is the function containing the assertion. Through the abstraction of the call environment no callers of the entry point functions have to be included.

Compared to the over-approximation of function calls, which can happen any number of times inside a module, the abstraction of the initial function call over-approximates the state only once. Furthermore, such an analysis can match user concepts. If a function is proven correct using this abstraction, the function is safe from error in every call environment. Such statements are recommended for library functions or functions that are accessible throughout the system.

Generate Preconditions for Entry Function. Similar to the previous refinement, we refine the abstraction using additional conditions that hold when the entry function is called. We create preconditions to restrict possible inputs to minimize the amount of false positives. To generate exhaustive preconditions for a function is a field of research on its own. The automatic generation of precise preconditions for large programs is currently not feasible in reasonable time. Preconditions that represent all possible call environments would have to encapsulate the complete prior program execution and are thus very costly. Nevertheless an automatic generation of such preconditions is possible using coarse approaches like abstract interpretation with an interval domain to generate value ranges for possible inputs.

Nevertheless, the approach we chose is to create preconditions not based on the prior program execution but based on the erroneous checks of our function f. First, we perform an analysis without preconditions possibly resulting in failed assertions of two kinds: *globally unsafe* and *locally unsafe*. Globally unsafe checks are such checks that will fail independent of the input, a simplified example would be the statement (x = y/0). The locally unsafe status is given to checks for which an error is found that dependents on input values of f (parameters and memory state). The precondition generation only regards locally unsafe checks. For every check, we create a precondition representing the input for which the error arises.

Bounded model checking can create an exact error trace for a failed assertion in the abstracted program. Using a symbolic execution approach can generate preconditions by following constraints backwards from the location of the failed assertion up to the start of function f. The transition relation τ is therefore inverted and symbolically executed. The symbolic execution is built upon the earlier executed bounded model checking attempt. The program is already inlined and the loops are unrolled up to a given bound. Furthermore, the exact error trace gives restrictions on branching possibilities. After the creation of such a (partial) precondition for a trace, the function has to be re-verified and the procedure to be repeated until all traces that lead to a failed assertion are covered. The amount of traces are assumed to be small because simple errors that occur on all traces are found earlier and marked globally unsafe while only locally unsafe locations, which only appear for a subset of traces, are checked for false positives. The conjunction of the resulting constraints is negated to form the precondition for f and thereby represents all input values for which there is no error in the module M_P. After generating such an over-approximating precondition for a check, the precondition is inserted into the initial state formula for module M_P. The approach iteratively chooses all modules containing the precondition and verifies the module while deactivating all internal checks. If the precondition holds, we have proven that the check is globally safe. If the precondition does not hold, the process is repeated iteratively until we reached the main function.

Extension and Combination of Abstractions. The four modularization approaches were described by starting with a single function in which checks are inserted. As mentioned earlier, the approach works the same way when starting with modules of bigger size. These enlargements of modules reduce the amount of abstractions and thereby the amount of false positives generated. The cost of such larger modules is the scalability of the approach. In reality an upper bound for the module size is manually given (dependent on the program code and time and memory constraints of the user). An algorithm for generating larger initial modules is given in Sect. 4.1.

Furthermore, a combination of the above abstractions is possible to improve scalability or to refine the verification. For programs with a deep call graph the inclusion of either the functions calling the module or all the called functions can still lead to formulas which are too large to be handled by an SMT solver. Thus, we can separate the program into three parts based on the call graph to further improve scalability: Top level modules are verified using the postcondition abstractions and bottom level modules are solved using the precondition abstraction. For modules found in the middle part of the call graph both pre- and post-conditions are necessary. Another possibility is to run the different approaches one after each other to refine the analysis result stepwise. For every analysis only the checks which are marked locally unsafe are rechecked using a different abstraction.

3.2   Properties of Modularization

We want to define properties that every module and the total modularization should strive towards. We divide them into *mandatory properties* that are necessary to guarantee the soundness of the verification approach and *success properties* that every module should strive towards for a high probability of optimal modularization for verification.

Mandatory Properties: Given a program P and a modularization $\mathcal{M}_P$. Following properties have to hold for every valid modularization.

Total-Coverage: The union of all modules has to cover the whole program, and each check has to be included at least once in every function. Every function has to appear in at least one module and thus the union of all functions included in modules represent the complete function set of P. The same is not required for the set of global variable symbols, because of, e.g., unused symbols that do not influence the program.

Single-Entry: Every module $M_i \in \mathcal{M}_P$ should have one single entry point from which the verification starts. For verification methods like bounded model checking the encoding of the program has to start at one entry point. When verifying a program with multiple entry functions, for example a library with a number of API functions, several verification jobs have to be run. These jobs can be run independently and also in parallel. To make the modules larger and to simplify the human understanding of the modularization, one could summarize modules with more then one entry point.

Information-Principle: All information that is needed for the sound verification of the module is included in the module itself. Meaning that all functions and global variables that are written to or read from are included in the verification task. Furthermore, the input of the entry point function or an abstraction of it has to be included.

Computable: The modularization should be computable in polynomial time with respect to the size of the input program. The separation of graphs into a fixed number of partitions that have minimal amount of edges between them is closely related to our partitioning. Edges in this case can be regarded as call or data dependencies. The so-called k-partitioning problem itself is NP-hard and thus one can assume that also precise algorithms for the efficient modularization of a program will have a similar complexity. Most likely, as in the case of the k-partitioning problem, we have to use abstractions and approximations of an ideal modularization that are computable in reasonable time.

Success Properties: Given a program P and a modularization $\mathcal{M}_P$. The following properties should be striven towards by every *efficient* modularization.

Solvable: The size and complexity of a module should be manageable by the chosen verification approach, in our case bounded model checking. The module size that is manageable by a given approach depends on the programming style and the design of single functions. The scalability of bounded model checking approaches limits at program sizes of about 10–100 KLoC of C code. On the other hand there are examples where a single function containing only a few lines of code is not manageable in reasonable time [2].

Minimal Dependencies: The second success property addresses the amount of dependencies between modules and thus the quantity of pre-/post-conditions or `nondet`-abstractions generated. We distinguish between call and data dependencies based on a graph structure. Let there be a node for every function in P, and let edges describe either call or data dependencies, then a directed edge in graph G_P from function f_1 to function f_2 represents one of the following: (1) function call from f_1 to f_2, (2) memory read in f_2 after a memory write in f_1 at the same location. The modularization of a program summarizes nodes and thereby also incoming and outgoing edges into modules. The minimal dependencies property states that the overall number of edges between modules should be as low as possible.

It should not be the aim of any modularization to minimize the dependencies for large programs. For a modularization $\mathcal{M}_P = \{P\}$, there would be no dependencies, but $\mathcal{M}_P$ would not be solvable in reasonable time. With equal intention one should be careful optimizing only scalability by analyzing every function by itself, which would lead to the maximal number of dependencies between the modules. One has to find a balance between these two properties. Current practical implementations for modularization have a tendency towards regarding every function by itself. Furthermore, while the sizes of modules can vary considerably, so can the complexity of the included functions. Finding heuristics for optimal module sizes considering both properties is part of future work.

4   Evaluation

For the evaluation, we have implemented a global analysis without any modularization. Additionally, we have implemented the abstraction of the call environment as described in Sect. 3.1 for every function and for modules of chosen size based on the call graph. The approaches will be compared in this section based on a real-world embedded software project of around 160 KLoC.

4.1   Implementation

All implementations are incorporated in the tool QPR-Verify, which is based on the bounded model checker LLBMC. There are several optimizations, parameters and features not relevant for the comparison to other approaches and are thus not described here. Further details can be found in [17].

Global Analysis. At first, the LLVM IR program is generated with the clang compiler. The global analysis then encodes the program starting at a given entry point. The entry point is normally set to the main function. Starting at the entry point, the whole program is encoded from the LLVM IR into an SMT formula containing both the program semantics and all inserted checks (Fig. 3). During encoding, loops are unrolled and functions inlined up to a bound b. Also checks (assertions) are added as special function calls into the bitcode. This formula is then given to an SMT solver. If the SMT solver finds a model, a possible program error has been detected. After finding the model, the specific check is deactivated and the altered formula is checked again. The check states are set to either safe, loopbound safe (safe up to loop bound), loopbound unsafe, unsafe or undecidable.

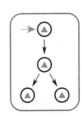

Fig. 3. Global analysis

Local Analysis. The local analysis implements the call context abstraction from Sect. 3.1. It starts a verification job for every function while abstracting input parameters and memory content at the beginning of the function. For every function f, the analysis sets f as the entry point and starts encoding of the program at f. All called function are thereby automatically included. The approach then activates only the checks in f, one by one. Every check is individually inserted into the program and checked. Additional to the states of the global analysis, the status locally unsafe can be taken by a check for which an error was found. To further optimize the analysis, we implemented a slicing algorithm. Starting at the individual check that is to be verified the algorithm collects statements influencing the check statement. The algorithm thus traverses the program backwards, up to the entry point. The encoding of the program is then optimized by only regarding collected statements.

Call Graph Analysis. The third implemented approach extends the local analysis to modules of size m based on a created call graph G_P. Nodes are functions and edges are call dependencies as described in Sect. 3.2. First, the approach removes "utility-functions" (functions that have a high amount of incoming edges from all parts of the graph). The filtered call graph G'_P has a tree-like structure starting at the **main** function. We decided to take advantage of this property by running our modularization algorithm in a bottom-up fashion from the leaves of the tree, and looking for subtrees that are smaller then a given bound $b_{G'}$. Furthermore, we chose not to enforce the tree-property by cutting edges but accepting the imperfections of the tree-approximation and considering them in our module creation by putting functions into more then one module if needed. If a leaf is called for example from two different functions f_1 and f_2 and f_1 and f_2 do not have a joint parent within bound $b_{G'}$, we have to verify the leaf starting from both functions. The adjustments of entry points and module size can still be improved using abstraction refinement techniques [1].

4.2   Evaluation Results

For the evaluation of global, local and call-graph analysis, we selected an open-source project from the embedded system domain, Connection Manager (ConnMan) [13]. This library handles internet connections within embedded systems. The tool is mainly developed by Intel Cooperation and further used by big automotive manufactures like BMW CarIT GmbH [4]. While, in general, bounded model checking is optimized for arithmetic operations, which are more common in systems like motor controls, the connection manager contains a high number of checks to be verified.

We base our evaluation on ConnMan version 1.36 with 471 files, approx. 160 KLoC, and 3,025 functions. In our experiments, we determined the number of checks that could be solved by the three implemented approaches. First, our tool builds and compiles the application while inserting **27,402 checks** for typical runtime errors, including 11,164 checks for overflows on implicit type casts and 2,405 checks for overflow on arithmetic operations. In a preprocessing phase, QPR-Verify handles simple checks that can be solved by constant propagation and bit-width reasoning without the use of an SMT solver. This analysis was able to prove safe 25,833 out of the given 27,402 checks. 13 checks were shown to be unsafe by the preprocessor, and **1,556 checks** remained open. These remaining checks are hard verification problems that we handled with our different modularization approaches. Table 2 shows the summarized results.

For the **global analysis** we chose 1 as a loop bound and gave a timeout of 1,200 s for all three approaches. The global approach was not able to transform the program into an SMT formula even for the loop bound of one (due to out-of-memory situations). (We tested the global analysis on a range of smaller programs up to 20 KLoC with success, but larger programs are often not feasible for a global analysis.) Thus the global analysis produces the same result as the preprocessor-only analysis.

Table 2. Results of three different solving approaches.

Results/approach	Global	Local	Call graph
Safe	0	108	212
Safe up to loop bound	0	43	43
Locally unsafe	0	1,351	1,247
Unsafe	0	0	0
Undecided	1,556	54	54

The **local analysis** was performed with a loop bound of 6 and was able to handle most of the open checks. Out of the 1,556 open problems 108 could be verified as safe. 43 checks are verified to be *loop bound safe* meaning that within the given loop bound of 6 there is no error. To label these checks as `safe`, one would have to increase the loop bound incrementally. Furthermore, 1,351 checks were moved to the category *locally unsafe*, meaning that the approach found an error while abstracting all input parameters. For some checks in the `main` function or other high level functions most of the program has to be encoded, and thus there are still 54 open checks that could not be classified. The local analysis creates good results, where a global approach was not able to verify a single property. The disadvantage lies in locally unsafe checks. Potential false positives have been generated due to our abstraction being quite coarse.

Finally, the **call graph analysis** tries to classify locally unsafe checks by extending the context of the functions containing a check. The modularization, as described in Sect. 4.1, is created based on the bitcode created by the LLVM compiler. We chose a bound $b_{G'} = 15$ for the creation of entry points. Our pursuing ambition is to set bounds up to hundreds of functions, but the transformation of the program into SMT formulas is still limited. A bound of 15 produced best results for our approach. The modularization regarded 2,961 functions after filtering. For these functions 1,103 entry points for modules were created including 2,074 functions and leaving 887 functions in a single-function module (i.e. local analysis is applied). The analysis was able to move 104 locally safe checks to the category of (globally) safe. Yet being a moderate improvement, one can see the advantage of the call graph modularization.

5   Conclusion and Future Work

We defined a denotational program semantics for LLVM as well as notions for modularization of LLVM programs. Based on these notions, we developed four fully automatic modularization approaches. The discussion of mandatory and success properties for a modularization in the context of software verification is a foundation for further future modularization approaches. We implemented a global analysis and compared it to a local analysis (abstracting away the call context of a function) and a call graph analysis (extending the local verification approach). We show, that for moderately-sized real-world software the global approach is not sufficient. The modularization approaches, in comparison, can deliver much more successful verification results.

To further improve automatic verification of large programs, future work includes implementation of the remaining two modularization approaches described above. The automatic creation of pre- and postconditions will likely reduce the amount of false positives. Additionally, we want to develop a customized alias analysis to argue about and refine data dependencies of programs.

References

1. Ball, T., Bounimova, E., Kumar, R., Levin, V.: SLAM2: static driver verification with under 4% false alarms. In: Proceedings of the 2010 Conference on Formal Methods in Computer-Aided Design, pp. 35–42. FMCAD Inc. (2010)
2. Balyo, T., Heule, M.J., Järvisalo, M. (eds.): Proceedings of SAT Competition 2017: Solver and Benchmark Descriptions. University of Helsinki (2017)
3. Beckert, B., Hähnle, R., Schmitt, P.H.: Verification of Object-Oriented Software: The KeY Approach. Springer, Heidelberg (2007). https://doi.org/10.1007/978-3-540-69061-0
4. BMW CarIT GmbH: Open Source ConnMan (2019). http://www.bmw-carit.de/open-source/connman.php. Accessed 10 June 2019
5. Clarke, E.M., Long, D.E., McMillan, K.L.: Compositional model checking. In: Fourth Annual Symposium on Logic in Computer Science, pp. 353–362 (1989)
6. Cobleigh, J.M., Giannakopoulou, D., PǍsǍreanu, C.S.: Learning assumptions for compositional verification. In: Garavel, H., Hatcliff, J. (eds.) TACAS 2003. LNCS, vol. 2619, pp. 331–346. Springer, Heidelberg (2003). https://doi.org/10.1007/3-540-36577-X_24
7. Cousot, P., Cousot, R.: Abstract interpretation: a unified lattice model for static analysis of programs by construction or approximation of fixpoints. In: Proceedings of the 4th Annual Symposium on Principles of Programming Languages, pp. 238–252 (1977)
8. Giannakopoulou, D., Pasareanu, C.S., Cobleigh, J.M.: Assume-guarantee verification of source code with design-level assumptions. In: Proceedings of 26th International Conference on Software Engineering, pp. 211–220. IEEE (2004)
9. Grumberg, O., Long, D.E.: Model checking and modular verification. In: Baeten, J.C.M., Groote, J.F. (eds.) CONCUR 1991. LNCS, vol. 527, pp. 250–265. Springer, Heidelberg (1991). https://doi.org/10.1007/3-540-54430-5_93
10. Hardekopf, B., Lin, C.: Flow-sensitive pointer analysis for millions of lines of code. In: Proceedings of the 9th Annual IEEE/ACM International Symposium on Code Generation and Optimization, pp. 289–298. IEEE Computer Society (2011)
11. Hawblitzel, C., et al.: Ironclad apps: end-to-end security via automated full-system verification. In: 11th Symposium on Operating Systems Design and Implementation, pp. 165–181 (2014)
12. Henzinger, T.A., Qadeer, S., Rajamani, S.K.: You assume, we guarantee: methodology and case studies. In: Hu, A.J., Vardi, M.Y. (eds.) CAV 1998. LNCS, vol. 1427, pp. 440–451. Springer, Heidelberg (1998). https://doi.org/10.1007/BFb0028765
13. Intel Corporation: Connection Manager (2019). https://git.kernel.org/pub/scm/network/connman/connman.git/tag/?h=1.36. Accessed 10 June 2019

14. Kaiser, J.O., Dang, H.H., Dreyer, D., Lahav, O., Vafeiadis, V.: Strong logic for weak memory: reasoning about release-acquire consistency in Iris. In: 31st European Conference on Object-Oriented Programming (2017)
15. Koopman, P.: A case study of Toyota unintended acceleration and software safety. Carnegie Mellon University Presentation, September 2014
16. Le Lann, G.: An analysis of the Ariane 5 flight 501 failure-a system engineering perspective. In: Proceedings of International Conference and Workshop on Engineering of Computer-Based Systems, pp. 339–346 (1997)
17. Merz, F., Falke, S., Sinz, C.: LLBMC: bounded model checking of C and C++ programs using a compiler IR. In: Joshi, R., Müller, P., Podelski, A. (eds.) VSTTE 2012. LNCS, vol. 7152, pp. 146–161. Springer, Heidelberg (2012). https://doi.org/10.1007/978-3-642-27705-4_12
18. Müller, P.: Modular Specification and Verification of Object-Oriented Programs. Springer, Heidelberg (2002). https://doi.org/10.1007/3-540-45651-1
19. Müller, P.: The binomial heap verification challenge in Viper. In: Müller, P., Schaefer, I. (eds.) Principled Software Development, pp. 203–219. Springer, Cham (2018). https://doi.org/10.1007/978-3-319-98047-8_13
20. Westland, J.C.: The cost of errors in software development: evidence from industry. J. Syst. Softw. **62**(1), 1–9 (2002)

PDNet: A Programming Language for Software-Defined Networks with VLAN

Shuangqing Xiang[1]($\boxtimes$), Marcello Bonsangue[2], and Huibiao Zhu[1]

[1] Shanghai Key Laboratory of Trustworthy Computing,
East China Normal University, Shanghai, China
xiangsqing@aliyun.com, hbzhu@sei.ecnu.edu.cn
[2] LIACS, Leiden University, Niels Bohrweg 1, 2333CA Leiden, The Netherlands
m.m.bonsangue@liacs.leidenuniv.nl

Abstract. Software-Defined Networking (SDN) is an emerging networking paradigm, which separates the network's control logic from the underlying routers and switches, providing the ability to program network, simplifying network management and creating an environment for network evolution. NetKAT is a domain-specific language for specifying and verifying packet-processing functions in software-defined networks (SDNs). This paper proposes a more powerful programming language, PDNet, extending NetKAT to specify the behaviors of SDNs that support virtual local area network (VLAN) tags. We present the operational semantics of PDNet in terms of automata and a syntactic derivatives. When comparing PDNet and NetKAT we show that PDNet is strictly more expressive than NetKAT. As expected, we also show that PDNet is as expressive as NetKAT when describing SDNs without VLAN.

Keywords: Software Defined Networks · VLAN · Pushdown systems · NetKAT

1 Introduction

Traditional network devices, such as switches, routers, firewalls, etc. are built by different vendors out of special purposes. Due to all kinds of custom hardware and interfaces, it is hard to configure traditional networks. Besides, the control plane (that decide how to handle network traffic) and the data plane (that forwards traffic) are bundled inside the networking devices, reducing flexibility and hindering innovation and evolution of the networking infrastructure [1]. The emergence of Software-Defined Networking (SDN) [2], a new network paradigm, has brought a foundational shift on this respect.

It is impossible to reason precisely about legacy network behaviors, which makes it hard to apply formal methods to verify network correctness. SDN offers the Internet community another chance to develop the right kind of architecture and abstractions. This has also led to a great resurgence in interest of applying formal methods to specification, verification, and synthesis of networking protocols and applications [3]. NetKAT [4] is a network programming language, which

© Springer Nature Switzerland AG 2019
Y. Ait-Ameur and S. Qin (Eds.): ICFEM 2019, LNCS 11852, pp. 203–218, 2019.
https://doi.org/10.1007/978-3-030-32409-4_13

is used for specifying and verifying the packet-processing behavior of software-defined networks (SDNs). The operational semantic of NetKAT has been presented in [5] in terms of deterministic NetKAT automata. Given a NetKAT expression, a corresponding deterministic NetKAT automaton can be built following the syntactic derivative. The language accepted by a NetKAT automaton is a regular language, which makes it possible to reason about the correctness of a NetKAT program using the equational theory presented in [4].

However, regular expressions are not enough to describe some network behaviors especially when it include the usage of virtual local area network (VLAN). A VLAN is a broadcast domain that is partitioned and isolated in a computer network at the data link layer (OSI layer 2) [6]. It is commonly used in all network virtualization technologies because of its dynamic character. VLAN tags are a useful mechanism for limiting the scope of broadcast traffic, enforcing security and privacy policies, simplifying access control, decentralizing network management, and enabling host mobility [7]. In a SDN, network administrators can configure and manage VLANs more flexibly and efficiently using the OpenFlow protocol [8], the de-facto standard communication protocol between a controller and a switch. The newest edition of the OpenFlow protocol supports adding, modifying and removing VLAN tags. A packet may have one or more VLAN tags stored in a stack so that only the outermost (newest) tag can be modify or delete.

In this paper we extend NetKAT with packets supporting a stack to store VLAN tags. We use three actions in PDNet ($push(v)$, $f_0 \leftarrow v$, and pop) to add, modify and remove a tag separately. The main contributions of our work are listed as below:

- Propose a new programming language, PDNet, to describe the behaviors of SDNs based on NetKAT. The ability to describe VLANs makes our language more expressive than NetKAT.
- Study the operational semantics of PDNet, presented in terms of PDNet automata. A PDNet automaton can be built from a PDNet expression following the syntactic derivatives.
- Prove that PDNet is as expressive as NetKAT when restricting the syntax to no VLAN stack manipulating actions.
- Show that PDNet is more expressive than NetKAT.

To help the proofs, we will give a novel definition of nondeterministic NetKAT automata and the corresponding syntactic derivatives.

2   Preliminaries

2.1   SDN and OpenFlow

As shown in Fig. 1, a SDN has three layers. A single-controller OpenFlow-based network has one controller, some switches and some hosts. When a switch receives a packet, it will search its flow table to find a matching rule for the packet. If the matching rule exists, then the switch will forward the packet out through the port specified by the rule. Otherwise, the switch will inform the controller of receiving an unmatched packet, and then the controller will insert a rule into the flow table of the switch to tell the switch how to deal with the packet.

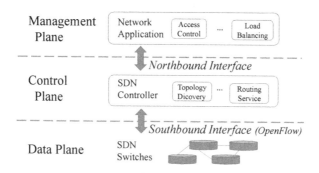

Fig. 1. SDN structure

2.2 VLAN

A VLAN allows to break one physical switch into smaller mini-switches, or extend a smaller virtual switch across multiple physical switches. In Fig. 2 we show an example of a network where there are two physical switches and three VLANs (VLAN 10, VLAN 20, and VLAN 30). Notice that VLAN 10 has been extended onto a second switch, which enables Host B and Host C to exist in the same VLAN, despite being connected to different physical switches. Assuming that host C is sending a packet to host B. The packet header C|B|(VLAN)|Type is a standard Layer 2 header. At first, the packet enters VLAN 10 through the access port on switch Y (Y:1), and a tag #10 is added into its header. Then the tagged packet is flooded to all the ports inside the red circle of switch Y except the port that received the packet. Port Y:2 is an access port that connects to

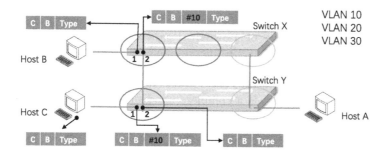

Fig. 2. An example of VLANs

switch X, the VLAN tag of every packet that leaves VLAN 10 through Y:2 will be removed. When the packet from host C to host B arrives at port X:2, the tag #10 is added into its header again.

Notice that, in nested VLANs, it is possible that a packet has more than one VLAN tag, and any action on VLAN tags only acts on the outermost (newest) tag. In the OpenFlow protocol, there are three actions that are related to VLAN.

- *Push_tag:* Push a new VLAN tag onto the packet. A newly pushed tag should always be inserted in the outermost valid location of the VLAN field.
- *Pop_tag:* Pop the outermost VLAN tag from the packet.
- *Set_tag:* Set the ID of the outermost VLAN tag.

2.3   Syntax of NetKAT

Forwarding a packet from node to node in a network can be seen as moving from state to state in an automaton. Therefore, it is natural to use regular expression to describe the forwarding behavior of a network. For example, the concatenation of a series of forwarding behaviors specifies a path. Moreover, Kleene algebra (KA) [9], a sound and complete equational theory for regular expressions, can be used to reason about properties of networks.

NetKAT is an instance of Kleene algebra with tests (KAT) [10]. KAT is a two-sorted algebra $(K, B, +, \cdot, *, \bar{\ }, 0, 1)$, where $B \subseteq K$:

$$(K, +, \cdot, *, 0, 1) \text{ is a Kleene algebra and}$$
$$(B, +, \cdot, \bar{\ }, 0, 1) \text{ is a Boolean algebra .}$$

A Kleene algebra consists of three operators and two constants: choice $(+)$, sequential composition operator $(\cdot)$, iteration $(*)$, fail (0) and skip (1). $(\cdot)$ is usually elided in expressions. B is the set of tests. When applied to tests, $(+)$ and $(\cdot)$ act as disjunction and conjunction respectively. $(\bar{\ })$ is the Boolean negation operator defined only on B. We let p, q, r, s, t range over arbitrary elements of K and a, b, c, d over tests in.

The syntax of NetKAT is shown in Table 1. A packet pk is a packet record that composes of k fields, including the header values and the location information. A sequence of packet forms a history, which records the states of a packet as it travels in the network. A policy specifies the behaviors of a switch. A predicate models the filtering process of a switch. Predicates may have true (1), false (0), test $(f = v)$, conjunctions, disjunction, and negation $(\neg a)$. An assignment $(f \leftarrow v)$ assigns value v to the field f. A test $(f = v)$ checks whether the field f is equal to v. (dup) records the current state of a packet into the history. α is a complete test, and π is a complete assignment. $f_1, \cdots, f_k$ are in some arbitrary but fixed order. α_π is the complete test corresponding to the complete assignment π, and π_α is the complete assignment corresponding to the complete test α. The operator precedence is: $(*) > (\cdot) > (+)$.

Table 1. Syntax and operational semantics of NetKAT

NetKAT Syntax

$$
\begin{aligned}
Fields \quad & f ::= f_1 \mid \ldots \mid f_k \\
Packets \quad & pk ::= \{f_1 = v_1, \ldots, f_k = v_k\} \\
Histories \quad & h ::= pk ::<> \mid pk :: h \\
Predicates \quad & b ::= 1 \mid 0 \mid f = n \mid b \cdot b \mid b + b \mid \neg b \\
Policies \quad & p ::= b \mid f \leftarrow n \mid dup \mid p^* \mid p + p \mid p \cdot p \\
Complete\ Test \quad & \alpha ::= f_1 = v_1 \cdot f_2 = v_2 \cdots f_k = v_k \\
Complete\ Assignment \quad & \pi ::= f_1 \leftarrow v_1 \cdot f_2 \leftarrow v_2 \cdots f_k \leftarrow v_k
\end{aligned}
$$

Deterministic NetKAT automata

$M_d = (S, \delta, \varepsilon, s_0)$	$Language : L_d \subseteq At \times At \times At^*$
$\delta : S \times At \times At \to S$	$Accept_d : S \times I \to 2 :$
$\varepsilon : S \times At \times At \to 2$	$Accept_d(s, \alpha\beta) = \varepsilon(s, \alpha, \beta)$
$s_0 \in S$	$Accept_d(s, \alpha\beta w) = Accept_d(\delta(t, \alpha, \beta), \beta w)$
	where $w \in At \times At^*$ $\alpha, \beta \in At$

Example 1. As shown in Fig. 3, Host H_0 sends packets to host H_1 via two switches: S_0 and S_1. A packet is composed of source address (src), destination address and two fields: switch (sw) and port (pt). The policy for switch S_0 is encoded as:

$$
p_0 \triangleq (sw = S_0 \cdot pt = P_1 \cdot dst = H_1 \cdot pt \leftarrow P_2)
$$

It specifies that for a packet whose current location is port P_1 of switch S_0, and its destination address is H_1, forward the packet out through port P_2.

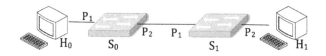

Fig. 3. Example network for NetKAT

2.4   Operational Semantics of NetKAT

The definition of deterministic NetKAT automata is illustrated in Table 1.

- S is a finite set of states;
- δ is a continuation map, which specifies transitions from one state to another state;

- ε is an observation map, which records information of each state;
- s_0 is a distinguished start state.

Every NetKAT expression (policy) p can be interpreted as a subset of $At \cdot \Pi \cdot (dup \cdot \Pi)^*$. Here At is the set of complete tests, and Π is the set of complete assignments. The language $G(p)$ of a NetKAT expression p is the set of strings accepted by the finite NetKAT automaton associated with p [5].

Observing the string $\alpha \pi_1 dup \pi_2$, we can think of it as $\alpha \beta_{\pi_1} \beta_{\pi_2}$, where α is the precondition and β_{π_1} denotes the postcondition after doing the assignment π_1. The placeholder dup is used to record the postcondition after the first assignment. We can write postconditions explicitly and omit assignments as well as duplications, and as a result, the language accepted by a deterministic NetKAT automaton is just a subset of $At \times At \times At^*$.

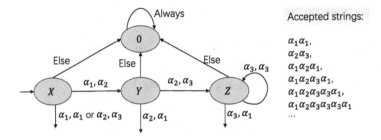

Fig. 4. An example of deterministic NetKAT automata

Example 2. Figure 4 shows a simple deterministic NetKAT automaton and the strings it accepts. There are four states $(X, Y, Z, 0)$. The three vertical arrows without subsequent states represent observation map, and the other arrows stand for continuation map. Assuming the packet consists of two fields, and each field has two possible values, then there are four possible complete tests $(\alpha_1, \alpha_2, \alpha_3, \alpha_4)$.

- $Accept_d(X, \alpha_1\alpha_1) = \varepsilon(X, \alpha_1, \alpha_1) = 1$, and thus the string $\alpha_1\alpha_1$ is accepted.
- $Accept_d(X, \alpha_1\alpha_2\alpha_1) = Accept_d(\delta(X, \alpha_1, \alpha_2), \alpha_2\alpha_1) = Accept_d(Y, \alpha_2\alpha_1) = \varepsilon(Y, \alpha_2, \alpha_1) = 1$, and hence the string $\alpha_1\alpha_2\alpha_1$ is accepted.

3 Nondeterministic NetKAT Automata

In order to prove the relation between NetKAT and PDNet in Sect. 5, next we propose a novel definition of nondeterministic NetKAT automata as well as a corresponding syntactic derivatives. An example of nondeterministic NetKAT automata presented in this section will help understand the semantics of PDNet.

3.1 Automata Definition

As shown in Table 2, a nondeterministic NetKAT automaton (M_n) is a 4-tuple (T, Δ, E, t_0) where

- T is a finite set of states;
- Δ is a continuation map;
- E is a observation map;
- t_0 is a distinguished start state.

Table 2. Nondeterministic NetKAT automata

Automata definition	
$M_n = (T, \Delta, E, t_0)$	$Accept_n : T \times I \to 2 :$
$\Delta : T \times At \to \mathcal{P}(T \times At)$	$Accept_n(t, \alpha\beta) = E(t, \alpha, \beta)$
$E : T \times At \times At \to 2$	$Accept_n(t, \alpha\beta v) = 1$
$Language : L_n \subseteq At \times At \times At^*$	where $v \in At \times At^*$ $\alpha, \beta \in At$
	$\Longleftrightarrow$
	$\exists(t', \beta) \in \Delta(t, \alpha) \cdot Accept_n(t', \beta v) = 1$

Syntactic derivatives	
$D_n : Exp \times At \to \mathcal{P}(Exp \times At)$	$E_n : Exp \times At \times At \to 2$
$D_n(b, \alpha) = \{\}$ $D_n(\pi, \alpha) = \{\}$	$E_n(b, \alpha, \beta) = [\alpha = \beta \leq b]$
$D_n(dup, \alpha) = \{(\alpha, \alpha)\}$	$E_n(\pi, \alpha, \beta) = [\pi = \pi_\beta]$
$D_n(e_1 + e_2, \alpha) = D_n(e_1, \alpha) \cup D_n(e_2, \alpha)$	$E_n(dup, \alpha, \beta) = 0$
$D_n(e_1 \cdot e_2, \alpha) =$	$E_n(e_1 + e_2, \alpha, \beta) = E_n(e_1, \alpha, \beta)$
$\{(e \cdot e_2, \beta) | (e, \beta) \in D_n(e_1, \alpha)\}$	$+ E_n(e_2, \alpha, \beta)$
$\cup \{(1 \cdot e', \xi) | \exists \eta \bullet E_n(e_1, \alpha, \eta) = 1$	$E_n(e_1 \cdot e_2, \alpha, \beta) = \sum_\eta (E_n(e_1, \alpha, \eta)$
$\wedge (e', \xi) \in D_n(e_2, \eta)\}$	$\cdot E_n(e_2, \eta, \beta))$
$D_n(e^*, \alpha) =$	$E_n(e^*, \alpha, \beta) = [\alpha = \beta]$
$\{(e_1 \cdot e^*, \beta) | (e_1, \beta) \in D_n(e, \alpha)\}$	$+ \sum_\eta (E_n(e, \alpha, \eta) \cdot E_n(e^*, \eta, \beta))$
$\cup \{(1 \cdot e_2, \xi) | \exists \eta \bullet E_n(e, \alpha, \eta) = 1$	
$\wedge (e_2, \xi) \in D_n(e^*, \eta))\}$	

3.2 Syntactic Derivatives

In the bottom of Table 2, we define the non deterministic automata generated by the syntactic derivatives of a NetKAT expression. Exp is a superset of reduced NetKAT expressions that include arbitrary tests b. Every NetKAT expression is provable equivalent to a reduced NetKAT expression, where each assignment is a complete assignment and each test is a complete test.

Example 3. An example is shown below to explain how to build a corresponding nondeterministic automaton from a reduced NetKAT expression. Let the packet have two fields (f_1, f_2), and each field has two possible values ($\{0, 1\}$). Thus the set of possible complete tests is $At = \{f_1 = 0 \cdot f_2 = 0, f_1 = 1 \cdot f_2 = 0, f_1 = 0 \cdot f_2 = 1, f_1 = 1 \cdot f_2 = 1\}$. Let the start expression be $\alpha_1 \pi_1 dup \pi_2$, where the complete test α_1 is $f_1 = 1 \cdot f_2 = 0$, the complete assignment π_1 denotes $f_1 \leftarrow 0 \cdot f_2 \leftarrow 0$, and π_2 is $f_1 \leftarrow 0 \cdot f_2 \leftarrow 1$. Note that α_π represents the complete test that is corresponding to π. When we use α without any subscript, it stands for any complete test that belongs to At.

The first step is to compute all the states. The computing process is given as below. The start expression $\alpha_1 \pi_1 dup \pi_2$ is the initial state, and its subsequent state is the expression $\alpha_{\pi_1} \pi_2$.

$$D_n(\alpha_1 \pi_1 dup \pi_2, \alpha) = \{(e \cdot \pi_1 dup \pi_2, \beta) | (e, \beta) \in D_n(\alpha_1, \alpha)\}$$
$$\cup \{(e', \xi) | \exists \eta \bullet E_n(\alpha_1, \alpha, \eta) = 1 \wedge (e', \xi) \in D_n(\pi_1 dup \pi_2, \eta)\}$$

For $D_n(\alpha_1, \alpha) = \{\}$, $E_n(\alpha_1, \alpha, \eta) = 1 \iff \alpha = \eta = \alpha_1$

Thus $D_n(\alpha_1 \pi_1 dup \pi_2, \alpha) = \{\} \cup D_n(\pi_1 dup \pi_2, \alpha_1)$

Then

$$D_n(\pi_1 dup \pi_2, \alpha_1) = \{(e \cdot dup \pi_2, \beta) | (e, \beta) \in D_n(\pi_1, \alpha_1)\}$$
$$\cup \{(e', \xi) | \exists \eta \bullet E_n(\pi_1, \alpha_1, \eta) = 1 \wedge (e', \xi) \in D_n(dup \pi_2, \eta)\}$$

For $D_n(\pi_1, \alpha_1) = \{\}$, $E_n(\pi_1, \alpha_1, \eta) = 1$ IFF $\alpha_{pi_1} = \eta$

Thus $D(\pi_1 dup \pi_2, \alpha_1) = \{\} \cup D_n(dup \pi_2, \alpha_{\pi_1})$

Then

$$D_n(dup \pi_2, \alpha_{\pi_1}) = \{(e \cdot \pi_2, \beta) | (e, \beta) \in D_n(dup, \alpha_{\pi_1})\}$$
$$\cup \{(e', \xi) | \exists \eta \bullet E_n(dup, \alpha_{\pi_1}, \eta) = 1 \wedge (e', \xi) \in D_n(\pi_2, \eta)\}$$

For $D_n(dup, \alpha_{\pi_1}) = \{(\alpha_{\pi_1}, \alpha_{\pi_1})\}$, $E_n(dup, \alpha, \eta) = 0$

Thus $D(dup \pi_2, \alpha_{\pi_1}) = \{(\alpha_{\pi_1} \pi_2, \alpha_{\pi_1})\} \cup \{\}$

Then

$$D_n(\alpha_{\pi_1} \pi_2, \alpha_{\pi_1}) = \{(e \cdot \pi_2, \beta) | (e, \beta) \in D_n(\alpha_{\pi_1}, \alpha_{\pi_1})\}$$
$$\cup \{(e', \xi) | \exists \eta \bullet E_n(\alpha_{\pi_1}, \alpha, \eta) = 1 \wedge (e', \xi) \in D_n(\pi_2, \eta)\}$$

For $D_n(\alpha_{\pi_1}, \alpha) = \{\}$, $E_n(\alpha_{\pi_1}, \alpha_{\pi_1}, \eta) = 1$ IFF $\alpha_{\pi_1} = \eta = \alpha_{\pi_1}$

Thus $D_n(\alpha_{\pi_1} \pi_2, \alpha) = \{\} \cup D_n(\pi_2, \alpha_{\pi_1}) = \{\}$

The second step is to check whether a state can accept the string that is associated with the state. $E_n(dup, \alpha, \beta) = 0$, and therefore the computation result for any string that combines with dup using the composition operator is 0. Thus, $E_n(\alpha_1 \pi_1 dup \pi_2, \alpha, \beta) = 0$, and it means that the start state does not accept any string. The computation for the second state is as follows:

$$E_n(\alpha_{\pi_1} \pi_2, \alpha, \beta) = \sum_\eta (E_n(\alpha_{\pi_1}, \alpha, \eta) \cdot E_n(\pi_2, \eta, \beta)) = 1 \; IFF \; \beta = \alpha_{\pi_2}$$

Finally, according to the computations above, we illustrate the nondeterministic automata for the expression $\alpha_1 \pi_1 \, dup \, \pi_2$ in Fig. 5. We only draw those arrows that lead to accepted strings. The two complete tests on the transition arrow can be thought of the precondition and the postcondition after the assignment π_1. The postcondition of the first state should be passed to the subsequent state and that is, α_{π_1} is passed to the second state as its precondition.

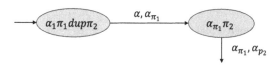

Fig. 5. The nondeterministic NetKAT automaton for $\alpha_1 \pi_1 \, dup \, \pi_2$

4   PDNet

4.1   PDNet Syntax

When the network to be programmed is simple, regular expressions are able to specify VLAN fields as long as the programmer remembers the indexes and orders of all the operations on VLAN tags. However, when the network topology is more complex, or there are some changes that need be made (switch functionalities or network structures that involve operations of VLAN tags) in the network, it is tedious to modify all the related policies, since the index of the field that denotes the outermost VLAN tag always needs to be counted carefully.

Instead of using regular expressions, we use a more intuitive and flexible structure to model VLAN tags, and that is stack. As shown in the top of Table 2, we add a field named f_0 to store VLAN tags for each packet. Fields f_1 to f_k are mapping to integers, while field f_0 is mapping to a stack. When a packet traverses VLANs, it at least has one VLAN tag, and therefore, the stack has at least one element. $f_0 = v$ denotes checking the top (outermost) tag of the stack, and $f_0 \leftarrow v$ stands for assigning v to the top tag. We also have $push(v)$ and pop that are corresponding to adding and removing of a VLAN tag respectively. Note that a complete test or a complete assignment excludes the VLAN field.

4.2   Operational Semantics of PDNet

Just like NetKAT expressions, each PDNet expression is equivalent to a reduced PDNet expression in which all assignments are complete assignments, and all tests are complete tests. Because there is a stack in each packet, the intuitive thought of developing the operational semantics of PDNet is to use pushdown automata. To take a step further, in order to design model checking algorithms for PDNet, we adopt pushdown system [11] to present the operational semantics. Formally, a pushdown system $\mathcal{P} = (R, \Gamma, \Phi, c_0)$ is a transition system with 4-tuple where:

Table 3. Syntax and semantics of PDNet

Syntax of PDNet

$$Fields\ f ::= f_0\,|\,\ldots\,|f_k \qquad Stacks\ \ \vec{vl} ::= v\,|\,v \cdot \vec{vl}$$
$$Packets\ pkt ::= \{f_0 = \vec{vl}, f_1 = v_1, \ldots, f_k = v_k\}$$
$$Predicates\ b ::= 1\,|\,0\,|\,f = v\,|\,b \cdot b\,|\,b + b\,|\,\neg b$$
$$Policies\ p ::= b\,|\,f \leftarrow v\,|\,dup\,|\,push(v)\,|\,pop\,|\,p + p\,|\,p \cdot p\,|\,p^*$$
$$Complete\,Test\ \alpha ::= f_1 = v_1 \cdot f_2 = v_2 \cdots f_k = v_k$$
$$Complete\,Assignment\ \pi ::= f_1 \leftarrow v_1 \cdot f_2 \leftarrow v_2 \cdots f_k \leftarrow v_k$$

PDNet automata

$M_p = (R \cup \{*\}, \Gamma, \phi, c_0)$

$\phi : R \times At \times \Gamma \longrightarrow \mathcal{P}((R \cup \{*\}) \times At \times (\{\epsilon\} \cup \Gamma \cup \Gamma \times \Gamma))$

Configuration:

$r \in R \quad o \in R \cup \{*\} \quad \alpha, \beta \in At \quad \gamma \in \Gamma \quad \xi \in \Gamma^* \quad \omega \in \{\epsilon\} \cup \Gamma \cup \Gamma \times \Gamma$

$< r, \alpha, \gamma\xi > \hookrightarrow < o, \beta, \omega\xi > \quad If\ (o, \beta, \omega) \in \phi(r, \alpha, \gamma)$

Language: $L_p \subseteq At \times At \times At^*$

$Accept_p : S \times I \longrightarrow 2 \ Where\ I = At \times At \times At^* :$

$Accept_p(< *, u, \Lambda) = 1$

$Accept_p(< r, u >, \alpha\beta x) = Accept_p(< o, v >, \beta x) \quad If\ < r, \alpha, u > \hookrightarrow < o, \beta, v >$

$Where\ \alpha, \beta \in At,\ x \in At \times At^*,\ u, v \in \Gamma \times \Gamma^*$

PDNet automata from syntactic derivatives

$\Phi(b, \alpha, \gamma) = \{(*, \alpha, \gamma)\,|\,If\ (f_0 = \gamma) \cdot \alpha \le b\}$

$\Phi(\pi, \alpha, \gamma) = \{(*, \beta_\pi, \gamma)\}$

$\Phi(f_0 \leftarrow v, \alpha, \gamma) = \{*, \alpha, \gamma[v]\}$

$\Phi(dup, \alpha, \gamma) = \{(\alpha, \alpha, \gamma)\}$

$\Phi(push(v), \alpha, \gamma) = \{(*, \alpha, v \cdot \gamma)\}$

$\Phi(pop, \alpha, \gamma) = \{(*, \alpha, \epsilon)\}$

$\Phi(e_1 + e_2, \alpha, \gamma) = \Phi(e_1, \alpha, \gamma) \cup \Phi(e_2, \alpha, \gamma)$

$\Phi(e_1 e_2, \alpha, \gamma) = \{(e \cdot e_2, \beta, \xi)\,|\,(e, \beta, \xi) \in \Phi(e_1, \alpha, \gamma)\}$

$\qquad \cup \{(e_2, \beta, \epsilon)\,|\,(*, \beta, \epsilon) \in \Phi(e_1, \alpha, \gamma)\}$

$\qquad \cup \{(e_2, \beta, \gamma_1\gamma_2)\,|\,(*, \beta, \gamma_1\gamma_2) \in \Phi(e_1, \alpha, \gamma)\}$

$\qquad \cup \{(e, \beta, \gamma_2)\,|\,(*, \beta_1, \gamma_1) \in \delta(e_1, \alpha, \gamma) \wedge (e, \beta, \gamma_2) \in \Phi(e_2, \beta_1, \gamma_1)\}$

$\qquad \cup \{(*, \beta, \gamma_2)\,|\,(*, \beta_1, \gamma_1) \in \delta(e_1, \alpha, \gamma) \wedge (*, \beta, \gamma_2) \in \Phi(e_2, \beta_1, \gamma_1)\}$

$\Phi(e^*, \alpha, \gamma) = \{(e' \cdot e^*, \beta, \xi)\,|\,(e', \beta, \xi) \in \Phi(e, \alpha, \gamma)\}$

$\qquad \cup \{(e^*, \beta, \epsilon)\,|\,(*, \beta, \epsilon) \in \Phi(e, \alpha, \gamma)\}$

$\qquad \cup \{(e^*, \beta, \gamma_1\gamma_2)\,|\,(*, \beta, \gamma_1\gamma_2) \in \Phi(e, \alpha, \gamma)\}$

$\qquad \cup \{(e, \beta, \gamma_2)\,|\,(*, \beta_1, \gamma_1) \in \delta(e, \alpha, \gamma) \wedge (e, \beta, \gamma_2) \in \Phi(e^*, \beta_1, \gamma_1)\}$

$\qquad \cup \{(*, \beta, \gamma_2)\,|\,(*, \beta_1, \gamma_1) \in \delta(e, \alpha, \gamma) \wedge (*, \beta, \gamma_2) \in \Phi(e^*, \beta_1, \gamma_1)\}$

- R is a finite set of states (control locations);
- Γ is a finite stack alphabet;
- Φ is a finite subset of $(R \times \Gamma) \times (R \times \Gamma^*)$, if $((r, \gamma), (r', \omega))$ in Φ, we can also write it as $<r, \gamma> \hookrightarrow <r', \xi>$, where $\xi \in \Gamma^*$.
- c_0 is the initial configuration with the form of $<r, \xi>$, where $r \in R$ and $\xi \in \Gamma^*$.

As shown in the middle of Table 3, a PDNet automaton is a nondeterministic pushdown system M_p. R is the set of non-terminated states, while $\{*\}$ denotes the termination state. Besides the stack in the input data, we also need to consider the precondition and postcondition of an expression. Therefore a configuration is composed of three elements: state, precondition (or postcondition), and stack symbols, which is slightly different from the standard pushdown system. $\gamma \xi$ denotes the whole stack, and γ stands for the top element of the stack. In a PDNet program, there are four actions that involve actions on stack:

- $f_0 = v$: the stack is unchanged, and $\omega \in \Gamma$;
- $f_0 \leftarrow v$: the top element of the stack is modified, and $\omega \in \Gamma$;
- $push(v)$: a new element is added onto the top of the stack, and $\omega \in \Gamma \times \Gamma$;
- pop: the top element of the stack is removed, and $\omega \in \{\epsilon\}$.

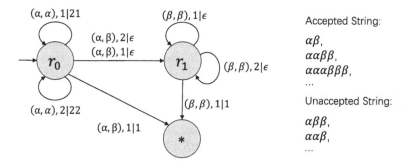

Fig. 6. An example of PDNet automata

Example 4. Figure 6 presents a simple PDNet automaton with three states. The set of possible complete tests is $\{\alpha, \beta\}$, and $\Gamma = \{1, 2\}$. The two transitions from r_0 to r_0 denote $push(1)$ and $push(2)$ respectively. The transitions from r_0 to r_1 stand for pop. The strings accepted by the automaton have the form of $\alpha^n \beta^n$.

4.3   Syntactic Derivatives

As shown in Table 3, we also give a syntactic derivative for PDNet, which is an instance of PDNet automata. The syntactic derivative is defined as:

$$\Phi : Exp_p \times At \times \Gamma \longrightarrow \mathcal{P}((Exp_p \cup \{*\}) \times At \times (\{\epsilon\} \cup \Gamma \cup \Gamma \times \Gamma))$$

Where Exp_p is the set of all the strings with the syntax:

$$e ::= b \mid \pi \mid dup \mid f_0 \leftarrow v \mid push(v) \mid pop \mid e + e \mid e \cdot e \mid e^*$$

b is an arbitrary test that is defined in the top of Table 1, while π is a complete assignment.

Since Exp and Exp_p are similar, most of the derivation rules are similar to the rules of the syntactic derivative of nondeterministic NetKAT automata. To make the derivation rules simpler, we combine D_n and E_n together to get Φ. Besides, we delete all the branches that lead to 0. The conversion formula from the syntactic derivative of nondeterministic NetKAT automata to the syntactic derivative of PDNet automata is:

$$\Phi(e, \alpha, \gamma) = \{(e_1, \beta, \gamma) | (e_1, \beta) \in D_n(e, \alpha)\} \cup \{(*, \beta, \gamma) | E_n(e, \alpha, \beta) = 1\}$$

Where e does not contain any element of $\{push(v), f_0 \leftarrow v, pop, f_0 = v\}$.

5   Comparing NetKAT and PDNet

After introducing the syntax and operational semantics of PDNet, we compare NetKAT and PDNet in this section, and it concerns two parts. One is that PDNet can describe some network behaviors that NetKAT cannot, and another one is that PDNet without actions on VLAN tags can specify the same network behaviors as NetKAT.

Theorem 1 (Expressiveness).   *There are languages accepted by PDNet automata that cannot be accepted by any NetKAT automata.*

Proof sketch. As mentioned before, the strings accepted by PDNet automata may have the form of $\alpha^n \beta^n$. For example, the PDNet expression $e \triangleq f_0 = 1 \cdot f_1 = 0 \cdot push(2)^* \cdot f_1 = 1 \cdot pop^* \cdot f_0 = 1$ denotes the behavior of letting a packet enter $k(k \geq 0)$ nested VLANs and then leave the k VLANs in the reverse order. The stack alphabet is $\{1, 2\}$ and the complete tests are $\{f_1 = 0, f_1 = 1\}$. The corresponding PDNet automaton is shown in Fig. 6, where r_0 corresponds to p, while r_1 corresponds to the subexpression pop^*; $f_0 = 1$. In fact the PDNet automaton for the expression e, although finite, generates an infinite number of configurations, and they are all needed to define the language accepted.

However, it can be proved that a NetKAT automaton cannot recognize this language using standard language theoretical techniques such as distinguishability classes or the pumping lemma [12].   □

Then, we prove the second part: PDNet is as expressive as NetKAT when specifying networks without VLANs. The proof consists of three steps:

1. Deterministic NetKAT automata and nondeterministic NetKAT automata are language equivalent.
2. The syntactic derivative of deterministic NetKAT automata and the syntactic derivative of nondeterministic NetKAT automata are language equivalent.
3. The syntactic derivative of nondeterministic NetKAT and the syntactic derivative of PDNet automata are isomorphic for all PDNet expressions that do not contain $push(v)$, $f_0 \leftarrow v$, pop, or $f_0 = v$.

Lemma 1 *(step 1). Given a nondeterministic NetKAT automaton (T, Δ, E, t_0), we define a deterministic NetKAT automaton $(\mathcal{P}(T), \delta, \varepsilon, s_0)$:*

- $\delta(X, \alpha, \beta) = \{(t \in T | \exists x \in X \cdot (t, \beta) \in \Delta(x, \alpha)\}$
- $\varepsilon(X, \alpha, \beta) = 1 \iff \exists x \in X \cdot E(x, \alpha, \beta) = 1$
- $s_0 = \{t_0\}$, where $X \in \mathcal{P}(T)$.

Then $\forall X \in \mathcal{P}(T)$, $Accept_d(X, \alpha\beta\mathsf{w}) = 1 \iff \exists x \in X \cdot Accept_n(x, \alpha\beta\mathsf{w}) = 1$.

Proof. $\mathsf{w} = \Lambda$:

$Accept_d(X, \alpha\beta) = \varepsilon(X, \alpha\beta) = 1 \iff$
$\exists x \in X \cdot E(x, \alpha, \beta) = Accept_n(x, \alpha\beta) = 1$
$\mathsf{w} = \sigma \cdot \mathsf{w}'$, where $\sigma \in At$, $\mathsf{w}' \in At^*$
$Accept_d(X, \alpha\beta\sigma\mathsf{w}') = Accept_d(\delta(X, \alpha\beta), \beta\sigma\mathsf{w}') = 1 \iff$
$\exists t \in \delta(X, \alpha\beta) \cdot Accept_n(t, \beta\sigma\mathsf{w}') = 1 \iff$
$\exists x \in X \cdot \exists(t, \beta) \in \Delta(x, \alpha) \cdot Accept_n(t, \beta\sigma\mathsf{w}') = 1 \iff$
$\exists x \in X \cdot Accept_n(x, \alpha\beta\sigma\mathsf{w}') = 1$ □

Lemma 2 *(step 1). Given a deterministic NetKAT automaton $(S, \delta, \varepsilon, s_0)$, we define a nondeterministic NetKAT automaton (S, Δ, E, s_0):*

- $\Delta(s, \alpha) = \{(s', \beta) | \delta(x, \alpha, \beta) = s'\}$, where $s \in S$
- $E(s, \alpha, \beta) = 1$ IFF $\varepsilon(s, \alpha, \beta) = 1$, where $s \in S$
- Then $\forall s \in S$, $Accept_n(s, \alpha\beta\mathsf{w}) = 1 \iff Accept_d(s, \alpha\beta\mathsf{w}) = 1$

Proof. $\mathsf{w} = \Lambda$:
$Accept_n(s, \alpha\beta) = E(s, \alpha, \beta) = 1 \iff \varepsilon(s, \alpha, \beta) = Accept_d(s, \alpha\beta) = 1$
$\mathsf{w} = \sigma \cdot \mathsf{w}'$, where $\sigma \in At$, $\mathsf{w}' \in At^*$
$Accept_n(s, \alpha\beta\sigma\mathsf{w}') = 1 \iff$
$\exists(t, \beta) \in \Delta(s, \alpha) \cdot Accept_n(t, \beta\sigma\mathsf{w}') = 1 \iff$
$\exists(t, \beta) \in \{(s', \eta) | \delta(s, \alpha, \eta) = s'\} \cdot Accept_n(t, \beta\sigma u) = 1 \iff$
$\exists t = \delta(s, \alpha, \beta) \textbf{.} Accept_n(t, \beta\sigma u) = 1 \iff$
$\exists t = \delta(s, \alpha, \beta) \textbf{.} Accept_d(t, \beta\sigma u) = 1 \iff$ (hypothesis)
$Accept_d(\delta(s, \alpha, \beta), \beta\sigma u) = Accept_d(s, \alpha\beta\sigma u) = 1$ □

Similar to the syntactic derivative of nondeterministic NetKAT automata shown in Table 2, the syntactic derivative of deterministic NetKAT automata is composed of a continuous map D_d and a observation map E_d.

Lemma 3 *(step 2). The automaton (Exp, D_d, E_d, e_0) and the automaton (Exp, D_n, E_n, e_0) are language equivalent.*

Proof. By induction of the length of the string.

w = Λ:

- $e = b$:
  $Accept_d(b, \alpha\beta) = E_d(b, \alpha, \beta) = [\alpha = \beta \leq b] = E_n(b, \alpha, \beta) = Accetp_n(b, \alpha\beta)$
- $e = \pi$:
- $Accept_d(\pi, \alpha\beta) = E_d(b, \alpha, \beta) = [\pi = \pi_\beta] = E_n(\pi, \alpha, \beta) = Accetp_n(\pi, \alpha\beta)$
- $e = dup,\ e_1 + e_1,\ e_1e_2,\ or\ e_1^*$: $\cdots$

When $e = dup$, $e_1 + e_1$, e_1e_2, $or\ e_1^*$, the proofs are similar, and we do not list them here.

w = $\sigma \cdot$ w′, where $\sigma \in At$, w′ $\in At^*$:

- $e = b$:
  $Accept_d(b, \alpha\sigma u) = Accept_d(D_d(b, \alpha, \beta), \beta\sigma u) = Accept_d(0, \beta\sigma u) = 0$
  $Accept_n(b, \alpha\sigma u) = 1 \iff \exists(e', \beta) \in D_n(b, \alpha) \cdot Accept_n(e', \beta\sigma u)$
  Since $D_n(b, \alpha) = \{\}$, $Accept_n(b, \alpha\sigma u) = 0$
- $e = \pi$:
  $Accept_d(\pi, \alpha\beta\sigma w') = Accept_d(D_d(\pi, \alpha\beta), \beta\sigma w') = Accept_d(0, \beta\sigma w') = 0$
  $Accept_n(\pi, \alpha\beta\sigma w') = 1 \iff \exists(e', \beta) \in D_n(\pi, \alpha) \cdot Accept_n(e', \beta\sigma w') = 1$
  Since $D_n(\pi, \alpha) = \{\}$, $Accept_n(\pi, \alpha\beta\sigma w') = 0 = Accept_d(\pi, \alpha\beta\sigma w')$
- $e = dup,\ e_1 + e_1,\ e_1e_2,\ or\ e_1^*$: $\cdots$

The same like before, we omit the proofs for the situations where $e = dup$, $e_1 + e_1$, e_1e_2, $or\ e_1^*$. □

Lemma 4 *(step 3). Given a PDNet automaton (Exp, Γ, Φ, e) and a nondeterministic NetKAT automaton (Exp, D_n, E_n, e), we define:*

$\varphi(D_n, E_n)(e, \alpha) = \{(e', \beta)|(e', \beta) \in D_n(e, \alpha) \wedge e \neq 0\} \cup \{(*, \beta)|E_n(e, \alpha, \beta) = 1\}$
$\psi_{D_n}(\Phi)(e, \alpha) = \{(e', \beta)|(e', \beta) \in \Phi(e, \alpha)\}$
$\psi_{E_n}(\Phi)(e, \alpha, \beta) = 1 \iff (*, \beta) \in \Phi(e, \alpha)$.

Then φ is an isomorphism for all the PDNet expressions (e) that do not contain $push(v)$, $f_0 \leftarrow v$, pop, or $f_0 = v$.

Proof.

$$\varphi(\psi_{D_n}(\Phi), \psi_{E_n}(\Phi))(e, \alpha) = \{(e', \beta)|(e', \beta) \in \psi_{D_n}(\Phi)(e, \alpha) \wedge e \neq 0\}$$
$$\cup \{(*, \beta)|E_n(e, \alpha, \beta) = 1\}$$
$$= \{(e', \beta)|(e', \beta) \in \Phi(e, \alpha) \wedge e \neq 0\}$$
$$\cup \{(*, \beta)|(*, \beta) \in \Phi(e, \alpha)\}$$
$$= \Phi(e, \alpha), \text{ where } e \neq 0$$

$$\psi_{D_n}(\varphi(D_n, E_n))(e, \alpha) = \{(e', \beta)|(e', \beta) \in \varphi(D_n, E_n)(e, \alpha)\}$$
$$= \{(e', \beta)|(e', \beta) \in \{(e'', \eta)|(e'', \eta) \in D_n(e, \alpha) \wedge e \neq 0\}$$
$$\cup \{(*, \eta)|E_n(e, \alpha, \beta) = 1\}\}$$
$$= \{(e'', \eta)|(e'', \eta) \in D_n(e, \alpha) \wedge e \neq 0\}$$
$$= D_n(e, \alpha), \text{ where } e \neq 0$$

$$\psi_{E_n}(\varphi(D_n, E_n))(e, \alpha, \beta) = 1 \iff (*, \beta) \in \varphi(D_n, E_n)(e, \alpha)$$
$$\iff (*, \beta) \in \{(e', \eta) | (e', \eta) \in D_n(e, \alpha) \wedge e \neq 0\}$$
$$\cup \{(*, \eta) | E_n(e, \alpha, \beta) = 1\}$$
$$\iff E_n(e, \alpha, \beta) = 1$$

$\square$

From Lemmas 1–4, we can conclude Theorem 2.

Theorem 2 (Compatibility). *Automata of NetKAT and PDNet without* $push(v)$, $f_0 \leftarrow v$, *pop, or* $f_0 = v$ *recognize the same class of languages.*

6   Conclusion and Future Work

This paper develops a new programming language (PDNet) based on NetKAT to specify the behaviors of software-defined networks. The novel aspect of the language proposed is that PDNet is able to describe the behaviors of adding, removing and modifying VLAN tags. We use a stack in each packet to store VLAN tags and three new actions to handle them. We also give an operational semantics of PDNet based on pushdown system. Each PDNet expression can be transformed into a corresponding PDNet automaton following the rules of the syntactic derivatives.

PDNet automata are not a standard pushdown automata, as the stack is in the input data and not part of the automaton itself. This explains why there is no full recursion in PDNet expressions, but only tail recursion via Kleene star.

The deterministic NetKAT automata have been proposed in [5]. We give here a novel definition of nondeterministic NetKAT automata as well as the syntactic derivative. Finally, we compare PDNet and NetKAT. First, it is possible to construct expressions like $p^n q^n$ in PDNet, which makes the language of a PDNet automaton a context-free language. However, a NetKAT automaton cannot recognize such language. Therefore, PDNet is more expressive than NetKAT. Second, it is proved that PDNet without $push(v)$, pop, $f_0 \leftarrow v$ or $f_0 = v$ is as expressive as NetKAT.

Other work on NetKAT are mainly concern with probabilistic extension, fast compiler or coalgebraic decision procedure [5,13,14]. We do not expect problems with a probabilistic or weighted extension of PDNet, because these already have been well studied in the context of pushdown systems [15,16]. In the future, we will develop a modeling checking algorithm for PDNet, and then we may check some interesting properties in software-defined networks with VLANs.

Acknowledgement. This work was partly supported by National Natural Science Foundation of China (Grant No. 61872145), National Key Research and Development Program of China (Grant No. 2018YFB2101300), Shanghai Collaborative Innovation Center of Trustworthy Software for Internet of Things (Grant No. ZF1213) and the Fundamental Research Funds for the Central Universities of China.

References

1. Kreutz, D., Ramos, F.M.V., Veríssimo, P.E., Rothenberg, C.E., Azodolmolky, S., Uhlig, S.: Software-defined networking: a comprehensive survey. Proc. IEEE **103**(1), 14–76 (2015)
2. Xia, W., Wen, Y., Foh, C.H., Niyato, D., Xie, H.: A survey on software-defined networking. IEEE Commun. Surv. Tutor. **17**(1), 27–51 (2015)
3. Qadir, J., Hasan, O.: Applying formal methods to networking: theory, techniques, and applications. IEEE Commun. Surv. Tutor. **17**(1), 256–291 (2015)
4. Anderson, C.J., et al.: NetKAT: semantic foundations for networks. In: The 41st Annual ACM SIGPLAN-SIGACT Symposium on Principles of Programming Languages, POPL 2014, San Diego, CA, USA, 20–21 January 2014, pp. 113–126 (2014)
5. Foster, N., Kozen, D., Milano, M., Silva, A., Thompson, L.: A coalgebraic decision procedure for NetKAT. In: Proceedings of the 42nd Annual ACM SIGPLAN-SIGACT Symposium on Principles of Programming Languages, POPL 2015, Mumbai, India, 15–17 January 2015, pp. 343–355 (2015)
6. IEEE standard for local and metropolitan area networks–bridges and bridged networks. IEEE 802.1Q-2018 (2018)
7. Minlan, Y., Rexford, J., Sun, X., Rao, S.G., Feamster, N.: A survey of virtual LAN usage in campus networks. IEEE Commun. Mag. **49**(7), 98–103 (2011)
8. McKeown, N., et al.: OpenFlow: enabling innovation in campus networks. Comput. Commun. Rev. **38**(2), 69–74 (2008)
9. Kozen, D.: A completeness theorem for kleene algebras and the algebra of regular events. Inf. Comput. **110**(2), 366–390 (1994)
10. Kozen, D.: Kleene algebra with tests. ACM Trans. Program. Lang. Syst. **19**(3), 427–443 (1997)
11. Schwoon, S.: Model checking pushdown systems. Ph.D. thesis, Technical University Munich, Germany (2002)
12. Martin, J.C.: Introduction to languages and the theory of computation (1997)
13. Foster, N., Kozen, D., Mamouras, K., Reitblatt, M., Silva, A.: Probabilistic NetKAT. In: Proceedings of Programming Languages and Systems - 25th European Symposium on Programming, ESOP 2016, Held as Part of the European Joint Conferences on Theory and Practice of Software, ETAPS 2016, Eindhoven, The Netherlands, 2–8 April 2016, pp. 282–309 (2016)
14. Smolka, S., Eliopoulos, S.A., Foster, N., Guha, A.: A fast compiler for NetKAT. In: Proceedings of the 20th ACM SIGPLAN International Conference on Functional Programming, ICFP 2015. ACM New York (2015)
15. Brázdil, T., Esparza, J., Kiefer, S., Kucera, A.: Analyzing probabilistic pushdown automata. Formal Methods Syst. Des. **43**(2), 124–163 (2013)
16. Minamide, Y.: Weighted pushdown systems with indexed weight domains. Log. Methods Comput. Sci. **12**(2), 1–27 (2016)

Consistency Enforcement for Static First-Order Invariants in Sequential Abstract State Machines

Klaus-Dieter Schewe[(✉)]

Zhejiang University, UIUC Institute, Haining, China
kdschewe@acm.org

Abstract. Given a program specification P and a first-order static invariant I the problem of consistency enforcement is to determine a modified program specification P_I that is consistent with respect to I, i.e. whenever I holds in a state S it also holds in the successor states determined by P_I, and at the same time only minimally deviates from P. We formalise this problem by the notion of the *greatest consistent specialisation* (GCS) adapting and generalising this 20 year old concept to sequential Abstract State Machines (ASMs) with emphasis on bounded parallelism. In a state satisfying I such that P is repairable the notion of consistent specialisation will require an enlargement of the update set, which defines a partial order with respect to which a GCS is defined. We show that GCSs are compositional in two respects: (1) the GCS of an ASM with a complex rule can be obtained from the GCSs of the involved assignments, and (2) the GCS with respect to a set of invariants can be built using the GCSs for the individual invariants in the set.

Keywords: Consistency enforcement · Static invariant · Consistent specialisation · Abstract State Machine · Compositionality

1 Introduction

State-based formal methods for the development of software systems place emphasis on correctness proofs, most of which are concerned with *consistency* and *refinement*. For the former ones we consider static invariants I that are to hold in every state S of a program specification P. Such invariants are expressed as logical formulae, most importantly using first-order logic (though not restricted to this), and consistency verification splits the problem into showing that consistency holds for the initial state(s) and is preserved by state transitions defined by P, i.e. whenever I holds in a state S it also holds in the successor state(s) determined by P. If such a proof fails, P has to be modified, but there is very little methodological support for this.

A remedy to this lack of methodology is provided by *consistency enforcement*, which has already been studied in the 1990s, in particular in the field of databases [13]. The emphasis was mainly on the use of rule triggering systems,

© Springer Nature Switzerland AG 2019
Y. Ait-Ameur and S. Qin (Eds.): ICFEM 2019, LNCS 11852, pp. 219–235, 2019.
https://doi.org/10.1007/978-3-030-32409-4_14

but in view of many problems associated with the active database approach (see [14]) the interest has somehow died out. Unfortunately, this also stopped further investigation of alternative approaches in rigorous state-based methods such as *greatest consistent specialisations* (GCSs, see [15]), which were grounded in Dijkstra's guarded commands with predicate transformer semantics [5] in an extended form [12] (also used at that time in the upcoming B method [1]).

In a nutshell, the problem of consistency enforcement is to determine a modified program specification P_I that is consistent with respect to I, i.e. whenever I holds in a state S it also holds in the successor states determined by P_I, and at the same time only minimally deviates from P, where "minimal deviation" is formalised by a specialisation order, i.e. P_I is maximal with respect to this order among all consistent specialisations of P with respect to I. In the theory of GCSs it could be shown that compositionally with respect to sets of invariants holds, i.e. a GCS for the conjunction of invariants in a set can be essentially built by taking the GCSs with respect to the individual invariants in arbitrary order. It could further be shown that compositionality with respect to the composition of P can also be achieved.

Nonetheless, the research remained uncompleted and still not fully satisfactory. The notion of state space was adopted from B, and thus refers to a finite set of state variables. When these are bound to bulk data such as sets or relations, the notion of specialisation becomes too restricted as already observed in [11]. Furthermore, the compositional GCS construction does not take parallelism into account, not even bounded parallelism, and the handling of GCSs for assignments has not been addressed.

In this paper, we pick up the thread from the 20 year old research and investigate consistency enforcement in the context of Abstract State Machines (ASMs, [3]). In doing so we emphasise Tarski structures as states with much more fine-grained locations, as well as non-determinism and parallelism, but we still restrict our investigation to bounded parallelism as in sequential ASMs [10]. We also restrict static invariants to formulae in first-order logic. As predicate transformers are not suited to capture parallelism, we redefine the notion of GCS—this will be done in Sect. 2 dedicated to preliminaries—but for simple state variables and specifications without parallelism the new definition will cover the old one. We will show that it is still possible to characterise specialisation using the logic of non-deterministic ASMs [8,9]. With this we are able to prove again compositionality with respect to the structure of ASM rules—this gives the main content of Sect. 3 dedicated to compositionality with respect to rules. This compositionality result allows us to concentrate on GCSs for assignments.

In Sect. 4 we address compositionality with respect to sets of invariants. It is easy to see that with the fine-grained notion of location compositionality for sets of invariants as in the guarded-command-based GCS theory cannot be achieved. However, as only assignments have to be taken into consideration, we can exploit *critical paths* as in [14], where they were used to show the limitations of rule triggering systems for consistency enforcement. Here we will use them, again in connection with *local stratification* to obtain a canonical form for the

GCS of an assignment with respect to a set of invariants. For the latter ones we exploit a representation in clausal form, where skolemised variables give rise to **choose**-rules. We conclude with a brief summery and outlook in Sect. 5.

2 Consistent Specialisations

As stated above consistency enforcement starts from a program specification P and a static invariant I. For the former one we will concentrate on specifications of *sequential algorithms*, and we know from [10] that these are captured by sequential ASMs, so our specifications will be based on ASMs (see [3] for a detailed introduction).

Thus, let Σ denote a *signature*, i.e. a finite set of function symbols. Each $f \in \Sigma$ has a fixed arity $ar_f \in \mathbb{N}$ (including 0). A *structure* S over Σ is given by a base set B and an interpretation of the function symbols, i.e. for $ar_f = n$ the structure contains a function $f_S : B^n \rightarrow B \cup \{\bot\}$, where $\bot$ denotes a value outside B representing undefinedness, by means of which partial functions are captured. An *isomorphism* between Σ-structures S and S' is a bijection $\sigma : B \rightarrow B'$ between the corresponding base sets of S and S', respectively (extended by $\sigma(\bot) = \bot$) such that $f_{S'}(\sigma(v_1), \ldots, \sigma(v_n)) = \sigma(f_S(v_1, \ldots, v_n))$.

Usually, we assume an implicit background, i.e. fixed constant values and operations on them, e.g. truth values and their junctors, or natural numbers. The background together with Σ allows us to define terms and formulae (using equality as predicate symbol) in the usual way. Their interpretation in a structure S is then defined as usual assuming that the constants are interpreted by themselves and the operations on them have a fixed interpretation, with their fixed interpretation in a structure S.

A (static) *invariant* over Σ is a closed first-order formula I in a logic with equality and only the function symbols in Σ (and the background). A structure S *satisfies* the invariant I (denoted as $S \models I$) iff the interpretation of I in S yields **true**.

2.1 Sequential Abstract State Machines

ASMs provide means for the specification of computations on isomorphism classes of structures. Thus, an ASM is defined by a signature Σ and an ASM closed rule r. The signature defines a *set $\mathcal{S}$ of states*, out of which a subset $\mathcal{I}$ is declared as *set of initial states*. Both $\mathcal{S}$ and $\mathcal{I}$ must be closed under isomorphisms.

Each state defines a set of locations. A *location* ℓ of S is given by a function symbol $f \in \Sigma$ (say of arity n) and a tuple $(v_1, \ldots, v_n) \in B^n$, where B is the base set of S. We write $val_S(\ell) = v_0$ for a location $\ell = (f, (v_1, \ldots, v_n))$ iff $f_S(v_1, \ldots, v_n) = v_0$ holds.

An *update* is a pair (ℓ, v_0) comprising a location ℓ and a value $v_0 \in B \cup \{\bot\}$. An *update set* is a finite set Δ of updates. Δ is called *clash-free* iff there cannot be two updates $(\ell, v), (\ell, v') \in \Delta$ with the same location ℓ and $v \neq v'$. If Δ is a clash-free update set on state S, then there is a well-defined *successor state*

$S' = S + \Delta$ with $val_{S'}(\ell) = v_0$ for $(\ell, v_0) \in \Delta$ and $val_{S'}(\ell) = val_S(\ell)$ otherwise. For completeness we further let $S + \Delta = S$ in case Δ is not clash-free.

The rule gives rise to state transitions. Sequential *ASM rules r* are defined as follows:

- Each *assignment* $f(t_1, \ldots, t_n) := t_0$ with a function symbol $f \in \Sigma$ of arity n and terms t_i for $i = 0, \ldots, n$ is an ASM rule.
- If φ is a Boolean term (i.e. it evaluates to a truth value) and r_1 and r_2 are ASM rules, then also **if** φ **then** r_1 **else** r_2 **endif** is an ASM rule (branching).
- If $r_1, \ldots, r_k$ are ASM rules, then also **par** $r_1 \ldots r_k$ **endpar** is an ASM rule (bounded parallelism).
- If x is a variable, $\varphi(x)$ is a Boolean term with free x and $r(x)$ is an ASM rule with free x, then also **choose** x **with** $\varphi(x)$ **do** r(x) **enddo** is an ASM rule (choice).

For completeness we also permit rules of the form **let** $x = t$ **in** $r(x)$, **skip** and **fail**. The former one is just a shortcut for **choose** x **with** $x = t$ **do** r(x) **enddo** emphasising that the "choice" is deterministic, **skip** can be seen as a shortcut for some $f(t_1, \ldots, t_n) := f(t_1, \ldots, t_n)$, i.e. a rule that does not change the state, and **fail** represents **choose** x **with** $x \neq x$ **do** r(x) **enddo**, i.e. it is a rule that is always undefined.

We use parentheses freely as well as the usual abbreviations for branching rules. We also mention the unbounded parallelism rule **forall** x **with** $\varphi(x)$ **do** r(x) **enddo**, which is permitted in general in ASMs, but not in sequential ASMs.

Given a state S a rule r together with a valuation ζ of its free variables yields a set of update sets, which we denote as $\Delta_r(S)$:

- For an assignment rule $f(t_1, \ldots, t_n) := t_0$ there is exactly one update set, so we have $\Delta_r(S) = \{\{((f, (val_{S,\zeta}(t_1), \ldots, val_{S,\zeta}(t_n))), val_{S,\zeta}(t_0))\}\}$.
- For a branching rule **if** φ **then** r_1 **else** r_2 **endif** we have $\Delta_r(S) = \Delta_{r_1}(S)$ for $val_{S,\zeta}(\varphi) = \mathbf{true}$, and $\Delta_r(S) = \Delta_{r_2}(S)$ for $val_{S,\zeta}(\varphi) = \mathbf{false}$.
- For a bounded parallel rule **par** $r_1 \ldots r_k$ **endpar** we have $\Delta_r(S) = \{\Delta_1 \cup \cdots \cup \Delta_k \mid \Delta_i \in \Delta_{r_i}(S)$ for $i = 1, \ldots, k\}$.
- For a choice rule **choose** x **with** $\varphi(x)$ **do** r(x) **enddo** we have $\Delta_r(S) = \bigcup_{val_{S,\zeta}(\varphi(x)) = \mathbf{true}} \Delta_{r(x)}(S)$.

Then we also have $\Delta_{\mathbf{skip}}(S) = \{\emptyset\}$ and $\Delta_{\mathbf{fail}}(S) = \emptyset$.

Definition 1. An ASM is *consistent* with respect to an invariant I iff every initial state $S_0 \in \mathcal{I}$ satisfies I, and for every state $S \in \mathcal{S}$ satisfying I also every successor state $S' = S + \Delta$ with $\Delta \in \Delta_r(S)$ satisfies I.

2.2   Greatest Consistent Specialisations

Recall from the introduction that the idea is to replace a specification P (i.e. a sequential ASM) by a modified specification P_I that is consistent with respect to a given invariant I subject to some minimality condition. Let us tacitly assume that the given initial states S_0 always satisfy $S_0 \models I$, so we can concentrate on the state transitions. That is, we have to modify the rule r of a given sequential ASM. Therefore, in the following we always consider such a rule r.

Update sets in a state S represent the intention behind the specification. It therefore appears natural to request that the modification should preserve the updates, i.e. update sets should be (minimally) enlarged. The question is whether this is always possible, and the next example shows that this is not the case (see also [14]).

Example 1. Consider an ASM with a rule **par** $p(a) :=$ **true** $q(a) :=$ **false endpar** and an invariant $I \equiv \forall x.p(x) \Rightarrow q(x)$. Assume a is a constant evaluated to itself, so the only update set in an arbitrary state S will be $\Delta = \{((p,(a)),\textbf{true}),((q,(a)),\textbf{false})\}$. Hence in every successor state $S' = S + \Delta$ we will have $val_{S'}(p(a)) =$ **true** and $val_{S'}(q(a)) =$ **false**, which violates I, and no enlargement of Δ can repair this. So the specification has to be considered to be non-repairable.

Example 1 shows that there are situations, where consistency enforcement by means of enlarging update sets is not possible, so we need a notion of a repairable update set. For this we consider a clash-free update set $\Delta \in \boldsymbol{\Delta}_r(S)$ as a structure, i.e. we let $val_{\Delta}(\ell) = v$ for $(\ell, v) \in \Delta$ and $val_{\Delta}(\ell) = \bot$ otherwise.

Definition 2. An update set $\Delta \in \boldsymbol{\Delta}_r(S)$ is *non-repairable* with respect to an invariant I iff $\Delta \models \neg I$ holds. An ASM is *repairable* in state S with respect to I iff there is at least one repairable update set $\Delta \in \boldsymbol{\Delta}_r(S)$.

Now we can approach a definition of consistent specialisation.

Definition 3. Consider an ASM $\mathcal{A}$ with a rule r and an invariant I. An ASM $\mathcal{A}_I$ with rule r_I is a *consistent specialisation* of $\mathcal{A}$ iff for all states S the following holds:

(i) If $S \models I$, then
    (a) for all repairable $\Delta \in \boldsymbol{\Delta}_r(S)$ there exists some $\Delta' \in \boldsymbol{\Delta}_{r_I}(S)$ with $\Delta \subseteq \Delta'$, and
    (b) for all $\Delta' \in \boldsymbol{\Delta}_{r_I}(S)$ there exists a repairable $\Delta \in \boldsymbol{\Delta}_r(S)$ with $\Delta \subseteq \Delta'$.
(ii) If $S \not\models I$, then $\boldsymbol{\Delta}_{r_I}(S) = \emptyset$.
(iii) If $S \models I$, then for $\Delta' \in \boldsymbol{\Delta}_{r_I}(S)$ we have $S + \Delta' \models I$.

Note that (i) and (iii) in Definition 3 together imply that if $\boldsymbol{\Delta}_r(S)$ only contains non-repairable update sets, then $\boldsymbol{\Delta}_{r_I}(S)$ will be empty.

We can define a partial order $\leq$ on consistent specialisations of $\mathcal{A}$ with respect to an invariant I. If $\mathcal{A}_1$ and $\mathcal{A}_2$ are two consistent specialisations of $\mathcal{A}$ with rules r_1 and r_2, respectively, then we have $\mathcal{A}_1 \leq \mathcal{A}_2$ iff for all states S and all $\Delta_1 \in \boldsymbol{\Delta}_{r_1}(S)$ there exists a $\Delta_2 \in \boldsymbol{\Delta}_{r_2}(S)$ with $\Delta_2 \subseteq \Delta_1$.

Clearly, if an update set is repairable, then the greatest consistent specialisation will contain all minimal extensions (exploit unbounded choice for this), which justifies the following definition.

Definition 4. Consider an ASM $\mathcal{A}$ with a rule r and an invariant I. An ASM $\mathcal{A}_I$ with rule r_I is the *greatest consistent specialisation* (GCS) of $\mathcal{A}$ iff it is a consistent specialisation and maximal with respect to the partial order $\leq$.

Remarks. Note that our definition of GCS is an ASM $\mathcal{A}_I$ over the same signature as the given ASM $\mathcal{A}$. Thus, states of $\mathcal{A}_I$ are also states of $\mathcal{A}$ and vice versa. Furthermore, the definition is based on the assumption that the invariant is confirmed to be valid, which is different from work as e.g. in [16], where invariants are allowed to be weakened to achieve consistency. GCS are also "universal" in the sense that all possible ways of minimal repair (as defined in Definition 3) are taken into account leaving decisions, which of these might be preferred to a human-driven refinement process. This differs from work of others, e.g. [4], where machine learning methods are applied to detect the "best" repair.

Example 2. Consider a simple invariant $I \equiv f \neq \bot \Rightarrow g(f) \neq \bot$, so the signature Σ contains at least function symbols f and g of arity 0 and 1, respectively. Take the rule r_1 defined by $f := a$ with a constant a. Then the GCS will be defined by a rule

    if $f = \bot \vee g(f) \neq \bot$
    then choose y **do par** $f := a \; g(a) := y$ **endpar enddo**
    else fail endif

This is easily verified using directly Definition 3. Note that the outermost branching rule and the **fail** is only needed to capture the case of the rule being applied in a state S not satisfying I.

Next take a rule r_2 defined by $g(a) := b$ with another constant b. Then the GCS is defined by

    if $f = \bot \vee g(f) \neq \bot$ **then** $g(a) := b$ **else fail endif**

Clearly, the GCS of **par** $r_1 \; r_2$ **endpar** is

    if $f = \bot \vee g(f) \neq \bot$ **then par** $f := a \; g(a) := b$ **endpar else fail endif**

This is different from **par** $r_{1I} \; r_{2I}$ **endpar**.

Example 3. Let us consider another simple, yet slightly more complicated example with an invariant $I \equiv f \neq \bot \Rightarrow \exists y.g(f, y) = f$. Let r_1 be as in Example 2 and let r_2 be defined as $g(a, b) := a$. Then the GCS of r_1 is defined by

    if $f = \bot \vee \forall y.g(f, y) \neq f$
    then choose y **do par** $f := a \; g(a, y) := a$ **endpar enddo**
    else fail endif

For r_2 the GCS will be defined by the rule

    if $f = \bot \vee \forall y.g(f, y) \neq f$ **then** $g(a, b) := a$ **else fail endif**

Clearly, the GCS of **par** r_1 r_2 **endpar** is

if $f = \bot \vee \forall y.g(f,y) \neq f$
then par $f := a$ $g(a,y) := a$ **endpar**
else fail endif

Again, this is different from **par** r_{1I} r_{2I} **endpar**.

Remark. In principle, the new definition of a GCS follows the idea of the definition given in [15], but as we want to deal with parallelism, the use of predicate transformers is excluded. In addition, there are a few more subtle differences. Definition 4 is based on update sets, which are grounded on the fine-tuned notion of location in ASMs. For instance, every tuple in a relation defines a location, whereas in the "old" work the whole relation would be considered as a single value with the consequence that preserving "effects" (now updates) is much more restrictive. We will see that this has consequences on compositionality with respect to sets of invariants, but in Sect. 4 we will be able to achieve results that are even more convincing than those for the "old" notion of GCSs.

3   Compositionality with Respect to Rule Composition

The key result in [15] states that the GCS can be built by first replacing elementary commands, i.e. assignments and **skip**, by their respective GCSs, and then adding preconditions to ensure that the result is indeed a specialisation. This reduces GCS construction to the case of assignments. The most difficult parts of the decisive "upper bound theorem" are concerned with sequences and recursion. In our modernised theory we can dispense with recursion, as the semantics of ASMs includes the iteration of the rule, so we have a finer-grained notion of consistency. Nonetheless, an extension to recursive ASMs (see [2]) is likewise possible. As we deal with sequential algorithms there is also no need to bother about sequences, as they are not needed (see the proof of the sequential ASM thesis in [10] and the corresponding behavioural theory of unbounded parallel algorithms in [7]; sequences can be easily expressed using bounded parallelism and branching). However, we now have to deal at least with bounded parallelism, to which the theory in [15] does not apply.

   In this section we will nonetheless show that compositionality holds for sequential ASM rules, and the most difficult part of the proof will concern the case of the bounded parallel rule. This will reduce GCS construction again to assignments, which we will handle in the next section.

3.1   Branching and Choice

First consider the cases of branching and choice rules.

Proposition 1. *Let $\mathcal{A}$ be an ASM with a rule of the form **if** φ **then** r_1 **else** r_2 **endif**. Then the rule of its GCS $\mathcal{A}_I$ with respect to an invariant I can be written as **if** φ **then** r_{1I} **else** r_{2I} **endif**, where r_{iI} is the rule of the GCS of the ASM defined by r_i.*

Due to space and time restrictions we omit the proof here. We only have to check the conditions of Definitions 3 and 4 using the definition of update sets yielded by branching rules. This is rather straightforward.

Proposition 2. *Let $\mathcal{A}$ be an ASM with a rule of the form **choose** x **with** $\varphi(x)$ **do** $r(x)$ **enddo**. Then the rule of its GCS $\mathcal{A}_I$ with respect to an invariant I can be written as **choose** x **with** $\varphi(x)$ **do** $r_I(x)$ **enddo**, where $r_I(x)$ is the rule of the GCS of the ASM defined by $r(x)$.*

Same as for the proof of Proposition 1 the proof of Proposition 2 is rather straightforward based on the definition of update sets yielded by a choice rule and Definitions 3 and 4.

3.2   Bounded Parallelism

Next consider the case of a bounded parallel rule. As Examples 2 and 3 already show, we cannot obtain a simple compositional result as in Proposition 1 or 2. If we build the GCSs of the different parallel branches of an unbounded parallel rule separately and recombine them using unbounded parallelism, then we may have additional branches that subsume those in the real GCS. There may also be **fail** branches. Both have to be excluded.

In order to do this we need to exploit the logic of non-deterministic ASMs [8,9], which is defined as a fragment of second-order logic, in which quantification over update sets is permitted. However, as we are not yet dealing with unbounded parallelism, we can simplify the logic discarding multiset functions and thus also update multisets. We can also dispense with the difficult handling of meta-finite structures.

Terms of the logic are the terms defined by the given ASM. *Formulae* of the logic are built inductively using the following rules:

- If s and t are terms, then $s = t$ is a formula.
- If $t_1, \ldots, t_r$ are terms and X is a second-order variable of arity r, then $X(t_1, \ldots, t_r)$ is a formula.
- If r is a rule and X is a second-order variable of arity 3, then $\mathrm{upd}(r, X)$ is a formula.
- If φ and ψ are formulae, then also $\neg\varphi$, $\varphi \vee \psi$ are formulae.
- If φ is a formula, x is a first-order variable and X is a second-order variable, then also $\forall x.\varphi$ and $\forall X.\varphi$ are formulae.

- If φ is a formula and X is a second-order variable of arity 3, then $[X]\varphi$ is a formula.

Additional junctors and quantifiers such as $\wedge$, $\rightarrow$ and $\exists$ are defined as shortcuts in the usual way. We also use $\langle X \rangle \varphi$ as shortcut for $\neg[X]\neg\varphi$ as common in dynamic logic.

In [8] a Henkin semantics for the logic was defined, in which the interpretation of second-order quantifiers is part of the specification of a structure.

Definition 5. A *Henkin prestructure* over signature Σ is a state S with nonempty base set B extended by sets of n-ary relations $D_n \subseteq \mathcal{P}(B^n)$ for each $n \geq 1$.

Variable assignments ζ for a Henkin prestructure S are defined as usual. We have $\zeta(x) \in B$ for first-order variables x, and $\zeta(X) \in D_n$ for second-order variables X of arity n. Given a variable assignment, formulae can be interpreted in a Henkin prestructure. As we want to obtain update sets, we introduce new constant symbols c_f for each function symbol $f \in \Sigma$. For a second-order variable X of arity 3 we write $val_{S,\zeta}(X) \in \Delta(r, S, \zeta)$, meaning that there is a set $\Delta \in \Delta(r, S, \zeta)$ such that $(f, a_0, a_1) \in U$ iff $(c_f^S, a_0, a_1) \in val_{S,\zeta}(X)$.

If φ is a formula, then the truth value of φ on S under ζ is determined as follows:

- If φ is of the form $s = t$, then $[\![\varphi]\!]_{S,\zeta} = \mathbf{true}$ iff $val_{S,\zeta}(s) = val_{S,\zeta}(t)$.
- If φ is of the form $X(t_1, \ldots, t_r)$, then $[\![\varphi]\!]_{S,\zeta} = \mathbf{true}$ iff $(val_{S,\zeta}(t_1), \ldots, val_{S,\zeta}(t_n)) \in val_{S,\zeta}(X)$.
- If φ is of the form $\mathrm{upd}(r, X)$, then $[\![\varphi]\!]_{S,\zeta} = \mathbf{true}$ iff $val_{S,\zeta}(X) \in \Delta(r, S, \zeta)$.
- If φ is of the form $\neg\psi$, then $[\![\varphi]\!]_{S,\zeta} = \mathbf{true}$ iff $[\![\psi]\!]_{S,\zeta} = \mathbf{false}$.
- If φ is of the form $(\alpha \vee \psi)$, then $[\![\varphi]\!]_{S,\zeta} = \mathbf{false}$ iff $[\![\alpha]\!]_{S,\zeta} = [\![\psi]\!]_{S,\zeta} = \mathbf{false}$.
- If φ is of the form $\forall x.\psi$, then $[\![\varphi]\!]_{S,\zeta} = \mathbf{true}$ iff $[\![\psi]\!]_{S,\zeta[x \mapsto a]} = \mathbf{true}$ for all $a \in B$.
- If φ is of the form $\forall X.\psi$, where X is a second-order variable of arity n, then $[\![\varphi]\!]_{S,\zeta} = \mathbf{true}$ iff $[\![\psi]\!]_{S,\zeta[X \mapsto R]} = \mathbf{true}$ for all $R \in D_n$.
- If φ is of the form $[X]\psi$, then $[\![\varphi]\!]_{S,\zeta} = \mathbf{false}$ iff $\zeta(X)$ represents a clash-free update set Δ such that $[\![\psi]\!]_{S+\Delta,\zeta} = \mathbf{false}$ holds.

We can use the logic to define $\mathrm{con}(r, X)$ to express that X represents one of the possible update sets generated by the rule r, and that X is clash-free. This can be expressed in the logic by the formula $\mathrm{con}(r, X) \equiv \mathrm{upd}(r, X) \wedge \mathrm{conUSet}(X)$, where

$$\mathrm{conUSet}(X) \equiv \bigwedge_{f \in \Sigma} \forall x, y, z. X(c_f, x, y) \wedge X(c_f, x, z) \rightarrow y = z.$$

Furthermore, in accordance with [15, Prop.7] we can use $\chi(r, r')$ to express that r' subsumes r. This can be expressed in the logic by

$$\chi(r, r') \equiv \{L' \mapsto L\}.[r'']\langle r \rangle (L = L'),$$

where L represents the common locations used by rules r and r', L' is a disjoint copy of L, and r'' results from r' by replacing all locations in L by the corresponding ones in L'.

Proposition 3. *Let $\mathcal{A}$ be an ASM with a rule of the form* **par** $r_1 \dots r_k$ **endpar.** *Then the rule of its GCS $\mathcal{A}_I$ with respect to an invariant I can be written as*

$$\textit{choose } y_1, \dots, y_k \textit{ with } \bigwedge_{1 \le i \le k} \psi_i(y_i) \wedge \exists X_i . con(r'_i(y_i), X_i)$$
$$\textit{do par} \dots \hat{r}_i(y_i) \dots \textit{ endpar enddo,}$$

where $\hat{r}_i(y_i)$ is defined to be the rule

$$\textit{if } \bigwedge_{j \ne i} \neg\chi(r'_j(y_j), r'_i(y_i)) \textit{ then } r'_i(y_i) \textit{ else fail endif}$$

using the GCSs with the rules r_{iI} of the form

$$\textit{choose } y_i \textit{ with } \psi_i(y_i) \textit{ do } r'_i(y_i) \textit{ enddo.}$$

For the proof, which we have to omit due to space and time restrictions, we look again directly at Definitions 3 and 4. It is easy to see that the parallel composition of GCSs r_{iI} defines a consistent specialisation, but in general not the GCS. Conditions $con(r'_i(y_i), X_i)$ remove branches with clashes in update sets, and conditions $\neg\chi(r'_j(y_j), r'_i(y_i))$ discard parallel branches yielding update sets that contain update sets from other branches.

Note that in Proposition 3 we assume that the GCSs r_{iI} of the rules r_i have a specific form. This is in accordance with Propositions 1, 2 and (inductively) 3 as well as with the key result (see Theorem 1 in Sect. 4), on GCSs of assignments.

Example 4. Let us reconsider Examples 2 and 3. In the former case the parallel composition of r_{1I} and r_{2I} leads to the rule

if $f = \bot \vee g(f) \ne \bot$
then choose y **do par** $f := a$ $g(a) := b$ $g(a) := y$ **endpar enddo else**
fail endif

Each parallel branch with $y \ne b$ defines only update sets that are not clash-free. The requirement in Proposition 3 that there must exist a clash-free update set removes these branches, so only the correct GCS remains.

In Example 3 the parallel composition of r_{1I} and r_{2I} leads to the rule

if $f = \bot \vee \forall y.g(f, y) \ne f$
then choose y **do par** $f := a$ $g(a, b) := a$ $g(a, y) := a$ **endpar enddo**
else fail endif

Here a parallel branch with $y \ne b$ leads to update sets with an additional update $((g, (a, y)), a)$, hence $\chi(r'(b), r'(y))$ holds (using $r'(y)$ as name for the rules inside the **par**-block). Then the condition in Proposition 3 excludes such branches, and we obtain the correct GCS.

4 Compositionality with Respect to Sets of Invariants

Propositions 1, 2 and 3 allow us to build the GCS in a compositional way, provided the GCSs of assignments are known. We will address assignments in this section. We will combine this directly with the treatment of sets of invariants. Clearly, consistency with respect to such a set is equivalent to consistency with respect to the conjunction of the invariants in the set, so the results of the previous section can be preserved.

In [15, Prop.12] it could be shown that with the coarse notion of GCS defined there compositionality with respect to conjunctions can be easily obtained. In other words, a GCS with respect to a set of invariants can be built step-by-step using the invariants in the set in arbitrary order. This does no longer hold in our modernised and fine-grained case, as the following example shows.

Example 5. Consider two invariants $I_1 \equiv \forall x.p(x) \Rightarrow q(x)$ and $I_2 \equiv \forall x.p(x) \Rightarrow p(f(x))$. Taking an ASM with a rule $p(a) := true$, its GCS with respect to I_1 is defined by the rule **par** $p(a) := true \; q(a) := true$ **endpar** on states satisfying I_1. Building for this the GCS with respect to I_2 gives a rule, which on states satisfying $I_1 \wedge I_2$ takes the form **par** $p(a) := true \; q(a) := true \; p(f(a)) := true$ **endpar**, which is not the GCS with respect to $I_1 \wedge I_2$.

The reason for the discrepancy between Example 5 and the "old" theory in [15] is again due to the changed treatment of locations. Using the theory in [15] p and q would be state variables bound to unary relations, i.e. sets, and a GCS for an assignment such as $p(a) := true$—in fact an insertion—cannot make further changes to p, and only use preconditions to enforce I_2.

Fortunately, there is away to deal simultaneously with several invariants mutually influencing each other. This is inspired by the handling of rule triggering systems in [14]. We will adopt this theory here exploiting the fact that it is only required for consistency enforcement for a single assignment. In fact, single assignments are almost always repairable, unless the invariant contains a single literal.

4.1 Clausal Form and Atomic Repairs

We assume that invariants I are first-order formulae, so we can write them in *prenex normal form*

$$\forall \boldsymbol{x}_1 \exists \boldsymbol{y}_1 \forall \boldsymbol{x}_2 \exists \boldsymbol{y}_2 \ldots .\varphi(\boldsymbol{x}_1, \boldsymbol{y}_1, \boldsymbol{x}_2, \boldsymbol{y}_2, \ldots).$$

Then the existentially quantified variables can be replaced by Skolem functions $y_{1j} = sk_{1j}(\boldsymbol{x}_1)$, $y_{2j} = sk_{2j}(\boldsymbol{x}_1, sk_{11}(\boldsymbol{x}_1), \ldots, sk_{1n_1}(\boldsymbol{x}_1), \boldsymbol{x}_2)$, etc.

We can further assume that the quantifier-free formula $\varphi(\boldsymbol{x}_1, \boldsymbol{y}_1, \boldsymbol{x}_2, \boldsymbol{y}_2, \ldots)$ is written in conjunctive normal form, so it gives rise to a set of clauses, i.e. disjunctions of literals $\neg L_1 \vee \neg L_2 \vee \cdots \vee \neg L_k \vee L_{k+1} \vee \cdots \vee L_{k+\ell}$ with the variables x_{ij} and y_{ij} appearing in the atoms. Furthermore, atoms are simply equations.

A violation of an invariant I is always linked to a violation of one of its clauses, so we concentrate on the clauses. As in the relational case treated in [14] we may define an *atomic repair* by means of a trigger. In case a positive literal t_1 or a negative literal $\neg t_2$ is violated by an assignment changing the value of either t_1 or t_2 and this leads to the whole clause to become false, we can use another assignment making a positive literal $t'_1 \neq t'_2$ to become **true** or a negative literal $\neg t'_1 \neq \neg t'_2$ become **false**. Any variable appearing in t_1 or t_2 must also be bound to the same value in the triggered update, and all other variables must be selected by embedding the assignment into a **choose**-rule. Any such possibility defines an *atomic repair rule* comprising an *event E*, i.e. an assignment rule leading to an invariant violation, a *clause I* that is violated, and a *repair R*, which is an assignment embedded in a choice-rule. In analogy to rule triggering system we write **on** E **if** $\neg I$ **do** R for such an atomic repair rule.

Example 6. Let us consider a simple example adopted from [14, Ex.5] with three clauses:

$$I_1 \equiv \neg p(x) \vee \neg r(x) \vee q(x) \quad I_2 \equiv \neg q(x) \vee p(x) \quad I_3 \equiv \neg p(x) \vee r(x)$$

Then we obtain the following ten atomic repair rules:

$$R_1 : \textbf{on } p(x) := \textbf{true if } \neg I_1 \textbf{ do } q(x) := \textbf{true}$$
$$R_2 : \textbf{on } q(x) := \textbf{false if } \neg I_1 \textbf{ do } p(x) := \textbf{false}$$
$$R_3 : \textbf{on } r(x) := \textbf{true if } \neg I_1 \textbf{ do } q(x) := \textbf{true}$$
$$R_4 : \textbf{on } q(x) := \textbf{false if } \neg I_1 \textbf{ do } r(x) := \textbf{false}$$
$$R_5 : \textbf{on } q(x) := \textbf{true if } \neg I_2 \textbf{ do } p(x) := \textbf{true}$$
$$R_6 : \textbf{on } p(x) := \textbf{false if } \neg I_2 \textbf{ do } q(x) := \textbf{false}$$
$$R_7 : \textbf{on } p(x) := \textbf{true if } \neg I_3 \textbf{ do } r(x) := \textbf{true}$$
$$R_8 : \textbf{on } r(x) := \textbf{false if } \neg I_3 \textbf{ do } p(x) := \textbf{false}$$
$$R_9 : \textbf{on } p(x) := \textbf{true if } \neg I_1 \textbf{ do } r(x) := \textbf{false}$$
$$R_{10} : \textbf{on } r(x) := \textbf{true if } \neg I_1 \textbf{ do } p(x) := \textbf{false}$$

It is easy to see that all possible atomic repair rules—assuming a single assignment causing a violation—can be derived from a clause, the **on**-part refers to the violating assignment, the **if**-part is the negation of the clause, and the **do**-part is an assignment corresponding to another literal in the clause, by means of which the violation would be disabled.

A set of atomic repair rules is said to be *complete* for an assignment rule r iff for every possible violation of an invariant clause I defined by a set of invariants there is at least one atomic repair rule with event r and clause I, and the same holds for all assignment rules appearing as repair in at least one atomic repair rule. A complete set of repair rules for r defines a sequential ASM rule, which we call a *complete repair* and denote as r_{rep}.

4.2 Critical Paths

We will now provide the means to reduce a system of atomic repair rules in such a way that we can obtain a GCS. For this we adapt the notions of *rule graph* and *critical trigger path*.

Definition 6. Let Σ be a signature and $\mathcal{R}$ a set of atomic repair rules on Σ. Then the associated *rule graph* (V, E) is defined as follows:

- The set V of vertices is the disjoint union of Σ and $\mathcal{R}$. We then talk of Σ-vertices and $\mathcal{R}$-vertices, respectively.
- If $R \in \mathcal{R}$ has event E affecting a location of $p \in \Sigma$ and a repair on $q \in \Sigma$, then we have an edge from p to R labelled by $+$ or $-$ depending on E leading to a violation of a negative or a positive literal, respectively, and an edge from R to q analogously labelled by $+$ or $-$ depending on whether the repair assignment on a q-location refers to a positive or negative literal.

Definition 7. Let (V, E) be the rule graph associated with a system $\mathcal{R}$ of atomic repair rules. A *trigger path* is a sequence $v_0, e_1, v'_1, e'_1, \ldots, e'_\ell, v_\ell$ of vertices and edges such that $v_i \in \Sigma$ for all $i = 0, \ldots, \ell$, $v'_i \in \mathcal{R}$ holds for all $i = 1, \ldots, \ell$, e_i is an edge from v_{i-1} to v'_i, and e'_i is an edge from v'_i to v_i with the same label as e_{i+1}.

For a trigger path assign to each vertex $v_i \in \Sigma$ a formula φ_i that is the negation of a clause such that the following conditions hold:

(i) φ_i implies the negation of the clause associated with v'_{i+1};
(ii) the application of the repair in v'_{i+1} will lead to a state satisfying φ_{i+1}.

Definition 8. A trigger path $v_0, e_1, v'_1, e'_1, \ldots, e'_\ell, v_\ell$ is *critical* iff it has maximum length and $\models \neg(\varphi_0 \vee \varphi_\ell)$ holds.

Intuitively, a critical trigger path corresponds to a sequence of applications of atomic repair rules, each initialised by a violation of a clause, which finally lead to a state, where the intended update is undone. Thus, such trigger paths cannot define an extension of a repairable update set.

Proposition 4. *Let S be a consistent state with respect to a given set of invariants, let r be an assignment affecting a location with function symbol $p \in \Sigma$, and assume $S + \Delta_r(S) \models \varphi_0$, where φ_0 is a conjunction of literals. Then for a complete repair r_{rep} the sequence $r; r_{rep}$ is a consistent specialisation with respect to the conjunction of the given invariants iff there is no critical trigger path starting with a vertex p labelled by φ_0.*

The proof, which we cannot present here, basically follows the arguments used in the proof of [14, Prop.4]. If there were such a critical trigger path, it would lead to a state, in which one of the updates in $\Delta_r(S)$ would be discarded, which is contained in the definition of a critical trigger path. Conversely, if there is no such trigger path, r_{rep} will lead to a state satisfying φ_ℓ.

4.3 Locally Stratified Sets of Invariants

We now look for sufficient and necessary conditions on the set of clauses derived from a set of invariants that will allow us to obtain a complete repair satisfying the conditions in Proposition 4, i.e. the absence of critical paths. The intuition behind this procedure is that non-critical trigger paths give rise to cumulative updates, by means of which a repairable update set can be extended to achieve consistency, whereas critical trigger paths would undo some of the given updates. A complete repair then defines a consistent specialisation as shown by Proposition 4.

Definition 9. Let C be a set of clauses on Σ derived from a set of invariants. Then C is called *stratified* iff there is a partition $C = C_1 \cup \ldots \cup C_n$ with pairwise disjoint sets of clauses C_i called *strata* such that the following conditions are satisfied:

(i) If L is a negative (or positive, respectively) literal of some clause $c \in C_i$, then all clauses $c' \in C$ containing a positive (or negative, respectively) literal L' such that L and L' are unifiable also lie in stratum C_i.

(ii) All clauses c, c' containing unifiable literals L and L' either both positive or both negative must lie in different strata.

Stratified sets of clauses give rise to complete repairs without critical trigger paths.

Proposition 5. *Let C be a set of clauses on Σ derived from a set of invariants, and assume that C is stratified. Then there exists a complete repair r_{rep} such that the sequence $r; r_{rep}$ is a consistent specialisation with respect to the conjunction of the given invariants.*

For the proof, which we omit again due to space and time restrictions, we construct the set of all atomic repair rules from C. Then assume the existence of a critical trigger path initiated by r, i.e. r affects a location with function symbol $p \in \Sigma$, $S + \Delta_r(S) \models \varphi_0$ holds for a conjunction of literals, and the critical trigger path starting with a vertex p labelled by φ_0. Then φ_0 and φ_ℓ must contain a literal and its negation, respectively, and the corresponding rules must involve clauses in different strata, which leads to a contradiction.

Stratified sets of invariant clauses are sufficient for the construction of consistent specialisation, and stratification can be checked effectively and efficiently (see Algorithm 8 and Propositions 9 and 10 in [14]), but stratification is no necessary condition. We will now look at the weaker notion of local stratification, which will give us also a necessary condition.

Definition 10. Let C be a set of clauses on Σ derived from a set of invariants. A *labelled subsystem* consists of a literal L (the *label*), a subset $C' = \{c \in C \mid \rho_L(c)$ is defined$\}$, and a set of clauses $C'' = \{\rho_L(c) \mid c \in C'\}$ such that each clause $c \in C'$ can be written as the disjunction $\rho_L(c) \vee c'$ with $\models c' \Rightarrow L$.

Here $\rho_L(c)$ is defined iff the negation $\sim L$ does not occur in the clause c. Then $\rho_L(c)$ results from c by omission of the literal L, if the result contains at least two literals. Otherwise $\rho_L(c)$ is simply c. We call c' the *label part* and $\rho_L(c)$ the *label-free part* of the clause c. If L is understood from the context, we drop the subscript and write ρ instead of ρ_L.

A labelled subsystem (C', C'', L) is called *stratified* iff the set C'' is stratified in the sense of Definition 9 or locally stratified as defined below.

Definition 11. Let C be a set of clauses on Σ derived from a set of invariants. Then C is called *locally stratified* iff $C = C_1' \cup \cdots \cup C_n'$ with stratified labelled subsystems (C_i', C_i'', L_i) $(i = 1, \ldots, n)$ such that for each clause $c \in C_i'$ and each literal L occurring in its label part with respect to C_i there exists another j with $c \in C_j'$ and L occurring in its label-free part of c with respect to C_j.

Proposition 6. *Let C be a set of clauses on Σ derived from a set of invariants. Then there exists a complete repair r_{rep} such that the sequence $r; r_{rep}$ is a consistent specialisation with respect to the conjunction of the given invariants iff C is locally stratified.*

For the proof of sufficiency we can proceed analogously to the proof of Proposition 5, i.e. we take the local strata to define sets of atomic repair rules and build the union of these. Then the assumption of a critical trigger path leads again to a contradiction to the set of clauses being locally stratified.

Conversely, if we have a consistent specialisation $r; r_{rep}$ Proposition 4 implies the absence of critical trigger paths. From this it is possible to construct a local stratification (see also the proof of [14, Thm.12].

Example 7. Reconsider the invariants in Example 6. It is easy to see that this set is locally stratified leading to the atomic repair rules in the example without R_9 and R_{10}.

Finally, we can obtain the GCS of an assignment r by a choice between all possible complete repairs defined by local stratifications of the given set of invariants.

Theorem 1. *Let C be a locally stratified set of clauses on Σ derived from a set of invariants. Then the GCS of an assignment r with respect to the set of invariants is defined by the sequence $r; rep$, where rep is defined by the choice among all complete repairs r_{rep} defined by different local stratifications of C.*

5   Conclusion

In this paper we picked up the 20 year old theory of greatest consistent specialisation for consistency enforcement with respect to static invariants. We generalised the definition in the context of sequential Abstract State Machines with finer grained locations and bounded parallelism. Then we obtained generalised compositionality results with respect to the composition of ASM rules and sets of invariants. The new theory supports the systematic *construction* of consistent specifications, which is not bound to ASMs.

However, we still excluded unbounded parallelism from our investigation. Extending the theory in this direction is an open, non-trivial task for continued research. We also emphasised only invariants expressed in first-order logic as well as only static invariants, though this covers the vast majority of specifications using state-based rigorous methods. Nonetheless, extensions to more complex invariants as well as a theory for transition or general dynamic invariants would make sense. For instance, in [6] the importance of higher-order logic constructs in formal methods was emphasised. Furthermore, in a database context many classes of static constraints have been studied [17]. These give rise to important classes of static invariants that could be used to derive a catalogue of GCSs for them, and this could be further extended to classes of invariants in other contexts giving even more support for the construction of consistent specifications.

References

1. Abrial, J.-R.: The B-Book - Assigning Programs to Meanings. Cambridge University Press, Cambridge (2005)
2. Börger, E., Schewe, K.-D.: A behavioural theory of recursive algorithms (2019). Submitted for publication
3. Börger, E., Stärk, R.: Abstract State Machines. Springer, Heidelberg (2003). https://doi.org/10.1007/978-3-642-18216-7
4. Cai, C., Sun, J., Dobbie, G.: B-repair: repairing B-models using machine learning. In: 23rd International Conference on Engineering of Complex Computer Systems (ICECCS 2018), pp. 31–40. IEEE Computer Society (2018)
5. Dijkstra, E.W., Scholten, C.S.: Predicate Calculus and Program Semantics. Texts and Monographs in Computer Science. Springer, New York (1990). https://doi.org/10.1007/978-1-4612-3228-5
6. Ferrarotti, F., González, S., Schewe, K.-D., Turull-Torres, J.M.: Systematic refinement of abstract state machines with higher-order logic. In: Butler, M., Raschke, A., Hoang, T.S., Reichl, K. (eds.) ABZ 2018. LNCS, vol. 10817, pp. 204–218. Springer, Cham (2018). https://doi.org/10.1007/978-3-319-91271-4_14
7. Ferrarotti, F., Schewe, K.-D., Tec, L., Wang, Q.: A new thesis concerning synchronised parallel computing - simplified parallel ASM thesis. Theor. Comput. Sci. **649**, 25–53 (2016)
8. Ferrarotti, F., Schewe, K.-D., Tec, L., Wang, Q.: A complete logic for database abstract state machines. Log. J. IGPL **25**(5), 700–740 (2017)
9. Ferrarotti, F., Schewe, K.-D., Tec, L., Wang, Q.: A unifying logic for non-deterministic, parallel and concurrent abstract state machines. Ann. Math. Artif. Intell. **83**(3–4), 321–349 (2018)
10. Gurevich, Y.: Sequential abstract state machines capture sequential algorithms. ACM Trans. Comput. Logic **1**(1), 77–111 (2000)
11. Link, S., Schewe, K.-D.: Towards an arithmetic theory of consistency enforcement based on preservation of delta-constraints. Electr. Notes Theor. Comput. Sci. **61**, 64–83 (2002)
12. Nelson, G.: A generalization of Dijkstra's calculus. ACM Trans. Program. Lang. Syst. **11**(4), 517–561 (1989)

13. Schewe, K.-D.: Consistency enforcement in Entity-Relationship and object-oriented models. Data Knowl. Eng. **28**(1), 121–140 (1998)
14. Schewe, K.-D., Thalheim, B.: Limitations of rule triggering systems for integrity maintenance in the context of transition specifications. Acta Cybern. **13**(3), 277–304 (1998)
15. Schewe, K.-D., Thalheim, B.: Towards a theory of consistency enforcement. Acta Inf. **36**(2), 97–141 (1999)
16. Schmidt, J., Krings, S., Leuschel, M.: Repair and generation of formal models using synthesis. In: Furia, C.A., Winter, K. (eds.) IFM 2018. LNCS, vol. 11023, pp. 346–366. Springer, Cham (2018). https://doi.org/10.1007/978-3-319-98938-9_20
17. Thalheim, B.: Dependencies in Relational Databases. Springer, Wiesbaden (1991). https://doi.org/10.1007/978-3-663-12018-6

Probably Approximate Safety Verification of Hybrid Dynamical Systems

Bai Xue[1,2,3(✉)], Martin Fränzle[4], Hengjun Zhao[5], Naijun Zhan[1,2], and Arvind Easwaran[6]

[1] State Key Laboratory of Computer Science, Institute of Software, CAS, Beijing, China
{xuebai,znj}@ios.ac.cn
[2] University of Chinese Academy of Sciences, Beijing, China
[3] Beijing Institute of Control Engineering, Beijing, China
[4] Carl von Ossietzky Universität Oldenburg, Oldenburg, Germany
fraenzle@informatik.uni-oldenburg.de
[5] Southwest University, Chongqing, China
zhaohj2016@swu.edu.cn
[6] Nanyang Technological University, Singapore, Singapore
arvinde@ntu.edu.sg

Abstract. In this paper we present a method based on linear programming that facilitates reliable safety verification of hybrid dynamical systems subject to perturbation inputs over the infinite time horizon. The verification algorithm applies the probably approximately correct (PAC) learning framework and consequently can be regarded as statistically formal verification in the sense that it provides formal safety guarantees expressed using error probabilities and confidences. The safety of hybrid systems in this framework is verified via the computation of so-called PAC barrier certificates, which can be computed by solving a linear programming problem. Based on scenario approaches, the linear program is constructed by a family of independent and identically distributed state samples. In this way we can conduct verification of hybrid dynamical systems that existing methods are not capable of dealing with. Some preliminary experiments demonstrate the performance of our approach.

Keywords: Hybrid systems · Probably approximately safe · Linear program

1 Introduction

The complexity of today's technological applications induces a quest for automation, leading to autonomous cyber-physical systems [9]. Many of these systems operate in safety-critical contexts and hence become safety-critical systems themselves. Being safety-critical, they have to reliably sustain safety despite perturbations. The propagation of these perturbations however tends to be highly nonlinear and combine continuous and discrete dynamics. Such combined dynamics yield a hybrid dynamical system involving interacting discrete-event and

© Springer Nature Switzerland AG 2019
Y. Ait-Ameur and S. Qin (Eds.): ICFEM 2019, LNCS 11852, pp. 236–252, 2019.
https://doi.org/10.1007/978-3-030-32409-4_15

continuous-variable dynamics. Hybrid dynamical systems are important in applications such as robotics, manufacturing systems and bio-molecular networks, and have been at the center of intense research activity in computer-aided verification, control theory, and applied mathematics [2].

The process of verifying with mathematical rigor that a hybrid dynamical system behaves correctly is a well-established branch of formal methods in computer science [1]. Unfortunately, many decision problems underlying formal verification of hybrid systems are undecidable [17]. Even surprisingly simple dynamical systems combining discrete and continuous dynamics feature undecidable state-reachability problems, like multi-priced timed automata with stopwatch prices [13] or three-dimensional piecewise constant derivative systems [3]. General undecidability renders sound yet incomplete automatic verification methods as well as methods providing a controlled approximation error attractive, e.g. [10,14,26], which nevertheless are computationally expensive. Although sophisticated heuristics have been developed to improve scalability of the techniques, automatic key-press formal verification of real-world systems is still considered to be impractical [30]. Techniques for simulation-based verification can prove fruitful in this regard for systems over finite time horizons, as they combine the scalability of simulation with rigorous coverage criteria supporting either a complete or a statistical verification through generalization from samples [23,38].

In this paper we propose a linear programming based method that facilitates reliable, in the sense of featuring a rigorously quantified confidence in the verification verdict, safety verification of hybrid systems subject to perturbations over the infinite time horizon. Akin to [11], the verification algorithm applies the framework of PAC learning theory [15] to adjust the effort invested in generating samples to a desired confidence in the verification verdict. Given a confidence $\beta \in (0,1)$, the objective is to compute a probability $\epsilon \in (0,1)$ such that the probability of initial continuous states leading to the satisfiability of safety properties is larger than $1-\epsilon$, with at least $1-\beta$ confidence. Such verification in our method is studied by learning a so-called PAC barrier certificate with respect to ϵ and β, which with at least $1 - \beta$ confidence is indeed a barrier certificate with probability larger than $1 - \epsilon$. The computation is based on scenario approaches [6] and linear interval inequalities [28], which encodes as a linear programming problem. The linear program is constructed using linear interval inequalities and a family of independent and identically distributed state samples extracted from the initial set. Based on the computed solution to this linear program, confidence level $\beta \in (0,1)$ and number of samples, we compute a probability measure ϵ based on scenario approaches such that the computed solution to the linear program forms a PAC barrier certificate with respect to ϵ and β. Consequently we conclude that the probability of initial continuous states leading to the satisfiability of safety properties is larger than $1-\epsilon$, with confidence higher than $1-\beta$. Some examples demonstrate the performance and merits of our approach.

2   Preliminaries

In this section we introduce hybrid systems, the safety verification problem, scenario approaches and linear interval inequalities. The following notations are used throughout this paper: $C^1(\mathbb{R}^n)$ is the set of continuously differentiable functions from $\mathbb{R}^n$ to $\mathbb{R}$. $\mathbb{R}_{\geq 0}$ denotes the set of nonnegative real values and $\mathbb{R}_{>0}$ denotes the set of positive reals. Vectors are denoted by boldface letters.

2.1   Hybrid Systems

A hybrid system is a tuple $H = (\mathcal{X}, L, X, X_0, \text{Inv}, \boldsymbol{F}, T)$ [24]:

- $\mathcal{X} \subseteq \mathbb{R}^n$ is the continuous state space;
- L is a finite set of locations and we will in the sequel denote its cardinality by $M = |L|$ with $L = \{1, \ldots, M\}$;
- The overall state space of the system is $X = L \times \mathcal{X}$, and a state of the system is denoted by $(l, \boldsymbol{x}) \in L \times \mathcal{X}$;
- $X_0 \subseteq X$ is the set of initial states;
- $\text{Inv} : L \to 2^{\mathcal{X}}$ is the invariant, which assigns to each location l a set $\text{Inv}(l) \subseteq \mathcal{X}$ that contains all possible continuous states while at location l;
- $\boldsymbol{F} : X \to 2^{\mathbb{R}^n}$ is a set of vector fields. $\boldsymbol{F}$ assigns to each $(l, \boldsymbol{x}) \in X$ a set $\boldsymbol{F}(l, \boldsymbol{x}) \subseteq \mathbb{R}^n$ which constrains the evolution of the continuous state according to the differential inclusion $\dot{\boldsymbol{x}} \in \boldsymbol{F}(l, \boldsymbol{x})$;
- $T \subseteq X \times X$ is a relation capturing discrete transitions between two locations. Here a transition $((l', \boldsymbol{x}'), (l, \boldsymbol{x})) \in T$ indicates that from the state $(l', \boldsymbol{x}')$ the system can undergo a discrete jump to the state $(l, \boldsymbol{x})$.

We assume that the uncertainty in the continuous flow is caused by some perturbation inputs in the manner: $\boldsymbol{F}(l, \boldsymbol{x}) = \{\dot{\boldsymbol{x}} \in \mathbb{R}^n \mid \dot{\boldsymbol{x}} = \boldsymbol{f}_l(\boldsymbol{x}, \boldsymbol{d}), \text{ for some } \boldsymbol{d} \in D(l)\}$, where $\boldsymbol{f}_l(\boldsymbol{x}, \boldsymbol{d})$ is a vector field that governs the flow of the system at location l, and $\boldsymbol{d}$ is a vector of perturbation inputs that takes value in $D(l) \subset \mathbb{R}^r$.

Trajectories of the hybrid system H starting from some initial state $(l_0, \boldsymbol{x}_0) \in X_0$ are concatenations of steps, with each step either being a continuous flow or a discrete transition, with the endpoint of each step matching the startpoint of the next step, and with the first step starting in $(l_0, \boldsymbol{x}_0) \in X_0$. During a continuous flow, the discrete location l is maintained and the continuous state evolves according to the differential inclusion $\dot{\boldsymbol{x}} \in \boldsymbol{F}(l, \boldsymbol{x})$, as long as $\boldsymbol{x}$ remains inside the invariant set $\text{Inv}(l)$. At a state $(l_1, \boldsymbol{x}_1)$ a discrete transition to $(l_2, \boldsymbol{x}_2)$ can occur iff $((l_1, \boldsymbol{x}_1), (l_2, \boldsymbol{x}_2)) \in T$. We then say that $\boldsymbol{x}_1 \in \mathsf{G}_{l_1, l_2} = \{\boldsymbol{x}_1 \in \mathcal{X} \mid ((l_1, \boldsymbol{x}_1), (l_2, \boldsymbol{x})) \in T \text{ for some } \boldsymbol{x} \in \mathcal{X}\}$ and $\boldsymbol{x}_2 \in \mathsf{R}_{l_1, l_2}(\boldsymbol{x}_1)$, where $\mathsf{R}_{l_1, l_2} : \boldsymbol{x}_1 \to \{\boldsymbol{x} \in \mathcal{X} \mid ((l_1, \boldsymbol{x}_1), (l_2, \boldsymbol{x})) \in T\}$. If $\mathsf{G}_{l', l}$ is empty then no discrete transition from location l' to location l is possible and the associated reset map undefined. Although not explicitly stated, it is assumed that the description of the hybrid system given above is well-posed. For example, $(l, \boldsymbol{x}) \in X_0$ automatically implies that $\boldsymbol{x} \in \text{Inv}(l)$, and $((l', \boldsymbol{x}'), (l, \boldsymbol{x})) \in T$ implies that $\boldsymbol{x}' \in \text{Inv}(l')$ and $\boldsymbol{x} \in \text{Inv}(l)$.

Given a system H and a set of unsafe states $X_u \subseteq X$, the classical *safety verification problem* is concerned with proving that no trajectory of the hybrid system H originating from the set X_0 of initial states can ever enter the unsafe region X_u. If this property holds, the hybrid system H is safe. Unfortunately, such safety verification problem is undecidable generally and consequently is challenging, even for systems with simple dynamics. In this paper we relax the notion of safety, replacing qualitative safety (no trajectory may ever reach an unsafe state) by quantitative safety (the probability of unsafe behaviors stays below a quantitative safety target with some specified confidence). We call a system satisfying the latter property *probably approximately safe*. Its concept is formally introduced in Definition 1. The probably approximate safety verification applies the PAC learning framework [15] and consequently can be regarded as statistically formal verification in the sense that it provides formal safety guarantees expressed using error probabilities and confidence.

Suppose $\mathtt{Ini}(l) = \{x \mid (l, x) \in X_0\}$ is endowed with a $\sigma-$algebra $\mathcal{D}_l$ and that a probability $\mathtt{Pr}_l$ over $\mathtt{Ini}(l)$ is assigned, where $l \in L$. In addition, we assume $\mathtt{Ini} = \mathtt{Ini}(1) \times \ldots \times \mathtt{Ini}(M)$ is endowed with a $\sigma-$algebra $\mathcal{D}'$ and that a probability $\mathtt{Pr}$ over $\mathcal{D}'$ is assigned. Obviously, $\mathtt{Pr} = \mathtt{Pr}_1 \times \ldots \times \mathtt{Pr}_M$.

Definition 1. *A hybrid system H is probably approximately safe with respect to the set* $\mathtt{Ini}$, $\epsilon \in (0, 1)$ *and* $\beta \in (0, 1)$ *(or, $\mathtt{PAS}(\epsilon, \beta)$) if with at least $1 - \beta$ confidence, $\mathtt{Pr}(C) \geq 1 - \epsilon$, where $C = \mathtt{Ini}'(1) \times \ldots \times \mathtt{Ini}'(M)$ is a subset of the set $\mathtt{Ini}$ and $\mathtt{Ini}'(l) \subseteq \mathtt{Ini}(l)$ is a set of continuous states xs in the location $l \in L$ such that trajectories of H starting from (l, x) never enter the unsafe region X_u.*

Besides, we in this paper restrict the invariant set $\mathtt{Inv}(l)$, disturbance set $D(l)$, unsafe set $\mathtt{Uns}(l)$, guard set $\mathtt{G}_{l',l}$ and initial set $\mathtt{Ini}(l)$ to the interval form for $l \in L$, where $\mathtt{Uns}(l) = \{x \mid (l, x) \in X_u\}$. The probability distribution $\mathtt{Pr}_l$ is assumed to be uniform distribution over $\mathtt{Ini}(l)$ for $l \in L$. We need to point out here that our method is not limited to this particular probability distribution. This feature is reflected in scenario approaches, which will be introduced in Subsect. 2.2. To some extent, the assumption of uniform distribution over $\mathtt{Ini}(l)$ for $l \in L$ is reasonable since every continuous state in $\mathtt{Ini}(l)$ is of equal importance especially for safety-critical systems. Any state leading to a violation of the safety property will result in a systems failure. Ideally, we wish that the hybrid system is safe for every initial state. As mentioned before, this is challenging to verify with mathematical rigor. Inspired by machine learning theory, we attempt to use a family of random finite states in $\mathtt{Ini}(l)$ to learn safety information of hybrid systems in the PAC framework and would expect to verify systems that existing verification methods are not capable of dealing with.

2.2 Scenario Approaches

The scenario optimization has been shown as an intuitive and effective way to deal with chance-constrained optimization [4,5] based on finite randomization of the constraints at the expense of giving probabilistic guarantees on the robustness of the solution. Concretely, consider the chance-constrained optimization:

$$\min_{\boldsymbol{x}\in\mathbb{R}^m} J(\boldsymbol{x})$$
$$\text{s.t. } P\big(\{\boldsymbol{\delta}\in\Delta \mid \max_{j=1,\dots,n_m} g_j(\boldsymbol{x},\boldsymbol{\delta}) \le 0\}\big) \ge 1-\epsilon, \tag{1}$$

where $\boldsymbol{\delta}\in\Delta\subseteq\mathbb{R}^r$, $J:\mathbb{R}^m\rightarrow\mathbb{R}$ is a convex function and $g_j:\mathbb{R}^m\times\mathbb{R}^r\rightarrow\mathbb{R}$ for $j=1,\dots,n_m$. Besides, $\{\boldsymbol{x}\in\mathbb{R}^m \mid \max_{j=1,\dots,n_m} g_j(\boldsymbol{x},\boldsymbol{\delta})\le 0\}$ is convex and closed for fixed $\boldsymbol{\delta}$. Any $\boldsymbol{x}$ satisfying the chance constraint of (1) is referred to as an ϵ−level feasible solution. It is assumed that Δ is endowed with a σ−algebra $\mathcal{D}$ and that P is a probability measure defined over $\mathcal{D}$.

The scenario approach substitutes the chance constraint in (1) with a finite number of hard constraints, each corresponding to a different realization $\boldsymbol{\delta}^{(k)}$, $k=1,\dots,N$ of the uncertain parameter $\boldsymbol{\delta}$, extracted independently according to the probability distribution P. This leads to the convex optimization:

$$\min_{\boldsymbol{x}\in\mathbb{R}^m} J(\boldsymbol{x})$$
$$\texttt{s.t.}\ \max_{j=1,\dots,n_m} g_j(\boldsymbol{x},\boldsymbol{\delta}^{(i)}) \le 0, i=1,\dots,N. \tag{2}$$

Assumption 1. *The convex optimization* (2) *is feasible for all possible multi-sample extractions* $(\boldsymbol{\delta}^{(1)},\dots,\boldsymbol{\delta}^{(N)})\in\Delta^N$ *and its feasibility region has a non-empty interior. Moreover, the solution* $\boldsymbol{x}^*$ *of* (2) *exists and is unique.*

One can allow for violating part of the sample constraints to improve the optimal value by removing some sample constraints. Any removal algorithm $\mathcal{A}$ can be used when removing constraints in (2) [4]. The randomized program (2) where k constraints are removed by $\mathcal{A}$ is expressed as

$$\min_{\boldsymbol{x}\in\mathbb{R}^m} J(\boldsymbol{x})$$
$$\texttt{s.t.}\ \max_{j=1,\dots,n_m} g_j(\boldsymbol{x},\boldsymbol{\delta}^{(i)}) \le 0, i\in\{1,\dots,N\}\setminus\mathcal{A}(\boldsymbol{\delta}^{(1)},\dots,\boldsymbol{\delta}^{(N)}) \tag{3}$$

and its solution is indicated as $\boldsymbol{x}^{**}$. We assume the following:

Assumption 2. $\boldsymbol{x}^{**}$ *almost surely violates all the* k *removed constraints.*

Theorem 1 [4,5]. *Let* $\beta\in(0,1)$ *be any small confidence value. If* N *and* k *are such that* $\binom{k+m-1}{k}\sum_{i=0}^{k+m-1}\binom{N}{i}\epsilon^i(1-\epsilon)^{N-i}\le\beta$, *where* m *is the number of optimization variables, then with probability at least* $1-\beta$, *we have that* $P\big(\{\boldsymbol{\delta}\in\Delta \mid \max_{j=1,\dots,n_m} g_j(\boldsymbol{x}^{**},\boldsymbol{\delta})\le 0\}\big)\ge 1-\epsilon.$

In Theorem 1, $1-\beta$ is the N-fold probability P^N in $\Delta^N=\Delta\times\Delta\times\cdots\times\Delta$, i.e., the set to which the extracted sample $(\boldsymbol{\delta}^{(1)},\dots,\boldsymbol{\delta}^{(N)})$ belongs.

2.3 Linear Interval Inequalities

A system of linear interval inequalities is formulated as $A^I y \le b^I$, where $A^I = \{A:\underline{A}\le A\le\overline{A}\}$ (component-wise inequalities) is an $m\times n$ interval matrix and $b^I=\{b:\underline{b}\le b\le\overline{b}\}$(component-wise inequalities) is an m−dimensional interval vector. A $\boldsymbol{y}_0$ is called a strong solution to the system of linear interval inequalities if it satisfies $A\boldsymbol{y}_0 \leq \boldsymbol{b}$ for each $A \in A^I$ and $\boldsymbol{b} \in \boldsymbol{b}^I$. We denote the set of all strong solutions by Y, and Y is given as follows.

Theorem 2 [28]. $Y = \{\boldsymbol{y}_1 - \boldsymbol{y}_2 : \overline{A}\boldsymbol{y}_1 - \underline{A}\boldsymbol{y}_2 \leq \underline{b}, \boldsymbol{y}_1 \geq \boldsymbol{0}, \boldsymbol{y}_2 \geq \boldsymbol{0}\}.$

A strong solution can be computed by solving a linear programming problem based on Theorem 2. Based on this, for a parametric polynomial of the form $B(\boldsymbol{x}, \boldsymbol{c}) = \sum_{\alpha \in \mathcal{M}} c_\alpha \boldsymbol{x}^\alpha$, where c_α's are parametric coefficients making $B(\boldsymbol{x}, \boldsymbol{c})$ non-positive over an interval $\boldsymbol{x} \in I$, can be obtained in the way: (1) For each monomial $\boldsymbol{x}^\alpha (\alpha \in \mathcal{M})$, we use interval arithmetic to obtain its lower and upper bounds $I^{\alpha-}$ and $I^{\alpha+}$ respectively over the interval I, and yield a linear interval inequality $\sum_{\alpha \in \mathcal{M}} [I^{\alpha-}, I^{\alpha+}] c_\alpha \leq 0$. (2) According to Theorem 2, by replacing each variable c_α with a difference of two variables $c_{\alpha 1}$ and $c_{\alpha 2}$, where $c_{\alpha 1} \geq 0$ and $c_{\alpha 2} \geq 0$, we can replace $[I^{\alpha-}, I^{\alpha+}] c_\alpha$ by $I^{\alpha+} c_{\alpha 1} - I^{\alpha-} c_{\alpha 2}$ and arrive at a linear inequality $\sum_{\alpha \in \mathcal{M}} [I^{\alpha+} c_{\alpha 1} - I^{\alpha-} c_{\alpha 2}] \leq 0$, denoted as $\psi[c_{\alpha 1}, c_{\alpha 2}]$. We denote the above procedure as `linear_interval_inequalities` $(B(\boldsymbol{x}, \boldsymbol{c}), I)$. For more details, please refer to [27,29,35]. If $(c_{\alpha 1}, c_{\alpha 2})_{\alpha \in \mathcal{M}}$, where there exists an $\alpha \in \mathcal{M}$ such that $c_{\alpha 1} - c_{\alpha 2} \neq 0$, is found, the polynomial B is obtained by substituting c_α with $c_{\alpha 1} - c_{\alpha 2}$.

3   Probably Approximate Safety Verification

In this section we detail our approach for conducting probably approximate safety verification of hybrid systems via the computation of so-called PAC barrier certificates. The concept of PAC barrier certificates is introduced in Subsect. 3.1. The computation method is formulated in Subsect. 3.2.

3.1   PAC Barrier Certificates

A popular approach to safety verification for hybrid systems employs barrier certificates, which partition the state space X into two regions containing forward reachable states of the initial states and backward reachable states of the unsafe states, respectively. There are several variants of barrier certificates and accordingly diverse methods for computing them, e.g., [7,20–22,24,32,37]. In this paper we employ exponential-condition-based barrier certificates from [21] as an instance serving to illustrate our method, which however is not confined to this particular variant of barrier certificates. Exponential-condition-based barrier certificates form the core of Theorem 3 underneath.

Theorem 3 ([21]). *Let $H = (\mathcal{X}, L, X, X_0, \text{Inv}, \boldsymbol{F}, T)$ be a hybrid system. Given $S_\lambda = \{\lambda_l \in \mathbb{R} \mid l \in L\}$ and $S_\sigma = \{\sigma_{l',l} \in \mathbb{R}_{\geq 0} \mid ((l, \cdot), (l', \cdot)) \in T\}$, if there exists a family of functions $(B_l(\boldsymbol{x}) \in C^1(\mathbb{R}^n))_{l \in L}$ such that for all $l \in L$, the following constraints hold*

$(1)\ B_l(\boldsymbol{x}) > 0, \forall \boldsymbol{x} \in \text{Uns}(l),\ (2)\ B_l(\boldsymbol{x}) \leq 0, \forall \boldsymbol{x} \in \text{Ini}(l),$

$(3)\ \dfrac{\partial B_l}{\partial \boldsymbol{x}}(\boldsymbol{x}) \boldsymbol{f}_l(\boldsymbol{x}, \boldsymbol{d}) + \lambda_l B_l(\boldsymbol{x}) \leq 0, \forall (\boldsymbol{x}, \boldsymbol{d}) \in \text{Inv}(l) \times D(l), \qquad (4)$

$(4)\ B_l(\boldsymbol{x}) - \sigma_{l',l} B_{l'}(\boldsymbol{x}') \leq 0, \forall (\boldsymbol{x}', \boldsymbol{x}) \in \mathsf{G}_{l',l} \times \mathsf{R}_{l',l}(\boldsymbol{x}'),$

then the safety of the hybrid system H is guaranteed, i.e., no trajectories starting from $(l, \boldsymbol{x})$ for $l \in L$ and $\boldsymbol{x} \in \mathtt{Ini}(l)$ will enter the unsafe state set X_u.

Based on Theorem 3, semi-definite programming based methods were proposed in [21] to synthesize barrier certificates for polynomial hybrid systems. In order to be able to automatically compute similar certificates for a much wider class of systems, we verify probably approximate safety of hybrid systems and provide a proof of this property via the computation of *PAC barrier certificates*. The concept of PAC barrier certificates is formally presented in Definition 2.

Definition 2. *Let $H = (\mathcal{X}, L, X, X_0, \mathtt{Inv}, \boldsymbol{F}, T)$ be a hybrid system. Given $S_\lambda = \{\lambda_l \in \mathbb{R} \mid l \in L\}$ and $S_\sigma = \{\sigma_{l',l} \in \mathbb{R}_{\geq 0} \mid ((l, \cdot), (l', \cdot)) \in T\}$, a family of functions $(B_l(\boldsymbol{x}) \in \mathcal{C}^1(\mathbb{R}^n))_{l \in L}$ is a family of PAC barrier certificates with respect to $\epsilon \in (0, 1)$ and $\beta \in (0, 1)$ (or, PACBC(ϵ, β)), if they satisfy the following constraints:*

1. for each $l \in L$ and $l' \in L$,

(1) $B_l(\boldsymbol{x}) > 0, \forall \boldsymbol{x} \in \mathtt{Uns}(l)$, (2) $B_l(\boldsymbol{x}) - \sigma_{l',l} B_{l'}(\boldsymbol{x}') \leq 0, \forall (\boldsymbol{x}', \boldsymbol{x}) \in \mathtt{G}_{l',l} \times \mathtt{R}_{l',l}(\boldsymbol{x}')$,

(3) $\dfrac{\partial B_l}{\partial \boldsymbol{x}}(\boldsymbol{x}) \boldsymbol{f}_l(\boldsymbol{x}, \boldsymbol{d}) + \lambda_l B_l(\boldsymbol{x}) \leq 0, \forall (\boldsymbol{x}, \boldsymbol{d}) \in \mathtt{Inv}(l) \times D(l)$.

$$(5)$$

2. with confidence of at least $1 - \beta$, $\Pr(C) \geq 1 - \epsilon$, where $C = \{\boldsymbol{y} \in \mathtt{Ini} \mid B_l(\boldsymbol{x}_l) \leq 0, l \in L\}$ with $\boldsymbol{y} = (\boldsymbol{x}_1, \ldots, \boldsymbol{x}_M)$ and $\boldsymbol{x}_l \in \mathtt{Ini}(l)$.

The PACBC(ϵ, β) is an exact barrier certificate for the system H with the initial set $\cup_{l \in L} \{(l, \boldsymbol{x}) \mid \boldsymbol{x} \in \mathtt{Ini}(l) \wedge B_l(\boldsymbol{x}) \leq 0\}$. That is, no trajectories starting from $\cup_{l \in L} \{(l, \boldsymbol{x}) \mid \boldsymbol{x} \in \mathtt{Ini}(l) \wedge B_l(\boldsymbol{x}) \leq 0\}$ will enter X_u, and the set $\cup_{l \in L} \{(l, \boldsymbol{x}) \mid \boldsymbol{x} \in \mathtt{Ini}(l) \wedge B_l(\boldsymbol{x}) \leq 0\}$ is an under-approximation of the set of initial states rendering H safe, e.g.,[33,34,36]. However, it is just a PAC barrier certificate for the system H with the initial set X_0.

Theorem 4. *If $(B_l(\boldsymbol{x}) \in \mathcal{C}^1(\mathbb{R}^n))_{l \in L}$ is PACBC(ϵ, β), the system H is PAS(ϵ, β).*

Proof. Let $C = \{\boldsymbol{y} \in \mathtt{Ini} \mid B_l(\boldsymbol{x}_l) \leq 0, l \in L\}$, where $\boldsymbol{y} = (\boldsymbol{x}_1, \ldots, \boldsymbol{x}_M)$ with $\boldsymbol{x}_l \in \mathtt{Ini}(l)$. From constraint (5) in Definition 2, we have that trajectories starting from $\cup_{l \in L} \{(l, \boldsymbol{x}) \mid \boldsymbol{x} \in \mathtt{Ini}(l) \wedge B_l(\boldsymbol{x}) \leq 0\}$ cannot enter X_u. Also, since $\Pr(C) \geq 1 - \epsilon$ with at least $1 - \beta$ confidence, H is PAS(ϵ, β) from Definition 1. □

Corollary 1 is an immediate consequence of Definition 2 and Theorem 3.

Corollary 1. *Suppose that $(B_l(\boldsymbol{x}) \in \mathcal{C}^1(\mathbb{R}^n))_{l \in L}$ is PACBC(ϵ, β). If $\mathtt{Ini}(l) \subseteq \{\boldsymbol{x} \in \mathtt{Ini}(l) \mid B_l(\boldsymbol{x}) \leq 0\}$ for $l \in L$, the hybrid system H is safe.*

Another benefit of computing PACBC(ϵ, β) is to conduct probabilistic safety verification of hybrid systems.

Corollary 2. *Suppose that $(B_l(\boldsymbol{x}) \in \mathcal{C}^1(\mathbb{R}^n))_{l \in L}$ is PACBC(ϵ, β). If $\Pr(C) \geq 1 - \epsilon$, where $C = \{\boldsymbol{y} \in \mathtt{Ini} \mid B_l(\boldsymbol{x}_l) \leq 0 \text{ for } l \in L\}$ with $\boldsymbol{y} = (\boldsymbol{x}_1, \ldots, \boldsymbol{x}_M)$ and $\boldsymbol{x}_l \in \mathtt{Ini}(l)$, then $\Pr_l(C_l) \geq 1 - \epsilon$ for $l \in L$, where C_l is a set of states $\boldsymbol{x}s$ in $\mathtt{Ini}(l)$ such that trajectories starting from $(l, \boldsymbol{x})$ never enter X_u.*

Proof. Since $\mathtt{Pr} = \mathtt{Pr}_1 \times \ldots \times \mathtt{Pr}_l$, we have that $\mathtt{Pr}_l(C_l') \geq 1 - \epsilon$, where $C_l' = \{\boldsymbol{x} \in \mathtt{Ini}(l) \mid B_l(\boldsymbol{x}) \leq 0\}$. Also, since $C_l' \subseteq C_l$, we have the conclusion. $\qquad\square$

[31] developed a tool ProbReach to address the probabilistic safety verification problem in Corollary 2 for hybrid systems. Since reachable set computation based techniques are used in [31], it is limited to safety verification of hybrid systems over finite time horizons. [19] proposed a bilinear semidefinite programming based method to compute probabilistic barrier certificates for polynomial hybrid systems. Unfortunately, the bilinear semidefinite program falls within nonlinear programming framework and is notoriously hard to solve.

3.2   Probably Approximate Safety Verification

In this section we present our linear programming based method for synthesizing $\mathtt{PACBC}(\epsilon, \beta)$ and thus conducting probably approximate safety verification of hybrid systems. The linear program is constructed based on linear interval inequalities and scenario approaches.

We first select barrier certificate templates $(B_l(c_{l,1}, \ldots, c_{l,i_l}, \boldsymbol{x}))_{l \in L}$ such that (1) $B_l(c_{l,1}, \ldots, c_{l,i_l}, \boldsymbol{x}) \in \mathcal{C}^1(\mathbb{R}^n)$ is a linear function in $c_{l,1}, \ldots, c_{l,i_l}$ for $\boldsymbol{x} \in \mathbb{R}^n$, where $(c_{l,j})_{j=1}^{i_l}$ are unknown parameters and $i_l \geq 1$ is a positive integer. For convenience c_l is used to denote $(c_{l,1}, \ldots, c_{l,i_l})$ in the rest of this paper. (2) Let $C_r = \{\boldsymbol{x} \in \mathtt{Ini}(l) \mid B_l(c_l, \boldsymbol{x}) = r\}$ for $r \in \mathbb{R}$,

$$\mathtt{Pr}_l(C_r) = 0, \forall l \in L, \forall r \in \mathbb{R}. \tag{6}$$

This requirement is to ensure that the solution computed by scenario approaches satisfies Assumption 2, which will be reflected in Lemma 1. Generally, polynomial functions satisfy the requirement (6).

Under the assumption that ϵ is given (later, we will introduce how to give an appropriate ϵ), we try to compute $(c_l)_{l \in L}$ by solving the following chance-constrained optimization:

$$\min_{c_l, l \in L, \theta} \theta + \sum_{l=1}^{M} w_l \int_{\mathtt{Ini}(l)} B(c_l, \boldsymbol{x})d\boldsymbol{x}, \tag{7}$$

$$\mathtt{s.t.} \mathtt{Pr}(\{\boldsymbol{y} \in \mathtt{Ini} \mid \max_{l \in L} B(c_l, \boldsymbol{x}_l) \leq \theta\}) \geq 1 - \epsilon, \tag{8}$$

$$0 \leq \theta \leq U_\theta, \tag{9}$$

$$\text{for each } l \in L \text{ and } l \in L' : \tag{10}$$

$$B_l(\boldsymbol{x}) - \zeta_l \geq 0, \forall \boldsymbol{x} \in \mathtt{Uns}(l), \tag{11}$$

$$\frac{\partial B_l}{\partial \boldsymbol{x}}(\boldsymbol{x})f_l(\boldsymbol{x}, d) + \lambda_l B_l(\boldsymbol{x}) \leq 0, \forall(\boldsymbol{x}, d) \in \mathtt{Inv}(l) \times D(l), \tag{12}$$

$$B_l(\boldsymbol{x}) - \sigma_{l',l} B_{l'}(\boldsymbol{x}') \leq 0, \forall(\boldsymbol{x}', \boldsymbol{x}) \in \mathtt{G}_{l',l} \times \mathtt{R}_{l',l}(\boldsymbol{x}'), \tag{13}$$

where $\boldsymbol{y} = (\boldsymbol{x}_1, \ldots, \boldsymbol{x}_M)$ with $\boldsymbol{x}_l \in \mathtt{Ini}(l)$, $\sigma_{l',l} \in \mathbb{R}_{\geq 0}$, $\zeta_l \in \mathbb{R}_{>0}$ and $\lambda_l \in \mathbb{R}$ are given, and U_θ is a user-defined positive bound for θ. w_ls, $l = 1, \ldots, M$, are given positive values such that $\sum_{l=1}^{M} w_l = 1$. In (7), w_l for $l \in L$ represents the relative significance of the l_{th} set $\texttt{Ini}(l)$. The minimum operator on $\int_{\texttt{Ini}(l)} B(c_l, x) dx$ aims to find c_l such that $\{x \in \texttt{Ini}(l) \mid B(c_l, x) \leq 0\}$, which is a set of states xs such that trajectories starting from (l, x) never enter X_u, is as large as possible.

Solving the chance-constrained optimization (7)–(13) directly is notoriously hard. It generally falls within the nonlinear programming framework and is an NP-hard problem. Below we show the use of scenario approaches and linear interval inequalities to encode (7)–(13) as a linear programming problem, whose solution provides a family of PAC barrier certificates with respect to ϵ and β.

We first relax constraints (11)–(13) to linear constraints over c_l using linear interval inequalities. For this sake, we first construct a family of interval boxes $(I_{\texttt{U}(l)}^i)_{i=1}^{k_{1,l}}$, $(I_{\texttt{Inv}(l)}^i)_{i=1}^{k_{2,l}}$ and $(I_{\texttt{G}_{l',l}}^i)_{i=1}^{k_{3,l}}$ such that $\texttt{Uns}(l) \subseteq \cup_{i=1}^{k_{1,l}} I_{\texttt{U}(l)}^i$, $\texttt{Inv}(l) \times D(l) \subseteq \cup_{i=1}^{k_{2,l}} I_{\texttt{Inv}(l)}^i$ and $\texttt{G}_{l',l} \subseteq \cup_{i=1}^{k_{3,l}} I_{\texttt{G}_{l',l}}^i$, respectively. Then, for $i = 1, \ldots, k_{1,l}$, we obtain a linear relaxation $\psi_{1,i}[c_{1,l}, c_{2,l}]$ of the constraint $-B_l(c_l, x) + \zeta_l \leq 0$ for $x \in \texttt{Uns}(l)$ based on $\texttt{linear\_interval\_inequalities}(-B_l(c_l, x) + \zeta_l, I_{\texttt{U}(l)}^i)$, where $\zeta_l \in \mathbb{R}_{>0}$ is a user-defined small positive value. If $(c_{1,l}, c_{2,l})$ satisfies $\wedge_{i=1}^{k_{1,l}} \psi_{1,i}[c_{1,l}, c_{2,l}]$, $-B_l(c_{1,l} - c_{2,l}, x) < 0$ for $x \in \texttt{Uns}(l)$. Analogously, we obtain linear relaxations $\wedge_{i=1}^{k_{2,l}} \psi_{2,i}[c_{1,l}, c_{2,l}]$ and $\wedge_{i=1}^{k_{3,l}} \psi_{3,i}[c_{1,l}, c_{2,l}]$ of constraints (12) and (13), respectively. Therefore, if $(c_{1,l}, c_{2,l})_{l \in L}$ satisfies

$$\wedge_{i=1}^{k_{1,l}} \psi_{1,i}[c_{1,l}, c_{2,l}] \bigwedge \wedge_{i=1}^{k_{2,l}} \psi_{2,i}[c_{1,l}, c_{2,l}] \bigwedge \wedge_{i=1}^{k_{3,l}} \psi_{3,i}[c_{1,l}, c_{2,l}], \tag{14}$$

$(B_l(c_{1,l} - c_{2,l}, x))_{l \in L}$ satisfies constraints (11), (12) and (13). For ease of exposition, we denote (14) by $\psi_l[c_{1,l}, c_{2,l}]$.

Next, we substitute the chance constraint (8) with N hard constraints, which are constructed based on N independent and identically distributed samples $(y_i)_{i=1}^N$ with $y_i = (x_{1,i}, \ldots, x_{M,i})$ extracted from the set $\texttt{Ini}$ according to the probabilistic distribution $\texttt{Pr}$, where $x_{l,i} \in \texttt{Ini}(l)$ for $l = 1, \ldots, M$. The N hard constraints over c_l and θ are $\max_{l \in L} B_l(c_l, x_{l,i}) \leq \theta, i = 1, \ldots, N$. Obviously, $B_l(c_l, x_{l,i}) \leq \theta$ is a linear function in c_l and θ.

Finally, we obtain a linear relaxation (15) over $(c_{i,l})$ and θ for solving (7)–(13),

$$\min_{c_{i,l}, i=1,2, l \in L, \theta} \theta + \sum_{l=1}^{M} w_l \int_{\texttt{Ini}(l)} B(c_{1,l} - c_{2,l}, x) dx$$

$\texttt{s.t. for each } i = 1, \ldots, N : \max_{l \in L} B_l(c_{1,l} - c_{2,l}, x_{l,i}) \leq \theta,$

$\texttt{for each } l \in L : (1) \; \psi_l[c_{1,l}, c_{2,l}], (2) \; 0 \leq \theta \leq U_\theta, c_{i,l} \leq U_c, i = 1, 2,$
$$\tag{15}$$

where $U_c \in \mathbb{R}_{>0}$ is a pre-specified upper bound for $c_{i,l}$ for $l \in L$ and $i = 1, 2$, and $U_\theta \in \mathbb{R}_{>0}$ is pre-specified upper bound for θ. Let $(c_{1,1}^*, c_{2,1}^*, \ldots, c_{1,M}^*, c_{2,M}^*, \theta^*)$ be an optimal solution to the linear program (15).

Remark 1. After obtaining $(c_{1,1}^*, c_{2,1}^*, \ldots, c_{1,M}^*, c_{2,M}^*, \theta^*)$, $\texttt{Pr}(C)$ can be estimated based on the Chernoff-Hoeffding Bound [18] in the statistical context.

The Chernoff-Hoeffding Bound formulates that with a confidence of at least $1 - e^{-2N\epsilon'^2}$, $\mathtt{Pr}(C) \geq p - \epsilon'$ with $p = \frac{N'}{N}$, where C is defined in Definition 1 and N' is the number of sample states $\boldsymbol{y}_i$s such that $\max_{l \in L} B_l(\boldsymbol{c}^*_{1,l} - \boldsymbol{c}^*_{2,l}, \boldsymbol{x}_{l,i}) \leq 0$. In the following we give a different estimation based on scenario approaches. The difference between these two estimations will be presented in examples.

Based on the computed solution $(\boldsymbol{c}^*_{1,1}, \boldsymbol{c}^*_{2,1}, \ldots, \boldsymbol{c}^*_{1,M}, \boldsymbol{c}^*_{2,M})$, we further relax the linear program (15) as a new linear program over the single variable θ:

$$\min_{\theta} \theta + \sum_{l=1}^{M} w_l \int_{\mathtt{Ini}(l)} B(\boldsymbol{c}^*_{1,l} - \boldsymbol{c}^*_{2,l}, \boldsymbol{x}) d\boldsymbol{x}$$

$$\text{s.t. for each } i = 1, \ldots, N : \max_{l \in L} B_l(\boldsymbol{c}^*_{1,l} - \boldsymbol{c}^*_{2,l}, \boldsymbol{x}_{l,i}) \leq \theta,$$

$$\text{for each } l \in L : (1) \; \psi_l[\boldsymbol{c}^*_{1,l}, \boldsymbol{c}^*_{2,l}], \; (2) \; 0 \leq \theta \leq U_\theta, \boldsymbol{c}^*_{i,l} \leq U_c, i = 1, 2.$$

$$(16)$$

Obviously, (16) is feasible. Also, the optimal value of θ is unique and equal to θ^*. Assumption 1 is satisfied.

Then we remove samples from $(\boldsymbol{x}_{1,i}, \ldots, \boldsymbol{x}_{M,i})_{i=1}^{N}$ such that $\max_{l \in L} B_l(\boldsymbol{c}^*_{1,l} - \boldsymbol{c}^*_{2,l}, \boldsymbol{x}_{l,i}) > 0$, and denote the indexes of removed constraints by $\{i_1, \ldots, i_k\}$, leading eventually to the following linear program,

$$\min_{\theta} \theta + \sum_{l=1}^{M} w_l \int_{\mathtt{Ini}(l)} B(\boldsymbol{c}^*_{1,l} - \boldsymbol{c}^*_{2,l}, \boldsymbol{x}) d\boldsymbol{x}$$

$$\text{s.t. for each } i = 1, \ldots, N \setminus \{i_1, \ldots, i_k\} : \max_{l \in L} B_l(\boldsymbol{c}^*_{1,l} - \boldsymbol{c}^*_{2,l}, \boldsymbol{x}_{l,i}) \leq \theta,$$

$$\text{for each } l \in L : (1) \; \psi_l[\boldsymbol{c}^*_{1,l}, \boldsymbol{c}^*_{2,l}], \; (2) \; 0 \leq \theta \leq U_\theta, \boldsymbol{c}^*_{i,l} \leq U_c, i = 1, 2.$$

$$(17)$$

Let θ^{**} be an optimal solution to the linear program (17). Obviously, $\theta^{**} = 0$.

Remark 2. Although the removed sample $(x_{1,j}, \ldots, x_{M,j})$ satisfies $\max_{i \in L} B_l (\boldsymbol{c}^*_{1,i} - \boldsymbol{c}^*_{2,i}, \boldsymbol{x}_{l,j}) > 0$, where $j \in \{i_1, \ldots, i_k\}$, it does not indicate that the hybrid system H starting from $(l, \boldsymbol{x}_{l,j})$ will enter X_u, since the existence of barrier certificates satisfying (4) is just a sufficient condition for justifying the safety of the system.

The constraint removal algorithm $\mathcal{A}$ for obtaining (17) can be chosen as $\mathcal{A}(\boldsymbol{y}_1, \ldots, \boldsymbol{y}_N) = \{i_1, \ldots, i_k\}$, where $\left(\max_{l \in L} B_l(\boldsymbol{c}^*_{1,l} - \boldsymbol{c}^*_{2,l}, \boldsymbol{x}_{l,i_j}) \right)_{j=1}^{k}$ are the first k largest values in $\left(\max_{l \in L} B_l(\boldsymbol{c}^*_{1,l} - \boldsymbol{c}^*_{2,l}, \boldsymbol{x}_{l,i}) \right)_{i=1}^{N}$. Let $\boldsymbol{z} = (\boldsymbol{y}_1, \ldots, \boldsymbol{y}_N)$. According to (6), $\mathtt{Pr}^N(\{\boldsymbol{z} \in \mathtt{Ini}^N | \theta^{**}(\boldsymbol{z}) \text{ violates the } k \text{ removed constraints}\}) = 1$, satisfying Assumption 2. This is formally stated in Lemma 1. Obviously, $\theta^{**}(\boldsymbol{z}) = \max_{l \in L} \max_{i \in \{1, \ldots, N\} \setminus \{i_1, \ldots, i_k\}} B_l(\boldsymbol{c}^*_{1,i} - \boldsymbol{c}^*_{2,i}, \boldsymbol{x}_{l,i})$. Herein, we shall write the optimal solutions to (17) as $\theta^{**}(\boldsymbol{z})$ to emphasize its stochastic nature.

Lemma 1. *Let* $\mathcal{A}(\boldsymbol{y}_1, \ldots, \boldsymbol{y}_N) = \{i_1, \ldots, i_k\}$ *in* (17) *and* $\big(\max_{l \in L} B_l(\boldsymbol{c}_{1,l}^*(\boldsymbol{z}) - \boldsymbol{c}_{2,l}^*(\boldsymbol{z}), \boldsymbol{x}_{l,i_j}) \big)_{j=1}^k$ *be the first* k *largest values in the family* $\big(\max_{l \in L} B_l(\boldsymbol{c}_{1,l}^*(\boldsymbol{z}) - \boldsymbol{c}_{2,l}^*(\boldsymbol{z}), \boldsymbol{x}_{l,i}) \big)_{i=1}^N$. *Then* $\mathrm{Pr}^N(S) = 1$, *where*

$$S = \big\{ \boldsymbol{z} \in \mathtt{Ini}^N \mid \theta^{**}(\boldsymbol{z}) \text{ violates the } k \text{ removed constraints} \big\}$$

and $\boldsymbol{z} = (\boldsymbol{y}_1, \ldots, \boldsymbol{y}_N)$, $\boldsymbol{y}_i = (\boldsymbol{x}_{1,i}, \ldots, \boldsymbol{x}_{M,i})$ *with* $\boldsymbol{x}_{l,i} \in \mathtt{Ini}(l)$ *for* $l \in L$ *and* $i \in \{1, \ldots, N\}$.

Proof. Let $A = \big\{ \boldsymbol{z} \in \mathtt{Ini}^N | \theta^{**}(\boldsymbol{z}) \text{ does not violate the } k \text{ removed constraints} \big\}$.

Let $\mathcal{M} = \{1, \ldots, N\}$, $\boldsymbol{z}_0 = (\boldsymbol{y}_{1,0}, \ldots, \boldsymbol{y}_{N,0}) \in A$ with $\boldsymbol{y}_{i,0} = (\boldsymbol{x}_{1,i,0}, \ldots, \boldsymbol{x}_{M,i,0})$ and $\boldsymbol{x}_{l,i,0} \in \mathtt{Ini}(l)$ for $l \in L$ and $i \in \mathcal{M}$, and $\mathcal{M}' = \{i_1, \ldots, i_k\}$. Consequently,

$$\max_{i \in \mathcal{M} \setminus \mathcal{M}'} \max_{l \in L} B_l(\boldsymbol{c}_{1,l}^*(\boldsymbol{z}_0) - \boldsymbol{c}_{2,l}^*(\boldsymbol{z}_0), \boldsymbol{x}_{l,i,0}) = \min_{j \in \mathcal{M}'} \max_{l \in L} B_l(\boldsymbol{c}_{1,l}^*(\boldsymbol{z}_0) - \boldsymbol{c}_{2,l}^*(\boldsymbol{z}_0), \boldsymbol{x}_{l,j,0}).$$

Let $B = \left\{ \boldsymbol{z} \in \mathtt{Ini}^N \middle| \begin{array}{l} \max_{i \in \mathcal{M} \setminus \mathcal{M}'} \max_{l \in L} B_l(\boldsymbol{c}_{1,l}^*(\boldsymbol{z}) - \boldsymbol{c}_{2,l}^*(\boldsymbol{z}), \boldsymbol{x}_{l,i}) \\ = \min_{j \in \mathcal{M}'} \max_{l \in L} B_l(\boldsymbol{c}_{1,l}^*(\boldsymbol{z}) - \boldsymbol{c}_{2,l}^*(\boldsymbol{z}), \boldsymbol{x}_{l,j}) \end{array} \right\}$. Obviously,

$A = B$. Also, since $\mathrm{Pr}_l(\{\boldsymbol{x} \in \mathtt{Ini}(l) \mid B_l(\boldsymbol{c}_{1,l}^* - \boldsymbol{c}_{2,l}^*, \boldsymbol{x}) = r\}) = 0$ for $r \in \mathbb{R}$ according to (6), we have that $\mathrm{Pr}(\{\boldsymbol{y} \in \mathtt{Ini} \mid \max_{l \in L} B_l(\boldsymbol{c}_{1,l}^* - \boldsymbol{c}_{2,l}^*, \boldsymbol{x}_l) = r\}) = 0$ for $r \in \mathbb{R}$. Therefore, $\mathrm{Pr}^N(B) = 0$ and consequently $\mathrm{Pr}^N(A) = 0$. □

Therefore, according to Theorem 1, if ϵ satisfies $\sum_{i=0}^k \binom{N}{i} \epsilon^i (1 - \epsilon)^{N-i} \le \beta$, $(B_l(\boldsymbol{c}_{1,l}^* - \boldsymbol{c}_{2,l}^*, \boldsymbol{x}))_{l \in L}$ is PACBC(ϵ, β).

Theorem 5. *If* ϵ *satisfies* $\sum_{i=0}^k \binom{N}{i} \epsilon^i (1 - \epsilon)^{N-i} \le \beta$, *the system* H *is* PAS(ϵ, β).

Proof. We reformulate (16) equivalently as the following linear program over θ,

$$\min_{\theta} \theta + \sum_{l=1}^M w_l \int_{\mathtt{Ini}(l)} B(\boldsymbol{c}_{1,l}^* - \boldsymbol{c}_{2,l}^*, \boldsymbol{x}) d\boldsymbol{x}$$

s.t.   for each $i = 1, \ldots, N : \max_{l \in L} B_l(\boldsymbol{c}_{1,l}^* - \boldsymbol{c}_{2,l}^*, \boldsymbol{y}_i) \le \theta$,

for each $l \in L$: (1) $\psi_l[\boldsymbol{c}_{1,l}^*, \boldsymbol{c}_{2,l}^*]$, (2) $0 \le \theta \le U_\theta, \boldsymbol{c}_{i,l}^* \le U_c, i = 1, 2$,
(18)

where $B_l(\boldsymbol{c}_{1,l}^* - \boldsymbol{c}_{2,l}^*, \boldsymbol{y}_i) = B_l(\boldsymbol{c}_{1,l}^* - \boldsymbol{c}_{2,l}^*, \boldsymbol{x}_{l,i})$ and $\boldsymbol{y}_i = (\boldsymbol{x}_{1,i}, \ldots, \boldsymbol{x}_{M,i})$ with $\boldsymbol{x}_{l,i} \in \mathtt{Ini}(l)$ and $l \in L$. The number of variables in (18) is 1.

Optimal solutions to (18) are optimal solutions to (17), and vice versa. Obviously, (18) is feasible and has unique solution. Also, according to Lemma 1, Assumption 2 holds. Thus, according to Definition 2 and Theorem 1, $(B_l(\boldsymbol{c}_{1,l}^* - \boldsymbol{c}_{2,l}^*, \boldsymbol{x}))_{l \in L}$ is PACBC(ϵ, β). Thus, the system H is PAS(ϵ, β) from Theorem 4. □

If $k > 0$, ϵ satisfying Theorem 5 can be explicitly relaxed as the following constraint according to inequation (8) in [5]:

$$\epsilon \ge \min\{1, \frac{1}{N}[k + \ln \frac{1}{\beta} + \sqrt{\ln^2 \frac{1}{\beta} + 2k \ln \frac{1}{\beta}}]\}. \tag{19}$$

If $k = 0$, ϵ satisfying Theorem 5 can be explicitly relaxed as the following constraint according to inequation (4) in [6]:

$$\epsilon \geq 1 - \beta^{\frac{1}{N}}. \tag{20}$$

Remark 3. One may compute the probability of continuous states leading to the satisfiability of safety properties via calculating $\int_C d\mathtt{Pr}$, where $C = \{x \in \mathtt{Ini}(1) \mid B_1(c^*_{1,l} - c^*_{2,l}, x) \leq 0\} \times \ldots \times \{x \in \mathtt{Ini}(M) \mid B_M(c^*_{1,l} - c^*_{2,l}, x) \leq 0\}$. Although there are methods, e.g. [16], to compute $\int_C d\mathtt{Pr}$, we have to point out that this computation is nontrivial generally, especially for high-dimensional systems.

4   Experiments

In this section we evaluate our method on some examples. Parameters that determine the performance of our method are presented in Table 1. All computations were performed on MATLAB installed on an i7-7500U 2.70 GHz CPU with 32G RAM running Windows 10. In our following computations, we adopt uniform grid spacings when partitioning continuous state spaces.

Example 1. Consider a pendulum described by differential equations

$$\dot{x} = y, \dot{y} = -d_0 \sin(x) - d_1 y,$$

where $\mathtt{Inv}(1) = [-10, 10] \times [-10, 10]$, $\mathtt{Ini}(1) = [-10, 5] \times [8, 10]$, $\mathtt{Uns}(1) = [9, 10] \times [7, 8]$ and $D(1) = \{(d_0, d_1) \mid d_0 \in [0.9, 1.1], d_1 \in [0.9, 1.1]\}$.
    The PAC barrier certificate template is $c_0 + c_1 x + c_2 y + c_3 x^2 + c_4 xy + c_5 y^2$. We first try to find a barrier certificate to verify whether this system is safe. The sets $\mathtt{Inv}(1)$, $\mathtt{Uns}(1)$ and $\mathtt{Ini}(1)$ are partitioned into 10^4, 1 and 10^4 interval boxes, respectively. The system of linear constraints constructed by using

Table 1. $\dim_v$: dimension of the state space; $\dim_p$: dimension of the perturbation space; k: number of removed samples; ϵ: error level; β: confidence level; N: number of extracted samples; m: number of variables in (15); ζ: ζ_ls in (7)–(13); σ: $\sigma_{l',l}$s in (7)–(13); γ: γ_ls in (7)–(13); w: weights w_l in (15); U: upper bounds U_c and U_θ in (15); T: computation times (seconds)

Benchmarks	Dimension		Parameter												Time
	$\dim_v$	$\dim_p$	M	ϵ	β	N	k	m	ζ	σ	γ	w	U		T
Ex.3	2	2	1	0.05	10^{-12}	10^4	180	9	10^{-3}	–	1	1	10		19.10
Ex.4	2	0	2	0.47	10^{-12}	10^4	3559	25	10^{-3}	1	1	$\frac{1}{2}$	10		140.73
Ex.4	2	0	2	0.02	10^{-12}	10^4	9	25	10^{-3}	1	1	$\frac{1}{2}$	10		39.79
Ex.4	2	0	2	0.008	10^{-12}	10^4	0	25	10^{-3}	1	1	$\frac{1}{2}$	10		36.65
Ex.5	101	1	1	0.05	10^{-12}	10^4	0	203	10^{-3}	–	1	1	10		148.25

`linear_interval_inequalities`$(\cdot, \cdot)$ to encode the constraints in Theorem 3 is infeasible and consequently we have no knowledge of the safety of this system.

However, if we partition `Inv(1)` and `Uns(1)` into 400 and 1 interval boxes respectively, and then sample 10^4 states from `Ini(1)`, we obtain a PAC barrier certificate $B(x, y)$. $\{(x, y) \in \text{Ini}(1) \mid B(x, y) \leq 0\}$ is illustrated in Fig. 1. The number of removed samples is 180. Thus, the system is `PAS`$(0.021, 10^{-12})$. Note that the Chernoff-Hoeffding Bound indicates that the system is `PAS`$(0.052, 10^{-12})$.

This example also demonstrates that our approach can reduce the computational burden in safety verification of systems, albeit at the price of the computed barrier certificate being only probably approximately correct.

Example 2. We consider a hybrid model of a two-tank system, taken from [8]. The hybrid model has a continuous component of the state-space of dimension $n = 2$. It consists of 2 locations. The flow for each location is described by

$$f_1 \begin{pmatrix} x_1 \\ x_2 \end{pmatrix} = \begin{pmatrix} 1 - \sqrt{x_1} \\ \sqrt{x_1} - \sqrt{x_2} \end{pmatrix}, f_2 \begin{pmatrix} x_1 \\ x_2 \end{pmatrix} = \begin{pmatrix} 1 - \sqrt{x_1 - x_2 + 1} \\ \sqrt{x_1 - x_2 + 1} - \sqrt{x_2} \end{pmatrix}.$$

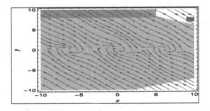

Fig. 1. An illustration of probably approximate safety verification for Example 1. Green, red and gray regions denote `Ini(1)`, `Uns(1)` and $\{(x, y) \in \text{Inv}(1) \mid B(x, y) \leq 0\}$, respectively. Blue curves denote vector fields when $(d_0, d_1) = (1, 1)$. (Color figure online)

The other parts of the hybrid automaton are:

1. Initial conditions: $\text{Ini}(1) = [5.25, 5.75] \times [0, 0.5]$ and $\text{Ini}(2) = [4, 6] \times [1, 1]$
2. Unsafe regions: $\text{Uns}(1) = [4, 4.5] \times [0, 0.5]$ and $\text{Uns}(2) = \emptyset$
3. Invariants: $\text{Inv}(1) = [4, 6] \times [0, 1]$ and $\text{Inv}(2) = [4, 6] \times [1, 2]$
4. Guards and resets: (a) $\text{G}_{1,2} = [4, 6] \times [0.99, 1]$ and $\text{R}_{1,2} \begin{pmatrix} x_1 \\ x_2 \end{pmatrix} = \begin{pmatrix} x_1 \\ 1 \end{pmatrix}$ (b) $\text{G}_{2,1} = \emptyset$ and $\text{R}_{2,1} \begin{pmatrix} x_1 \\ x_2 \end{pmatrix} = \begin{pmatrix} x_1 \\ x_2 \end{pmatrix}$.

The PAC barrier certificate templates are polynomials of this form $c_0 + c_1 x + c_2 y + c_3 x^2 + c_4 xy + c_5 y^2$. The sets `Inv(1)`, `Inv(2)`, $\text{G}_{1,2}$ are partitioned into 100, 1 and 1 interval boxes, respectively.

1. When no partition operator is implemented on `Uns(1)`, the number k of removed samples is 3559. According to (19), the system is `PAS`$(0.359, 10^{-12})$. Note that the Chernoff-Hoeffding Bound indicates that the system is `PAS`$(0.394, 10^{-12})$.

2. When the unsafe set $\mathtt{Uns}(1)$ is partitioned into 25 interval boxes, the number k of removed samples is 9. According to (19), the system is $\mathtt{PAS}(0.004, 10^{-12})$. The Chernoff-Hoeffding Bound indicates that the system is $\mathtt{PAS}(0.039, 10^{-12})$.

3. When the unsafe set $\mathtt{Uns}(1)$ is partitioned into 100 interval boxes, the number k of removed samples is 0. According to (20), the system is $\mathtt{PAS}(0.003, 10^{-12})$. The Chernoff-Hoeffding Bound indicates that the system is $\mathtt{PAS}(0.038, 10^{-12})$. For this case we use the satisfiability checker iSAT3 [12] to obtain that the computed PAC barrier certificate actually is a true barrier certificate satisfying (4), indicating that this system is safe.

The zero sublevel sets of the computed $\mathtt{PACBC}(\epsilon, \beta)$ for these three cases are illustrated in Fig. 2. From this example we observe that the size of linear program (15) depends on these two probability measures ϵ and β.

Example 3. To demonstrate applicability of our approach to high-dimensional systems, we consider a scalable non-polynomial example adapted from [25], which we instantiate with a rather high continuous dimension of 101.

$$\dot{x}_1 = d_0 + \frac{1}{100}\Big(\sum_{i \in \{1,\dots,l\}} x_{i+1} + x_{i+2}\Big),$$

$$\dot{x}_2 = x_3, \dot{x}_3 = -10\sin x_2 - x_2,$$

$$\dots$$

$$\dot{x}_{2l} = x_{2l+1}, \dot{x}_{2l+1} = -10\sin x_{2l} - x_2,$$

where $l = 50$, $D(1) = \{d_0 \mid d_0 \in [0.9, 1.1]\}$, $\mathtt{Inv}(1) = [-0.3, 0.3]^{2l+1}$, $\mathtt{Ini}(1) = [-0.30, 0.00] \times [-0.2, 0.30]^{2l}$ and $\mathtt{Uns}(1) = [-0.20, -0.15] \times [-0.30, -0.25]^{2l}$.

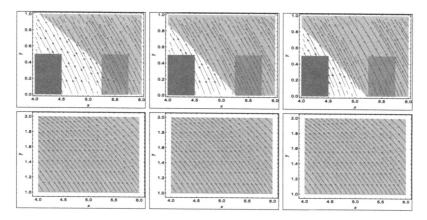

Fig. 2. An illustration of probably approximate safety verification for Example 2 with Case 1–3 (from left to right). Above: Gray region, Green region an Red region denote $\{(x, y) \in \mathtt{Inv}(1) \mid B_1(x, y) \leq 0\}$, $\mathtt{Ini}(1)$ and $\mathtt{Uns}(1)$, respectively. Below: Gray region and Green region denote $\{(x, y) \in \mathtt{Inv}(2) \mid B_2(x, y) \leq 0\}$ and $\mathtt{Ini}(2)$, respectively. (Color figure online)

The PAC barrier certificate template is chosen as $c_0 + \sum_{i=1}^{101} c_i x_i$. When no partition operator is implemented on the invariant set $\mathtt{Inv}(1)$, unsafe set $\mathtt{Uns}(1)$ and initial set $\mathtt{Ini}(1)$, the system of linear constraints constructed by using $\mathtt{linear\_interval\_inequalities}(\cdot, \cdot)$ to encode the constraints in Theorem 3 is infeasible. However, our method verifies that the system is $\mathtt{PAS}(0.003, 10^{-12})$ when no partition operator is implemented on $\mathtt{Inv}(1)$ and $\mathtt{Uns}(1)$. Note that the Chernoff-Hoeffding Bound indicates that the system is $\mathtt{PAS}(0.038, 10^{-12})$.

The dimensionality of this example demonstrates that our approach has great potential to open up a promising prospect for formal verification of industrial-scale (hybrid) systems by selecting appropriate ϵ, β and barrier certificate templates. In order to further enhance the scalability of our approach, we will encode constraint (5) using the scenario approach in our future work.

5   Conclusion

We have successfully leveraged the idea of scenario optimization to conduct safety verification of hybrid systems over the infinite time horizon in the framework of PAC learning theory. Based on scenario approaches and linear interval inequalities, a linear programming based method was proposed to compute PAC barrier functions and thus conduct probably approximate safety verification of hybrid systems in the sense that with at least $1 - \beta$ confidence, the probability that the system is safe is larger than $1 - \epsilon$. We have demonstrated the performance and merits of our approach on some benchmark examples.

Acknowledgements. Bai Xue was funded by CAS Pioneer Hundred Talents Program under grant No. Y8YC235015, NSFC under grant No. 61872341 and 61836005. Martin Fränzle was funded by Deutsche Forschungsgemeinschaft through grant FR 2715/4. Hengjun Zhao was funded by NSFC under grant No. 61702425. Naijun Zhan was funded by NSFC under grant No. 61625206 and 61732001. Arvind Easwaran was supported by the Energy Research Institute (ERI@N), NTU, Singapore.

References

1. Alur, R.: Formal verification of hybrid systems. In: EMSOFT 2011, pp. 273–278. IEEE (2011)
2. Alur, R., Courcoubetis, C., Henzinger, T.A., Ho, P.-H.: Hybrid automata: an algorithmic approach to the specification and verification of hybrid systems. In: Grossman, R.L., Nerode, A., Ravn, A.P., Rischel, H. (eds.) HS 1991-1992. LNCS, vol. 736, pp. 209–229. Springer, Heidelberg (1993). https://doi.org/10.1007/3-540-57318-6_30
3. Asarin, E., Maler, O.: Achilles and the tortoise climbing up the arithmetical hierarchy. J. Comput. Syst. Sci. **57**(3), 389–398 (1998)
4. Calafiore, G.C.: Random convex programs. SIAM J. Optim. **20**(6), 3427–3464 (2010)
5. Campi, M.C., Garatti, S.: A sampling-and-discarding approach to chance-constrained optimization: feasibility and optimality. J. Optim. Theory Appl. **148**(2), 257–280 (2011)

6. Campi, M.C., Garatti, S., Prandini, M.: The scenario approach for systems and control design. Annu. Rev. Control **33**(2), 149–157 (2009)
7. Dai, L., Gan, T., Xia, B., Zhan, N.: Barrier certificates revisited. J. Symb. Comput. **80**, 62–86 (2017)
8. Djaballah, A.: Computation of barrier certificates for dynamical hybrids systems using interval analysis. Université Paris-Saclay (2017)
9. Egyed, A.: Invited talk: a roadmap for engineering safe and secure cyber-physical systems. In: MEDI 2018, pp. 113–114 (2018)
10. Fränzle, M.: Analysis of hybrid systems: an ounce of realism can save an infinity of states. In: Flum, J., Rodriguez-Artalejo, M. (eds.) CSL 1999. LNCS, vol. 1683, pp. 126–139. Springer, Heidelberg (1999). https://doi.org/10.1007/3-540-48168-0_10
11. Fränzle, M., Gerwinn, S., Kröger, P., Abate, A., Katoen, J.-P.: Multi-objective parameter synthesis in probabilistic hybrid systems. In: Sankaranarayanan, S., Vicario, E. (eds.) FORMATS 2015. LNCS, vol. 9268, pp. 93–107. Springer, Cham (2015). https://doi.org/10.1007/978-3-319-22975-1_7
12. Fränzle, M., Herde, C., Teige, T., Ratschan, S., Schubert, T.: Efficient solving of large non-linear arithmetic constraint systems with complex boolean structure. J. Satisf. Boolean Model. Comput. **1**, 209–236 (2007)
13. Fränzle, M., Shirmohammadi, M., Swaminathan, M., Worrell, J.: Costs and rewards in priced timed automata. In: ICALP 2018, pp. 125:1–125:14 (2018)
14. Gao, S., Avigad, J., Clarke, E.M.: Delta-decidability over the reals. In: LICS 2012, pp. 305–314 (2012)
15. Haussler, D.: Probably approximately correct learning. Computer Research Laboratory, University of California, Santa Cruz (1990)
16. Henrion, D., Lasserre, J.B., Savorgnan, C.: Approximate volume and integration for basic semialgebraic sets. SIAM Rev. **51**(4), 722–743 (2009)
17. Henzinger, T.A., Kopke, P.W., Puri, A., Varaiya, P.: What's decidable about hybrid automata? J. Comput. Syst. Sci. **57**(1), 94–124 (1998)
18. Hoeffding, W.: Probability inequalities for sums of bounded random variables. J. Am. Stat. Assoc. **58**(301), 13–30 (1963)
19. Huang, C., Chen, X., Lin, W., Yang, Z., Li, X.: Probabilistic safety verification of stochastic hybrid systems using barrier certificates. ACM Trans. Embed. Comput. Syst. **16**(5), 186:1–186:19 (2017)
20. Kong, H., Bogomolov, S., Schilling, C., Jiang, Y., Henzinger, T.A.: Safety verification of nonlinear hybrid systems based on invariant clusters. In: HSCC 2017, pp. 163–172. ACM (2017)
21. Kong, H., He, F., Song, X., Hung, W.N.N., Gu, M.: Exponential-condition-based barrier certificate generation for safety verification of hybrid systems. In: Sharygina, N., Veith, H. (eds.) CAV 2013. LNCS, vol. 8044, pp. 242–257. Springer, Heidelberg (2013). https://doi.org/10.1007/978-3-642-39799-8_17
22. Lin, W., Wu, M., Yang, Z., Zeng, Z.: Exact safety verification of hybrid systems using sums-of-squares representation. Sci. China Inf. Sci. **57**(5), 1–13 (2014)
23. Nahhal, T., Dang, T.: Test coverage for continuous and hybrid systems. In: Damm, W., Hermanns, H. (eds.) CAV 2007. LNCS, vol. 4590, pp. 449–462. Springer, Heidelberg (2007). https://doi.org/10.1007/978-3-540-73368-3_47
24. Prajna, S., Jadbabaie, A.: Safety verification of hybrid systems using barrier certificates. In: Alur, R., Pappas, G.J. (eds.) HSCC 2004. LNCS, vol. 2993, pp. 477–492. Springer, Heidelberg (2004). https://doi.org/10.1007/978-3-540-24743-2_32
25. Ratschan, S.: Simulation based computation of certificates for safety of dynamical systems. In: Abate, A., Geeraerts, G. (eds.) FORMATS 2017. LNCS, vol. 10419, pp. 303–317. Springer, Cham (2017). https://doi.org/10.1007/978-3-319-65765-3_17

26. Ratschan, S., She, Z.: Safety verification of hybrid systems by constraint propagation-based abstraction refinement. ACM Trans. Embed. Comput. S. 6(1), 8 (2007)

27. Ratschan, S., She, Z.: Providing a basin of attraction to a target region of polynomial systems by computation of lyapunov-like functions. SIAM J. Control Optim. 48(7), 4377–4394 (2010)

28. Rohn, J.I., Kreslova, J.: Linear interval inequalities. Linear Multilinear Algebra 38, 79–82 (1994)

29. Sankaranarayanan, S., Chen, X., Ábrahám, E.: Lyapunov function synthesis using Handelman representations. In: NOLCOS 2013, pp. 576–581 (2013)

30. Schupp, S., et al.: Current challenges in the verification of hybrid systems. In: Berger, C., Mousavi, M.R. (eds.) CyPhy 2015. LNCS, vol. 9361, pp. 8–24. Springer, Cham (2015). https://doi.org/10.1007/978-3-319-25141-7_2

31. Shmarov, F., Zuliani, P.: ProbReach: verified probabilistic delta-reachability for stochastic hybrid systems. In: HSCC 2015, pp. 134–139 (2015)

32. Sogokon, A., Ghorbal, K., Tan, Y.K., Platzer, A.: Vector barrier certificates and comparison systems. In: Havelund, K., Peleska, J., Roscoe, B., de Vink, E. (eds.) FM 2018. LNCS, vol. 10951, pp. 418–437. Springer, Cham (2018). https://doi.org/10.1007/978-3-319-95582-7_25

33. Xue, B. Fränzle, M., Zhan, N.: Inner-approximating reachable sets for polynomial systems with time-varying uncertainties. IEEE Trans. Autom. Control (2019)

34. Xue, B., She, Z., Easwaran, A.: Under-approximating backward reachable sets by polytopes. In: Chaudhuri, S., Farzan, A. (eds.) CAV 2016. LNCS, vol. 9779, pp. 457–476. Springer, Cham (2016). https://doi.org/10.1007/978-3-319-41528-4_25

35. Xue, B., She, Z., Easwaran, A.: Underapproximating backward reachable sets by semialgebraic sets. IEEE Trans. Autom. Control 62(10), 5185–5197 (2017)

36. Xue, B., Wang, Q., Zhan, N., Fränzle, M.: Robust invariant sets generation for state-constrained perturbed polynomial systems. In: HSCC 2019, pp. 128–137 (2019)

37. Zhang, Y., Yang, Z., Lin, W., Zhu, H., Chen, X., Li, X.: Safety verification of nonlinear hybrid systems based on bilinear programming. IEEE Trans. CAD Integr. Circuits Syst. 37(11), 2768–2778 (2018)

38. Zuliani, P., Platzer, A., Clarke, E.M.: Bayesian statistical model checking with application to simulink/stateflow verification. In: HSCC 2010, pp. 243–252 (2010)

A Formally Verified Algebraic Approach for Dynamic Reliability Block Diagrams

Yassmeen Elderhalli$^{(\boxtimes)}$, Osman Hasan, and Sofiène Tahar

Electrical and Computer Engineering, Concordia University, Montréal, Canada
{y_elderh,o_hasan,tahar}@ece.concordia.ca

Abstract. Dynamic reliability block diagrams (DRBDs) are introduced to overcome the modeling limitations of traditional reliability block diagrams, such as the inability to capture redundant components. However, so far there is no algebraic framework that allows conducting the analysis of a given DRBD based on its structure function. In this paper, we propose a new algebra to formally express the structure function and the reliability of a DRBD with spare constructs based on basic system blocks and newly introduced DRBD operators. We present several simplification properties that allow reducing the structure of a given DRBD. We formalize the proposed algebra in higher-order logic to ensure its soundness, and formally verify its corresponding properties using the HOL4 theorem prover. This includes formally verifying generic reliability expressions of the spare costruct, series, parallel and deeper structures in an extensible manner that allows verifying the reliability of complex systems. Finally, we demonstrate the applicability of this algebra by formally analyzing the reliability of two real-world systems in HOL4.

Keywords: Dynamic reliability block diagrams · Algebra · Theorem proving · HOL4

1 Introduction

Reliability of a system is the probability that it will continue to provide its desirable service in a given period of time. Fault trees (FTs) [14] and reliability block diagrams (RBDs) [8] are the most commonly used reliability modeling techniques. FTs graphically model the sources of failure of a system using FT gates. An RBD, on the other hand, is a graphical representation of the reliability of a system. The components of a system are modeled as blocks and are connected using connectors (lines) to create a path or multiple paths from the RBD input to its output. These paths represent the required working blocks (system components) for the system to have a successful operation. The modeled system fails when components fail in such a manner that leads to the disconnection of all the paths between the input and the output. RBDs can be connected in a *series, parallel, series-parallel* or *parallel-series* fashion to create the appropriate modeling structure depending on the behavior and the components redundancy

© Springer Nature Switzerland AG 2019
Y. Ait-Ameur and S. Qin (Eds.): ICFEM 2019, LNCS 11852, pp. 253–269, 2019.
https://doi.org/10.1007/978-3-030-32409-4_16

of the modeled system, which provides flexible and extensible modeling configurations to represent complex systems. However, both the traditional RBDs and FTs are unable to model the dynamic behavior of system components, where the change of state of one component can affect the state of other components.

Dynamic fault trees (DFTs) [14] are proposed as an extension to traditional FTs by introducing DFT gates, such as spare gates, to overcome the above-mentioned limitation. However, the only behavior that is captured by DFTs is the dynamic failure effect of one system component in the failure or activation of other components. To overcome the modeling limitations of DFTs, RBDs are extended to *dynamic reliability block diagrams* (DRBDs) to model the dynamic dependency among system components by introducing new DRBD blocks [4], which enable capturing the effect of sharing a load and spare constructs that model the reliability of spare parts in a DRBD.

Formal methods have been used in the analysis of RBDs and DRBDs. In [16], the formal semantics of DRBD constructs in Object-Z formalism [15] have been proposed. However, analyzing and verifying the behavior of DRBDs based on this formalism are not feasible due to the non-availability of tool support. Thus, the DRBDs have been proposed to be converted into a Colored Petri Net (CPN) to be analyzed using Petri nets tools [15]. An algorithm to automatically convert a DRBD into a CPN has been also proposed in [13]. However, due to the usage of CPNs, only a few state-based properties of the modeled system can be analyzed. In [1], Ahmed *et al.* used the HOL4 theorem prover [9] to formalize several configurations of static RBDs. However, this formalization can only analyze the combinatorial behavior of systems and cannot be extended to formalize and reason about the dynamic aspects, and hence DRBDs. One of the main reasons for this deficiency is the lists based formalization of independence between multiple failure events. In this paper, we propose a completely new and different formalization from [1] that supersedes these deficiencies. In particular, we propose a more generic formalization of dynamic failure dependencies [7], based on a set-theoretic definition of independence [12] and Lebesgue integral. Thus, our proposed formalization can model and analyze both dynamic and static RBDs.

In system engineering, it is important to be able to analyze DRBDs qualitatively to identify the sources of system vulnerability, and quantitatively to evaluate the system reliability. However, to the best of our knowledge, there is no algebraic approach that mathematically models a given DRBD and enables expressing its function based on basic components just like the DFT algebra [10]. Using such algebra in the reliability analysis will result in simpler and fewer proof steps than the DFT-based algebraic analysis [10], since the probabilistic principle of inclusion and exclusion will not be invoked. In this paper, we propose, for the first time, a new algebraic approach for DRBD analysis that allows having a DRBD expression to be used for both qualitative and quantitative analyses. We introduce new operators to mathematically model the dynamic behavior in DRBD structures and constructs. In particular, we use these operators to model a DRBD spare construct besides traditional series, parallel, series-parallel and parallel-series structures. Moreover, we provide simplification theorems that allow reducing the structure of a given DRBD. This DRBD structure can be then analyzed to obtain a generic expression of the system reliability.

The reliability expressions obtained using this approach are generic and independent of the distribution and density functions that represent the system components. Although basic operators, such as OR and AND, were introduced in [4], they are only useful to model parallel and series constructs of dependent components. In addition, these constructs [4] are quite complex, which makes the modeling of large systems quite difficult. Therefore, we use the constructs proposed in [16] as they are much simpler. Leveraging upon the expressive nature of HOL, we formally verify the soundness of the proposed DRBD algebra using HOL theorem proving. We choose the HOL4 theorem prover for our work to benefit from our existing formalization of DFT algebra. Our ultimate goal is to develop a formally verified algebra that follows the traditional reliability expressions of the series and parallel structures in an easily extensible manner and at the same time can capture the dynamic behavior of real-world systems. Our formalization totally differs from and overcomes the formalization of static RBDs presented in [1] in the sense that it can formally express the structure function of a DRBD using the introduced DRBD operators. In addition, it can formally model and analyze DRBD spare constructs. Furthermore, we model the static RBD structures, i.e., series, parallel and deeper structures in a way similar to the mathematical models available in the literature, which makes it easily understood and followed by reliability engineers that are not familiar with HOL theorem proving. Finally, we illustrate the usefulness of the proposed developments in conducting the formal analysis of two real-world systems: the terminal reliability of a shuffle-exchange network and the reliability of a drive-by-wire system.

2   DRBD Algebra

In this section, we present, for the first time, an algebra for DRBD analysis that allows modeling the structure function of DRBDs with spare constructs. Moreover, we present some simplification properties that enable reducing the structure function when possible. Throughout this work, we assume that system components or blocks are represented by random variables that in turn represent their time-to-failures. In addition, we assume that system components are non-repairable, i.e., we are interested in expressing the reliability of the system considering that the failed components will not be repaired. It is worth mentioning that our proposed algebra follows the general lines for the DFT algebra [10].

The reliability of a single component, which time-to-failure function is represented by random variable X, is mathematically defined as [8]:

$$R_X(t) = Pr\{s \mid X(s) > t\} = 1 - Pr\{s \mid X(s) \leq t\} = 1 - F_X(t) \quad (1)$$

where $F_X(t)$ is the cumulative distribution function (CDF) of X. We call $\{s \mid X(s) > t\}$ as a DRBD event as it represents the set that we are interested in finding the probability of until time t:

$$event\ (X,\ t)\ =\ \{s \mid X(s)\ >\ t\} \quad (2)$$

2.1 Identity Elements, Operators and Simplification Properties

Similar to the identity elements of ordinary Boolean algebra and DFT algebra [10], we introduce two identity elements, i.e., ALWAYS and NEVER, that represent two states of any system block. The *ALWAYS* element represents a system component that stops working from time 0 ($ALWAYS = 0$). While the *NEVER* element represents a component that continues to work until $+\infty$, i.e., its failure time is $+\infty$ ($NEVER = +\infty$). These identity elements play an important role in the reduction process of the structure functions of DRBDs. We introduce operators to model the relationship between the various blocks in a DRBD. These operators can be divided into two categories: (1) The AND and OR operators that are not concerned with the dependencies among system components. (2) Temporal operators, i.e., *After*, *Simultaneous* and *Inclusive After*, that can capture the dependencies between system components. DRBDs are concerned with modeling the several paths of success of a given system. Thus, if we are concerned in the success behavior of a DRBD until time t, it means that we are interested in how the system would not fail until time t. As a result, we can use the time-to-failure random variables in modeling the time-to-failure of a given DRBD, i.e., its structure function. It is assumed that for any two system components that possess continuous failure distribution functions, the possibility that these components fail at the same time can be neglected.

In [4], AND and OR operators were introduced to model the parallel and series constructs between dependent components only without providing any mathematical model to these operators. We propose to use the AND ($\cdot$) and OR ($+$) operators to model series and parallel blocks in a DRBD, respectively, without any restriction. We provide a mathematical model for each operator based on the time of failure of its inputs, as listed in Table 1, to be used in the proposed algebra. The AND operator models the series connection between two or more system blocks. For example, the 2-block series DRBD in Table 1 continues to work only if components X and Y are working. We model the AND operator as the minimum time of its input arguments. Similarly, the OR operator models the connection between parallel components in a DRBD, i.e., all the components in a parallel structure should fail for this DRBD to fail. We model the OR operator as the maximum time of failure of its input arguments that represent basic system blocks or sub-DRBDs. This approach facilitates using these operators to model even the complex structures. If X and Y are independent, then the reliability of the 2-block systems can be expressed as given in Table 1. To reach these expressions, we need to express the DRBD events as the intersection and union for the AND and OR operators, respectively.

Table 1. Mathematical and reliability expressions of AND and OR operators

Operator	Math. Model	Reliability	2-block Structure
AND	$X{\cdot}Y = min\ (X,Y)$	$R_{(X{\cdot}Y)}(t) = R_X(t) \times R_Y(t)$	Series $\cdot\boxed{X}\text{-}\boxed{Y}\cdot$
OR	$X{+}Y = max\ (X,Y)$	$R_{(X+Y)}(t) = 1-((1-R_X(t)) \times (1-R_Y(t)))$	Parallel $\boxed{X} \atop \boxed{Y}$

Table 2. Mathematical expressions of temporal operators

After ($\triangleright$)	Simultaneous (Δ)	Inclusive after ($\unrhd$)
$X \triangleright Y = \begin{cases} X, & X > Y \\ +\infty, & X \leq Y \end{cases}$	$X \Delta Y = \begin{cases} X, & X = Y \\ +\infty, & X \neq Y \end{cases}$	$X \unrhd Y = \begin{cases} X, & X \geq Y \\ +\infty, & X < Y \end{cases}$

$$event\ ((X \cdot Y),\ t)\ =\ event\ (X,\ t)\ \cap\ event\ (Y,\ t) \tag{3}$$

$$event\ ((X + Y),\ t)\ =\ event\ (X,\ t)\ \cup\ event\ (Y,\ t) \tag{4}$$

In order to model the dynamic behavior of systems in DRBDs, we introduce new temporal operators: *after* ($\triangleright$), *simultaneous* (Δ), and *inclusive after* ($\unrhd$), as listed in Table 2. The *after* operator represents a situation where it is required to model a component that continues to work after the failure of another. The time of failure of the after operator equals the time of failure of the last component, which is required to fail. However, if the required sequence does not occur, then the output can never fail, i.e., the time of failure equals $+\infty$. The behavior of the simultaneous operator is similar to the one introduced in the DFT algebra [10]. The output of this operator fails if both its inputs fail at the same time, otherwise it can never fail. Finally, the inclusive after operator encompasses the behavior of both the after and simultaneous operators, i.e, it models a situation where it is required that one component continues to work after another one or fail at the same time, otherwise it can never fail. When dealing with basic components, the inclusive after will behave in a similar way as the after operator. Therefore, their probabilities can be expressed for independent random variables as:

$$R_{(X \triangleright Y)}(t) = 1 - \int_0^t f_X(x) \times F_Y(x)\ dx \tag{5}$$

where f_X is the probability density function (PDF) of X and F_Y is the CDF of Y. We introduce several simplification properties to reduce the structure function of a DRBD. These simplification properties range from simple ones, such as the associativity and idempotence of the operators, to more complex theorems. The idea of these properties is to reduce the algebraic expressions based on the time of failure. For example, $X \cdot ALWAYS = ALWAYS$ means that if a component in a series structure is not working, i.e., always fails, then the series structure is not working. The full list of simplification theorems is available at [6].

2.2   DRBD Constructs and Structures

The spare construct, shown in Table 3 [16], is introduced in DRBDs to model situations where a spare part is activated and replaces the main part, after its failure, by introducing a spare controller to activate the spare [16]. Depending on the failure behavior of the spare part, we can have three variants, i.e., hot, warm and cold ($H|W|C$) spares. For the hot spare (HSP) construct, the spare possesses the same failure behavior in both its active and dormant states.

Table 3. Mathematical and reliability expressions of spare constructs

Math. Model	Reliability	
$Q_{WSP}=(X_a \triangleright Y)\cdot(Y \triangleright X_d)$	$R_{WSP}(t)=1-\int_0^t \int_y^t f_{(X_a|Y=y)}(x)\, f_Y(y)dxdy$ $-\int_0^t f_Y(y)F_{X_d}(y)dy$	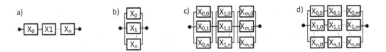
$Q_{CSP}=X_a \triangleright Y$	$R_{cold\ spare}(t)=1-\int_0^t \int_y^t f_{(X_a|Y=y)}(x)\, f_Y(y)\, dx\, dy$	
$Q_{HSP}=X+Y$	$R_{HSP}(t) =1-((1-R_X(t))\times(1-R_Y(t)))$	

a) X_0—$X1$—X_n b) X_0 X_1 X_n c) $X_{0,0}$ $X_{1,0}$ $X_{m,0}$ / $X_{0,1}$ $X_{1,1}$ $X_{m,1}$ / $X_{0,n}$ $X_{1,n}$ $X_{m,n}$ d) $X_{0,0}$ $X_{0,1}$ $X_{0,m}$ / $X_{1,0}$ $X_{1,1}$ $X_{1,m}$ / $X_{n,0}$ $X_{n,1}$ $X_{n,m}$

Fig. 1. DRBD Structures: (a) Series, (b) Parallel, (c) Series-Parallel (d) Parallel-Series

The cold spare (CSP) cannot fail in its dormant state and is only activated after the failure of the main part. The failure behavior of the warm spare (WSP) in the dormant state is attenuated by a dormancy factor from the active state. In order to distinguish between the dormant and active states of the spare, just like the DFT algebra [10], we use two different symbols to model the spare part of the DRBD spare construct, one for the dormant state and the other for the active one. For the WSP construct, in Table 3, the spare X is represented by X_a and X_d for the active and dormant states, respectively. After the failure (F) of the main part Y, X will be activated (A) by the spare controller. We model the structure function of the WSP construct (Q_{WSP}) using the DRBD operators based on the description of its behavior as given in Table 3. Thus, we need two conditions to be satisfied in order for the spare to work. Firstly, the active state of the spare will continue to work after the failure of the main part $(X_a \triangleright Y)$. Secondly, the main part will continue to work after the failure of the spare in its dormant state $(Y \triangleright X_d)$. However, since the spare part can only fail in one of its states (X_a, X_d) but not both as it is non-repairable, only one of the terms of the Q_{WSP} affects the behavior and the other can never fail, i.e., it fails at $+\infty$.

Since the DRBD spare construct and the DFT spare gate exhibit complementary behavior, i.e., the DRBDs consider the success and the DFTs consider the failure, we can use the probability of failure of the warm spare DFT gate [10] to find the reliability of the WSP DRBD construct. It is assumed that the dormant spare and the main part are independent since the failure of one does not affect the failure of the other. However, the failure of the active spare is affected by the time of failure of the main part, since it will be activated after the failure of the main part. Thus, we express the reliability of the WSP as given in Table 3, where $f_{(X_a|Y=y)}$ is the conditional density function of X_a given that Y failed at time y. Q_{WSP} and R_{WSP} represent the general behavior of the spare, i.e., the warm spare. The hot and cold spares represent its special cases and can be expressed as given in Table 3. For Q_{HSP}, the spare part X has the same behavior in both states and thus there is no need to distinguish both states. The reliability of CSP and HSP (using the OR operator) can be expressed as given in Table 3.

Table 4. Mathematical and reliability expressions of DRBD structures

Structure	Math. Model	Reliability expression
Series	$\bigcap_{i=1}^{n}(event\ (X_i,\ t))$	$\prod_{i=1}^{n} R_{X_i}(t)$
Parallel	$\bigcup_{i=1}^{n}(event\ (X_i,\ t))$	$1-\prod_{1=1}^{n}(1-R_{X_i}(t))$
Series-Parallel	$\bigcap_{i=1}^{m}\bigcup_{j=1}^{n}(event\ (X_{(i,j)},\ t))$	$\prod_{i=1}^{m}(1-\prod_{j=1}^{n}(1-R_{X_{(i,j)}}(t)))$
Parallel-Series	$\bigcup_{i=1}^{n}\bigcap_{j=1}^{m}(event\ (X_{(i,j)},\ t))$	$1-(\prod_{i=1}^{n}(1-\prod_{j=1}^{m}(R_{X_{(i,j)}}(t))))$

The series structure (Fig. 1(a)) represents a collection of blocks that are connected in series. The system continues to work until the failure of one of these blocks. We define a series structure that represents the intersection of all events of the blocks in this structure as in Table 4, where X_i represents the ith block in the series structure and n is the number of blocks. Interestingly, any block in our proposed algebra can represent a basic system component or a complex structure, such as a spare construct. Moreover, since we are dealing with the events, we can use the ordinary reliability expressions for the series structure assuming the independence of the individual blocks. The parallel structure (Fig. 1(b)) represents a system that continues to work until the failure of the last block in the structure. The behavior of the parallel structure can be expressed using the OR operator. We represent the parallel structure as the union of the individual events of the blocks. The series-parallel structure (Fig. 1(c)) represents a series structure, where the blocks of the series structure are parallel structures. The structure function of this structure can be expressed using AND of ORs operators. Table 4 lists the model for this structure with its reliability expression, where n is the number of blocks in the parallel structure and m is the number of parallel structures that are connected in series. The parallel-series structure (Fig. 1(d)) represents a group of series structures that are connected in parallel. Its structure function can be expressed using OR of ANDs operators.

3   Formalization of DRBDs in HOL

In this section, we present our formalization for the newly proposed DRBD algebra including DRBD events, operators, constructs, simplification theorems and reliability expressions. First, we review some HOL probability theory preliminaries required for understanding the rest of the paper.

3.1   HOL Probability Theory

The probability space is defined in HOL as a measure space, where the measure (probability) of the entire space is 1. It is defined as a triplet $(\Omega, \mathcal{A}, \mathcal{P}r)$, where Ω is the space, $\mathcal{A}$ are the probability events and $\mathcal{P}r$ is the probability [11]. Two functions are defined in HOL; p_space p and events p, that return the space

(Ω) of the above triplet and the events ($\mathcal{A}$), respectively. A random variable is a measurable function that maps the probability space p to another space [11].

The cumulative distribution function (CDF) is defined as [7]:

Definition 1. ⊢ ∀p X t. CDF p X t = distribution p X {y | y ≤ (t:real)}

where p is a probability space, X is a real-valued random variable, t is a variable of type real that represents time and `distribution` is defined as the probability that a random variable belongs to a certain set; {y|y≤(t:real)} in this case.

Independence of random variables is an important property that ensures that the probability of the intersection of the events of these random variables equals the product of the probability of the individual events. We use `indep_vars p M X ii` [12] to ensure that a group X is composed of random variables indexed by the elements in set ii and that the events represented by the preimage of these random variables are independent using `indep_sets`. `indep_var` is defined, based on `indep_vars`, to capture the behavior of independence for two random variables [12]. More details about these definitions can be found in [6].

Finally, the Lebesgue integral is defined in HOL4 based on positive simple functions and then extended for positive functions and functions with positive and negative values [11]. Throughout this work, we use the Lebesgue integral for positive functions, i.e., `pos_fn_integral`, since we are integrating distribution and density functions, which are always positive. The integration is over the real line and thus we use the Lebesgue-Borel measure (`lborel`) [12] for this purpose. For the ease of understanding, we use the regular mathematical expressions.

3.2 DRBD Event

In our formalization, we define the inputs, or the random variables representing the time-to-failure of system components, as lambda abstracted functions with a return datatype of extended-real (`extreal`), which represents real numbers and ±∞. We define the DRBD event of Eq. (2) as:

Definition 2. ⊢ ∀p X t. DRBD_event p X t = { s | Normal t < X s} ∩ p_space p

where `Normal` typecasts the real value of t from real to `extreal`. This type conversion is required since we need real-valued random variables. However, we need to deal with `extreal` datatype to model the `NEVER` element. Thus, we define the time-to-failure functions to return `extreal` and typecast the values from `extreal` to real using the function `real` and vice versa using `Normal`.

We define the reliability as the probability of the DRBD event (Eq. (1)):

Definition 3. ⊢ ∀p X t. Rel p X t = prob p (DRBD_event p X t)

We verify the reliability-CDF relationship (Eq. (1)) as:

Theorem 1. ⊢ ∀p X t. rv_gt0_ninfinity [X] ∧
random_variable (real o X) p borel ⇒ (Rel p X t = 1- CDF p (real o X) t)

where `real` typecasts the values of the random variable from `extreal` to real as the CDF is defined for real-valued random variables, `random_variable (real o X) p borel` ensures that `(real o X)` is a random variable over the real line represented by the `borel` space [12], and `rv_gt0_ninfinity` ensures that the random variable is greater than or equal to 0 and not equal to $+\infty$, which means that the time of failure of any component cannot be negative or $+\infty$. Theorem 1 is verified based on the fact that the `DRBD_event` and the set of the CDF are the complement of each other. Therefore, the probability of one of them equals one minus the other. For the rest of the paper, we will denote `CDF p (real o X) t` by $F_X(t)$ to facilitate the understanding of the theorems.

3.3   Identity Elements, Operators and Simplification Theorems

Our formalization of the identity elements and DRBD operators is listed in Table 5, where `extreal` is the extended-real datatype in HOL4, `PosInf` represents $+\infty$, and `min` and `max` return the minimum and maximum values of their arguments, respectively. This formalization follows the proposed definitions in Tables 1 and 2. However, we define the operators as lambda abstracted functions to be able to conduct the probabilistic analysis later. We verify several simplification theorems based on the properties of `extreal` numbers in HOL. The full list of these theorems and the proof script are available at [6] and [5], respectively.

In order to verify the reliability of the DRBD constructs, such as the spare, we need first to verify the reliability of the DRBD operators that are used to express the structure function of these constructs. For the AND and OR operators, we verify their reliability expressions as in Theorems 2 and 3, respectively.

Theorem 2. $\vdash$ $\forall$p X t. `rv_gt0_ninfinity [X;Y]` $\wedge$
    `indep_var p lborel (real o X) lborel (real o Y)` $\Rightarrow$
    `(Rel p (X·Y) t = Rel p X t * Rel p Y t)`

Theorem 3. $\vdash$ $\forall$p X t. `rv_gt0_ninfinity [X;Y]` $\wedge$
    `indep_var p lborel (real o X) lborel (real o Y)` $\Rightarrow$
    `(Rel p (X + Y) t = 1 - (1 - Rel p X t) * (1 - Rel p Y t))`

We verify Theorem 2 by first rewriting using Definition 3. Then, we prove that `DRBD_event` of the AND operator equals the intersection of the individual events, as in Eq. (3). Utilizing the independence of the real-valued random variables `(real o X)` and `(real o Y)`, the probability of intersection of their events equals the product of the probability of the individual events. Since X and Y are greater than 0 and are not equal to $+\infty$, based on the function `rv_gt0_ninfinity`, the events in the probability space that correspond to X and Y are equal to the ones that correspond to `real o X` and `real o Y`. As a result, the `DRBD_events` of X and Y are independent. Hence, the probability of their intersection equals the product of the probability of the individual events, i.e., their reliability. Theorem 3 is verified in a similar way. However, we prove that the `DRBD_event` of the OR operator equals the union of the individual events, as in Eq. (4).

Table 5. Definitions of identity elements and DRBD operators

Element/Operator	Mathematical expression	Formalization
Always element	$ALWAYS = 0$	⊢ R_ALWAYS = (λs. (0:extreal))
Never element	$NEVER = +\infty$	⊢ R_NEVER = (λs. PosInf)
AND	$X \cdot Y = min(X,Y)$	⊢ ∀X Y. R_AND X Y =(λs. min (X s) (Y s))
OR	$X + Y = max(X,Y)$	⊢ ∀X Y. R_OR X Y = (λs. max (X s) (Y s))
After	$X \triangleright Y = \begin{cases} X, & X > Y \\ +\infty, & X \leq Y \end{cases}$	⊢ ∀X Y. R_AFTER X Y = (λs. if Y s < X s then X s else PosInf)
Simultaneous	$X \triangle Y = \begin{cases} X, & X = Y \\ +\infty, & X \neq Y \end{cases}$	⊢ ∀X Y. R_SIMULT X Y = (λs. if X s = Y s then X s else PosInf)
Inclusive After	$X \trianglerighteq Y = \begin{cases} X, & X \geq Y \\ +\infty, & X < Y \end{cases}$	⊢ ∀ X Y. R_INCLUSIVE_AFTER X Y = (λs. if Y s ≤ X s then X s else PosInf)

We verify that this union of events equals to the complement of the intersection of the complements of the individual events. Then, Theorem 3 can be proven using the independence of random variables.

We extend the definition of the AND and OR operators to n-ary operators, nR_AND and nR_OR, that can be used to represent the relationship between an arbitrary number of elements. We formally define nR_AND and nR_OR as:

Definition 4.
⊢ ∀X s. nR_AND X s = ITSET (λe acc. R_AND (X e) acc) s R_NEVER

Definition 5.
⊢ ∀X s. nR_OR X s = ITSET (λe acc. R_OR (X e) acc) s R_ALWAYS

where ITSET is the HOL function to iterate over sets. These definitions apply the R_AND and R_OR over the elements of X indexed by the numbers in s. R_NEVER and R_ALWAYS are the identity elements of the R_AND and R_OR operators, respectively. The reliability of these operators is similar to the reliability of the series and parallel structures, respectively, as will be described in the following section.

Finally, we verify the reliability expression of the after operator as:

Theorem 4. ⊢ ∀X Y p f_x t. rv_gt0_ninfinity [X; Y] ∧ 0 ≤ t ∧
indep_var p lborel (real o X) lborel (real o Y) ∧
distributed p lborel (real o X) f_x ∧ (∀x. 0 ≤ f_x x) ∧
cont_CDF p (real o Y) ∧ measurable_CDF p (real o Y) ⇒
(Rel p (X ▷ Y) t = 1- $\int_0^t f_x(x) \times F_Y(x)\ dx$)

where distributed p lborel (real o X) f_x ensures that random variable real o X has a PDF f_x, cont_CDF and measurable_CDF ensure that F_y is continuous and measurable [7]. The proof of this theorem is based on $Pr(Y < X < t) = \int_0^t f_X(x) \times F_Y(x)\ dx$, which is verified in [7] using the properties of the Lebesgue integral and independence of random variables. As the DRBD and DFT events complement one another, the above expression allows us to verify the reliability expression of the *after* operator, since it represents a situation where the system continues to work until two components fail in sequence.

3.4   DRBD Constructs and Their Reliability Expressions

We present the formalization of the warm spare (WSP) construct. The expressions of the rest of the spares; hot and cold, can be found in [6].

Definition 6. $\vdash \forall Y\ X_a\ X_d.\ R\_WSP\ Y\ X_a\ X_d\ =\ (X_a\ \triangleright\ Y)\ \cdot\ (Y\ \triangleright\ X_d)$

Since the DRBD and DFT events complement one another, we use our formalization of the probability of failure of the warm spare gate [7] to verify the reliability of the WSP construct:

Theorem 5. $\vdash \forall p\ Y\ X_a\ X_d\ t\ f_Y\ f_{X_aY}\ f_{X_a|Y}.\ 0 \le t\ \wedge$
$(\forall s.\ \texttt{ALL\_DISTINCT}\ [X_a\ s;\ X_d\ s;\ Y\ s])\ \wedge\ \texttt{DISJOINT\_WSP}\ Y\ X_a\ X_d\ t\ \wedge$
$\texttt{rv\_gt0\_ninfinity}\ [X_a;\ X_d;\ Y]\ \wedge\ \texttt{den\_gt0\_ninfinity} f_{X_aY}\ f_Y\ f_{X_a|Y}\ \wedge$
$\forall y.\ \texttt{cond\_density lborel lborel p (real o } X_a) \texttt{(real o Y) } y\ f_{X_aY}\ f_Y\ f_{X_a|Y})\ \wedge$
$\texttt{indep\_var p lborel (real o } X_d) \texttt{ lborel (real o Y)}\ \wedge$
$\texttt{cont\_CDF p (real o } X_d)\ \wedge\ \texttt{measurable\_CDF p (real o } X_d)\ \Rightarrow$
$\left(\texttt{Rel p (R\_WSP Y } X_a\ X_d)\ t\right)=1-\left(\int_0^t f_Y(y)*\left(\int_y^t f_{(X_a|Y=y)}(x)\ dx\right)dy+\int_0^t f_Y(y)F_{X_d}(y)dy\right)$

where ALL_DISTINCT ensures that the main and spare parts cannot fail at the same time, DISJOINT_WSP $Y\ X_a\ X_d$ t ensures that until time t, the spare can only fail in one of its states and den_gt0_ninfinity ascertains the proper values of the density functions; joint $(0 \le f_{XY})$, marginal $(0 < f_Y)$ and conditional $(0 \le f_{X_a|Y})$ [7]. Theorem 5 is verified by first defining a conditional density function $f_{X_a|Y}$ for random variables (real o X_a) and (real o Y) using cond_density. This is required as the failure of the spare part is affected by the time of failure of the main part. Therefore, it is required to define this conditional density function then prove the expression based on the probability of failure of the DFT spare gate, which is verified based on the properties of the Lebesgue integral.

The formal definitions of the series and parallel structures are listed in Table 6. We define the series structure as a function that accepts a group of sets, Y, that are indexed by the numbers in set s and returns the intersection of these sets. The parallel structure is defined in a similar way but it returns the union of the sets rather than the intersection. The group of sets, Y, in both structures represents a family of events, i.e, Y will be instantiated later with DRBD events. We verify the reliability expressions of the series and parallel structures, given in Table 4, as shown in Table 6, where $s \neq \{\} \wedge$ FINITE s ensures that the set of indices, s, is nonempty and finite. The reliability of the series structure is verified based on the independence of the input events using indep_sets, which ensures that for the probability space p, the given group of sets $((\lambda i.\ \{\texttt{rv\_ti\_event p X t i}\})$ indexed by the numbers in set s are independent. The family of sets $((\lambda i.\ \{\texttt{rv\_to\_event p X t i}\})$ represents the DRBD events of the group of time-to-failure functions, X, where rv_to_event is defined as:

Definition 7. $\vdash \forall p\ X\ t.\ \texttt{rv\_to\_event p X t}\ =\ (\lambda i.\ \texttt{DRBD\_event p (X i) t})$

This function enables us to create the group of DRBD_event of time-to-failure functions of system blocks (X). Based on the independence of these sets and the definition of the series structure (intersection of sets), we verify that the probability of the series structure equals to the product of the reliability of the individual blocks (`Rel p (X i) t`), where i∈s. The product function (Π) in HOL4 returns a real value and the probability returns `extreal`, therefore, it is required to typecast the product function to `extreal` using `Normal`. Similarly, the product function finds the product of real-valued functions, thus, it is required to typecast the reliability function (`Rel`) to real using the `real` function. Similarly, we replace the parallel structure (the union of events) with the complement of the intersection of the complements of the events. Then, we verify that the probability of this complement equals one minus the probability of the intersection of the complements. This requires the condition that all DRBD events created using `rv_to_event` belong to the events of the probability space p.

We verify that the series and parallel structures are equal to the DRBD events of the `nR_AND` and `nR_OR`, respectively.

Table 6. Formal definitions and reliability of the series and parallel structures

	Series Structure	Parallel Structure
Definition	⊢ ∀Y s. DRBD_series Y s = $\cap_{i \in s}$ (Y i)	⊢ ∀Y s. DRBD_parallel Y s = $\cup_{i \in s}$ (Y i)
Reliability	⊢ ∀p X t s. s ≠ {} ∧ FINITE s ∧ indep_sets p (λi. {rv_to_event p X t i}) s ⇒ (prob p (DRBD_series (rv_to_event p X t) s) = Normal ($\Pi_{i \in s}$ (real (Rel p (X i) t))))	⊢ ∀p X t s. s ≠ {} ∧ FINITE s ∧ indep_sets p (λi. {rv_to_event p X t i}) s ∧ (∀i. i ∈ s ⇒ rv_to_event p X t i ∈ events p) ⇒ (prob p (DRBD_parallel (rv_to_event p X t) s) = 1 - Normal ($\Pi_{i \in s}$ (real (1 - Rel p (X i) t))))

Theorem 6. ⊢ ∀p X t s. FINITE s ∧ s ≠ {} ⇒
    (DRBD_event p (nR_AND X s) t = DRBD_series (rv_to_event p X t) s)

Theorem 7. ⊢ ∀p X t s. FINITE s ∧ 0 ≤ t ⇒
    (DRBD_event p (nR_OR X s) t = DRBD_parallel (rv_to_event p X t) s)

We verify Theorems 6 and 7 by inducting on set s using `SET_INDUCT_TAC` that creates two subgoals to be solved; one for the empty set and another one for inserting an element to a finite set. Then, we use the fact that the DRBD events of the AND and OR operators equal the intersection and the union of the individual events, respectively. For Theorem 7, an additional condition is required, $0 \leq t$, to be able to manipulate the sets and reach the final form of the theorem.

These structures can be easily extended to model and verify more complex structures, such as two-level structures, i.e., series-parallel and parallel-series structures, as shown in Table 7. The main idea in building these two-level structures is to partition the family of blocks into distinct groups, where we use a set, J, to index these partitions, i.e., it has the number of groups in the first top level. For each group in this top level, we have another set, {s j| j ∈ J}, that has the indices of the blocks in the second level, i.e. the subgroups. For example, for the parallel-series structure of Fig. 1(d), if $n = m = 1$, then the outer parallel structure has two series structures, where each series structure has two blocks. Thus, J = {0;1}. For each j ∈ J, we have a certain set s j that has the indices of the blocks in the inner series structure. Thus, s = (λj. if j = 0 then {0;1} else {2;3}). This also applies to the series-parallel structure. Therefore, the structure of the DRBD can be determined based on the given sets of indices.

We verify the theorems in Table 7 by extending the proofs of the series and parallel structures. However, it is required to deal with the intersection of unions in case of the series-parallel structure and the union of intersections in case of parallel-series structure. Therefore, we need to extend the independence of sets properties to include the independence of union and intersection of partitions of the events. We verify the independence of union of partitions as:

Theorem 8. ⊢ ∀p s J Y. indep_sets p (λi. {Yi}) $\bigcup_{j \in J}$ (s j) ∧ J ≠ {} ∧
(∀i. i ∈ J ⇒ countable (s i)) ∧ FINITE J ∧ disjoint_family_on s J ⇒
indep_sets p (λj. {$\bigcup_{i \in s\ j}$ (Y i)}) J

where sets J and s have the indices of the partitions and the individual blocks of each partition, respectively, disjoint_family_on ensures that the indices of the blocks in different partitions are disjoint and indep_sets p (λi. {Y i}) $\bigcup_{j \in J}$ (s j) ensures the independence of the family of blocks {Y i} where the indices of the individual blocks are given by the union of s. Similarly, we verify the independence of intersection of partitions and the details can be found in [6].

In order to verify the reliability of the series-parallel structure, we need to ensure the independence of the individual blocks. Therefore, we combine the indices of all blocks into a single set using $\bigcup_{j \in J}$ (s j) to be used with indep_sets. To be able to use the reliability of the series structure in this proof, we use Theorem 8 to verify the independence of the unions of partitions of events. This means verifying that the parallel structures are independent, i.e., the probability of intersection of these parallel structures equals the product of the reliability of the parallel structures. Several assumptions related to sets {s

Table 7. Verified reliability of the series-parallel and parallel-series structures

Reliability of Series-Parallel Structure	Reliability of Parallel-Series Structure

⊢ ∀p X t s J.
indep_sets p
(λi. {rv_to_event p X t i}) ($\bigcup_{j \in J}$(s j)) ∧
(∀i. i ∈ J ⇒ s i ≠ {} ∧ FINITE (s i)) ∧
FINITE J ∧ J ≠ {} ∧ disjoint_family_on s J ⇒
(prob p
  (DRBD_series
   (λj. DRBD_parallel
    (rv_to_event p X t) (s j)) J) =
Normal
  ($\Pi_{j \in J}$
   (1 − $\Pi_{i \in (s\ j)}$ (real (1 − Rel p (X i) t)))))
	⊢ ∀p X t s J.
	indep_sets p
	(λi. {rv_to_event p X t i}) ($\bigcup_{j \in J}$(s j))∧
	(∀i. i ∈ $\bigcup_{j \in J}$(s j) ⇒
	  rv_to_event p X t i ∈ events p) ∧
	(∀i. i ∈ J ⇒ s i ≠ {} ∧ FINITE (s i)) ∧
	FINITE J ∧ J ≠ {} ∧
	disjoint_family_on s J ⇒
	(prob p
	  (DRBD_parallel
	   (λj. DRBD_series
	    (rv_to_event p X t) (s j)) J) =
	1 −
	Normal
	  ($\Pi_{j \in J}$
	   (1 − $\Pi_{i \in (s\ j)}$ (real (Rel p (X i) t)))))

i| i ∈ J} and J are required, i.e., these sets are finite and nonempty. Finally, disjoint_family_on ensures that every block has a unique index. The reliability of the parallel-series structure is verified in a similar manner based on the reliability of the parallel structure and the independence of the intersection of partitions of events rather than the union. In addition, it is required that all DRBD events belong to the events of the probability space.

We extend the reliability of the series-parallel structure to verify the reliability of a four-level nested structure, i.e., series-parallel-series-parallel. For this, we have four sets (indexed sets) that determine the structure of the DRBD. We verify the four-level nested structure using two main steps. We first verify the reliability of the outer series-parallel, which requires verifying the independence of the intersection of union of partitions of the DRBD blocks, i.e., the inner series-parallel structures are independent. Then, we verify the reliability of the inner series-parallel structures based on some set manipulation. This way, we can verify even deeper structures, which would require verifying the independence of more nested structures. We use the nested four-level structure to verify the reliability of the series-parallel-series structure as it represents a special case of the series-parallel-series-parallel, where each of the innermost parallel structures has only one block. More details about this proof can be found in [6]. Our formalization follows the natural definitions of parallel and series structures. Moreover, our verified lemmas of independence allow verifying deeper structures, which makes our formalization flexible and applicable to model the most complex systems.

4   Applications

To demonstrate the applicability of our proposed DRBD algebra, we formally analyze the reliability of a drive-by-wire system (DBW) [2] and a shuffle-exchange network (SEN) [3] (Fig. 2) to verify generic expressions that are independent of the failure distribution of system components, i.e., we can use different types of distributions to model the failure of components as long as they satisfy the required conditions, such as the continuity. We present here the details of the SEN system due to space limitations and the details of the formal reliability analysis of the DBW system is available at [6].

A SEN is a single-path multistage interconnection network (MIN) that provides the necessary switching in multi-processor systems [3]. It consists of sources (inputs) and destinations (outputs), where only one possible path is available between each source and destination. To increase the reliability of such network,

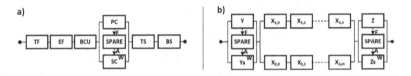

Fig. 2. DRBD of: (a) DBW and (b) SEN with spare constructs

additional switching elements are added to provide additional paths between each source and destination. A SEN having two paths between each source and destination is usually called SEN+. The terminal reliability analysis, which is the reliability of the connection between a given source and destination, is usually conducted using static RBDs [3]. However, each source and destination are always connected to single switches, where their failure leads to the failure of the connection. Therefore, we propose to further enhance the reliability of this connection by using spare parts that replace these single switches after failure. Thus, we model the reliability of the modified SEN+ system using DRBDs, as shown in Fig. 2(b), where Y and Z are the main single switches that are connected to the source and destination with their spares Ys and Zs, respectively. The parallel structure in the middle represents the reliability model of the two alternative paths between the source and the destination. We formally express the structure function of this DRBD as:

$$Q_{SEN} = nR\_AND \ (\lambda i. \ \text{if } i = 0 \text{ then } R\_WSP \ Y \ Ys_a \ Ys_d$$
$$\text{else if } i = 1 \text{ then } \big((nR\_AND \ X \ L1) + (nR\_AND \ X \ L2)\big)$$
$$\text{else } R\_WSP \ Z \ Zs_a \ Zs_d) \ \{0; \ 1; \ 2\}$$

Thus, the outer series structure is expressed using the nR_AND operator over the set $\{0; 1; 2\}$ as this structure has three different structures; i.e., two spare constructs and one parallel structure, and L1 and L2 are the sets that have the indices of the components in the inner series structures. In order to re-utilize the verified expressions of reliability, we verify that the DRBD event of the Q_{SEN} is equal to a nested series-parallel-series structure to verify a generic expression for the reliability of the SEN+ system:

Theorem 9. $\vdash \forall p \ X \ Y \ Ys_a \ Ys_d \ Z \ Zs_a \ Zs_d \ t \ L1 \ L2.$
SEN_set_req p L1 L2 (ind_set [{0}; L1; L2; {3}])
  (ind_set [{0}; {1; 2}; {3}]) {0; 1; 2}
  (event_set [(DRBD_event p (R_WSP Y Ys_a Ys_d) t,0);
              (DRBD_event p (R_WSP Z Zs_a Zs_d) t,3)] (rv_to_event p X t)) $\Rightarrow$
(prob p (DRBD_event p Q_{SEN} t) =
Rel p (R_WSP Y Ys_a Ys_d) t * Rel p (R_WSP Z Zs_a Zs_d) t *
(1 - (1 - Normal ($\prod_{l \in L1}$ (real (Rel p (X 1) t)))) *
     (1 - Normal ($\prod_{l \in L2}$ (real (Rel p (X 1) t)))))))

where SEN_set_req ensures that the input sets are finite and nonempty. It also ensures the independence of the input events over the probability space and that they belong to the probability events. ind_set and event_set generate the proper indices for the blocks in the structure. Their description can be found in [6]. The reliability of the spare constructs can be further rewritten using Theorem 5 given that the required conditions are ensured. The final theorem with the expressions of the reliability of the spare constructs is available in [5]. The proof scripts of the DBW and SEN required around 150 and 1020 lines, respectively, and are available at [5]. Finally, we evaluate, using MATLAB, the reliability of the DBW assuming exponential distribution with failure rates as given in Fig. 3. We also evaluate the reliability of the SEN system (Fig. 3) assuming the same

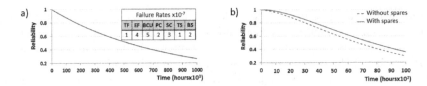

Fig. 3. Reliability of (a) DBW (b) SEN with/without spare constructs

failure rate of 1×10^{-5} for all switching elements with 16 switching elements in each series structure. We evaluate the SEN reliability without and with spares with a dormancy factor of 0.1. This result shows that considering the spares in the reliability analysis leads to having a more reliable and realistic system than static RBDs that are usually used for the analysis of similar SENs.

To sum up, we are able to provide generic expressions of reliability of the DBW and SEN+ systems that are verified in HOL theorem proving, which cannot be done using other formal tools. These expressions can be instantiated with different failure distributions without the need to repeat the analysis. In addition, we demonstrated that our formalization is flexible and can be used to model more complex systems of an arbitrary number of blocks by implementing its hierarchy using sets that can be instantiated later to model a specific system structure, which is an added feature of our formalized algebra.

5   Conclusion

In this paper, we proposed a new algebra to analyze dynamic reliability block diagrams (DRBDs). We developed the HOL formalization of this algebra in HOL4, which ensures its correctness and allows conducting the analysis within a theorem prover. Furthermore, this algebra provides formalized generic expressions of reliability that cannot be verified using other formal tools. This HOL formalization is the first of its kind that takes into account the system dynamics by providing the HOL formal model of spare constructs and temporal operators. The proposed algebra is compatible with the reliability expressions of traditional RBDs as demonstrated by the reliability expressions of the series and parallel structures. It also facilitates extending the verified reliability expressions to model complex systems using nested structures. Finally, we demonstrated the usefulness of this work by formally conducting the analysis of a drive-by-wire and a shuffle-exchange network systems to verify generic expressions of reliability, which are independent of the failure probability distribution of system components. We plan to extend this algebra to include other DRBD constructs, such as load sharing, in order to provide a more complete framework to algebraically analyze DRBDs in HOL.

References

1. Ahmed, W., Hasan, O., Tahar, S.: Formalization of reliability block diagrams in higher-order logic. J. Appl. Logic **18**, 19–41 (2016). https://doi.org/10.1016/j.jal.2016.05.007
2. Altby, A., Majdandzic, D.: Design and Implementation of a Fault-tolerant Drive-by-wire System. Master's thesis, Chalmers University of Technology, Sweden (2014)
3. Bistouni, F., Jahanshahi, M.: Analyzing the reliability of shuffle-exchange networks using reliability block diagrams. Reliab. Eng. Syst. Saf. **132**, 97–106 (2014). https://doi.org/10.1016/j.ress.2014.07.012
4. Distefano, S.: System Dependability and Performances: Techniques, Methodologies and Tools. Ph.D. thesis, University of Messina, Italy (2005)
5. Elderhalli, Y.: DRBD Formal Analysis: HOL4 Script (2019). http://hvg.ece.concordia.ca/code/hol/DRBD/index.php
6. Elderhalli, Y., Hasan, O., Tahar, S.: A Formally Verified HOL Algebra for Dynamic Reliability Block Diagrams. Technical report, Concordia University, Canada (2019). http://arxiv.org/abs/1908.01930
7. Elderhalli, Y., Ahmad, W., Hasan, O., Tahar, S.: Probabilistic analysis of dynamic fault trees using HOL theorem proving. J. Appl. Logics **2631**(3), 469 (2019)
8. Hasan, O., Ahmed, W., Tahar, S., Hamdi, M.S.: Reliability block diagrams based analysis: a survey. In: Numerical Analysis and Applied Maths, vol. 1648, pp. 850129.1-4 (2015). https://doi.org/10.1063/1.4913184
9. HOL4: (2019). https://hol-theorem-prover.org/
10. Merle, G.: Algebraic Modelling of Dynamic Fault Trees, Contribution to Qualitative and Quantitative Analysis. Ph.D. thesis, ENS, France (2010)
11. Mhamdi, T., Hasan, O., Tahar, S.: Formalization of entropy measures in HOL. In: van Eekelen, M., Geuvers, H., Schmaltz, J., Wiedijk, F. (eds.) ITP 2011. LNCS, vol. 6898, pp. 233–248. Springer, Heidelberg (2011). https://doi.org/10.1007/978-3-642-22863-6_18
12. Qasim, M., Hasan, O., Elleuch, M., Tahar, S.: Formalization of normal random variables in HOL. In: Kohlhase, M., Johansson, M., Miller, B., de de Moura, L., Tompa, F. (eds.) CICM 2016. LNCS (LNAI), vol. 9791, pp. 44–59. Springer, Cham (2016). https://doi.org/10.1007/978-3-319-42547-4_4
13. Robidoux, R., Xu, H., Xing, L., Zhou, M.: Automated modeling of dynamic reliability block diagrams using colored petri nets. IEEE Trans. Syst. Man Cybern. **40**(2), 337 (2010). https://doi.org/10.1109/TSMCA.2009.2034837
14. Ruijters, E., Stoelinga, M.: Fault tree analysis: a survey of the state-of-the-art in modeling. Anal. Tools. Comput. Sci. Rev. **15–16**, 29–62 (2015). https://doi.org/10.1016/j.cosrev.2015.03.001
15. Smith, G.: The Object-Z Specification Language, vol. 1. Springer, New York (2012)
16. Xu, H., Xing, L.: Formal semantics and verification of dynamic reliability block diagrams for system reliability modeling. In: Software Engineering and Applications, pp. 155–162 (2007)

Reasoning About Universal Cubes in MCMT

Sylvain Conchon$^{(\boxtimes)}$ and Mattias Roux

LRI, Université Paris Sud, CNRS, 91405 Orsay, France
conchon@lri.fr

Abstract. The Model Checking Modulo Theories (MCMT) framework is a powerful model checking technique for verifying safety properties of parameterized transition systems. In MCMT, logical formulas are used to represent both transitions and sets of states and safety properties are verified by an SMT-based backward reachability analysis. To be fully automated, the class of formulas handled in MCMT is restricted to *cubes*, i.e. existentially quantified conjunction of literals. While being very expressive, cubes cannot define properties with a global termination condition, usually described by a universally quantified formula.

In this paper we describe BRWP, an extension of the backward reachability of MCMT for reasoning about validity properties expressed as *universal cubes*, that is formulas of the form $\exists i \forall j. \mathcal{C}(i,j)$, where $\mathcal{C}(i,j)$ is a conjunction of literals. Our approach consists in a tight cooperation between the backward reachability loop and a deductive verification engine based on weakest-precondition calculus (WP). To provide evidence for the applicability of our new algorithm, we show how to make Cubicle, a model checker based on MCMT, cooperates with the Why3 platform for deductive program verification.

1 Introduction

In this paper, we consider the problem of verifying safety properties of parameterized systems. The systems we are interested in are called *array-based* transition systems. This is a syntactically restricted class of parameterized systems, introduced by Ghilardhi and Ranise [9] where states are represented as arrays indexed by an arbitrary number of processes. Distributed systems with consensus or commitment protocols are typical examples modeling with array-based systems.

The verification of array-based systems as proposed in [8] led to a powerful model checking technique called *Model Checking Modulo Theories* (MCMT). This is a symbolic SMT-based model checking technique where logical formulas (expressed in a fragment of first-order logic) are used to represent both transitions and sets of states, and safety properties are verified by backward reachability analysis. A safety property to be verified in MCMT is expressed in its negated form as a formula that represents unsafe states. Each unsafe formula must be a *cube*, i.e., have the form $\exists i. \mathcal{C}(i)$, where $\mathcal{C}(i)$ is a conjunction of literals.

© Springer Nature Switzerland AG 2019
Y. Ait-Ameur and S. Qin (Eds.): ICFEM 2019, LNCS 11852, pp. 270–285, 2019.
https://doi.org/10.1007/978-3-030-32409-4_17

While the expressiveness of cubes is sufficient to encode a large class of *safety invariants*, it is usually too weak for describing safety properties with a *global* termination condition. For instance, in a consensus algorithm, one would like to check that, at the end of the consensus, there is no process deciding a value distinct from the value chosen by the others. Unfortunately, the "at the end of the consensus" part of the sentence must take the form of a *universally* quantified formula defining the condition for the processes to terminate. To cope with such properties, MCMT must be extended to reason about *universal cubes*, that is formulas of the form $\exists i \forall j . \mathcal{C}(i, j)$, where $\mathcal{C}(i, j)$ is a conjunction of literals.

To handle such formulas, one can try to encode universal cubes as transitions with *universal guards*, i.e., guards containing universally quantified global conditions that check the state variables of all processes. However, since universal quantifiers in guards prevents the backward reachability algorithm to be fully automated, solutions based on over approximations techniques have been proposed [1–3]. One of the best solution is proposed in [3] as a syntactic transformation which can be seen as the implementation of a crash-failure model where an unbounded number of processes can die at any time. Unfortunately, while very efficient, this over approximation technique results in false positives for non fault-tolerant systems which are very common in distributed systems.

Another way to handle universal cubes would consist to give up model checking techniques and instead to use a more expressive and powerful Hoare-style reasoning. For instance, translating Cubicle systems to the input language of the TLA+ system [12] is straightforward and would allow the user to use a proof system like TLAPS [6]. Similarly, one can translate Cubicle's input language to DVF [10], a deductive verification framework dedicated to transition systems which uses SMT solvers to prove the generated verification conditions. However, while those frameworks offer automatic backends to discharge proof obligations, an important and very painful part of the proof effort consists in finding *manually* the auxiliary invariants of the system which are mandatory for the safety property to be proved.

In this paper, we propose to bridge the gap between model checking and deductive verification. Our technique consists in a tight cooperation between the backward reachability loop of MCMT and a deductive verification engine based on weakest-precondition calculus. To provide evidence for the applicability of our technique, we show how to make Cubicle, a model checker based on MCMT, cooperate with the Why3 platform for deductive program verification [7]. Our contributions are as follows:

- A new algorithm, called BRWP, that extends the backward reachability algorithm to handle universal cubes (Sect. 4).
- A translation schema from Cubicle to Why3 (Sect. 5).

In Sect. 2, we illustrate the problem of handling universal cubes in MCMT on a simplified version of a splitter, a basic building block of renaming algorithms in shared memory. We give an overview of our approach in Sect. 3.

2   The Problem of Universal Quantifiers in MCMT

Throughout this paper, we use a simplified version of a splitter algorithm to illustrate the problems and solutions we are presenting.

Splitters have been first introduced by Lamport [11] to implement fast mutual-exclusion algorithms, then used by Moir and Anderson to solve the renaming problem in shared memory [13]. A splitter can be depicted graphically by the schema in Fig. 1. It is a concurrent object used to distinguish an arbitrary number (n) of callers. Each process that calls the splitter gets a decision value among stop, down and right. The decision values respect the following rules:

- There are only three possible decisions : Stop, Right and Down
- At most one process ends in Stop
- At most $n-1$ processes end in Down
- At most $n-1$ processes end in Right

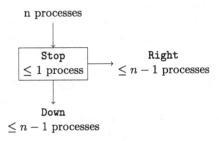

Fig. 1. Splitter

The splitter algorithm for each process p is represented in Fig. 2 as an automaton with seven states (PC$_0$ to PC$_3$, Stop, Down and Right) and two boolean variables X and Y. The initial state is PC$_0$ where Y is supposed to be initialised to false and X can contain any value. The first transition should be read as follows: a process p in state PC$_0$ can go to PC$_1$ and assign X to p. Similarly, if Y is false then a process p can go from PC$_1$ to PC$_2$ else it can go to state Right. A transition from PC$_2$ to PC$_3$ assigns Y to true ($\top$). Finally, the process p can go from PC$_3$ to Stop if X $= p$, otherwise it can go to Down.

Modeling this (simplified) splitter algorithm is immediate using array-based transition systems. We assume given an enumeration type state with seven constructors (PC$_0$, ..., PC$_3$, Stop, Down and Right), two variables X and Y and an array PC such that, for each process p, PC$[p]$ contains a value of type state. Initially, each process is in state PC$_0$ and Y $= \bot$, which is described by the following universal formula $\mathcal{I}nit$:

$$\mathcal{I}nit : \forall p.\mathrm{PC}[p] = \mathrm{PC}_0 \wedge \mathrm{Y} = \bot$$

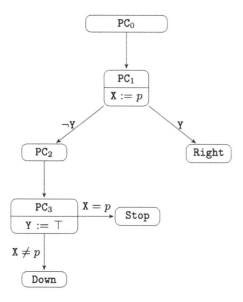

Fig. 2. Automaton for a process p representing the splitter with updates to shared variables attached to the nodes and conditions labeled to edges

The six transitions of the automaton are described by the six formulas spl_{xxx} given in Fig. 3. Each formula relates the values of state variables before and after the transition. We denote by X' the value of the variable X after the execution of the transition. For instance, transition spl_0 should read as: if there exists a process p such that $PC[p]$ contains PC_0, then update $PC[p]$ to PC_1 and variable X to p.

According to the conditions previously stated, proving the safety of the splitter amounts to checking that states satisfying one of the following three formulas are not reachable:

$$\varphi_1 : \exists ij.\ i \neq j \ \wedge \ PC[i] = \texttt{Stop} \ \wedge \ PC[j] = \texttt{Stop}$$
$$\varphi_2 : \forall i.PC[i] = \texttt{Down}$$
$$\varphi_3 : \forall i.PC[i] = \texttt{Right}$$

The reachability analysis in MCMT is performed by running a symbolic backward algorithm. Starting from a formula describing the system's unsafe condition, its pre-images are iteratively computed for all transitions. Pre-images that are subsumed by already visited nodes are not expanded anymore. This process ends either when a formula in a node intersects the initial formula $\mathcal{I}nit$ or when there is no more pre-image to compute.

An important result about array-based systems is that pre-images of cubes (existentially quantified conjunction of literals) are computable and can be represented as union (disjunction) of cubes [9]. Thus, starting from a cube, the backward reachability analysis produces only cubes and is therefore automatable. For instance, the pre-image of the cube φ_1 by spl_{stop} is the following

$$spl_0 : \quad \exists p. \quad \begin{array}{l} \text{PC}[p] = \text{PC}_0 \ \wedge \\ \text{PC'}[p] = \text{PC}_1 \ \wedge \ \text{X'} = p \end{array}$$

$$spl_{right} : \exists p. \quad \begin{array}{l} \text{PC}[p] = \text{PC}_1 \ \wedge \ \text{Y} \ \wedge \\ \text{PC'}[p] = \text{Right} \end{array}$$

$$spl_1 : \quad \exists p. \quad \begin{array}{l} \text{PC}[p] = \text{PC}_1 \ \wedge \ \neg \text{Y} \ \wedge \\ \text{PC'}[p] = \text{PC}_2 \end{array}$$

$$spl_2 : \quad \exists p. \quad \begin{array}{l} \text{PC}[p] = \text{PC}_2 \ \wedge \\ \text{PC'}[p] = \text{PC}_3 \ \wedge \ \text{Y'} = \top \end{array}$$

$$spl_{stop} : \exists p. \quad \begin{array}{l} \text{PC}[p] = \text{PC}_3 \ \wedge \ \text{X} = p \ \wedge \\ \text{PC'}[p] = \text{Stop} \end{array}$$

$$spl_{down} : \exists p. \quad \begin{array}{l} \text{PC}[p] = \text{PC}_3 \ \wedge \ \text{X} \neq p \ \wedge \\ \text{PC'}[p] = \text{Down} \end{array}$$

Fig. 3. Splitter transition system

formula φ_1' which describes the states from which a state characterized by φ_1 can be reached by taking the transition $spl_{stop}(i)$ (where the parameter i indicates which process is concerned by the transition) :

$$\varphi_1' : \exists ij. \ i \neq j \ \wedge \ \text{X} = i \ \wedge \ \text{PC}[i] = \text{PC}_3 \ \wedge \ \text{PC}[j] = \text{Stop}$$

The termination of this reachability analysis is guaranteed as long as one can exhibit a well-quasi-ordering on the set of cubes generated during the algorithm [9].

Concerning the second and third formulas φ_2 and φ_3, they are not cubes as they contain universal quantifiers. The computation of their pre-images will introduce existential quantifiers. For example, the pre-image of φ_2 by $spl_{down}(j)$ is the following φ_2' formula:

$$\varphi_2' : \exists j \forall i. \ i \neq j \implies \text{X} \neq j \ \wedge \ \text{PC}[j] = \text{PC}_3 \ \wedge \ \text{PC}[i] = \text{Down}$$

and the pre-image of φ_2' by the same transition will give the new formula φ_2'':

$$\varphi_2'' : \exists jk \forall i. \ \begin{array}{l} i \neq j \neq k \implies \text{X} \neq j \ \wedge \ \text{X} \neq k \ \wedge \\ \text{PC}[j] = \text{PC}_3 \ \wedge \ \text{PC}[k] = \text{PC}_3 \ \wedge \ \text{PC}[i] = \text{Down} \end{array}$$

From φ_2' and φ_2'', it may seem obvious that the reachability analysis of φ_2 will generate an infinite sequence of formulas where new existentially quantified processes will be piled up, leading to the impossibility of reaching a fixpoint and thus terminating.

For those reasons, the MCMT framework is restricted to the analysis of cubes. However, as illustrated by the properties φ_2 or φ_3, some problems involve formulas that are not cubes and that need to be handled.

As mention in the introduction, there exists techniques for extending MCMT to universal quantifiers. In [3], a syntactic transformation is proposed which can be interpreted as the implementation of a crash-failure model. The main idea is to view a universal formula $\forall i.\varphi$ as an infinite conjunction and to over approximate it as a *finite* conjunction $\exists i_1, \ldots, i_n.\varphi(i_1) \wedge \cdots \wedge \varphi(i_n)$, by considering that, except for those n processes, all other processes crashed before reaching the states described by this formula. For instance, using this technique, φ_2 could be seen as a cube ψ_2 of the form

$$\psi_2 : \exists i.PC[i] = \texttt{Down}$$

by considering that the number of processes that did not crash is exactly one. Computing the pre-image of ψ_2 is immediately simpler but we can see with utter certainty that this state is not unsafe if more than one processes are involved in subsequent transitions. From this example it is obvious that protocols that are not fault-tolerant (like the splitter) would produce wrong results.

3   Reasoning About Universal Cubes in MCMT

In this section, we illustrate BRWP, an extended version of the backward reachability of MCMT for reasoning about universal quantifiers using the splitter given in Sect. 2. Our extension applies to *universal cubes* (u-cubes) which are formulas of the form $\exists i \forall j.\mathcal{C}(i, j)$, where $\mathcal{C}(i, j)$ is a conjunction of literals parameterized by two vectors i and j of distinct process variables. We proceed in three steps to reason about u-cubes.

Step 1: Reachability Analysis in a Finite Domain. Instead of considering the parameterized case, we first restrict the domain of processes to a finite set of process identifiers (denoted in the rest of the paper by the symbols $\#_1$, $\#_2$, ...). The number chosen for the cardinality of the domain is arbitrary, but in our case studies we fix the domain to contain only 3 or 4 processes.

Fixing the cardinality allows us to instantiate the universal part of u-cubes and convert them to cubes. For instance, in a domain restricted to 3 distinct processes $\#_1$, $\#_2$ and $\#_3$, the formula φ_2 is transformed in the following cube $\varphi_2^{\#3}$ (with no quantifiers):

$$\varphi_2^{\#3} : PC[\#_1] = \texttt{Down} \ \wedge \ PC[\#_2] = \texttt{Down} \ \wedge \ PC[\#_3] = \texttt{Down}$$

From these cubes, we run the (traditional) backward reachability algorithm of MCMT, bounded by the finite cardinality of the domain of processes. Thereby, for instance, the first pre-image of $\varphi_2^{\#3}$ by $spl_{down}(\#_1)$ is the following $\varphi'^{\#3}_2$ formula:

$$\varphi'^{\#3}_2 : PC[\#_1] = PC_3 \ \wedge \ X \neq \#_1 \ \wedge \ PC[\#_2] = \texttt{Down} \ \wedge \ PC[\#_3] = \texttt{Down}$$

It is important to remark that $\varphi'^{\#3}_2$ has the same number of processes as $\varphi_2^{\#3}$. Indeed, the cardinality of the domain prevents us to add new (existential) quantifiers.

If the reachability algorithm terminates with a pre-image that intersects the initial formula, then we can conclude that the system is unsafe in the parameterized case. Otherwise, if a fixpoint is reached (which is the case for the splitter), we can only conclude that the property is valid for the chosen number of processes, and we proceed to Step 2.

Step 2: Generalising Invariants. To go further and prove the properties defined by u-cubes for the parameterized case, we try to exploit (a subset of) the pre-images computed in Step 1 by trying to generalise those formulas for an infinite domain. This is done by abstracting process constants by existential or universal quantified variables.

The problem of generalising a pre-image computed in Step 1 is that it can characterize unreachable states in a finite domain but reachable ones in an infinite domain (which seems normal since this kind of algorithms are not fault-tolerant). For instance, consider the previous formula $\varphi'^{\#3}_2$ obtained by computing the pre-image of $\varphi^{\#3}_2$ by $spl_{down}(\#_1)$. The states described by this formula are unsafe (and unreachable from $\mathcal{I}nit$) if the domain is limited to three processes, but they becomes safe if a fourth process exists as it could be in any state of the automaton (PC_0, PC_1, $Right$,...) as shown by the graph in Fig. 4.

To check if a pre-image represents unreachable states in an infinite domain, we first transform it into a cube by replacing process constants with existential variables, then we replay the reachability algorithm of MCMT. If this cube is shown to be unreachable, then we keep it for Step 3. Otherwise, we transform the pre-image as a u-cube by only abstracting with existential variables the process constants involved in a transition and using universal quantifiers for abstracting the other constants. The u-cubes generated by this generalisation technique are safe (but nevertheless less informative) invariants that we keep for Step 3.

For instance, the pre-image $\varphi'^{\#3}_2$ is first generalised as a cube by abstracting the process constants $\#_1$, $\#_2$ and $\#_3$ by three existentially quantified variables p_1, p_2 and p_3:

$$\varphi'^{\exists}_2 : \exists p_1 p_2 p_3 \quad \begin{aligned} &p_1 \neq p_2 \neq p_3 \,\wedge\, X \neq p_1 \,\wedge\, PC[p_1] = PC_3 \,\wedge\, \\ &PC[p_2] = \text{Down} \,\wedge\, PC[p_3] = \text{Down} \end{aligned}$$

Running a backward reachability from $\varphi'^{\exists}_2$ shows that it describes states reachable from $\mathcal{I}nit$. Therefore, we can filter this formula out as it is actually safe and can't be treated as an invariant of the system.

Now, when looking closely at the pre-image $\varphi'^{\#3}_2$, it appears that process $\#_1$ has been used by a transition when $\#_2$ and $\#_3$ remained untouched. In terms of quantifiers, this can be semantically captured by (1) adding a fresh existential variable p_1 for representing $\#_1$ and (2) by representing processes $\#_2$ and $\#_3$ with the same universally quantified variable p_2. Therefore, $\varphi'^{\#3}_2$ can be generalised by the following u-cube

$$\varphi'^{\exists\forall}_2 : \exists p_1.\forall p_2.p_1 \neq p_2 \implies X \neq p_1 \,\wedge\, PC[p_1] = PC_3 \,\wedge\, PC[p_2] = \text{Down}$$

which represents states that are unsafe if there exists a process p_1 in PC_3 such that $X \neq p_1$ and that all other processes are in Down.

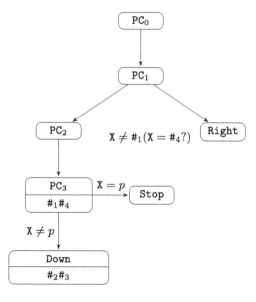

Fig. 4. Processes $\#_2$ and $\#_3$ are in **Down** and process $\#_1$ is in PC_3, ready to go in **Down**, but a fourth process $\#_4$ could be in all other states

Step 3: Deductive Verification. Given a property φ, the result of Steps 1 and 2 is a set of (u-)cubes $\{\mathcal{I}_{k_1}^{\exists\forall}, \ldots, \mathcal{I}_{k_p}^{\exists\forall}\}$ representing invariants of the original system computed from the finite backward reachability of φ.

To prove φ, our last step consists in proving the following conjunction ψ using a deductive verification technique.

$$\psi : \varphi \wedge \mathcal{I}_{k_1}^{\exists\forall} \wedge \cdots \wedge \mathcal{I}_{k_p}^{\exists\forall}$$

For that, we translate the array-based parameterized transition system, as well as the formula ψ, in the input language of a deductive verification engine.

Considering the impressive number of back-ends (SMT or TPTP solvers) supported by the Why3 platform, we have chosen to translate array-based systems to WhyML, the input language of Why3. However, the translation requires great attention as (1) the semantic gap between array-based systems and WhyML is important, and (2) the way transition systems are represented may have a strong impact on the deductive engine (see Sect. 5).

4   Formalising BRWP

The implementation of BRWP is given in Algorithm 1. It's an extended version of the backward reachability procedure of MCMT for reasoning about universal cubes.

This algorithm takes as input a formula φ and an integer c. It starts by initiating two variables, $\mathcal{V}$, the set of the visited nodes initially empty and $\mathcal{Q}$, the queue of pending nodes initialised with the instantiated version $\varphi^{\#c}$ of φ. The formula $\varphi^{\#c}$ is instantiated as seen in Step 1 with a cardinality fixed to c. BRWP iteratively computes the transitive closure of pre-images $\text{FINITEPRE}^*(\varphi^{\#c})$ until it reaches one of the two following termination conditions:

- the safety check (line 7) fails which means that the treated node corresponds to a possible initial state and thus that the system is unsafe
- there are no more nodes in $\mathcal{Q}$ which means that a fixpoint has been reached and the system is safe (for a finite domain)

If the first termination condition has been reached, the system is not safe for a finite number of processes and can not be safe for an infinite number of them. However, if the second condition has been reached, the visited nodes need to be treated to correspond to the infinite domain as seen in Step 2. When these filtering and generalisation have been computed (see next subsections for a description of this step), the new invariants are delivered to a deductive verification engine by calling the function Check_inductive_invariant(see Sect. 5).

4.1   Generalisation and Filtering

The code of the generalisation and filtering function Generalize_and_filter is given in the Algorithm 2. It takes as input the set $\mathcal{V}^{\#c}$ of instantiated formulas computed during the finite backward reachability. Its goal is to transform those formulas in cubes by renaming the processes and binding them to existential quantifiers. However, before doing so, a simplification step (function Simplify) is performed since the finitness of our domain allows us to transform multiple differences in an equality. For example, considering again the formula $\varphi'^{\#3}_2$ seen in Sect. 3:

$$\varphi'^{\#3}_2 : PC[\#_1] = PC_3 \ \wedge \ X \neq \#_1 \ \wedge \ PC[\#_2] = \text{Down} \ \wedge \ PC[\#_3] = \text{Down}$$

Its pre-image by transition $spl_{down}(\#_2)$ gives the following formula:

$$X \neq \#_1 \ \wedge \ X \neq \#_2 \ \wedge \ PC[\#_2] = PC_3 \ \wedge \ PC[\#_3] = \text{Down}$$

In this case, the fact that we're facing a finite domain actually helps us. Since there are only three processes, the literals $X \neq \#_1$ and $X \neq \#_2$ implies that $X = \#_3$. This formula is thus transformed first as follows:

$$X = \#_3 \ \wedge \ PC[\#_2] = PC_3 \ \wedge \ PC[\#_3] = \text{Down}$$

then, it is generalised as the following cube:

$$\exists p_2, p_3. \ \ X = p_3 \ \wedge \ PC[p_2] = PC_3 \ \wedge \ PC[p_3] = \text{Down}$$

After this generalisation and simplification transformation has been performed, the cube φ thus obtained is given to the same backward reachability engine (BWD), but this time without the finite domain constraint. If the model checker returns safe, φ is saved in the set variable $\mathcal{S}_1$ for the deductive verification engine and the instantiated formula $\varphi^{\#c}$ is filtered out from the set $\mathcal{V}$ of formulas to be given to the second generalisation algorithm implemented in Universal_Generalization.

Algorithm 1: Backward reachability and deductive verification

Variables :
    $\mathcal{V}$: visited nodes
    $\mathcal{Q}$: work queue

1 **function** BRWP(φ, c) : **begin**
2     $\varphi^{\#c}$:= Instantiate (φ, c);
3     $\mathcal{V}$:= $\emptyset$;
4   push($\mathcal{Q}$, $\varphi^{\#c}$);
5   **while** not_empty($\mathcal{Q}$) **do**
6        $\varphi^{\#c}$:= pop($\mathcal{Q}$);
7   **if** *(I $\wedge$ $\varphi^{\#c}$ sat)* **then**
8   **return** *unsafe*
9   **else if** $(\varphi^{\#c} \not\models \mathcal{V})$ **then**
10          $\mathcal{V}$:= $\mathcal{V} \cup \{\varphi^{\#c}\}$;
11   push($\mathcal{Q}$, FINITEPRE($\varphi^{\#c}$, c));
12   **end**
13   **end**
14     $\mathcal{S}_1$, $\mathcal{V}'$:= Generalize_and_filter($\mathcal{V}$);
15     $\mathcal{S}_2$:= Universal_Generalization($\mathcal{V}'$);
16   Check_inductive_invariant($\varphi \wedge \mathcal{S}_1 \wedge \mathcal{S}_2$)
17 **end**

4.2 Universal Generalisation

The code of the function Universal_Generalization is given in Algorithm 3. Similarly to the previous generalisation function, Universal_Generalization takes as input the set $\mathcal{V}^{\#c}$ of instantiated cubes.

To explain the main part of this algorithm, we illustrate its uses in Fig. 5, starting from the following property φ of the splitter

$$\varphi : \forall p.\mathrm{PC}[p] = \mathsf{Down}$$

which, after instantiation (for instance when c is 3), is given to the generalisation function as the following formula:

$$\varphi^{\#c} : \mathrm{PC}[\#_1] = \mathsf{Down} \wedge \mathrm{PC}[\#_2] = \mathsf{Down} \wedge \mathrm{PC}[\#_3] = \mathsf{Down}$$

This formula is first tagged with a vector of processes $\overrightarrow{V}^{\#c}$ describing which processes are from the same quantifier. Here, $\overrightarrow{V}^{\#3} = \{\#_1, \#_2, \#_3\}_\forall$, where the meaning of the annotation $\forall$ is that the 3 processes come from the universal quantifier. When computing the pre-image from the transition spl_{down} : $\exists i.\mathrm{PC}[i] = \mathrm{PC}_3 \wedge \mathrm{X} \neq i \wedge \mathrm{PC}'[i] = \mathsf{Down}$, we end up with the new formula

$$\varphi_1^{\#3} = \mathrm{PC}[\#_1] = \#_3 \wedge \mathrm{X} \neq \#_1 \wedge \mathrm{PC}[\#_2] = \mathsf{Down} \wedge \mathrm{PC}[\#_3] = \mathsf{Down}$$

and the new vector $\overrightarrow{V}^{\#3} = \{\#_1\}_\exists, \{\#_2, \#_3\}_\forall$. The reasoning behind this comes from the fact that transitions in Cubicle are existentially quantified. Thus, since processes $\#_2$ and $\#_3$ have not been involved in the transition, they remain attached to the universal quantifier. On the contrary, process $\#_1$ becomes attached to a new existential quantifier.

Algorithm 2: Generalise and filter

```
 1 function Generalize_and_filter(V#c) : begin
 2     V := V#c;
 3     S1 := ∅;
 4     forall φ#c ∈ V#c do
 5         Δ∃ := ⊤ ;
 6         forall p ∈ V#c do
 7             v := Fresh_Variable();
 8             Δ∃ := Δ∃ ∧ v;
 9             Replace(p, v, φ#c);        /* Replace all occurrences of the
                   process p with the fresh process v */
10         end
11         D = Distinct(Δ∃);             /* All variables are different */
12         φ = Δ∃ ∧ D ∧ φ#c;
13         Simplify(φ);
14         if BWD(φ) safe then
15             S1 := S1 ∪ {φ};
16             V := V \ {φ#c}
17         end
18     end
19     return (S1, V)
20 end
```

When generalised, all literals containing an existential-tagged processes (we use the notation $\overrightarrow{V}^{\#3_\exists}$ to denote this set of variables) are kept with their processes being renamed in new distinct existential processes and all the literals containing an universal-tagged process (we use the notation $\overrightarrow{V}^{\#3_\forall}$ to denote this set of variables) are merged into one literal quantified by a fresh universal process. For instance, the formula $\varphi_1^{\#3}$ is generalised as follows:

$$\exists p_1.\forall p_2.p_1 \neq p_2 \implies PC[p_1] = PC_6 \wedge PC[p_2] = \text{Down}$$

Algorithm 3: Universal Generalisation

```
1  function Universal_Generalization(𝒱#c) : begin
2      𝒱:= ∅;
3      forall φ#c (tagged by V⃗#n) ∈ 𝒱#c do
4          Δ∃ := ⊤ ;
5          Δ∀ := ⊤ ;
6          forall p ∈ V⃗#n∃ do
7              v := Fresh_Variable();
8              Δ∃ := Δ∃∧ v;                                        ·
9              Replace(p, v, φ#c);          /* Replace all occurrences of the
                 process p with the fresh process v */
10         end
11         if V⃗#n∀ ≠ ∅ then
12             v := Fresh_Variable();
13             Δ∀ := v;
14             Remove_and_Replace(p, v, φ#c);   /* Remove all the literals
                 parameterized by processes from V⃗#n∀ and adds a new
                 literal parameterized by v */
15         end
16         binop := if Δ∀ = ⊤ then ∧ else ⟹ ;
17         𝒟 = Distinct(Δ∃, Δ∀);            /* All variables are different */
18         φ = Δ∃ ∧ Δ∀ ∧ 𝒟 binop φ#c;
19         𝒱:= 𝒱 ∪{φ};
20     end
21 end
```

---

5 Deductive Verification

The last function call Check_inductive_invariant($\varphi \wedge \mathcal{S}_1 \wedge \mathcal{S}_2$) of BRWP requires the help of a deductive verification engine. In our implementation, we are using the Why3 platform [7].

Given a program $\mathcal{P}$ and its specification $\mathcal{T}$ (a set of theories, program invariants and properties), Why3 tries to check that $\mathcal{P}$ satisfies $\mathcal{T}$ by performing an inductive invariant check with a compositional reasoning and a weakest-precondition (WP) engine. Verification conditions generated by the WP calculus of Why3 are discharged to a large number of automatic or interactive solvers (SMT, TPTP, Coq, etc.).

The implementation of Check_inductive_invariant is essentially based on the translation of array-based transition systems to WhyML, the input language of Why3. However, the gap between the semantics of MCMT and WhyML is important. Indeed, Why3 is a platform designed to work with sequential, deterministic and terminating programs, while the semantics of array-based transition systems is concurrent, non-deterministic and non-terminating. To see how to bridge the gap between these two languages, we illustrate our translation using the splitter example (Sect. 2).

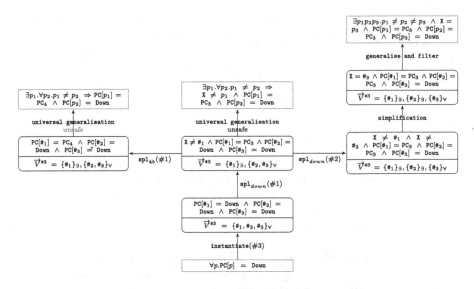

Fig. 5. First nodes and their simplification, filtration and generalisation for the splitter

State Declaration. Our encoding starts with types declarations. The type `proc` of processes is represented by integers (`int` in WhyML). The system's state is encoded by a record with two mutable variables x and y, as well as an array pc (implicitly indexed by integers) containing values of type `state`.

```
type proc = int
type system = {
  mutable x : proc;
  mutable y : bool;
  pc : array state;
}
```

Initial States. The initial formula of the splitter defines initial states with the following formula $\mathcal{I}nit$

$$\mathcal{I}nit : \forall p.\text{PC}[p] = \text{PC}_0 \wedge \text{Y} = \bot$$

where only Y and PC[] are given a value, the other variable x can contain an arbitrary value. Since Why3 expects every variable to be initialised, we give to x a random value in the range of possible values.

```
let s = {
  y = false;
  pc = Array.make _n PC0;
  x = Random.random_int _n;
} in
```

Infinite Execution. The semantics of an array-based transition system is given by a single infinite loop which repeatedly execute two steps:

1. evaluate all the guards of transitions, given the current values of the global state
2. arbitrarily choose one of the commands whose guard is true and execute it, updating the variables

Translating *infinite* loops in Why3 is problematic, in particular when one want to check invariants when exiting it. A solution to this problem is to consider that the loop ends when it reaches a bound given as a parameter of our system. The resulting program in Why3 is then bounded by the number of processes and the number of steps allowed in the loop.

```
let splitter1 (_n : int) (maxsteps : int) : system
  requires { 0 < _n }
  ...
  =
  (* ... *)
  while ( !nbsteps < maxsteps ) do
    variant { maxsteps - !nbsteps }
    incr nbsteps;
    (* ... *)
  done;
  s
end
```

Nondeterminism. There are two sources of nondeterminism in array-based systems. The first one can be illustrated by considering the following transitions t_1 and t_2:

$$t_1 : \exists p.\text{PC}[p] = \text{PC0} \wedge \text{PC'}[p] = \text{PC1}$$
$$t_2 : \exists p.\text{PC}[p] = \text{PC0} \wedge \text{PC'}[p] = \text{PC2}$$

If $\text{PC}[p] = \text{PC0}$ for some process p, then both transition can be triggered, resulting in a state where $\text{PC}[p]$ equals to PC1 or PC2.

In order to mimic this nondeterminism in Why3, we add a coin toss to each translation of a transition's guard. This coin toss does not need to be specified, it just allows Why3 to explore all the possibilities.

```
val coin () : bool
if coin () && pc.[i] = PC0
then pc.[i] <- PC1
if coin () && pc.[i] = PC0
then pc.[i] <- PC2
```

The second source of nondeterminism comes from the fact that, at each step of the loop, transitions need to be taken by random unique processes. The Why3 program thus needs to know that it can take the transition of its choice with the processes of its choice if the guards hold true with such processes.

This is done by specifying a function that takes two arguments, the max number of processes n and the number of needed processes k (*e.g.* the max number of processes involved in transition guards, updates, etc.). This function ensures that all the processes it creates will be different. There is no need to implement it as we just use its specification to help the deductive verification. Why3 having difficulty with lists and algebraic data types to reason inductively, the result returned by this function is an array of the size of the number of processes needed. The value k is determined by the maximum number of parameters (processes) in a transition. In the splitter case, k will then be equal to 1.

```
val k_random (k:int) (n:int) : (result:array int)
  requires { 0 <= k }
  requires { k <= n }
  ensures { length result = k }
  ensures { forall i j:int. 0 <= i < n /\ 0 <= j < n /\ i <> j ->
            result[i] <> result[j] }
  ensures { forall i:int. 0 <= i < n -> 0 <= result[i] < n }
```

Invariants. Finally, as it is (when all the transitions have been added), this file can not be proven by Why3 since it lacks important loop invariants. The algorithms to find such invariants are independent of BRWP and by lack of space, we omit to describe them. In our implementation, these invariants are found during the backward reachability loop using the BRAB technique of Cubicle [4,5], a model checker based on MCMT. Those invariants are automatically added to the Why3 file as invariant formulas.

```
while ( !nbsteps < maxsteps ) do
  invariant { 0 <= s.x < _n }
  invariant { forall _p1 : int. 0 <= _p1 < _n /\
                        s.x = _p1 -> s.pC[_p1] <> Down }
  invariant { exists _p1 : int. 0 <= _p1 < _n /\ s.pC[_p1] <> Down }
  (* ... *)
```

6   Conclusion and Perspectives

In this paper, we have presented an extension of the MCMT framework for reasoning about universal cubes, that formulas with both existential and universal quantifiers. Our approach tightly combines the backward reachability algorithm of MCMT with a deductive verification engine.

We have implemented our framework in the Cubicle model checker, with the help of the Why3 platform for program verification. Our first experiments are very promising as we have been able to prove automatically algorithms like the splitter which were out of scope the Cubicle model checker.

As future work, we plan to design an even more tight integration between our backward reachability algorithm and a weakest-precondition calculus in order to implement a complete roundtrip loop between these algorithms.

References

1. Abdulla, P.A., Delzanno, G., Rezine, A.: Parameterized verification of infinite-state processes with global conditions. In: Damm, W., Hermanns, H. (eds.) CAV 2007. LNCS, vol. 4590, pp. 145–157. Springer, Heidelberg (2007). https://doi.org/10.1007/978-3-540-73368-3_17

2. Abdulla, P.A., Ben Henda, N., Delzanno, G., Rezine, A.: Handling parameterized systems with non-atomic global conditions. In: Logozzo, F., Peled, D.A., Zuck, L.D. (eds.) VMCAI 2008. LNCS, vol. 4905, pp. 22–36. Springer, Heidelberg (2008). https://doi.org/10.1007/978-3-540-78163-9_7

3. Alberti, F., Ghilardi, S., Pagani, E., Ranise, S., Rossi, G.P.: Universal guards, relativization of quantifiers, and failure models in model checking modulo theories. JSAT **8**(1/2), 29–61 (2012)

4. Conchon, S., Goel, A., Krstić, S., Mebsout, A., Zaïdi, F.: Cubicle: a parallel SMT-based model checker for parameterized systems. In: Madhusudan, P., Seshia, S.A. (eds.) CAV 2012. LNCS, vol. 7358, pp. 718–724. Springer, Heidelberg (2012). https://doi.org/10.1007/978-3-642-31424-7_55

5. Conchon, S., Goel, A., Krstic, S., Mebsout, A., Zaidi, F.: Invariants for finite instances and beyond. In: FMCAD 2013, Portland, OR, USA, October 20–23 (2013)

6. Cousineau, D., Doligez, D., Lamport, L., Merz, S., Ricketts, D., Vanzetto, H.: TLA$^+$ proofs. In: Giannakopoulou, D., Méry, D. (eds.) FM 2012. LNCS, vol. 7436, pp. 147–154. Springer, Heidelberg (2012). https://doi.org/10.1007/978-3-642-32759-9_14

7. Filliâtre, J.-C., Paskevich, A.: Why3—where programs meet provers. In: Felleisen, M., Gardner, P. (eds.) ESOP 2013. LNCS, vol. 7792, pp. 125–128. Springer, Heidelberg (2013). https://doi.org/10.1007/978-3-642-37036-6_8

8. Ghilardi, S., Nicolini, E., Ranise, S., Zucchelli, D.: Towards SMT model checking of array-based systems. In: Armando, A., Baumgartner, P., Dowek, G. (eds.) IJCAR 2008. LNCS (LNAI), vol. 5195, pp. 67–82. Springer, Heidelberg (2008). https://doi.org/10.1007/978-3-540-71070-7_6

9. Ghilardi, S., Ranise, S.: Backward reachability of array-based systems by SMT solving: Termination and invariant synthesis. LMCS **6**(4) (2010)

10. Goel, A., Krstic, S., Leslie, R., Tuttle, M.R.: SMT-based system verification with DVF. In: SMT 2012, Manchester, UK, June 30 - July 1

11. Lamport, L.: A fast mutual exclusion algorithm. ACM Trans. Comput. Syst. **5**(1), 1–11 (1987)

12. Lamport, L.: Specifying Systems: The TLA+ Language and Tools for Hardware and Software Engineers. Addison-Wesley Longman Publishing Co., Inc., Boston (2002)

13. Moir, M., Anderson, J.H.: Wait-free algorithms for fast, long-lived renaming. Sci. Comput. Program. **25**(1), 1–39 (1995)

sCompile: Critical Path Identification and Analysis for Smart Contracts

Jialiang Chang[1($\boxtimes$)], Bo Gao[2], Hao Xiao[2], Jun Sun[3], Yan Cai[4], and Zijiang Yang[1]

[1] Department of Computer Science, Western Michigan University,
Kalamazoo, MI 49009, USA
{jialiang.chang,zijiang.yang}@wmich.edu
[2] Pillar of Information System Technology and Design,
Singapore University of Technology and Design, Singapore, Singapore
bo_gao@mymail.sutd.edu.sg, hao_xiao@sutd.edu.sg
[3] School of Information Systems,
Singapore Management University, Singapore, Singapore
junsun@smu.edu.sg
[4] State Key Laboratory of Computer Science, Institute of Software,
Chinese Academy of Sciences, Beijing, China
ycai.mail@gmail.com

Abstract. Ethereum smart contracts are an innovation built on top of the blockchain technology, which provides a platform for automatically executing contracts in an anonymous, distributed, and trusted way. The problem is magnified by the fact that smart contracts, unlike ordinary programs, cannot be patched easily once deployed. It is important for smart contracts to be checked against potential vulnerabilities. In this work, we propose an alternative approach to automatically identify critical program paths (with multiple function calls including *inter-contract* function calls) in a smart contract, rank the paths according to their criticalness, discard them if they are infeasible or otherwise present them with user friendly warnings for user inspection. We identify paths which involve monetary transaction as critical paths, and prioritize those which potentially violate important properties. For scalability, symbolic execution techniques are only applied to top ranked critical paths. Our approach has been implemented in a tool called sCompile, which has been applied to 36,099 smart contracts. The experiment results show that sCompile is efficient, i.e., 5 s on average for one smart contract. Furthermore, we show that many known vulnerabilities can be captured if user inspects as few as 10 program paths generated by sCompile. Lastly, sCompile discovered 224 unknown vulnerabilities with a false positive rate of 15.4% before user inspection.

Keywords: Blockchain · Symbolic testing · Smart contract

1 Introduction

Built on top of cryptographic algorithms [1–3] and the blockchain technology [4–6], cryptocurrency like Bitcoin has been developing rapidly in recent years.

© Springer Nature Switzerland AG 2019
Y. Ait-Ameur and S. Qin (Eds.): ICFEM 2019, LNCS 11852, pp. 286–304, 2019.
https://doi.org/10.1007/978-3-030-32409-4_18

Many believe it has the potential to revolutionize the banking industry by allowing monetary transactions. Smart contracts bring it one step further by providing a framework which allows any contract to be executed in an autonomous, distributed, and trusted way. Smart contracts thus may revolutionize many industries. Ethereum [7], an open-source, blockchain-based cryptocurrency, is the first to integrate the functionality of smart contracts. Due to its enormous potential, its market cap reached at $29.1 billion as of Jun 17th, 2019.

In essence, smart contracts are computer programs which are automatically executed on a distributed blockchain infrastructure. A majority of smart contracts in Ethereum are written in a programming language called Solidity [8]. Like ordinary programs, Solidity programs may contain vulnerabilities, which potentially lead to attacks. The problem is magnified by the fact that smart contracts, unlike ordinary programs, cannot be patched easily once they are deployed on the blockchain.

In recent years, these attacks exploit security vulnerabilities in Ethereum smart contracts and often result in monetary loss. One notorious example is the DAO attack [9], i.e., an attacker stole more than 3.5 million Ether (about $45 million USD at the time) from the DAO contract on June 17, 2016.

The problem of analyzing and verifying smart contracts is far from being solved. Some believe that it will never be, just as the verification problem of traditional programs. Solidity is designed to be Turing-complete which intuitively means that it is very expressive and flexible. The price to pay is that almost all interesting problems associated with checking whether a smart contract is vulnerable are undecidable [10]. Consequently, tools which aim to analyze smart contracts *automatically* either are not scalable or produce many false alarms. For instance, Oyente [11] is designed to check whether a program path leads to a vulnerability or not using a constraint solver to check whether the path is feasible or not. Due to the limitation of constraint solving techniques, if Oyente is unable to determine whether the path is feasible or not, the choice is either to ignore the path (which may result in a false negative, i.e., a vulnerability is missed) or to report an alarm (which may result in a false alarm).

Besides, we believe that manual inspection is unavoidable given the expressiveness of Solidity. However, given that smart contracts often enclose many behaviors (which manifest through different paths), manually inspecting every path is overwhelming. Thus, sCompile further aims to reduce the manual effort by identifying a small number of critical paths and presenting them to the user with easy-to-digest information.

Overall, sCompile works as follows:

- sCompile firstly constructs a control flow graph (CFG) which captures all possible control flow including those due to the *inter-contract* function calls. sCompile then systematically generates paths (with a bounded sequence of function calls).
- To address path explosion, sCompile then statically identifies paths which are 'critical'. In this work, we define paths involving monetary transactions as critical paths, which is often sufficient in capturing vulnerabilities in smart contracts.

- We then define a set of (configurable) money-related properties based on existing vulnerabilities and identify all paths that potentially violate our properties. Considering that different properties have different criticalness and a long path may be unlikely feasible than a short one, sCompile ranks all paths by computing a criticalness score for each path based on the two factors.
- Finally, for top ranked paths, sCompile automatically checks whether it is feasible using symbolic execution techniques. And, the feasible paths are presented to the user for inspection.

We have implemented sCompile and applied it to 36,099 smart contracts gathered from EtherScan [12]. Our experiment shows that sCompile can efficiently analyze smart contracts, i.e., it spends 5 s on average to analyze a smart contract (with a bound on the number of function calls 3). Furthermore, we show that sCompile effectively prioritizes programs paths which reveal vulnerabilities in smart contracts, i.e., it is often sufficient to capture the vulnerability by inspecting the reported 10 or fewer critical paths. Overall, sCompile identified 224 vulnerabilities. The false positive rate of sCompile (before the results are reported for user inspection) is 15.4%, which is also generally acceptable. A further user study result shows that with sCompile's help, users are more likely to identify vulnerabilities in smart contracts.

```
contract toyDAO{
    address owner;
    mapping (address => uint) credit;
    function toyDAO() payable public {
        owner = msg.sender;
    }
    function donate() payable public{
        credit[msg.sender] = 100;
    }
    function withdraw() public {
0       uint256 value = 20;
1       if (msg.sender.call.value(value)()) {
2           credit[msg.sender] = credit[msg.sender] - value;
        }
    }
}
contract Bitway is ERC20 {
    function () public payable {
        createTokens();
    }
    function createTokens() public payable {
        require(msg.value > 300);
        ...
    }
    ...
}
```

Fig. 1. Illustrative contracts

The rest of the paper is organized as follows. Section 2 illustrates how sCompile works through a few simple examples. Section 3 presents the details of our approach step-by-step. Section 4 shows evaluation results on sCompile. Section 5 reviews related work and lastly Sect. 6 concludes with a discussion on future work.

2 Illustrative Examples

In this section, we present multiple examples to illustrate vulnerabilities in smart contracts and how sCompile helps to reveal them. The contracts are shown in Fig. 1.

Example 1: Contract *toyDAO* is an invariant one of DAO contract. Mapping *credit* is a map which records a user's credit amount. Function *donate()* allows user to top up its credit with 100 wei (which is a unit of Ether). Function *withdraw()* by design sends 20 wei to message sender (at line 1) and then updates *credit*. However, when line 1 is executed, message sender could call function *withdraw()* through its fallback function, before line 2 is executed. Line 1 is then executed again and another 20 wei is sent to message sender. Eventually, all Ether in this contract's wallet is sent to message sender.

In sCompile, inspired by common practice in banking industry, assume that the user sets the limit to be 30. Given the contract, a critical path reported by sCompile is one which executes line 0, 1, 0, and 1. The path is associated with a warning message stating that the accumulated amount transferred along the path is more than the limit. We remark that existing approaches often check such vulnerability through a property called reentrancy, which often results in false alarms [11,13].

Example 2: Contract *Bitway* is another token management contract. It receives Ether (i.e., cryptocurrency in Ethereum) through function *createTokens()*. Note that this is possible because function *createTokens()* is declared as *payable*. However, there is no function in the contract which can send Ether out. Given this contract, sCompile identifies a list of critical paths for user inspection. The most critical one is a path where function *createTokens()* is invoked. Furthermore, it is labeled with a warning message stating that the smart contract appears to be a "black hole" contract as there is no path for sending Ether out, whereas this path allows one to transfer Ether into the wallet of the contract. By inspecting this path and the warning message, the user can capture the vulnerability. In comparison, existing tools like Oyente [11] and MAIAN [14] report no vulnerability given the contract. We remark that even although MAIAN is designed to check similar vulnerability, it checks whether a contract can receive Ether through testing[1] and thus results in a false negative in this case.

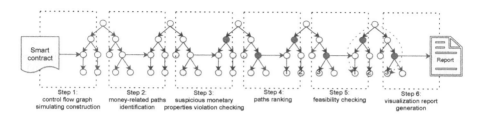

Step 1:	Step 2:	Step 3:	Step 4:	Step 5:	Step 6:
control flow graph simulating construction	money-related paths identification	suspicious monetary properties violation checking	paths ranking	feasibility checking	visualization report generation

Fig. 2. Overall workflow of sCompile

---

[1] MAIAN sends a value of 256 wei to the contract deployed in the private blockchain network.

3   Approach

Figure 2 shows the overall work flow of sCompile. Firstly, given a smart contract, sCompile constructs a control flow graph (CFG) [15] and systematically enumerates all paths. Secondly, we identify the monetary paths based on the CFG up to a user-defined bound on the number of function calls. Thirdly, we analyze each path in order to check whether it potentially violates any of the pre-defined monetary properties. Next, we compute a criticalness score for each and rank the paths accordingly. Afterwards, we apply symbolic execution to filter infeasible critical paths. Lastly, we present the results along with the associated paths to the user for inspection.

3.1   Constructing CFG

sCompile constructs a CFG for a smart contract (the compiled EVM opcode with a single entrance for whole and for each function) to capture all possible paths. Formally, a CFG is a tuple $(N, root, E)$ such that

- N is a set of nodes, where each node is a basic block of opcodes.
- $root \in N$ is the first basic block of opcodes.
- $E \subseteq N \times N$ is a set of edges, where each edge (n, n') corresponds to exactly a control directly from flow n to n'.

We also consider inter-contract functions calls, where there is a CALL to a foreign function that is assumed to call the current function including third-part contract.

For instance, Fig. 3 shows the CFG of contract *toyDAO* shown in Fig. 1. Each node is in the form of $Node\_m\_n$, where m and n are indices of the first and the last opcodes of the basic block, respectively. The red diamond node at the top is the *root* node; the blue rectangle nodes represent the first node of a function. Note that a black oval represents a node that can be redirected to the root due to inter-contract function calls. The black solid edges represent the normal control flow. The red dashed edges represent control flow due to a new function call, e.g., the edge from $Node\_88\_91$ to $Node\_0\_12$. That is, for every node n such that n ends with a terminating opcode instruction (i.e., STOP, RETURN), we introduce an edge from n to *root*. The red dotted edges represent control flow due to the inter-contract function call. That is, for every node which ends with a CALL instruction to an external function, an edge is added from the node to the root.

Given a bound b on the number of function calls, we can systematically unfold the CFG so as to obtain all paths during which only b or fewer functions are called. For instance, with a bound 2, the set of paths include all of those which visit $Node\_81\_87$ or $Node\_102\_109$ no more than twice.

Statically constructing the CFG is non-trivial due to *indirect jumps* in the bytecode generated by the Solidity compiler. For instance, part of bytecode for contract *toyDAO* is shown as follows.

```
 ...........        |     .......
 92 JUMPDEST        |     300 SHA3
 93 PUSH2 0x0064  // 100  |     301 DUP2
```

```
96 PUSH2 0x0070  //  112  |      303 SSTORE
99 JUMP                   |      304 POP
                          |
100 JUMPDEST              |      305 JUMPDEST
101 STOP                  |      306 POP
......                    |      307 JUMP
112 JUMPDEST              |      ........
113 PUSH1 0x00            |
115 PUSH1 0x14            |
......                    |
```

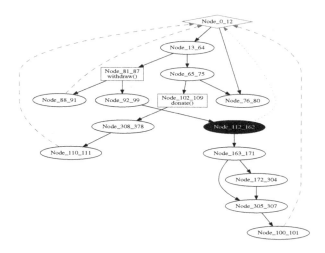

Fig. 3. Control flow graph of the contract *toyDAO* (Color figure online)

Considering that Solidity compiler use templates and often introduces indirect jumps (e.g., PUSH), we actually construct CFGs from EVM opcode as follows:

- Disassemble the bytecode to a sequence of opcode instructions.
- Identify all basic blocks (BBL) from the opcode instructions as nodes of a CFG, where the boundaries among BBLs are branching instructions JUMP and JUMPI, JUMPDEST, call instructions CALL, and terminal instructions such as RETURN, STOP, and REVERT.)
- Connect basic blocks with edges (e.g., direct jumps) which are statically decided from the opcode instructions.
- Use stack simulation to complete the CFG with edges for indirect jumps.

In the above, whenever there are indirect jumps, their targets cannot be decided by checking proceeding instructions and we have missing edges. These nodes are known as *dangling blocks* and we introduce *stack simulation* to find the successor of them. Stack simulation is similar to define-use analysis except that dangling blocks which are reachable from the entry BBL are processed first. That is, we find all paths from entry BBL to dangling blocks (e.g., the two paths from $Node\_0\_12$ to $Node\_305\_307$) and simulate instructions in each path following semantics of the instruction on the stack. Note that a dangling block ends with JUMP may have multiple successors in the CFG. When we reach the JUMP or JUMPI in the dangling block, the content of the top stack entry shall be determined and we connect the dangling block with BBL which starts at the address as in the top stack entry. For instance, for dangling block $Node\_305\_307$, there is only one successor $Node\_100\_101$ in both paths which is pushed by the instruction at address 093. We repeat above steps until all dangling blocks are processed.

3.2 Identifying Monetary Paths

Given a bound b on the number of call depth (i.e., the number of function calls) and a bound on the loop iterations, there are still many paths in the CFG to be analyzed. For instance, there are 6 paths in the *toyDAO* contract with a call depth bound of 1 (and a loop bound of 5) and 1296 with a call depth bound of 4. This is known as the path explosion problem [16]. In this work, we focus on money-related paths to avoid path explosion as almost all vulnerabilities [17] are 'money'-related.

A node is money-related if and only if its BBL contains any of following opcode instructions: CALL, CREATE, DELEGATECALL or SELFDESTRUCT. In general, one of these instructions must be used when Ether is transferred from one account to another. A path which traverses through a money-related node is considered money-related.[2]

3.3 Identifying Property-Violating Paths

Next, sCompile prioritizes paths that violate critical properties. The objective is to prioritize those paths which may trigger violation of critical properties for user inspection. The properties are designed based on previously known vulnerabilities and they can be configured and extended in sCompile.

Property: Respect the Limit. In sCompile, we allow users to set a limit on the amount of Ether transferred out of the contract's wallet. For each path, we statically check whether Ether is transferred out of the wallet and whether the transferred amount is potentially beyond the limit. To do so, for each path, we use a symbolic variable to simulate the remaining limit. Each time an amount is transferred out, we decrease the variable accordingly and check whether the remaining limit is less than zero. If so, the path potentially violates the property. Note that if we are unable to determine the exact amount to be transferred, we conservatively assume the limit may be broken.

Property: Avoid Non-existing Addresses. Any hexadecimal string of length no greater than 40 is considered a valid (well-formed) address in Ethereum. If a

---

[2] Note that each opcode instruction in EVM is associated with some gas consumption which technically makes them money-related. Gas [7] is the cost of any transaction that can be utilized to measure actions on Ethereum platform. However, the gas consumption alone in most cases does not constitute vulnerabilities and therefore we do not consider them money-related. In Fig. 3, we visualize money-related nodes with black background (e.g., the node $Node\_112\_162$ with a CALL statement msg.sender.call.value(value)()).

non-existing address is used as the receiver of a transfer, the Solidity compiler does not generate any warning and the contract can be deployed on Ethereum successfully. If a transfer to a non-existing address is executed, Ethereum automatically registers a new address (after padding 0s in front of address so that its length becomes 160bits). Because this address is owned by nobody, no one can withdraw Ether in it since no one has the private key.

For every path which contains instruction CALL or SELFDESTRUCT, sCompile checks whether the address in the instruction exists or not. This is done with the help of EtherScan Ethereum [12] (which can check whether an address is registered or not). A path which sends Ether to a non-existing address is considered to be violating the property. Currently, to minimize the number of requests to EtherScan, we only query external transactions, thus may lead to false positives when the address has only internal transactions. Of course, users can configure sCompile to also check internal transactions.

Property: Guard Suicide. sCompile checks whether a path would result in destructing the contract without constraints on the date or block number, or the contract ownership. A contract may be designed to "suicide" (with the opcode SELFDESTRUCT) after certain date or reaching certain number of blocks, and often by transferring the Ether in the contract wallet to the owner. A notorious example is Parity Wallet which resulted in an estimated loss of tokens worthy of $155 million [18].

We thus check whether there exists a path which executes SELFDESTRUCT and whether its path condition is constituted with constraints on date or block number and contract owner address. While checking the former is straightforward, checking the latter is achieved by checking whether the path contains constraints on instruction TIMESTAMP or BLOCK, and checking whether the path condition compares the variables representing the contract owner address with other addresses. A path which calls SELFDESTRUCT without such constraints is considered a violation of the property.

```
  contract StandardToken is Token {
1     function destroycontract(address _to) {
2         require(now > start + 10 days);
3         require(msg.sender != 0);
4         selfdestruct(_to);
5     }
6     ...
7 }
8 contract Problematic is StandardToken { ... }
```

Fig. 4. Guardless suicide

One example is the *Problematic* contract[3] shown in Fig. 4. Contract *Problematic* inherits contract *StandardToken*, where one of functions is *destroycontract()* allowing one to destruct contract. sCompile can report that line 4 potentially violates the property.

---

[3] We hide the names of the contracts as some of them are yet to be fixed.

Property: Be No Black Hole. In a few cases, sCompile analyzes paths which do not contain CALL, CREATE, DELEGATECALL or SELFDESTRUCT. For instance, if a contract has no money-related paths (i.e., never sends any Ether out), sCompile then checks whether there exists a path which allows contract to receive Ether. The idea is to check whether contract acts like a black hole for Ether. If it does, it is considered a vulnerability.

To check whether the contract can receive Ether, we check whether there is a *payable* function. Since Solidity version 0.4.x, a contract is allowed to receive Ether only if one of its public functions is declared with the keyword *payable*. When the Solidity compiler compiles a non-payable function, the following sequence of opcode instructions are inserted before the function body.

```
1  CALLVALUE
2  ISZERO
3  PUSH XX
4  JUMPI
5  PUSH1 0x00
6  DUP1
7  REVERT
```

At line 1, the instruction CALLVALUE retrieves the message value (to be received). Instruction ISZERO then checks if the value is zero, if it is zero, it jumps (through the JUMPI instruction at line 4) to the address which is pushed into stack by the instruction at line 3; or it goes to the block starting at line 5, which reverts the transaction (by instruction REVERT at line 7). Thus, to check whether the contract is allowed to receive Ether, we go through every path to check whether it contains the above-mentioned sequence of instructions. If all of them do, we conclude that the contract is not allowed to receive Ether. Otherwise, it is.

If the contract can receive Ether but cannot send any out, we identify the path for receiving Ether as potentially violating the property and label it with a warning messaging stating that the contract is a black hole.

Above properties are designed based on reported vulnerabilities. Of course, sCompile is designed to be extensible, i.e., new properties can be easily supported by providing a function which takes a path as input and reports whether the property is violated.

To further help users understand paths of a smart contract, sCompile supports additional analysis. For instance, sCompile provides analysis of gas consumption of paths.

However, without trying out all possible inputs, users may not be aware of the existence of certain particularly gas consuming paths. The gas consumption of a path is estimated based on each opcode instruction in the path statically.

3.4   Ranking Program Paths

To allow user to focus on most critical paths and to save analyses efforts, we prioritize paths according to the likelihood they reveal critical vulnerability. For each path, we calculate a criticalness score and rank paths according to scores. Criticalness scores are calculated as follows: let pa be a path and V be the set of properties which pa violates.

$$criticalness(pa) = \frac{\Sigma_{pr \in V} \alpha_{pr}}{\epsilon * bound(pa)} \tag{1}$$

where α_{pr} is a constant which denotes the criticalness of violating property pr, $bound(pa)$ is the depth bound of path pa (i.e., the number of function calls) and

ϵ is a positive constant. Intuitively, the criticalness is designed such that the more critical a property the path violates, the larger the score is; and the more properties it violates, the larger the score is. Furthermore, it penalizes long paths so that short paths are presented first for user inspection.

Table 1. Definition of α_{pr}

	Transfer limit	Non-existing addr.	Suicide	Black hole
Likelihood	1	1	2	3
Severity	2	3	3	2
Difficulty	2	2	3	2
α_{pr}	4	6	18	12

To assess the criticalness of each property, we use the technique called failure mode and effects analysis (FMEA [19]) which is a risk management tool widely used in a variety of industries. FMEA evaluates each property with 3 factors, i.e., *Likelihood*, *Severity* and *Difficulty*. Each factor is a value rating from 1 to 3, i.e., 3 for *Likelihood* means the most likely; 3 for *Severity* means the most severe and 3 for *Difficulty* means the most difficult to detect. The criticalness α_{pr} is then set as the product of the three factors. After ranking, only paths which have a criticalness score larger than certain threshold are subject to further analysis, reducing the number of paths significantly.

In order to identify the threshold for criticalness, we adapt the k-fold cross-validation [20,21] idea in statistical area. We collected a large set of smart contracts and split them into a training data set (10,452 contracts) and a test data set (25,678 contracts). We repeated the experiments 20 times which took more than 5,700 total hours of all machines and optimizes those parameters. The adapted parameters are shown in Table 1, and ϵ is set to be 1 and the threshold for criticalness is set to be 10.

3.5 Feasibility Checking

Not all the paths are feasible. To avoid such false alarms, we filter infeasible paths through symbolic execution [22]. The basic idea is to symbolically execute a given program. Symbolic execution has been previously applied to Solidity programs in Oyente [11] and MAIAN [14]. In this work, we apply symbolic execution to reduce the paths which are to be presented for users' inspection. Only if a path is found to be infeasible by symbolic execution, we remove it. In comparison, both Oyente and MAIAN aim to fully automatically analyze smart contracts and thus when a path cannot be determined by symbolic execution, the result may be a false positive or negative.

For instance, Fig. 5 shows a contract which is capable of receiving (since the function is *payable*) and sending Ether (due to *owner.transfer(msg.value)* at line 5), and thus sCompile does not flag it to be a black hole contract. MAIAN however claims that it is. A closer investigation reveals that because MAIAN

```
contract GigsToken {
1    function createTokens() payable {
2      require(msg.value > 0);
3      uint256 tokens = msg.value.mul(RATE);
4      balances[msg.sender] = balances[msg.sender].add(tokens);
5      owner.transfer(msg.value);
6    }
7    ...
   }
```

Fig. 5. A non-greedy contract

has trouble in solving path conditions for reaching line 5, and thus mistakenly assumes the path is infeasible. As a result, it believes there is no way Ethers can be sent out and thus the contract is a black hole.

4   Implementation and Evaluation

4.1   Implementation

sCompile is implemented in C++ with about 8 K lines of code. The symbolic execution engine in sCompile is built based on the Z3 SMT solver [23].

4.2   Experiment

We aim to answer research questions (RQ) regarding sCompile's efficiency, effectiveness and usefulness in practice. Our test subjects contain all 36,099 contracts (including both the training set and the test set) with Solidity source code downloaded from EtherScan. sCompile can directly take EVM code as input and the source code is used for our manual inspection for experiment purpose.

All experiment are done on an Amazon EC2 C3 xlarge instance installed with Ubuntu 16.04 and gcc 5.4. The timeout set for sCompile is: global wall time is 60 s and Z3 solver timeout is 100 milliseconds. The limit on the maximum number of blocks for a single path is set to be 60, and the limit on the maximum iterations of loops is set to be 5, i.e., each loop is unfolded at most five times.

RQ1: Is sCompile Efficient Enough for Practical Usage? In this experiment, we evaluate sCompile in terms of its execution time. We systematically apply sCompile to all the benchmark programs in the training set.

The results are summarized in Fig. 6. In sub-table of Fig. 6, the second, third and fourth row show the execution of sCompile with call depth bound 1, 2, and 3 respectively. For comparison, the fifth row shows the execution time of Oyente (the latest version 0.2.7) with the same timeout. We remark that the comparison should be taken with a grain of salt. Oyente does not consider sequences of function calls, i.e., its bound on function calls is 1. Furthermore, it does not consider initialization of variables in the constructor (or in the contract itself). The next columns show the execution time of MAIAN (the latest commit version on Mar 19). Although MAIAN is designed to analyze paths with multiple (by default, 3) function calls, it does not consider the possibility of a third-party contract calling any function in the contract through inter-contract function calls and thus often explores much fewer paths than sCompile. Furthermore, MAIAN checks only one of the three properties (i.e., suicidal, prodigal and greedy) each time. Thus, we must run MAIAN three times to check all three properties. The different bounds used in all three tools are summarized in Table 2.

Table 2. Loop bound definitions among three tools

Tool	Call bound	Loop bound	Timeout	Other bound
sCompile	3	5	60 s	60 cfg nodes
Oyente	1	10	60 s	N.A
MAIAN	3 (no inter-contract)	N.A	60 s	60 cfg nodes

In sub-table of Fig. 6, the second column shows the median execution time and the third column shows the number of times the execution time exceeds the global wall time (60 s). We observe that sCompile almost always finishes its analysis within 10 second. Furthermore, the execution time remains similar with different call depth bounds. This is largely due to sCompile's strategy on applying symbolic execution only to a small number of top ranked critical paths. We do however observe that the number of timeouts increases with an increased call depth bound. A close investigation shows that this is mainly because the number of paths extracted from CFG is much larger and it takes more time to extract all paths for ranking. In comparison, although Oyente has a call depth bound of 1, it times out on more contracts and spends more time on average. MAIAN spends more time on each property than the total execution of sCompile. For some property (such as *Greedy*), MAIAN times out fewer times, which is mainly because it does not consider inter-contract function calls and thus works with a smaller CFG.

The sub-figure in Fig. 6 visualizes the distribution of execution time of the tools in plot-box. The x-axis represents the execution time (in seconds). From the figure, we can conclude that sCompile is efficient.

Table 3 shows the statistics on the number of processed paths, including the estimated total number of paths on average (in the second column), the number of symbolic-executed (based on CFG), and the number passed to users. It can be observed that only a small fraction of the paths are symbolically analyzed. Furthermore, the number of symbolically executed paths remain small even when the call depth bound is increased. This is because only the top ranked critical paths are analyzed by symbolic execution.

RQ2: Is sCompile Effective to Practical Usage? In the second experiment, we aim to investigate the effectiveness of sCompile. We apply sCompile to all 36,099 contracts and manually inspect the critical paths reported by sCompile to check whether the path, together with the associated warning message, reveals a true vulnerability in the contract. Note that not all properties checked by sCompile readily signals a vulnerability. We only focus on those results produced by sCompile which are directly related to vulnerabilities in the following, i.e., paths which are deemed to violate property "avoid non-existing addresses",

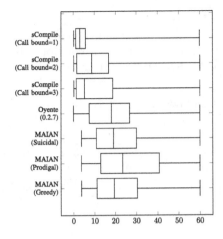

	median(s)	timeout #
sCompile (Call bound = 1)	3.106	1145
sCompile (Call bound = 2)	8.717	1737
sCompile (Call bound = 3)	5.267	2597
Oyente	18.015	2223
MAIAN (Suicidal)	19.053	1561
MAIAN (Prodigal)	23.472	6186
MAIAN (Greedy)	19.397	1081

Fig. 6. Execution time of *sCompile* vs. Oyente vs. MAIAN

Table 3. Average number of program paths

	In total	Symbolic-executed	To user
Call depth 1	48.92	37.51	1.49
Call depth 2	6177.21	144.24	12.46
Call depth 3	31346.62	121.23	12.62

Table 4. Comparison on vulnerable contracts

	sCompile			MAIAN		
	Alarmed	True positive	False positive	Alarmed	True positive	False positive
Avoid non-existing address	37	32	5	N.A	N.A	N.A
Be no black hole	57	57	0	141	56	85
Guard suicide	42	38	4	66	30	36

"be no black hole" and "guard suicide". Note that two of the properties (i.e., the latter two) analyzed by sCompile are supported by MAIAN as well. We can thus compare sCompile's performance with that of MAIAN for these two properties. The results are shown in Table 4. In the following, we discuss the detailed findings[4].

For *Property: Be no Black Hole*, there are 57 contracts in the training set are marked vulnerable by sCompile. We manually confirmed that they are all

---

[4] We have informed all developers whose contact info are available about the vulnerabilities in their contracts and several have confirmed the vulnerabilities and deployed new contracts to substitute the vulnerable ones. Some are yet to respond, although the balance in their contracts are typically small.

true positives. In comparison, MAIAN identified 141 black hole contracts and 56 contracts among them are true positives, 43 of which overlap with sCompile's results. For 13 missed contracts by sCompile but detected by MAIAN, all of them took more than 60 s and thus sCompile timed out before finishing analyzing.

The other 85 identified by MAIAN are false positives and 62 of them are library contracts. We randomly choose 5 contracts from the remaining for further investigation. We find Z3 could not finish solving the path condition in time and thus MAIAN conservatively marks the contract as vulnerable. After extending the time limit for Z3 and total timeout, 4 of the 5 false positives are still reported. The reason is that these contracts can only send Ether out after certain period, and MAIAN could not find a feasible path to send Ether out for such cases, and mistakenly flags contract as a black hole.

For *Property: Guard Suicide*, sCompile reports a program path if it leads to SELFDESTRUCT, without a constraint on the ownership of the contract or the date or the block number, i.e., a guard to prevent an unauthorized users from killing the contract. Among the analyzed contracts, sCompile identified 42 contracts which contain at least one path which violates the property. Many of the identified contracts violate the property due to contract inheritance as shown in Fig. 4.

The remaining 4 cases reported by sCompile are false positives. We manually investigated into them and found that they belong to two uncommon coding cases (where 3 of them are originated from the same contract) and three of them can be detected by sCompile by slightly revising its implementation.

MAIAN identified 66 contracts violating the property. 30 of them are true positives, 13 of which are also identified by sCompile. The other 36 are false positives. The contract *MiCarsToken* shown in Fig. 7 shows a typical false alarm. There are 2 constraints before SELFDESTRUCT in the contract. sCompile considers such a contract safe for there is a guard of *msg.sender == owner* (or the other condition), whereas MAIAN reports a vulnerability as the contract can also be killed if the msg.sender is not the owner when the second condition is satisfied.

```
contract MiCarsToken {
    function killContract () payable external {
        if (msg.sender==owner ||
            msg.value >=howManyEtherInWeiToKillContract)
        selfdestruct(owner);
    }
    ...
}
```

Fig. 7. Ambiguous cases between sCompile and MAIAN

We further analyzed the 17 cases which were neglected by sCompile. 6 of them are alarmed for owner change as exemplified in Fig. 8. In this contract, *selfdestruct* is well guarded, but the developer makes a mistake so that the constructor becomes a normal function, and anyone can invoke *mortal()* to make himself the owner of this contract and kill the contract.

For *Property: Avoid Non-existing Address.* For the contracts in the training set, all addresses identified are of length 160 bits. However, there are 37

```
contract Mortal {
    address public owner;
    function mortal() { owner = msg.sender; }
    function kill() {
        if (msg.sender == owner) suicide(owner); }
}
```

Fig. 8. Contract of owner change

contracts identified as non-existing addresses (i.e., not registered in Ethereum mainnet). They may be used for different reasons. For example, in contract *AmbrosusSale*, the address of TREASURY does not exist before the function `specialPurchase()` or `processPurchase()` is invoked (which will cost more gas for its first user). And there are 5 addresses registered by internal transactions.

We further analyzed 25,647 contracts newly uploaded in EtherScan from February 2018 to July 2018. For *"Be no Black Hole"*, there are 109 vulnerabilities out of 139 alarms generated by sCompile. Applying MAIAN on these contracts, 84 of them are marked vulnerable, 77 of which are true vulnerabilities overlapping with those found by sCompile and 7 library contracts are marked vulnerable mistakenly. Among the 139 contracts, 25 vulnerable ones are missed by MAIAN according to our manual check. For *"Guard Suicide"*, there are 83 vulnerabilities out of 114 alarms generated by sCompile. Applying MAIAN on these contracts, 42 are marked vulnerable, all of which overlap with those found by sCompile. For *"Avoid Non-existing Addresses"*, there are 80 vulnerabilities out of 87 alarms generated by sCompile. The 7 false alarms are due to internal transactions.

In total, sCompile identifies 224 vulnerabilities from the 36,099 contracts consisting of 46 *Black Hole* vulnerabilities, 66 *Guardless Suicide* vulnerabilities and 112 *Non-existing Address* vulnerabilities.

RQ3: Is sCompile Useful to Contract Users? Different from other tools which aim to fully automatically analyze smart contracts, sCompile is designed to facilitate human users. We thus conduct a user study to see whether sCompile is helpful to them.

The study takes the form of an online test. Once a user starts the test, first the user is briefed with necessary background on smart contract vulnerabilities (with examples). Then, 6 smart contracts (selected at random each time from a pool of contracts) are displayed one by one. For each contract, the source code is first shown. Afterwards, the user is asked to analyze the contract and answer the two questions. The first question asks what is the vulnerability the contract has. The second question requires user to identify the most gas consuming path in contract (with one function call).

For the first three contracts, the outputs from sCompile are shown alongside the contract source code as a hint to the user. For the remaining 3 contracts, the hints are not shown. The contracts are randomized so that not the same contracts are always displayed with the hint. The goal is to check whether users can identify the vulnerabilities correctly and more efficiently with sCompile's results.

We distribute the test through social networks and online professional forums. We also distribute it through personal contacts who we know have some experience with Solidity smart contracts. In three weeks we collected 48 successful responses to the contracts (without junk answers)[5]. Table 5 summarizes the results. Recall that sCompile's results are presented for the first three contracts. Column LOC and #paths shows the number of lines and paths in each contract. Note that in order to keep the test manageable, we are limited to relatively small contracts in this study. Columns Q1 and Q2 show the number of correct responses (the numerator) out of the number of valid responses (the denominator). We collect the time (in seconds) taken by each user in the Time column to answer all the questions. In the end of the survey we ask the user to give us a score (on the scale of 1 to 7, the higher the score the more useful our tool is) on how useful the hints in helping them answer the questions. The value in column Usefulness is the average score over all responses because all responses are shown half the hints.

Table 5. Statistics and results of surveyed contracts

Contract	LOC	#paths	Q1	Q2	Time	Usefulness
C1 (w)	33	8	7/8	3/8	119	5
C2 (w)	52	16	7/8	2/8	98	
C3 (w)	67	38	7/8	2/8	233	
C4 (w/o)	87	59	2/8	1/8	414	
C5 (w/o)	103	13	3/8	1/8	397	
C6 (w/o)	107	27	4/8	1/8	420	

The results show that for the first three contracts for which sCompile's analysis results are shown, almost all users are able to answer Q1 correctly using less time. For the last three contracts without the hints, most of the users cannot identify the vulnerability correctly and it takes more time for them to answer the question. For identifying the most gas-consuming path, even with the hints on which function takes the most gas, most of the users find it difficult in answering the question, although with sCompile's help, more users are able to answer the question correctly. The results show that gas consumption is not a well-understood problem and highlight the necessity of reporting the condition under which maximum gas consumption happens. All the users think our tool is useful (average score is 5/7) in helping them identify the problems.

5   Related Work

sCompile is related to existing work on identifying vulnerabilities in smart contracts that can be roughly categorized into 3 groups according to the level at

---

[5] There are about 80 people who tried the test. Most of the respondents however leave the test after the first question, which perhaps evidences the difficulty in analyzing smart contracts.

which the vulnerability resides at: Solidity-level, EVM-level, and blockchain-level [17]. In addition, existing work can be categorized according to the techniques they employ to find vulnerabilities: symbolic execution [11,14,24–26], static-analysis based approaches [27] and formal verification [13,28]. Our approach works at the EVM-level and is based on static analysis and symbolic execution, and is thus closely related to the following work.

Oyente [11] formulates the security bugs as intra-procedural properties and uses symbolic execution to check these properties. However, Oyente does not perform inter-procedural analyses to check inter-procedural or trace properties as did in sCompile.

MAIAN [14] is recently developed to find three types of problematic contracts in the wild: prodigal, greedy and suicidal. It formulates the three types of problems as inter-procedural properties and performs bounded inter-procedural symbolic execution. It builds a private testnet to valid whether the contracts found by it are true positives by executing the contracts with data generated by symbolic execution. However, sCompile differs from MAIAN in following aspects. First, sCompile makes a much more conservative assumption about a call to third-party contract which we assume can call back a function in current contract. sCompile is designed to reduce user effort rather than to analyze smart contracts fully automatically. Secondly, sCompile supports more properties than MAIAN. Thirdly, sCompile checks properties in ways which are different from MAIAN. Other symbolic execution based tools [24,25] perform intra-procedural symbolic analysis directly on the EVM bytecode as what Oyente does.

The tool Securify [27] is based on static analysis to analyze contracts. It specifies both compliance and violation patterns for the property. The vulnerability detection problem is then reduced to search the patterns on the inferred data and control dependencies information. The use of compliance pattern reduces the number of false positives in the reported warnings. In the ranking algorithm, our approach rely on syntactic information to reduce paths for further symbolic analysis to improve performance. We analyze the extracted paths with symbolic execution which is more precise than the pure static analysis as adopted by Securify.

Other attempts on analyzing smart contracts include formal verification using either model-checking techniques [13] or theorem-proving approaches [28]. They in theory can check arbitrary properties specified manually in a form accepted by the model checker or the theorem prover. It is known that model checking has limited scalability whereas theorem proving requires an overwhelming amount of user effort.

6   Conclusion

We proposed a practical approach named sCompile to reveal "money-related" paths in smart contract and to further detect vulnerabilities among critical ones. In our experiment among 36,099 smart contracts, it detected 224 new vulnerabilities. All the new vulnerabilities are well defined in our approach and could be presented to the user in well-organized information within a reasonable time frame. A comparison with two existing approaches also demonstrated that sCompile is both efficient and effective.

Acknowledgement. This work is supported by the Singapore Ministry of Education (MOE) Academic Research Fund (AcRF) Tier 1 grant, the Youth Innovation Promotion Association of the Chinese Academy of Sciences (YICAS) (Grant No. 2017151), the Young Elite Scientists Sponsorship Program by CAST (Grant No. 2017QNRC001), and the Blockchain Technology and Application Joint Laboratory, Guiyang Academy of Information Technology (Institute of Software Chinese Academy of Sciences Guiyang Branch).

References

1. Diffie, W., Hellman, M.: New directions in cryptography. IEEE Trans. Inf. Theor. **22**(6), 644–654 (2006)
2. Diffie, W., Hellman, M.E.: Multiuser cryptographic techniques. In: Proceedings of the June 7–10, 1976, National Computer Conference and Exposition, AFIPS 1976, pp. 109–112. ACM, New York (1976)
3. Jorstad, N.D., Landgrave, T.S.: Cryptographic algorithm metrics. In: 20th National Information Systems Security Conference (1997)
4. Haber, S., Stornetta, W.S.: How to time-stamp a digital document. In: Menezes, A.J., Vanstone, S.A. (eds.) CRYPTO 1990. LNCS, vol. 537, pp. 437–455. Springer, Heidelberg (1991). https://doi.org/10.1007/3-540-38424-3_32
5. Brito , J., Castillo, A.: Bitcoin: a primer for policymakers. Mercatus Center at George Mason University (2013)
6. Narayanan, A., Bonneau, J., Felten, E., Miller, A., Goldfeder, S.: Bitcoin and Cryptocurrency Technologies: A Comprehensive Introduction. Princeton University Press, Princeton (2016)
7. Wood, G.: Ethereum: a secure decentralised generalised transaction ledger. Ethereum Proj. Yellow Pap. **151**, 1–32 (2014)
8. Solidity, the contract-oriented programming language. https://github.com/ethereum/solidity. Accessed 12 June 2019
9. Attack - the dao - the dao. https://daowiki.atlassian.net/wiki/spaces/DAO/pages/7209155/Attack. Accessed 12 June 2019
10. Turing, A.M.: On computable numbers, with an application to the Entscheidungs problem. Proc. London Math. Soc. **42**, 230–265 (1937)
11. Luu, L., Chu, D.-H., Olickel, H., Saxena, P., Hobor, A.: Making smart contracts smarter. In: Proceedings of the 2016 ACM SIGSAC Conference on Computer and Communications Security, pp. 254–269. ACM (2016)
12. Ethereum (eth) blockchain explorer. https://etherscan.io/. Accessed 30 June 2018
13. Kalra, S., Goel, S., Dhawan, M., Sharmar, S.: Zeus: analyzing safety of smart contracts. In: Network and Distributed Systems Security Symposium 2018, pp. 1–12. internetsociety (2018)
14. Nikolic, I., Kolluri, A., Sergey, I., Saxena, P., Hobor, A.: Finding the greedy, prodigal, and suicidal contracts at scale. arXiv preprint arXiv:1802.06038 (2018)
15. Allen, F.E.: Control flow analysis. In: ACM Sigplan Notices, vol. 5, pp. 1–19. ACM (1970)
16. Anand, S., Godefroid, P., Tillmann, N.: Demand-driven compositional symbolic execution. In: Ramakrishnan, C.R., Rehof, J. (eds.) TACAS 2008. LNCS, vol. 4963, pp. 367–381. Springer, Heidelberg (2008). https://doi.org/10.1007/978-3-540-78800-3_28
17. Atzei, N., Bartoletti, M., Cimoli, T.: A survey of attacks on ethereum smart contracts (SoK). In: Maffei, M., Ryan, M. (eds.) POST 2017. LNCS, vol. 10204, pp. 164–186. Springer, Heidelberg (2017). https://doi.org/10.1007/978-3-662-54455-6_8

18. Another parity wallet hack explained. https://medium.com/@Pr0Ger/another-parity-wallet-hack-explained-847ca46a2e1c. Accessed 06 June 2018
19. Stamatis, D.H.: Failure Mode and Effect Analysis: FMEA from Theory to Execution. ASQ Quality Press, Hardcover (2003)
20. Devijver, P.A., Kittler, J.: Pattern Recognition: A Statistical Approach. Prentice hall, Englewood Cliffs (1982)
21. Kohavi, R., et al.: A study of cross-validation and bootstrap for accuracy estimation and model selection. In: Ijcai, vol. 14, pp. 1137–1145. Montreal, Canada (1995)
22. King, J.C.: Symbolic execution and program testing. Commun. ACM **19**(7), 385–394 (1976)
23. de Moura, L., Bjørner, N.: Z3: an efficient SMT solver. In: Ramakrishnan, C.R., Rehof, J. (eds.) TACAS 2008. LNCS, vol. 4963, pp. 337–340. Springer, Heidelberg (2008). https://doi.org/10.1007/978-3-540-78800-3_24
24. ConsenSys. Mythril: Security analysis of ethereum smart contracts (2018). https://github.com/ConsenSys/mythril. Accessed 30 May 2018
25. trailofbits. Manticore: Symbolic execution tool (2018). https://github.com/trailofbits/manticore. Accessed 30 May 2018
26. Jiang, B., Liu, Y., Chan, W.K.: Contractfuzzer: Fuzzing smart contracts for vulnerability detection. arXiv preprint arXiv:1807.03932 (2018)
27. Tsankov, P., Dan, A., Cohen, D.D., Gervais, A., Buenzli, F., Vechev, M.: Securify: practical security analysis of smart contracts. arXiv preprint arXiv:1806.01143 (2018)
28. Bhargavan, K., et al.: Formal verification of smart contracts: short paper. In: Proceedings of the 2016 ACM Workshop on Programming Languages and Analysis for Security, PLAS 2016, pp. 91–96. ACM (2016)

A Mechanized Theory of Program Refinement

Boubacar Demba Sall[(✉)], Frédéric Peschanski, and Emmanuel Chailloux

Sorbonne Université, CNRS, LIP6, 75005 Paris, France
{boubacar.sall,frederic.peschanski,emmanuel.chailloux}@lip6.fr

Abstract. We present a mechanized theory of program refinement that allows for the stepwise development of imperative programs in the Coq proof assistant. We formalize a design language with support for gradual refinement and a calculus which enforces *correctness-by-construction*. A notion of *program design* captures the hierarchy of refinement steps resulting from a development. The underlying theory follows the *predicative programming* paradigm where programs and specifications are both easily expressed as predicates, which fit naturally in the dependent type theory of the proof assistant.

Keywords: Stepwise refinement · Program verification · Predicative programming · Correctness-by-construction · Type theory · Proof assistant · Coq

1 Introduction

Program development by *stepwise refinement* [8,25,26] is inherently an interactive activity where programming steps and proof steps alternate and feed back on each other. It therefore makes sense to perform refinement steps within an interactive proof assistant (p.a.) whose very purpose is to help in specification, proof composition and mechanical proof verification. This however requires that a theory of program refinement be embedded in the formalism of the p.a. Most theories of refinement fall in two groups. The theories (e.g. [9,19]) in the first group are based upon the calculus of relations, and represent programs as well as specifications uniformly as set-theoretic relations on program states. In the second group, the theories (e.g. [2,21]) are underpinned by Hoare logic or the wp-calculus[1]. The view there is that programs relate sets of program states represented in logic as predicates, while specifications are pairs of predicates. In this paper, we investigate the *predicative programming* [10,22] approach to refinement which can be viewed as an expression of the relational point of view in predicative terms rather than in set theory. This investigation lead to the development of a mechanized theory of stepwise refinement towards imperative programs (similar to those studied in [21]) in the realm of the Coq p.a. [24]. We make the following contributions.

---

[1] Calculus of weakest preconditions.

© Springer Nature Switzerland AG 2019
Y. Ait-Ameur and S. Qin (Eds.): ICFEM 2019, LNCS 11852, pp. 305–321, 2019.
https://doi.org/10.1007/978-3-030-32409-4_19

Firstly, we formalize in type theory a language of stepwise program design, and a calculus which enforces correctness-by-construction. The language is a simple imperative language (with assignment, sequence, if statements and iteration) which we enrich to allow the expression of a hierarchy of refinement steps, each step associating a specification to an implementation. The calculus stems from a synthesis of ideas from predicative and relational theories of refinement. On the one hand, the relational point of view unifies the usual assertions (e.g. precondition, post-condition, invariant) under a single and more general notion of specification, hence simplifying the formulation of the theory. On the other hand, the predicative point of view makes it easier to write specifications and handle proof obligations (p.o.s).

Secondly, we uncover necessary and sufficient conditions for a while statement to refine a given specification. In particular, the loop body must be given an adequate relational specification. The advantage is that these specifications are more flexible than invariants.

Finally, we have mechanized the aforementioned calculus as well as the underlying theory in the Coq p.a. so that the declaration of a refinement step automatically triggers the generation of p.o.s (in the language of the p.a.) to ensure the correctness of the refinement. All the artifacts presented in the paper (definitions and theorem statements), as well as all the proofs, have been formalized in about 4000 lines of Coq script and made available in a companion repository[2]. This framework thus enables certified imperative program design by gradual refinement, and demonstrates that, in terms of mechanized semantics in type theory, the relational point of view is a viable alternative to Hoare-logic style semantics. Moreover, the Coq p.a. provides a full-blown functional language to write specifications with the benefit of type checking, type inference and parametric polymorphism for free.

The outline of the paper is as follows. In Sect. 2 we give an overview of program development by stepwise refinement in our proposed framework. In Sect. 3 we introduce the language of program designs, we describe the rules of the calculus, and we formulate the main correctness theorem. In Sect. 4 we formalize the semantics of our language, we define the refinement relation based on this semantics, and we justify the design rules introduced in Sect. 3. In Sect. 5 we turn our attention to making the framework more practical by applying some automatic simplifications to the p.o.s. A discussion of related work and the conclusion follow.

2 An Overview of Stepwise Program Design

To give an overview of our framework as experienced by the user, we consider a classical example: the (integer) square root computation. We begin by declaring the following abstract definition of the square root computation:

Program Definition Sqrt $:= \langle r'^2 \leq x < (r' + 1)^2 \rangle_x.$

---

[2] https://github.com/bsall/AMToPR-ICFEM-2019.

With the Definition keyword we have named our computation Sqrt, and declared its high level specification. The role of the Program keyword will be clarified shortly, its purpose is to invoke a built-in feature [23] of the p.a. which will help us to manage the p.o.s. Most specifications we will write are akin to *before-after predicates* which describe relations between the initial and final states of a program. We use the usual convention that variables are primed to mean their value after execution, and unprimed to mean their value before execution. The specification of the square root computation reads as follows: from the initial value of variable x we aim to compute its square root and make the result available as the final value of r (denoted by r'). Additionally, the value of x is required to remain unchanged. The notation $\langle S \rangle_{x_1,\dots,x_n}$ used in the definition is a shorthand for $\langle S \wedge x'_1 = x_1 \wedge \cdots \wedge x'_n = x_n \rangle$. Our objective is to elaborate, incrementally, a program to fulfill this specification. Once we have decided on a more precise implementation, we open braces to write this implementation. In our example, this first refinement step leads to the following situation:

(1) **Program Definition** Sqrt $:= \langle\, r'^2 \leq x < (r' + 1)^2 \,\rangle_x \,\{$
$\qquad r := 0;$
$\qquad h := x + 1;$
$\qquad \langle\, r^2 \leq r'^2 \leq x < h'^2 \leq h^2 \,\wedge\, r' + 1 = h' \,\rangle_x$
$\quad \}.$

Our initial specification has developed into a *specified block* [11] whose header is the initial specification. The body of the block introduces a new variable h so that $[r..h]$ delimits the search space. The last statement specifies the search strategy we intend to implement, i.e. narrow the search space around x (first conjunct), up to the point where the initial specification is fulfilled (second conjunct). The notations being used to design the square root computation (e.g. $\langle...\rangle$ $\{...\}$, ;) are syntactic sugar for invoking specific constructions rules defined in Sect. 3.2. These rules ensure the correctness of our design with respect to the semantics defined in Sect. 4. Specifically, the rules stipulate that to construct the specified block above, one must provide a proof that the body of the block refines (in the sense of Sect. 4.2) the header of the block. Thanks to the Program keyword we can mimic the construction of a specified block and let the p.a. save the p.o. corresponding to the missing proof for later. This p.o. is to be discharged separately so that our design is not cluttered with the details of the proofs. At this point, even though the p.a. has performed some type checking automatically, the Sqrt definition is not yet complete: for example it cannot be referred to in other definitions. To complete our definition, we must provide the missing proof by writing a proof script which is generally of the following form:

Next Obligation. $t_1. \ ... \ t_i.$ nia. $... \ t_j. \ ... \ t_k.$ Qed.

The Next Obligation command is to fetch and display the next p.o. among those left to be discharged. The following sequence of t_i commands invoke built-in proof tools called *tactics*. For example, the nia tactic used to deal with non linear arithmetic is very helpful in our case. Finally, the Qed command instructs the p.a. to check our proof for validity. By repeating the process we have just described to make specifications more and more precise, we ultimately obtain the design of Listing 1.1 below after three more refinement steps (labeled (2), (3) and (4)).

(1) **Program Definition** Sqrt := $\langle\, r'^2 \le x < (r'+1)^2\, \rangle_x$ {
    $r := 0;$
    $h := x + 1;$
(2) $\langle\, r^2 \le r'^2 \le x < h'^2 \le h^2 \;\wedge\; r'+1 = h'\, \rangle_x$ {
        while $r + 1 \ne h$ **do**
(3) $\langle\, r^2 \le r'^2 \le x < h'^2 \le h^2 \;\wedge\; (r < r' \;\vee\; h > h')\, \rangle_x$ {
(4) $\langle\, r < m' < h\, \rangle_{x,r,h}$ {
                $m := r + (h - r)/2$
            };
            if $m^2 \le x$ **then** $r := m$ **else** $h := m$ **end**
        }
        done
    }}.

Listing 1.1. The square root program design with refinement steps (1) to (4)

The second refinement step has consisted in deciding to implement the search strategy as a loop. The body of the loop required two more refinement steps (numbered (3) and (4)). An important remark is that all the successive steps are visible in the final design: one can imagine collapsing specified blocks showing only the associated specifications, or instead expanding blocks to dig into the implementation details. Once all p.o.s are discharged we have built an object carrying programming instructions, the design decisions (refinement steps) that lead to those instructions, and the proofs of correctness of all refinements. We call this object a *program design*. Keeping all refinement steps around is important because, in their absence, the design decisions they materialize tend to be lost as time passes, rendering program evolution ever more harder. Thanks to the proofs carried by the program design, our framework is able to assemble a global certificate of design correctness. To assemble such a certificate we write the following script:

Definition sqrt_proof := CbC.soundness Sqrt.

In other words, the sqrt_proof term results from applying the soundness theorem of our design rules (the CbC.soundness term) to the Sqrt design. This term is a proof that can be independently checked for validity. The soundness theorem of the design rules is formulated in Sect. 3. We refer the reader to the companion repository for a detailed example[3] of how the refinement process is carried out for the square root computation.

3   The Calculus of Program Designs

In this section we formally present the calculus of program designs. We begin with the language of program designs. Then, we formulate the construction rules of the calculus whose purpose is to enforce *correctness-by-construction*.

---

[3] https://github.com/bsall/AMToPR-ICFEM-2019/tree/master/src/examples/.

Statement $S ::=$
    effect f (state transformer with $f : T \to T$)
    $\mid \langle R \rangle$ (specification statement with $R : T \to T \to \mathsf{Prop}$))
    $\mid S_1 \; ; \; S_2$ (sequence)
    $\mid$ **if** C **then** S_1 **else** S_2 **end** (if statement with condition $C : T \to \mathsf{Prop}$)
    $\mid S_1 \; \{ \; S_2 \; \}$ (specified block with S_1 block-free)
    $\mid$ **while** C **do** S **done**   (iteration with condition $C : T \to \mathsf{Prop}$)

Fig. 1. The language of program designs w.r.t. the type T of program states (Prop is the built-in type of logical propositions in the Coq p.a.)

3.1   The Language of Program Designs

To design programs in the way described previously, we need a language with support for gradual refinement. Moreover, adhering to the correctness-by-construction [18] paradigm, our objective is to impose further restrictions so that only correct program designs can be constructed. The syntax of the core language we study is given in Fig. 1. It is a very classical imperative language, close in spirit to the language studied in [20], but embedded in the Coq p.a. Since Coq is underpinned by a dependent type theory, type checking, type inference and parametric polymorphism are for free. In the p.a., the syntax is encoded as an inductive type implicitly parameterized by the type T of program states.

The Statements of the Language. Sequential composition as well as the statements related to the if and while keywords are self-explanatory. The effect statement reflects the notion of state transformation as a syntactic constructor. This provides a nice generalization of various kinds of effects. Notably, the **skip** instruction is defined as **effect** $(\lambda \, s \Rightarrow s)$. Assignment statements are also derivable. For example, the instruction $v := v + w$ (where v and w are variables of type Nat) translates to **effect** $(\lambda \, (v, w) \Rightarrow (v + w, w))$ where T is Nat $\times$ Nat.

The $\langle R \rangle$ construct is a *specification statement* [21]. It can be thought of as standing for a "program fragment yet to be implemented" [21], or alternatively as a procedure call to a program specified by R. The notation $\langle ... \rangle$ is from [17]. The encoding in Coq of before-after predicates is straightforward. For example $\lambda \, (i \, i' : \mathsf{nat}) \Rightarrow i' > i$ specifies a program that increases variable i. More generally, $\langle R \rangle$ designates a program P such that: (1) when started in state s the set of possible outputs of P is $\{ \; s' \mid R \, s \, s' \; \}$, and (2) P terminates on input s exactly when $(\exists \, s' \cdot R \, s \, s')$ is true (i.e. the set of possible outputs is not empty). Non deterministic behavior is reflected by a number of possible outputs greater than one. Following [22], we equate abnormal termination in an error state with non termination, therefore **abort** $\equiv \langle \; \lambda \, (s \, s' : T) \Rightarrow \mathsf{False} \; \rangle$.

The specified block $S_1 \; \{ \; S_2 \; \}$ represents a pair of statements resulting from the refinement of S_1 by S_2 as explained in Sect. 2. This is the feature enabling gradual refinement. S_1 is called the *abstraction* of the block and S_2 is called its *concretization*. During program design, when we write $S_1 \; \{ \; S_2 \; \}$, we record a

$$\varphi(\textbf{effect } f) \qquad\qquad\qquad \overset{\text{def}}{=} (\textbf{effect } f) \ \{ \ (\textbf{effect } f) \ \}$$

$$\varphi(\langle R \rangle) \qquad\qquad\qquad\qquad \overset{\text{def}}{=} \langle R \rangle \ \{ \ \langle R \rangle \ \}$$

$$\varphi(S_1;S_2) \qquad\qquad\qquad \overset{\text{def}}{=} \varphi_a(S_1) \ ; \ \varphi_a(S_2) \ \{ \ \varphi_c(S_1) \ ; \ \varphi_c(S_2) \ \}$$

$$\varphi(\textbf{if } C \textbf{ then } S_1 \textbf{ else } S_2 \textbf{ end}) \overset{\text{def}}{=} \textbf{if } C \textbf{ then } \varphi_a(S_1) \textbf{ else } \varphi_a(S_2) \textbf{ end } \{$$
$$\textbf{if } C \textbf{ then } \varphi_c(S_1) \textbf{ else } \varphi_c(S_2) \textbf{ end}$$
$$\}$$

$$\varphi(S_1 \ \{ \ S_2 \ \}) \qquad\qquad \overset{\text{def}}{=} S_1 \ \{ \ \varphi_c(S_2) \ \}$$

$$\varphi(\textbf{while } C \textbf{ do } S \textbf{ done}) \qquad \overset{\text{def}}{=} \textbf{if } C \textbf{ then } \langle \ \lambda \ s \ s' \Rightarrow [\![\varphi_a(S)]\!] \ s \ s' \wedge \neg C \ s' \ \rangle \textbf{ end } \{$$
$$\textbf{while } C \textbf{ do } \varphi_c(S) \textbf{ done}$$
$$\}$$

Fig. 2. The design projection function φ

design decision which communicates an abstract intent (S_1), and some (hopefully more concrete and correct) means of realizing it (S_2). We assume that the abstraction S_1 does not itself contain specified blocks, we say that it is *block-free*. This restriction is justified by the fact that we are interested in refining specifications of programs, not in refining blocks which stand for a record of design decisions. Note that programming constructs are allowed in the abstraction of specified blocks. For example, the abstraction of a block can be of the if-then-else form.

Projection Function. We now define the projection function φ, which will be used in the formulation of the rules and properties of the calculus. The definition is given in Fig. 2 above. From a statement S, φ computes an abstraction $\varphi_a(S)$, and a (generally distinct) concretization $\varphi_c(S)$, such that both statements are block-free. We write $\varphi(S) = \varphi_a(S) \ \{ \ \varphi_c(S) \ \}$ to match the syntax of the language. For example, if we consider the program design of Listing 1.1, the aforesaid abstraction is the outermost specification $\langle \ r'^2 \leq x < (r'+1)^2 \ \rangle_x$, and the concretization is the statement resulting from the intermediary specifications (lines in blue labeled (1) up to (4)) being ignored.

φ is defined so that the effect and $\langle R \rangle$ statements are respectively their own abstraction. Concerning sequential composition and the if-the-else construct, φ simply extracts the (abstraction, concretization) pairs from the inner statements and combines them in parallel.

In the case of the specified block the corresponding abstraction is just S_1 by definition, and the concretization is the one of the body of the block.

The abstraction of a loop is constructed from the abstraction of its body which, in consequence, must be specified with care. We come back to this in Sect. 4.3. The $[\![\cdot]\!]$ operator refers to the interpretation of statements as binary relations on program states. This interpretation is detailed in Sect. 4.1. To give an example, $[\![i := i+1]\!]$ denotes the predicate $i' = i+1$ (encoded as $(\lambda \ i \ i' \ \Rightarrow i' = i+1)$ in the p.a.).

$$\dfrac{}{\text{Design } (\textbf{effect } f)} \qquad \dfrac{}{\text{Design } \langle R \rangle} \qquad \dfrac{\text{Design } S_1 \ \wedge \ \text{Design } S_2}{\text{Design } S_1 ; S_2}$$

$$\dfrac{\text{Design } S_1 \ \wedge \ \text{Design } S_2}{\text{Design } (\textbf{if } C \textbf{ then } S_1 \textbf{ else } S_2 \textbf{ end})} \qquad \dfrac{\text{Design } S_2 \ \wedge \ \varphi_a(S_2) \sqsubseteq S_1}{\text{Design } (S_1 \ \{ \ S_2 \ \})}$$

$$\dfrac{\text{Design } S \ \wedge \ K;K \sqsubseteq K, \quad \text{with } K \overset{\text{def}}{=} (\textbf{if } C \textbf{ then } \varphi_a(S) \textbf{ end}) \ \wedge \text{ well\_founded } (\lambda \ s \ s' \Rightarrow C \ s' \wedge (\llbracket \varphi_a(S) \rrbracket \ s' \ s) \wedge C \ s)}{\text{Design } (\textbf{while } C \textbf{ do } S \textbf{ done})}$$

Fig. 3. The calculus of program designs

Actually we compute $\varphi_a(S)$ to reason about S at an abstract level, and we compute $\varphi_c(S)$ to get a block-free statement which can be translated into a programming language provided S is precise enough (i.e. no specification statements among the leaves of the syntax tree). The calculus we define in Sect. 3.2 allows to characterize a family of statements S which have the property that $\varphi_c(S)$ is truly a refinement of $\varphi_a(S)$.

3.2 Enforcing Correctness-by-Construction

The usefulness of a program design rests upon the correctness of what this design communicates. In order to enforce design correctness, we restrict our language by imposing strict construction rules. We say that a program design S is correct if and only if the predicate Design S can be derived from the rules of Fig. 3. The goal of these rules is to ensure that when the refinement process is completed we indeed have that $\varphi_c(S)$ refines $\varphi_a(S)$. The refinement relation ($\sqsubseteq$) will be formally defined in Sect. 4.2, but its informal meaning is as follows: we say that S_2 refines S_1 (denoted by $S_2 \sqsubseteq S_1$) if and only if every specification satisfied by S_1 is also satisfied by S_2. In fact, when S_1 and S_2 are block-free, our formalization allows to derive that latter description of refinement in terms of Hoare triples, i.e. we have established the following equivalence:

$$S_2 \sqsubseteq S_1 \ \leftrightarrow \ \forall P \ Q \cdot \{P\} \ S_1 \ \{Q\} \ \rightarrow \ \{P\} \ S_2 \ \{Q\}$$

The two basic instructions effect and $\langle R \rangle$ are, unsurprisingly, the axioms of the proof system. All the statements involved in the other compound instructions must *already* be correct designs. The requirements for a block $S_1 \ \{ \ S_2 \ \}$ to be a correct design are as follows. First, it must be the case that S_2 is a correct design, and moreover that $\varphi_a(S_2)$ refines S_1. In the conjunct involving the refinement relation, we can abstract away from the implementation details of S_2 and only consider $\varphi_a(S_2)$ because at the same time we require S_2 to be a correct program design (i.e. $\varphi_c(S_2) \sqsubseteq \varphi_a(S_2)$). This requirement entails that ultimately $\varphi_c(S_2)$ is guaranteed to refine S_1 since the refinement relation is transitive. The rule for while loops is more intricate. The requirement that $K;K$ refines K is to ensure that K is a correct over-approximation of the loop's behavior. As usual,

$$[\![\text{effect } f]\!] \qquad \overset{\text{def}}{=} \lambda\, s\, s' \Rightarrow s' = (f\ s)$$

$$[\![\langle R \rangle]\!] \qquad \overset{\text{def}}{=} R$$

$$[\![S_1; S_2]\!] \qquad \overset{\text{def}}{=} [\![S_1]\!] \Box [\![S_2]\!]$$

$$[\![\text{if } C \text{ then } S_1 \text{ else } S_2 \text{ end}]\!] \overset{\text{def}}{=} [\![S_1]\!] \lhd C \rhd [\![S_2]\!]$$

$$[\![S_1 \{ S_2 \}]\!] \qquad \overset{\text{def}}{=} [\![S_2]\!]$$

$$[\![\text{while } C \text{ do } S \text{ done}]\!] \qquad \overset{\text{def}}{=} \text{least fixpoint of } (\lambda\, \mathcal{X} \Rightarrow ([\![S]\!]\Box\mathcal{X}) \lhd C \rhd [\![\text{skip}]\!])$$

Fig. 4. The predicative semantics of the language of program designs

the well-foundedness requirement ensures that the loop terminates on all inputs of interest. Here again, the fact that S is required to be an already correct design allows us to only consider $\varphi_a(S)$ in the other requirements. Ultimately, the central theorem of our proposed framework is the following one.

Theorem 1 (Correctness of program designs).
(soundness) $\forall\, S \cdot \text{Design } S \rightarrow \varphi_c(S) \sqsubseteq \varphi_a(S)$
(completeness) $\forall\, S_1\, S_2 \cdot\ S_2 \sqsubseteq S_1 \rightarrow \exists\, S \cdot \text{Design } S\ \wedge\ \varphi(S) = S_1 \{ S_2 \}$

This theorem explains that whenever we are able to derive Design S for some program design, the associated concretization refines the associated abstraction. Clearly it is possible to have $\varphi_c(S) \sqsubseteq \varphi_a(S)$ while Design S is not derivable. For example consider the following program design

$$S \overset{\text{def}}{=} \text{skip} \{ \langle \lambda\, s\, s' \Rightarrow \text{False} \rangle \{ \text{skip} \} \}.$$

We have skip $\sqsubseteq$ skip, and yet Design S cannot be derived. So as one would expect the design rules are not complete in the absolute sense. However they are complete in the weaker sense that for any concretization S_2 and abstraction S_1 such that $S_2 \sqsubseteq S_1$, it is possible to come up with a correct design S whose associated concretization and abstraction are respectively S_2 and S_1. When we complete a design, the soundness part of Theorem 1 allows to construct a tangible lambda-term certifying that our design is doubtlessly correct: this lambda-term is the certificate of correctness we alluded to in Sect. 2. The completeness part of Theorem 1 reassures us that the design rules we restrict ourselves to use do not limit the kind of programs that can be obtained by applying these rules.

4   Predicative Semantics and Refinement Relation

In this section we discuss the key properties justifying the design rules of our calculus. First we present the predicative interpretation of statements and define the refinement relation in terms of this interpretation. Then, we examine the particular case of loops.

4.1 Predicative Semantics

Except for loops and specified blocks, our interpretation of statements as predicates coincide with the predicative semantics of [22]. We denote by Spec the type of specifications, i.e. the type of binary relations on the type T of program states.

$$\mathsf{Spec} \overset{\text{def}}{=} T \to T \to \mathsf{Prop}$$

The predicative interpretation of statements associates to each statement a specification of type Spec. This interpretation is inductively defined on the syntax of statements as indicated in Fig. 4 above with the semantic function $[\![\cdot]\!] : \mathsf{Statement} \to \mathsf{Spec}$.

State Transformation, Specification Statements and Specified Blocks. The specification associated to the state transformer (effect f) explains that the after state is the image by f of the before state. The interpretation of the specification statement $\langle R \rangle$ is just R since R is already a specification. For specified blocks, we choose the interpretation to be the one of the supposedly better implementation among the statements composing the block.

Alternative. The if-then-else statement denotes the specification described in Eq. (1) below. Here, A and B are of type Spec and C has type $T \to \mathsf{Prop}$.

$$A \lhd C \rhd B \overset{\text{def}}{=} \lambda\,(s\ s' : T) \Rightarrow C\ s \wedge (A\ s\ s') \ \vee \ \neg(C\ s) \wedge (B\ s\ s') \qquad (1)$$

The notation used is borrowed from [15], and expresses a selection between two specifications depending on C, i.e. either C is true ($\lhd$) of the input state and A is selected, or C is false ($\rhd$) of the input state and B is selected.

Sequence. For sequential composition, we need a notion of composition for specifications. We define below the *angelic* and *demonic* composition of specifications.

Definition 1 (Composition of specifications). *Let S_1 and S_2 be of type Spec. The angelic and demonic composition operators are respectively defined as follows:*

$$S_1 \boxdot S_2 \overset{\text{def}}{=} \lambda\ s\ s' \Rightarrow \exists\ s_x \cdot S_1\ s\ s_x \ \wedge\ S_2\ s_x\ s'$$
$$S_1 \boxempty S_2 \overset{\text{def}}{=} \lambda\ s\ s' \Rightarrow (S_1 \boxdot S_2)\ s\ s' \ \wedge\ \forall\ s_x \cdot S_1\ s\ s_x \ \to \exists\ s' \cdot S_2\ s_x\ s'$$

Angelic composition is just relational composition. Demonic composition is relational composition further restricted to account for the fact that the interpretation of $\langle S_1 \rangle;\langle S_2 \rangle$ is defined only on those states s such that S_2 is defined for all possible outputs of S_1 on s. As an illustration of the difference between the two operators, consider the following example:

$$\{(1,2),(1,3)\} \boxdot \{(2,4)\} = \{(1,4)\}, \text{ but } \{(1,2),(1,3)\}\boxempty\{(2,4)\} = \{\}$$

We see that angelic composition does not properly capture the possibility of failure because the input 1 should not be present in the domain of the composition since it may cause an error if the output is 3. Therefore, as in [9], we use demonic composition [3,4] to formalize the sequential composition of specifications. Consequently, the specification associated to the sequential composition of statements is the demonic composition of their interpretations. The $\square$ notation for demonic composition is from [9]. For angelic composition, we use a similar notation rather than (;) to prevent confusion with sequential composition of statements.

Iteration. The while statement is interpreted as the least fixpoint (lfp for short) of a function from specifications to specifications. The lfp operator is encoded in type theory as follows:

$$\mathsf{lfp}\ (F : \mathsf{Spec} \to \mathsf{Spec}) \overset{\mathrm{def}}{=} \lambda\ s\ s' \Rightarrow \forall\ X \cdot (\forall\ s\ s' \cdot F\ X\ s\ s' \to X\ s\ s') \to X\ s\ s'$$

This encoding explains that a pair $(s, s') \in \mathsf{lfp}(F)$ iff (s, s') is in all specifications X such that $(F\ X \subseteq X)$. Let $F = (\lambda\ \mathcal{X} \Rightarrow (\llbracket S \rrbracket \square \mathcal{X}) \lhd C \rhd \llbracket \mathsf{skip} \rrbracket)$, then F is monotonic since demonic composition is right-monotonic w.r.t. inclusion of specifications. Hence, by the Knaster-Tarski fixpoint theorem, the interpretation of the while statement is indeed the least fixpoint of F as predicates ordered by implication (i.e. relations ordered by inclusion) form a complete lattice.

Note 1. The conditions C of the if and while statements send states to Prop. In the logic of Coq, this means that the conditions may be undecidable on some inputs. However, the predicative semantics of the if-then-else and while statements implicitly address this decidability issue since such a statement S cannot be defined on a state s unless $(C\ s)$ is decidable (i.e. $\forall\ s\ s' \cdot \llbracket S \rrbracket\ s\ s' \to (C\ s) \lor \neg(C\ s)$).

4.2   The Refinement Relation

The refinement relation occupies unsurprisingly a central place in our development. To formalize this relation, we choose a classical relational interpretation (as found in e.g. [7]) which we translate in predicative terms. In particular, this formulation amounts to a first-order predicate as long as the relations involved can be expressed in first-order logic.

Definition 2 (Predicative refinement). *We say that S_2 refines S_1 if and only if whenever S_1 terminates on some state s, S_2 terminates on s and all observable behaviors of S_2 on s are observable behaviors of S_1 on s:*

$$S_2 \sqsubseteq S_1 \overset{\mathrm{def}}{=} \forall\ s\ s' \cdot \llbracket S_1 \rrbracket\ s\ s' \to (\forall\ s' \cdot \llbracket S_2 \rrbracket\ s\ s' \to \llbracket S_1 \rrbracket\ s\ s') \land (\exists\ s' \cdot \llbracket S_2 \rrbracket\ s\ s')$$

This definition reflects the fact that reducing non-determinism or enlarging the domain of a statement moves it down the refinement ordering. The correctness of the design rules relies on important properties of the refinement relation, some of which are stated in the following Lemma.

Lemma 1 (Properties of refinement). *Let P and Q designate statements, and let C designate a condition. The following properties hold:*

1. $P \sqsubseteq P$
2. $P \sqsubseteq Q \;\rightarrow\; Q \sqsubseteq R \;\rightarrow\; P \sqsubseteq R$
3. $P_1 \sqsubseteq Q_1 \rightarrow P_2 \sqsubseteq Q_2 \rightarrow$ if C then P_1 else P_2 end $\sqsubseteq$ if C then Q_1 else Q_2 end
4. $P_1 \sqsubseteq Q_1 \rightarrow P_2 \sqsubseteq Q_2 \rightarrow P_1;P_2 \sqsubseteq Q_1;Q_2$
5. $P \sqsubseteq Q \;\rightarrow\;$ while C do P done $\sqsubseteq$ while C do Q done

Essentially, this lemma states that the refinement relation is a preorder, and that the control structures of our language are monotonic w.r.t. refinement. Property (2) justifies the design rule for specified blocks, whereas properties (3) and (4) justify the design rules for the if statement and sequential composition. It is worth mentioning that these properties of refinement need never be explicitly used to discharge p.o.s. In practice, the properties are seamlessly applied during the composition of program designs. For example, the nesting of specified blocks implicitly invokes the transitivity of refinement. In fact, the composition of program designs feels like programming, but also consists in constructing (behind the scenes) the main frame of the proof of correctness.

4.3 The Special Case of Loops

The predicative semantics of loops is defined as the least fixpoint of a rather complex function. Even though it is possible to prove refinements by applying the least fixpoint axioms directly, we prefer to avoid that method because it proves to be rather impractical. Also, we would like to be as uniform as possible and rely on the notion of specification only. Note that Lemma 2 below provides an alternative characterization of loops as if statements under some conditions.

Lemma 2 (Loop Summarization).
well_founded $(\lambda \ s \ s' \Rightarrow C \ s' \wedge [\![P]\!] \ s' \ s \wedge C \ s)$
$\rightarrow$ (if C then P end; if C then P end) $\sqsubseteq$ if C then P end
$\rightarrow$ while C do P done $\equiv$ if C then $\langle \ \lambda \ s \ s' \Rightarrow [\![P]\!] \ s \ s' \wedge \neg(C \ s') \ \rangle$ end

This summarization lemma is inspired by the relational approach described in [9], and suggests the following design method for loops. First, one should start with a loop body satisfying the conditions of Lemma 2. This first step consists in finding an abstract specification of what the loop body is intended to achieve. Then, one applies the summarization lemma and checks that the loop summary refines the desired specification. Finally, the loop body may be further refined with a more precise implementation. In this way, the lfp definition never appears explicitly in refinement statements to prove. This method rests on the following theorem, which builds on the previous lemma to give necessary and sufficient conditions for a while statement to refine a given specification.

Theorem 2 (Loop refinement rule).

$$\textbf{while } C \textbf{ do } P \textbf{ done} \sqsubseteq R$$
$$\leftrightarrow \exists\, L \cdot P \sqsubseteq L \wedge \textit{well\_founded } (\lambda\, s\, s' \Rightarrow C\, s' \wedge [\![L]\!]\, s'\, s \wedge C\, s)$$
$$\wedge\ (\textbf{if } C \textbf{ then } L \textbf{ end ; if } C \textbf{ then } L \textbf{ end}) \sqsubseteq\ \textbf{if } C \textbf{ then } L \textbf{ end}$$
$$\wedge\ \textbf{if } C \textbf{ then } \langle\, \lambda\, s\, s' \Rightarrow [\![L]\!]\, s\, s' \wedge \neg(C\, s')\, \rangle \textbf{ end} \sqsubseteq\ R$$

Combined with properties (2) and (5) of Lemma 1, this theorem justifies the design rule for the while statement in Fig. 3. To see why this is the case take $P = \varphi_c(S)$ and $L = \varphi_a(S)$. The soundness (only-if part) and completeness (if part) of the theorem follow from Lemmas 1 and 2. Notably, the proof of completeness uses, as a witness for L, the transitive closure of the following relation:

$$\prec_P^C \overset{\text{def}}{=} \lambda\, s\, s' \Rightarrow C\, s \wedge [\![P]\!]\, s\, s' \wedge (\exists\, s' \cdot [\![\textbf{while } C \textbf{ do } P \textbf{ done}]\!]\, s\, s')$$

The fact that the relation $\prec_P^C$ fulfills the well-foundedness requirement is a by-product of the least fixpoint semantics given to the while statement. A closer look at Lemma 2 shows that the second hypothesis implies the transitivity of the relation ($\lambda\, s\, s' \Rightarrow C\, s \wedge [\![P]\!]\, s\, s'$). This means that in general the loop body must have a non deterministic specification for loop summarization to apply. Hence, the ability to specify non deterministic behavior is key even when the end goal is a deterministic program.

Note 2. The most common way of dealing with loops is through the use of invariants and variants. In the case of the square root algorithm presented in Sect. 2, one can prove correctness in Hoare logic using ($r^2 \leq x < h^2$) as invariant and ($h - r$) as variant. If we consider that the intention of the programmer is to have the loop body maintain the invariant and decrease the variant, then the corresponding specification is the following:

$$\langle\, (r^2 \leq x < h^2\ \wedge\ r'^2 \leq x' < h'^2)\ \wedge\ (h - r > h' - r')\, \rangle_x$$

This specification states that the invariant is true at the beginning of execution as well as at the end of execution, and also that the variant is lower at the end than it was at the beginning. From the invariant and the variant, one can reason to deduce that the objective is to shrink the search interval and make progress by either increasing r or decreasing h. However, the intention to implement this objective is not so well conveyed by the specification of the loop body when it is written under the invariant-variant mindset. Because specifications are more flexible, the programmer has the opportunity to convey his intentions in a more intelligible way as we did in our example of Sect. 2. In that alternative specification of the loop body, one better sees the search interval closing up around x.

5   Refinement in a Calculus of Weakest Prespecifications

In this section we turn our attention to the simplification of p.o.s. Consider the typical situation where a specified block $S_1 \{ S_2 \}$ is introduced. As required by the design rules, the p.a. should prompt us to prove the statement $\varphi_a(S_2) \sqsubseteq S_1$. However, the current definition of the refinement relation $\sqsubseteq$ is too primitive as a means to compute such p.o.s. This is mostly due to demonic composition, i.e. the $\square$ operator. For example, the statement $\langle P_1 \rangle;...;\langle P_n \rangle \sqsubseteq \langle Q_1 \rangle;...;\langle Q_n \rangle$ yields, after unfolding the $\sqsubseteq$ and $\square$ operators, a formula containing a profusion of existential quantifiers, and whose size is exponential in n. To avoid such a situation and simplify p.o.s, we recast the definition of the refinement relation in a calculus akin to the classical wp-calculus.

We begin by observing that in Definition 2 the right hand side (r.h.s.) of the implication is $(\kappa([\![S_2]\!], [\![S_1]\!]))\ s\ s$, where κ is a relational operator called the *conjugate kernel* in [7] and the *the weakest prespecification* in [14, 16]. We now translate this operator in a predicative form.

Definition 3 (The weakest prespecification). *Let R_1 and R_2 be two specifications. The weakest prespecification of R_2 w.r.t. R_1 is defined as follows:*

$$\kappa(R_2, R_1) \overset{\text{def}}{=} \lambda\ s\ s' \Rightarrow (\forall\ s'' \cdot R_2\ s'\ s'' \rightarrow R_1\ s\ s'') \wedge (\exists\ s'' \cdot R_2\ s'\ s'')$$

If it exists, the weakest K such that $\langle K \square R_2 \rangle \sqsubseteq \langle R_1 \rangle$ is $\kappa(R_2, R_1)$. Let $K = \kappa(R_2, R_1)$. The output state s' of K on some input state s is such that R_2 terminates on s', and for every s'' produced by R_2 from s', the overall outcome (s, s'') of $K \square R_2$ is a behavior of R_1. Specializing κ to the statements of our language and simplifying the resulting expressions, leads to the following specification transformer.

Definition 4. (The wpr transformer). *We define, by induction on the syntax, the function wpr of type $\textsf{Statement} \rightarrow \textsf{Spec} \rightarrow \textsf{Spec}$ as follows:*

$$wpr(\textbf{effect}\ f,\ R) \overset{\text{def}}{=} \lambda\ s\ s' \Rightarrow R\ s\ (f\ s')$$
$$wpr(S_1;S_2,\ R) \overset{\text{def}}{=} wpr(S_1,\ wpr(S_2,\ R))$$
$$wpr(\textbf{if}\ C\ \textbf{then}\ S_1\ \textbf{else}\ S_2\ \textbf{end},\ R) \overset{\text{def}}{=} (wpr(S_1,\ R)^{-1} \lhd C \rhd wpr(S_2,\ R)^{-1})^{-1}$$
$$wpr(\textbf{while}\ C\ \textbf{do}\ S\ \textbf{done},\ R) \overset{\text{def}}{=} \textit{lfp}\,\big(\lambda\ \mathcal{X} \Rightarrow (wpr(S,\ \mathcal{X})^{-1} \lhd C \rhd R^{-1})^{-1}\big)$$
$$wpr(S_1\ \{\ S_2\ \},\ R) \overset{\text{def}}{=} wpr(S_2,\ R)$$
$$wpr(\langle R_2 \rangle,\ R_1) \overset{\text{def}}{=} \kappa(R_2, R_1)$$

where $R^{-1} \overset{\text{def}}{=} \lambda\ s\ s' \Rightarrow R\ s'\ s$

In fact $wpr(S, R)$ is equivalent to $\kappa([\![S]\!], R)$. Also, wpr is monotonic in its second argument, therefore the least fixpoint in the definition of wpr for the while statement is defined. The wpr transformer is encoded as a Coq fixpoint definition by pattern matching on the first argument. The following theorem shows that refinement can be defined in terms of wpr. The definition is a translation of the relational definition in terms of κ from [7].

Theorem 3. $\forall\ S_1\ S_2 \cdot S_2 \sqsubseteq S_1 \quad \leftrightarrow \quad \forall s \cdot (\exists s' \cdot [\![S_1]\!]\ s\ s') \rightarrow wpr(S_2, [\![S_1]\!])\ s\ s$

By using this wpr-based definition of refinement, we get simpler p.o.s for the same reasons that wp computes simpler p.o.s. In some way we have dealt with the $\square$

operator on the l.h.s. of $\sqsubseteq$ (i.e. S_2 in Theorem 3). More precisely, the expression $\mathsf{wpr}(\langle P_1 \rangle;...;\langle P_n \rangle, R)$ simplifies to a formula whose size is linear in n after unfolding definitions, and $\mathsf{wpr}(\mathbf{effect}\ f, R)$ simplifies to a formula with no additional quantifiers. Remains the r.h.s. of $\sqsubseteq$ to consider (i.e. $[\![S_1]\!]$ in Theorem 3). We observe that:

$$
\begin{aligned}
[\![(\mathbf{effect}\ f);R]\!] &\equiv \lambda\, s\, s' \Rightarrow R\ (f\ s)\ s' \\
[\![(\mathbf{if}\ C\ \mathbf{then}\ S_1\ \mathbf{else}\ S_2\ \mathbf{end});R]\!] &\equiv [\![S_1;R]\!] \lhd C \rhd [\![S_2;R]\!] \\
[\![(S_1;S_2);R]\!] &\equiv [\![S_1;(S_2;R)]\!]
\end{aligned}
$$

By recursively applying the equations above, $[\![S_1]\!]$ may in some cases simplify to a formula with no additional quantifiers. In our development these simplifications are done automatically each time a p.o. is computed. Of course the size of p.o.s may still become unmanageable. But, by refining in small steps, one also keeps the size of p.o.s in check. It is the case that the wpr transformer is not of much help when loops are involved, but thanks to Theorem 3 we can fall back on Theorem 2 to avoid having to manipulate the least fixpoint definition.

Note 3. One might wonder whether it would be possible to achieve the simplification of p.o.s by using the wp-calculus. Indeed this is possible, based on the following connection between wpr and wp from [16]: $\forall\, s \cdot \mathsf{wpr}(S, R)\ s\ s \leftrightarrow \mathsf{wp}(S, (R\ s))\ s$. However, as far as uniformity is concerned, we found the concept of weakest-prespecification quite appealing: weakest-prespecifications deal with a single kind of object (specifications), whereas weakest-preconditions involve two types of objects (specifications and conditions).

6   Related Work

In this section we put our research work in the context of mainly three areas: the notion of program design, the use of predicative and relational semantics and the more specific comparison with related Coq developments. By lack of space, we limit that last discussion to the Coq p.a., but there are many works of mechanization in the framework of other theorem provers. One example is the *Refinement Calculator* [6] developed on top of the HOL system.

On Program Designs. A similar notion of program *development* is proposed in [20] to capture the refinement history. A development is defined as a "multiway branching tree" of refinement steps. In this language each specification statement is given an identifier, and refinement steps reference the specifications they refine by these identifiers. This is very much in the spirit of *literate programming* [17] with the important difference that formal specifications replace informal ones. Comparatively, our program designs are based on the notion of specified blocks introduced in [11]. Since specified blocks can be nested they naturally represent a tree of design decisions without the need for explicit identifiers: the abstract syntax tree provides enough structure to capture the relevant information. This also means that unlike in [20] we have no need to structure a specific database of program and specification fragments.

On the Predicative and Relational Approaches. The semantics of our language of program designs is close to the predicative interpretation of programming constructs of [10–12], with important differences. Firstly, we follow [22] by using demonic composition to represent sequential composition, and by equating non termination, termination in an error state, and relational undefinedness instead of using a time variable or a fictitious program state to distinguish between terminating and non-terminating behaviors as in [10,15]. Representing non termination by undefinedness means however that we cannot for example, specify a program choosing nondeterministically to either terminate or loop forever on a given input. The second difference has to do with our refinement proof rule for loops which is closer to [9] where the focus is on assigning abstract specifications to loop bodies rather than on attaching outer specifications to loops as in [11]. A loop proof rule similar to ours follows from the results presented in [9], but our rule has weaker requirements and is provably complete.

On Refinement in the Coq Proof Assistant. There are other works of mechanization of refinement theories in the Coq p.a., in particular [5] and [1], both based on the refinement calculus [21]. The goal of the development presented in [1] is to derive imperative programs by applying validated refinement rules in proof mode. As a consequence the final program design entangles the intermediary refinement steps together with their proof of correctness. The mechanization of the refinement calculus presented in [5] supports a quite expressive language (with pattern matching and structural recursion), however the language does not include features to structure the refinement steps. Our work also differs with existing approaches in the way we treat loops. In [1] one must specify loop invariants while our formalization allows to specify loop bodies as input-output relations, which is more general. In [5] one has to work with the fixpoint characterization of loops while we use a more convenient rule. Moreover, we use weakest prespecifications (wpr) instead of weakest preconditions (wp) to compute p.o.s.

7   Conclusion and Future Works

We have presented a formalized theory of stepwise refinement. The formalization is the result of our study of both relational and predicative points of view on stepwise refinement, which lead us to a calculus benefiting from some cross-fertilization between the two points of view. We have mechanized this formalization thus allowing for correct-by-construction imperative program design in the Coq p.a., even though the scalability of our framework is yet to be improved by extending our language with local variables, procedures and simple modules.

Another thing that needs improvement is how the p.o.s are related to refinement steps. Presently, changing the refinement strategy may require the reordering of the proof scripts. To avoid this, the programmer must be offered an explicit mechanism for associating p.o.s with their respective refinement steps.

To take this work further, we are currently extending our mechanization to *data refinement* [13] in order to be able to prove correctness when data representations change to become more restricted or efficient. For example, this will enable certified refinements from mathematical unbounded data structures (e.g. Peano integers) to implementable data structures (e.g. machine integers), thereby opening the way for a completely faithful translation of the final refinement into an efficient programming language such as C.

Acknowledgment. We are very grateful to Sylvain Boulmé and Pierre-Évariste Dagand for all the insightful discussions we had about this work. We also thank the anonymous referees for their useful suggestions.

References

1. Alpuim, J., Swierstra, W.: Embedding the refinement calculus in Coq. Sci. Comput. Program. **164**, 37–48 (2018)
2. Back, R.J., Wright, J.: Refinement Calculus: A Systematic Introduction. Springer, New York (2012). https://doi.org/10.1007/978-1-4612-1674-2
3. Backhouse, R., Van Der Woude, J.: Demonic operators and monotype factors. Math. Struct. Comput. Sci. **3**(4), 417–433 (1993)
4. Berghammer, R., Zierer, H.: Relational algebraic semantics of deterministic and nondeterministic programs. TCS. **43**, 123–147 (1986)
5. Boulmé, S.: Intuitionistic refinement calculus. In: Della Rocca, S.R. (ed.) TLCA 2007. LNCS, vol. 4583, pp. 54–69. Springer, Heidelberg (2007). https://doi.org/10.1007/978-3-540-73228-0_6
6. Butler, M., Långbacka, T.: Program derivation using the refinement calculator. In: Goos, G., Hartmanis, J., van Leeuwen, J., von Wright, J., Grundy, J., Harrison, J. (eds.) TPHOLs 1996. LNCS, vol. 1125, pp. 93–108. Springer, Heidelberg (1996). https://doi.org/10.1007/BFb0105399
7. Desharnais, J., Jaoua, A., Mili, F., Boudriga, N., Mili, A.: A relational division operator: the conjugate kernel. TCS **114**(2), 247–272 (1993)
8. Dijkstra, E.: Notes on structured programming. In: Dahl, O.J., Dijkstra, E.W., Hoare, C.A.R. (eds.) Structured Programming. Academic Press, London (1972)
9. Frappier, M., Mili, A., Desharnais, J.: A relational calculus for program construction by parts. Sci. Comput. Program. **26**(1–3), 237–254 (1996)
10. Hehner, E.C.: Predicative programming Part I. Commun. ACM **27**(2), 134–143 (1984)
11. Hehner, E.C.: Specified blocks. In: Meyer, B., Woodcock, J. (eds.) VSTTE 2005. LNCS, vol. 4171, pp. 384–391. Springer, Heidelberg (2008). https://doi.org/10.1007/978-3-540-69149-5_41
12. Hehner, E.C.: A Practical Theory of Programming. Springer, New York (2012). https://doi.org/10.1007/978-1-4419-8596-5
13. Hoare, C.A.R.: Proof of correctness of data representations. In: Gries, D. (ed.) Programming Methodology, pp. 269–281. Springer, New York (1978). https://doi.org/10.1007/978-1-4612-6315-9_20
14. Hoare, C.A.R., He, J.: The weakest prespecification. Inf. Process. Lett. **24**(2), 127–132 (1987)
15. Hoare, C.A.R., Jifeng, H.: Unifying Theories of Programming, vol. 14. Prentice Hall, Englewood Cliffs (1998)
16. Josephs, M.B.: An introduction to the theory of specification and refinement. In: IBM research Report RC 12993. IBM Thomas J. Watson Research Division (1987)

17. Knuth, D.E.: Literate programming. Comput. J. **27**(2), 97–111 (1984)
18. Kourie, D.G., Watson, B.W.: The Correctness-by-Construction Approach to Programming. Springer, Heidelberg (2012). https://doi.org/10.1007/978-3-642-27919-5
19. Mili, A.: A relational approach to the design of deterministic programs. Acta Informatica **20**(4), 315–328 (1983)
20. Morgan, C.: The refinement calculus, and literate development. In: Möller, B., Partsch, H., Schuman, S. (eds.) Formal Program Development. LNCS, vol. 755, pp. 161–182. Springer, Heidelberg (1993). https://doi.org/10.1007/3-540-57499-9_20
21. Morgan, C., Robinson, K., Gardiner, P.: On the Refinement Calculus (Formal Approaches to Computing and Information Technology (FACIT)). Springer, London (1994)
22. Sekerinski, E.: A calculus for predicative programming. In: Bird, R.S., Morgan, C.C., Woodcock, J.C.P. (eds.) MPC 1992. LNCS, vol. 669, pp. 302–322. Springer, Heidelberg (1993). https://doi.org/10.1007/3-540-56625-2_20
23. Sozeau, M.: Subset coercions in Coq. In: Altenkirch, T., McBride, C. (eds.) TYPES 2006. LNCS, vol. 4502, pp. 237–252. Springer, Heidelberg (2007). https://doi.org/10.1007/978-3-540-74464-1_16
24. The Coq Development Team: The Coq proof assistant, version 8.8.0, April 2018
25. Wirth, N.: Program development by stepwise refinement. Commun. ACM **14**(4), 221–227 (1971)
26. Woodcock, J., Davies, J.: Using Z. Prentice Hall International (1996)

A Relational Static Semantics for Call Graph Construction

Xilong Zhuo and Chenyi Zhang[(✉)]

College of Information Science and Technology, Jinan University, Guangzhou, China
chenyi_zhang@jnu.edu.cn

Abstract. The problem of resolving virtual method and interface calls in object-oriented languages has been a long standing challenge to the program analysis community. The complexities are due to various reasons, such as increased levels of class inheritance and polymorphism in large programs. In this paper, we propose a new approach called type flow analysis that represent propagation of type information between program variables by a group of relations without the help of a heap abstraction. We prove that regarding the precision on reachability of class information to a variable, our method produces results equivalent to that one can derive from a points-to analysis. Moreover, in practice, our method consumes lower time and space usage, as supported by the experiment result.

1 Introduction

For object-oriented programming languages, virtual methods (or functions) are those declared in a base class but are meant to be overridden in different child classes. Statically determine a set of methods that may be invoked at a call site is important to program analysis, from which a subsequent optimization may reduce the cost of virtual function calls by performing method inlining if the target method forms a singleton set, remove methods that are never called by any call sites, or produce a call graph which can be useful in other optimization processes.

Efficient solutions, such as Class Hierarchy Analysis (CHA) [8,9], Rapid Type Analysis (RTA) [4] and Variable Type Analysis (VTA) [23], conservatively assign each variable a set of class definitions, with relatively low precision. Alternatively, with the help of an abstract heap, one may take advantage of a points-to analysis (e.g. [3]) to compute a set of object abstractions that a variable may refer to, and resolve the receiver classes in order to find associated methods at call sites.

The algorithms used by CHA, RTA and VTA are conservative, which aim to provide an efficient way to resolve calling edges, and which usually take linear-time in the size of a program by focusing on the types that are collected at the receiver of a call site. For instance, let x be a variable of declared class A, then at a call site $x.m()$, CHA will draw a call edge from this call site to method $m()$ of class A and every definition $m()$ of a class that extends A. In case class

Y. Ait-Ameur and S. Qin (Eds.): ICFEM 2019, LNCS 11852, pp. 322–335, 2019.
https://doi.org/10.1007/978-3-030-32409-4_20

```
class A{
    A f;
    void m(){
        return this.f;
    }
}
class B extends A{}
class C extends A{}
```

```
1:    A x = new A();   //O_1
2:    B b = new B();   //O_2
3:    A y = new A();   //O_3
4:    C c = new C();   //O_4
5:    x.f = b;
6:    y.f = c;
7:    z = x.m();
```

Fig. 1. An example that compares precision on type flow in a program.

Statement	VTA fact
$A\ x = $ new $A()$	$x \leftarrow A$
$B\ b = $ new $B()$	$b \leftarrow B$
$A\ y = $ new $A()$	$y \leftarrow A$
$C\ c = $ new $C()$	$c \leftarrow C$
$x.f = b$	$A.f \leftarrow b$
$y.f = c$	$A.f \leftarrow c$
	$A.m.this \leftarrow x$
$z = x.m()$	$A.m.return \leftarrow A.f$
	$z \leftarrow A.m.return$

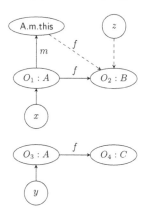

Fig. 2. VTA facts on the example

Fig. 3. Points-to results on the example

A does not define $m()$, a call edge to an ancestor class that defines $m()$ will also be included. For a variable x of declared interface I, CHA will draw a call edge from this call site to every method of name $m()$ defined in class X that implements I. We write $CHA(x,m)$ for the set of methods that are connected from call site $x.m()$ as resolved by Class Hierarchy Analysis (CHA). Rapid Type Analysis (RTA) is an improvement from CHA which resolves call site $x.m()$ to $CHA(x,m) \cap inst(P)$, where $inst(P)$ stands for the set of methods of classes that are instantiated in the program.

Variable Type Analysis (VTA) is a further improvement. VTA defines a node for each variable, method, method parameter and field. Class names are treated as values and propagation of such values between variables work in the way of value flow. As shown in Fig. 2 (example code in Fig. 1), the statements on line 1–4 initialize type information for variables x, y, b and c, and statements on line 5–7 establish value flow relations. Since both x and y are assigned type A, $x.f$ and $y.f$ are both represented by node $A.f$, thus the set of types reaching $A.f$ is now $\{B, C\}$. (Note this is a more precise result than CHA and RTA which assign $A.f$ with the set $\{A, B, C\}$.) Since $A.m.this$ refers to x, $this.f$ inside method $A.m()$ now refers to $A.f$. Therefore, through $A.m.return$, z receives $\{B, C\}$ as its final set of reaching types.

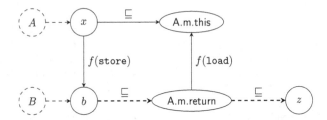

Fig. 4. Type Flow Analysis for variable z in the example

The result of a context-insensitive subset based points-to analysis [3] creates a heap abstraction of four objects (shown on line 1−4 of Fig. 1 as well as the ellipses in Fig. 3). These abstract objects are then inter-connected via field store access defined on line 5−6. The derived field access from $A.m.this$ to O_2 is shown in dashed arrow. By return of the method call $z = x.m()$, variable z receives O_2 of type B from $A.m.this.f$, which gives a more precise set of reaching types for variable z.

From this example, one may conclude that the imprecision of VTA in comparison with points-to analysis is due to the over abstraction of object types, such that O_1 and O_3, both of type A, are treated under the same type. Nevertheless, points-to analysis requires to construct a heap abstraction, which brings in extra information, especially when we are only interested in the set of reaching types of a variable.

In this paper we introduce a relational static semantics called Type Flow Analysis (TFA) on program variables and field accesses. Different from VTA, in addition to the binary value flow relation "$\sqsubseteq$" on the variable domain VAR, where $x \sqsubseteq y$ denotes all types that flow to x also flow to y, we also build a ternary field store relation $\rightarrow \, \subseteq$ VAR $\times \mathcal{F} \times$ VAR to trace the *load* and *store* relationship between variables via field accesses. This provides us additional ways to extend the relations $\sqsubseteq$ as well as $\rightarrow$. Taking the example from Fig. 1, we are able to collect the store relation $x \xrightarrow{f} b$ from line 5. Since $x \sqsubseteq$ A.m.this, together with the implicit assignment which loads f of A.m.return, we further derives $b \sqsubseteq$ A.m.return and $b \sqsubseteq z$ (dashed thick arrows in Fig. 4). Therefore, we assign type B to variable z. The complete reasoning pattern is depicted in Fig. 4. Nevertheless, one cannot derive $c \sqsubseteq z$ in the same way.

We have proved that in the context-insensitive inter-procedural setting, TFA is as precise as the subset based points-to analysis regarding type related information. Since points-to analysis can be enhanced with various types of context-sensitivity on variables and objects (e.g., call-site-sensitivity [13,20], object-sensitivity [16,21,25] and type-sensitivity [21]), extending type flow analysis with context-sensitivity will only require to consider contexts on variables, which is left for future work. The context-insensitive type flow analysis has been implemented in the Soot framework [1], and the implementation has been tested on a collection of benchmark programs from SPECjvm2008 [2] and DaCapo [5]. Our preliminary experimental result has shown that TFA spends similar or sometimes less runtime than CHA [8], but has precision comparable to that of a points-to analysis.

2   Type Flow Analysis

We define a core calculus consisting of most of the key object-oriented language features, shown in Fig. 5, which is designed in the same spirit as Featherweight Java [11]. A program is defined as a code base $\overline{C}$ (i.e., a collection of class definitions) with statement s to be evaluated. To run a program, one may assume that s is the default (static) entry method with local variable declarations $\overline{D}$, similar to e.g., Java and C++, which may differ in specific language designs. We define a few auxiliary functions. Let function $fields$ maps class names to their fields, $methods$ maps class names to their defined or inherited methods, and $type$ provides types (or class names) for objects. Given class c, if $f \in fields(c)$, then $ftype(c, f)$ is the defined class type of field f in c. Similarly, give an object o, if $f \in fields(type(o))$, then $o.f$ may refer to an object of type $ftype(type(o), f)$ or any of its subclass at runtime. Write $\mathcal{C}$ for the set of classes, OBJ for the set of objects, $\mathcal{F}$ for the set of fields and VAR for the set of variables that appear in a program.[1]

$$
\begin{array}{lll}
C & ::= & \text{class } c \; [\text{extends } c] \; \{\overline{F}; \; \overline{M}\} \\
F & ::= & c \; f \\
D & ::= & c \; z \\
M & ::= & m(x) \; \{\overline{D}; s; \text{return } x'\} \\
s & ::= & e \mid x{=}\text{new } c \mid x{=}e \mid x.f{=}y \mid s; s \\
e & ::= & \text{null} \mid x \mid x.f \mid x.m(y) \\
prog & ::= & \overline{C}; \overline{D}; s
\end{array}
$$

Fig. 5. Abstract syntax for the core language.

In this simple language we do not model common types (e.g., int and float) that are irrelevant to our analysis, and we focus on the reference types which form a class hierarchical structure. Similar to Variable Type Analysis (VTA), we assume a context insensitive setting, such that every variable can be uniquely determined by its name together with its enclosing class and methods. For example, if a local variable x is defined in method m of class c, then $c.m.x$ is the unique representation of that variable. Therefore, it is safe to drop the enclosing the class and method name if it is clear from the context. In general, we have the following types of variables in our analysis: (1) local variables, (2) method parameters, (3) this reference of each method, all of which are syntactically bounded by their enclosing methods and classes.

---

[1] Sometimes we mix-use the terms *type* and *class* in this paper when it is clear from the context.

We enrich the variable type analysis with the new type flow analysis by using three relations, a partial order on variables $\sqsubseteq \subseteq \text{VAR} \times \text{VAR}$, a type flow relation $\dashrightarrow \subseteq \mathcal{C} \times \text{VAR}$, as well as a field access relation $\longrightarrow \subseteq \text{VAR} \times \mathcal{F} \times \text{VAR}$, which are initially given as follows.

Definition 1 *(Base Relations). We have the following base facts for the three relations.*

1. *$c \dashrightarrow x$ if there is a statement $x = \mathsf{new}\ c$;*
2. *$y \sqsubseteq x$ if there is a statement $x = y$;*
3. *$x \xrightarrow{f} y$ if there is a statement $x.f = y$.*

Intuitively, $c \dashrightarrow x$ means variable x may have type c (i.e., c flows to x), $y \sqsubseteq x$ means all types flow to y also flow to x, and $x \xrightarrow{f} y$ means from variable x and field f one may access variable y.[2] These three relations are then extended by the following rules.

Definition 2 *(Extended Relations).*

1. *For all statements $x = y.f$, if $y \xrightarrow{f\ *} z$, then $z \sqsubseteq^* x$.*
2. *$c \dashrightarrow^* y$ if $c \dashrightarrow y$, or $\exists x \in \text{VAR} : c \dashrightarrow^* x \wedge x \sqsubseteq^* y$;*
3. *$y \sqsubseteq^* x$ if $x = y$ or $y \sqsubseteq x$ or $\exists z \in \text{VAR} : y \sqsubseteq^* z \wedge z \sqsubseteq^* x$;*
4. *$y \xrightarrow{f\ *} z$ if $\exists x \in \text{VAR} : x \xrightarrow{f} z \wedge (\exists z' \in \text{VAR} : z' \sqsubseteq^* y \wedge z' \sqsubseteq^* x)$;*
5. *The type information is used to resolve each method call $x = y.m(z)$.*

$$
\begin{aligned}
&\forall\, c \dashrightarrow^* y : \\
&\forall\, m(z')\{\ldots \mathsf{return}\ x'\} \in methods(c) :
\end{aligned}
\quad
\left\{
\begin{array}{l}
z \sqsubseteq^* c.m.z' \\
c \dashrightarrow^* c.m.this \\
c.m.x' \sqsubseteq^* x
\end{array}
\right.
$$

The final relations are the least relations that satisfy constraints of Definition 2. Comparing to VTA [23], we do not have field reference $c.f$ for each class c defined in a program. Instead, we define a relation that connects the two variable names and one field name. Although the three relations are inter-dependent, one may find that without method call (i.e., Definition 2.5), a smallest model satisfying the two relations $\rightarrow^*$ (field access) and $\sqsubseteq^*$ (variable partial order) can be uniquely determined without considering the type flow relation $\dashrightarrow^*$.

In order to compare the precision of TFA with points-to analysis, we present a brief list of the classical subset-based points-to rules for our language in Fig. 6, in which Ω (the var-points-to relation) maps a reference to a set of objects it may points to, and Φ (the heap-points-to relation) maps an object and a field to a set of objects. The points-to rules are mostly straightforward, except that $param(type(o), m))$, $this(type(o), m))$ and $return(type(o), m)$ refer to the formal parameter, this reference and return variable of method m of the class for which object o is declared, respectively.

---

[2] Note that VTA treats statement $x.f = y$ as follows. For each class c that flows to x which defines field f, VTA assigns all types that flow to y also to $c.f$.

statement	Points-to constraints
$x = \text{new } c$	$o_i \in \Omega(x)$
$x = y$	$\Omega(y) \subseteq \Omega(x)$
$x = y.f$	$\forall o \in \Omega(y) : \Phi(o, f) \subseteq \Omega(x)$
$x.f = y$	$o \in \Omega(x) : \Omega(y) \subseteq \Phi(o, f)$
$x = y.m(z)$	$\begin{cases} (z) \subseteq \Omega(param(type(o), m)) \\ \Omega(this(type(o), m)) = \{o\} \\ \forall x' \in return(type(o), m) : \\ \qquad \Omega(x') \subseteq \Omega(x) \end{cases}$

Fig. 6. Constraints for points-to analysis.

To this end we present the first result of the paper, which basically says type flow analysis has the same precision regarding type based check, such as call site resolution and cast failure check, when comparing with the points-to analysis.

Theorem 1. *In a context-insensitive analysis, for all variables x and classes c, $c \dashrightarrow^* x$ iff there exists an object abstraction o of c such that $o \in \Omega(x)$.*

Proof (sketch). For a proof sketch, first we assume every object creation site $x = \text{new } c_i$ at line i defines a mini-type c_i, and if the theorem is satisfied in this setting, a subsequent merging of mini-types into classes will preserve the result.

Moreover, we only need to prove the intraprocedural setting which is the result of Lemma 1. Because if in the intraprocedural setting the two systems have the same smallest model for all methods, then at each call site $x = y.m(a)$ both analyses will assign y the same set of classes and thus resolve the call site to the same set of method definitions, and as a consequence, each method body will be given the same set of extra conditions, thus all methods will have the same initial condition for the next round iteration. Therefore, both inter-procedural systems will eventually stabilize at the same model.   □

The following lemma focuses on the key part of the proof for Theorem 1, which shows that TFA and points-to are equivalent regarding call site resolution locally within a function.

Lemma 1. *In a context-insensitive intraprocedural analysis where each class c only syntactically appears once in the form of $\text{new } c$, for all variables x and classes c, $c \dashrightarrow^* x$ iff there exists an object abstraction o of type c such that $o \in \Omega(x)$.*

Proof. Since the points-to constraints define the smallest model (Ω, Φ) with $\Omega : \text{VAR} \rightarrow \text{OBJ}$ and $\Phi : \text{OBJ} \times \mathcal{F} \rightarrow \mathcal{P}(\text{OBJ})$, and the three relations of type flow analysis also define the smallest model that satisfies Definitions 1 and 2, we prove that every model of points-to constraints is also a model of TFA, and vice versa. Then the least model of both systems must be the same, as otherwise it would lead to contradiction.

($\star$) For the 'only if' part ($\Rightarrow$), we define $Reaches(x) = \{c \mid c \dashrightarrow^* x\}$, and assume a bijection $\xi : C \to$ OBJ that maps each class c to the unique (abstract) object o that is defined (and $type(o) = c$). Then we construct a function $Access : C \times \mathcal{F} \to \mathcal{P}(C)$ and show that $(\xi(Reaches), \xi(Access))$ satisfies the points-to constraints. Define $Access(c, f) = \{c' \mid x \xrightarrow{f\ *} y \wedge c \in Reaches(x) \wedge c' \in Reaches(y)\}$. We prove the following cases according to the top four points-to constraints in Fig. 6.

- For each statement $x =$ new c, we have $\xi(c) \in \xi(Reaches(x))$;
- For each statement $x = y$, we have $Reaches(y) \subseteq Reaches(x)$ and $\xi(Reaches(y)) \subseteq \xi(Reaches(x))$;
- For each statement $x.f = y$, we have $x \xrightarrow{f} y$, then by definition for all $c \in Reaches(x)$, and $c' \in Reaches(y)$, we have $c' \in Access(c, f)$, therefore $\xi(c') \in \xi(Reaches(y))$ we have $\xi(c') \in \xi(Access(\xi(c), f))$.
- For each statement $x = y.f$, let $c \in Reaches(y)$, we need to show $\xi(Access(c, f)) \subseteq \xi(Reaches(x))$, or equivalently, $Access(c, f) \subseteq Access(x)$. Let $c' \in Access(c, f)$, then by definition, there exist z, z' such that $c \in Reaches(z)$, $c' \in Reaches(z')$ and $z \xrightarrow{f\ *} z'$. By $c \in Reaches(y)$ and Definition 2.4, we have $y \xrightarrow{f\ *} z'$. Then by Definition 2.1, $z' \sqsubseteq^* x$. Therefore $c' \in Reaches(x)$.

($\star$) For the 'if' part ($\Leftarrow$), let (Ω, Φ) be a model that satisfies all the top four constraints defined in Fig. 6, and a bijection $\xi : C \to$ OBJ, we show the following constructed relations satisfy value points-to.

- For all types c and variables x, $c \dashrightarrow^* x$ if $\xi(c) \in \Omega(x)$;
- For all variables x and y, $x \sqsubseteq^* y$ if $\Omega(x) \subseteq \Omega(y)$;
- For all variables x and y, and for all fields f, $x \xrightarrow{f\ *} y$ if for all $o_1, o_2 \in$ OBJ such that $o_1 \in \Omega(x)$ and $o_2 \in \Omega(y)$ then $o_2 \in \Phi(o_1, f)$.

We check the following cases for the three relations $\dashrightarrow^*$, $\sqsubseteq^*$ and $\to$ that are just defined from the above.

- For each statement $x =$ new c, we have $\xi(c) \in \Omega(x)$, so $c \dashrightarrow^* x$ by definition.
- For each statement $x = y$, we have $\Omega(y) \subseteq \Omega(x)$, therefore $y \sqsubseteq^* x$ by definition.
- For each statement $x.f = y$, we have for all $o_1 \in \Omega(x)$ and $o_2 \in \Omega(y)$, $o_2 \in \Phi(o_1, f)$, which derives $x \xrightarrow{f\ *} y$ by definition.
- For each statement $x = y.f$, given $y \xrightarrow{f\ *} z$, we need to show $z \sqsubseteq^* x$. Equivalently, by definition we have for all $o_1 \in \Omega(y)$ and $o_2 \in \Omega(z)$, $o_2 \in \Phi(o_1, f)$. Since points-to relation gives $\Phi(o_1, f) \subseteq \Omega(x)$, we have $o_2 \in \Omega(x)$, which derives $\Omega(z) \subseteq \Omega(x)$, the definition of $z \sqsubseteq^* x$.
- The proof for the properties in the rest of Definition 2 are related to transitivity of the three TFA relations, which are straightforward. We leave them for interested readers.   □

3 Implementation and Optimization

The analysis algorithm is written in Java, and is implemented in the Soot framework [1], the most popular static analysis framework for Java. The three base relations (i.e., $\dashrightarrow$, $\sqsubseteq$ and $\rightarrow$) of Definition 1 are extracted from Soot's intermediate representation and the extended relations (i.e., $\dashrightarrow^*$, $\sqsubseteq^*$ and $\rightarrow^*$) of Definition 2 are then computed considering the mutual dependency relations between them. Since we are only interested in reference types, we do not carry out analysis on basic types such as boolean, int and double. We also do not consider more advanced Java features such as functional interfaces and lambda expressions, as well as usages of Java Native Interface (JNI), nor method calls via Java reflective API. We have not tried to apply the approach to Java libraries, all invocation of methods from JDK are treated as end points, thus all possible call back edges will be missed in the analysis. Array accesses are treated conservatively—all type information that flows to one member of a reference array flows to all members of that array, so that only one node is generated for each array.

Since call graph information may be saved and be used for subsequent analyses, we propose the following two ways to reduce storage for computed result. If a number of variables are similar regarding type information in a graph representation, they can be merged and then referred to by the merged node.

1. If $x \sqsubseteq^* y$ and $y \sqsubseteq^* x$, we say x and y form an *alias pair*, written $x \sim y$. Intuitively, $\mathsf{VAR}/\sim$ is a partition of VAR such that each $c \in \mathsf{VAR}/\sim$ is a strongly connected component (SCC) in the variable graph edged by relation $\sqsubseteq$, which can be quickly collected by using Tarjan's algorithm [24].
2. A more aggressive compression can be achieved in a way similar to bisimulation minimization of finite state systems [12,17]. Define $\approx \subset \mathsf{VAR} \times \mathsf{VAR}$ such that $x \approx y$ is symmetric and if
   - for all class c, $c \dashrightarrow^* x$ iff $c \dashrightarrow^* y$, and
   - for all $x \xrightarrow{f\ *} x'$ there exists $y \xrightarrow{f\ *} y'$ and $x' \approx y'$.

It is straightforward to see that $\approx$ is a more aggressive merging scheme.

Lemma 2. *For all $x, y \in \mathsf{VAR}$, $x \sim y$ implies $x \approx y$.*

We have implemented the second storage minimization scheme by using Kanellakis and Smolka's algorithm [12] which computes the largest bisimulation relation for a given finite state labelled transition system. In our interpretation, the variables are treated as states and the field access relation is treated as the state transition relation. The algorithm then merges equivalent variables into a single group. As a storage optimization process, this implementation has been tested and evaluated in the next section.

4 Experiment and Evaluation

We evaluate our approach by measuring its performance on 13 benchmark programs. Among the benchmark programs, *compress*, *crypto* are from the classical SPECjvm2008 suite [2], and the other 11 programs are from the DaCapo suite [5]. We randomly selected these test cases from the two benchmark suites, in order to test code bases that are representative from a variety in size. All of our experiments were conducted on a Huawei Laptop equipped with an Intel i5-8250U processor at 1.60 GHz and 8 GB memory, running Ubuntu 16.04LTS with OpenJDK 1.8.0.

We compare our approach against the default implementation of Class Hierarchy Analysis (CHA) and context-insensitive points-to analysis [14] that are implemented by the Soot team. We use Soot as our basic framework to extract the SSA based representation of the benchmark code. We also generate automata representation for the resulting relations which can be visualized in a subsequent user-friendly manual inspection. The choice of the context-insensitive points-to analysis is due to our approach also being context-insensitive, thus the results will be comparable. In the following tables we use CHA, PTA and TFA to refer to the results related to class hierarchy analysis, points-to analysis and type flow analysis, respectively. During the evaluation the following three research questions are addressed.

RQ1 How efficient is our approach compared with the traditional class hierarchy analysis and points-to analysis?

RQ2 How accurate is the result of our approach when comparing with the other analyses?

RQ3 Does our optimization (or minimization) algorithm achieve significantly reduce storage consumption?

4.1   RQ1: Efficiency

To answer the first research question, we executed each benchmark program 10 times with the CHA, PTA and TFA algorithms. We calculated the average time consumption (in seconds) as displayed at columns $T_{CHA}(s)$, $T_{PTA}(s)$ and $T_{TFA}(s)$ of the Table in Fig. 7. The sizes of each generated relation (i.e., the type flow relation '$--\rightarrow$', variable partial order '$\sqsubseteq$' and the field access '$\rightarrow$') are counted, which provides an estimation of size for the problem we are treating. One may observe that when the problem size increases, the execution time of the our algorithm also increases in a way similar to CHA, though in general the runtime of CHA is supposed to grow linearly in the size of a program. The reason that TFA sometimes outperforms CHA may be partially due to the size of the intrinsic complexity of the class and interface hierarchical structure that a program adopts. TFA is in general more efficient than the points-to analysis. The runtime cost in TFA basically depends on the size of generated relations, as well as the relational complexity as most of the time is consumed to calculate a fixpoint. For PTA it also requires extra time for maintaining and updating a heap abstraction. Taking a closer look at the benchmark *bootstrap*, CHA and PTA analyze the benchmark using about 23.97 and 34.62 s, respectively. As TFA only generated 773 relations, the analysis only takes 0.06 s.

In this preliminary study, we find TFA is in general more efficient than the subset based points-to analysis as implemented in Soot.

Benchmark	$T_{CHA}(s)$	$T_{PTA}(s)$	$T_{TFA}(s)$	$R_{\dashrightarrow}$	$R_{\sqsubseteq}$	$R_{\rightarrow}$
compress	0.02	0.11	0.01	89	207	24
crypto	0.01	0.13	0.03	94	226	18
bootstrap	23.97	34.62	0.06	201	555	17
commons-codec	0.008	0.12	0.12	316	3,360	49
junit	24.56	34.09	0.19	1,135	5,977	241
commons-httpclient	0.008	0.11	0.27	2,503	8,836	521
serializer	22.95	32.45	0.42	3,044	18,917	331
xerces	22.49	32.05	1.65	13,906	83,325	2,814
eclipse	22.80	41.34	1.15	8,434	40,932	1,618
derby	22.71	49.27	5.18	21,244	217,571	5,370
xalan	79.57	163.20	2.52	33,857	165,785	3,690
antlr	43.08	89.07	6.24	17,272	112,537	3,875
batik	48.85	97.22	2.77	30,473	127,430	6,053

Fig. 7. Runtime cost with different analysis

Benchmark	CS_{base}	CS_{CHA}	CS_{PTA}	CS_{TFA}
compress	153	160	18	73
crypto	302	307	62	121
bootstrap	657	801	539	328
commons-codec	1,162	1,372	270	557
junit	3,196	17,532	5,912	1,218
commons-httpclient	6,817	17,118	567	2,976
serializer	4,782	9,533	1,000	1,792
xerces	24,579	56,252	6,287	8,522
eclipse	23,607	95,073	28,201	9,925
derby	69,537	180,428	46,361	17,519
xalan	57,430	155,866	54,234	19,071
antlr	62,007	147,014	48,766	18,734
batik	56,877	235,085	52,486	21,791

Fig. 8. Call sites generated by different analyses

4.2 RQ2: Accurancy

We answer the second question by considering the number of generated call sites as an indication of accuracy. In type flow analysis, a method call $a.m()$ is resolved to $c.m()$ if class c is included in a's reaching type set and method $m()$ is defined for c. In general, a more accurate analysis often generates a smaller set of types for each calling variable, resulting fewer call edges in total in the call graph. The table included in Fig. 8 displays the number of call sites generated by different analyses. We also include the base call site counting, i.e., the number of call sites syntactically written in the source code, as the baseline at the CS_{base} column. It is not surprising that CHA usually has more call edges than call sites as it maps some call sites to more than one class.

Benchmark	Node$_{origin}$	Node$_{opt}$	Space Reduction	Time(s)
compress	205	163	20.49%	0.01
crypto	312	229	26.60%	0.02
bootstrap	517	328	36.56%	0.05
commons-codec	1,742	1,452	16.65%	0.40
junit	5,890	5,135	12.82%	1.93
commons-httpclient	9,748	7,611	21.92%	4.06
serializer	9,782	6,987	28.57%	7.42
xerces	42,085	33,375	20.70%	186.11
eclipse	34,899	28,347	18.77%	86.92
derby	112,496	96,962	13.81%	1765.74
xalan	103,941	75,699	27.17%	1827.75
antlr	57,518	42,475	26.15%	358.28
batik	90,014	71,476	20.59%	1090.97

Fig. 9. Optimization result

In comparison to CHA, our approach has reduced a significant amount of call site edges. In general, comparing to other two analyses, the number of call edges resolved by TFA are often larger than PTA and smaller than CHA on the same benchmark. The difference may be caused by our over approximation on analyzing array references, as well as the existence of unsolved call edges from e.g. JNI calls or reflective calls. If the points-to analysis implemented by the Soot team has made special treatment on arrays, JNI or Java reflection, then PTA may contain more call edges than TFA regarding these cases.

4.3 RQ3: Optimization

We apply bisimulation minimization to merge nodes that are of the same types as well as accessible types recursively through fields. Thus we can reduce the space consumption when there is a requirement to store the result for subsequent analysis processes. Regarding the third research question, we calculate the number of "effective" nodes before and after optimization process. Besides, time consumption is another factor that we consider. The results are shown in the table in Fig. 9. We evaluate our optimization algorithm on all benchmarks 10 times and find in general we can achieve about 12%−36% of space reduction. Considering the computation time which has become more significant for larger and more complex benchmarks such as derby and xalan, we suggest that compression of the intermediate result may not be viable to median to large sized target programs, as the benefit of space reduction seems limited regarding the extra time required to apply the reduction.

5   Related Work

There are not many works focusing on general purpose call graph construction algorithms, and we give a brief review of these works first.

As stated in the introduction, Class Hierarchy Analysis (CHA) [8,9], Rapid Type Analysis (RTA) [4] and Variable Type Analysis (VTA) [23] are efficient algorithms that conservatively resolves call sites without any help from points-to analysis. Grove et al. [10] introduced an approach to model context-sensitive and context-insensitive call graph construction. They define call graph in terms of three algorithm-specific parameter partial orders, and provide a method called Monotonic Refinement, potentially adding to the class sets of local variables and adding new contours to call sites, load sites, and store sites. Tip and Palsberg [26] Proposed four propagation-based call graph construction algorithms, CTA, MTA, FTA and XTA. CTA uses distinct sets for classes, MTA uses distinct sets for classes and fields, FTA uses distinct sets for classes and methods, and XTA uses distinct sets for classes, fields, and methods. The constructed call graphs tend to contain slightly fewer method definitions when compared to RTA. It has been shown that associating a distinct set of types with each method in a class has a significantly greater impact on precision than using a distinct set for each field in a class. Reif et al. [18] study the construction of call graphs for Java libraries that abstract over all potential library usages, in a so-called *open world* approach. They invented two concrete call graph algorithms for libraries based on adaptations of the CHA algorithm, to be used for software quality and security issues. In general they are interested in analyzing library without knowing client application, which is complementary to our work that has focus on client program while treating library calls as end nodes.

Call graphs may serve as a basis for points-to analysis, but often a points-to analysis implicitly computes a call graph on-the-fly, such as the context insensitive points-to algorithm implemented in Soot using SPARK [14]. Most context-sensitive points-to analysis algorithms (e.g., [16,21,22,25]) progress call edges together with value flow, to our knowledge. The main distinction of our approach from these points-to analysis is the usage of an abstract heap, as we are only interested in the actual reaching types of the receiver of a call. Nevertheless, unlike CHA and VTA, our methodology can be extended to context-sensitive settings.

Regarding the treatment of flow analysis in our algorithm, downcast analysis has been studied in region inference which is a special memory management scheme for preventing dangling pointers or improving precision in garbage collection in object-oriented programming languages [6,7]. These works are type-based analysis, while our methodology belongs to traditional static program analysis. Similar ideas regarding value flow can also be found in the graph-reachability based formulation (e.g. [15,19]) to which all distributed data flow analyses can be adopted.

6   Conclusion

In this paper we have proposed Type Flow Analysis (TFA), an algorithm that constructs call graph edges for Object-Oriented programming languages. Different from points-to based analysis, we do not require a heap abstraction, so the computation is purely relational. We have proved that in the context-insensitive setting, our result is equivalent to that would be produced by a subset-based points-to analysis, regarding the core Object-Oriented language features. We have implemented the algorithm in the Soot compiler framework, and have conducted preliminary evaluation by comparing our results with those produced by the built-in CHA and points-to analysis algorithms in Soot on a selection of 13 benchmark programs from SPECjvm2008 and DaCapo benchmark suites, and achieved promising results. In the future we plan to develop context-sensitive analysis algorithms based on TFA.

Acknowledgment. We thank Bernhard Scholz for his guidance in our experiment regarding JVM configurations. We also thank anonymous reviewers of ICFEM 2019 for their helpful suggestions to improve the quality of the paper. However due to limited time left before the camera ready deadline we are unable to finish all suggested improvements.

References

1. Soot. https://sable.github.io/soot/. Accessed 10 June 2019
2. SPECjvm2008. https://www.spec.org/jvm2008/. Accessed 18 June 2019
3. Andersen, L.O.: Program analysis and specialization for the C programming language. Ph.D. thesis, DIKU, University of Copenhagen, May 1994
4. Bacon, D.F., Sweeney, P.F.: Fast static analysis of C++ virtual function calls. In: Proceedings of the 11th ACM SIGPLAN Conference on Object-oriented Programming, Systems, Languages, and Applications, OOPSLA 1996, pp. 324–341 (1996)
5. Blackburn, S.M., et al.: The DaCapo benchmarks: Java benchmarking development and analysis. In: Proceedings of the 21st Annual ACM SIGPLAN Conference on Object-oriented Programming Systems, Languages, and Applications, OOPSLA 2006, pp. 169–190 (2006)
6. Boyapati, C., Salcianu, A., W. Beebee, J., Rinard, M.: Ownership types for safe region-based memory management in real-time Java. In: Proceedings of the ACM SIGPLAN 2003 Conference on Programming Language Design and Implementation, PLDI 2003, pp. 324–337 (2003)
7. Chin, W., Craciun, F., Qin, S., Rinard, M.: Region inference for an object-oriented language. In: Proceedings of the ACM SIGPLAN 2004 Conference on Programming Language Design and Implementation, PLDI 2004, pp. 243–254 (2004)
8. Dean, J., Grove, D., Chambers, C.: Optimization of object-oriented programs using static class hierarchy analysis. In: Tokoro, M., Pareschi, R. (eds.) ECOOP 1995. LNCS, vol. 952, pp. 77–101. Springer, Heidelberg (1995). https://doi.org/10.1007/3-540-49538-X_5
9. Fernández, M.F.: Simple and effective link-time optimization of Modula-3 programs. In: Proceedings of the ACM SIGPLAN 1995 Conference on Programming Language Design and Implementation, PLDI 1995, pp. 103–115 (1995)
10. Grove, D., DeFouw, G., Dean, J., Chambers, C.: Call graph construction in object-oriented languages. In: Proceedings of the 12th ACM SIGPLAN Conference on Object-oriented Programming, Systems, Languages, and Applications, OOPSLA 1997, pp. 108–124 (1997)
11. Igarashi, A., Pierce, B.C., Wadler, P.: Featherweight Java: a minimal core calculus for Java and GJ. ACM Trans. Program. Lang. Syst. **23**(3), 396–450 (2001)

12. Kanellakis, P.C., Smolka, S.A.: CCS expressions, finite state processes, and three problems of equivalence. Inf. Comput. **86**, 43–68 (1990)
13. Kastrinis, G., Smaragdakis, Y.: Hybrid context-sensitivity for points-to analysis. In: Proceedings of the 34th ACM SIGPLAN Conference on Programming Language Design and Implementation, PLDI 2013, pp. 423–434 (2013)
14. Lhoták, O., Hendren, L.: Scaling Java points-to analysis using spark. In: Proceedings of the 12th International Conference on Compiler Construction, CC 2003, pp. 153–169 (2003)
15. Lu, Y., Shang, L., Xie, X., Xue, J.: An incremental points-to analysis with CFL-reachability. In: Proceedings of the 22nd International Conference on Compiler Construction, CC 2013, pp. 61–81 (2013)
16. Milanova, A., Rountev, A., Ryder, B.G.: Parameterized object sensitivity for points-to analysis for Java. ACM Trans. Softw. Eng. Methodol. **14**(1), 1–41 (2005)
17. Paige, R., Tarjan, R.E.: Three partition refinement algorithms. SIAM J. Comput. **16**, 973–989 (1987)
18. Reif, M., Eichberg, M., Hermann, B., Lerch, J., Mezini, M.: Call graph construction for Java libraries. In: Proceedings of the 2016 24th ACM SIGSOFT International Symposium on Foundations of Software Engineering, FSE 2016, pp. 474–486 (2016)
19. Reps, T.: Program analysis via graph reachability. In: Proceedings of the 1997 International Symposium on Logic Programming, ILPS 1997, pp. 5–19 (1997)
20. Shivers, O.G.: Control-flow analysis of higher-order languages or taming lambda. Ph.D. thesis (1991)
21. Smaragdakis, Y., Bravenboer, M., Lhoták, O.: Pick your contexts well: understanding object-sensitivity. In: Proceedings of the 38th Annual ACM SIGPLAN-SIGACT Symposium on Principles of Programming Languages, POPL 2011, pp. 17–30 (2011)
22. Sridharan, M., Bodík, R.: Refinement-based context-sensitive points-to analysis for Java. In: Proceedings of the 27th ACM SIGPLAN Conference on Programming Language Design and Implementation, PLDI 2006, pp. 387–400 (2006)
23. Sundaresan, V., et al.: Practical virtual method call resolution for Java. In: Proceedings of the 15th ACM SIGPLAN Conference on Object-oriented Programming, Systems, Languages, and Applications, OOPSLA 2000, pp. 264–280. (2000)
24. Tarjan, R.E.: Depth-first search and linear graph algorithms. SIAM J. Comput. **1**, 146–160 (1972)
25. Tan, T., Li, Y., Xue, J.: Making k-object-sensitive pointer analysis more precise with still k-limiting. In: Rival, X. (ed.) SAS 2016. LNCS, vol. 9837, pp. 489–510. Springer, Heidelberg (2016). https://doi.org/10.1007/978-3-662-53413-7_24
26. Tip, F., Palsberg, J.: Scalable propagation-based call graph construction algorithms. In: Proceedings of the 15th ACM SIGPLAN Conference on Object-Oriented Programming, Systems, Languages, and Applications. OOPSLA 2000, pp. 281–293 (2000)

Solution Enumeration Abstraction: A Modeling Idiom to Enhance a Lightweight Formal Method

Allison Sullivan[1(✉)], Darko Marinov[2], and Sarfraz Khurshid[3]

[1] North Carolina A&T State University, Greensboro, USA
aksullivan@ncat.edu
[2] University of Illinois at Urbana-Champaign, Urbana, USA
marinov@illinois.edu
[3] University of Texas at Austin, Austin, USA
khurshid@utexas.edu

Abstract. Formal methods are a key to engineering more reliable systems. In this paper, we focus on an important application of formal methods — enumerating solutions to logical formulas that encode properties of interest. Solution enumeration has many uses, e.g., in systematic software testing, model counting, or hardware analysis. We introduce *solution enumeration abstraction*, a novel idiom that allows users to define data abstractions to enhance solution enumeration by specifying how the solutions must differ, so enumeration creates a high quality set of solutions of a manageable size. We embody the idiom as a technique built on top of Alloy, a well-known lightweight formal method, which is comprised of a first-order relational logic with transitive closure, and a SAT-based analysis engine. Experimental results show that our technique supports a variety of data abstractions, and can substantially reduce the number of solutions enumerated and the time to enumerate them.

1 Introduction

Enumerating solutions to logical formulas that describe properties of interest is a highly useful application of formal methods in many domains. For example, solution enumeration enables validation of software designs [19,33,36,44], systematic testing of implementations [30,35], model counting for reliability analysis of systems [12], or program synthesis for security analysis of hardware [5,46,47]. While solution enumeration has found many uses, its effectiveness relies heavily on the quality and number of solutions enumerated. Creating too similar or too many solutions can lead to redundancy and inefficiency in the supported application, and harm scalability [5,19,30,33,35,36,44,46,47].

In this paper, we introduce *solution enumeration abstraction*, a novel idiom that allows users to define data abstractions to enhance solution enumeration by specifying how the solutions must differ. As a result, the collection of solutions enumerated is a tailored subset that focuses on solutions explicitly of value to

© Springer Nature Switzerland AG 2019
Y. Ait-Ameur and S. Qin (Eds.): ICFEM 2019, LNCS 11852, pp. 336–352, 2019.
https://doi.org/10.1007/978-3-030-32409-4_21

the user. We implement our idiom for Alloy [19], a declarative, first-order modeling language that is deployed with the analyzer and a solution enumeration toolset. Given an Alloy model and a *scope*, i.e., bound on the universe of discourse, the analyzer creates a constraint-solving problem in propositional logic and uses off-the-shelf SAT technology [9,11,16,27,42] to solve it.

Alloy has been used in academia and industry for design and modeling of software systems [3,6,20,22,48,51], and for various forms of analyses of code, including deep static checking [13,21], systematic testing [30], data structure repair [41,50], and automated debugging [17]. To illustrate one application domain in more detail, Alloy has been recently used to model and analyze not only software but hardware systems. Trippel et al. [5,46,47] in the *CheckMate* project use Alloy to model program executions valid in a given microarchitecture in order to explore memory consistency and security properties of such microarchitecture. Their work found new variants of security exploits such as Meltdown and Spectre. From the Alloy perspective, their models are highly interesting as they employ some key structures. In particular, they build graphs (called μhb graphs—for "microarchitectural happens-before" graphs) that capture the precise valid ordering of events on a given microarchitecture. These graphs often give rise to structures that the domain modeling considers equivalent and, as such, it is not needed to explore all those equivalent structures.[1]

Our idiom is founded on the principles of *data abstraction*, e.g., as embodied by *abstraction functions*, which map concrete data structures to abstract entities that the structures represent [28]. Abstraction functions naturally occur when abstract data types are used. To illustrate, consider a height-balanced binary search tree that implements a set of integers. An abstraction function can map trees to sets of integers, e.g., a tree with 3 nodes — where 2 is the value in the root, and 1 and 3 are, respectively, the values in the left and the right child of the root — can be mapped to the set {1,2,3}.

Traditional abstraction functions have many well-known uses. They document the key relationships that form the foundation of the implementation of the abstract data type; the implementation must provide behaviors that are correct with respect to the corresponding operations on the abstract data type. Moreover, abstraction functions facilitate analysis of code, e.g., using modular reasoning [26]. Furthermore, they enable synthesis of code, e.g., to synthesize *equals* or *hashCode* methods [38], or iterators over collections [39].

Our newly proposed idiom allows Alloy users to define abstraction functions in their models, and lays the foundation for a novel technique for *abstraction-directed solution enumeration* that restricts the enumeration to only create solutions that are mutually different at the level of the abstract domain, thereby providing the user vital control over solution enumeration. To illustrate, if a binary search tree implements a set, and two trees contain the same set of values, only one of them is generated. In general, an abstraction function maps

---

[1] We thank Caroline Trippel for pointing out specific examples of the equivalence properties in the domain of μhb graphs. We abstract these architecture-specific models into more general cases that are easier to present for a broader audience.

many concrete structures to one abstract structure. Hence, enumerating (concrete) structures that map to unique abstract values can substantially reduce the number of solutions.

Our technique generalizes beyond traditional abstraction functions. For example, the user can simply enumerate solutions that differ with respect to a *subset* of existing relations in their model, e.g., creating a set of binary trees where no two trees have the exact same parent pointers. Another example is where the users want to reduce the number of solutions based on a criteria they desire, e.g., create graphs that do not have the same transitive closure in the context of hardware modeling (see Footnote 1); the users can encode the criteria using our idiom, and then use our technique to focus enumeration on the relations that are introduced to define the criteria. Another example in the context of hardware modeling is when the user writes an alternative model with the goal to reduce the number of solutions even if doing so impacts some other quality attribute (e.g., readability) of the model (see Footnote 1); the user can instead embed the alternative model in the abstraction and use it without modifying the original model.

Our technique is complementary to existing approaches for reducing the number of solutions. One such well-known approach is *symmetry breaking*, where additional constraints are added to the formula to remove *isomorphic* solutions to help the solvers prune more [8, 23, 43], e.g., to remove isomorphic graphs when enumerating binary search trees. Our enumeration technique allows defining and utilizing abstraction functions even in the presence of symmetry breaking constraints. Moreover, our technique can completely *subsume* symmetry breaking, and allows writing symmetry breaking constraints directly as abstractions.

Overall, our new technique enables a key *separation of concerns* in software modeling, where the user can build the model without worrying about refining it to facilitate solution enumeration, which can then be guided by defining an appropriate abstraction using our idiom. We make the following contributions:

- **Idiom.** We introduce an idiom to model abstraction functions in Alloy;
- **Abstraction-Directed Solution Enumeration.** We present an abstraction technique to direct solution enumeration, so the solutions enumerated differ at the abstract level, or stated dually, some solutions that differ at the concrete level are not generated if they map to the same abstract values;
- **Generalization.** We present a generalization of our core technique to support various forms of abstractions to direct solution enumeration; and
- **Evaluation.** We present an experimental evaluation using several subject models; the results show that our technique can substantially reduce the number of solutions and the generation time. Our prototype and the subject models are available online: "https://github.com/Allisonius/Seabs".

Related Work. Abstraction functions are a central concept in data abstraction [28]. They have been supported by many systems for writing formal specifications, e.g., by the Larch family [18, 25]. Various analyses leverage abstraction functions [26, 38, 39], or more general forms of abstraction [14, 29, 34, 37, 49] for

```
module list
one sig List { header: lone Node }
sig Node { elem: Int, link: lone Node }

pred Acyclic { /* no directed cycle */
  all n: List.header.*link | n !in n.^link }
pred NoRepetition { /* unique nodes have unique elements */
  all disj m, n: List.header.*link | m.elem != n.elem }
pred RepOk { Acyclic and NoRepetition }
fact Reachability { List.header.*link = Node } /* no disconnected node */

run RepOk for 3 but 2 int
```

Fig. 1. Alloy model of a singly-linked list of integers.

increased efficacy. A key difference between previous work and this paper is our use of abstraction functions in the context of logical formulas to direct solution enumeration using propositional satisfiability solvers.

In the context of Alloy, solution enumeration is commonly used for *scenario exploration* where the user inspects the solutions to validate the Alloy models. Several past projects improve solution enumeration by focusing it using different criteria, e.g., symmetry [23], minimality [33], field exhaustiveness [35], and coverage [36,44]. Our approach is orthogonal to these techniques and can work in tandem with them, e.g., as we show for symmetry breaking (Sect. 3.3.2).

More generally, solution enumeration is a technique that enables a number of software analyses, e.g., test input generation for automated testing [30] and model counting for reliability analysis [12]. Researchers have developed various optimizations, e.g., dedicated search [4], mixing of generators and solvers [15,24], solver-aided languages [40], and sampling [10,31] for more effective enumeration. We believe our approach can also combine with some of these optimizations, and we plan to explore the integration in future work.

2 Overview

This section describes two illustrative examples to provide an overview of our approach for controlling solution enumeration in Alloy by utilizing abstraction functions. The first example shows a traditional abstraction function for an abstract data type (Sect. 2.1). The second example shows how our approach addresses a problem in the context of recent work [5,46,47] on hardware modeling using Alloy (Sect. 2.2). We describe the basics of Alloy as needed.

2.1 Singly-Linked List and Set

Consider modeling in Alloy an implementation of a set of integers using a singly-linked acyclic list of nodes that contain integers without repetition (Fig. 1).

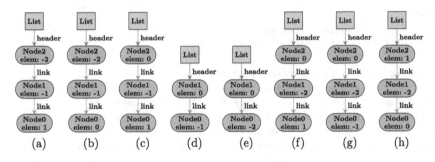

Fig. 2. First 8 solutions generated by the Alloy analyzer. For each structure, the square box is the list atom (*List*), and each ellipse is a node atom and is labeled with its identity (*Node0*, *Node1*, or *Node2*) and integer element (*elem*).

The `module` keyword names the model, which contains a set (`sig`) of lists (`List`) and a set of nodes (`Node`). Each element in an Alloy set is an atom. The keyword `one` declares the set of lists to contain only one element — each solution will contain exactly one list. The *field* `header` (in `List`) declares a binary relation of type `List` × `Node`. The keyword `lone` makes `header` a partial function; thus, each list has at most one header. The field `elem` (in `Node`) models the node elements and introduces a total function `Node` × `Int`, where `Int` is the built-in Alloy type that models primitive integers; `link` models the linking structure of the list and is a partial function of type `Node` × `Node`.

Each predicate (`pred`) defines a formula that can be *invoked* elsewhere. The predicate `Acyclic` defines acyclicity of a linked list using universal quantification (`all`). The expression `List.header.*link` uses relational composition ('.') and reflexive transitive closure ('*') to represent the set of all nodes reachable from the list's header node. The operator '^' is transitive closure; the expression `n.^link` represents the set of all nodes reachable from n following one or more traversals along the `link` field. The operator '!' is logical negation, and the keyword `in` represents the subset operation. Thus, the predicate `Acyclic` requires the list not to contain a directed cycle. The predicate `NoRepetition` also uses universal quantification; the keyword `disj` makes m and n distinct. Thus, the predicate `NoRepetition` requires distinct list nodes to contain unique elements and the list to not contain any duplicates. The predicate `RepOk` uses logical conjunction to require the list to be acyclic and free of duplicates.

Each fact defines a constraint that must be satisfied by every solution. The fact `Reachability` requires every node to be in the list so there are no disconnected components in any solution. This fact helps create more meaningful solutions that do not contain parts that are not relevant to the properties modeled.

The `run` command instructs the Alloy analyzer to create a solution with respect to the `RepOk` predicate, the predicates it transitively invokes, and the facts. The command specifies a scope of 3 for all the sigs in the model, i.e., *up to* 3 atoms in each sig, and a bit-width of 2 for integers, i.e., 4 integer values {-2, -1, 0, 1}. The analyzer can enumerate multiple (and if desired, all) solutions.

```
module listAF
open list
one sig AbsFun { af: set Int }
fact AbsFunDef { AbsFun.af = List.header.*link.elem }
```

Fig. 3. An abstraction function modeled using our idiom.

Figure 2 shows the first 8 solutions created by the analyzer. In total, the analyzer creates 41 solutions for the given scope. All these solutions are *non-isomorphic* with respect to the identity of atoms. The Alloy analyzer automatically adds *symmetry-breaking predicates* [8,43] which, in general, remove many but not all isomorphic solutions. For this scope, these predicates remove all symmetries. While these solutions are non-isomorphic, more than one solution contains the same *set* of node values. For example, the two lists in Figs. 2(f) and 2(h) represent the same set {-2, 0, 1} with 3 values. In fact, of the 41 solutions found, 6 represent the set {-2, 0, 1}.

2.1.1 Idiom for Modeling Abstraction Functions

Next, consider modeling the abstraction function for the list representing a set. The abstraction function $\alpha : \mathcal{C} \rightarrow \mathcal{A}$ maps each concrete data structure (in the concrete domain $\mathcal{C}$) to an abstract value (in the abstract domain $\mathcal{A}$). In general, each value in the abstract domain may itself be a structure. In this example, we describe our idiom for the special case when the abstract domain contains sets of integers; Sect. 3.1 presents a more general treatment. Our modeling idiom has 2 basic steps: (1) add a new singleton sig, e.g., called *AbsFun*, that introduces a field, e.g., af, that models $\mathcal{A}$; and (2) add a new fact that defines the value of the field af (in *AbsFun*) in terms of the fields that model the concrete structure.

Figure 3 shows an Alloy model that defines the abstraction function for our list example. The keyword **open** allows importing another model, which, in this case, is our list model (Fig. 1). The sig **AbsFun** and field **af** model the abstraction function. Specifically, **af** introduces a binary relation **AbsFun** × **Int**; the keyword **set** declares **af** to be an arbitrary relation that maps to a *set* of integers. The expression **List.header.*link.elem** represents the set of all integer elements in the list nodes. The fact **AbsFunDef** constrains the field **af**'s value to equal the set of integers in the list and hence defines the abstraction function.

Our model of the abstraction function introduces a new sig and a new binary relation. Any solution for **RepOk** that is generated with respect to this new model contains a solution for the original model (**list**), i.e., in the concrete domain, and in addition, contains the corresponding value in the abstract domain (given by the value of the field **af**), which allows observing applications of the abstraction function (as well as inspecting concrete structures as before). The number of solutions for the old model (**list**, Fig. 1) is the same as the number of solutions for new model (**listAF**, Fig. 3) because each solution to **listAF** is a pair that contains a solution to **list** and its abstract value, and each abstract value has at least one corresponding concrete structure.

2.1.2 Using Abstraction Functions to Direct Solution Enumeration

Next, we describe how our idiom enables directing solution enumeration to reduce the number of solutions. Observe that many solutions to the original model (list, Fig. 1) can map to the same abstract value, e.g., there are 6 lists $l_1, \ldots, l_6$ with exactly 3 nodes with elements -1, 0, and 1, and each $l_i (1 \leq i6)$ maps to the same set $\{-1, 0, 1\}$. Our key insight is that if we require enumeration to create solutions that *differ with respect to the fields that model the abstraction function*, the set of all solutions created will not contain any two solutions that have the same value in the abstract domain. We embody this insight into a new solution enumeration technique built on top of the Alloy analyzer's Kodkod back-end (Sect. 3.2).

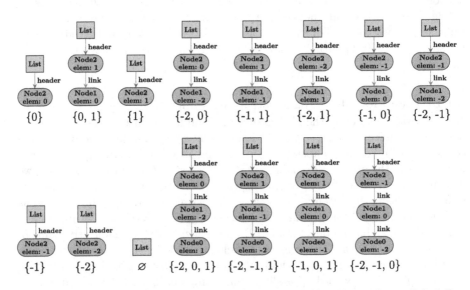

Fig. 4. All 15 solutions enumerated by our technique. Each solution has a linked list (in the concrete domain) and a set (in the abstract domain).

To illustrate, enumerating all solutions for the command "run RepOk for 3 but 2 int" with respect to the model listAF (Fig. 3) using our new technique for directed enumeration creates 15 solutions (Fig. 4) instead of the 41 that default enumeration creates for the model list (Fig. 1). As the scope increases, the reduction in the number of solutions increases. For the command "run RepOk for 6 but 3 int" (i.e., up to 6 nodes and 8 integers $\{-4, -3, \ldots, 2, 3\}$), our directed approach creates 247 solutions whereas the default enumeration creates 28,961 solutions. Generating fewer solutions also takes much less time; for this latter command, our directed approach takes 1.2 s (total) whereas the default enumeration takes 35.1 s (total).

```
module graph
sig Node { edges: set Node }
```

Fig. 5. Alloy model of a graph simplified from CheckMate [46].

2.2 Graph and Transitive Closure

Recent work [5,46,47] used Alloy to model *microarchitectural happens-before* graphs in the context of hardware modeling, and introduced a number of custom techniques to reduce the number of solutions enumerated by the Alloy analyzer since each solution contributed to a security litmus test. Figure 5 shows a minimal Alloy model that represents the nodes and edges of the graph. For this model, the Alloy analyzer enumerates 152 solutions using the default scope of 3.

One reduction the authors desired was to create one representative graph from each class that has the same transitive closure (see Footnote 1). Figure 6 shows how our technique allows defining an *abstraction function*, which basically *is* transitive closure, to direct enumeration as desired. Our technique enumerates only 59 solutions for this model (using the default scope), which reduces the number of enumerated solutions by over 2.5x.

Moreover, if self-loops are not relevant in differentiating solutions, the abstraction function can instead be the *reflexive* transitive closure: "`AbsFun.af = *edges`". Our technique then enumerates 26 solutions for the resulting model (using the default scope), reducing the number over 5.8x over the original model.

```
module graphAF
open graph
one sig AbsFun { af: Node -> Node }
fact AbsFunDef { AbsFun.af = ^edges }
```

Fig. 6. Directing enumeration to create one representative graph from each class that has the same transitive closure.

3 Abstraction-Directed Solution Enumeration

Our basic approach has two parts: (1) an idiom for writing an abstraction function in Alloy (Sect. 3.1); and (2) a technique for using it for solution enumeration (Sect. 3.2). Therefore, to utilize our approach, a user first writes an abstraction function for their model and then invokes our solution enumeration technique. While we focus on abstraction functions, our approach supports more general forms of abstractions to guide solutions enumeration (Sect. 3.3). In future work, we plan to generalize our approach to other solvers, e.g., SMT solvers that allow enumeration [32].

3.1   Idiom

The abstraction function $\alpha : \mathcal{C} \to \mathcal{A}$ maps structures in the concrete domain $\mathcal{C}$ to values in the abstract domain $\mathcal{A}$. In general, each abstract value may itself be a structure. Assume the abstract domain is modeled using k relations $a_1, \ldots, a_k$ ($k \geq 1$). Our idiom for modeling the abstraction function has two basic steps:

1. Add a new singleton sig A with fields $a_1, \ldots, a_k$ that model $\mathcal{A}$; and
2. Add a new fact F to constrain $a_1, \ldots, a_k$ (in A) with respect to the relations that model the concrete domain (to define the abstraction).

Given an initial model m that characterizes the concrete domain, our idiom results in a model m' that consists of m and, in addition, has a new sig A, k new relations $a_1, \ldots, a_k$, and a new fact F. Some examples are shown in Figs. 3 and 6 in Sect. 2. Because F simply *defines* the values for the new relations in terms of the relations in m, and the abstraction function α should be total, any solution to m can be extended to a solution for m'. In other words, the number of solutions for m and m' is identical; there is a bijection between solutions of m (each solution is only a concrete structure) and solutions of m' (each solution is a *pair* of a concrete structure and an abstract value). Therefore, simply writing the abstraction function does *not* by itself reduce the number of solutions enumerated using the Alloy analyzer. However, our new directed enumeration technique enables the reduction (Sect. 3.2).

There are other ways to model abstraction functions in Alloy. Perhaps the simplest is to use the *function* (`fun`) paragraph, which introduces a named expression. For example, for the singly-linked list model (Fig. 1), we can write "`fun AbstractionFunction(): set Int { List.header.*link.elem }`" to define the abstraction function. An advantage is that no new sig (or field) must be added. A disadvantage is that the *return* type (i.e., the type of the expression in the function body), which models the abstract domain, can be just one relation (of arity 1, i.e., a set, or higher). This approach can be extended to support more general return types, e.g., by adding a new sig and fields that model the abstract domain, but doing so reduces this approach to our idiom.

3.2   Directed Enumeration

We next describe our key technique for directing solution enumeration to reduce the number of solutions. Our insight is to require solution enumeration to create solutions that each *differ from all previous solutions with respect to the fields that model the abstraction function*, so the set of all solutions created will not contain two different solutions with the same value in the abstract domain.

In Alloy, solution enumeration is provided by the Kodkod [45] back-end, which uses enumerating SAT solvers [9,11,16,27,42]. When the user desires another solution after a solution, say s, is generated, Kodkod follows the standard practice in modern SAT solvers [11] for solution enumeration and adds a new clause c to the propositional formula in conjunctive normal form (CNF) such that any solution to the new formula will differ from s for at least one

---

Algorithm 1. Abstraction-directed solution enumeration.

Input: Formula ϕ, Scope s, Set of relations Abs.
Output: Solutions enumerated with respect to the given abstraction.

1 $absVars = \{\}$ // empty set of unique ids for variables
2 **foreach** $\rho \in Abs$ **do**
3 |___ $absVars = absVars \cup primaryVariables(\rho)$

4 $solver =$ new Solver(ϕ, s)   // instatiate Kodkod for solution enumeration
5 **while True do**
6 | $solution = solver$.solve()
7 | **if** $solution ==$ **null then break** // no (new) solution found
8 | output($solution$)
9 | // add the negation of the current solution w.r.t. absVars
10 | $negSolAbsVars =$ new int[$absVars$.size()]
11 | int $j = 0$
12 | **for** $i \leftarrow 1$ **to** $solver.numPrimaryVars$ **do**
13 | | **if** $i \in absVars$ **then**
14 | | |___ $negSolAbsVars[j] = solultion$.valueOf($i$) ? $-i$: i
15 | |___ j++

16 |___ $solver$.addClause($negSolAbsVars$)

---

boolean variable. This difference is only with respect to the *primary variables*, which Kodkod creates when it translates the model m to a propositional formula p but before p is translated to a CNF formula, because the translation to CNF introduces auxiliary variables, and only the primary variables directly model the relations in m. Different assignments to auxiliary variables may represent the same assignment for primary variables. However, different assignments to primary variables always represent different solutions to the model.

To direct enumeration using the abstraction function, we adapt Kodkod's enumerator to *require the solutions to differ with respect to only the boolean variables that correspond to the fields that model the abstraction function* (and not all fields in the model as done traditionally). Algorithm 1 shows the pseudocode of our directed enumeration. The inputs are a formula ϕ, a scope s, and a set of all relations Abs that model the abstract domain. For each relation ρ, *primaryVariables* (in Kodkod) returns the set of primary variables that model ρ; Kodkod represents each variable using a unique integer id. The method $solve()$ returns a solution if one exists and *null* otherwise. Lines 10–16 show the logic for adding a new clause $negSolAbsVars$ that ensures the next solution differs from the previous ones *with respect to the abstract domain*.

The guard on Line 13 is the key for restricting solutions to differ at the abstract level; without this guard, we get the Kodkod's traditional enumeration (hence we show the guard explicitly rather than iterating over $absVars$). Kodkod's $numPrimaryVars$ returns the number of priary variables. The new clause only contains *literals* for the primary variables that represent the relations in Abs; for each such variable v, the clause contains literal v, resp. !v, if the value of v is *false*, resp. *true* in the last solution.

3.3 Generalization

We next describe how our approach generalizes to support a wide range of scenarios for directing solution enumeration to create higher quality solutions. Our approach is not restricted to just abstraction functions. In fact, it does not even require the use of the idiom (Sect. 3.1) for modeling abstraction functions! In particular, our directed enumeration algorithm does not require the existence of an abstraction function in the Alloy model. The set of relations *Abs* can be *any* relations that already exist in the model. The user simply marks this set, e.g., in our current tool, as a comma-separated list of relations in the command-line arguments (e.g., −−absRels this/AbsFun,this/AbsFun.af). Thus, our approach embodies a general technique for directed enumeration where the goal is to create solutions that must differ with respect to a given set of relations. Next, we briefly describe how our approach supports three scenarios that differ from traditional abstraction functions.

3.3.1 Focused Enumeration

Consider supporting a *goal* or *criterion*, e.g., a *test purpose*, that the enumerated solutions should meet [2]. For example, Alloy users often write additional constraints in their models to focus enumeration, say to create structures with no disconnected components (as illustrated in Fig. 1). Our approach provides a new way for users to actively focus enumeration, where solution differences that do not matter can be explicitly defined and utilized. To illustrate, the user can define the abstraction function List.header.*link for the model in Fig. 1 to direct enumeration to not create two solutions where the list has the same set of nodes (regardless of whether or not the disconnected components differ).

As another example of focused enumeration, consider enumerating *red-black trees* that are height-balanced binary search trees where each node is colored either red or black [7]. Two red-black trees may be identical as binary search trees and differ only in the node colors. If it is desirable to create solutions that must differ as binary search trees modulo color, our approach directly supports this requirement by using the existing set of relations except color to define the abstraction and direct enumeration of desired red-black trees.

3.3.2 Symmetry Breaking

Symmetry breaking is a widely used technique for helping SAT solvers prune their search or create fewer solutions [8,23,43,52]. Our approach has a three-fold interaction with symmetry breaking.

Abstraction functions in the presence of symmetry breaking constraints for the concrete domain — our idiom is orthogonal to the use of symmetry breaking and can be used regardless of whether the original Alloy model uses symmetry breaking constraints or not;

Symmetry breaking constraints for the abstract domain — our idiom allows defining symmetry breaking constraints for the abstract domain, e.g., to remove isomorphism at the abstract level. The user simply applies the standard practice of adding symmetry breaking constraints but does so only for the relations that model the abstract domain.

Symmetry breaking constraints as abstraction functions — a model m that has explicit symmetry breaking constraints, e.g., as a fact sb, can be augmented using our idiom such that (1) the abstract domain contains new relations that correspond to the relations that are originally in m, and (2) the abstraction function constrains the abstract domain values to equal the concrete domain structures, and lifts the symmetry breaking constraints sb to the abstract domain, which are no longer enforced at the concrete domain. Doing so gives a clean separation of symmetry breaking constraints from the base model because the purpose of these constraints is only to assist the back-end solvers and direct solution enumeration, and they would otherwise not be a part of the model.

3.3.3   Modeling Alternatives

An Alloy model typically evolves through different stages, some of which resemble how code evolves. Specifically, the Alloy user has to balance multiple concerns (correctness, analyzability, readability, etc.) when creating their model. Our approach allows a key separation of concerns that enables the user to consider analyzability — with regards to solution enumeration — as a separate concern when writing the model.

To illustrate, recent work on using Alloy for hardware modeling [46] introduced an initial model that is natural to write but leads to too many solutions. They then used an alternative model to make it more useful for solution enumeration, although the alternative made it cumbersome to write and reason about some key expressions that involved transitive closure (see Footnote 1). The original model used a binary relation "$edges : Node \times Node$" to model edges, where each node is an $\langle Event, Location\rangle$ pair; this model allows the user to simply write "$^\wedge edges$" for transitive closure. The alternative model removed the indirection of using node atoms in the definition of edges, and used a different relation "$edges' : Event \times Location \times Event \times Location$", to ensure the Alloy analyzer does not enumerate the many combinations that relate node atoms to $\langle Event, Location\rangle$ pairs. While the use of $edges'$ reduces the number of solutions enumerated, the use of transitive closure becomes cumbersome because it can only be applied to a homogeneous binary relation, which the user must now construct from $edges'$ before using the transitive closure operator.

With our approach, the user simply defines the alternative formulation using the abstraction without having to rewrite the original constraints, which are written using natural and intuitive formulas. To illustrate, for the $edges$ and $edges'$ example, the user states how the *values* of $edges$ and $edges'$ relate. (The model is available online: https://github.com/Allisonius/Seabs.) Thus, the abstraction function definition simply relates the structures in the original model to the values in the alternative model — without any need to transform or adapt the original structural constraints to the alternative model.

4   Evaluation

This section presents an experimental evaluation of our approach. We use a suite of 15 Alloy models, including data structures that implement abstract data types [7], models from the standard Alloy distribution [1], and models based on recent work that used Alloy for hardware security analysis (see Footnote 1) [5,46,47].

For each model, Table 1 lists the relations in the original model, the relations that define the abstract domain, and the form of abstraction used. The abstract domain relations are either a subset of the relations in the original model, e.g., for *rbt*, or new relations that we introduced for abstraction-directed enumeration and list with their types. The form of abstraction is either traditional abstraction function, e.g., a set implemented as a dynamic data structure (Sect. 2.1), focused enumeration (Sect. 3.3.1), symmetry breaking (Sect. 3.3.2), or modeling alternatives (Sect. 3.3.3).

The models include object arrays (*objarray*), multi-sets of integers (*multiset*), singly-linked lists (*list*, *listsymbr*), doubly-linked lists (*dll*), binary search trees (*bst*, *bstsymbr*), search trees with parent pointers (*bstp*), min-heaps (*minheap*), red-black trees (*rbt*), general directed trees with integers (*dtree*), general directed graphs (*graph* and *graph2*), and specialized modeling of edges as a map between $\langle Event, Location \rangle$ pairs (*graphsym* and *graphsym2*). The *graph*, *graph2*, *graphsym*, and *graphsym2* subjects are based on models from CheckMate [46].

Table 2 presents the results of our experimental evaluation. We consider two versions of Alloy: (1) the latest stable release, i.e., Alloy 4.2; and (2) the latest (possibly unstable) build, i.e., Alloy 5.0 [1]. We use each version to compare, for each model, the two techniques: (1) Alloy analyzer's default enumeration for the original Alloy model (*Original*) and (2) our abstraction-directed enumeration for the augmented model that includes the desired abstraction (*Abstraction-directed enumeration*). For each technique, the table lists the number of all (boolean) variables in the SAT encoding (*#Var*), the number of primary variables (*#PVar*), the number of all clauses (*#Cls*), the number of solutions (*#Sol*), and the time taken to find all solutions ($T_{v.4}$ using Alloy 4.2 and $T_{v.5}$ using Alloy 5.0). For each model, the table also lists the scope (*Scope*), which we selected as the minimum of 10 and the largest scope for which the default enumeration can enumerate all solutions in under 1 minute (so that all experiments finish in a reasonable time).

For all but 2 cases, the number of primary variables is smaller for the original model than the model that includes the abstraction to guide solution enumeration. Being smaller is expected, as modeling the abstraction introduces a new sig and relation(s). For 2 cases (*bstp* and *rbt*), the numbers are the same because the abstraction is simply a subset of the *existing* relations.

As expected, the number of solutions enumerated by our technique is no more than the number enumerated by the default enumeration. For one case (*objarray*), the numbers are the same, because the Alloy's default symmetry breaking behaves the same as the abstraction function we defined. Across all cases, the number of solutions can be reduced by up to 405.3x (*dtree*).

Table 1. Models used in our evaluation.

Model	Relations - Original Model	Relations - Abstract Domain	Abstraction
objarray	ObjectArray.array	AbsFun.af: set Object	Traditional − set of objects
list	List.header, Node.elem Node.link	AbsFun.af: set Int	Traditional − set of integers
bst	BST.root, BST.size, Node.key, Node.left, Node.right	AbsFun.af: set Int	Traditional − set of integers
minheap	MinHeap.root, Node.key, Node.left, Node.right	AbsFun.af: set Int	Traditional − set of integers
dll	DLL.header, Node.pre, Node.nxt, Node.elem	AbsFun.af: set Int	Traditional − set of integers
dtree	Tree.root, Node.edges, Node.elem,	AbsFun.af: set Int	Traditional − set of integers
graph	Node.edges	AbsFun.af: Node×Node	Focused enumeration − transitive closure
graph2	Node.edges	AbsFun.af: Node×Node	Focused enumeration − reflexive transitive closure
bstp	BST.root, BST.size, Node.key, Node.left, Node.right, Node.parent	Node.parent	Focused enumeration − parent must differ
rbt	RBT.root, RBT.size Node.key, Node.left, Node.right, Node.color	RBT.root, RBT.size Node.key, Node.left, Node.right	Focused enumeration − search tree must differ
listsymbr	List.header, Node.elem Node.link	AbsFun.af1: List×Node, AbsFun.af2: Node×Int, AbsFun.af3: Node×Node	Symmetry breaking − non-isomorphic structures
bstsymbr	BST.root, BST.size, Node.key, Node.left, Node.right	AbsFun.af: set Int	Symmetry breaking and traditional
multiset	MultiSet.array, MultiSet.length	AbsFun.array: Int×Int, AbsFun.length: Int	Modeling alternatives − sorted array of integers
graphsym	Node.event, Node.location, Node.edges	AbsFun.af: Event×Location× Event×Location	Modeling alternatives − map between $\langle E, L \rangle$ pairs
graphsym2	Node.event, Node.location Node.edges	AbsFun.af1: Event×Location AbsFun.af2: Event×Location× Event×Location	Modeling alternatives − two maps to allow isolated nodes

For Alloy 4.2 (the latest stable release), for all cases, enumerating all solutions using our technique takes less time than the default enumeration. The time speedup using our technique is between 1.1x (*rbt*) to 74.9x (*dtree*). For Alloy 5.0 (the latest, possibly unstable, build), the relative performance results are

Table 2. Performance comparison between the techniques. Times are in seconds.

Model	Original						Abstraction-directed enumeration						Scope
	#Var	#PVar	#Cls	#Sol	$T_{v.4}$	$T_{v.5}$	#Var	#PVar	#Cls	#Sol	$T_{v.4}$	$T_{v.5}$	
bst	14036	341	34936	2179	40.9	40.2	13779	357	34099	9	2.9	2.5	9
bstp	8200	290	18954	625	4.6	7.7	8018	290	18211	429	3.6	7.6	7
bstsymbr	12780	332	34220	626	13.4	8.5	12523	348	33383	9	4.0	13.9	9
dtree	1244	75	2751	88769	59.9	59.3	1319	83	3254	219	0.8	0.7	5
dll	2113	132	5119	28961	22.6	24.9	2196	140	5354	247	0.5	0.5	6
list	1874	96	4742	28961	24.0	24.7	1957	104	4977	247	0.5	0.6	6
listsymbr	1874	96	4742	28961	24.0	24.7	1696	180	4232	20160	9.1	8.9	6
minheap	2322	100	5033	15913	13.0	12.0	2397	108	5236	219	0.6	0.6	5
multiset	306	72	489	585	1.0	1.0	1662	144	4257	165	0.3	0.6	3
graph	138	20	200	6344	4.9	4.3	448	36	994	671	0.6	0.9	4
graph2	138	20	200	6344	4.9	4.3	460	36	994	190	0.3	0.9	4
graphsym	360	36	500	915	1.7	1.6	4323	126	7319	148	0.8	0.6	3
graphsym2	360	36	500	915	1.7	1.6	4515	126	7652	170	1.0	0.5	3
objarray	1398	110	3716	11	0.5	0.5	1478	120	3843	11	0.2	0.1	10
rbt	8639	255	20648	84	4.5	11.0	8373	255	19737	65	4.1	13.4	7

different for 2 cases (*bstsymbr* and *rbt*) where our technique has a slowdown of 1.6x and 2.9x for *bstsymbr* and *rbt*, respectively; however, the number of solutions is not impacted by the choice of the Alloy version and is still substantially reduced. Moreover, because each solution may be used for expensive post-processing [46] (e.g., to test long-running code executed on each solution), the number of solutions can be more important than the time to generate them. Across the remaining 13 cases, the time speedup using our technique is between 1.7x (*graphsym2*) to 84.7x (*dtree*). Overall, the performances of Alloy 4.2 and Alloy 5.0 are similar.

5   Conclusions

We introduced solution enumeration abstraction, a new modeling idiom that allows Alloy users to define abstractions to enhance solution enumeration. The user specifies how the solutions must differ, so enumeration creates a high quality set of solutions of a manageable size. We implemented our technique on top of the Alloy tool-set and evaluated using a variety of abstractions to show the generality and usefulness of the proposed idiom. The experimental results show that the technique can substantially reduce the number of solutions and the time taken to enumerate them.

Acknowledgments. We thank Caroline Trippel for sharing some of her excellent Alloy models and commenting on an earlier paper draft. This work was partially supported by NSF grants. CNS-1646305, CCF-1718903, CNS-1740916, and CCF-1918189, and an Intel ISRA grant for research on hardware security.

References

1. Alloy analyzer Website (2019). http://alloytools.org
2. Ammann, P., Offutt, J.: Introduction to Software Testing. Cambridge University Press, Cambridge (2008)
3. Bagheri, H., Kang, E., Malek, S., Jackson, D.: A Formal Approach for Detection of Security Flaws in the Android Permission System. Formal Aspects of Computing. Springer, London (2018). https://doi.org/10.1007/s00165-017-0445-z
4. Boyapati, C., Khurshid, S., Marinov, D.: Korat: Automated testing based on Java predicates. In: ISSTA (2002)
5. CheckMate GitHub (2019). https://github.com/ctrippel/checkmate
6. Chong, N., Sorensen, T., Wickerson, J.: The semantics of transactions and weak memory in x86, Power, ARM, and C++. In: PLDI (2018)
7. Cormen, T.H., Leiserson, C.E., Rivest, R.L., Stein, C.: Introduction to Algorithms, 3rd edn. The MIT Press, Cambridge (2009)
8. Crawford, J.: A theoretical analysis of reasoning by symmetry in first-order logic (extended abstract). In: AAAI 1992 Workshop on Tractable Reasoning (1992)
9. CryptoMiniSat Solver Website (2019). https://www.msoos.org/cryptominisat5/
10. Dutra, R., Bachrach, J., Sen, K.: SMTSampler: efficient stimulus generation from complex SMT constraints. In: ICCAD (2018)
11. Een, N., Sorensson, N.: An extensible SAT-solver. In: SAT (2003)
12. Filieri, A., Pasareanu, C.S., Visser, W.: Reliability analysis in Symbolic PathFinder. In: ICSE (2013)
13. Galeotti, J.P., Rosner, N., Pombo, C.G.L., Frias, M.F.: TACO: efficient SAT-based bounded verification using symmetry breaking and tight bounds. TSE **39**(9), 1283–1307 (2013)
14. Ghiya, R., Hendren, L.J.: Is it a tree, a DAG, or a cyclic graph? a shape analysis for heap-directed pointers in C. In: POPL (1996)
15. Gligoric, M., Gvero, T., Jagannath, V., Khurshid, S., Kuncak, V., Marinov, D.: Test generation through programming in UDITA. In: ICSE (2010)
16. Glucose Solver Website (2019). https://www.labri.fr/perso/lsimon/glucose/
17. Gopinath, D., Malik, M.Z., Khurshid, S.: Specification-based program repair using SAT. In: TACAS (2011)
18. Guttag, J.V., Horning, J.J.: Larch: Languages and Tools for Formal Specification (1993)
19. Jackson, D.: Software Abstractions: Logic, Language, and Analysis. The MIT Press, Cambridge (2006)
20. Jackson, D., Sullivan, K.J.: COM revisited: Tool-assisted modelling of an architectural framework. In: SIGSOFT FSE (2000)
21. Jackson, D., Vaziri, M.: Finding bugs with a constraint solver. In: ISSTA (2000)
22. Khurshid, S., Jackson, D.: Exploring the design of an intentional naming scheme with an automatic constraint analyzer. In: ASE (2000)
23. Khurshid, S., Marinov, D., Shlyakhter, I., Jackson, D.: A case for efficient solution enumeration. In: SAT (2003)
24. Kuraj, I., Kuncak, V., Jackson, D.: Programming with enumerable sets of structures. In: OOPSLA (2015)
25. Leavens, G.T., Baker, A.L., Ruby, C.: Preliminary design of JML: a behavioral interface specification language for Java. Softw. Eng. Notes **31**(3), 1–38 (2006)
26. Leino, K.R.M., Müller, P.: A verification methodology for model fields. In: ESOP (2006)

27. Lingeling, Plingeling, and Treengeling Website (2019). http://fmv.jku.at/lingeling/
28. Liskov, B., Guttag, J.: Program development in Java: Abstraction, Specification, and Object-Oriented Design (2000)
29. Manevich, R., Yahav, E., Ramalingam, G., Sagiv, M.: Predicate abstraction and canonical abstraction for singly-linked lists. In: VMCAI, pp. 181–198 (2005)
30. Marinov, D., Khurshid, S.: TestEra: a novel framework for automated testing of Java programs. In: ASE (2001)
31. Meel, K.S., et al.: Constrained sampling and counting: universal hashing meets SAT solving. In: Beyond NP, AAAI Workshop (2016)
32. de Moura, L., Bjorner, N.: Z3: an efficient SMT solver. In: TACAS (2008)
33. Nelson, T., Saghafi, S., Dougherty, D.J., Fisler, K., Krishnamurthi, S.: Aluminum: principled scenario exploration through minimality. In: ICSE, pp. 232–241 (2013)
34. Pacheco, C., Ernst, M.D.: Randoop: feedback-directed random testing for Java. In: OOPSLA Companion, pp. 815–816 (2007)
35. Ponzio, P., Aguirre, N., Frias, M.F., Visser, W.: Field-exhaustive testing. In: SIGSOFT FSE (2016)
36. Porncharoenwase, S., Nelson, T., Krishnamurthi, S.: CompoSAT: specification-guided coverage for model finding. In: FM (2018)
37. Păsăreanu, C.S., Pelánek, R., Visser, W.: Concrete model checking with abstract matching and refinement. In: CAV (2005)
38. Rayside, D., Benjamin, Z., Singh, R., Near, J.P., Milicevic, A., Jackson, D.: Equality and hashing for (almost) free: generating implementations from abstraction functions. In: ICSE (2009)
39. Rayside, D., Montaghami, V., Leung, F., Yuen, A., Xu, K., Jackson, D.: Synthesizing iterators from abstraction functions. In: GPCE (2012)
40. Ringer, T., Grossman, D., Schwartz-Narbonne, D., Tasiran, S.: A solver-aided language for test input generation. In: PACMPL OOPSLA (2017)
41. Samimi, H., Aung, E.D., Millstein, T.D.: Falling back on executable specifications. In: ECOOP (2010)
42. SAT4J Solver Website (2019). https://www.sat4j.org/
43. Shlyakhter, I.: Generating effective symmetry-breaking predicates for search problems. In: SAT (2001)
44. Sullivan, A., Wang, K., Zaeem, R.N., Khurshid, S.: Automated test generation and mutation testing for Alloy. In: ICST (2017)
45. Torlak, E., Jackson, D.: Kodkod: a relational model finder. In: TACAS (2007)
46. Trippel, C., Lustig, D., Martonosi, M.: CheckMate: automated synthesis of hardware exploits and security litmus tests. In: MICRO (2018)
47. Trippel, C., Lustig, D., Martonosi, M.: Security verification via automatic hardware-aware exploit synthesis: The CheckMate approach. In: IEEE Micro (2019)
48. Wickerson, J., Batty, M., Sorensen, T., Constantinides, G.A.: Automatically comparing memory consistency models. In: POPL (2017)
49. Xie, T., Marinov, D., Notkin, D.: Rostra: a framework for detecting redundant object-oriented unit tests. In: ASE (2004)
50. Zaeem, R.N., Khurshid, S.: Contract-based data structure repair using Alloy. In: ECOOP (2010)
51. Zave, P.: Reasoning about identifier spaces: how to make chord correct. IEEE Trans. Softw. Eng. **43**(12), 1144–1156 (2017)
52. Zhang, J.: The generation and application of finite models. Ph.D. thesis, Institute of Software, Academia Sinica, Beijing (1994)

Formal Analysis of Qualitative Long-Term Behaviour in Parametrised Boolean Networks

Nikola Beneš, Luboš Brim, Samuel Pastva, Jakub Poláček,
and David Šafránek$^{(\boxtimes)}$

Faculty of Informatics, Masaryk University, Brno, Czech Republic
{xbenes3,brim,xpastva,xpolace3,safranek}@fi.muni.cz

Abstract. Boolean networks offer an elegant way to model the behaviour of complex systems with positive and negative feedback. The long-term behaviour of a Boolean network is characterised by its attractors. Depending on various logical parameters, a Boolean network can exhibit vastly different types of behaviour. Hence, the structure and quality of attractors can undergo a significant change known in systems theory as attractor bifurcation. In this paper, we establish formally the notion of attractor bifurcation for Boolean networks. We propose a semi-symbolic approach to attractor bifurcation analysis based on a parallel algorithm. We use machine-learning techniques to construct a compact, human-readable, representation of the bifurcation analysis results. We demonstrate the method on a set of highly parametrised Boolean networks.

Keywords: Attractor analysis · Machine learning · Boolean networks

1 Introduction

Complex systems appearing in biology, chemistry, physics, and engineering are composed of hundreds to thousands of components whose *interactions* give rise to systems collective behaviours. *Regulatory networks* (RNs), also known as gene regulatory networks [15], Thomas' networks [35], discrete or logical regulatory networks, offer an elegant, holistic, and mathematically rigorous way to model these complicated interactions [26]. In regulatory networks, the long-term behaviour of a system is characterised by the so-called *attractors*. For example, in biology such attractors can represent the phenotypes of a living cell. The typical types of attractors are sinks, cycles, or chaotic attractors. Identification and classification of attractors in the state space of a RN is thus a very important step towards understanding of systems behaviour.

In this paper, we focus on a basic form of RNs represented by *Boolean networks* (BNs). In BNs, systems components are modelled as Boolean variables. Edges in BNs represent positive or negative interactions between variables.

D. Šafránek—This work has been supported by the Czech Science Foundation grant No. 18-00178S.

Y. Ait-Ameur and S. Qin (Eds.): ICFEM 2019, LNCS 11852, pp. 353–369, 2019.
https://doi.org/10.1007/978-3-030-32409-4_22

The behaviour of Boolean networks is sensitive to various *logical parameters*. To that end, in this paper, we primarily work with *parametrised Boolean networks* (PBNs). It is worth noting that the method can be straightforwardly extended to general (multi-valued) RNs. Due to their binary character, BNs have significantly smaller states space and parameter space allowing, in combination with parallel algorithms, more efficient analysis of large-scale networks. Despite its simplicity, BNs are frequently used to model important phenomena in genetics or biology.

The structure and quality (types) of attractors may undergo a significant change when parameters vary their values. In the literature of continuous dynamical systems, such dramatic changes are called *bifurcations* and the parameter values for which a bifurcation occurs are termed *bifurcation points* [25]. As attractors represent the long-term behaviours, the focus on *attractor bifurcation* analysis is fundamental to a full understanding of diverse properties of BNs, e.g., their structural stability.

We consider two central sub-problems related to the attractor bifurcation analysis in PBNs. The first one is the computation of the so-called *bifurcation function*, which maps parameter values to a multi-set of attractor types that are present in the system for the given parameter value. The second, and in some sense equally serious, sub-problem is the presentation of the multi-dimensional bifurcation function to the end-user in the form of a *bifurcation diagram* which visually summarises the succession of bifurcations as parameters change and identifies the bifurcation points.

One might attempt using the methods of bifurcation analysis as known from continuous-time dynamical systems [25]. However, the study of bifurcations in discrete-time discrete-space systems, as is the case of PBNs, requires an entirely different framework. The reasons are twofold: First, the parameters, variables and behaviours in these systems are not continuous, so the concept of a small, smooth change does not exist. However, even if we consider other measures of closeness, such as Hamming distance between parametrisations, we still have to overcome the second issue: multi-dimensionality. While the traditional continuous view on bifurcation also suffers from dimensional blow-up, it is generally accepted that performing bifurcation analysis even for one or two parameters can be beneficial. In PBNs, the parameter domains are much simpler, so considering just one or two parameters is often not enough to uncover interesting behaviour. Moreover, it also significantly complicates presenting the results concisely to the user.

Our contribution to the bifurcation analysis for PBNs is threefold: (i) We establish the notion of attractor bifurcation for PBNs, (ii) we propose a semi-symbolic approach for computing the bifurcation function, (iii) we employ machine learning techniques to efficiently construct and visualise bifurcation diagrams.

In discrete systems, attractors are typically understood as terminal strongly connected components (TSCC) of the system [22,24]. This corresponds to the intuitive notion of states where the behaviour eventually stays forever. To compute the bifurcation function, we employ the *asynchronous semantics* of BNs and introduce its extension to PBNs. Subsequently, we use an on-the-fly parallel semi-symbolic algorithm for computing TSCCs which itself is based on ideas from [5]. Instead of using SMT to decide over real-valued parameters in differential models, we employ BDDs that are more efficient for PBNs with asynchronous update. The identified TSCCs are classified and collected into a bifurcation function. The bifurcation diagram is then represented in the form of a *bifurcation decision tree*, which provides an *exact* description of the bifurcation function and is learned from its symbolic representation using machine learning techniques. This way we tackle the problem of presenting the many-dimensional analysis result in a concise and human-readable format.

Related Work. Attractor identification has been recently studied with non-parametric BNs (see [2] for an overview). Some of the existing algorithms take advantage of synchronous update semantics that significantly simplifies the problem [15]. This allows for efficient exact solutions in terms of SAT [13,34], constraint programming [12], or integer-programming [4]. A BDD-based representation is employed, e.g., in [15,37]. In [16] it is shown that SMT-based techniques work well in PBNs with synchronous update. However, it is known that synchronous update can produce unrealistic attractors [22,31]. Models with asynchronous update cover in most cases the real attractors quite well, though it has been recently shown that some exceptions exist [10]. Nevertheless, the problem of attractor identification becomes more difficult due to the non-deterministic nature of the state transitions. Most of the works for asynchronous models target the non-parametric case only. Various techniques have been employed including BDDs [15,28], optimisation [20,21], algebraic-based methods [18], SAT [17], answer set programming [27], concurrency theory [9], sampling [38], or network structure decomposition [11]. Here we focus on the parametric case with the asynchronous update semantics.

The parameter space of a biological system explodes combinatorially with the arity of component interactions. To that end, attractor detection in parametrised models remains to be a grand challenge in general. It is worth noting that parametrised network semantics can be entirely encoded using the BDD framework [28]. However, then the problem is that algorithms efficiency and scalability entirely rely on concrete construction procedures of BDDs. In this paper, we combine explicit state representation with symbolic BDD representation of parameters. This allows us to adapt the existing sequential SCC-detection algorithms and also to develop new on-the-fly and parallel algorithms fine-tuned for the specific needs of attractor analysis.

To the best of our knowledge, this paper introduces bifurcation analysis to PBNs for the first time. Most of the mentioned techniques focus primarily on attractor detection in non-parametric settings. A distinct feature of our approach is a fully-automatised classification of the attractors characterising the attractor structure at the semantics level. In [3,24] the authors elaborate at the level of the network structure to study the systems behaviour and its stability using (manual) analytical methods in non-parametric cases.

2   Parametrised Boolean Networks

We start this section with the definition of (non-parametrised) Boolean networks and their asynchronous semantics, together with the notion of attractors. We then follow with the description of the parametrised version and a means of restricting the parametrisation space using static constraints.

Definition 1. *A* Boolean network (BN) *is a tuple* $\mathcal{B} = (\mathcal{V}, R, \mathcal{F})$ *such that:*

- $\mathcal{V} = \{A, B, \ldots\}$ *is a finite set of Boolean state variables.*
- $R \subseteq \mathcal{V} \times \mathcal{V}$ *is a set of* regulations. *For* $A \in \mathcal{V}$, *we say that* $\mathcal{C}(A) = \{B \in \mathcal{V} \mid (B, A) \in R\}$ *is the* context *of* A, *i.e. the subset of* $\mathcal{V}$ *regulating* A.
- $\mathcal{F} = \{F_A \mid A \in \mathcal{V}\}$ *is a family of* logical update functions. *The signature of each* F_A *is given by the context of* A *as* $F_A : \{0,1\}^{|\mathcal{C}(A)|} \to \{0,1\}$.

The state space *of* $\mathcal{B}$, $\Pi(\mathcal{B}) = \{0,1\}^{|\mathcal{V}|}$, *is then the set of all possible Boolean configurations of the variables (assuming some arbitrary fixed variable ordering).*

For $(A, B) \in R$, we say that A is a *regulator* of B. For a state $s \in \Pi(\mathcal{B})$ and a variable $A \in \mathcal{V}$, we write $s(A)$ to denote the value of A in s. We use $s[A \mapsto k]$ for some $k \in \{0, 1\}$ to denote a copy of the state s with the value of variable A set to k. Finally, for a state s and an update function F_A, we abuse the notation and write $F_A(s)$ to denote F_A applied to s restricted to the context of A.

In Boolean networks, one also often describes various properties of the network regulations. Here, we focus on three most basic types of regulation:

Observability: We say that $(A, B) \in R$ is observable if there exists a configuration where changing the value of A also changes the value of F_B, formally:

$$\exists s \in \Pi(\mathcal{B}) : F_B(s[A \mapsto 0]) \neq F_B(s[A \mapsto 1])$$

Activation and *Inhibition:* We say that a regulation $(A, B) \in R$ is activating if by increasing A, one cannot decrease the value of F_B. Symmetrically, the regulation is inhibiting if by increasing A, one cannot increase the value of F_B:

$$\text{Activation: } \forall s \in \Pi(\mathcal{B}) : F_B(s[A \mapsto 0]) \Rightarrow F_B(s[A \mapsto 1])$$
$$\text{Inhibition: } \forall s \in \Pi(\mathcal{B}) : F_B(s[A \mapsto 0]) \Leftarrow F_B(s[A \mapsto 1])$$

A regulation which is not observable has no effect in the network. On the other hand, activation and inhibition in biological models can be viewed as a positive or negative feedback, where presence of one biochemical substance enables or disables production of another substance.

The semantics of a Boolean network can be described using a directed graph, where the vertices of the graph are the states of the network and edges represent the evolution of the network state. We consider the state of the Boolean network to evolve in an *asynchronous* manner, i.e. each variable is updated independently:

Definition 2. *Let $\mathcal{B} = (\mathcal{V}, R, \mathcal{F})$ be a BN. The* asynchronous semantics *of $\mathcal{B}$ is a directed graph $Async(\mathcal{B}) = (\Pi(\mathcal{B}), E)$, where $E \subseteq \Pi(\mathcal{B}) \times \Pi(\mathcal{B})$ such that $(u, v) \in E$ if and only if $u \neq v$ and there exists a variable $\mathtt{A} \in \mathcal{V}$ for which $v = u[\mathtt{A} \mapsto F_{\mathtt{A}}(u)]$.*

For two states s and t of a BN $\mathcal{B}$, we write $s \to t$ if $(s, t) \in E$ of $Async(\mathcal{B})$ and $s \to^* t$ if $(s, t) \in E^*$, where E^* is the reflexive and transitive closure of E.

The long-term behaviour that we are interested in is captured by the notion of *attractors*. As explained in the introduction, in discrete-state systems represented by graphs, attractors are understood as terminal strongly connected components of the graph. In the following, we use the two terms interchangeably.

Definition 3. *Let $\mathcal{B} = (\mathcal{V}, R, \mathcal{F})$ be a BN. We define an* attractor *of $\mathcal{B}$ to be a terminal strongly connected component (TSCC) of $Async(\mathcal{B}) = (\Pi(\mathcal{B}), E)$, i.e. a maximal subset $A \subseteq \Pi(\mathcal{B})$ such that for all $s, t \in A$, $s \to^* t$, and for all $s \in A$ and $t \in \Pi(\mathcal{B})$, $s \to t$ implies $t \in A$.*

Parametrised Boolean Networks. For complex networks, fully determining the update function family $\mathcal{F}$ from data or literature can be very challenging. To deal with this uncertainty, we extend the Boolean network with a set of logical parameters which determine the exact behaviour of each update function. The parametrised logical update functions then either return a Boolean value or a logical parameter representing the uncertainty of the behaviour. Formally, we define the parametrised Boolean network as follows:

Definition 4. *We define a* parametrised Boolean network (PBN) *to be a tuple $\widehat{\mathcal{B}} = (\mathcal{V}, \mathcal{P}, R, P, \mathfrak{F})$. Here, $\mathcal{V}$ and R are the same as in Definition 1. Additionally:*

- $\mathcal{P} = \{\mathtt{P}, \mathtt{Q}, \ldots\}$ *is a finite set of Boolean logical parameters;*
- $P \subseteq \{0, 1\}^{\mathcal{P}}$ *is a subset of valid parametrisations;*
- $\mathfrak{F} = \{\widehat{F}_{\mathtt{A}} \mid \mathtt{A} \in \mathcal{V}\}$ *is a family of parametrised logical update functions. The signature of each $\widehat{F}_{\mathtt{A}}$ is given as $\widehat{F}_{\mathtt{A}} : \{0, 1\}^{|\mathcal{C}(\mathtt{A})|} \to (\{0, 1\} \cup \mathcal{P})$.*

Similar to states, for a parametrisation $p \in P$, we write $p(\mathtt{P})$ to denote the value of $\mathtt{P}$ in p and we also use the same notation $p[\mathtt{P} \mapsto k]$ for substitution. The notion of state space of a PBN is identical to that of a BN. By fixing a concrete $p \in P$, we get a family of (non-parametrised) logical update functions $\mathfrak{F}_p = \{F_{\mathtt{A}} \mid \mathtt{A} \in \mathcal{V}\}$ such that $F_{\mathtt{A}}(s) = \widehat{F}_{\mathtt{A}}(s)$ if $\widehat{F}_{\mathtt{A}}(s) \in \{0, 1\}$ and $F_{\mathtt{A}}(s) = p(\widehat{F}_{\mathtt{A}}(s))$ otherwise. We thus obtain a standard BN $\widehat{\mathcal{B}}_p = (\mathcal{V}, R, \mathfrak{F}_p)$. We can then generalize the definition of attractors to PBNs, saying that a subset $A \subseteq \Pi(\widehat{\mathcal{B}})$ is an *attractor in parametrisation* $p \in P$ if A is an attractor of $\widehat{\mathcal{B}}_p$. For different parametrisations, the attractors do not have to overlap, thus it is important to always specify the exact parametrisations for which A represents an attractor. The asynchronous semantics of a PBN can be described using an edge-coloured graph:

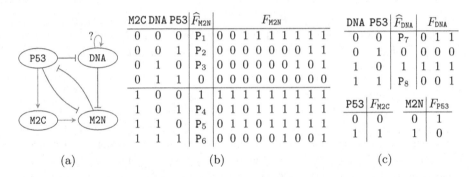

Fig. 1. (a) A simplified PBN describing the DNA damage mechanism adapted from [1]. Every regulation is either activating (green) or inhibiting (red) and observable, except for (DNA, DNA), which is not necessarily observable. (b) Valid update functions F_{M2N} satisfying the static constraints. (c) Valid update functions F_{DNA}, F_{M2C} and F_{P53} satisfying the static constraints. (Color figure online)

Definition 5. *Let $\widehat{\mathcal{B}} = (\mathcal{V}, \mathcal{P}, R, P, \mathfrak{F})$ be a PBN. The asynchronous semantics of $\widehat{\mathcal{B}}$ is an edge-coloured directed graph $Async(\widehat{\mathcal{B}}) = (\Pi(\widehat{\mathcal{B}}), E, P)$ where P is a set of edge colours and $E \subseteq \Pi(\widehat{\mathcal{B}}) \times P \times \Pi(\widehat{\mathcal{B}})$ is a set of coloured edges such that $(u, p, v) \in E$ if and only if $u \to v$ in $Async(\widehat{\mathcal{B}}_p)$.*

Obviously, by fixing $p \in P$ in $Async(\widehat{\mathcal{B}})$, one can obtain the directed graph $Async(\widehat{\mathcal{B}}_p)$. Given a fixed $Async(\widehat{\mathcal{B}}) = (\Pi(\widehat{\mathcal{B}}), E, P)$, we also write $\mathbb{C}(u, v) = \{p \in P \mid (u, p, v) \in E\}$ to denote the set of colours which enable the edge $u \to v$. In the following we assume that the set $\mathbb{C}(u, v)$ is represented symbolically while the state space is considered explictly. For that reason, we speak about a *semi-symbolic* graph.

Static Parameter Constraints. In general, the set of possible parametrisations can be even doubly-exponential in the size of the network [36]. It is thus critical to restrict the parameter space as much as possible. Furthermore, a fully parametrised network can be prone to overfitting. To that end, it is useful to supplement regulations with static constraints limiting their outcomes [19,33].

We already presented observability, activation and inhibition as specific properties of regulations. In a parametrised setting, these properties can be used as constraints to restrict the parametrisation space. We assume that every regulation in a PBN can be marked with a subset of these three constraints. Then for all $p \in P$ of $\widehat{\mathcal{B}}$, $\widehat{\mathcal{B}}_p$ must adhere to these constraints, e.g. a regulation marked observable in $\widehat{\mathcal{B}}$ must be observable in $\widehat{\mathcal{B}}_p$ and the same for activation and inhibition.

In Fig. 1a, we show such parametrised Boolean network where all regulations are marked as either activating or inhibiting. Figures 1b and 1c then show the possible update functions satisfying these static constraints together with the corresponding logical parameters. Note that the fully parametrised model would have 16 parameters and 65536 parametrisations, but by applying the static constraints, only 27 parametrisations remain valid, significantly reducing the size of the associated coloured graph.

3   Attractor Bifurcation Using Component Analysis

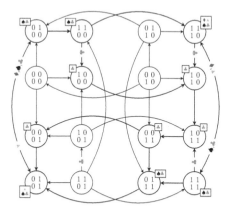

While PBNs allows us to capture the uncertainty of interactions between individual components of the network, the long-term behaviour of a PBN can vary drastically depending on parametrisation. Consider the coloured graph in Fig. 2, depicting the asynchronous semantics and attractors of four specific parametrisations of the PBN in Fig. 1a. All parametrisations are very similar, yet the long-term behaviour of the network is clearly very different in each case. This brings up a natural question: Which parameter values influence the long-term behaviour of the network and in what way?

Fig. 2. The asynchronous semantics of the PBN given in Fig. 1a, restricted to $P = \{\blacklozenge, \vartriangle, \spadesuit, \clubsuit\}$. Here, $\blacklozenge = \{P_{2,3,6} : 0, P_{1,4,5,7,8} : 1\}$, $\vartriangle = \blacklozenge[P_3 \mapsto 1]$, $\spadesuit = \blacklozenge[P_6 \mapsto 1]$, and $\clubsuit = \spadesuit[P_8 \mapsto 0]$. The unlabelled edges are enabled for all parametrisations. The highlighted vertices represent attractors for indicated parametrisations. (Color figure online)

3.1   Attractor Bifurcation

In continuous systems, one typically refers to this type of change in long-term behaviour due to parameter variation as *bifurcation*, we thus utilise this term as well. In accordance with the continuous case, we also consider three primary types of long-term behaviour:

Stability ($\odot$): An attractor A of $\mathcal{B}$ is considered stable if $|A| = 1$, i.e. the attractor consists of a single state in which the network stays forever. Observe that for parametrisation $\blacklozenge$, we have one stable attractor (1110) whereas for $\vartriangle$, there are two stable attractors (0101 and 1110).

Oscillation ($\circlearrowright$): An attractor A of $\mathcal{B}$ is considered oscillating if it is not stable and if A can be partitioned into pairwise disjoint sets $A_1, \ldots A_k$ such that for all $s \in A_i$, if $s \to t$, then $t \in A_{(i+1) \bmod k}$. The simplest example of an oscillating attractor is a *cycle*, where $|A_i| = 1$ for each A_i. A cycle is also present in our example under parametrisation $\spadesuit$, consisting of states $0101 \to 0100 \to 1100 \to 1110 \to 1111 \to 0111$.

Disorder ($\rightleftarrows$): Finally, attractor A is considered disordered if it is not stable nor oscillating. This means that due to non-determinism, the network will stay in A forever, but behave unpredictably. In our example graph, such attractor is visible for parametrisation $\clubsuit$.

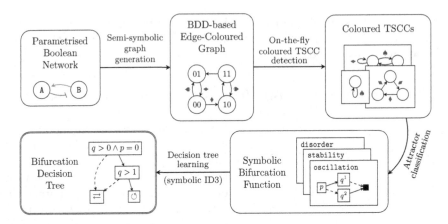

Fig. 3. Overview of the proposed method for computing the bifurcation function and the construction of the bifurcation decision tree of a PBN.

The long-term behaviour of a BN is then characterised by a multi-set over the universe of the three behaviours $\{\odot, \circlearrowleft, \rightleftarrows\}$. We call such multi-set a *behavioural class* c and we denote the set of all behavioural classes $\mathfrak{C}$. We say that c is a behavioural class of G, where G is a directed graph, if the multiplicity and types of attractors in G match c. The problem of attractor bifurcation for PBN is then defined as follows:

Definition 6. *The problem of attractor bifurcation for a PBN $\widehat{\mathcal{B}} = (\mathcal{V}, \mathcal{P}, R, P, \mathfrak{F})$ is to compute a bifurcation function $\mathcal{A} : P \to \mathfrak{C}$ which assigns to each parametrisation P the behavioural class of $Async(\widehat{\mathcal{B}}_p)$.*

3.2 Computing Bifurcation Function

Our approach is illustrated in Fig. 3. In this section, we address the construction of the bifurcation function. First, we take a PBN $\widehat{\mathcal{B}}$ and compute a BDD-based semi-symbolic graph of its asynchronous semantics $Async(\widehat{\mathcal{B}})$. This allows us to utilise efficient parallel algorithms while maintaining the advantages of the symbolic representation. We then use a parallel TSCC detection algorithm based on [5], extracting the attractors of $Async(\widehat{\mathcal{B}})$ on-the-fly. Each attractor is classified as stable, oscillating, or disordered and this information is used to incrementally build the bifurcation function $\mathcal{A}$. The problem of visualising the bifurcation function using machine learning is then addressed in the next section.

BDD-Based Parameter Representation. While the static parameter constraints typically provide a significant reduction of parameter space, real-world parametrised networks are still too large to represent explicitly. We thus rely on symbolic representation of parametrisation sets to handle large models. As the symbolic data structure, we use reduced ordered binary decision diagrams [7].

Given a $\widehat{\mathcal{B}} = (\mathcal{V}, \mathcal{P}, P, R, \mathfrak{F})$, the logical parameters $\mathsf{P} \in \mathcal{P}$ serve as the Boolean variables in the BDD representation. Each BDD represents a unique Boolean formula over $\mathcal{P}$ which we also view as a set of parametrisations satisfying this formula. We assume that P is also given as a BDD. We can then implement standard operations over parametrisation sets: $B_1 \cap B_2$ becomes $B_1 \wedge B_2$, $B_1 \cup B_2$ becomes $B_1 \vee B_2$, $B_1 \setminus B_2$ becomes $B_1 \wedge \neg B_2$, and emptiness checking becomes satisfiability checking. From now on, we will thus use the terms BDD and parametrisation set interchangeably.

Algorithm 1. Attractor detection and classification procedures

---

Function TSCC$(\widehat{V})$

  if $\widehat{V}$ *is empty* **then return**;

  $\widehat{P} \leftarrow$ PIVOTS$(\widehat{V})$;

  $\widehat{F} \leftarrow$ FWD$(\widehat{V}, \widehat{P})$;

  $\widehat{B} \leftarrow$ BWD$(\widehat{F}, \widehat{P})$;

  $T \leftarrow P(\widehat{B}) \setminus P(\widehat{F} \setminus \widehat{B})$;

  parallel: CLASSIFY$(\widehat{B}|_T)$;

  parallel: TSCC$(\widehat{F} \setminus \widehat{B})$;

  parallel: TSCC$(\widehat{V} \setminus$ BWD$(\widehat{V}, \widehat{F}))$;

Function CLASSIFY$(\widehat{A})$

  $\widehat{A}_1 \leftarrow$ PIVOTS$(\widehat{A})$; $D \leftarrow \emptyset$;

  $k \leftarrow 1$; $\widehat{E} \leftarrow$ POST$(\widehat{A}_1)$;

  while $\widehat{E}$ *is not empty* **do**

    $\forall i \leq k : I_i \leftarrow P(\widehat{A}_i \cap \widehat{E})$;

    $D \leftarrow D \cup \{p \mid \exists i, j : p \in I_i \cap I_j\}$;

    $I_{k+1} \leftarrow P(\widehat{E}) \setminus \cup_{i \leq k} I_i$;

    if $I_{k+1} \neq \emptyset$ **then** $k \leftarrow k + 1$;

    $\widehat{E} \leftarrow \widehat{E}|_{(P \setminus D)} \setminus \cup_{i \leq k} \widehat{A}_i$;

    $\widehat{A}_i \leftarrow \widehat{A}_i \cup \widehat{E}|_{I_i}$;

    $\widehat{E} \leftarrow$ POST$(\widehat{E})$;

  end

  DISCOVERED$(\rightleftarrows, D)$;

  DISCOVERED$(\circlearrowleft, P(\widehat{A}) \setminus D)$;

Additionally, we define a *parametrised set of states* to be a mapping $\widehat{S} : \Pi(\widehat{\mathcal{B}}) \rightarrow 2^P$, i.e. each state is assigned a set of parametrisations (a BDD). By fixing $p \in P$ we obtain a standard set of states $\widehat{S}_p = \{s \in \Pi(\widehat{\mathcal{B}}) \mid p \in \widehat{S}(s)\}$. All standard set operations are applied element-wise. We use $P(\widehat{S})$ to denote all parametrisations for which $\widehat{S}$ contains some states, i.e. $P(\widehat{S}) = \{p \in P \mid \exists s \in \Pi(\widehat{\mathcal{B}}) : p \in \widehat{S}(s)\}$, and $\widehat{S}|_B$ to denote $\widehat{S}$ restricted to parametrisations B, i.e. $\widehat{S}|_B(s) = \widehat{S}(s) \cap B$. We say that $\widehat{S}$ is empty when $P(\widehat{S})$ is empty.

Finally, we define an operation PIVOTS which given $\widehat{S}$ computes some set $\widehat{S}'$ such that $\widehat{S}' \subseteq \widehat{S}$ and for every $p \in P(\widehat{S})$, there is exactly one s for which $p \in \widehat{S}'(s)$. Intuitively, PIVOTS selects some representant from $\widehat{S}$ for every parametrisation in $P(\widehat{S})$.

Semi-symbolic Graph. To represent $Async(\widehat{\mathcal{B}})$, we need to compute BDD $\mathbb{C}(u, v)$ for each potential $u \rightarrow v$. There is exactly one state variable $\mathsf{A} \in \mathcal{V}$ such that $v = u[\mathsf{A} \mapsto F_\mathsf{A}(u)]$. We thus need to inspect the value of $\widehat{F}_\mathsf{A}$ – if this value is a 0 or 1, the edge $u \rightarrow v$ does not depend on parameters and $\mathbb{C}(u, v)$ is therefore $\emptyset$ or P. If $F_\mathsf{A}(u)$ is the value of parameter P, we set $\mathbb{C}(u, v)$ to be $P \wedge (\mathsf{P} = v(\mathsf{A}))$. Note that due to the structure of $Async(\widehat{\mathcal{B}})$, for each $u \in \Pi(\widehat{\mathcal{B}})$, there are at most $|\mathcal{V}|$ states v such that $u \rightarrow v$.

Using this type of representation, we can define the parametrised next step PRE and POST operators as well as the conditional reachability operators FWD and BWD. Formally, $\text{PRE}(\widehat{S})(s) = \{p \in P \mid \exists t \in \Pi(\widehat{\mathcal{B}}) : p \in \widehat{S}(t) \cap \mathbb{C}(s,t)\}$ and $\text{POST}(\widehat{S})(s) = \{p \in P \mid \exists t \in \Pi(\widehat{\mathcal{B}}) : p \in \widehat{S}(t) \cap \mathbb{C}(t,s)\}$ while the reachability operators are the least fixed-points of $\text{FWD}(\widehat{C}, \widehat{S}) = \widehat{S} \cup (\widehat{C} \cap \text{POST}(\text{FWD}(\widehat{C}, \widehat{D})))$ and $\text{BWD}(\widehat{C}, \widehat{S}) = \widehat{S} \cup (\widehat{C} \cap \text{PRE}(\text{BWD}(\widehat{C}, \widehat{D})))$.

Note that we assumed P already satisfies the imposed static constraints. If this cannot be guaranteed, we can also construct the parametrisation sets satisfying individual static constraints in the form of BDDs and intersect them with P before the computation to ensure the set is valid.

Attractor Classification. This type of semi-symbolic representation can be then used by the function TSCC in Algorithm 1 to obtain the parametrised sets $\widehat{A}$ representing the attractors of our system. Specifically, the algorithm guarantees that $\widehat{A}_p$ is either empty, or a valid attractor of $Async(\widehat{\mathcal{B}}_p)$. The algorithm is initialized with $\widehat{V}(s) = P$ for all $s \in \Pi(\widehat{\mathcal{B}})$ and repeatedly removes strongly connected components with their backwards-reachable basins until the whole graph is processed while checking whether the discovered components are terminal. A more detailed description and correctness reasoning can be found in [5].

Since the exact subset of behavioural classes $\widehat{\mathcal{B}}$ exhibits is initially unknown, we construct the bifurcation function $\mathcal{A}$ incrementally. Initially, all parameters are assigned an empty class. Once a parametrised attractor $\widehat{A}$ is found, we partition $P(\widehat{A})$ as either $\odot$, $\circlearrowleft$ or $\rightleftarrows$ using the CLASSIFY function and update $\mathcal{A}$ accordingly, using DISCOVERED. Given a class c and parametrisation set B, DISCOVERED ensures that $\forall p \in B : \mathcal{A}(p) \leftarrow \mathcal{A}(p) + c$. In practice, the number of actual behavioural classes is typically very small, we can thus represent $\mathcal{A}$ as a collection of BDDs, each BDD specifying the parametrisation set of one class.

Finally, let us observe that detecting stable attractors is trivial – a state s is stable for all the parametrisations where it has no outgoing edges. In the CLASSIFY function, we thus assume that $\widehat{A}$ contains no stable attractors and only concern ourselves with the distinction between oscillation and disorder.

The classification algorithm picks some initial state for every parametrisation using the PIVOTS function and then iteratively computes a parametrised partition $\widehat{A}_1, \ldots, \widehat{A}_k$ of $\widehat{A}$. Here, $\widehat{E}$ is a frontier, moving one step further away from the initial states in every iteration. Observe that if $\widehat{A}_p$ is oscillating, $\widehat{E}_p$ must always be fully contained in some $\widehat{A}_i$. To test this, we compute the intersection sets I_i – if some parametrisation intersects two different $\widehat{A}_i$, it cannot be oscillating and is added to D. We then remove all disordered parametrisations from $\widehat{E}$ together with the state-parametrisation pairs already partitioned into some $\widehat{A}_i$. This ensures we do not loop forever. If a parametrisation is not oscillating, eventually it is wholly removed from $\widehat{E}$ due to a collision between I_i. If it is oscillating, eventually all states are partitioned into $\widehat{A}_i$ and are removed from $\widehat{E}$.

4   Bifurcation Diagrams as Decision Trees

Once we obtain the bifurcation function, we are left with an equally challenging task: constructing a concise representation that can be subsequently used to describe the behaviour of the system and present it to the user. For continuous dynamical systems, this is typically achieved using two or three dimensional plots of the bifurcation points, which partition the parameter space into regions with equivalent behaviour – *bifurcation diagrams*. In our case, the number of possible behaviours in the system is typically still quite small; however, the dimensionality of the parameter space prohibits us from using similar techniques.

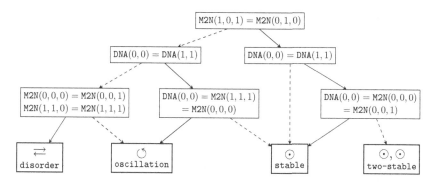

Fig. 4. Bifurcation decision tree of the PBN from Fig. 1a with all four modes of long-term behaviour. Solid arrows represent positive and dashed arrows negative decisions. When multiple conditions are present, they are assumed to be joined by a conjunction. Related update functions are highlighted with the same colour. For simplicity, we write just A instead of F_A. (Color figure online)

If we consider our running example, even after applying static constraints, we are left with 8 logical parameters. Drawing an 8-dimensional plot is infeasible. For this small system, we could consider presenting the full table of 27 parametrisations, however, such option is hard to read and completely infeasible for systems with thousands or millions of parametrisations.

Another option is to utilise the symbolic BDD representation as used during computations with the edge-coloured graph. While BDDs can often provide exponentially succinct representations of the underlying sets and can be efficiently manipulated, the size and readability of the BDD depends greatly on the corresponding attribute ordering. Determining the optimal (or close to optimal) ordering is in general a very hard problem [14,30]. Moreover, BDDs are limited to decisions solely based on the attribute valuation, not their relationships. These shortcomings are offset by the efficiency of the algorithmic BDD manipulation. However, efficient manipulation is not a priority in this situation, as we do not plan to compute logical combinations of our bifurcation diagrams. We are primarily concerned with user interpretation and understanding and therefore require a more human-friendly formalism.

4.1 Bifurcation Decision Trees

For this formalism, we propose *decision trees* as commonly used in machine learning [32]. Originally used to represent classifiers and decision strategies, a decision tree is a flowchart-like structure, where each node represents a test on some attribute(s) and each leaf represents one class or end-result. Furthermore, each leaf can have an assigned confidence level representing the precision of the result. In this context, we refer to these data structures as *bifurcation decision trees*. Compared to BDDs, decision trees have many advantages in terms of readability and succinctness:

- They are not bound by a fixed attribute ordering, meaning that in each branch, the most useful attribute can be chosen to test on.
- The test in each node can be essentially any logical formula of the attributes. This opens door for various reduction strategies (node chain merging) and combinations of attributes (equalities, logical combinations).
- There are efficient algorithms for learning decision trees from data based on information entropy.
- The learning algorithms can be configured to produce an exact decision tree for the whole dataset – in machine learning, this typically results in overfitting, but for us it is crucial to represent all of the edge cases reasonably.
- If needed, we can also use the precision mechanism to prune the corner cases of the tree and still give an exact result in the remaining branches. This produces an incomplete, but typically also much smaller bifurcation decision tree where the error is clearly bounded and can be further refined.

However, there are aspects in which decision trees are not ideal: The tree learning algorithms are not guaranteed to produce a minimal decision tree overall – the tree is only minimal with respect to the information gain in each decision. Furthermore, it is not always clear which attributes will be useful when learning the decision tree. Finally, the learning algorithms have to repeatedly explore the whole dataset which can be time consuming. Later in this section, we show how to learn decision trees directly from symbolic datasets, thus avoiding the need to repeatedly explore the whole dataset.

In Fig. 4, we present a bifurcation decision tree for our example BN from Fig. 1a, distinguishing between stable ($\odot$), two-stable ($\odot, \odot$), oscillating ($\circlearrowleft$) and disordered ($\rightleftarrows$) behaviour. For example, the right-most branch encodes the parameter settings leading to the bistable behaviour of the regulatory network. The tree has only 6 decision nodes – a significant reduction compared to BDDs for individual behavioural classes in $\mathcal{A}$, which on average have more than 30 decision nodes each for this model.

4.2 Learning Bifurcation Decision Trees

The main drawback of decision tree learning algorithms is the dimensional blow-up when increasing the number of dataset attributes. It is not possible for us to use the existing algorithms due to the sheer size of our parameter spaces. We already possess a compact, machine friendly representation of our dataset: BDDs. Specifically, for every relevant behavioural class $c \in \mathfrak{C}$, we posses a BDD B_c which describes all parametrisations p for which $\mathcal{A}(p) = c$. Our goal is to learn the decision tree from this symbolic representation instead of an explicit dataset.

To this end, we adapt the well known ID3 algorithm [29]. For a given dataset, the algorithm considers a set of decision attributes and selects the one with the highest information gain. Here, the information gain is computed as difference in information entropy before and after conditioning on the decision attribute.

Given our symbolic dataset specified as a sequence of BDDs, function ENTROPY in Algorithm 2 computes the overall information entropy of the dataset. Note that we use $|B|$ to denote the cardinality of the corresponding set of parametrisations – this can be easily computed by traversing the corresponding BDD. The learning algorithm LEARNTREE then considers a set of decision attributes $\mathfrak{A}$ such that every attribute is also a Boolean formula over $\mathcal{P}$ represented by a BDD A. This means the attributes can be the individual parameters of the PBN as well as more complex properties, such as static regulation constraints (observability, activation or inhibition of specific regulations) or combinations of parameters (equality or inequality between individual parameter pairs, etc.). By intersecting B_{c_i} with A and $\overline{A}$ (the complement of A), we condition the dataset on the attribute A (empty BDDs are automatically removed). Based on these values, we compute the information gain G_A for each attribute and select the split attribute S with the highest information gain. Finally, a decision tree node is created and the remaining datasets are processed recursively.

Algorithm 2. Symbolic ID3 algorithm

Function LEARNTREE($B_{c_1}, \ldots, B_{c_k}$)
 if $k = 1$ **then return** LEAF(c_1);
 $E \leftarrow$ ENTROPY($B_{c_1}, \ldots, B_{c_k}$);
 $\forall A \in \mathfrak{A} : G_A \leftarrow E - (\frac{1}{2}\text{ENTROPY}(\forall i : B_{c_i} \cap A) + \frac{1}{2}\text{ENTROPY}(\forall i : B_{c_i} \cap \overline{A}))$;
 $S \leftarrow A \in \mathfrak{A}$ with maximal G_A;
 return DECISION(S, LEARNTREE($\forall i : B_{c_i} \cap S$), LEARNTREE($\forall i : B_{c_i} \cap \overline{S}$));
Function ENTROPY($B_1, \ldots, B_k$)
 $B_{all} = \cup_{i \leq k} B_i$;
 return $\sum_{i=1}^{k} -\frac{B_i}{B_{all}} log_2(\frac{B_i}{B_{all}})$;

A leaf node is only created once a single behavioural class remains, meaning the tree has to correctly classify all parametrisations. We could also specify a desired precision and create a leaf node whenever the proportion of one class in the whole dataset is higher than this threshold. For example, if we specify precision 95%, a leaf node is created if 95% of parametrisations belong to one class. While this produces an inexact tree, it can also significantly reduce its size while preserving reasonable amount of information with a clearly bounded error.

Finally, we observe that the information gain property strongly prioritises fully classified datasets. As a result, the algorithm often produces chains of decision nodes leading to leaf nodes with the same class. We can greedily merge such a chain into a single decision node containing a conjunction of the chain conditions.

5   Case Study

We applied our workflow to several non-trivial real-world PBNs to assess its practicality. The models are taken from the GINsim model repository [8]. The workflow runs on a Java Virtual Machine (JVM) with the help of the algorithms from the Pithya model analysis tool [6]. The experiments were performed on a 32-core workstation with 32GB of memory. As tree attributes, we use individual parameters and their pair-wise equalities. The results are summarised in Fig. 5.

Model	$|\mathcal{V}|$	$|R|$	$|P|$	$\|\Pi(\mathcal{B})\| \cdot |P|$ (graph size)	$|X|$	$\sum \#B_c$	$\#D$	$\#D_{95\%}$
G2A	5	15	4.67e5	$> 2^{23}$	11	11054	3047	2534
Budding Yeast	9	19	2.07e5	$> 2^{26}$	6	3790	333	146
Fission Yeast	10	27	4.21e6	$> 2^{32}$	10	4265	135	87
Cell Cycle	10	38	1.21e10	$> 2^{43}$	29	49454	2396	275
Drosophila	14	42	5.52e10	$> 2^{49}$	18	38661	4653	2418

Fig. 5. The results of the experimental evaluation of our workflow. For each model, the table specifies the number of variables and regulations, the number of parametrisations valid under the static constraints, the overall size of the edge-coloured graph, the number of distinct behavioural classes ($|X|$), the total size of the BDDs for each class (in the number of decision nodes), the size of the exact bifurcation decision tree and finally the size of the bifurcation decision tree with confidence 95%.

The runtime of the experiments ranges between several seconds for the small instances to several hours for the largest models. Note that the decision tree learning algorithm required a significant portion of the runtime in each case. This further supports the necessity for learning bifurcation decision trees directly from symbolic instead of explicit datasets. If we were to use existing explicit techniques, the sizes of the data tables which we would have to construct would be hundreds to thousands of gigabytes for the largest models. While such dataset is not impossible to process, it would be certainly prohibitive for our machine.

As expected, even for systems with high amount of parametrisations, the number of behavioural classes is quite small. Additionally, in all instances, an exact bifurcation decision tree provides a much more compact representation of the attractors (5–30× smaller). Finally, in some instances (Cell Cycle), an approximate bifurcation decision tree with a reasonable precision (95%) can significantly reduce the size of the representation, specifically from 20× to almost 180×.

6   Conclusions

We have introduced a concise framework for fully-automatised attractor bifurcation analysis of PBNs, including a unique method based on formal methods and machine learning that allows us to compute bifurcation function and present the complex analysis results by means of human-readable bifurcation decision trees. The case study has shown that bifurcation decision trees are quite compact for large parametrisation sets. Their size can be reduced even more by employing approximation within a given confidence.

We would like to stress that our method is applicable to any discrete parameter-dependent system that has the form of a coloured graph. In particular, the approach can be applied to multi-valued regulatory networks. For future work we would like to improve scalability of our workflow by combining the enumerative approach with static analysis methods we have investigated in [23]. The results presented in this paper have been motivated by our long-time cooperation with biological research groups of CyanoTeam and National Infrastructure of Systems Biology (C4SYS). The method appears to be a promising tool that will help biologists to get understanding and to design control scenarios for important phenomena such as development of cell fates, circadian rhythms, or cell cycle.

References

1. Abou-Jaoudé, W., Ouattara, D.A., Kaufman, M.: From structure to dynamics: frequency tuning in the P53-MDM2 network: I logical approach. J. Theor. Biol. **258**(4), 561–577 (2009)
2. Abou-Jaoudé, W., et al.: Logical modeling and dynamical analysis of cellular networks. Front. Genet. **7**, 94 (2016)
3. Adiga, A., Galyean, H., Kuhlman, C.J., Levet, M., Mortveit, H.S., Wu, S.: Network structure and activity in Boolean networks. In: Kari, J. (ed.) AUTOMATA 2015. LNCS, vol. 9099, pp. 210–223. Springer, Heidelberg (2015). https://doi.org/10.1007/978-3-662-47221-7_16
4. Akutsu, T., Hayashida, M., Tamura, T.: Integer programming-based methods for attractor detection and control of boolean networks. CDC **2009**, 5610–5617 (2009)
5. Barnat, J., et al.: Detecting attractors in biological models with uncertain parameters. In: Feret, J., Koeppl, H. (eds.) CMSB 2017. LNCS, vol. 10545, pp. 40–56. Springer, Cham (2017). https://doi.org/10.1007/978-3-319-67471-1_3
6. Beneš, N., Brim, L., Demko, M., Pastva, S., Šafránek, D.: Pithya: a parallel tool for parameter synthesis of piecewise multi-affine dynamical systems. In: Majumdar, R., Kunčak, V. (eds.) CAV 2017. LNCS, vol. 10426, pp. 591–598. Springer, Cham (2017). https://doi.org/10.1007/978-3-319-63387-9_29
7. Bryant, R.E.: Graph-based algorithms for boolean function manipulation. Carnegie-Mellon Univ Pittsburgh PA, School of Computer Science, Technical report (2001)
8. Chaouiya, C., Naldi, A., Thieffry, D.: Logical modelling of gene regulatory networks with GINsim. Bacterial Molecular Networks, pp. 463–479. Springer, New York (2012). https://doi.org/10.1007/978-1-61779-361-5_23

9. Chatain, T., Haar, S., Jezequel, L., Paulevé, L., Schwoon, S.: Characterization of reachable attractors using petri net unfoldings. In: Mendes, P., Dada, J.O., Smallbone, K. (eds.) CMSB 2014. LNCS, vol. 8859, pp. 129–142. Springer, Cham (2014). https://doi.org/10.1007/978-3-319-12982-2_10
10. Chatain, T., Haar, S., Paulevé, L.: Boolean networks: beyond generalized asynchronicity. In: Baetens, J.M., Kutrib, M. (eds.) Cellular Automata and Discrete Complex Systems, pp. 29–42. Springer, Cham (2018). https://doi.org/10.1007/978-3-319-92675-9_3
11. Choo, S.M., Cho, K.H.: An efficient algorithm for identifying primary phenotype attractors of a large-scale Boolean network. BMC Syst. Biol. 10(1), 95 (2016)
12. Devloo, V., Hansen, P., Labbé, M.: Identification of all steady states in large networks by logical analysis. Bull. Math. Biol. 65(6), 1025–1051 (2003)
13. Dubrova, E., Teslenko, M.: A sat-based algorithm for finding attractors in synchronous Boolean networks. IEEE/ACM TCBB 8(5), 1393–1399 (2011)
14. Friedman, S.J., Supowit, K.J.: Finding the optimal variable ordering for binary decision diagrams. In: Proceedings of the 24th ACM/IEEE Design Automation Conference, pp. 348–356. ACM (1987)
15. Garg, A., Di Cara, A., Xenarios, I., Mendoza, L., De Micheli, G.: Synchronous versus asynchronous modeling of gene regulatory networks. Bioinformatics 24(17), 1917–1925 (2008)
16. Giacobbe, M., Guet, C.C., Gupta, A., Henzinger, T.A., Paixão, T., Petrov, T.: Model checking gene regulatory networks. In: Baier, C., Tinelli, C. (eds.) TACAS 2015. LNCS, vol. 9035, pp. 469–483. Springer, Heidelberg (2015). https://doi.org/10.1007/978-3-662-46681-0_47
17. Guo, W., Yang, G., Wu, W., He, L., Sun, M.I.: A parallel attractor finding algorithm based on Boolean satisfiability for genetic regulatory networks. PLOS ONE 9(4), 1–10 (2014)
18. Harvey, I., Bossomaier, T.: Time out of joint: attractors in asynchronous random Boolean networks. In: Proceedings of the Fourth European Conference on Artificial Life (ECAL 1997), pp. 67–75. MIT Press (1997)
19. Klarner, H.: Contributions to the Analysis of Qualitative Models of Regulatory Networks. Ph.D. thesis, Free University of Berlin (2015)
20. Klarner, H., Bockmayr, A., Siebert, H.: Computing symbolic steady states of Boolean networks. In: Was, J., Sirakoulis, G.C., Bandini, S. (eds.) ACRI 2014. LNCS, vol. 8751, pp. 561–570. Springer, Cham (2014). https://doi.org/10.1007/978-3-319-11520-7_59
21. Klarner, H., Bockmayr, A., Siebert, H.: Computing maximal and minimal trap spaces of Boolean networks. Nat. Comput. 14(4), 535–544 (2015)
22. Klemm, K., Bornholdt, S.: Stable and unstable attractors in Boolean networks. Phys. Rev. E 72(5), 055101 (2005)
23. Kolčák, J., Šafránek, D., Haar, S., Paulevé, L.: Parameter space abstraction and unfolding semantics of discrete regulatory networks. TCS 765, 120–144 (2019)
24. Kuhlman, C.J., Mortveit, H.S.: Attractor stability in nonuniform Boolean networks. Theor. Comput. Sci. 559, 20–33 (2014)
25. Kuznetsov, Y.A.: Elements of Applied Bifurcation Theory, vol. 112. Springer Science & Business Media, Berlin (2013)
26. Le Novere, N.: Quantitative and logic modelling of molecular and gene networks. Nat. Rev. Genet. 16(3), 146 (2015)
27. Mushthofa, M., Schockaert, S., De Cock, M.: Computing attractors of multi-valued gene regulatory networks using fuzzy answer set programming. FUZZ-IEEE 2016, 1955–1962 (2016)

28. Naldi, A., Thieffry, D., Chaouiya, C.: Decision diagrams for the representation and analysis of logical models of genetic networks. In: Calder, M., Gilmore, S. (eds.) CMSB 2007. LNCS, vol. 4695, pp. 233–247. Springer, Heidelberg (2007). https://doi.org/10.1007/978-3-540-75140-3_16
29. Quinlan, J.R.: Induction of decision trees. Mach. Learn. **1**(1), 81–106 (1986)
30. Rudell, R.: Dynamic variable ordering for ordered binary decision diagrams. In: ICCAD 1993, pp. 42–47. IEEE (1993)
31. Saadatpour, A., Albert, I., Albert, R.: Attractor analysis of asynchronous Boolean models of signal transduction networks. J. Theor. Biol. **266**(4), 641–656 (2010)
32. Safavian, S.R., Landgrebe, D.: A survey of decision tree classifier methodology. IEEE Trans. Syst., Man, and Cybern. **21**(3), 660–674 (1991)
33. Streck, A.: Toolkit for reverse engineering of molecular pathways via parameter identification. Ph.D. thesis, Free University of Berlin (2016)
34. Tamura, T., Akutsu, T.: Detecting a singleton attractor in a Boolean network utilizing sat algorithms. IEICE Trans. Fundam. Electron., Commun. Comput. Sci. **E92.A**(2), 493–501 (2009)
35. Thomas, R., d'Ari, R.: Biological Feedback. CRC Press, Boca Raton (1990)
36. Wang, R.S., Saadatpour, A., Albert, R.: Boolean modeling in systems biology: an overview of methodology and applications. Phys. Biol. **9**(5), 055001 (2012)
37. Yuan, Q., Qu, H., Pang, J., Mizera, A.: Improving BDD-based attractor detection for synchronous Boolean networks. Sci. China Inf. Sci. **59**(8), 212–220 (2016)
38. Zhang, S.Q., Hayashida, M., Akutsu, T., Ching, W.K., Ng, M.K.: Algorithms for finding small attractors in Boolean networks. EURASIP J. Bioinform. Syst. Biol. **2007**, 4–4 (2007)

Combining Parallel Emptiness Checks
with Partial Order Reductions

Denis Poitrenaud[1,2] and Etienne Renault[3(✉)]

[1] Sorbonne Université, CNRS, LIP6, 75005 Paris, France
[2] Université Paris Descartes, Paris, France
[3] LRDE, EPITA, Kremlin-Bicêtre, France
renault@lrde.epita.fr

Abstract. In explicit state model checking of concurrent systems, multi-core emptiness checks and partial order reductions (POR) are two major techniques to handle large state spaces. The first one tries to take advantage of multi-core architectures while the second one may decrease exponentially the size of the state space to explore.

For checking LTL properties, Bloemen and van de Pol [2] shown that the best performance is currently obtained using their multi-core SCC-based emptiness check. However, combining the latest SCC-based algorithm with POR is not trivial since a condition on cycles, the *proviso*, must be enforced on an algorithm which processes collaboratively cycles. In this paper, we suggest a pessimistic approach to tackle this problem for liveness properties. For safety ones, we propose an algorithm which takes benefit from the information computed by the SCC-based algorithm.

We also present new parallel provisos for both safety and liveness properties that relies on other multi-core emptiness checks. We observe that all presented algorithms maintain good reductions and scalability.

1 Introduction and Related Work

The automata-theoretic approach to explicit Linear-time Temporal Logic (LTL) model checking explores finite Labeled Transition Systems (LTS). Unfortunately, LTS are often too large to be fully explored in reasonable time and applying sequential algorithms becomes impractical. To tackle this well-known state explosion problem, various techniques have been suggested. In this paper we focus on the combination of two of them: Partial Order Reduction (POR) and multi-core emptiness checks.

POR exploits the interleaving semantics of concurrent systems by only considering representative executions [15, 22, 27] rather than all possible permutations of the execution of n independent actions (i.e. $n!$ possible interleavings). The selection of the representative executions is performed on-the-fly while exploring the LTS: for each state, the exploration algorithm only considers a nonempty (reduced) subset of all enabled actions, such that all omitted actions are "independent" from those in the reduced set. The execution of omitted actions is then postponed to a future state. The reduced LTS is sufficient to

© Springer Nature Switzerland AG 2019
Y. Ait-Ameur and S. Qin (Eds.): ICFEM 2019, LNCS 11852, pp. 370–386, 2019.
https://doi.org/10.1007/978-3-030-32409-4_23

check reachability problems (e.g. existence of a global deadlock). However, for LTL model checking,[1] only stuttering-invariant formula (e.g. not using the Next operator) can be verified. In addition to this restriction on formulas that can be checked, a complementary condition, called a *proviso*, must be enforced. If the same actions are consistently ignored along a cycle, the reduction may miss some undesirable behavior. When checking liveness properties, a sufficient condition is to force every cycle of the reduced LTS to contain at least one fully expanded state i.e. a state for which all actions are considered. When checking safety properties, forcing every (non-deadlock) state to have at least one fully expanded successor (direct or indirect) is sufficient.

An emptiness check for LTL model checking is an algorithm looking for a counterexample in the state space of the system. A counterexample is simply a lasso-shaped execution, i.e. a particular cycle reachable from the initial state.

The best multi-core emptiness checks are based on a Depth-First Search (DFS) exploration [2] and can be classified into two categories: those based on a Nested Depth First Search (NDFS) [10], and those based on an enumeration of Strongly Connected Components (SCC) [2,24]. While the algorithm of Renault et al. [24] performs a *state-based DFS exploration*, one can note that the one suggested by Bloemen and van de Pol [2] performs a DFS over SCCs rather than states which makes the detection of individual cycles more difficult. All these concurrent algorithms are based on the swarming technique [13]: multiple threads, with their own exploration order, are spawned from the initial state. Additionaly, in best concurrent emptiness checks [2,10,24], each thread shares information to prune the exploration of the others. Bloemen and van de Pol [2] have shown recently that their SCC-based algorithm provide actually the best results. This algorithm uses a (lock-free) concurrent union-find data structure that centralizes all the shared information. This structure is adapted with a work stealing mechanism.

In a sequential setting, provisos for emptiness checks have been well studied these last years [7,9,11,18,28]. The *in-stack* proviso introduced by Peled [22] and implemented in Spin has been improved by Evangelista and Pajault [9] with several mechanisms to reduce the number of expansions during a DFS exploration. Some of these mechanisms have then been deconstructed by Duret-Lutz et al. [7] to build new provisos (for liveness properties) that outperform the previous ones. These authors also proposed original provisos that can exploit the SCC information when the underlying emptiness check computes it. Other provisos have also been suggested (but not evaluated) in the more complex context of process algebra to consider τ-transitions [11,28]. Some works also focus on non-DFS based emptiness checks [4,5] thus defining new ways to detect potential ignoring cycles based on quadratic algorithms.

In a multi-core setting, POR has been less studied. Barnat et al. [1] suggested an approach based on a topological sort which sounds hard to combine efficiently with state-of-the-art parallel emptiness checks (see Laarman and Faragó [14]). Lerda and Sisto [17] proposed an adaptation of the *in-stack* proviso without knowing the entire DFS stack. More recently, Laarman and Wijs [16] worked

---

[1] See Peled [22] for a survey of POR reductions with LTL.

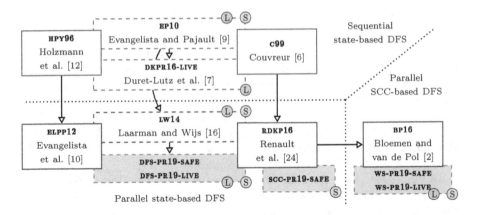

Fig. 1. Contributions of this paper are detailed in green. Red plain boxes correspond to sequential emptiness checks and blue plain boxes represent parallel emptiness checks. Dashed boxes are provisos. A proviso box is covered by a emptiness check box if the two are compatible. An edge links one box to another if the second one reuses ideas from the first one. Bullets tagged L represent liveness provisos and S the safety ones. (Color figure online)

on the adaption of the *in-stack* proviso with the best multi-core NDFS-based emptiness check [10] and achieved good reductions and good scalability.

Even if it has been shown that the best current performance is obtained using multi-core SCC-based emptiness checks, these algorithms have not yet be combined with POR due to several problems. For liveness properties, multi-core SCC-based emptiness checks compute SCCs rather than particular cycles while the proviso relies on detecting cycles. For safety properties, the expansion of a single state in each SCC without successor is enough but has never been realized in a multi-threaded context.

Figure 1 summarizes the contributions of this paper (in green). First, we aim at experimentally demonstrating that the improvements suggested in DKPR16 in a sequential setting can be shifted to multi-core one. DFS-PR19-LIVE and DFS-PR19-SAFE correspond to this adaptation. We can notice that both are compatible with the emptiness checks ELPP12 and RDKP16. After recalling necessary definitions in Sect. 2, we introduce in Sect. 3 these two new provisos and suggest a new one for safety properties SCC-PR19-SAFE. This last proviso exploits the underlying SCC computation of RDKP16. Section 4 introduces two last provisos WS-PR19-LIVE and WS-PR19-SAFE. These algorithms are the first provisos compatible with the BP16 emptiness check. Section 5 evaluates the performances of our provisos and shows that all of them achieve a reduction comparable to the state-of-the-art while maintaining a good scalability.

2 Preliminaries

A Labeled Transition System (LTS) is a tuple $L = \langle V, v_0, Act, \delta \rangle$ where V is a finite set of states, $v_0 \in V$ is a designated initial state, Act is a set of actions and

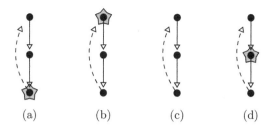

Fig. 2. Black nodes and plain edges represent the DFS stack, dashed edges represent (not yet visited) back edges, and starred states corresponds to already expanded states. In (a) and (b) CONDitional provisos do not require an expansion. In (c) and (d), the SOURCE or the DEST of the back edge should be preventively expanded. The liveness proviso of Evangelista and Pajault [9] will avoid the expansion in (d) since it is useless.

$\delta \subseteq V \times Act \times V$ is a (deterministic) transition relation where each transition is labeled by an action. If $(s, \alpha, d) \in \delta$, we say that d is a *successor* of s. We denote by $post(v)$ the set of all successors of $v \in V$.

A *path* between two states $v, v' \in V$ is a finite and non-empty sequence of adjacent transitions $\rho = (v_1, \alpha_1, v_2)(v_2, \alpha_2, v_3) \dots (v_n, \alpha_n, v_{n+1}) \in \delta^+$ with $v_1 = v$ and $v_{n+1} = v'$. When $v = v'$ the path is a *cycle*. Moreover, when all the states $v_1, \dots v_n$ are distinct states, then the cycle is said *elementary*.

A non-empty set $C \subseteq V$ is a Strongly Connected Component (SCC) iff any two different states $v, v' \in C$ are connected by a path, and C is maximal w.r.t. inclusion. If C is not maximal we call it a *partial* SCC.

For the purpose of partial-order reductions, an LTS is equipped with a function *reduced* : $V \to 2^V$ that returns a subset of successors reachable via a reduced set of actions. For any state $v \in V$, we have $reduced(v) \subseteq post(v)$ and $reduced(v) = \emptyset \implies post(v) = \emptyset$. The *reduced* function must satisfy other conditions depending on whether we use *ample set*, *stubborn set* or *persistent set* [see [15], for a survey]. The algorithms we present do not depend on the actual technique used to compute *reduced*.

The function *reduced* preserves only two properties on the corresponding reduced LTS: the presence of deadlocks, i.e. states without successors, and the presence of an infinite sequence, i.e. a cycle. When checking more complex properties, i.e. LTL formulae (safety or liveness), some additional conditions must be enforced. The *reduced* function must be restricted to reflect the variations of the Boolean values of the atomic propositions (appearing in the property). These extra conditions can easily be integrated in the computation of *reduced*.

However, the previous conditions do not prevent from continuously ignoring the same actions (in a cycle of the reduced LTS). This is the so-called *ignoring problem*. This problem can be solved using different *provisos* depending on the nature of the property, i.e. safety or liveness. These provisos rely on the presence of a *(fully) expanded states* in some cycles. A (fully) expanded state v is simply a state for which all the successors $post(v)$ are considered in the reduced LTS even if $reduced(v)$ is strictly included in $post(v)$.

3   Provisos for Emptiness Checks Applying a State-Based DFS

Liveness Properties. When checking liveness properties with POR and to ensure that no action will be ignored for ever, emptiness checks must ensure that *every cycle contains at least one expanded state (i.e. a state for which all actions are considered)*. Notice that this property is an over-approximation but ensures that the ignoring problem is tackled correctly. Thus it could lead to useless expansions while all actions have been seen during a particular cycle but not containing any fully expanded state.

Algorithm 1. State-based DFS equipped (highlighted in yellow) for checking liveness properties with POR

```
1   ∀v ∈ V : v.status ← UNKNOWN
2   VISITED ← ∅
3   ∀p ∈ [1 . . . n] : DFSₚ ← ∅
4   DFS-PR19-LIVE₁(v₀)|| . . . || DFS-PR19-LIVEₙ(v₀)

5   Procedure DFS-PR19-LIVEₚ(v ∈ V)
6       DFSₚ ← DFSₚ ∪ {v}
7       NEXT ← reduced(v)
8       if NEXT = post(v) then  cas(v.status, UNKNOWN, EXPANDED)
9       for v' ∈ mixₚ(NEXT) do
10          if v' ∉ DFSₚ ∪ VISITED then  DFS-PR19-LIVEₚ(v')
11          else if v' ∈ DFSₚ ∧ v.status = UNKNOWN ∧ v'.status = UNKNOWN then
12              ⌊ cas(v'.status, UNKNOWN, EXPANDED)
13          cas(v.status, UNKNOWN, NOT_EXPANDED)
14          if v.status = EXPANDED then
15              NEXT ← post(v) \ reduced(v)
16              for v' ∈ mixₚ(NEXT) do
17                  ⌊ if v' ∉ DFSₚ ∪ VISITED then  DFS-PR19-LIVEₚ(v')
18          VISITED ← VISITED ∪ {v}
19          DFSₚ ← DFSₚ \ {v}
```

Before diving into a multi-core setting, let us recall how this proviso property can be enforced for sequential DFS algorithms. Duret-Lutz et al. [7] suggested simple sequential provisos that are competitive with the state-of-the-art. During the DFS exploration of state v, the algorithm detects *back edges*, i.e. transitions $(v, \_, v')$ where v' is already in the DFS stack. When detecting such transitions, a cycle has been detected. Then, the algorithm (1) checks if v or v' is already expanded and if not (2) chooses to expand the source v, (exclusive) or the destination v'. In both cases, the expansion of v or v' ensures that the cycle closed by $(v, \_, v')$ contains at least one expanded state. Since all back edges discovered by the DFS cover all the elementary cycles, the property is respected. Figure 2 (a and b) describes cases where no expansion is required, while (c) describes a situation where an expansion is required (source or destination) and (d) a situation where a useless expansion is performed.

The aforementioned algorithms can be combined with a parallel swarmed exploration. Algorithm 1 (without highlighted lines) presents a swarmed exploration where all threads perform a state-based DFS exploration of the reduced state space.[2]

The n threads share a VISITED set (declared line 2) and each thread p maintains its own DFS set DFS_p (line 3). The threads are spawned line 4. When a new state v is visited by a thread p, it is first added in the local set DFS_p (line 6) and then a reduced set of successors is computed (line 7). These selected successors are explored in a randomized order (line 9). Each time a new state is discovered line 10, a recursive call is realized. After all the successors (not in DFS_p) has been inserted in VISITED, v can be itself added into VISITED and removed from DFS_p (lines 18 and 19).

Highlighted lines implement a new parallel proviso for liveness properties. It is based on the combination of two ideas: (1) the conditional destination expansion as suggested by Duret-Lutz et al. [7] since it achieves good results in sequential settings and, (2) the sharing of the state status (UNKNOWN, EXPANDED, NOT_EXPANDED) as presented by Laarman and Wijs [16].

Initially, all states are tagged UNKNOWN (line 1). When an UNKNOWN state yielding no reduction is encountered line 8, its status is fixed to EXPANDED by a compare-and-swap instruction. When a back-edge is detected between two UNKNOWN states (line 11), the destination is selected for expansion (line 12). Such an expansion is realized line 14 to 17 by considering the previously ignored successors. Before this expansion, the status of the state is checked. If this status is still UNKNOWN, no expansion is required for this state and its status can be fixed to NOT_EXPANDED (line 13).

Safety Properties. When checking safety properties with POR and to ensure that no action will be ignored at all, emptiness checks must ensure that *at least one expanded state is reachable from any visited state*. Here again, this property is an over-approximation. Thus it could lead to useless expansions while all actions have been seen during a bottom SCC not containing an expanded state.

As for Algorithm 1, the highlighted lines in Algorithm 2 correspond to a proviso equipping a state-based DFS. This new proviso implements a conditional destination expansion mixed with a sharing of the state status. During the DFS exploration, the proviso of Laarman and Wijs [16] systematically expands states having all its successors on the DFS stack. Here, we expand one of its destinations and only if the other destination are not already expanded. This is the first time that a safety proviso based on the expansion of a destination is proposed.

When visiting a state, the algorithm decides to expand it if its direct successors (in the reduced set) are all in its local DFS stack. The local variable *allin* (declared line 9) tracks if this condition holds. Initially, *allin* is true and set to false when the algorithm detects a direct successor not belonging to the DFS stack (lines 12 & 15). Line 14 implements the conditional expansion: *allin* stays true if all the direct successors are on the DFS stack but have an unknown status.

When a status has been fixed (different from UNKNOWN) for a state v, either v is itself expanded or an expanded state is reachable from it. In both cases, it is not necessary to expand its predecessor. Then, lines 17 and 18 are executed

---

[2] All instructions (excepted recursive calls) are considered to be atomic.

Algorithm 2. State-based DFS equipped (highlighted in yellow) for checking safety properties with POR

```
1  ∀v ∈ V : v.status ← UNKNOWN
2  VISITED ← ∅
3  ∀p ∈ [1...n] : DFSₚ ← ∅
4  DFS-PR19-SAFE₁(v₀)|| ... || DFS-PR19-SAFEₙ(v₀)
5  Procedure DFS-PR19-SAFEₚ(v ∈ V)
6  │  DFSₚ ← DFSₚ ∪ {v}
7  │  NEXT ← reduced(v)
8  │  if NEXT = post(v) then cas(v.status, UNKNOWN, EXPANDED)
9  │  allin ← ⊤
10 │  for v' ∈ mixₚ(NEXT) do
11 │  │  if v' ∉ DFSₚ ∪ VISITED then
12 │  │  │  allin ← ⊥
13 │  │  │  DFS-PR19-SAFEₚ(v')
14 │  │  else if v' ∉ DFSₚ ∨ v.status ≠ UNKNOWN ∨ v'.status ≠ UNKNOWN then
15 │  │  └  allin ← ⊥
16 │  if allin then
17 │  │  v' ← randomlyPick(reduced(s))
18 │  └  cas(v'.status, UNKNOWN, EXPANDED)
19 │  cas(v.status, UNKNOWN, NOT_EXPANDED)
20 │  if v.status = EXPANDED then
21 │  │  NEXT ← post(v) \ reduced(v)
22 │  │  for v' ∈ mixₚ(NEXT) do
23 │  └  └  if v' ∉ DFSₚ ∪ VISITED then DFS-PR19-SAFEₚ(v')
24 │  VISITED ← VISITED ∪ {v}
25 └  DFSₚ ← DFSₚ \ {v}
```

only if an expansion is required: a destination is chosen randomly and marked as to be expanded (just before the DFS will backtrack this state – line 20).

In the previous algorithm, multiple expansions can occur for a given SCC (see Fig. 3). The next algorithm avoids expansion in non bottom SCC and try to limit the expansions only to the entry point of each bottom SCC. In a sequential settings, this leads to have at most one expansion per bottom SCC. Recently, a state-based parallel swarmed DFS computing SCC has been proposed [24]. Here, we adapt this algorithm to implement the aforementioned idea while exploiting the status sharing as in the previous algorithm.

The unhighlighted lines of Algorithm 3 correspond to the one of Renault et al. [24]. The shared variable S maps to each state v, the set of states $S(v)$ belonging to the same (partial) SCC. The shared set DEAD contains all states belonging to fully visited SCCs. Initially, for any state v, the set $S(v) = \{v\}$. Each thread p maintains two local variables, a stack ROOTSₚ which contains the entry point of each traversed (partial) SCC and a set VISITEDₚ holding each state visited by thread p. A local unique number $v.num_p$ (called the live number in the SCC computation proposed by Tarjan [26]) is associated to each state v (line 8). Each newly discovered state is considered as the root of an SCC and then inserted in the stack ROOTSₚ line 9. This stack as well as the mapping S are updated each

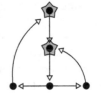

Fig. 3. Example where a useless expansion occurs in bottom-SCC for Algorithm 2. The two starred nodes will be expanded.

Algorithm 3. State-based DFS equipped (highlighted in yellow) for checking safety properties with POR - unhighlighted lines correspond to the SCC computation algorithm as presented in Renault et al. [24]

```
1   ∀v ∈ V : S(v) ← {v}
2   DEAD ← EXPANDED ← ∅
3   ∀p ∈ [1 . . . n] : VISITED_p ← ∅
4   ∀p ∈ [1 . . . n] : ROOTS_p ← ∅
5   SCC-PR19-SAFE_1(v_0)|| . . . || SCC-PR19-SAFE_n(v_0)
6   Function SCC-PR19-SAFE(v ∈ V) : Boolean
7       VISITED_p ← VISITED_p ∪ {v}
8       v.num_p ← |VISITED_p|
9       ROOTS_p.push(v)
10      NEXT ← reduced(v)
11      isTerm ← reduced(v) ≠ post(v)        // S(v) is a TSCC without exp. st.
12      if ¬isTerm then
13          EXPANDED ← EXPANDED ∪ {v}
14      for v' ∈ mix_p(NEXT) do
15          if v' ∈ DEAD then
16              isTerm ← ⊥
17          else if v' ∉ VISITED_p then
18              t ← SCC-PR19-SAFE(v')
19              isTerm ← isTerm ∧ t
20          else
21              while v'.num_p < ROOTS_p.top().num_p do
22                  r ← ROOTS_p.pop()
23                  S(r) ← S(v') ← S(r) ∪ S(v')
24      if isTerm ∧ v ∈ EXPANDED then
25          isTerm ← ⊥
26          NEXT ← post(v) \ reduced(v)
27          goto 14
28      if v = ROOTS_p.top() then
29          if isTerm then
30              EXPANDED ← EXPANDED ∪ {v}
31              isTerm ← ⊥
32              NEXT ← post(v) \ reduced(v)
33              goto 14
34          ROOTS_p.pop()
35          DEAD ← DEAD ∪ S(v)
36      return isTerm
```

time a closing edge, i.e. a transition $(v, \_, v')$ such that v' belongs t a partial SCC containing a state of the DFS stack, is detected (lines 21 to 23). The local unique number of states help to determine the effective root of the partial SCC: the stack is popped until this entry point becomes the top of the stack. The mapping S is updated to aggregate all the sets associated to popped states (line 23). Notice that the instruction line 23 must be atomic. When discovering the effective root v of a (complete) SCC (line 28), all states belonging (i.e. $S(v)$) to it are marked as DEAD atomically (line 35), thus restricting the visit by the other threads (line 15). The mapping S (and the set DEAD) can be efficiently implemented using a lock-free version of an union-find data structure.

To limit the number of expansions, the algorithm expands only the root of each bottom SCC not already containing an expanded state. The local variable *isTerm* tracks such an SCC (line 11, 16 and 19). When popping the root of a bottom SCC (line 28) for which no expanded state has been already discovered, an expansion is realized (lines 30–33). However, a same bottom SCC may have different entry points for different threads. To limit the number of expansions, the algorithm detects some of these situations line 24.

Notice that the two first provisos presented in this section are compatible with most of the optimizations presented by Evangelista and Pajault [9] as well as the one suggested by Duret-Lutz et al. [7]. Moreover, these provisos can be integrated in any emptiness checks based on a state-based DFS swarm exploration for instance CNDFS [10] or Renault et al. [24] algorithm. The latest presented proviso is only compatible with Renault et al. [24].

4   Provisos for SCC-Based DFS Emptiness Checks

Provisos presented in the previous section are not compatible with the best currently known parallel emptiness check [2]. Until now, there is no proviso, neither for safety nor for liveness properties, for this model-checking algorithm. This algorithm differs from the previous ones since it does not perform a DFS in terms of states but only in terms of SCCs: in particular, the states of a same SCC may be visited (and processed) in any order. One can note that SCCs are still marked DEAD in a DFS post-order (see Algorithm 4 without highlighted lines). We denote this kind of algorithms as *SCC-based DFS emptiness-checks*.

The algorithm of Bloemen and van de Pol [2] has been introduced to tackle the main drawback of the algorithm suggested by Renault et al. [24]. Indeed, in this last algorithm, each SCC must be completely processed by the same thread before it can be marked DEAD. To improve this, Bloemen and van de Pol [2] introduced a work-stealing mechanism to allow SCCs to be cooperatively treated (see the outer loop line 9 of Algorithm 4). Notice that this mechanism induces a more complex shared union-find data-structure (see [2]).

In this approach, all threads start a DFS until they reach a (partial) SCC which is currently processed by one (or more) other thread(s). The states belonging to this SCC (aggregated by the DFS) are then distributed among the various threads (line 10) and marked DONE (line 27) when all their successors are DEAD or detected to belong to the current SCC. When the last state of an SCC is marked DONE, the SCC itself is marked DEAD (line 29).

Liveness Properties. Implementing a proviso for liveness properties in this algorithm is complex since the work stealing mechanism removes all possible knowledge about cycles in this SCC. When checking liveness properties, the proviso must ensure that each elementary cycle contains (at least) one expanded state. In sequential and for such a cycle, the states can be marked DONE by the algorithm in any order. Our proviso consists to expand any state with at least one successor marked DONE. In a sequential setting, this approach ensures that all cycles or size $n > 1$ contains at least one expanded state ($n - 1$ for the worst case, $n/2$ in average).

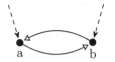

Fig. 4. Two threads cooperatively discovering a cycle. Dashed edges represent paths from the initial state while plain edges represent currently processed edges.

Algorithm 4. SCC-based DFS equipped (highlighted in yellow) for checking liveness properties with POR - unhighlighted lines correspond to the SCC computation algorithm as presented in Bloemen and van de Pol [2]

```
 1  ∀v ∈ V : S(v) ← {v}
 2  DEAD ← DONE ← EXPANDED ← ∅
 3  ∀p ∈ [1 . . . n] : Rₚ ← WIPₚ ← ∅
 4  WS-PR19-LIVE₁(v₀)|| . . . || WS-PR19-LIVEₙ(v₀)

 5  Procedure WS-PR19-LIVEₚ(v ∈ V)
 6      Rₚ.push(v)
 7      if v ∉ EXPANDED ∧ post(v) = reduced(v) then
 8          EXPANDED ← EXPANDED ∪ {v}
 9      while v′ ∈ (S(v) \ DONE) do
10          WIPₚ ← WIPₚ ∪ {v′}
11          NEXT ← v′ ∈ EXPANDED ? post(v′) : reduced(v′)
12          while NEXT ≠ ∅ do
13              w ← randomlyPick(NEXT)
14              if w ∈ DEAD then continue
15              else if ∄w′ ∈ Rₚ : w ∈ S(w′) then
16                  WIPₚ ← WIPₚ \ {v′}
17                  WS-PR19-LIVEₚ(w)
18                  goto 9
19              else
20                  if v′ ∉ EXPANDED ∧ w ∈ (DONE ∪ (⋃ᵢ∈[1...n] WIPᵢ)) \ EXPANDED then
21                      EXPANDED ← EXPANDED ∪ {w}
22                      NEXT ← NEXT ∪ (post(v′) \ reduced(v′))
23                  while w ∉ S(v) do
24                      r ← Rₚ.pop()
25                      t ← Rₚ.top()
26                      S(r) ← S(t) ← S(r) ∪ S(t)
27          DONE ← DONE ∪ {v′}
28          WIPₚ ← WIPₚ \ {v′}
29      if S(v) ⊄ DEAD then DEAD ← DEAD ∪ S(v)
30      if v = Rₚ.top() then Rₚ.pop()
```

However, in a parallel setting, this approach is not sufficient. Let us consider the example of Fig. 4 with two threads, one visiting state a, the second state b, and with a and b known to belong to the same SCC. Thread t_1 selects a line 9, while thread t_2 selects b and both a and b are not already DONE. The test line 15 prevents from a recursive call (for both t_1 and t_2). Since a and b will only be marked DONE line 27, t_1 as well as t_2 will not detect that an expansion is required. Indeed, the only successor of a (resp. b) is not DONE.

To solve this problem, we introduce the shared sets WIP_p that represent states currently processed by a thread p. Highlighted lines of Algorithm 4 detail this new proviso for liveness properties. A state is inserted into WIP_p when first discovered by a thread p (line 10) and removed either line 28 when the state has been marked DONE or line 16 before performing a recursive call. Doing a recursive call ensures that state $v′$ will not be marked by the current while loop line 12. Indeed, when backtracking from the recursive call, line 18 the thread will realize a jump to the outer loop. This jump implies that all the successors of a state must be seen without performing a recursive call before this state is marked DONE. This is the main difference between our algorithm and the one of Bloemen and van de Pol [2]. Line 20 checks when an expansion is required.

A state is expanded if one of its successors is DONE or belong to a WIP$_p$ sets and neither the source nor the destination is expanded.

Notice that the introduction of the WIP$_p$ sets also solves the expansion of the elementary cycles of size 1. As for the previous algorithms, the EXPANDED set allows to share expansions between threads.

Safety Properties. As for liveness properties, a proviso for safety properties has never been proposed for the algorithm of Bloemen and van de Pol [2]. The goal, like in Algorithm 3, is to limit expansions only to bottom SCCs and to minimize the number of expansions in such SCCs. Detecting that the SCC is a bottom

---

Algorithm 5. SCC-based DFS equipped (highlighted in yellow) for checking safety properties with POR - unhighlighted lines correspond to the SCC computation algorithm as presented in Bloemen et al. [3]

```
 1  ∀v ∈ V : S(v) ← {v}, S(v).isTerm ← ⊤
 2  DEAD ← DONE ← EXPANDED ← ∅
 3  ∀p ∈ [1 . . . n] : R_p ← ∅
 4  WS-PR19-SAFE₁(v₀)|| . . . || WS-PR19-SAFEₙ(v₀)
 5  Procedure WS-PR19-SAFE_p(v ∈ V)
 6      if v ∉ EXPANDED ∧ post(v) = reduced(v) then
 7          EXPANDED ← EXPANDED ∪ {v}
 8          S(v).isTerm ← ⊥
 9      R_p.push(v)
10      while pick v' from (S(v) \ DONE) do
11          isExpanded ← v' ∈ EXPANDED
12          NEXT ← isExpanded ? post(v') : reduced(v')
13          foreach w ∈ mix_p(NEXT) do
14              if w ∈ DEAD then
15                  S(v').isTerm ← ⊥
16              else if ∄w' ∈ R_p : w ∈ S(w') then
17                  WS-PR19-SAFE_p(w)
18                  if w ∉ S(v') then S(v').isTerm ← ⊥
19              else
20                  while w ∉ S(v) do
21                      r ← R_p.pop()
22                      t ← R_p.top()
23                      S(r) ← S(t) ← S(r) ∪ S(t)
24          while v' ∉ DONE do                          // Ensure good removing or expansion
25              nb ← |S(v') ∩ DONE|
26              // Expand the last element
27              if S(v') \ DONE = {v'} ∧ S(v').isTerm then
28                  EXPANDED ← EXPANDED ∪ {v'}
29                  S(v').isTerm ← ⊥
30                  break
31              else
32                  // v' is about to be DONE while another thread
33                  // requires an expansion
34                  if ¬isExpanded ∧ v' ∈ EXPANDED then
35                      break
36                  // Otherwise mark states DONE but only one by one
37                  else
38                      if nb = |S(v') ∩ DONE| then DONE ← DONE ∪ {v'}
39      if S(v) ⊄ DEAD then DEAD ← DEAD ∪ S(v)
40      if v = R_p.top() then R_p.pop()
```

one can be done as easily as for Algorithm 3. A Boolean *isTerm* is associated to each SCC and updated consequently (lines 1, 8, 15, 18 and 29 of algorithm 5). Notice that this Boolean is associated to an SCC rather than a state in order to propagate the information inside of the work stealing mechanism.

To implement the proviso, we can exploit a property of the original algorithm: when the last state of an SCC is marked DONE, the SCC is then marked DEAD. Capturing this instant could be useful to trigger an expansion in each bottom SCC. This approach, even if satisfying, does not work in the algorithm. Indeed, the algorithm is not aware that the state is the last one to be marked DONE.

To solve this problem, we propose a pessimistic approach (as previously). When a state is about to be marked DONE (lines 24 to 38), three situations may occur. First of all (line 27), the current state v' is the last one of the bottom (partial) SCC: in this case, the state is expanded line 28 and the SCC does not require any more expansion, i.e. *isTerm* is set to false. Second of all (line 34–35), the state is about to be marked DONE while another thread required the expansion of this state. In this case, new successors must be explored for this state, and the break line 35 will force this exploration. Finally, two (or more) states may be concurrently candidate for being DONE. Line 25 and 38 prevent concurrent multiple insertions in the set DONE (and thus potentially missing a required expansion). Each thread captures line 25 the current number of DONE states in the (partial) SCC while line 38 checks that this number has not changed in between. This leads to sequentialize the insertions in DONE. Notice that line 38 must be performed atomically even if it contains a conditional statement.

5 Evaluation

Benchmark Description. To evaluate the performance of the new provisos, we selected 21 models from the BEEM benchmark [20] that cover all types of models described by the classification of Pelánek [21]. All the models were selected such that Algorithm 1 with one thread and without applying POR would take at most 20 min on Intel(R) Xeon(R) @ 2.00 GHz with 250 GB of RAM. We fix the maximum running time to 40 min.[3] Here we compute only a reduced LTS explored by the algorithms presented in the previous sections. When applied in the context of a model checker, the visited reduced LTS will be larger due to the observation of visible transitions [23]. Experiments were run three times and only the median of the three values were kept.

According to Bloemen et al. [3], the performances of parallel emptiness checks may rely on the underlying graph structure. To evaluate this, the 21 models selected are divided into two categories: $\mathcal{M}_1$ (models with short cycles and many small SCCs) and $\mathcal{M}_2$ (models with long cycles and a small number of large SCCs). Bloemen et al. [3] observe that the performances for the algorithm suggested by Renault et al. [24] are degraded for $\mathcal{M}_2$ which is the motivation of the introduction of their new algorithm.

---

[3] For a description of our setup, including selected models, detailed results and code, see http://www.lrde.epita.fr/~renault/benchs/ICFEM-2019/results.html.

In this benchmark, we compared all the new algorithms presented in this paper with the only parallel provisos of the state-of-the-art, i.e LW14-LIVE (see Algorithm 1 in Laarman and Wijs [16]),[4] LW14-SAFE (see Algorithm 2 in Laarman and Wijs [16]). All the presented results have been computed using the same canvas and are then comparable. See Fig. 1 for an overview of our contributions and the compatibility with existing emptiness checks.

Implementation Details. Since all the presented algorithms rely on hashtables and linked lists, they can be implemented lock-free. The *reduced* function implements the stubborn set method from Valmari [27] as described by Pater [19] but in a deterministic way, i.e. for any state s, *reduced*(s) always returns the same set. However, because the computation of a reduced set[5] of enabled transitions can be costly, we opted for its memoization using mutexes. This is an implementation choice but a pure lock-free version remains possible. All the

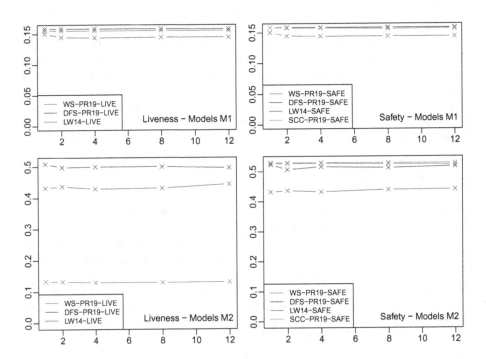

Fig. 5. Mean Reduction rates (in percent) on the whole benchmark, depicted for liveness and safety and for the two categories $\mathcal{M}_1$ and $\mathcal{M}_2$. The x-axis represents the number of threads when the y-axis the mean of the reduction rates.

---

[4] Notice that we only consider the blue DFS (without lines 33–37). When implementing an emptiness check the ignored lines could trigger complementary expansions. Thus the reported values here can be interpreted as the optimal bound (time, reduction, ...) for this algorithm.

[5] Our implementation uses *persistent sets* since a special attention must be paid when combining *ample sets* with on-the-fly exploration [25].

approaches proposed here have been implemented in Spot [8]. For a given model the corresponding Kripke structure is generated on-the-fly using DiVinE 2.4 patched by the LTSmin team.[6]

Reduction Rates. Figure 5 gives the mean of the reduction rates for the benchmark. It appears that the reduction rate of each algorithm is insensitive to the thread number. For $\mathcal{M}_1$, all algorithms tend to have a similar reduction rate even if LAARMAN (LIVE and SAFE) is slightly worse than the others (both for liveness and safety cases). For liveness and models $\mathcal{M}_2$, it appears that WS-PR19-LIVE significantly degrades the reduction rate. This is due to the pessimistic approach imposed by the lack of information from the DFS stack. This effect is minored for the safety case because expansions are limited to the bottom SCCs and by our strategy that minimizes the number of expansions in such SCCs.

Time Analysis. Tables 1 and 2 describe the measure for the two categories of model and all the algorithms running with 1 to 12 threads. For safety, LW14-SAFE and WS-PR19-SAFE have comparable running times. Since WS-PR19-SAFE has a smaller reduction rate than LW14-SAFE, the work-stealing mechanism implemented in WS-PR19-SAFE shows its efficiency. Nonetheless, SCC-PR19-SAFE and DFS-PR19-SAFE perform better. However, the complex data structure of SCC-PR19-SAFE impacts negatively its running time. For liveness, LW14-LIVE performs better than WS-PR19-LIVE. DFS-PR19-LIVE performs better than the two others regardless the category of models.

Finally, we can notice that the work-stealing mechanism of WS-PR19-LIVE particularly improves the speedup for models $\mathcal{M}_2$. The Fig. 6 displays the speedup curves for both liveness and safety and $\mathcal{M}_2$. For models $\mathcal{M}_1$, the speedup of all algorithms are comparable.

Table 1. States in 10^6, times in seconds and speedup for liveness provisos

		LW14-LIVE			DFS-PR19-LIVE			WS-PR19-LIVE		
		States	Time	Sp.	States	Time	Sp.	States	Time(s)	Sp.
$\mathcal{M}_1$	1 th.	412.3	3755	–	410.1	3732	–	411.5	4651	–
	2 th.	413.9	1983	1.89	410.1	1960	1.90	411.5	2505	1.86
	4 th.	415.2	1136	3.30	410.1	1124	3.32	411.5	1429	3.25
	8 th.	414.6	805	4.66	410.1	773	4.83	411.5	1021	4.55
	12 th.	414.6	691	5.43	410.1	678	5.50	411.5	829	5.60
$\mathcal{M}_2$	1 th	202.0	1372	–	181.5	1218	–	256.3	2761	–
	2 th.	199.3	718	1.91	182.2	632	1.93	256.2	1392	1.98
	4 th.	197.3	391	3.50	182.2	343	3.55	256.0	721	3.83
	8 th.	195.1	246	5.56	182.3	222	5.49	255.9	466	5.93
	12 th.	193.9	186	7.34	182.2	165	7.36	255.7	359	7.69

---

[6] See http://fmt.cs.utwente.nl/tools/ltsmin/#divine for more details.

Table 2. States in 10^6, times in seconds and speedup for safety provisos

		LW14-SAFE			DFS-PR19-SAFE			SCC-PR19-SAFE			WS-PR19-SAFE		
		State	Time	Sp.	State	Time	Sp.	State	Time	Sp.	State	Time	Sp.
$\mathcal{M}_1$	1 th.	412.3	5124	–	410.1	3734	–	410.1	4179	–	410.1	5041	–
	2 th.	413.9	2709	1.84	410.1	1961	1.90	410.4	2235	1.87	410.1	2744	1.84
	4 th.	414.6	1527	3.38	410.1	1124	3.32	410.3	1372	3.04	410.1	1493	3.38
	8 th.	414.5	1067	4.87	410.1	803	4.65	410.7	870	4.80	410.1	1034	4.87
	12 th.	414.7	809	6.23	410.1	641	5.82	410.5	784	5.33	410.1	809	6.23
$\mathcal{M}_2$	1 th.	202.0	1372	–	180.2	1214	–	179.1	1380	–	179.1	1935	–
	2 th.	199.6	724	1.90	180.5	633	1.92	179.2	713	1.93	179.1	997	1.94
	4 th.	197.2	391	3.50	180.7	339	3.58	179.2	336	4.10	179.1	543	3.56
	8 th.	195.1	263	5.21	180.8	214	5.67	179.5	257	5.37	179.2	362	5.35
	12 th.	194.0	187	7.32	180.7	165	7.32	179.5	205	6.72	179.2	296	6.52

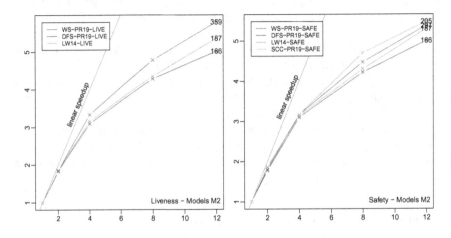

Fig. 6. Speedup on models $\mathcal{M}_2$

6 Conclusion

To our knowledge, only the work of Laarman and et al. proposes provisos designed for parallel model checking. Nonetheless, in sequential settings and for liveness properties, Duret-Lutz et al. [7] empirically shown that variations on the traditional proviso could improve performances. In this paper, we demonstrate that the application of the suggested provisos (in particular DFS-PR19-LIVE and DFS-PR19-SAFE) can also benefit to the parallel emptiness check based on a state-based DFS. During this investigation, we also proposed a new proviso also based on destination expansion but dedicated to safety properties.

However, the best existing parallel emptiness checks are based on an SCC computation. For the best of them (BP16 [2]), no existing provisos can be directly applied since it is based on a work-stealing mechanism breaking the

DFS post-order. In this paper, we proposed new provisos for this parallel emptiness check (for both liveness and safety properties). Moreover, we also presented a dedicated proviso for safety properties for Renault et al. [24]. Figure 1 summarizes the compatibility of the different provisos with respect to existing emptiness checks.

One of the challenging problems in parallelizing explicit state model checking is the model checking of stutter-free LTL properties on distributed systems. In this paper we propose, for the first time, several algorithms (that can be directly integrated into the best known emptiness checks) to tackle this problem. All provisos presented and evaluated in this paper achieve comparable speedups. However, the reduction rate of WS-PR19-LIVE for models with long cycles and a small number of large SCCs is significantly degraded compared to the other proposed algorithms. An open question remains: can we develop a liveness proviso for BP16 that preserves a good reduction rate for any category of models?

References

1. Barnat, J., Brim, L., Rockai, P.: Parallel partial order reduction with topological sort proviso. In: SEFM 2010, pp. 222–231. September 2010
2. Bloemen, V., van de Pol, J.: Multi-core SCC-based LTL model checking. In: Bloem, R., Arbel, E. (eds.) HVC 2016. LNCS, vol. 10028, pp. 18–33. Springer, Cham (2016). https://doi.org/10.1007/978-3-319-49052-6_2
3. Bloemen, V., Laarman, A., van de Pol, J.: Multi-core on-the-fly SCC decomposition. vol. 51, March 2016
4. Bošnački, D., Leue, S., Lafuente, A.L.: Partial-order reduction for general state exploring algorithms. In: Valmari, A. (ed.) SPIN 2006. LNCS, vol. 3925, pp. 271–287. Springer, Heidelberg (2006). https://doi.org/10.1007/11691617_16
5. Bošnaăźki, D., Leue, S., Lluch Lafuente, A.: Partial-order reduction for general state exploring algorithms. Int. J. Softw. Tools Technol. Transf. (STTT) 11(1), 39–51 (2009)
6. Couvreur, J.-M.: On-the-fly verification of linear temporal logic. In: Wing, J.M., Woodcock, J., Davies, J. (eds.) FM 1999. LNCS, vol. 1708, pp. 253–271. Springer, Heidelberg (1999). https://doi.org/10.1007/3-540-48119-2_16
7. Duret-Lutz, A., Kordon, F., Poitrenaud, D., Renault, E.: Heuristics for checking liveness properties with partial order reductions. In: Artho, C., Legay, A., Peled, D. (eds.) ATVA 2016. LNCS, vol. 9938, pp. 340–356. Springer, Cham (2016). https://doi.org/10.1007/978-3-319-46520-3_22
8. Duret-Lutz, A., Lewkowicz, A., Fauchille, A., Michaud, T., Renault, É., Xu, L.: Spot 2.0 — a framework for LTL and ω-automata manipulation. In: Artho, C., Legay, A., Peled, D. (eds.) ATVA 2016. LNCS, vol. 9938, pp. 122–129. Springer, Cham (2016). https://doi.org/10.1007/978-3-319-46520-3_8
9. Evangelista, S., Pajault, C.: Solving the ignoring problem for partial order reduction. Int. J. Softw. Tools Technol. Transf. 12(2), 155–170 (2010)
10. Evangelista, S., Laarman, A., Petrucci, L., van de Pol, J.: Improved multi-core nested depth-first search. In: Chakraborty, S., Mukund, M. (eds.) ATVA 2012. LNCS, pp. 269–283. Springer, Heidelberg (2012). https://doi.org/10.1007/978-3-642-33386-6_22

11. Hansen, H., Valmari, A.: Safety property-driven stubborn sets. In: Larsen, K.G., Potapov, I., Srba, J. (eds.) RP 2016. LNCS, vol. 9899, pp. 90–103. Springer, Cham (2016). https://doi.org/10.1007/978-3-319-45994-3_7

12. Holzmann, G.J., Peled, D.A., Yannakakis, M.: On nested depth first search. In: SPIN 1996, vol. 32, DIMACS: Series in Discrete Mathematics and Theoretical Computer Science. American Mathematical Society, May 1996

13. Holzmann, G.J., Joshi, R., Groce, A.: Swarm verification techniques. IEEE Trans. Softw. Eng. **37**(6), 845–857 (2011)

14. Laarman, A., Faragó, D.: Improved on-the-Fly livelock detection. In: Brat, G., Rungta, N., Venet, A. (eds.) NFM 2013. LNCS, vol. 7871, pp. 32–47. Springer, Heidelberg (2013). https://doi.org/10.1007/978-3-642-38088-4_3

15. Laarman, A., Pater, E., Pol, J., Hansen, H.: Guard-based partial-order reduction. STTT, pp. 1–22 (2014)

16. Laarman, A., Wijs, A.: Partial-order reduction for multi-core LTL model checking. In: Yahav, E. (ed.) HVC 2014. LNCS, vol. 8855, pp. 267–283. Springer, Cham (2014). https://doi.org/10.1007/978-3-319-13338-6_20

17. Lerda, F., Sisto, R.: Distributed-memory model checking with SPIN. In: Dams, D., Gerth, R., Leue, S., Massink, M. (eds.) SPIN 1999. LNCS, vol. 1680, pp. 22–39. Springer, Heidelberg (1999). https://doi.org/10.1007/3-540-48234-2_3

18. Nalumasu, R., Gopalakrishnan, G.: An efficient partial order reduction algorithm with an alternative proviso implementation. FMSD **20**(1), 231–247 (2002)

19. Pater, E.: Partial order reduction for pins, March 2011

20. Pelánek, R.: BEEM: benchmarks for explicit model checkers. In: Bošnački, D., Edelkamp, S. (eds.) SPIN 2007. LNCS, vol. 4595, pp. 263–267. Springer, Heidelberg (2007). https://doi.org/10.1007/978-3-540-73370-6_17

21. Pelánek, R.: Properties of state spaces and their applications. Int. J. Softw. Tools Technol. Transf. (STTT) **10**, 443–454 (2008)

22. Peled, D.: Combining partial order reductions with on-the-fly model-checking. In: Dill, D.L. (ed.) CAV 1994. LNCS, vol. 818, pp. 377–390. Springer, Heidelberg (1994). https://doi.org/10.1007/3-540-58179-0_69

23. Peled, D., Valmari, A., Kokkarinen, I.: Relaxed visibility enhances partial order reduction. Formal Meth. Syst. Des. **19**(3), 275–289 (2001)

24. Renault, E., Duret-Lutz, A., Kordon, F., Poitrenaud, D.: Variations on parallel explicit model checking for generalized Büchi automata. Int. J. Softw. Tools Technol. Transf. (STTT) **19**, 1–21 (2016)

25. Siegel, S.F.: What's wrong with on-the-fly partial order reduction. In: Dillig, I., Tasiran, S. (eds.) CAV 2019. LNCS, vol. 11562, pp. 478–495. Springer, Cham (2019). https://doi.org/10.1007/978-3-030-25543-5_27

26. Tarjan, R.: Depth-first search and linear graph algorithms. SIAM J. Comput. **1**(2), 146–160 (1972)

27. Valmari, A.: Stubborn sets for reduced state space generation. In: Rozenberg, G. (ed.) ICATPN 1989. LNCS, vol. 483, pp. 491–515. Springer, Heidelberg (1991). https://doi.org/10.1007/3-540-53863-1_36

28. Valmari, A.: More stubborn set methods for process algebras. In: Gibson-Robinson, T., Hopcroft, P., Lazić, R. (eds.) Concurrency, Security, and Puzzles. LNCS, vol. 10160, pp. 246–271. Springer, Cham (2017). https://doi.org/10.1007/978-3-319-51046-0_13

A Coalgebraic Semantics Framework for Quantum Systems

Ai Liu and Meng Sun$^{(\boxtimes)}$

School of Mathematical Sciences, Peking University, Beijing, China
{shaoai,sunm}@pku.edu.cn

Abstract. As a quantum counterpart of labeled transition system (LTS), quantum labeled transition system (QLTS) is a powerful formalism for modeling quantum programs or protocols, and gives a categorical understanding for quantum computation. With the help of quantum branching monad, QLTS provides a framework extending some ideas in non-deterministic or probabilistic systems to quantum systems. In this paper, we propose the notion of reactive quantum system (RQS), a variant of QLTS, and develop a coalgebraic semantics for both QLTS and RQS by an endofunctor on the category of convex sets, which has a final coalgebra. Such a coalgebraic semantics provides a unifying abstract interpretation for both QLTS and RQS. The notions of bisimulation and simulation can be employed to compare the behavior of different types of quantum systems and judge whether a coalgebra can be behaviorally simulated by another.

Keywords: Quantum labeled transition system · Reactive quantum system · Final coalgebra · Bisimulation · Simulation

1 Introduction

Quantum computation has been widely believed to bypass the end of Moore's Law and have an advantage over classical algorithms for certain problems. For instance, Grover's search algorithm can search an unordered array of size n in $O(\sqrt{n})$ time as opposed to the usual $O(n)$ time and Shor's factoring algorithm can factor numbers in polynomial time while no known classical algorithms can solve this problem in such time complexity [25]. There are not only theoretical curiosities for quantum computation, but also commercially available applications in quantum cryptography, which has a striking advantage over the classical cryptography in an *"unconditionally secure"* way [18]. Such advantages benefit from some prominent features of quantum mechanics, such as *superposition* and *entanglement*.

In order to develop quantum algorithms and protocols into concrete systems, foundations of quantum programming were investigated by Ying in [26], and a quantum programming language was introduced by Selinger in [22]. Beside implementing existing quantum algorithms and protocols, it is also important

© Springer Nature Switzerland AG 2019
Y. Ait-Ameur and S. Qin (Eds.): ICFEM 2019, LNCS 11852, pp. 387–402, 2019.
https://doi.org/10.1007/978-3-030-32409-4_24

to verify their correctness, which can be carried out by describing and analyzing theoretical models of quantum computation. *Quantum Turing machines* and *quantum circuits* are two fundamental models, which are computationally equivalent [16]. There have also been several high-level formalisms for quantum computation, such as *quantum functional programming* [9], *picturing quantum processes* [2] and qCCS, which is a variant of *Calculus of Communicating Systems* (CCS) with quantum flavor [28]. Moreover, quantum extensions of some classical computational models have been investigated recently, such as *quantum automata* [10], *quantum Markov chains* [15] and *communicating quantum processes* (CQP) which extends the pi-calculus with primitives for measurement and transformation of quantum states [8].

Equivalence checking has been a particularly relevant topic in quantum system verification. A technique using equivalence checking for verification of quantum protocols has been proposed in [1], which can go beyond stabilizer states and be used to verify protocols efficiently on all input states. It has been demonstrated that applicative bisimulation can be instantiated on the linear λ-calculi with quantum data in [14]. A probabilistic branching bisimulation for CQP has been proposed and shown to be a congruence in [3]. For qCCS, several kinds of bisimulation have been defined, such as open bisimulation [4], symbolic bisimulation [5], (approximate) strong bisimulation and weak bisimulation [6]. A software tool has been implemented to decide bisimilarity of qCCS configurations in [13]. Such bisimulations are defined concretely according to the labeled transition systems induced by the corresponding operational semantics of different quantum programming languages. In this paper, we propose a coalgebraic model of quantum systems and investigate a general notion of bisimulation naturally induced by it. This notion of bisimulation is defined in a highly abstract level, since only the acceptance probability of inputs is considered.

Coalgebra has emerged as a general framework for modeling *state-based transition systems* and covering different transition types: *non-deterministic*, *probabilistic* and so on [11]. There have been some coalgebraic models for quantum computation. For example, *Quantum labeled transition system* (QLTS) is defined in [20] to model quantum systems by using the *quantum branching monad* $\mathcal{Q}$ and following the principle of "*quantum data, classical control*". The abstract characterization of QLTS by coalgebras allows for applying the general trace and simulation theory [24] to quantum systems. A coalgebraic semantics for closed quantum systems (such as measure-once quantum finite automata [17]) is proposed in [21], which helps to relate the Schrödinger picture and Heisenberg picture of quantum mechanics with the dual concepts between algebras and coalgebras.

QLTS is a quantum extension of LTS whose transition structure is given by the coalgebra $X \to \mathcal{P}(\Sigma \times X)$. As well known, there is another type of LTS $X \to \mathcal{P}(X)^{\Sigma}$ capturing the behavior of reactive systems. This motivates us to develop the corresponding quantum extension of such reactive LTS types. In this paper, we propose the notion of *reactive quantum system* (RQS) based on the quantum branching monad [20]. Comparing with QLTS which is suitable for describing simple quantum programs and protocols, RQS provides an appropriate formalism for quantum systems with reactive behavior, like measure-many quantum automata [12]. We then employ the endofunctor F on the category of convex sets and convex maps [21], and show how both QLTS and RQS can be specified as F-coalgebras. Different from qCCS configurations which involve density matrices with the same dimension, a product of different dimensional density matrices is used to represent a configuration of a QLTS or a RQS, and the set of configurations is taken as the carrier set of the corresponding coalgebraic model. The dynamics of the coalgebra specifies the evolution of configurations and the acceptance probability of the current configuration. One advantage of using the functor F is the existence of final coalgebra, which makes it easy to verify whether two configurations in an F-coalgebra are behaviorally equivalent. We prove that two configurations are F-bisimilar if and only if they are behaviorally equivalent, and show how the forward/backward morphism can be used to explore whether one F-coalgebra can be behaviorally simulated by another.

The rest of this paper is organized as follows. Section 2 recalls the definition of QLTS. The notion of quantum reactive systems is proposed in Sect. 3. In Sect. 4, we investigate the endofunctor F and specify both QLTS and RQS as F-coalgebras. In Sect. 5, we prove that the bisimulation relationship is equivalent to behavioral equivalence on the final F-coalgebra. The notion of *(weak) simulation* for RQS is studied in Sect. 6. Finally, Sect. 7 concludes and discusses possible future work.

2   Quantum Labeled Transition System

In this section, we recall some concepts and notations in quantum computation [18,25,26]. In quantum computation, pure states are often represented by unit vector states while mixed states are often represented by density matrices.

Definition 1 (vector state). *An n-dimensional vector state s is a column vector in a Hilbert space $\mathbb{C}^n$, denoted by $|s\rangle = (c_1, \cdots, c_n)^T$. We denote the conjugate transpose of $|s\rangle$ by $\langle s|$, which is a row vector $(c_1^*, \cdots, c_n^*)$. A vector state $|s\rangle$ is called unit if $\langle s| |s\rangle = \sum_{i=1}^n c_i^* c_i = 1$.*

Definition 2 (density matrix). *An n-dimensional density matrix is a positive semi-definite matrix $\rho \in \mathbb{C}^{n \times n}$ with $\mathbf{tr}(\rho) \in [0,1]$, where $\mathbf{tr}(\rho)$ is the trace of ρ.*

The set of all n-dimensional density matrices is denoted by $\mathcal{DM}_n$. Note that density matrices are allowed to have a trace less than 1 in this paper, which represents the case when "some probability is missing". For any unit vector state $|s\rangle$, there is a corresponding density matrix $|s\rangle \langle s|$. Therefore, when it comes to quantum state transformations, we only consider the quantum operations acting on density matrices.

Definition 3 (quantum operation). *A quantum operation (QO) from a Hilbert space $\mathbb{C}^m$ to another Hilbert space $\mathbb{C}^n$ is a linear function $\Phi : \mathcal{DM}_m \to \mathcal{DM}_n$ satisfying the following conditions:*

- *(Trace non-increasing)* $\forall \rho \in \mathcal{DM}_m$, $\mathbf{tr}(\Phi(\rho)) \le \mathbf{tr}(\rho)$.
- *(Completely positive)* For any I_k, which is the identity map on $(k \times k)$-dimensional matrices, the form $I_k \otimes \Phi$ maps a positive semi-definite matrix to a positive semi-definite one, where $\otimes$ is the tensor product.

The set of quantum operations from $\mathbb{C}^m$ to $\mathbb{C}^n$ is denoted by $\mathcal{QO}_{m,n}$. Kraus' theorem ensures that any quantum operation $\Phi \in \mathcal{QO}_{m,n}$ on a density matrix $\rho \in \mathcal{DM}_m$ can always be written as

$$\Phi(\rho) = \sum_k B_k \rho B_k^\dagger$$

for some set of $n \times m$-dimensional matrices $\{B_k\}$ satisfying $\sum_k B_k^\dagger B_k \le I$, where $B_K^\dagger$ is the conjugate transpose of B_k. Thus, we can also denote a quantum operation Φ by $\{B_k\}$.

Now we recall the definition of quantum branching monad in [9], with which we can define QLTS and RQS.

Definition 4 (quantum branching monad [9]). *The quantum branching monad $\mathcal{Q}$ on the category of sets and functions is defined as follows:*

$$\mathcal{Q}(X) := \{c : X \to \prod_{m,n \in \mathbb{N}} \mathcal{QO}_{m,n} | \text{the trace condition}\}$$

$$(\mathcal{Q}(f)(c)(y))_{m,n} := \sum_{x \in f^{-1}(y)} (c(x))_{m,n}$$

where $\prod_{m,n \in \mathbb{N}}$ denotes a Cartesian product, $(c(x))_{m,n} \in \mathcal{QO}_{m,n}$ is the (m,n)-component of $c(x) \in \prod_{i,j} \mathcal{QO}_{i,j}$ and the trace condition is

$$\sum_{x \in X} \sum_{n \in \mathbb{N}} \mathbf{tr}((c(x))_{m,n}(\rho)) \le 1, \forall m \in \mathbb{N}, \forall \rho \in \mathcal{DM}_m.$$

The unit $\eta_X : X \to \mathcal{Q}(X)$ and the multiplication $\mu_X : \mathcal{Q}(\mathcal{Q}(X)) \to \mathcal{Q}(X)$ are:

$$(\eta_X(x)(x'))_{m,n} := \begin{cases} \{I_m\} & \text{if } x = x' \text{ and } m = n \\ 0 & \text{otherwise} \end{cases}$$

$$(\mu_X(h)(x'))_{m,n} := \sum_{c \in \mathcal{Q}(X)} \sum_{k \in \mathbb{N}} ((c(x))_{k,n} \circ (h(c))_{m,k})$$

Then we have the following definition for QLTS:

Definition 5 (QLTS [20]). *A quantum labeled transition system (X, s, c) consists of a set X and a pair of functions $s : 1 \to \mathcal{Q}(X)$ and $c : X \to \mathcal{Q}(\Sigma \times X + 1)$, where Σ is an alphabet and $1 = \{\sqrt{}\}$, which is a singleton.*

One possible execution of a QLTS is as follows. Given any initial density matrix $\rho \in \mathcal{D}\mathcal{M}_m$, ρ is taken into some state $x \in X$ of the system and evolves into some density matrix $\rho' = (s(x))_{m,n}(\rho) \in \mathcal{D}\mathcal{M}_n$. Then, in a transition between x and $x' \in X$, some action $a \in \Sigma$ occurs and ρ' evolves into $(c(x)(a, x')_{n,l})(\rho') \in \mathcal{D}\mathcal{M}_l$. After finite iterations of transitions, if the current state is x' and the current density matrix is ρ', the system terminates to $c(x')(\sqrt{})_{l,k}(\rho') \in \mathcal{D}\mathcal{M}_k$.

The trace semantics of a QLTS (X, s, c) is defined as an arrow $\mathbf{1} \to \mathcal{Q}(\Sigma^*)$, which can be calculated recursively as follows. First define the unique function $h_c : X \to \mathcal{Q}(\Sigma^*)$ as

$$(h_c(x)(\langle\rangle))_{m,n} = (c(x)(\sqrt{}))_{m,n}$$
$$(h_c(x)(a \cdot \sigma))_{m,n} = \sum_{x' \in X} \sum_{k \in \mathbb{N}} (h_c(x')(\sigma))_{k,n} \circ (c(x)(a, x'))_{m,k}$$

where $a \in \Sigma, \sigma \in \Sigma^*$. Then, the trace semantics is obtained:

$$(trace_{s,c}(\sigma))_{m,n} = \sum_{x \in X} \sum_{k \in \mathbb{N}} (h_c(x)(\sigma))_{k,n} \circ (s(x))_{m,k}.$$

This operator $(trace_{s,c}(\sigma))_{m,n}$ can be seen as an accumulated quantum operation along paths that leads to a sequence of observations σ through the system. The probability of observing σ at an initial state $\rho \in \mathcal{D}\mathcal{M}_m$ is represented as

$$P_{s,c}(\sigma, \rho) = \sum_{n \in \mathbb{N}} \mathbf{tr}((trace_{s,c}(\sigma))_{m,n}(\rho)) \in [0, 1].$$

Example 1. Here we show an example of QLTS for describing quantum programs with output taken from [27], where a discrete coined quantum walk on an n-cycle with an absorbing boundary at position 1 is depicted as a quantum. Let H_C be a 2-dimensional coin space with orthonormal basis states $|0\rangle$ and $|1\rangle$, and H_V be the n-dimensional principle space spanned by the position vectors $|i\rangle : i = 0, \cdots, n - 1$. We can formulate a quantum walk as a quantum loop:

$$\mathbf{while}(Mq \neq 1) \quad \{\mathbf{output} \quad Mq; \quad q := Uq\}$$

where

$$M = \sum_{i=0}^{n-1} i \, |i\rangle \, \langle i| \otimes I_2, \quad U = S(I_n \otimes H),$$

and q is a quantum register in $H_V \otimes H_C$. The program can be interpreted by the following three steps:

1. A 'coin-operator' $H = |+\rangle \langle 0| + |-\rangle \langle 1|$ is applied to the coin, where

$$|+\rangle = (|0\rangle + |1\rangle)/\sqrt{2}, |-\rangle = (|0\rangle - |1\rangle)/\sqrt{2}.$$

2. A shift operator

$$S = \sum_{i=0}^{n-1} |i \ominus 1\rangle \, \langle i| \otimes |0\rangle \, \langle 0| + \sum_{i=0}^{n-1} |i \oplus 1\rangle \, \langle i| \otimes |1\rangle \, \langle 1|$$

is performed on the space $H_V \otimes H_C$, which makes the quantum walk one step left or right according to the coin state. Here $\ominus$ and $\oplus$ denote subtraction and addition modulo n, respectively.

3. Measure the principle system to see if the current position of the walk is 1. If the result is 'yes' then the walk terminates, otherwise output the result and the walk continues.

The QLTS describing this program is constructed as $(X, s : 1 \rightarrow X, c : X \rightarrow Q(\Sigma \times X + 1))$, where $X = \{x\}$, $\Sigma = \{0, 2, \cdots, n - 1\}$ and

$$(s(x))_{2n,2n} = \{I_n \otimes I_2\}$$
$$(c(x)(k, x))_{2n,2n} = \{U(P_{|k\rangle} \otimes I_2)\}$$
$$(c(x)(\sqrt{}))_{2n,2n} = \{P_{|1\rangle} \otimes I_2\}$$

in which $P_{|k\rangle} = |k\rangle \langle k|$ is a projection matrix of $|k\rangle$. A trace $k_1 \cdots k_m$ records the path of the quantum walk and the trace semantics is

$$((trace_{s,c})(k_1 \cdots k_m))_{2n,2n}$$
$$= \{P_{|1\rangle} \otimes I_2\} \circ \{U(P_{|k_m\rangle} \otimes I_2)\} \cdots \{U(P_{|k_1\rangle} \otimes I_2)\} \circ \{I_n \otimes I_2\}.$$

If the initial position k is 1, there will be no valid trace (output); otherwise, the trace will start at $k_1 = k$ and end at $k_m = 0$ or $k_m = 2$. It is easy to prove that the probability of observing the trace $k_1 \cdots k_m$ with the initial position k_1 is $\frac{1}{2^m}$. Note that the initial state of the coin has no effect on the probability.

3   Reactive Quantum Systems

It is well known that LTS can be usually defined by one of the two transition structure types $\alpha : X \rightarrow P(X)^{\Sigma}$ and $\beta : X \rightarrow P(\Sigma \times X)$, where P is the powerset monad and Σ is an alphabet. Replacing the powerset monad P with the coproduct of distribution monad D and the termination possibility, $D + 1$, α and β are changed to $\alpha' : X \rightarrow (D(X) + 1)^{\Sigma}$ and $\beta' : X \rightarrow D(\Sigma \times X) + 1$, which capture the behavior of reactive and generative probabilistic systems, respectively [23]. Similarly, for the quantum case, if we replace P with $Q(\_ + 1)$, β changes to $c : X \rightarrow Q(\Sigma \times X + 1)$ constituting a QLTS, and we have a new transition structure $d : X \rightarrow Q(X + 1)^{\Sigma}$ corresponding to α, which motivates us to investigate on the notion of reactive quantum systems.

Definition 6. *A reactive quantum system (RQS) (X, s, d) is comprised of a set X and a pair of functions $s : 1 \rightarrow Q(X)$ and $d : X \rightarrow Q(X + 1)^{\Sigma}$, where Σ is an alphabet.*

The notion of RQS is similar to quantum Markov chains [15] but can involve different dimensional density matrices. Different from the trace semantics of QLTS, the trace semantics of RQS (X, s, d) can no longer be an arrow $1 :\rightarrow Q(\Sigma)$, but be a function

$$track_{s,d} : \Sigma^* \rightarrow \prod_{m,n \in \mathbb{N}} QO_{m,n}$$

which is defined as follows:

$$(track_{s,d}(\sigma))_{m,n} = \sum_{x \in X} \sum_{k \in \mathbb{N}} (h_d(x)(\sigma))_{k,n} \circ (s(x))_{m,k}.$$

where for all $a \in \Sigma$ and $\sigma \in \Sigma^*$:

$$(h_d(x)(\langle a \rangle))_{m,n} = (d(x)(a)(\sqrt{}))_{m,n}$$

$$(h_d(x)(a \cdot \sigma))_{m,n} = \sum_{x' \in X} \sum_{k \in \mathbb{N}} (h_d(x')(\sigma))_{k,n} \circ (d(x)(a)(x'))_{m,k},$$

Given an input sequence $\sigma \in \Sigma^*$, a RQS may terminate after receiving a finite prefix of σ which means the rest of the input sequence is invalid. The acceptance probability of a nonempty input sequence σa with an initial state $\rho \in \mathcal{DM}_m$ can be recursively defined as:

$$P_{s,d}(\sigma a, \rho) = \sum_{n \in \mathbb{N}} \mathbf{tr}((track_{s,d}(\sigma a))_{m,n}(\rho)) + P(\sigma, \rho),$$

and $P(\emptyset, \rho) = 0$.

Example 2. The following state diagram is an example of a quantum automaton over the input set $\Sigma = \{a, b\}$ and the state space $\mathbb{C}^2$ with the standard basis $\{|0\rangle, |1\rangle\}$.

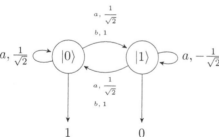

The transition matrices are

$$T_a = \frac{1}{\sqrt{2}} \begin{bmatrix} 1 & 1 \\ 1 & -1 \end{bmatrix} = H, T_b = \begin{bmatrix} 0 & 1 \\ 1 & 0 \end{bmatrix}.$$

The outcomes of states indicate whether they are final states: if the outcome is 1 then it is a final state. When receiving an input character $r \in \Sigma$, the automaton changes to a new state by the corresponding transition and measures the new state with the basis $\{|0\rangle, |1\rangle\}$. If the result is $\{|0\rangle\}$, the automaton will stop receiving inputs and doing transitions; otherwise, it will continue receiving the next input. The RQS for this automaton is $(X = \{x\}, s : 1 \to \mathcal{Q}(X), d : X \to$

$\mathcal{Q}(X+1)^{\Sigma})$ where

$$(s(x))_{2,2} = \{\mathcal{I}_2\}$$
$$(d(x)(a)(x))_{2,2} = \{P_{|1\rangle}H\}$$
$$(d(x)(a)(\sqrt{}))_{2,2} = \{P_{|0\rangle}H\}$$
$$(d(x)(b)(x))_{2,2} = \{P_{|1\rangle}T_b\}$$
$$(d(x)(b)(\sqrt{}))_{2,2} = \{P_{|0\rangle}T_b\}.$$

If the initial state is $|0\rangle$ and the input sequence is ab, then the acceptance probability is

$$\mathbf{tr}((track_{s,d}(ab))_{2,2})(|0\rangle\langle0|) + \mathbf{tr}((trace)_{s,d}(a)_{2,2})(|0\rangle\langle0|)$$
$$=\mathbf{tr}(P_{|0\rangle}T_bP_{|1\rangle}H|0\rangle\langle0|(P_{|0\rangle}T_bP_{|1\rangle}H)^{\dagger}) + \mathbf{tr}(P_{|0\rangle}H|0\rangle\langle0|(P_{|0\rangle}H)^{\dagger})$$
$$=\frac{1}{2} + \frac{1}{2} = 1.$$

Example 2 is a concrete instance of measure-many quantum finite automata (MM-QFA) [12], which is defined as follows:

Definition 7 (MM-QFA [12]). *A measure-many (1-way) quantum automaton (MM-QFA) is a sextuple $M = (H, \Sigma, \{U_a\}_{a\in\Sigma}, |s\rangle, H_{acc}, H_{rej})$ where H is a finite dimensional Hilbert space, Σ is a finite alphabet, U_a is a unitary operator on H, $|s\rangle \in H$ is the initial state, which is a unit ket, H_{acc} and H_{rej} are, respectively, the accepting subspace and the rejecting subspace of H, such that $H_{acc} \cap H_{rej} = \emptyset$.*

We now show how to construct the corresponding RQS for a MM-QFA.

Note that a bounded operator A on a Hilbert space H is a unitary operator if $A^{\dagger}A = AA^{\dagger} = I$ and a projection if $A = A^2$. The computation of a MM-QFA on an input sequence $w_1w_2\cdots w_n$ goes as follows. The operator U_{w_1} is first applied to the initial state $|s\rangle$ and then measure the resulting state $U_{w_1}|s\rangle$, which projects $U_{w_1}|s\rangle$ into a vector $|\phi'\rangle$ of one of the subspaces $H_{acc}, H_{rej}, H_{non}$, where H_{non} is the orthogonal complement of $H_{acc} \oplus H_{rej}$. In all cases the computation continues only if a projection P_{non} into H_{non} occurs. When no termination occurs, operators $U_{w_1}, \cdots, U_{w_n}$ are applied one after another, and after each such application the measurement is performed. The result of the computation can be seen as an application of the composed operator $U'_{w_n}\cdots U'_{w_1}|s\rangle$, where $U'_{w_i} = P_{non}U_{w_i}$. The probability that $w = w_1\cdots w_n$ is accepted can be recursively defined as

$$f(w) = \begin{cases} f(w') + \|P_{acc}U'_{w_n\cdots w_1}|s\rangle\|^2 & w' = w_1\cdots w_{n-1} \\ 0 & w = \emptyset \end{cases},$$

where P_{acc} is the projection into H_{acc}.

Given a MM-QFA $(H, \Sigma, \{U_a\}_{a\in\Sigma}, |s\rangle, H_{acc}, H_{rej})$ based on an n-dimensional Hilbert space, we can construct its corresponding RQS (X, s, d), where $X = \{x\}$ and for $a \in \Sigma$

$$(s(x))_{n,n} = \{\mathcal{I}_n\}$$
$$(d(x)(a)(x))_{n,n} = \{P_{non}U_a\}$$
$$(d(x)(a)(\sqrt{}))_{n,n} = \{P_{acc}U_a\}.$$

For any input sequence $\sigma \in \Sigma^*$, it is easy to verify the acceptance probability for the MM-QFA and the corresponding RQS are equal, which means

$$f(\sigma) = P_{s,d}(\sigma, |s\rangle \langle s|).$$

4   A Unifying Coalgebraic Framework for QLTS and RQS

Both QLTS and RQS follow the *"quantum data, classical control"* rule [22]. However, from the observers' perspective, the "classical control" part may be hidden from outside, and thus we focus on the change of "quantum data" and the probability of certain observational sequences. In this paper, we use the endofunctor

$$FX = X^{\Sigma} \times [0, 1] \tag{1}$$

on the category **Conv** consisting of convex sets and convex maps, where Σ is an alphabet. Both QLTS and RQS can be modeled as F-coalgebras.

The reason for working on the category **Conv** is to ensure that the transitions of coalgebras are valid and any convex combination of states is still a state. For any density matrices $\rho_1, \cdots, \rho_r$ in $\mathcal{DM}_m$ and any positive numbers $\lambda_1, \cdots, \lambda_r$ such that $\lambda_1 + \cdots + \lambda_r = 1$,

$$\mathbf{tr}(\sum_{i=1}^{r} \lambda_i \rho_i) = \sum_{i=1}^{r} \lambda_i \mathbf{tr}(\rho_i) \leq \sum_{i=1}^{k} \lambda_i = 1$$

Then we can get $\sum_{i=1}^{r} \lambda_i \rho_i \in \mathcal{DM}_m$. Therefore, $\mathcal{DM}_m(m \in \mathbb{N})$ is a convex set. We denote the product $\prod_{n \in \mathbb{N}} \mathcal{DM}_n$ by $\widehat{\mathcal{DM}}$. Due to the existence of infinite product in the category **Conv**, $\widehat{\mathcal{DM}}$ is also a convex set.

A configuration of a QLTS $(X, s : 1 \to X, c : X \to \mathcal{Q}(\Sigma \times X + 1))$ can be represented by an element γ in the convex set $\prod_{x \in X} \widehat{\mathcal{DM}} \cong \widehat{\mathcal{DM}}^{|X|}$. It means that the QLTS is likely to be in multiple positions with different density matrices simultaneously. Using $(\gamma)_{x,n}$ ($\gamma \in \prod_{x \in X} \widehat{\mathcal{DM}}$) to represent the $(n \times n)$-dimensional density matrix at the position x, we can have the corresponding F-coalgebra $CF_{s,c} = (\prod_{x \in X} \widehat{\mathcal{DM}}, \langle n_c, o_c \rangle)$, where for any $a \in \Sigma$,

$$(n_c(\gamma, a))_{x,n} = \sum_{k \in \mathbb{N}} \sum_{x' \in X} (c(x')(a, x))_{k,n}((\gamma)_{x',k})$$

$$o_c(\gamma) = \sum_{n \in \mathbb{N}} \sum_{k \in \mathbb{N}} \sum_{x \in X} \mathbf{tr}((c(x)(\sqrt{}))_{k,n}((\gamma)_{x,k}))$$

From the trace condition for quantum branching monad, it is easy to prove that n_c and o_c are convex maps. For $a \in \Sigma$ and $\sigma \in \Sigma^*$, let $n_c(\gamma, aw) = n_c(n_c(\gamma, a), w)$.

Lemma 1. *Given an initial density matrix $\rho \in \mathcal{DM}_m$, the initial configuration $(\gamma_0)_{x,n} = (s(x))_{m,n}(\rho)$. For any $\sigma \in \Sigma^*$, the following equations hold:*

$$(trace_{s,c}(\sigma))_{m,n}(\rho) = \sum_{k\in\mathbb{N}} \sum_{x'\in X} (c(x')(\sqrt{}))_{k,n}(n(\gamma_0, \sigma))$$

$$P_{s,c}(\sigma, \rho) = o_c(n_c(\gamma_0, \sigma))$$

Proof. The proof follows from the definition of trace semantics and mathematical induction.

Lemma 2. $\forall \gamma \in \prod_{x\in X} \widehat{\mathcal{DM}}. \sum_{\sigma\in\Sigma^*} o_c(n_c(\gamma, \sigma)) \leq \sum_{x\in X} \sum_{n\in\mathbb{N}} \mathbf{tr}((\gamma)_{x,n})$.

Proof. From the trace condition of quantum branching monad, we can assume that

$$\sum_{x\in X} \sum_{n\in\mathbb{N}} \mathbf{tr}((c(x))_{m,n}(\rho)) \leq \mathbf{tr}(\rho), \forall m \in \mathbb{N}, \forall \rho \in \mathcal{DM}_m.$$

If $\exists \rho \in \mathcal{DM}_m, \sum_{x\in X} \sum_{n\in\mathbb{N}} \mathbf{tr}((c(x))_{m,n}(\rho)) > \mathbf{tr}(\rho)$, let $\rho' = \frac{\rho}{\mathbf{tr}(\rho)} \in \mathcal{DM}_m$ and from linearity of quantum operations we can get

$$\sum_{x\in X} \sum_{n\in\mathbb{N}} \mathbf{tr}((c(x))_{m,n}(\rho')) > 1,$$

which is a contradiction with the trace condition. Combing the definitions of n_c and o_c, we can get

$$\sum_{x\in X} \sum_{n\in\mathbb{N}} \sum_{a\in\Sigma} \mathbf{tr}((n_c(\gamma, a))_{x,n}) + o_c(\gamma) \leq \sum_{x\in X} \sum_{n\in\mathbb{N}} \mathbf{tr}((\gamma)_{x,n}).$$

With this inequality, the lemma can be easily proved by using mathematical induction on the length of σ.

Theorem 1. $\forall \rho \in \mathcal{DM}_m. \sum_{\sigma\in\Sigma^*} P_{s,c}(\sigma, \rho) \leq \mathbf{tr}(\rho) \leq 1$.

Proof. The proof follows Lemmas 1 and 2.

In the case of RQS, since after receiving a finite prefix of the input sequence, the system may transform into some density matrix in the final state $\sqrt{}$, we need to record density matrices at $\sqrt{}$. Thus, a configuration of the RQS $(X, s : 1 \to X, d : X \to \mathcal{Q}(1 + X^\Sigma))$ can be represented by an element γ in the convex set $\prod_{x\in X\cup\{\sqrt{}\}} \widehat{\mathcal{DM}}$. The corresponding F-coalgebra $CF_{s,d} = (\prod_{x\in X\cup\{\sqrt{}\}} \widehat{\mathcal{DM}}, \langle n_d, o_d \rangle)$ is defined as follows where $x \in X$ and $a \in \Sigma$:

$$(n_d(\gamma, a))_{x,n} = \sum_{m\in\mathbb{N}} \sum_{x'\in X} (d(x')(a, x))_{m,n}((\gamma)_{x',m})$$

$$(n_d(\gamma, a))_{\sqrt{},n} = (\gamma)_{\sqrt{},n} + \sum_{m\in\mathbb{N}} \sum_{x\in X} (d(x)(\sqrt{}))_{m,n}((\gamma)_{x,m})$$

$$o_d(\gamma) = \sum_{n\in\mathbb{N}} \mathbf{tr}((\gamma)_{\sqrt{},n})$$

Lemma 3. *With an initial density matrix $\rho \in \mathcal{DM}_m$, we have the initial configuration*

$$(\gamma_0)_{x,n} = (s(x))_{m,n}(\rho)$$
$$(\gamma_0)_{\sqrt{},n} = 0$$

and for $\sigma \in \Sigma^*$,

$$(track_{s,d}(\sigma))_{m,n}(\rho) = \sum_{k \in \mathbb{N}} \sum_{x \in X} (d(x)(\sqrt{}))_{k,n}(n(\gamma_0, \sigma))$$
$$P_{s,d}(\sigma, \rho) = o_d(n_d(\gamma_0, \sigma)) \leq 1.$$

Proof. It can be proved by using the definition of the trace semantics and the mathematical induction.

5   Final Coalgebra and Bisimulation

For a functor T, a T-coalgebra $\omega : \Omega \to T\Omega$ is called a final coalgebra if it is a final object in the category of T-coalgebras and T-homomorphisms. The final coalgebra $([0,1]^{\Sigma^*}, \langle n_f, o_f \rangle)$ exists for the functor $FX = X^{\Sigma} \times [0,1]$, where $o_f(\beta) = \beta(\langle,\rangle)$ and $n_f(\beta)(a)(\sigma) = \beta(a\sigma)$. From any F-coalgebra $(X, \langle n, o \rangle)$ the unique behavior map $b : X \to [0,1]^{\Sigma^*}$ assigns to each state its behavior $b(x)(\sigma) = o(n(x, \sigma))$ and makes the following diagram commute:

$$
\begin{array}{ccc}
X & \xrightarrow{\quad b \quad} & [0,1]^{\Sigma^*} \\
{\scriptstyle \langle n,o \rangle} \downarrow & & \downarrow {\scriptstyle \langle n_f, o_f \rangle} \\
X^{\Sigma} \times [0,1] & \xrightarrow[b^{\Sigma} \times \mathrm{id}]{} & ([0,1^{\Sigma^*}])^{\Sigma} \times [0,1]
\end{array}
$$

We now come to the observational equivalence relationship for F-coalgebras. In coalgebra theory, there are two well-know notions of observational equivalence: *bisimulation* and *behavioral equivalence*. A bisimulation between two systems is intuitively a relation between their states together with a transition structure on it, while behavioral equivalence shows that two states can be mapped into the same state in another F-coalgebra by F-homomorphisms.

It has been demonstrated in [20] that, for the quantum branching monad $\mathcal{Q}$, $\mathcal{Q}$-bisimulation and behavioral equivalence do not coincide. However, for the functor F defined in (1), F-bisimulation coincides with behavioral equivalence.

Theorem 2. *Given two F-coalgebras $(X, \langle n_X, o_X \rangle)$ and $(Y, \langle n_Y, o_Y \rangle)$, $x \in X$ and $y \in Y$ are F-bisimlar iff they are behaviorally equivalent.*

Proof. ($\Rightarrow$) If x and y are F-bisimilar, there is a F-coalgebra $(R, \langle n_R, o_R \rangle)$ where $R \subseteq X \times Y$ such that the projection functions $\pi_1 : R \to X$ and $\pi_2 : R \to Y$ are F-homomorphisms and $(x, y) \in R$. Let b_X, b_Y, b_R be the behavioral maps from $(X, \langle n_X, o_X \rangle), (Y, \langle n_Y, o_Y \rangle), (R, \langle n_R, o_R \rangle)$ to the final coalgebra

$([0,1]^{\Sigma^*}, \langle n_f, o_f \rangle)$. Due to the uniqueness of the behavior map, $b_X \circ \pi_1 = b_R = b_Y \circ \pi_2$. Thus $b_X(x) = b_X \circ \pi_1(x, y) = b_Y \circ \pi_2(x, y) = b_Y(y)$.

($\Leftarrow$) If x and y are behaviorally equivalent, we have $b_X(x) = b_Y(y)$. Let $R' = \{(u, v) | b_X(u) = b_Y(v)\}$. Since b_X and b_Y are both F-homomorphisms, if $b_X(u) = b_Y(v)$, we have $o_X(u) = o_Y(v)$ and $b_X(n_X(u)) = b_Y(n_Y(u))$. Let $n_{R'}(u, v) = (n_X(u), n_Y(v))$ and $o_{R'}(u, v) = o_X(u) = o_Y(v)$. Then we have that R' is a F-bisimulaiton.

Theorem 3. *Let $(X_1, \langle n_1, o_1 \rangle)$ and $(X_2, \langle n_2, o_2 \rangle)$ be two F-coalgebras. Two states $x_1 \in X_1$ and $x_2 \in X_2$ are behaviorally equivalent, iff they are mapped into the same state in the final coalgebra $([0,1]^{\Sigma^*}, \langle n_f, o_f \rangle)$.*

Proof. ($\Leftarrow$) By definition.

($\Rightarrow$) If x_1 and x_2 are behaviorally equivalent, then there exists a F-coalgebra $(X_3, \langle n_3, o_3 \rangle)$ and two F-homomorphism $f : X_1 \to X_3$ and $g : X_2 \to X_3$ with $f(x_1) = g(x_2)$. Since $([0,1]^{\Sigma^*}, \langle n_f, o_f \rangle)$ is the final coalgebra, there exists a unique behavioral map b from $(X_3, \langle n_3, o_3 \rangle)$ to $([0,1]^{\Sigma^*}, \langle n_f, o_f \rangle)$. Due to the uniqueness of the behavior map b, $b \circ f$ and $b \circ g$ should be the behavioral maps from $(X_1, \langle n_1, o_1 \rangle)$ and $(X_2, \langle n_2, o_2 \rangle)$ to the final coalgebra $([0,1]^{\Sigma^*}, \langle n_f, o_f \rangle)$. Thus, $b \circ f(x_1) = b(f(x_1)) = b(g(X_2)) = b \circ g(x_2)$.

Theorem 4. *Given two QLTSs (X_1, s_1, c_1) and (X_2, s_2, c_2) with the same alphabet and their corresponding F-coalgebras CF_{s_1,c_1} and CF_{s_2,c_2}, if $trace_{s_1,c_1} = trace_{s_2,c_2}$ then for any density matrix $\rho \in \mathcal{DM}_m$, the corresponding initial configurations $(\gamma_0)_{x,n} = (s_1(x))_{m,n}(\rho), x \in X_1$ and $(\gamma_0')_{x,n} = (s_2(x))_{m,n}(\rho), x \in X_2$ are behaviorally equivalent.*

Proof. By definition.

Theorem 5. *Given two RQSs (X_1, s_1, d_1) and (X_2, s_2, d_2) with the same input alphabet and their corresponding F-coalgebras CF_{s_1,d_1} and CF_{s_2,d_2}, if $track_{s_1,d_1} = track_{s_2,d_2}$ then for any density matrix $\rho \in \mathcal{DM}_m$, the corresponding initial configurations*

$$(\gamma_0)_{x,n} = (s_1(x))_{m,n}(\rho), x \in X_1$$
$$(\gamma_0)_{\sqrt{},n} = 0$$
$$(\gamma_0')_{y,n} = (s_2(x))_{m,n}(\rho), x \in X_2$$
$$(\gamma_0')_{\sqrt{},n} = 0$$

are behaviorally equivalent.

Proof. By definition.

Theorem 6. *Given a QLTS (X, s, c) with the corresponding F-coalgebra $CF_{s,c}$ and a RQS (Y, t, d) with the corresponding F-coalgebra $CF_{t,d}$, $\gamma \in \prod_{x \in X} \widehat{\mathcal{DM}}$ and $\gamma' \in \prod_{y \in Y \cup \{\sqrt{}\}} \widehat{\mathcal{DM}}$ are behaviorally equivalent iff their behavior are both the empty map $\epsilon : \epsilon(\sigma) = 0, \sigma \in \Sigma^*$.*

Proof. ($\Leftarrow$) By definition.

($\Rightarrow$) Let b (b') be the behavior map from $CF_{s,c}$ ($CF_{t,d}$) to the final coalgebra $([0,1]^{\Sigma^*}, \langle n_f, o_f \rangle)$. If $b'(\gamma')$ is not ϵ, there exists σ' such that $b'(\gamma')(\sigma') > 0$. Since $b'(\gamma')(\sigma'a) \geq b'(\gamma')(\sigma')$, it is easy to get $\sum_{\sigma \in \Sigma^*} b'(\gamma')(\sigma) > 1$. If $b(\gamma) = b'(\gamma')$, then $\sum_{\sigma \in \Sigma^*} b(\gamma)(\sigma) > 1$, which is a contradiction with Lemma 2.

6   Simulation

Bisimulation relations require two bisimilar states to exhibit identical behavior. On the contrary, simulation relations are pre-orders on the state space which requires that whenever state y simulates state x, y can mimic all the behavior of x and the reverse is not guaranteed.

Definition 8 (Löwner partial order). *The order $\leq$ on the set $\mathcal{DM}_m$ of density matrices is defined by: $\rho_1 \leq \rho_2$ iff $\rho_2 - \rho_1$ is positive semi-definite.*

The following definition provides two possible orders for quantum operations, which is originally defined in [7].

Definition 9. *Let $\Phi, \Psi \in \mathcal{QO}_{m,n}$. There are two orders for quantum operations:*

- *$\Phi \sqsubseteq \Psi$ if $\forall \rho \in \mathcal{DM}_m$, $\Phi(\rho) \leq \Psi(\rho)$.*
- *$\Phi \lesssim \Psi$ if $\forall \rho \in \mathcal{DM}_m$, $\mathrm{tr}(\Phi(\rho)) \leq \mathrm{tr}(\Psi(\rho))$.*

Note that $\sqsubseteq$ is a partial order and thus also a pre-order, while $\lesssim$ is a pre-order.

Definition 10 (simulation for RQS). *Let (X, s, d) and (Y, t, e) be two RQSs with the same input alphabet Σ, for $a \in \Sigma$ and $m, n \in \mathbb{N}$:*

- *A forward simulation from (X, s, d) to (Y, t, e) is a function $f : X \to \mathcal{Q}Y$ that satisfies:*

$$\sum_{x \in X} \sum_{k \in \mathbb{N}} (f(x)(y))_{k,n} \circ (s(x))_{m,k} \sqsubseteq (t(y))_{m,n}$$

$$\sum_{x' \in X} \sum_{k \in \mathbb{N}} (f(x')(y))_{k,n} \circ (d(x)(a)(x'))_{m,k} \sqsubseteq \sum_{y' \in Y} \sum_{k \in \mathbb{N}} (e(y')(a)(y))_{k,n} \circ f(x)(y')_{m,k}$$

$$(d(x)(\sqrt{}))_{m,n} \sqsubseteq \sum_{y \in Y} \sum_{k \in \mathbb{N}} (e(y)(\sqrt{}))_{k,n} \circ (f(x)(y))_{m,k}.$$

- *A backward simulation from (X, s, d) to (Y, t, e) is a function $f : X \to \mathcal{Q}(Y)$ that satisfies:*

$$(t(y))_{m,n} \sqsubseteq \sum_{x \in X} \sum_{k \in \mathbb{N}} (f(x)(y))_{k,n} \circ (s(x))_{m,k}$$

$$\sum_{y' \in Y} \sum_{k \in \mathbb{N}} (e(y')(a)(y))_{k,n} \circ f(x)(y')_{m,k} \sqsubseteq \sum_{x' \in X} \sum_{k \in \mathbb{N}} (f(x')(y))_{k,n} \circ (d(x)(a)(x'))_{m,k}$$

$$\sum_{y \in Y} \sum_{k \in \mathbb{N}} (e(y)(\sqrt{}))_{k,n} \circ (f(x)(y))_{m,k} \sqsubseteq (d(x)(\sqrt{}))_{m,n}$$

If there exists a forward simulation (backward simulation) from (X, s, d) to (Y, t, e), we denote $(X, s, d) \sqsubseteq_F (Y, t, e)$ $((X, s, d) \sqsubseteq_B (Y, t, e))$.

Definition 11 (weak simulation for RQS). *By replacing the order $\sqsubseteq$ with $\lesssim$ in the inequations in Definition 10, we can get the corresponding notion of weak forward (backward) simulation from (X, s, d) to (Y, t, e), denoted $(X, s, d) \lesssim_F (Y, t, e)$ $((X, s, d) \lesssim_B (Y, t, e))$.*

Definition 12 (forward/backward morphism). *For two $\mathcal{F}$-coalgebras $(U, \alpha : U \to \mathcal{F}U)$ and $(V, \beta : V \to \mathcal{F}V)$, a forward morphism $h : \alpha \to \beta$ with respect to a simulation preorder $\leq$ is a homomorphism from U to V such that $\mathcal{F}h \cdot \alpha \leq \beta \cdot h$. Dually, h is called a backward morphism if $\beta \cdot h \leq \mathcal{F}h \cdot \alpha$.*

Theorem 7. *Given two RQSs (X, s, d) and (Y, t, e) with the same alphabet and their corresponding F-coalgebras $CF_{s,d} = (\prod_{x \in X \cup \{\surd\}} \widehat{\mathcal{DM}}, \langle n_d, o_d \rangle)$ and $CF_{t,e} = (\prod_{y \in Y \cup \{\surd\}} \widehat{\mathcal{DM}}, \langle n_e, o_e \rangle)$, if $(X, s, d) \sqsubseteq_F (Y, t, e)$ $((X, s, d) \sqsubseteq_B (Y, t, e))$, there exists a forward (backward) morphism from $CF_{s,d}$ to $CF_{t,e}$.*

Proof. If $(X, s, d) \sqsubseteq_F (Y, t, e)$, there exists a forward simulation $f : X \to Q(Y)$ from (X, s, d) to (Y, t, e). We define the function $\overline{f} : \prod_{x \in X \cup \{\surd\}} \widehat{\mathcal{DM}} \to \prod_{y \in Y \cup \{\surd\}} \widehat{\mathcal{DM}}$ as:

$$(\overline{f}(\gamma))_{y,n} = \sum_{x \in X} \sum_{k \in \mathbb{N}} (f(x)(y))_{k,n}((\gamma)_{x,k}), \quad (\overline{f}(\gamma))_{\surd,n} = (\gamma)_{\surd,n}.$$

Let $(g, r), (g', r') \in (\prod_{x \in X \cup \{\surd\}} \widehat{\mathcal{DM}})^{\Sigma} \times [0, 1]$. We define $(g, r) \leq (g', r')$ if for any $a \in \Sigma$, $(g(a))_{x,n} \leq (g'(a))_{x,n}$, $(g(a))_{\surd,n} \leq (g'(a))_{\surd,n}$ and $r \leq r'$. It is easy to verify this order is a pre-order and $\overline{f}$ is a forward morphism from $CF_{s,d}$ to $CF_{t,e}$. Analogously, if $(X, s, d) \sqsubseteq_B (Y, t, e)$, we can find a backward morphism from $CF_{s,d}$ to $CF_{t,e}$.

Theorem 8. *Given two RQSs (X, s, d) and (Y, t, e) with the same alphabet and their corresponding F-coalgebras $CF_{s,d} = (\prod_{x \in X \cup \{\surd\}} \widehat{\mathcal{DM}}, \langle n_d, o_d \rangle)$ and $CF_{t,e} = (\prod_{y \in Y \cup \{\surd\}} \widehat{\mathcal{DM}}, \langle n_e, o_e \rangle)$, if $(X, s, d) \lesssim_F (Y, t, e)$ $((X, s, d) \lesssim_B (Y, t, e))$, there exists a forward (backward) morphism from $CF_{s,d}$ to $CF_{t,e}$.*

Proof. The proof is similar to Theorem 7 except for the simulation order. Let $(g, r), (g', r') \in (\prod_{x \in X \{\surd\}} \widehat{\mathcal{DM}})^{\Sigma} \times [0, 1]$ and here we define $(g, r) \leq (g', r')$ if for any $a \in \Sigma$, $\mathbf{tr}((g(a))_{x,n}) \leq \mathbf{tr}((g'(a))_{x,n})$, $\mathbf{tr}((g(a))_{\surd,n}) \leq \mathbf{tr}((g'(a))_{\surd,n})$ and $r \leq r'$.

7   Conclusion and Future Work

In this paper we propose the notion of reactive quantum system as a variant of QLTS, and provide a unifying coalgebraic semantic framework for both QLTS and RQS. In fact, the coalgebraic models for QLTS and RQS have the same behavior shape captured by the functor $F = -^{\Sigma} \times [0, 1]$, for which the final coalgebra exists. Then we define the general notions of behavioral equivalence, bisimulation and simulation, with which we can compare the similarity of different quantum systems.

Besides QLTS and RQS, several other formalisms of quantum systems, such as quantum Turing machine [19], quantum process algebra [28] and quantum Markov decision processes [29], have been investigated in literature. On the other hand, a coalgebraic semantics of closed quantum systems has been proposed in [21]. One possible future work is to integrate more types of quantum systems into the unifying coalgebraic framework, then we can explore the relations between them coalgebraically.

Acknowledgement. We are indebted to Luis S. Barbosa and Renato Neves for helpful discussions regarding the coalgebraic framework. This work has been supported by the National Natural Science Foundation of China under grant no. 61772038, 61532019 and 61272160, and the Guangdong Science and Technology Department (Grant no.2018B010107004).

References

1. Ardeshir-Larijani, E., Gay, S.J., Nagarajan, R.: Equivalence checking of quantum protocols. In: Piterman, N., Smolka, S.A. (eds.) TACAS 2013. LNCS, vol. 7795, pp. 478–492. Springer, Heidelberg (2013). https://doi.org/10.1007/978-3-642-36742-7_33

2. Coecke, B., Kissinger, A.: Picturing Quantum Processes. Cambridge University Press, Cambridge (2017)

3. Davidson, T.A.S.: Formal verification techniques using quantum process calculus. PhD thesis, University of Warwick, Coventry, UK (2012)

4. Deng, Y., Feng, Y.: Open bisimulation for quantum processes. In: Baeten, J.C.M., Ball, T., de Boer, F.S. (eds.) TCS 2012. LNCS, vol. 7604, pp. 119–133. Springer, Heidelberg (2012). https://doi.org/10.1007/978-3-642-33475-7_9

5. Feng, Y., Deng, Y., Ying, M.: Symbolic bisimulation for quantum processes. ACM Trans. Comput. Logic **15**(2), 14:1–14:32 (2014)

6. Feng, Y., Duan, R., Ying, M.: Bisimulation for quantum processes. ACM Trans. Program. Lang. Syst. **34**(4), 17:1–17:43 (2012)

7. Feng, Y., Nengkun, Y., Ying, M.: Model checking quantum markov chains. J. Comput. Syst. Sci. **79**(7), 1181–1198 (2013)

8. Gay, S.J., Nagarajan, R.: Communicating quantum processes. In: Proceedings of POPL 2005, pp. 145–157. ACM (2005)

9. Hasuo, I., Hoshino, N.: Semantics of higher-order quantum computation via geometry of interaction. Ann. Pure Appl. Logic **168**(2), 404–469 (2017)

10. Hirvensalo, M.: Quantum automata theory – a review. In: Kuich, W., Rahonis, G. (eds.) Algebraic Foundations in Computer Science. LNCS, vol. 7020, pp. 146–167. Springer, Heidelberg (2011). https://doi.org/10.1007/978-3-642-24897-9_7

11. Jacobs, B.: Cambridge tracts in theoretical computer science. Introduction to Coalgebra: Towards Mathematics of States and Observation, vol. 59. Cambridge University Press, Cambridge (2016)

12. Kondacs, A., Watrous, J.: On the power of quantum finite state automata. In: Proceedings of FOCS 1997, pp. 66–75. IEEE Computer Society (1997)

13. Kubota, T., Kakutani, Y., Kato, G., Kawano, Y., Sakurada, H.: Application of a process calculus to security proofs of quantum protocols. In: Proceedings of the International Conference on Foundations of Computer Science (FCS), p. 1. The Steering Committee of The World Congress in Computer Science, Computer (2012)

14. Dal Lago, U., Rioli, A.: Applicative Bisimulation and Quantum λ-Calculi. In: Dastani, M., Sirjani, M. (eds.) FSEN 2015. LNCS, vol. 9392, pp. 54–68. Springer, Cham (2015). https://doi.org/10.1007/978-3-319-24644-4_4

15. Li, L., Feng, Y.: Quantum Markov chains: description of hybrid systems, decidability of equivalence, and model checking linear-time properties. Inf. Comput. **244**, 229–244 (2015)

16. Molina, A., Watrous, J.: Revisiting the simulation of quantum turing machines by quantum circuits. CoRR, abs/1808.01701 (2018)

17. Moore, C., Crutchfield, J.P.: Quantum automata and quantum grammars. Theor. Comput. Sci. **237**(1–2), 275–306 (2000)

18. Nielsen, M.A., Chuang, I.: Quantum Computation and Quantum Information. Cambridge University Press, Cambridge (2002)

19. Nishimura, H., Ozawa, M.: Perfect computational equivalence between quantum turing machines and finitely generated uniform quantum circuit families. Quant. Inf. Process. **8**(1), 13–24 (2009)

20. Ogawa, H.: Coalgebraic approach to equivalences of quantum systems. Master's thesis, University of Tokyo (2014)

21. Roumen, F.: Coalgebraic quantum computation. In: Proceedings of QPL 2012, vol. 158, EPTCS, pp. 29–38 (2014)

22. Selinger, P.: Towards a quantum programming language. Math. Struct. Comput. Sci. **14**(4), 527–586 (2004)

23. Sokolova, A.: Coalgebraic analysis of probabilistic systems. PhD thesis, Technische Universiteit Eindhoven (2005)

24. Urabe, N., Hasuo, I.: Generic forward and backward simulations III: quantitative simulations by matrices. In: Baldan, P., Gorla, D. (eds.) CONCUR 2014. LNCS, vol. 8704, pp. 451–466. Springer, Heidelberg (2014). https://doi.org/10.1007/978-3-662-44584-6_31

25. Yanofsky, N.S., Mannucci, M.: Quantum Computing for Computer Scientists. Cambridge University Press, Cambridge (2008)

26. Ying, M.: Foundations of Quantum Programming. Morgan Kaufmann, Burlington (2016)

27. Ying, M., Feng, Y.: Quantum loop programs. Acta Informatica **47**(4), 221–250 (2010)

28. Ying, M., Feng, Y., Duan, R., Ji, Z.-R.: An algebra of quantum processes. ACM Trans. Comput. Logic **10**(3), 191–1936 (2009)

29. Ying, S., Ying, M.: Reachability analysis of quantum Markov decision processes. Inf. Comput. **263**, 31–51 (2018)

Parameterized Hardware Verification Through a Term-Level Generalized Symbolic Trajectory Evaluation

Yongjian Li[1($\boxtimes$)] and Bow-yaw Wang[2]

[1] State Key Laboratory of Computer Science, Institute of Software,
Chinese Academy of Sciences, Beijing, China
lyj238@ios.ac.cn
[2] Institute of Information Science Academia Sinica, Taipei, Taiwan

Abstract. This paper proposes a term-level generalized symbolic trajectory evaluation (GSTE) to tackle parameterized hardware verification. We develop a theorem-proving technique for parameterized GSTE verification. In our technique, a constraint is associated with a node in GSTE graphs to specify reachable states. Generalized inductive relations between nodes of GSTE graphs are formulated; instantaneous implications are formalized on edges of GSTE graphs. Based on these formalization, parameterized GSTE are verified. We moreover formalize our techniques in Isabelle. We demonstrate the effectiveness of our techniques in case studies. Interestingly, subtleties between different implementations of FIFOs are discovered by our parameterized verification although these circuits have been extensively studied previously.

1 Introduction

Symbolic trajectory evaluation (STE) is an efficient formal hardware verification method which combines multi-valued simulation and symbolic simulation [1]. As a traditional simulator, it computes the result of executing a circuit from concrete Boolean test vectors as inputs. As a symbolic simulator, it computes symbolic expressions for circuits from arbitrary inputs. As a model checker, STE automatically checks a simple temporal logic formula for arbitrary inputs. The seamless connection between simulation and verification of STE is crucial to its success in industry [2].

Generalized STE (GSTE) extends STE so as to check properties over unbounded time [3,4]. It enhances the expressiveness of STE by GSTE assertion graphs. GSTE assertion graphs can specify any ω-regular properties. The complexity of GSTE algorithms however increases drastically due to fix-point computation. At Boolean level, a unique parameterization algorithm based on Binary Decision Diagrams (BDDs) builds canonical quaternary assignments to compute reachable states [3]. Both STE and GSTE have been implemented in the FORTE tool [5].

© Springer Nature Switzerland AG 2019
Y. Ait-Ameur and S. Qin (Eds.): ICFEM 2019, LNCS 11852, pp. 403–419, 2019.
https://doi.org/10.1007/978-3-030-32409-4_25

Many more hardware designs are done at term level. Hardware verification techniques have to be lifted up to term level as well. Yet many term-level hardware designs are parameterized in essence. Such parameterized circuit designs hence pose a challenging verification problem. When parameterized circuits are under verification, one wishes to demonstrate desired properties should hold for every instances of the circuits. Classical model checking however only verifies an instance of the given parameterized circuit at one run. It is not at all clear how to lift the classical technique to parameterized verification.

In this paper, we extend GSTE to parameterized circuit designs. We first define extended GSTE for parameterized circuits. We then propose a verification technique to perform extended GSTE. The main contributions of this paper are as follows:

- We propose a GSTE framework to model and specify parameterized circuits at term level. The key idea is to introduce uninterpreted functions and predicates to abstract unimportant details during parameterized verification.
- We develop a general proof method to parameterized GSTE verification. We associate each node in GSTE graphs with a constraint. These constraints specify reachable states up to the node. We formulate a generally inductive relation between nodes. We also formalize instantaneous implications over all edges based on constraints associated at their sources. Combining the inductive relation and instantaneous implication, we are able to prove GSTE specifications on parameterized circuits.
- Our techniques are formalized and certified in the proof assistant Isabelle [6]. We therefore provide a theorem-proving technique for parameterized verification on hardware designs.
- We demonstrate the effectiveness of our techniques by case studies on parameterized verification of data-dominated circuits such as FIFOs and dynamic shift memories. Interestingly, we reveal subtle differences between the two implementations of FIFOs and a boundary case condition of shift-register FIFO. Although these designs have been extensively studied previously, these subtitles have not been discovered to the best of our knowledge.

2   A Motivating Example

For example, we use a very simple example, a parameterized counter to show the hardness of parameterized circuit.

The variable *last* records the current value of the counter, and it is reset after the signal *rst*. *last* increases if it is less than $LAST$, and will be rest again if it is equal to $LAST$, where $LAST$ is a parameter. For such a counter, a simple property in parameterized form can be easily formulated: the counter is reset at time 0, the output *dout* is $n-1$ for any time point n for any $n < LAST$. Such a property can be formulated as a parameterized GSTE graph, as shown in Fig. 2, where both index i and $LAST$ are symbolic constants. We also use the dash line to informally indicate the symbolic essence of the parameterized verification.

```
module counter(clock,rst,d);          if (rst)
parameter LAST = 3;                         last= 0; end
parameter MSBD = 1;                    else begin
input clock;                                if (last =LAST) then last=last +1;
input rst;                                  else last=0 ;
output [MSBD:0] dout;                       end
reg [MSBD:0] last;                     end // always @ (posedge clock)
always @ (posedge clock)               assign dout = last;
begin                                  endmodule // counter
```

Fig. 1. A simple counter

Classical GSTE/STE (or most simulation/MC) techniques can only handle bound model and property, namely, we must fix the parameter $LAST$ and MSB, then we can use GSTE/STE to verify that the bound model satisfies the bound property. The circuit model in Fig. 1 and the GSTE assertion graph in Fig. 3 are special instances of the parameterized counter circuit and parameterized GSTE graph respectively with the settings $LAST = 3$ and $MSBA = 1$. Note that all indexes of vertexes are fixed value and we use a concrete line to informally indicate the concrete essence of the bound verification. The concrete GSTE verifications for a different setting of parameters of counter have to be done again. In the context of parameterized verification, parameters like $LAST$ are not needed to be fixed, and require that a GSTE graph instance should hold for an according circuit instance by instantiating these parameters with an arbitrary value $LAST$, where it is symbolic. Intuitively the gap from concrete verification to parameterized verification should be bridged easily, but it is surprisingly difficult to come up with a formal correctness argument for parameterized correctness of the simple counter manually.

Besides, practical GSTE/STE tool Forte [7] works in a netlist model (EXLIF) and specifies circuits in trajectory evaluation logic, which is essentially at low level. For instance, for the counter circuit in Fig. 3, the consequent $dout = 0$ must be a Boolean formula such as $dout_0 = false$ and $dout_1 = false$, where $dout_i (i \in \{0,1\}$ is one node bit of signal $dout$. Note thatwe can't write $dout = 0$ directly. In netlist based model, a bit is the basic unit in verification.Such a low level model and specification is difficult to be applied in high level verification of circuits like in Fig. 3, let alone parameterized verification of circuits.

Because a term instead of a bit is the basic unit at high level parameterized verification of circuits, which may be a concrete integer, or a symbolic constant of unbound integer variable like $last$, or function expressions such as $last + 1$, or array elements which model memories, and all these features are not available in netlist based model and specification, we must establish new circuit model and specification for STE/GSTE high level circuit verification in a parameterized way.

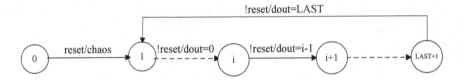

Fig. 2. Parameterized GSTE graph of a parameterized counter

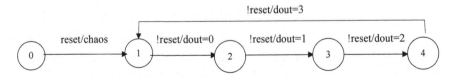

Fig. 3. A bound GSTE assertion graph of a bound counter with $LAST = 3$

3   An Extended GSTE Theory at Term Level

3.1   A Term-Level Circuit Model

We work in the context of hardware circuits, which usually are connected by wires, which we call nodes. We usually refer to some index or some value, which ranges from 0 to N; We explicitly let the number of nodes N vary, and we also allow a symbolic index i of type natural number; all these make the circuit parametric. Let $\mathbb{N}$ be the set of natural numbers, $\mathbb{I}$ be the set of all symbolic indexes. We consider the semantic domain $\mathbb{D} = \{X, \text{false}, \text{true}, \top\} \cup \mathbb{N} \cup \mathbb{I}$. The semantic domain $\mathbb{D}$ forms a lattice where X and $\top$ are the bottom and top elements respectively. Notice that the natural number constants can either be concrete (e.g., 0, 1) or symbolic (e.g., i, k). Allowing natural symbolic constants is the most important features in our extended GSTE work which are different from classical Boolean-level GSTE work.

We list the various syntactic categories and give a meta-variable that will be used to range over each category. There are three kinds of variables: (1) simple identifier, denoted by a string; (2) element of an array, denoted by a variable followed by an constant index. Notice that an index can be either concrete or symbolic. A symbolic index is the essential feature in parameterized verification; (3) field of a record, denoted by a variable followed by a string.

$$
\begin{array}{llllll}
c ::= & | n & | \text{true} & | \text{false} & | X & | \top \\
v ::= a & | v[n] & | v.a \\
e ::= v & | c & | f?e_1 : e_2 & | \text{Uif}(a, es) \\
f ::= e_1 = e_2 & | !f_1 & | f_1 \text{ Bop } f_2 & | \text{Uip}(a, es) & | \text{Chaos} & | \text{Miracle}
\end{array}
$$

A simple expression is either a variable v or a constant c, while a compound expression is constructed with the ite (if-then-else) form $f?e_1 : e_2$, uninterpreted function called $\text{Uif}(opr, es)$, where opr is a string to identify the operator and es a list of expressions. A formula can be an atomic formula or a compound formula.

An atomic formula can be a constant chaos, or miracle, or just a Boolean variable, or an equivalence formula $e_1 = e_2$, or an uninterpreted predicate Uip(opr, es). A formula can also be constructed from formulas using the logic connectives, including negation (!), binary connectives Bop such as conjunction (&), disjunction (|), implication ($\longrightarrow$).

In this work, a circuit is just a statement. We regard them to be the same.

$$S ::= \mathsf{Parallel}([v_i := e_i]_{i=1}^{n}) \mid \mathsf{IF}\ f\ \mathsf{THEN}\ S_1\ \mathsf{ELSE}\ S_2$$

An assignment assigns an expression e to a variable x, and is abbreviated as $x := e$. A statement S is either a set of parallel assignments Parallel $[x_1 := e_1, ; ..., x_k := e_n]$, which is abbreviated as $x_1 := e_1; ...; x_k := e_k$, or a conditional statement IF f THEN S_1 ELSE S_2. Specially, Parallel [] is denoted by Skip.

For convenience, we define case expressions and case statements as follows:

$$\mathsf{caseE}([f_1 \rightarrow e_1, f_2 \rightarrow e_2, \cdots, f_n \rightarrow e_n])\mathsf{end} \equiv$$
$$f_1?e_1 : (f_2?e_2 : \cdots (f_n?e_n : \mathsf{X})) \cdots)$$
$$\mathsf{caseS}([f_1 \rightarrow S_1, f_2 \rightarrow S_2, \cdots, f_n \rightarrow S_n])\mathsf{end} \equiv$$
$$\mathsf{IF}\ f_1\ \mathsf{THEN}\ S_1\ \mathsf{ELSE}\ \cdots \mathsf{IF}\ f_n\ \mathsf{THEN}\ S_n\ \mathsf{ELSE}\ \mathsf{Skip}$$

caseE ges and caseS gSs are switch-case expressions and statements respectively, where ges and gS are lists of guarded expressions and statements. In our modelling language, index is only a natural number. In order to model $mem[e]$ in the left and right side of an assignment in Verilog. We define:
read$(a, n, e) \equiv$ caseE($[e = i \rightarrow a[i]]_{i=0}^{n}$)end;
write$(a, n, le, re) \equiv$ caseS($[le = i \rightarrow a[i] := re]_{i=0}^{n}$)end.

Example 1. Let us model the counter circuit in Fig. 2. *LAST* is a symbolic parameter of natural number:

$S_1 \equiv last := 0;$

$S_2(LAST) \equiv tail := (last = LAST)?0 : \mathsf{Uif}(`` + ", [tail, 1]);$

counter$(LAST) \equiv$ CaseS$[rst = \mathsf{H} \rightarrow S_1, !rst = \mathsf{H} \rightarrow S_2(LAST)]$end

3.2   GSTE Graph

Definition 1. *An assertion graph is a five-tuple $G(N) \equiv (V(N), init, E(N), ant(N), cons(N))$, where $V(N)$ is a set of vertices containing a vertex init which is called the initial vertex; $E(N)$ is a set of edges. Each edge is a pair of vertices. Finally, $ant(N)$ and $cons(N)$ are two functions from edge to formula. $\mathsf{ant}(N)(e)$ is the antecedent of e, $\mathsf{cons}(N)(e)$ the consequent of e. For an edge $e = (n_1, n_2)$, we define $\mathsf{source}(e) \equiv n_1$, and $\mathsf{sink}(e) \equiv n_2$*

In Definition a vertex represents a symbolic state which can be reached from the initial vertex, and an edge a symbolic transition. The antecedent of the edge formulates the stimulus enforced to the input nodes of the circuit, and the consequent of the edge specifies the values expected on circuit nodes as a response.

However, notice that the assertion graph can be parameterized, namely, either the number of the nodes or those of the edges the graph can be a parameter, or a symbolic one. This is the most important feature which distinguishes our semantic theory from the classical GSTE theory. Figure 4 formalizes a parameterized assertion graph for the parameterized counter where $LAST$ are symbolic parameters, while Fig. 2 intuitively depict the parameterized graph.

---

vertexL$(LAST) \equiv [0, \cdots, LAST + 1]$
edgeL$(LAST) \equiv (LAST + 1, 1)\#[(i, i + 1).0 \le i \le LAST]$
antOfConuter$(LAST)(e) \equiv$
    let $from = $ source(e) in let $to = $ sink(e) in
    if $(from = 0)$ then $rst = H$ else $!rst = H$
consOfCounter$(LAST)(e) \equiv$
    let $from = $ source(e) in let $to = $ sink(e) in
    (if $(from = 0)$ then $chaos$ else $to - 1$
CounterGsteSpec$(LAST) \equiv (0, $vertexL$(LAST), $edgeL$(LAST), $antOfFifo$(LAST), $consOfFifo$(LAST))$

Fig. 4. Parameterized counter GSTE graph

3.3   Semantics

A circuit state s is an instantaneous snapshot of a circuit behavior given by an assignment of values to variables. In order to deal with parameterized verification, we allow both value and variable can be symbolic. A state sequence assigns a state to a time point. Here we still use a natural number t to define the type time. Thus, a state sequence is a mapping from time to a state.

A function f in our semantic domain is one mapping from a list of values to a value. An interpretation $\mathbb{I}$ of an operator opr is a mapping from opr to a function. Formal semantics of expressions and formulas at a state s w.r.t. an interpretation $\mathbb{I}$, are given in Table 1.

For convenience, we define tautology$(\mathbb{I}, f) \equiv \forall s.s \models_{\mathbb{I}} f$, and write tautology $\mathbb{I} f$ as $\models_{\mathbb{I}} f$. Next we formally define a state transition $s \overset{\mathbb{I},S}{\to} s$ caused by a statement S. Rule Par $- 1$ defines a skip transition of an NIL assignment list; Rule Par $- 2$ a state update to s' which replaces v with an evaluation of e at state s under interpretation $\mathbb{I}$, where s' is the result state from s after assignment $asgn$ is executed, note that we use $[\![e]\!]^{\mathbb{I}}_s$ instead of $[\![e]\!]^{\mathbb{I}}_{s'}$, thus all assignments in $(v := e)\#asgn$ are executed in parallel; Rule IF $- 1$ and IF $- 2$ defines the semantics of IF statement: the former says that S_1 branch is executed if b is satisfied; the latter says that branch S_2 is executed otherwise.

Definition 2. *We define the set of trajectories of a circuit M:*$[M]^{\mathbb{I}}$ *under an interpretation* $\mathbb{I}$ *inductively: (1)* $[] \in [M]^{\mathbb{I}}$*; (2)* $[s] \in [M]^{\mathbb{I}}$*; (3)* $(s\#s'\#sq) \in [M]^{\mathbb{I}} \equiv (s \overset{\mathbb{I},M}{\to} s' \wedge s'\#sq \in [M]^{\mathbb{I}})$

Table 1. Sematic of expressions and formulas

$$[\![v]\!]^I_s \equiv s(v), \text{ where } v \text{ is a variable}$$
$$[\![c]\!]^I_s \equiv c, \text{ where } c \text{ is a constant}$$
$$[\![f?e_1 : e_2]\!]^I_s \equiv$$
$$\text{if } s \models_I f \text{ then } [\![e_1]\!]^I_s \text{ else } [\![e_2]\!]^I_s$$
$$[\![\mathsf{Uif}(opr, opds)]\!]^I_s \equiv$$
$$\mathbb{I}(opr)([\![opds_1]\!]^I_s, \ldots, [\![opds_n]\!]^I_s)$$

$$s \models_I e_1 = e_2 \equiv [\![e_1]\!]^I_s = [\![e_2]\!]^I_s$$
$$s \models_I \,!f \equiv s \not\models_I f$$
$$s \models_I f_1 \& f_2 \equiv s \models_I f_1 \text{ and } s \models_I f_2$$
$$s \models_I f_1 \mid f_2 \equiv s \models_I f_1 \text{ or } s \models_I f_2$$
$$s \models_I f_1 \longrightarrow f_2 \equiv s \models_I f_1 \text{ implies } s \models_I f_2$$
$$s \models_I \mathsf{Uip}(opr, opds) \equiv$$
$$([\![opds_1]\!]^I_s, \ldots, [\![opds_n]\!]^I_s) \in \mathbb{I}(opr)$$
$$s \models_I \mathsf{chaos}$$
$$s \not\models_I \mathsf{miracle}$$

Table 2. Sematics of statements

$$\text{Par-1} \frac{}{s \xrightarrow{\mathbb{I}, \mathsf{Parallel}([])} s}$$

$$\text{Par-2} \frac{s \xrightarrow{\mathbb{I}, \mathsf{Parallel}(asgns)} s'}{s \xrightarrow{\mathbb{I}, \mathsf{Parallel}((v:=e)\#asgns)} s'(v \leftarrow [\![e]\!]^I_s)}$$

$$\text{IF-1} \frac{s \xrightarrow{\mathbb{I}, S_1} s' \quad s \models_I b}{s \xrightarrow{\mathbb{I}, \mathsf{IF}\ b\ \mathsf{THEN}\ S1\ \mathsf{ELSE}\ S2} s'}$$

$$\text{IF-2} \frac{s \xrightarrow{\mathbb{I}, S_2} s' \quad s \models_I !b}{s \xrightarrow{\mathbb{I}, \mathsf{IF}\ b\ \mathsf{THEN}\ S1\ \mathsf{ELSE}\ S2} s'}$$

Definition 3. *A list of edges p is one of the set of all the paths of $G \equiv (V, init, E, ant, cons)$, denoted by $\mathsf{pathOf}(G)$, if and only if (1) $[] \in \mathsf{pathOf}(G)$ or (2) $e\#es \in \mathsf{pathOf}(G) \equiv e \in E \wedge es \in \mathsf{pathOf}(G) \wedge (es = [] \vee \mathsf{source}((\mathsf{hd}(es)) = \mathsf{sink}(e))$*

Usually we consider a path starting from the initial node of a GSTE graph, and call it a GSTE path. Namely, we define: $p \in \mathsf{gstePath}(G)$ if $p \in \mathsf{pathOf}(G) \wedge (p \neq [] \longrightarrow \mathsf{source}(\mathsf{hd}(p) = init))$. E.g., $[(0,1),(1,2),(2,3)]$ is a GSTE path in Fig. 3.

Definition 4. *A state sequence sq satisfies a path p under a mapping ρ from edges to assertions if and only if the following conditions are satisfied: (1) $[] \models^\rho_I es$ (2) $sq \models^\rho_I []$ (3) $s\#sq \models^\rho_I e\#es \equiv sq \models^\rho_I es \wedge s \models_I \rho(e)$*

Now we can define the semantics of an assertion graph: a circuit M satisfies the specification formalized in an assertion graph under an interpretation.

Definition 5. *A circuit M satisfies an assertion graph $G = (V, init, E, ant, cons)$ under an interpretation $\mathbb{I}$, written $M \Vdash_I G$, if for any state sequence sq s.t. $sq \in [M]^I$, any path p s.t. $p \in \mathsf{gstePath}(G)$, $sq \models^{ant}_I p$ implies $sq \models^{cons}_I p$.*

4   Proving Assertion Graphs

In this section, we will introduce our main techniques which can be used to prove $M \Vdash_I G$. In order to do this, we need some preliminary definitions.

Definition 6. *Let* $[x_i \mapsto e_i]_{i=1}^n$ *denote a list of substitutions. Define*

$$c[x_i \mapsto e_i]_{i=1}^n = c$$

$$y[x_i \mapsto e_i]_{i=1}^n = \begin{cases} e_i \text{ if } y = x_i \text{ for some } i \\ y \text{ otherwise} \end{cases}$$

$$f?e_1 : e_2[x_i \mapsto e_i]_{i=1}^n =$$
$$f[x_i \mapsto e_i]_{i=1}^n ? e_1[x_i \mapsto e_i]_{i=1}^n : e_2[x_i \mapsto e_i]_{i=1}^n)$$
$$\mathsf{Uif}(fn, t_1, t_2, \dots, t_k)[x_i \mapsto e_i]_{i=1}^n =$$
$$\mathsf{Uif}(fn, t_1[x_i \mapsto e_i]_{i=1}^n, t_2[x_i \mapsto e_i]_{i=1}^n, \dots, t_k[x_i \mapsto e_i]_{i=1}^n)$$

Substitutions for formulas are defined similarly.

$$(t = t')[x_i \mapsto e_i]_{i=1}^n = t[x_i \mapsto e_i]_{i=1}^n = t'[x_i \mapsto e_i]_{i=1}^n$$
$$(!f)[x_i \mapsto e_i]_{i=1}^n = !f[x_i \mapsto e_i]_{i=1}^n$$
$$(f\&f')[x_i \mapsto e_i]_{i=1}^n = f[x_i \mapsto e_i]_{i=1}^n \& f'[x_i \mapsto e_i]_{i=1}^n$$
$$(f \mid f')[x_i \mapsto e_i]_{i=1}^n = f[x_i \mapsto e_i]_{i=1}^n \mid f'[x_i \mapsto e_i]_{i=1}^n$$
$$(f \longrightarrow f')[x_i \mapsto e_i]_{i=1}^n = f[x_i \mapsto e_i]_{i=1}^n \longrightarrow f'[x_i \mapsto e_i]_{i=1}^n$$
$$\mathsf{Uip}(pn, t_1, t_2, \dots, t_k)[x_i \mapsto e_i]_{i=1}^n =$$
$$\mathsf{Uip}(pn, t_1[x_i \mapsto e_i]_{i=1}^n, t_2[x_i \mapsto e_i]_{i=1}^n, \dots, t_k[x_i \mapsto e_i]_{i=1}^n)$$
$$\mathsf{Miracle}[x_i \mapsto e_i]_{i=1}^n = \mathsf{Miracle}$$
$$\mathsf{Chaos}[x_i \mapsto e_i]_{i=1}^n = \mathsf{Chaos}$$

$e[x_i \mapsto e_i]_{i=1}^n$ substitutes each occurrence of v_i in e by e_i; while $f[x_i \mapsto e_i]_{i=1}^n$ substitutes each occurrence of v_i in f by e_i. Basing on the substitution to expressions and formulas, we define the so-called the weakest precondition and pre-expression:

Definition 7. *The weakest precondition of a property f w.r.t. a statement and the pre-expression of an expression e w.r.t. a statement are defined as follows:*

$$preCond(f, Parallel[x_i := e_i]_{i=1}^n) = f[x_i \mapsto e_i]_{i=1}^n$$
$$preCond(f, \mathsf{IF}\ b\ \mathsf{THEN}\ S_1\ \mathsf{ELSE}\ S_2) =$$
$$b \longrightarrow preCond(f, S_1) \wedge \neg b \longrightarrow preCond(f, S_2)$$

$$preExp(e, Parallel[x_i := e_i]_{i=1}^n) = e[x_i \mapsto e_i]_{i=1}^n$$
$$preExp(e, \mathsf{IF}\ b\ \mathsf{THEN}\ S_1\ \mathsf{ELSE}\ S_2) =$$
$$b?preExp(e, S_1) : preExp(e, S_2)$$

4.1 General Induction

A tag function μ assigns a formula to a vertex n. Namely $\mu(n)$ stands for constraint specifications for states which are represented by n. Given a tag function μ to nodes, and a state sequence sq, a path p, we define a function $sq \Vdash_\mu^I p$, which specifies that sq and p have the same length, and sq_i satisfies $\mu(\text{source}(p_i))$ for any i s.t. $0 \leq i < |sq|$. Here sq_i denotes the i-th element of sq.

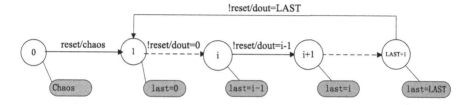

Fig. 5. An intuitive explaining of Example. 2

Definition 8. *Given a tag function μ to nodes, and a state sequence sq, and an interpretation $\mathbb{I}$, we define $sq \Vdash_\mu^\mathbb{I} p$ where (1) $[] \Vdash_\mu^\mathbb{I} []$ (2) $s\#sq \Vdash_\mu^\mathbb{I} e\#p \equiv sq \Vdash_\mu^\mathbb{I} p\&s \models_\mathbb{I} \mu(\mathsf{source}(e))$*

Intuitively, a tag function of a node n in a GSTE graph G represents a formula to characterize the reachable states at n after transitions specified transitions given by paths of G each of which starts from the initial vertex to n. Let us define a generally inductive relation:

Definition 9. *Let $G = (V, init, E, ant, cons)$ be an assertion graph, M be a circuit. G is called to be generally inductive w.r.t. M under an interpretation $\mathbb{I}$ if the following condition holds:* $\mathsf{induct}(G, M, \mu, \mathbb{I})$ *if and only if for all $e \in E$, for any s, $s \models_\mathbb{I} ant(e)$ and $s \models_\mathbb{I} \mu(\mathsf{source}(e))$, implies $s \models_\mathbb{I} \mathsf{preCond}(\mu(\mathsf{sink}(e)), M)$.*

Example 2. We define μ to be a tag function for the counter specification where $LAST > 0$ shown in Fig. 4 s.t. (1) $\mu(0) = \mathsf{Chaos}$; (2) $\forall i.0 \leq i \leq LAST, \mu(i+1) = last = i$.

Figure 5 illustrates the tag function in Example 2. Each tag function of a vertex formalizes its state in a symbolic way, namely a formula containing symbolic constant i or $LAST$.

In order to illustrate Definition 8 further, we need interpret the meaning of "$+$" operator occurring in the statements. Let us use only two axioms to specify $\mathbb{I}$ on the addition and subtraction operators:

Definition 10. axiomOnAdd: $\mathbb{I}("+")([i, 1]) = (i + 1)$

Here $\mathsf{axiomOnAdd}$ models the addition operation of 1 to an operand i.

Example 3. According to the definition of μ in Example 2 and Definition 10, where $0 < LAST$. Let $M = \mathsf{counter}(LAST)$. We have $\mathsf{induct}(G, M, \mu, \mathbb{I})$. Because

1. for $e = (0, 1)$, for any s, $s \models_\mathbb{I} \mathsf{preCond}(\mu(\mathsf{sink}(e)), M)$ if and only if $s \models_\mathbb{I} 0 = 0$.
2. for $e = (i + 1, i + 2)$ s.t. $0 \leq i < LAST - 1$, for any s, $s \models_\mathbb{I} last = i$ and $s \models_\mathbb{I} !rst = \mathsf{H}$, implies $s \models_\mathbb{I} last + 1 = i + 1$ which also implies $s \models_\mathbb{I} \mathsf{preCond}(\mu(\mathsf{sink}(e)), M)$;
3. for $e = (LAST + 1, 1)$, for any s, $s \models_\mathbb{I} last = LAST$ and $s \models_\mathbb{I} !rst = \mathsf{H}$, implies $s \models_\mathbb{I} 0 = 0$ which also implies $s \models_\mathbb{I} \mathsf{preCond}(\mu(\mathsf{sink}(e)), M)$;

Here the generally inductive relation means that characterization of the tag function μ to nodes can be preserved under the sequential behaviors (or transition relation) defined by an edge e of the graph $G = (V, init, E, ant, cons)$, where $ant(e)$ is the stimuli of the transition. Namely, For an edge $e = (n, n') \in E$, if $s \models_{\mathbb{I}} \mu(n)$, and $s \models_{\mathbb{I}} ant(e)$, and $s \overset{\mathbb{I},M}{\rightarrow} s'$, then $s' \models_{\mathbb{I},M} \mu(n')$.

Lemma 1. *Let $G = (V, init, E, ant, cons)$ be an assertion graph, M be a circuit, and* $\mathsf{induct}(G, M, \mu, \mathbb{I})$, *for any edge $e \in E$, for any state s, if $s \models_{\mathbb{I}} ant(e)\&\mu(\mathsf{source}(e))$ and $s \overset{\mathbb{I},M}{\rightarrow} s'$, then $s' \models_{\mathbb{I}} \mu(\mathsf{sink}(e))$.*

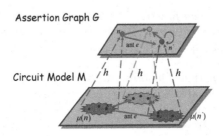

Fig. 6. GSTE graph M is an abstraction of the state space of M under the tag function μ

Remark 1. In fact, Lemma 1 shows the intuition behind the tag function μ and the generally inductive relation, which reveals the simulation relation from an assertion graph G to state space of the circuit model M, as shown in Fig. 6. Notice that $\mu(n)$ clusters a set of states. Here we can regard G as a high-level transition system, where an edge e is a transition from a node n to another one n' under a stimulus labeled by ant e. The edge e simulates any transition form s to s' under a stimulus ant e, where $s \in \mu(n)$ and $s \in \mu(n')$. In the other side, basing on the function μ, we can naturally derive an abstraction function h from a state s to a node n which is not the initial node of G s.t. $h\,s$ is the unique node n such that $s \in \mu(n)$ and $n \neq initial\ G$. In this sense, the subgraph of G, which excludes the initial node of G, is an abstraction of behaviours of the state space of M.

Consider a path p of a GSTE-graph G and a trajectory of a circuit M such that $\mathsf{induct}(G, M, \mu, \mathbb{I})$, if $sq \models_{\mathbb{I}}^{ant} p$, which means that each state of sq satisfies the stimulus constraint posed by the antecedent of G, then $sq \Vdash_{\mu}^{\mathbb{I}} p$.

Lemma 2. *Let $G = (V, init, E, ant, cons)$ be an assertion graph, M be a circuit. If* $\mathsf{induct}(G, M, \mu, \mathbb{I})$, *and for any state sequence sq s.t. $sq \in [M]^{\mathbb{I}}$, for any path p s.t. $p \in \mathsf{pathOf}(G)$, if $\mathsf{hd}(sq) \models_{\mathbb{I}} \mu(\mathsf{source}(\mathsf{hd}(p)))$, and $sq \models_{\mathbb{I}}^{ant} p$, then $sq \Vdash_{\mu}^{\mathbb{I}} p$.*

Example 4. Let sq is a state sequence with length $LAST + 3$ and p is a path length $LAST + 2$ in Fig. 5 s.t. (1) $sq_1 = [last \mapsto 0]$; (2) $sq_{1+i} = [last \mapsto i]$, where $0 < i \leq LAST$; (3) $p_0 = (0, 1)$, (4) $p_i = (i, i + 1)$, where $0 < i \leq LAST$ Notice that we need not specify anything about sq_0. We can check $sq \models_{\mathbb{I}}^{ant} p$, thus $sq \Vdash_{\mu}^{\mathbb{I}} p$.

4.2 Instantaneous Implication

Before we give our main theorem, we define a predicate which formalizes the instantaneous characterization decided by a combinational part of a circuit.

Definition 11. *Let* $G = (V, init, E, ant, cons)$ *be an assertion graph.* $\mathsf{instImply}(G, \mu, \mathbb{I})$ *if and only if for all* $e \in E$, *for all states* s, $s \models_{\mathbb{I}} ant(e)$ *and* $s \models_{\mathbb{I}} \mu(\mathsf{source}(e))$, *implies* $s \models_{\mathbb{I}} cons(e)$.

Lemma 3. *Let* $G = (V, init, E, ant, cons)$ *be an assertion graph, M be a circuit. If* $\mathsf{induct}(G, M, \mu, \mathbb{I})$, *and* $\mathsf{instImply}(G, \mu, \mathbb{I})$. *For any state sequence sq s.t.* $[M]^{\mathbb{I}} sq$, *for any path p s.t.* $p \in \mathsf{pathOf}(G)$, *if* $\mathsf{hd}(sq) \models_{\mathbb{I}} \mu(\mathsf{source}(\mathsf{hd}(p)))$, *and* $sq \models_{\mathbb{I}}^{ant} p$, *then* $sq \models_{\mathbb{I}}^{cons} p$.

　　If both the induction relation $\mathsf{induct}(G, M, \mu, \mathbb{I})$ and the instantaneous implication $\mathsf{instImply}(G, \mu, \mathbb{I})$ hold, and the initial vertex is assigned to chaos, then $M \Vdash_{\mathbb{I}} G$.

Theorem 1. *Let* $G = (V, init, E, ant, cons)$ *be an assertion graph, M be a circuit. If there is a tagging function s.t.* $\mathsf{induct}(G, M, \mu, \mathbb{I})$, *and* $\mathsf{instImply}(G, \mu, \mathbb{I})$, *and* $\mu(init) = \mathsf{chaos}$, *then* $M \Vdash_{\mathbb{I}} G$.

We have formalize all the theory in an Isabelle theory file, `paraGste.thy` [8], which has 1326 lines. In particular, we have formally proved all the lemmas and the main theorem in Isabelle. Thus we have a sound and formal base to do further case studies.

5 Case Studies

5.1 An Overview of Axiomatic Approach in Case Studies

Generally speaking, we need do the things in the case study as follows:

- We need interpret the semantics of uninterpreted function or predicate symbols used in the case study by introducing axioms. Namely, an axiomatic approach is adopted to formalize a semantic interpretation function $\mathbb{J}$.
- We shall construct a tag function μ which maps a node in G to a formula. Usually, the returned value of μ is a formula of conjunction of a list of formulas. These formulas are obtained by the intuition of the design principle of the circuit under design.
- We prove that $\mathsf{induct}(G, M, \mu, \mathbb{J})$. That is to say, the inductive relation should hold. Then we prove that $\mathsf{instImply}(G, \mu, \mathbb{I})$. At last by the main theorem 1, we can conclude $M \Vdash_{\mathbb{I}} G$.

　　Due to limitation of space, we only list the tag function μ, which are the most creative part of all parts of the case study. Interesting readers can refer to [8] for detailed Isabelle formalization and proofs.

5.2 Verification of a Ring Buffer Based FIFO

In this section, we consider the verification of the ring buffer based implementation of FIFO, which is taken from the examples of VIS [9]. The FIFO is shown in Fig. 7 (a) and the assertion graph is formalized in Fig. 7 (b). The *head* pointer points to the insertion point unless the buffer is full, and the *tail* one points to the first element in the queue unless the buffer is empty. On a *push* operation, the data is put to the entry indexed by the head pointer which is then incremented by 1 (modulo 3). On a *pop* operation, the data in the entry pointed by the tail pointer is read out and the tail pointer is incremented by 1. Initially, both pointers have value 0. A push on a full buffer is a NOOP. A pop from an empty buffer is a NOOP too. If both *push* and *pop* are asserted at the same clock cycle, only the push operation is performed. *dout* gives the first element of the queue unless the buffer is empty, in which case its value is arbitrary. The *full* is set when the tail pointer meets the head pointer from behind, indicating that the FIFO is full.

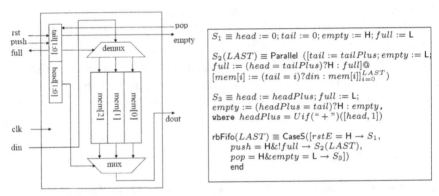

(a) Structure of Ring Buffer Based FIFO   (b) Formal model of Ring Buffer Based FIFO

Fig. 7. Ring buffer based FIFO

In Fig. 7(b), Branch 1 represents the resetting statement guarded by $rst =$ H. Branch 2 is the push action S_2 guarded by *push* and *!full* signals, where S_2 is composed of parallel actions of increase of *tail* , assigning L to *empty*, and assigning each *mem[i]* with a case expression $(i = tail)?din : mem[i])$ to *mem[i]*, and assigning *din* to *mem[0]*. Here we notice that *mem[tail]* := *din* is transformed into a list of parallel assignments to each *mem[i]*, among which only the *mem[i]* is assigned by *din* if *tail* = *i*. Note that the execution of S_2 causes only one update to one element of *mem[i]* such as *i* = *tail*. Less update to storage element causes less power consumption. So ring buffer based FIFO is more suitable for low-power computation environment such as mobile computing. Branch 3 is the pop action S_3 guarded by *push* and *!full* signals, where *head* is increased with one if *tail* is 0 and *full* is set L and *empty* is set if *headPlus* is equal to *tail*.

Because operator "+" in $rbFifo$ with a parameter $LAST$ is interpreted as addition modulo to $LAST+1$, thus we use the following axiom to interpret "+":

Definition 12. axiomOnAdd $\mathbb{I}("+")([i,1]) = (i+1)\%(LAST+1)$

Next we define plusN(e,n) to be an expression that is adding e with n.

Definition 13. *Definition of addition with n. (1)* plusN$(e,0) \equiv e$, *(2)* plusN$(e, (n+1)) \equiv$ Uif$("+", [$plusN$(e,n),1])$

The GSTE assertion graph with the tagging function is shown in Definition 14, which specifies the intuitive design principle of a ring-buffered FIFO.

Definition 14. *We define μ to be a tag function for the Fifo specification where $LAST > 0$ shown in Fig. 4 s.t.*

- $\mu(0) \equiv$ chaos;
- $\mu(1) \equiv tail = head \& empty = $ H$\& full = $ L;
- $\mu(2i+1) \equiv tail = $ plusN$(head, i) \& empty = $ L$\& full = $ L, *if* $1 \leq i \leq LAST$;
- $\mu(2i + 2) \equiv tail = $ plusN$(head, i) \& empty = $ L$\&$read$(mem, LAST, $ plusN$(head, i-1)) = $ D$\& full = $ L, *if* $1 \leq i \leq LAST$;
- $\mu(2 * LAST + 3) \equiv tail = head \& empty = $ L$\& full = $ H,
- $\mu(2 * LAST + 4) \equiv tail = head \& empty = $ L$\& full = $ H$\&$read$(mem, LAST, $ plusN$(head, LAST)) = $ D

Vertexes 0 is the initial node which is labelled with chaos, namely empty constraints. Vertex 1 is the state after resetting or being popped as empty. For all $1 \leq i \leq LAST$, vertex $(2i + 1)$ is a state that is neither empty nor full, and maintains an invariant that $tail = ($plusN $head\ i)$; vertex $(2i+2)$ is a state that is neither empty nor full, and maintains an invariant that $tail = $ plusN$(head, i-1)$, and *data* is stored in $mem[$plusN$(head, i-1)]$. vertex $2 * LAST + 3$ is a state that tail is the same as head, and the tag $full$ is set. vertex $2 * LAST + 4$ is almost the same as $2 * LAST + 3$ in addition to D is stored in $mem[$plusN$(head, LAST)$. Notice that at vertexes 1 and $2 * LAST + 3$ and $2 * LAST + 4$, $tail$ is the same as $head$ (because plusN$(head, (LAST+1))$ is equal to $head$ under our interpretation $\mathbb{I}$ which is specified in Definition 12. At vertex 1, $empty$ signal is set, while at vertex $2 * LAST + 3$ (or $2 * LAST + 4$) $full$ sinal is set. At a state where the queue is neither empty nor full, the number of elements is the difference between $tail$ and $head$ then modulo to $LAST + 1$ (Fig. 8).

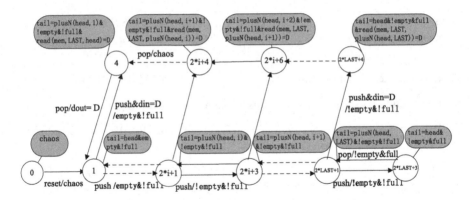

Fig. 8. An intuitive explaining of Definition. 14

5.3   Experiment Results

Besides the ring buffer FIFO, we also do case study on shift register FIFO and dynamic shift memory (also known as sequential shift) which are frequently used in FPGA (Field-Programmable Gate Array) designs.

All of the proof scripts of the three case studies are based on a public theory of parameterized GSTE `paraGste.thy`. We run Isabelle [6] to do proof checking of the proof theories in a workstation with an Intel Xeon processor, 8 GiB memory and 64-bit ubuntu 16.4. Experiment results are summarized in Table 3.

In our experiment, we find a subtle difference between the shifting-register FIFO and ring-buffer FIFO, the latter explicitly uses a register variable $full$ to indicate whether the FIFO is full. Even when $LAST = 0$ (namely the depth of the FIFO is 1), the FIFO still can be pushed into an element, and $full$ is set and $empty$ is reset; then with the data being popped out, the $full$ is reset

Table 3. Experiment results

theory	lines	Times
counter	202	8
srfifo	468	32
rbfifo	1388	49
dsmemory	475	8
paraGste	1326	22

and $empty$ is set. At all the time, head will be equal to tail. However, the output signal $full$ of the shift register based FIFO is assigned by the expression $tail = LAST$, the FIFO can't be pushed into any element if $LAST = 0$. That is to say, the shifting-register based design can't implement an instance with $LAST = 0$. So there is subtle difference between the two different kinds of designs of FIFO.

Although the two kinds of FIFOs in concrete size have been verified many times, our work has revealed the subtle difference between them, which has never been known by previous work. Besides, from our result, we know that the design of register shifting based FIFO is just correct when its length is greater than 1. From this, we know the importance of the parameterized verification of hardware design. Indeed, for the vast majority concrete size, a circuit design is correct.

But it is not valid for a special size. The case studies further demonstrate the novel features of our work.

6   Related Work

Techniques such as symbolic indexing and parametric representation of Boolean constraints have been integrated into STE [1,10–12]. STE is also enriched with lightweight theorem proving to have more expressive assertions through a strongly typed higher-order functional programming language called FL [5]. These are all implemented in the tool Forte.

STE/GSTE has relatively limited exposure in academics [13–15]. The work in [13] proposed an automatic abstraction algorithm for symbolic indexing. The counterexample-guided abstraction refinement framework was developed in [14]. The work proposed an algorithm to identify causes of imprecision through counterexamples from GSTE. It also developed two algorithms for model and specification refinements respectively. These algorithms are implemented in the tool AutoGSTE. Symmetry reduction has been applied to GSTE in order to alleviate the state explosion problem [15]. These work is all done at the Boolean level.

A word-level STE is developed to verify properties of System Verilog designs recently [16]. The idea is to derive more abstract lattices from RTL descriptions. The technique is essentially model checking via SMT. It does not consider parameterized designs.

7   Conclusion

In this work, we extend GSTE to the term level and develop a framework for parameterized hardware verification. We formalize assertion graphs and sufficient conditions to verify parameterized designs in the proof assistant Isabelle. Compared to Boolean-level STE/GSTE, our term-level assertion graphs give a more concise abstraction of parameterized designs (Fig. 6). Using our method, verifiers can get more insights to the correctness of parameterized hardware designs through assertion graphs. In our case studies, we demonstrate how to apply our method to identify subtleties in different designs of FIFOs.

In the future, we hope to extend our automatic proof technique [17] to automate the parameterized GSTE proof. The auxiliary invariants and the corresponding dependency relations among the discovered invariants can be found automatically. Besides, we will link our GSTE at term level with classical GSTE at Boolean level. The key is to instantiate the parameterized GSTE assertion graph with tagging functions, and an inductive invariants of an node will be fed into an SMT-slover, and all the solutions will be computed, and the disjunction of the concrete solutions will be transformed into bit level and tagged with the nodes of GSTE graph at Boolean level. The linkage can make the GSTE at Boolean level more efficient, which also can furthermore the correctness of the bound low level netlist synthesized by EDA tool. We also want to link our work with more advanced SMT-solver in order to make the verification more efficient.

Acknowledgements. Yongjian Li is supported by grant 61672503 from National Natural Science Foundation and grant 2017YFB0801900 from the National Key Research and Development Program in China.

References

1. Seger, C.J.H., Bryant, R.E.: Formal verification by symbolic evaluation of partially-ordered trajectories. Formal Meth. Syst. Des. **6**(2), 147–189 (1995)
2. Gordon, M.: Directions in formal and semi-formal verification (2011). http://www.cl.cam.ac.uk/~mjcg/Research00/
3. Yang, J., Seger, C.J.H.: Introduction to generalized symbolic trajectory evaluation. IEEE Trans. VLSI Syst. **11**(3), 345–353 (2003)
4. Yang, J., Goel, A.: GSTE through a case study. In: Pileggi, L.T., Kuehlmann, A. (eds.) ICCAD, pp. 534–541. ACM (2002)
5. Seger, C.J.H., et al.: An industrially effective environment for formal hardware verification. IEEE Trans. Comput. -Aided Des. Integrated Circ. Syst. **24**(9), 1381–1405 (2005)
6. Nipkow, T., Paulson, L.C., Wenzel, M.: Isabelle/HOL — A Proof Assistant for Higher-Order Logic. LNCS, vol. 2283. Springer, Heidelberg (2002). https://doi.org/10.1007/3-540-45949-9
7. Technical Publications and Training, Intel Corporation: Forte/fl user guide, 2003 edn (2003)
8. Parameterized generalized symbolic trajetory eveluation. https://github.com/raphelIos/parametricGste
9. Brayton, R.K., et al.: VIS: A system for verification and synthesis. In: Alur, R., Henzinger, T.A. (eds.) CAV 1996. LNCS, vol. 1102, pp. 428–432. Springer, Heidelberg (1996). https://doi.org/10.1007/3-540-61474-5_95
10. Adams, S., Bjork, M., Melham, T., Seger, C.J.: Automatic abstraction in symbolic trajectory evaluation. In: FMCAD 2007: Proceedings of the Formal Methods in Computer Aided Design, pp. 127–135. IEEE Computer Society, Washington, DC, USA (2007)
11. Pandey, M., Raimi, R., Bryant, R.E., Abadir, M.S.: Formal verification of content addressable memories using symbolic trajectory evaluation. In: DAC 1997: Proceedings of the 34th annual Design Automation Conference. pp. 167–172. ACM, New York, NY, USA (1997)
12. Jones, R.B.: Applications of symbolic simulation to the formal verification of microprocessors. Ph.D. thesis, Stanford, CA, USA (1999). AAI9958122
13. Adams, S., Björk, M., Melham, T., Seger, C.J.: Automatic abstraction in symbolic trajectory evaluation. In: Baumgartner, J., Sheeran, M. (eds.) Formal Methods in Computer Aided Design: FMCAD 2007: November 11–14 2007, Austin, Texas, USA. pp. 127–135. IEEE Computer Society (2007). http://www.cs.ox.ac.uk/tom.melham/pub/Adams-2007-AAS.pdf
14. Chen, Y., Xie, F., Yang, J.: Optimizing automatic abstraction refinement for generalized symbolic trajectory evaluation. In: Proceedings of the 45th Annual Design Automation Conference, pp. 143–148. DAC 2008, ACM, New York, NY, USA (2008). http://doi.acm.org/10.1145/1391469.1391508
15. Li, Y., Zeng, N., Hung, W.N.N., Song, X.: Combining symmetry reduction with generalized symbolic trajectory evaluation. Comput. J. **57**(1), 115–128 (2014)

16. Chakraborty, S., et al.: Word-Level Symbolic Trajectory Evaluation. In: Kroening, D., Păsăreanu, C.S. (eds.) CAV 2015. LNCS, vol. 9207, pp. 128–143. Springer, Cham (2015). https://doi.org/10.1007/978-3-319-21668-3_8
17. Li, Y., et al.: An automatic proving approach to parameterized verification. ACM Trans. Comput. Logic **19**(4), 27:1–27:25 (2018)

An Axiomatisation of the Probabilistic μ-Calculus

Junnan Xu[1,2], Wanwei Liu[3], David N. Jansen[1,4], and Lijun Zhang[1,2,4(✉)]

[1] Institute of Software, Chinese Academy of Sciences, Beijing, China
zhanglj@ios.ac.cn
[2] University of Chinese Academy of Sciences, Beijing, China
[3] College of Computer Science, National University of Defense Technology,
Changsha, China
[4] Institute of Intelligent Software, Guangzhou, China

Abstract. The probabilistic μ-calculus (PμTL) is a simple and succinct probabilistic extension of the propositional μ-calculus, by extending the 'next'-operator with a probabilistic quantifier. We extend the approach developed by Walukiewicz for propositional μ-calculus and provide an axiomatisation of PμTL. Our main contributions are a sound axiom system for PμTL, and a proof of its completeness for aconjunctive formulae.

1 Introduction and Summary

In the seminal paper [16], Kozen has introduced propositional μ-calculus, named μTL, as an extension of modal logic with the least fixpoint operator μ. He also investigated the axiomatisation of μTL, and presented an axiom system, inspired by [24]. Kozen showed that his axiomatisation is sound, and also complete for a subset of formulae, called *aconjunctive formulae*. In detail, it proves the negations of all unsatisfiable aconjunctive formulae. Completeness for the full logic seems to be rather intricate. Based on some deep investigations including [5,22,23], it was finally proven in [27] by Walukiewicz after more than a decade. Tamura [26] reformulated the proof by introducing wide tableaux and providing a more suitable definition of a tableau consequence.

In this paper we consider the probabilistic extension of μTL. Semantics for probabilistic programs have already been studied by Kozen in [15]. [22] have proposed an expectation-based logic for reasoning about probabilistic programs. Probabilistic CTL (PCTL), first introduced in [13], has gained popularity in recent years [4]. There are long lines of research into the model checking problem and satisfiability problem for PCTL* (and sublogics PCTL and PLTL), as in [1,3,4,6,7]. Recently, in [11], a complex deductive approach for PCTL* was introduced, which is however not complete.

Several probabilistic extensions of μTL have been studied, for example in [2,14,19,20,22]. In [21], a different extension of μ-calculus was proposed by Mio. He interpreted a formula as a function from states to real values in [0, 1]. The extension encodes full PCTL, however, model checking and satisfiability

© Springer Nature Switzerland AG 2019
Y. Ait-Ameur and S. Qin (Eds.): ICFEM 2019, LNCS 11852, pp. 420–437, 2019.
https://doi.org/10.1007/978-3-030-32409-4_26

algorithms are still unknown, as these calculi are known to be far from trivial. Another probabilistic μ-calculus was introduced in [10] along with a model checking algorithm for it. It is able to encode PCTL formulae as well. However, the calculus only allows alternation-free formulae.

Recently, direct extensions of μTL have been introduced independently in [8] and [18]. The logic PμTL in [18] uses the "next" operator X with a probability bound p to replace the "existential-next" operator $\Diamond$ and the "forall-next" operator $\Box$ (often parameterized with an action). The logic in [8] subsumes the one in [18]. The model checking problem is studied in both papers, and the satisfiability problem has been proven in [18] to be (at worst) double exponential. In [9], the complexity is improved to single exponential, meeting the lower bound for the satisfiability problem of μTL. Most recently, in [17], a probabilistic μ-calculus incomparable with PCTL* is introduced. An axiom system is proven to be sound and complete for its alternation-free fragment.

In this paper, we aim at establishing an axiomatisation for PμTL in [18]. Our approach is based on the work of [16,27]. The simple axioms $\langle a\rangle f \vee \langle a\rangle g \leftrightarrow \langle a\rangle (f \vee g)$ and $\langle a\rangle f \wedge [a]g \rightarrow \langle a\rangle (f \wedge g)$ suffice for μTL, but they do not suffice in the probabilistic setting. A naïve extension is incomplete, as it cannot prove sophisticated probability deductions such as $X^{>0.7}f \wedge X^{>0.7}g \wedge X^{>0.7}h \rightarrow X^{>0.1}(f \wedge g \wedge h)$.

Our first contribution is a sound axiom system. The main difficulty is to prove a conjunction of formulae whose outermost operator is X. Satisfiability of conjunctions of formulae gained by discarding the outermost X operator needs to be taken into account. We introduce an extra inference rule (EXT) described in cover notation. Axioms and inference rules for μTL are amended. We prove that the axiom system is sound.

On completeness, let us first recall the three main proof steps in [27] for μTL:

1. The first step is a tableau construction proposed by Streett and Emerson [25]. The *tableau* captures satisfiability of a formula: one can construct a model from a tableau of a satisfiable formula, and it was shown in [23] that if the formula is unsatisfiable then one can construct for the formula a tableau-like structure called a *refutation*. Parity games are introduced on tableaux. Starting at the root node, two players (called Satisfier and Devil) choose one child node in each step. A formula is satisfiable iff Satisfier has a winning strategy in the corresponding parity game. The existence of refutations plays an important role in the completeness proof.
2. The second step is a slight extension of Kozen's argument in [16]. For a given formula if there is a so-called *thin* refutation then its negation is provable. Now, a (weakly) aconjunctive formula has the property that every refutation for it is thin.
3. The third step is a reduction of an arbitrary formula to a special one. It cannot be proven that there is a semantically equivalent aconjunctive formula f' such that $f \rightarrow f'$ is provable for every formula f. Thus Walukiewicz introduced the notion of *disjunctive formulae* in a way that it is easier to show that the negation of an unsatisfiable disjunctive formula is provable. A technique called *tableau equivalence/consequence* is proposed to establish the last step of the proof.

Our second contribution is to establish the first two steps above, proving the completeness of PμTL on aconjunctive formulae. Tableaux/refutations and games on them are adapted to match probabilistic formulae. A new type of nodes, (COV) nodes, is added. We prove that a PμTL formula is satisfiable iff there is a tableau, and there is a refutation iff it is not satisfiable. In non-probabilistic tableau games, (MOD) nodes are played by Devil to indicate satisfiability of a conjunction of formulae whose outermost operator is $\langle \cdot \rangle$ or $[\cdot]$. Due to the complexity of the probabilistic setting, it is refined into two levels. Each (MOD) node is played by Satisfier followed by (COV) nodes played by Devil. Finally, we show that a formula is satisfiable iff Satisfier has a winning strategy.

Then we prove for a given PμTL formula with a thin refutation that its negation is provable. In our conservative extension, the concept *thin* still works, and still a refutation of an aconjunctive PμTL formula is thin. We follow Kozen's argument in a converse negative way, introduce counters and assign a formula on each node of the refutation. Counters record regeneration steps of the corresponding variable in the tableau. We prove that on each path some counter gets arbitrary big. It implies that there is a node equipped with a formula which can be reduced to a propositional tautology. By tracing back to the root node, we show the negation of the initial formula is provable.

The proof for the third step is quite involved, and it does not look like any direct modification can help for our probabilistic extension. We can still define disjunctiveness in PμTL, but constructing a semantically equivalent formula for an arbitrary formula fails. In μTL, we wind a tableau into a designated finite tree with back edges and construct a disjunctive formula so that its winding has the same shape. Then we confirm that the disjunctive formula is semantically equivalent to the original one. This step does not work in PμTL because given the shape of a (COV) node, we cannot always create a disjunctive formula with this exact shape. We leave this part as our future work.

In Sect. 3 we adapt the tableau construction for PμTL and the parity game. The main contributions of this paper are an axiom system for the logic PμTL and the soundness and completeness results for the class of aconjunctive formulae (Sect. 4).

Related Work. We have discussed some related work above. One of the key difficulties of probabilistic deduction is probability computation. If the logic contains an "until" operator, we may have to calculate infinite sums to characterize satisfiability, which significantly increases the difficulty to find a complete axiom system (see e.g. [11]). On the other side, our succinct system only needs to compute one-step probabilities and is hence easier, but the cover technique and tableau construction are rather intricate.

The axiomatisation in [17] uses a patch of rules to figure out the precise border of deduction with one-step probability computation, while our (EXT) rule does a similar job. Their (consistent) marking technique can be rewritten into our game terminology. Due to usage of (in-)equational modalities and blocks, their axiomatisation only handles the alternation-free fragment. Our axiomatisation does not have these constraints and has potential to reach full completeness.

In [9], the satisfiability of PμTL is discussed, and we shall discuss the relations in the paper.

2   Preliminaries

In this section we recall PμTL in the style of [18].

Syntax. Let us fix a countable set $\mathscr{A}$ of *atomic propositions* and fix a countable set $\mathscr{Z}$ of *formula variables*. We will use a, a_1, a_2 etc. to range over $\mathscr{A}$ and Z, Z_1, Z_2 etc. to range over $\mathscr{Z}$. We also use p, p_1, p_2, etc. to denote *probabilities*, i.e., real numbers in the interval of $[0,1]$. For convenience, we use $\rhd$ to range over $\{>,\geq\}$, and we use $\overline{\rhd}$ to represent the other inequality sign, i.e. $\overline{\rhd} \in \{>,\geq\} \setminus \{\rhd\}$.

Formulae of PμTL, denoted f, g etc., can be constructed by the following grammar:

$$f ::= \bot \mid a \in \mathscr{A} \mid Z \in \mathscr{Z} \mid f \rightarrow f \mid \mathsf{X}^{>p} f \mid \mu Z.f$$

We say that an occurrence of Z in f is *bound* if it is in the scope of some μZ; otherwise, this occurrence is *free*. In addition, in $\mu Z.f$ we require that all free occurrences of Z in f are *positive*. Formally: If $f = Z$, then Z occurs positively in f. – If $f = f_n \rightarrow f_p$, $f = \mathsf{X}^{>p} f_p$ or $f = \mu Z.f_p$, then variables occurring negatively in f_n or positively in f_p occur positively in f and vice versa.

Given a formula f and a variable Z, replacing each free occurrence of Z in f by a formula g, we can get a *substitution* of Z by g on f, denoted by $f[g/Z]$. As usual, we use the following derived operators as syntactic sugar:

$$\top \stackrel{\text{def}}{=} \neg \bot$$

$$\neg f \stackrel{\text{def}}{=} f \rightarrow \bot \qquad\qquad f_1 \vee f_2 \stackrel{\text{def}}{=} \neg f_1 \rightarrow f_2$$

$$f_1 \wedge f_2 \stackrel{\text{def}}{=} \neg(\neg f_1 \vee \neg f_2) \qquad f_1 \leftrightarrow f_2 \stackrel{\text{def}}{=} (f_1 \rightarrow f_2) \wedge (f_2 \rightarrow f_1)$$

$$\nu Z.f \stackrel{\text{def}}{=} \neg \mu Z.\neg f[\neg Z/Z] \qquad \mathsf{X}^{\geq p} f \stackrel{\text{def}}{=} \neg \mathsf{X}^{>1-p} \neg f$$

$$\mathsf{X}^{\rhd r} f \stackrel{\text{def}}{=} \mathsf{X}^{>1} f \text{ for } r > 1 \qquad \mathsf{X}^{\rhd r} f \stackrel{\text{def}}{=} \mathsf{X}^{\geq 0} f \text{ for } r < 0$$

The last two formulas extend the $\mathsf{X}^{\rhd r}$ operator to "probabilities" outside the range $[0,1]$.

With these derived operators, we may transform a formula into *positive normal form* (*PNF*, for short). That is, we write formulas using the grammar:

$$f ::= \bot \mid \top \mid a \mid \neg a \mid Z \mid \neg Z \mid f_1 \vee f_2 \mid f_1 \wedge f_2 \mid \mathsf{X}^{>p} f \mid \mathsf{X}^{\geq p} f \mid \mu Z.f \mid \nu Z.f$$

Note that in PNF, f can have a subformula $\neg Z$ only if this occurrence of Z is free.

We denote the (free and bound) variables in f by $\mathsf{Var}(f)$ and the subformulae of f by $\mathsf{Sub}(f)$. We classify a PμTL formula in PNF referring to its outermost operator, e.g., we call $\mathsf{X}^{>0} g$ a X-formula while $\mu Z.g$ a μ-formula. In addition, we collectively call a μ-formula or a ν-formula a σ-formula. Further, we recall the following definitions:

1. A formula of the form a or $\neg a$ and $\top, \bot$ is called *literal*. We denote the set of literals in a set of formulae Γ, by $\mathsf{Lit}(\Gamma)$.
2. A formula f is *well-named* if each bound variable is bound exactly once, and bound variables and free variables do not share the same names.
3. Assume that f is well-named and is in PNF. Then, the *binder function* $\mathscr{D}_f$ of f is a function that maps each bound variable of f to the σ-subformula of f with the variable. Note that each bound variable Z occurring in a well-named f has a unique fixpoint operator $\sigma_Z \in \{\mu, \nu\}$ whose scope is g_Z, forming a subformula $\sigma_Z Z.g_Z$ of f. Thus the binder function is unique.
4. Suppose a PμTL formula f is well-named and in PNF. It is *guarded* if for each bound variable Z, each of its occurrences is in some X-subformula of $\mathscr{D}_f(Z)$.

We call Z a *μ-variable* (resp. *ν-variable*) if $\mathscr{D}_f(Z) = \mu Z.g_Z$ (resp. $\mathscr{D}_f(Z) = \nu Z.g_Z$).

Definition 1 (Dependency order). *Assume that f is well-named. We define the dependency relation $\sqsubset_f$ over its bound variables, which is the minimal partial order fulfilling that Z_1 is free in $\mathscr{D}_f(Z_2)$ implies $Z_1 \sqsubset_f Z_2$.*

Let f be a formula with a binder function $\mathscr{D}_f$ consistent with $\sqsubset_f$, i.e. Z_1 is free in $\mathscr{D}_f(Z_2)$ implies $Z_1 \sqsubset_f Z_2$. For every $g \in \mathsf{Sub}(f)$ we define the *expansion* of g with respect to $\mathscr{D}_f$ as $\langle [g] \rangle_{\mathscr{D}_f} = g[\mathscr{D}_f(Z_n)/Z_n] \cdots [\mathscr{D}_f(Z_1)/Z_1]$, where the order $(Z_1, Z_2, \ldots, Z_n)$ is an arbitrary linearisation of $\sqsubset_f$, i.e. $Z_i \sqsubset_f Z_j$ implies $i < j$. This is well-defined since the expansion is independent of the choice of linearisation. The set of expansions of the subformulae of f, $\{\langle [g] \rangle_{\mathscr{D}_f} \mid g \in \mathsf{Sub}(f)\}$, is the so-called Fisher–Ladner closure of f.

The expansions may be not well-named. However we can fix this by proper variable renaming. That is, for each variable, rename occurrences introduced by each substitution (of some $\sqsubset_f$-larger variable) and native occurrences of the same bound variable to different variables, but all free variables are still candidates for later substitutions.

Example 2. Let $f = \mu Z_1.(a_1 \vee \mu Z_2.(Z_1 \vee Z_2 \vee a_2))$, $g = Z_1 \vee Z_2 \vee a_2 \in \mathsf{Sub}(f)$. We have

$$\langle [g] \rangle_{\mathscr{D}_f} = (Z_1 \vee Z_2 \vee a_2)[\mathscr{D}_f(Z_2)/Z_2][\mathscr{D}_f(Z_1)/Z_1]$$
$$= \big(Z_1 \vee \underbrace{\mu Z_2.(Z_1 \vee Z_2 \vee a_2)}_{\mathscr{D}_f(Z_2)} \vee a_2\big)[\mathscr{D}_f(Z_1)/Z_1] \tag{2a}$$
$$= \underbrace{\mu Z_1.(a_1 \vee \mu Z_2.(Z_1 \vee Z_2 \vee a_2))}_{\mathscr{D}_f(Z_1)}$$
$$\vee \mu Z_2.\big(\underbrace{\mu Z_1.(a_1 \vee \mu Z_2.(Z_1 \vee Z_2 \vee a_2))}_{\mathscr{D}_f(Z_1)} \vee Z_2 \vee a_2\big) \vee a_2 \tag{2b}$$

Of the two occurrences of Z_1 in (2a), the first is native, and the second is introduced by substitution. Their expansions should be assigned different names, meanwhile both of them will be substituted in (2b) as they are free. The final result after making this well-named is something like

$$\langle[g]\rangle_{\mathscr{D}_f} = \mu Z_1.(a_1 \vee \mu Z_2.(Z_1 \vee Z_2 \vee a_2))$$
$$\vee \mu Z_3.\Big(\mu Z_4.(a_1 \vee \mu Z_5.(Z_4 \vee Z_5 \vee a_2)) \vee Z_3 \vee a_2\Big) \vee a_2.$$

Semantics. A *Markov chain* is a tuple $M = (S, P, L_M)$, where S is a finite set of states; $P : S \times S \to [0, 1]$ is a *distribution function*, fulfilling that $\sum_{s' \in S} P(s, s') = 1$ for each $s \in S$; and $L_M : S \to 2^{\mathscr{A}}$, is the *labelling function*. Indeed, PμTL is insensitive to whether the Markov chain is finite, but it is needed in the completeness proof, as in the classical non-probabilistic setting.

The *semantics* of a PμTL formula f is defined w.r.t. a Markov chain $M = (S, P, L_M)$ and a *valuation* $e : \mathscr{Z} \to 2^S$, denoted by $[\![f]\!]_M^e$, which returns a subset of S. Inductively:

1. $[\![\bot]\!]_M^e = \varnothing$;
2. $[\![a]\!]_M^e = \{s \in S \mid a \in L_M(s)\}$;
3. $[\![Z]\!]_M^e = e(Z)$;
4. $[\![f_1 \to f_2]\!]_M^e = (S \setminus [\![f_1]\!]_M^e) \cup [\![f_2]\!]_M^e$;
5. $[\![\mathsf{X}^{>p} f]\!]_M^e = \{s \in S \mid \sum_{s' \in [\![f]\!]_M^e} P(s, s') > p\}$;
6. $[\![\mu Z.f]\!]_M^e = \bigcap \{S' \subseteq S \mid [\![f]\!]_M^{e[Z \mapsto S']} \subseteq S'\}$.

   Here, $e[Z \mapsto S']$ is a valuation which agrees with e except that it assigns S' to Z.

For convenience, we denote by $M, s \models_e f$ in the case of $s \in [\![f]\!]_M^e$. When f is *closed* (i.e. no free variable occurs in f), we may abbreviate it to $M, s \models f$.

We say that f is a *valid formula*, denoted by $\models f$, iff $M, s \models f$ for every Markov chain M and each state s of M. In addition, we say that f is *satisfiable* if $f \to \bot$ is not valid. A set of formulae Γ is *satisfiable* if there exists some Markov chain M and a state s, such that $M, s \models f$ for every $f \in \Gamma$.

3   Tableau

In this section we adapt the tableau construction of μTL to our logic. As for μTL, we assume the input formula f to be well-named, in PNF and guarded.

We first recall the notions of modal sets, cover and parse function.

Definition 3 (Modal set). *A set Γ of formulae of the form $\{\mathsf{X}^{\triangleright p_1} f_1, \ldots, \mathsf{X}^{\triangleright p_n} f_n, l_1, \ldots, l_s\}$ where $l_1, \ldots, l_s$ are literals (or free variables), is called a* modal set. *Further, we define* $\mathsf{Post}(\Gamma) = \{f_1, \ldots, f_n\}$.

A modal set is called consistent *iff it doesn't contain $\bot$ nor conflicting literals.*

Definition 4 (Cover). *Given a modal set $\Gamma \subseteq \mathsf{Sub}(f)$, a* cover *$\mathscr{C}$ of Γ is a non-empty subset of $2^{\mathsf{Post}(\Gamma)} \setminus \{\varnothing\}$ such that there exists a weight function $w : \mathscr{C} \to [0, 1]$ satisfying $\sum_{\Delta \in \mathscr{C}} w(\Delta) \leq 1$ and for all $\mathsf{X}^{\triangleright p} g \in \Gamma$, it holds that $\sum_{\Delta \ni g} w(\Delta) \triangleright p$.*

Denote the covers of Γ by $\mathsf{Cov}(\Gamma)$. Denote the covers induced by subformulae of f by $\mathsf{Cov}_f := \{\mathscr{C} \mid \Gamma \subseteq \mathsf{Sub}(f) \text{ is a modal set}, \mathscr{C} \in \mathsf{Cov}(\Gamma)\}$.

We recall the definition of tableau and game from [9]. A tableau is a tree whose nodes are labelled with either a set of formulae or a cover to satisfy. Intuitively, the labels store requirements on satisfiability. The nodes labelled with a set of formulae are called T_0-nodes whereas the nodes labelled with a cover are called T_1-nodes. At every T_0-node, if its label is not a modal set, then some formula g is composite and can be simplified; if its label is a consistent modal set, we construct T_1-nodes as its children, one for each cover. At every T_1-node, we construct a T_0-node labelled with Δ, for each member Δ of the cover. Branches may be infinite, or end in a T_0 leaf with inconsistent labels, or end in a T_0 leaf without covers (either because the X formulae are inconsistent or because the modal set does not contain any X formulae).

Definition 5 (Tableau). *Given a formula f, a tableau is a labelled tree $\mathscr{T} = (T, R, r, L_T)$ where T is a set of nodes, $R \subseteq T \times T$ is the children relation, r is the root node, $L_T : T \to 2^{\mathsf{Sub}(f)} \cup \mathsf{Cov}_f$ is a labelling function satisfying the conditions below.*

For each node m, $R_m = \{n \mid (m, n) \in R\}$ denotes the children of m. We use $T_0 = \{m \mid m \in T, L_T(m) \in 2^{\mathsf{Sub}(f)}\}$ and $T_1 = \{m \mid m \in T, L_T(m) \in \mathsf{Cov}_f\}$ to denote the two disjoint kinds of nodes. We define the function $A : T \setminus \{r\} \to T_0$ that maps m to its closest ancestor in T_0. Additionally, we define the following functions:

1. *A function $\mathsf{Hook} : T \to 2^{\mathsf{Sub}(f)}$ that maps each node m to a subset of $L_T(m)$,*
2. *For each node $m \in T_0 \setminus \{r\}$, a function $\mathsf{Target}_m : \mathsf{Hook}(m) \to L_T(A(m))$.*

The labelling function and functions Hook, Target_m satisfy the following conditions: (i) $L_T(r) = \{f\}$. (Thus $r \in T_0$, which ensures the well-definedness of A). (ii) For all $m \in T$, it is always one of the following cases:

1. *$m \in T_0$, $g = g_1 \vee g_2 \in L_T(m)$, $R_m = \{n_1, n_2\}$, $L_T(n_1) = L_T(m) \cup \{g_1\} \setminus \{g\}$ and $L_T(n_2) = L_T(m) \cup \{g_2\} \setminus \{g\}$.*
   In this case, we call m a (OR)-node and define $\mathsf{Hook}(n_1) = \{g_1\}$, $\mathsf{Hook}(n_2) = \{g_2\}$, $\mathsf{Target}_{n_1}(g_1) = \mathsf{Target}_{n_2}(g_2) = g$.
2. *$m \in T_0$, $g = g_1 \wedge g_2 \in L_T(m)$, $R_m = \{n\}$, $L_T(n) = L_T(m) \cup \{g_1, g_2\} \setminus \{g\}$.*
   In this case, we call m an (AND)-node and define $\mathsf{Hook}(n) = \{g_1, g_2\}$, $\mathsf{Target}_n(g_1) = \mathsf{Target}_n(g_2) = g$.
3. *$m \in T_0$, $g = \sigma_Z Z.g_Z \in L_T(m)$, $R_m = \{n\}$, $L_T(n) = L_T(m) \cup \{g_Z\} \setminus \{g\}$.*
   In this case, we call m a (σ_Z)-node and define $\mathsf{Hook}(n) = \{g_Z\}$, $\mathsf{Target}_n(g_Z) = g$.
4. *$m \in T_0$, $g = Z \in L_T(m)$, $R_m = \{n\}$, $L_T(n) = L_T(m) \cup \{g_Z\} \setminus \{g\}$.*
   In this case, we call m a (REG)-node and define $\mathsf{Hook}(n) = \{g_Z\}$, $\mathsf{Target}_n(g_Z) = g$.
5. *$m \in T_0$, $L_T(m)$ is a consistent modal set, $R_m = \{n_{\mathscr{C}} \mid \mathscr{C} \in \mathsf{Cov}(L_T(m))\}$ and $L_T(n_{\mathscr{C}}) = \mathscr{C}$ for every $\mathscr{C} \in \mathsf{Cov}(L_T(m))$. (If $L_T(m)$ only contains literals then $R_m = \varnothing$.)*
6. *$m \in T_0$, $L_T(m)$ is an inconsistent modal set, $R_m = \varnothing$, i.o.w. m is a leaf node.*
   In the above two cases, we call m a (MOD)-node.

7. $m \in T_1$, $L_T(m) = \mathscr{C}$, $R_m = \{n_\Delta \mid \Delta \in \mathscr{C}\}$, $L_T(n_\Delta) = \Delta$ *for every* $\Delta \in \mathscr{C}$.
In this case, we call m a (COV)-*node and claim that for every $g \in \Delta$ and $\Delta \in C$ there is a unique formula of the form* $\mathsf{X}^{\triangleright p}g \in L_T(A(n_\Delta))$, *define* $\mathsf{Hook}(n_\Delta) = \Delta$, $\mathsf{Target}_{n_\Delta}(g) = \mathsf{X}^{\triangleright p}g$.

For a given formula f, multiple tableaux may exist. This is because, in a top-down construction, when we are at some node $m \in T_0$, several of the first four cases may be available to construct child nodes. We can choose any of them and this leads to different (but equivalent) tableaux. If neither of the first four cases is available, then $L_T(m)$ must be a modal set. Thus either Case 5 or Case 6 is available. If it is Case 5, then each of its child nodes n_C is a T_1-node. Then Case 7 is available and each grandchild node n_Δ belongs to T_0 so we can continue with the construction of the tableau.

Note that according to the definition above, for every T_0-node m and $g \in L_T(m) \setminus \mathsf{Hook}(m)$, we have $g \in L_T(A(m))$. Hence we can extend the domain of every Target_m to the whole $L_T(m)$, denoted by Target_m^+, by mapping each element $g \in L_T(m) \setminus \mathsf{Hook}(m)$ to itself. Formally: $\mathsf{Target}_m^+(g)$ equals to $\mathsf{Target}_m(g)$ if $g \in \mathsf{Hook}(m)$, and to g otherwise.

Definition 6 (Trace). *Given an infinite path $\mathscr{P}$ of a tableau $\mathscr{T} = (T, R, r, L_T)$, a trace on $\mathscr{P}$ will be a function π assigning a formula to every node $n \in T_0$ along $\mathscr{P}$ satisfying:*

1. $\pi(n) \in L_T(n)$. *Particularly,* $\pi(r) = f$.
2. *If* $n \neq r$, $\pi(A(n)) = \mathsf{Target}_n^+(\pi(n))$.

Definition 7 (Regeneration on a trace/path). *Given a trace π on an infinite path $\mathscr{P}$, we say that there is a* regeneration *of a variable Z on $\mathscr{P}$ at a node n if $\mathsf{Hook}(n) = \{g_Z\}$ and $\mathsf{Target}_n(g_Z) = Z$. The regeneration of Z at n is on π if $\pi(A(n)) = Z$ and $\pi(n) = g_Z$.*

Note that moving down along a path $\mathscr{P}$, the size of the formulae in the labels on T_0-nodes decreases except when a regeneration occurs. Hence regenerations occur infinitely often on an infinite path. Since f is guarded and each subformula cannot regenerate before losing its X-operator, there are infinitely many (MOD)-nodes too. Thus on every trace, the size of the formula decreases infinitely often, which implies that there are infinitely many regenerations on the trace. Let $\mathsf{Inf}_R(\pi)$ denote the set of variables which regenerate infinitely often on π. As it can be easily proven [27], there exists a unique least variable $Z_0 \in \mathsf{Inf}_R(\pi)$ with respect to $\sqsubseteq_f$, i.e. $\forall Z \in \mathsf{Inf}_R(\pi)$, $Z_0 \sqsubseteq_f Z$.

Definition 8 (μ-trace and ν-trace). *We call a trace a μ-trace (resp. ν-trace) iff the least variable (w.r.t. $\sqsubseteq_f$) regenerated infinitely often is a μ-variable (resp. ν-variable).*

We call a path $\mathscr{P}$ an odd path *if either it is infinite and there exists a μ-trace on it or it is finite and ends in an inconsistent leaf node, else we call it an even path.*

Definition 9 (Tableau game). *A tableau game G for a formula f is a game played on a tableau $\mathscr{T}$ of f by two players, say* Satisfier *and* Devil. *Intuitively,* Satisfier *intends to show that f is satisfiable whereas* Devil *that it is not. They play the game as follows:*

1. *The game starts at the root node r,*
2. *In any* (COV) *node* Devil *chooses one of the children, in any other node* Satisfier *chooses one of the children.*
3. *The result of such a game is either a finite or an infinite path of the tableau $\mathscr{T}$.* Satisfier *wins iff the path is even.*

Theorem 10. *Let G be a tableau game for a formula f. There is always a player who has a winning strategy in G.*

To show the above theorem, similar as in [9], we exploit the *determinacy result* [12] for parity games. This is accomplished by defining a parity game $\mathscr{G}$ which is a product of G and a deterministic parity automaton $\mathscr{A}$. It follows then that one has a winning strategy in G iff he/she has a winning strategy in $\mathscr{G}$.

Remark 11. Deviating slightly from [9], we label the tableau nodes with subformulae rather than expansions (i.e., members of the Fisher–Ladner closure). The purpose of labelling with subformulae is to simplify the completeness proof.

Theorem 12. *For a given formula f, let $\mathscr{T}$ and G be the tableau and tableau game, respectively. Then,* Satisfier *has a winning strategy in G iff f is satisfiable.*

The winning tree of Devil will be referred to as *refutation*, which will play an important role in the completeness proof.

Definition 13 (Refutation). *The winning tree of* Devil *in a tableau game G on $\mathscr{T}$ is called a refutation $\mathscr{R}$. That is, a subtree of $\mathscr{T}$ which contains all child nodes at each T_0-node but only one child node at each T_1-node according to the winning strategy.*

Corollary 14. *If f is unsatisfiable then every tableau for f has a refutation.*

4   The Axiom System

Now we give a Kozen-style axiom system for PμTL. Given a set of formulae Γ, we denote $\bigvee_{g \in \Gamma} g$ by $\bigvee \Gamma$, and we use $\bigwedge \Gamma$ analogously. The system consists of the following axioms: (K1) all tautologies of propositional logic; (K2) $X^{>1} f \to \bot$; (K3) $f[\mu Z.f/Z] \to \mu Z.f$; and the inference rules

$$(\text{K4}) \qquad \frac{f \to g \quad f}{g}$$

$$(\text{K5}) \qquad \frac{f[g/Z] \to g}{(\mu Z.f) \to g}$$

$$(\text{Ext}) \qquad \frac{\bigwedge B \to \bot, \forall B \in \mathscr{B}}{\bigwedge \Gamma \to \bot},$$

where Γ is a modal set, $\mathscr{B} \subseteq 2^{\text{Post}(\Gamma)}$
and for all $\mathscr{C} \in \text{Cov}(\Gamma)$, $\mathscr{B} \cap \mathscr{C} \neq \varnothing$.

Axioms (K1), (K3), (K4), (K5) are the same as the axioms for μTL. The simple axiom (K2) will be used frequently to derive contradictions in the probabilistic setting.

The innovative (EXT) rule closely corresponds to the (MOD)–(COV) structure in a tableau. For a set of X-formulae Γ, it may happen that the probabilities of mutually exclusive formulas in $\mathsf{Post}(\Gamma)$ are so high that no cover of Γ exists. Then, a complete proof system should allow to infer $\bigwedge \Gamma \to \bot$. The antecedents of (EXT) describes the mutually exclusive formulas: every $B \subseteq \mathsf{Post}(\Gamma)$ in $\mathscr{B}$ is such a set of formulas.

Example 15. Let $\Gamma = \{\mathsf{X}^{>0.7}a, \mathsf{X}^{>0.7}b, \mathsf{X}^{>0.7}(\neg a \vee \neg b)\}$. Then $\mathsf{Post}(\Gamma) = \{a, b, \neg a \vee \neg b\}$. Let $\mathscr{B} = \{\mathsf{Post}(\Gamma)\}$. Note that $\{\{a, b\}, \{a, \neg a \vee \neg b\}, \{b, \neg a \vee \neg b\}\}$ (all maximal proper subsets of $\mathsf{Post}(\Gamma)$) is not a cover of Γ because there is no weight function for this set. Therefore, every element $\mathscr{C} \in \mathsf{Cov}(\Gamma)$ must contain $\mathsf{Post}(\Gamma)$, so $\mathscr{B} \cap \mathscr{C} \neq \varnothing$. Thus the requirements for (EXT) are fulfilled, and we can conclude:

$$\frac{a \wedge b \wedge (\neg a \vee \neg b) \to \bot}{\mathsf{X}^{>0.7}a \wedge \mathsf{X}^{>0.7}b \wedge \mathsf{X}^{>0.7}(\neg a \vee \neg b) \to \bot}$$

A *proof* of f is a sequence $f_0, f_1, \ldots, f_n = f$ where each f_i is either an instance of some axiom or obtained via applying some inference rule. We say that f is *provable*, denoted $\vdash f$, if there exists a proof of f. f is *consistent* if $\neg f$ is not provable.

4.1 An Equivalent Formulation of the (EXT) Rule

Although (EXT) looks neat, it is rather tedious to calculate all the covers of a modal set. Below we present an equivalent (EXT$'$) rule, which reduces it to a linear programming problem that is easier to solve in practice. This will be used later in proving the soundness result and other properties.

(EXT$'$) $\dfrac{\bigwedge B \to \bot, \forall B \in \mathscr{B}}{\bigwedge \Gamma \to \mathsf{X}^{\triangleright q} \bigvee \mathsf{Post}(\Gamma)}$

           where Γ is a modal set, $\mathscr{B} \subseteq 2^{\mathsf{Post}(\Gamma)}$

           and $\triangleright q$ is decided by the linear programming problem below.

First we calculate the optimal value of the following linear programming problem.

$$\mathsf{Opt} = \inf \sum_{\Delta : \Delta \subseteq \mathsf{Post}(\Gamma)} w_\Delta$$

$$\text{s.t.} \quad w_\Delta \geq 0, \quad \forall \Delta \subseteq \mathsf{Post}(\Gamma)$$

$$w_\Delta = 0, \quad \forall \Delta \in \mathscr{B} \qquad (*)$$

$$\sum_{\Delta : g \in \Delta} w_\Delta \triangleright p, \quad \forall \mathsf{X}^{\triangleright p} g \in \Gamma$$

We determine $\rhd q$ by:

- If (*) does not have a valid solution, (this instance of) (EXT′) cannot be applied.
- If the infimum in (*) is achievable, we set $\rhd q$ to $\geq$ Opt.
- If the infimum in (*) is not achievable, we set $\rhd q$ to $>$ Opt.

Example 16. Still let $\Gamma = \{\mathsf{X}^{>0.7}a, \mathsf{X}^{>0.7}b, \mathsf{X}^{>0.7}(\neg a \vee \neg b)\}$, $\mathscr{B} = \{\mathsf{Post}(\Gamma)\}$. The corresponding linear programming problem is:

$$\mathsf{Opt} = \inf_{\Delta : \Delta \subseteq \mathsf{Post}(\Gamma)} \sum w_\Delta$$
$$\text{s.t. } w_\Delta \geq 0, \quad \forall \Delta \subseteq \mathsf{Post}(\Gamma)$$
$$w_{\{a,b,\neg a \vee \neg b\}} = 0$$
$$w_{\{a\}} + w_{\{a,b\}} + w_{\{a,\neg a \vee \neg b\}} + w_{\{a,b,\neg a \vee \neg b\}} > 0.7$$
$$w_{\{b\}} + w_{\{a,b\}} + w_{\{b,\neg a \vee \neg b\}} + w_{\{a,b,\neg a \vee \neg b\}} > 0.7$$
$$w_{\{\neg a \vee \neg b\}} + w_{\{a,\neg a \vee \neg b\}} + w_{\{b,\neg a \vee \neg b\}} + w_{\{a,b,\neg a \vee \neg b\}} > 0.7$$

The solution $\mathsf{Opt} = 1.05$ is not achievable, so the application of (EXT′) gives:

$$\frac{a \wedge b \wedge (\neg a \vee \neg b) \rightarrow \bot}{\mathsf{X}^{>0.7}a \wedge \mathsf{X}^{>0.7}b \wedge \mathsf{X}^{>0.7}(\neg a \vee \neg b) \rightarrow \mathsf{X}^{>1}(a \vee b \vee \neg a \vee \neg b)}$$

(Remember that $\mathsf{X}^{>1.05}$ was defined to be syntactic sugar for $\mathsf{X}^{>1}$).

Compare this with Example 15. Informally speaking, an application of (EXT) can be replaced by (EXT′) with the same Γ and $\mathscr{B}$, followed by some application of (K2).

For the other direction, an application of (EXT′) with Γ and $\mathscr{B}$ can be simulated by modifying Γ and $\mathscr{B}$ slightly such that the premises of (EXT) are fulfilled; then, the result of applying (EXT) with the modified sets is syntactically equivalent to the result of the original (EXT′), up to $\neg\neg f \leftrightarrow f$ and the removal of syntactic sugar.

Now we give the detailed proof:

Lemma 17. *[Equivalence of* (EXT) *and (*EXT′*)]*

1. *The system* (K1)–(K5)+(EXT) *can derive (*EXT′*),*
2. *The system* (K1)–(K5)+(*EXT′*) *can derive* (EXT).

Proof. We frequently use the following simple equivalence:

$$\mathsf{X}^{\rhd p}g \Leftrightarrow \neg\mathsf{X}^{\overline{\rhd}1-p}\neg g$$

Proof of Part 1. Let Γ be a modal set, $\mathscr{B} \subseteq 2^{\mathsf{Post}(\Gamma)}$ such that for all $B \in \mathscr{B}, \bigwedge B \rightarrow \bot$. Let $\rhd q$ be decided by the LP problem (*). We have to prove $\bigwedge \Gamma \rightarrow \mathsf{X}^{\rhd q} \bigvee \mathsf{Post}(\Gamma)$. We exploit the equivalence above and prove instead:

$$\bigwedge \Gamma \wedge \left(\mathsf{X}^{\overline{\rhd}1-q} \bigwedge_{g \in \mathsf{Post}(\Gamma)} \neg g\right) \rightarrow \bot \qquad (\dagger)$$

To use (EXT), we consider the following construction and prove the premises of (EXT):

$$\Gamma' = \Gamma \cup \{X^{\triangleright 1-q}h\} \quad \text{with} \quad h = \bigwedge_{g \in \mathsf{Post}(\Gamma)} \neg g$$

and $\mathscr{B}' = \mathscr{B} \cup \{\Delta \mid h \in \Delta, \Delta \subseteq \mathsf{Post}(\Gamma')\} \setminus \{\{h\}\}$. First, every $\Delta \in \mathscr{B}' \setminus \mathscr{B}$ contains some $g \in \mathsf{Post}(\Gamma)$ and $h = \bigwedge_{g \in \mathsf{Post}(\Gamma)} \neg g$. Hence $\forall \Delta \in \mathscr{B}', \bigwedge \Delta \to \bot$. Second, for an arbitrary cover $\mathscr{C}$ of Γ' there is a weight function $w : \mathscr{C} \to [0,1]$ such that

$$\sum_{\Delta \in \mathscr{C}} w(\Delta) = 1 \tag{a}$$

$$\sum_{h \in \Delta, \Delta \in \mathscr{C}} w(\Delta) \overline{\triangleright} 1 - q \tag{b1}$$

$$\forall X^{\triangleright p} g \in \Gamma, \sum_{g \in \Delta, \Delta \in \mathscr{C}} w(\Delta) \triangleright p \tag{b2}$$

We define the expansion $w^+ : 2^{\mathsf{Post}(\Gamma')} \to [0,1]$ by: $w^+(\Delta) = w(\Delta)$ if $\Delta \in \mathscr{C}$, and equals to 0 otherwise. Then these assertions can be rewritten to

$$\sum_{\Delta \in 2^{\mathsf{Post}(\Gamma')}} w^+(\Delta) = 1 \tag{a'}$$

$$\sum_{h \in \Delta} w^+(\Delta) \overline{\triangleright} 1 - q \tag{b1'}$$

$$\forall X^{\triangleright p} g \in \Gamma, \sum_{g \in \Delta} w^+(\Delta) \triangleright p \tag{b2'}$$

Next we prove that $\mathscr{C} \cap \mathscr{B}' \neq \varnothing$ by contradiction. Suppose $\mathscr{C} \cap \mathscr{B}' = \varnothing$.

Note that the summation in (b1') accounts for those Δ that either belong to $2^{\mathsf{Post}(\Gamma)}$ or contain h. In the second case, Δ must be in $\widetilde{\mathscr{B}}$, so it does not belong to the cover $\mathscr{C}$. By the definition of w^+, $w^+(\Delta) = 0$. Hence we have $\forall X^{\triangleright p} g \in \Gamma, \sum_{g \in \Delta, \Delta \in 2^{\mathsf{Post}(\Gamma)}} w^+(\Delta) \triangleright p$.

It is obvious that the restriction of w^+ to $2^{\mathsf{Post}(\Gamma)}$ also satisfies the first two groups of conditions of the LP problem in (*). Thus it is a valid solution, which implies $\sum_{\Delta \in 2^{\mathsf{Post}(\Gamma)}} w^+(\Delta) \triangleright q$. However, from (a') and (b2') one derives $\sum_{\Delta \in 2^{\mathsf{Post}(\Gamma)}} w^+(\Delta) \not\triangleright q$. Contradiction! So we cannot have $\mathscr{C} \cap \mathscr{B}' = \varnothing$, and hence $\forall \mathscr{C} \in \mathsf{Cov}(\Gamma'), \mathscr{C} \cap \mathscr{B}' \neq \varnothing$. Now we can apply (EXT) with Γ' and $\mathscr{B}'$, and get (†) immediately.

Proof of Part 2. We are given a modal set $\Gamma \subseteq \mathsf{Sub}(f)$ and $\mathscr{B} \subseteq 2^{\mathsf{Post}(\Gamma)}$ such that for all $\mathscr{C} \in \mathsf{Cov}(\Gamma)$, we have $\mathscr{C} \cap \mathscr{B} \neq \varnothing$. With (K2), it suffices to prove that the optimal value of the LP problem in (*) is greater than 1.

If not, then there exists a solution such that $\sum_\Delta w_\Delta = 1$. Hence $\mathscr{C} = \{\Delta \mid w_\Delta > 0\}$ is a cover of Γ. By assumption, $\mathscr{C} \cap \mathscr{B} \neq \varnothing$. This contradicts $w_\Delta = 0$ for all $\Delta \in \mathscr{B}$. $\square$

With the equivalence formulation, we can establish some properties below.

Lemma 18. *With the axiom system, we can show the following:*

1. $\vdash \mathsf{X}^{>p}f \wedge \mathsf{X}^{>p'}g \to \mathsf{X}^{>p+p'-1}(f \wedge g)$.
2. $\vdash \mathsf{X}^{>p}f \wedge \neg\mathsf{X}^{>p'}g \to \mathsf{X}^{>p-p'}(f \wedge \neg g)$.
3. $\vdash \neg\mathsf{X}^{>p}f \wedge \neg\mathsf{X}^{>p'}g \to \mathsf{X}^{\geq 1-p-p'}(\neg f \wedge \neg g)$.
4. $\vdash \mathsf{X}^{>p}f \to \mathsf{X}^{\geq p}f$.
5. $\vdash \mathsf{X}^{>p}f \to \mathsf{X}^{>p-p'}f$.
6. $\vdash \mathsf{X}^{\geq p}f \to \mathsf{X}^{\geq p-p'}f$.
7. $\vdash \mathsf{X}^{\geq p}f \to \mathsf{X}^{>p-p'}f$ *where* $p' > 0$.
8. *If* $\vdash f \to \bot$ *then* $\vdash \mathsf{X}^{\geq p}f \to \bot$.
9. *If* $\vdash f$ *then* $\vdash \mathsf{X}^{\geq 1}f$.
10. *If* $\vdash f \to g$ *then* $\vdash \mathsf{X}^{>p}f \to \mathsf{X}^{>p}g$ *and* $\vdash \mathsf{X}^{\geq p}f \to \mathsf{X}^{\geq p}g$.

4.2   Soundness and Completeness

Theorem 19 (Soundness). *The axiom system is sound, i.e.,* $\vdash f$ *implies* $\models f$.

The completeness result restricts to aconjunctive formulae, initially introduced in [16]:

Definition 20 (Aconjunctive formulae). *Given a $P\mu TL$ formula f, we say that a variable Z is active in g, a subformula of f, iff there is a variable Z' appearing in g and $Z \sqsubseteq_f Z'$. Let Z be a variable with its natural binder function $\mathscr{D}_f(Z) = \mu Z.g(Z)$. The variable Z is called aconjunctive iff for all subformulae of g of the form $g_1 \wedge g_2$ it is not the case that Z is active in g_1 as well as in g_2.*

We call a refutation *thin* iff whenever a formula of the form $g_1 \wedge g_2$ is reduced in some node of the refutation then no variable is active in g_1 as well as in g_2. Similar to μTL, since variables cannot be active in both conjuncts of an aconjunctive formula, the refutation of any aconjunctive formula is thin.

First recall some basic properties without probabilities (hence same as for μTL):

Lemma 21 ([16]). *Suppose that all occurrences of Z in f and g are positive, and let $\sigma_Z \in \{\mu, \nu\}$. Then:*

2. *If* $\vdash f \to g$ *then* $\vdash f[h/Z] \to g[h/Z]$.
3. *If* $\vdash f_1 \to f_2$ *then* $\vdash g[f_1/Z] \to g[f_2/Z]$.
4. *If* $\vdash f \to g$ *then* $\vdash \sigma_Z Z.f \to \sigma_Z Z.g$.

5. $\vdash \sigma_Z Z.f \leftrightarrow f[\sigma_Z Z.f/Z]$.
6. If $\vdash f[\mu Z.(g \wedge f)/Z] \rightarrow g$ then $\vdash \mu Z.f \rightarrow g$.

Given an aconjunctive PμTL tautology f, we can build a thin refutation of its negation (which is also aconjunctive), so the following theorem allows us to prove $\neg\neg f$.

Theorem 22. *If a formula has a thin refutation then its negation is provable.*

Proof. The proof idea is taken from Walukiewicz's argument [27] for μTL. It involves technical markings to track the formula unwindings. Using our conservative probabilistic extensions, we are able to adapt the proof to our setting in a very natural manner.

We assign a formula to each node of the refutation and prove that there is a finite path down to some node whose assigned formula is a propositional tautology. Further, we can build a proof of the formula assigned to a node from a proof of the formula assigned to the successor on the path. This implies that the formula we assigned to root node, which happens to be f, is provable. But for (AND) nodes, it is unclear which of the successors is relevant, so we have to constrain to thin refutations to ensure correctness.

To handle infinite paths, we use some tokens to store information about regenerations of bound variables. The counter in a token records how often a variable was regenerated since the last regeneration of some variable smaller than it (w.r.t. $\sqsubset_f$). If we find two nodes whose counters fulfil some requirement, the formula assigned to the latter will turn out to be a propositional tautology. We maintain a list of tokens: we can remove tokens from the list and add tokens to the right end of the list. Removed tokens are never used again. Each token has its own *counter*. The counter of a new token is set to 0. We also assign a pair (formula, bound variable of f) to every token on the list.

Let us first introduce some operations on labelled lists of tokens. We say that g is *replaceable* by h in some list of tokens if either of the conditions holds:

1. h does not appear in the labels of tokens in the list
2. the smallest variable Z_g such that (g, Z_g) is the label of some token is smaller than the smallest variable Z_h such that (h, Z_h) is the label of some token
3. variables Z_g and Z_h are the same but the token labelled (g, Z_g) is to the left of the token labelled (h, Z_h).

If g is replaceable by h then to *replace* g by h means, first, to delete all the tokens labelled (h, Z), for all variable Z, and next replace each label of the form (g, Z) by (h, Z).

If g is not replaceable by h then we can *delete* g from the list by removing all the tokens labelled (g, Z) for all variables Z.

To the root of $\mathcal{R}$ we assign an empty list of tokens. Suppose we have a list of tokens for a node m which is not a (MOD) node, we construct the list of tokens of its child node n. We construct the list of tokens of each of its grandchildren instead when m is a (MOD) node (again we don't need to consider (COV) nodes) according to the following rules:

1. Suppose (OR) is applied in m to $g \vee h$ and, say g is the result of the reduction which appears in the label of n. The token list for n is obtained by replacing $g \vee h$ by g if $g \vee h$ is replaceable by g.
2. Suppose (REG) is applied in m to Z where $\mathscr{D}_f(Z) = \sigma_Z Z.g$. If Z is replaceable by g then replace Z by g. In case Z is a μ-variable also increase the counter of the token now labelled (g, Z) and set the counters of all tokens to the right of it to 0.
3. Suppose (μ) or (ν) is applied in m to $\sigma_Z Z.g$. If $\sigma_Z Z.g$ is replaceable by g then we replace $\sigma_Z Z.g$ by g. In case Z is a μ-variable we additionally put a new token labelled (g, Z) at the end of the list.
4. Suppose (AND) is applied in m to $g \wedge h$. As the refutation is thin, every variable is active in at most one of g or h. If $g \wedge h$ is replaceable by g and Z is active in g, then in every token labelled $(g \wedge h, Z)$, replace its label by (g, Z), and analogously for h.
5. Suppose (MOD) is applied in m followed by an application of the (COV) rule (recall that in a refutation there is exactly one premise in a (COV) node). Let $L_T(m) = \{\mathsf{X}^{\rhd p_1} f_1, \ldots, \mathsf{X}^{\rhd p_n} f_n, l_1, \ldots, l_s\}$ and $L_T(n) \subseteq \mathsf{Post}(L_T(m))$. For every token labelled $(\mathsf{X}^{\rhd p_i} f_i, Z)$ for some Z and f_i appears in $L_T(n)$, replace this label by (f_i, Z).
6. After the above steps remove tokens which are either (i) labelled with pairs (g, Z) with Z not active in g or (ii) labelled with formulae not appearing in the node label.

Remark 23. According to the rules above, for each node m, for every pair (g, Z) such that $g \in L_T(m)$ and Z is active in g, there is exactly a token labelled by (g, Z).

We need the following two lemmas to continue our proof, note that Lemma 25 differs slightly from the proof for the non-probabilistic version:

Lemma 24. *For every path $\mathscr{P}$ of $\mathscr{R}$ there is a counter which gets arbitrarily big on $\mathscr{P}$.*

Next we assign a formula to every node of $\mathscr{R}$. To do this for every node n of $\mathscr{R}$ and every formula $g \in L_T(n)$ we define a binder function $\mathscr{D}_{n,g}$ depending on the token list for n. These binder functions will be obtained from $\mathscr{D}_f$ by modifications of one kind. For some μ-variables instead of $\mathscr{D}_f(Z) = \mu Z.g_Z$ we will have $\mathscr{D}_{n,g}(Z) = \mu Z.\neg\gamma_1 \wedge \ldots \wedge \neg\gamma_k \wedge g_Z$, where formulae $\gamma_1, \ldots, \gamma_k$ are determined in the following way: Consider ancestors of n up to the nearest node where a token now labelled (g, Z) is created or its counter is reset to zero. Among these ancestors choose all $n_1, \ldots, n_k$ where the counter of the token was increased(the child node of a (REG) node, including n itself), then for $i = 1, \ldots, k$,

$$\gamma_i = \bigwedge\{\langle[h]\rangle_{\mathscr{D}_{n_i,h}} \mid h \in L_T(n_i), h \neq g_Z\}$$

The formula assigned to the node n is

$$\neg\bigwedge\{\langle[g]\rangle_{\mathscr{D}_{n,g}} \mid g \in L_T(n)\} \qquad (**)$$

Lemma 25. *If for some node m formula $\neg \bigwedge \{\langle [g] \rangle_{\mathscr{D}_{m,g}} \mid g \in L_T(m)\}$ is unprovable then either (i) m is a* (MOD) *node and there is a grandchild n of m that $\neg \bigwedge \{\langle [g] \rangle_{\mathscr{D}_{n,g}} \mid g \in L_T(n)\}$ is unprovable or (ii) m is not a* (MOD) *node and there is a child n of m that $\neg \bigwedge \{\langle [g] \rangle_{\mathscr{D}_{n,g}} \mid g \in L_T(n)\}$ is unprovable.*

Back to Theorem 22, for the root r of $\mathscr{R}$ we have $\mathscr{D}_{r,f} = \mathscr{D}_f$. Using the assumption that $\neg f$ is unprovable and the above observation we obtain an infinite path $\mathscr{P}$ of $\mathscr{R}$ such that for every node n of $\mathscr{P}$ the formula $\neg \wedge \{\langle [g] \rangle_{\mathscr{D}_{n,h}} \mid h \in L_T(n)\}$ is unprovable.

Let t be a token whose counter can be arbitrarily big on $\mathscr{P}$. Let Z be the variable from the label of t and let $\mathscr{D}_f(Z) = \mu Z.g$ be its original definition. Because the counter of t is unbounded there must be two (REG) nodes n_1, n_2 on $\mathscr{P}$ such that

1. $L_T(n_1) = L_T(n_2)$,
2. in both nodes the parts of the lists to the left of t are identical,
3. t is labelled by (Z, Z),
4. the counter of t was increased and it was not reset between n_1 and n_2.

Let us assume that n_2 is a descendant of n_1. We will show that $\neg \bigwedge \{\langle [h] \rangle_{\mathscr{D}_{n_2,h}} \mid h \in L_T(n_2)\}$ is provable. As binder functions are established by $(**)$ we have that $\mathscr{D}_{n_2,h} = \mathscr{D}_{n_1,h}$ for every formula $h \in L_T(n_1)$, $h \neq Z$. This is because by (3) and (4) the counters of all the tokens to the right of t are 0 and all the counters to the left of t are the same in n_1 and n_2. Of course, the counter of t in n_1 is strictly smaller than in n_2. We have:

$$\mathscr{D}_{n_1,Z}(Z) = \mu Z. \neg \gamma_1 \wedge \ldots \wedge \neg \gamma_i \wedge g_Z$$
$$\mathscr{D}_{n_2,Z}(Z) = \mu Z. \neg \gamma_1 \wedge \ldots \wedge \neg \gamma_j \wedge g_Z$$

where $j > i$ and formulae $\gamma_1, \ldots, \gamma_j$ are determined by the rule $(**)$. We know that γ_{i+1} is $\bigwedge \{\langle [h] \rangle_{\mathscr{D}_{n_1,h}} \mid h \in L_T(n_1), h \neq Z\}$. It is the same as $\bigwedge \{\langle [h] \rangle_{\mathscr{D}_{n_2,h}} \mid h \in L_T(n_2), h \neq Z\}$.

Finally we have that

$$\neg \bigwedge \{\langle [g] \rangle_{\mathscr{D}_{n_2,g}} \mid g \in L_T(n_2)\}$$
$$= \neg \Big(\bigwedge \{\langle [h] \rangle_{\mathscr{D}_{n_2,h}} \mid h \in L_T(n_2), h \neq Z\} \wedge \langle [Z] \rangle_{\mathscr{D}_{n_2,Z}} \Big)$$
$$= \neg (\gamma_{i+1} \wedge \mu Z. \neg \gamma_1 \wedge \ldots \wedge \neg \gamma_j \wedge g_Z)$$

which is just an instance of (K5) and the propositional tautology $\neg \gamma_1 \wedge \ldots \wedge \neg \gamma_j \wedge g_Z \to \neg \gamma_{i+1}$, a contradiction with the choice of $\mathscr{P}$. $\square$

For an aconjunctive formula f, if f is unsatisfiable, there exists a thin refutation $\mathscr{R}$. Hence $\neg f$ is provable by Theorem 22. Thus we have the completeness result:

Theorem 26. *If f is an unsatisfiable aconjunctive formula, then $\neg f$ is provable.*

Acknowledgement. This work is supported by the National Natural Science Foundation of China (Grants Nos. 61761136011,61532019), and the Guangdong Science and Technology Department (Grant No. 2018B010107004).

References

1. de Alfaro, L.: Formal verification of probabilistic systems. Ph.D. thesis, Stanford University (1997), Technical report STAN-CS-TR-98-1601
2. de Alfaro, L., Majumdar, R.: Quantitative solution of omega-regular games. In: 33rd ACM Symposium on Theory of Computing, STOC 2001, pp. 675–683. ACM, New York (2001). https://doi.org/10.1145/380752.380871
3. Baier, C.: On algorithmic verification methods for probabilistic systems. Habilitationsschrift, Universität Mannheim: Fakultät für Mathematik und Informatik (1998)
4. Baier, C., Katoen, J.-P.: Principles of Model Checking. MIT Press, Cambridge (2008)
5. Banieqbal, B., Barringer, H.: Temporal logic with fixed points. In: Banieqbal, B., Barringer, H., Pnueli, A. (eds.) Temporal Logic in Specification. LNCS, vol. 398, pp. 62–74. Springer, Heidelberg (1989). https://doi.org/10.1007/3-540-51803-7_22
6. Bianco, A., de Alfaro, L.: Model checking of probabilistic and nondeterministic systems. In: Thiagarajan, P.S. (ed.) FSTTCS 1995. LNCS, vol. 1026, pp. 499–513. Springer, Heidelberg (1995). https://doi.org/10.1007/3-540-60692-0_70
7. Brázdil, T., Forejt, V., Křetínský, J., Kučera, A.: The satisfiability problem for probabilistic CTL. In: Twenty-Third Annual IEEE Symposium on Logic in Computer Science, Los Alamitos, Calif, pp. 391–402. IEEE (2008). https://doi.org/10.1109/LICS.2008.21
8. Castro, P., Kilmurray, C., Piterman, N.: Tractable probabilistic μ-calculus that expresses probabilistic temporal logics. In: Mayr, E.W., Ollinger, N. (eds.) 32nd International Symposium on Theoretical Aspects of Computer Science: STACS 2015. LIPIcs, vol. 30, pp. 211–223. Schloss Dagstuhl-Leibniz-Zentrum für Informatik, Dagstuhl, Germany (2015). https://doi.org/10.4230/LIPIcs.STACS.2015.211
9. Chakraborty, S., Katoen, J.-P.: On the satisfiability of some simple probabilistic logics. In: ACM (ed.) LICS, New York, pp. 56–65 (2016). https://doi.org/10.1145/2933575.2934526
10. Cleaveland, R., Iyer, S.P., Narasimha, M.: Probabilistic temporal logics via the modal mu-calculus. Theor. Comput. Sci. **342**(2–3), 316–350 (2005). https://doi.org/10.1016/j.tcs.2005.03.048
11. Dimitrova, R., Ferrer Fioriti, L.M., Hermanns, H., Majumdar, R.: Probabilistic CTL*: the deductive way. In: Chechik, M., Raskin, J.-F. (eds.) TACAS 2016. LNCS, vol. 9636, pp. 280–296. Springer, Heidelberg (2016). https://doi.org/10.1007/978-3-662-49674-9_16
12. Emerson, E.A., Jutla, C.S.: Tree automata, mu-calculus and determinacy (extended abstract). In: Proceedings 32nd Annual Symposium of Foundations of Computer Science: FOCS, pp. 368–377. IEEE (1991). https://doi.org/10.1109/SFCS.1991.185392
13. Hansson, H., Jonsson, B.: A logic for reasoning about time and reliability. Formal Asp. Comput. **6**(5), 512–535 (1994). https://doi.org/10.1007/BF01211866
14. Huth, M., Kwiatkowska, M.: Quantitative analysis and model checking. In: 12th Annual IEEE Symposium on Logic in Computer Science, Los Alamitos, Calif, pp. 111–122. IEEE (1997). https://doi.org/10.1109/LICS.1997.614940
15. Kozen, D.: Semantics of probabilistic programs. J. Comput. Syst. Sci. **22**(3), 328–350 (1981). https://doi.org/10.1016/0022-0000(81)90036-2

16. Kozen, D.: Results on the propositional μ-calculus. Theor. Comput. Sci. **27**(3), 333–354 (1983). https://doi.org/10.1016/0304-3975(82)90125-6
17. Larsen, K.G., Mardare, R., Xue, B.: Probabilistic mu-calculus: decidability and complete axiomatization. In: Lal, A., Akshay, S., Saurabh, S., Sen, S. (eds.) 36th IARCS Annual Conference on Foundations of Software Technology and Theoretical Computer Science: FSTTCS. LIPIcs, vol. 65, pp. 25:1–25:18. Schloss Dagstuhl-Leibniz-Zentrum für Informatik, Dagstuhl, Germany (2016). https://doi.org/10.4230/LIPIcs.FSTTCS.2016.25
18. Liu, W., Song, L., Wang, J., Zhang, L.: A simple probabilistic extension of modal mu-calculus. In: Proceedings of the Twenty-Fourth International Joint Conference on Artificial Intelligence, Palo Alto, Calif, pp. 882–888. AAAI Press (2015). https://www.ijcai.org/Abstract/15/129
19. McIver, A.K., Morgan, C.C.: Games, probability, and the quantitative μ-calculus $qM\mu$. In: Baaz, M., Voronkov, A. (eds.) LPAR 2002. LNCS (LNAI), vol. 2514, pp. 292–310. Springer, Heidelberg (2002). https://doi.org/10.1007/3-540-36078-6_20
20. McIver, A., Morgan, C.: Results on the quantitative μ-calculus $qM\mu$. ACM Trans. Comput. Log. **8**(1), 3 (2007). https://doi.org/10.1145/1182613.1182616
21. Mio, M.: Probabilistic modal μ-calculus with independent product. In: Hofmann, M. (ed.) FoSSaCS 2011. LNCS, vol. 6604, pp. 290–304. Springer, Heidelberg (2011). https://doi.org/10.1007/978-3-642-19805-2_20
22. Morgan, C., McIver, A.: A probabilistic temporal calculus based on expectations. In: Proceedings of Formal Methods Pacific. Citeseer (1997)
23. Niwiński, D., Walukiewicz, I.: Games for the μ-calculus. Theor. Comput. Sci. **163**(1–2), 99–116 (1996). https://doi.org/10.1016/0304-3975(95)00136-0
24. Pratt, V.R.: A decidable mu-calculus: Preliminary report. In: 22nd Annual Symposium on Foundations of Computer Science, Los Angeles, pp. 421–427. IEEE (1981). https://doi.org/10.1109/SFCS.1981.4
25. Streett, R.S., Emerson, E.A.: An automata theoretic decision procedure for the propositional mu-calculus. Inf. Comput. **81**(3), 249–264 (1989). https://doi.org/10.1016/0890-5401(89)90031-X
26. Tamura, K.: Completeness of Kozen's axiomatization for the modal mu-calculus: A simple proof. CoRR abs/1408.3560 (2014). http://arxiv.org/abs/1408.3560
27. Walukiewicz, I.: Completeness of Kozen's axiomatisation of the propositional μ-calculus. Inf. Comput. **157**(1–2), 142–182 (2000). https://doi.org/10.1006/inco.1999.2836

Synthesizing Nested Ranking Functions for Loop Programs via SVM

Yi Li[1], Xuechao Sun[2,3], Yong Li[2,3], Andrea Turrini[2,4(✉)], and Lijun Zhang[2,3,4]

[1] Chongqing Key Laboratory of Automated Reasoning and Cognition, Automated Reasoning and Cognition Center, Chongqing Institute of Green and Intelligent Technology, Chinese Academy of Sciences, Chongqing, China
[2] State Key Laboratory of Computer Science, Institute of Software, Chinese Academy of Sciences, Beijing, China
turrini@ios.ac.cn
[3] University of the Chinese Academy of Sciences, Beijing, China
[4] Institute of Intelligent Software, Guangzhou, Guangzhou, China

Abstract. Termination of programs is probably the most famous undecidable problem in computer science. Despite this undecidability result, a lot of effort has been spent on improving algorithms that prove termination of loops, which is one of the building blocks of software reliability analysis. These algorithms are usually focused on finding an appropriate ranking function for the loop, which proves its termination. In this paper, we consider nested ranking functions for loop programs and show that the existence problem of a nested ranking function is equivalent to the existence problem of a hyperplane separating classes of data. This allows us to leverage Support-Vector Machines (SVM) techniques for the synthesis of nested ranking functions. SVM are supervised learning algorithms that are used to classify data; they work by finding a hyperplane separating data points parted into two classes. We show how to carefully define the data points so that the separating hyperplane gives rise to a nested ranking function for the loop. Experimental results confirm the effectiveness of our SVM-based synthesis of nested ranking functions.

1 Introduction

Analyzing software properties such as in reachability analysis often requires to prove the termination of programs. However, termination of programs is probably the most famous problem in computer science which has been proven to be undecidable [24,25]. In theory, the termination problem is closed and not so much can be done with it; in practice, however, things are different: as remarked in [10], undecidability does not imply that we are always unable to prove termination, simply we are unable to always prove termination. This means that we can require a termination proving tool to always return an answer, which has to be correct, just it can be "unknown" instead of only "terminating" or "nonterminating", with the aim to avoid "unknown" as much as possible.

© Springer Nature Switzerland AG 2019
Y. Ait-Ameur and S. Qin (Eds.): ICFEM 2019, LNCS 11852, pp. 438–454, 2019.
https://doi.org/10.1007/978-3-030-32409-4_27

For instance, ULTIMATE AUTOMIZER [15], one of the leading tools in program analysis according to the outcomes of the SV-COMP competitions[1], gives definitive answers to a large amount of termination problems in the termination category.

The termination of loops is at the core of the termination analysis techniques used in ULTIMATE AUTOMIZER; to show termination, it covers the whole set of executions of a program by means of certified modules, each one covering a subset of executions sharing the same termination argument, e.g., a *ranking function*.

Ranking functions, which are nowadays a standard technique to prove the termination of a loop, map a program state into an element of some well-founded ordered set, such that their value decreases whenever the loop completes an iteration. While termination of programs is undecidable, ranking function detection problems can well be decidable, given certain classes of ranking functions and program representations. Motivated by that, the synthesis of linear ranking functions has attracted a lot of attention [2,8,9,13,16,20,23]. In [8,9], Colón and Sipma synthesize linear ranking functions for linear-constraint loops. For this type of loops, it is possible to find a linear ranking function by exploiting linear programming (LP) techniques. Many researchers have worked on solutions based on LP methods: in 2004, a complete and efficient solution for linear ranking function synthesis for single-path linear loops over rationals was proposed by Podelski and Rybalchenko [20]. The complexity of a complete solution for single-path linear loops with integer variables was finally settled by [2] in 2014.

Unfortunately, not all terminating loops have a linear ranking function, so several researchers proposed ways to combine multiple linear ranking functions to capture more complex scenarios. Bradley et al. [5,6] showed how to synthesize lexicographic linear ranking functions (LLRFs); Ben-Amram and Genaim [2] proposed a complete algorithm on the notion of LLRFs; and Leike and Heizmann [16] presented templates for many different ranking functions with affine linear components similar to LLRFs, including nested ranking functions considered in this paper. In addition, Bagnara and Mesnard [1] analyzed the existence of eventual linear ranking functions, which are multi-phase linear ranking functions (MΦRFs) of depth 2. A complete solution for d-depth eventual linear ranking functions was proposed in [18]; Ben-Amram and Genaim [3] further provided a complete polynomial-time solution for MΦRFs with bounded depth.

Since linear-constraint loops with linear ranking functions comprise a very limited class of loop behaviors, to capture more behaviors, a different line of research [7,12,21] focuses on detecting polynomial ranking functions for loops with polynomial guards and polynomial updates. For instance, in [7] the detection of ranking functions is reduced to the solution of semi-algebraic systems problems. All polynomial ranking functions can be obtained with the given degree bounds by cylindrical algebraic decomposition with double exponential complexity. In [12], Cousot made use of parametric abstraction, Lagrangian relaxation, and semi-definite programming (SDP) to compute ranking functions of loops. While being efficient, the obtained actual function may be not a rank-

---

[1] https://sv-comp.sosy-lab.org/.

ing function due to numerical errors. This problem was addressed in [21] by Shen et al.: they used a symbolic-numeric hybrid method to derive the rational coefficients of the exact ranking function from the numerical coefficients of the function obtained by the SDP algorithm. Yuan et al. [26] proposed a ranking function detection method exploiting Support-Vector Machines (SVM) [11] which is even able to handle loops with radical and fractional variable assignment updates. Their method is only applicable to the synthesis of global ranking functions.

In this paper, we move a step further by exploiting SVM to synthesize nested ranking functions of loops. It turns out that the ranking functions considered in [26] are a special class of ours. A nested ranking function is defined by means of multiple functions, each one used in a different phase, such that the value in one phase is allowed to increase, but less than the value of the previous phase. Differently from standard nested ranking functions, where the functions involved are linear, our algorithm supports nonlinear functions out of the box. The main contribution of this work is an equivalence reduction between the existence of a nested ranking function of a loop program (possibly with radical and fractional variable assignment updates) and the existence of a hyperplane separating the origin O and a subset S of the Euclidean space defined by the program. Based on this equivalence, our synthesis algorithm for nested ranking functions works as follows. We first give a definition of k-nested ranking function, equivalent but slightly different from its original definition in [3], in order to fit the SVM input data space. We then sample points from S as the training set S', and then derive a candidate separating hyperplane between O and S' by usual SVM algorithms. We finally check whether the candidate nested ranking function derived from the separating hyperplane is a correct ranking function by means of the tool Z3 [19].

To evaluate the effectiveness of our SVM-based synthesis algorithm, we compare our prototype tool SVMRANKER with LASSORANKER, which is part of ULTIMATE AUTOMIZER and its core component responsible for finding ranking functions or proving nontermination. LASSORANKER implements a wide range of techniques (see, e.g., [14–17]) which are very effective, making ULTIMATE AUTOMIZER the winner of the 2019 SV-COMP competition [4] in the Termination category, as well as of the previous two editions of the SV-COMP Termination category. The experimental results show that our tool has been able to prove termination for 65% more programs than LASSORANKER proved to terminate. This confirms that the SVM-based algorithm we propose for the synthesis of k-nested linear and nonlinear ranking functions is an effective technique that complements well the large set of techniques available in LASSORANKER.

Organization of the Paper. The rest of the paper is organized as follows. Section 2 gives some basic background necessary for this work. Section 3 introduces the SVM-based method to synthesize a nested ranking function for a given program. Section 4 presents the experimental results and discusses our lessons learned. Section 5 concludes the paper with some final remark.

$$\textbf{while } q > 0:$$
$$q := q - y;$$
$$y := y + 1;$$

Fig. 1. A looping program

2   Preliminaries

In this paper we use subscripts to restrict standard number sets, like $\mathbb{R}_{\geq 0}$ for non-negative real numbers. Given $\mathbf{x} \in \mathbb{R}^n$, we denote by $|\mathbf{x}| = n$ the size of $\mathbf{x}$.

We denote by $A \cdot B$ the usual multiplication between matrices A and B.

A relation $\mathcal{R} \subseteq X \times X$ is *well-founded* if each subset $\emptyset \neq X' \subseteq X$ has an $\mathcal{R}$-minimal element, i.e., there is $m \in X'$ such that $\neg \mathcal{R}(m, x)$ for each $x \in X'$.

2.1   Program Specification

In this paper, we focus on programs that consist of only loops. We use binary relations over the program's states to the executions of programs. We denote by $\mathbf{x}$ a vector of n variables $(x_1, \cdots, x_n)^T \in \mathbb{R}^n$ corresponding to the current program state, and by $\mathbf{x}' = (x'_1, \cdots, x'_n)^T \in \mathbb{R}^n$ the variables of after the execution. Let $\mathbb{R}[\mathbf{x}]$ be the polynomial ring on real numbers.

Definition 1 (Loop Program). *A loop program* $\mathsf{Loop}(\mathbf{x}, \mathbf{x}')$ *is a binary relation defined by a formula with free variables* $\mathbf{x}$ *and* $\mathbf{x}'$ *of the form*

$$\bigvee_{i=1}^{d} \left(\left(\bigwedge_{j=1}^{k_i} g_{i,j}(\mathbf{x}) \geq 0 \right) \wedge \left(\bigwedge_{j=1}^{m_i} f_{i,j}(\mathbf{x}, \mathbf{x}') \geq 0 \right) \right)$$

for finite numbers $k_i, m_i, d \geq 1$ *where* $\bigwedge_{j=1}^{k_i} g_{i,j}(\mathbf{x}) \geq 0$ *is the i-th loop guard condition and* $\bigwedge_{j=1}^{m_i} f_{i,j}(\mathbf{x}, \mathbf{x}') \geq 0$ *the i-th nondeterministic update assignment statement.*

In a loop program defined as above, the loop body is given by means of a relation between the updated values $\mathbf{x}'$ and the previous values $\mathbf{x}$. The update is called deterministic if, for a given $\mathbf{x}$ satisfying the loop condition $\bigwedge_{j=1}^{k_i} g_{i,j}(\mathbf{x}) \geq 0$, there is at most one $\mathbf{x}'$ satisfying the update constraint $\bigwedge_{j=1}^{m_i} f_{i,j}(\mathbf{x}, \mathbf{x}') \geq 0$. Otherwise, such an update is called nondeterministic. Let $\Omega_i = \{ (\mathbf{x}, \mathbf{x}') \in \mathbb{R}^{2n} \mid \bigwedge_{j=1}^{k_i} g_{i,j}(\mathbf{x}) \geq 0, \bigwedge_{j=1}^{m_i} f_{i,j}(\mathbf{x}, \mathbf{x}') \geq 0 \}$ denote the set of executions of the loop body with respect to the i-th alternative, where each execution is represented by the value $\mathbf{x}$ of the state variables satisfying the guard condition $\bigwedge_{j=1}^{k_i} g_{i,j}(\mathbf{x}) \geq 0$ and the corresponding value $\mathbf{x}'$ as updated by the body $\bigwedge_{j=1}^{m_i} f_{i,j}(\mathbf{x}, \mathbf{x}') \geq 0$. In this way we can represent a loop program by means of the binary relation $\Omega = \Omega_1 \vee \Omega_2 \vee \cdots \vee \Omega_d$. Since a loop can be specified by Ω, in the following, we identify the loop with Ω.

As an example of looping program, consider the code in Fig. 1 originally proposed in [16]. We can represent its executions by the formula

$$\Omega = (q > 0) \wedge (q' = q - y \wedge y' = y + 1)$$

which corresponds to the loop guard $(q > 0)$ in conjunction with the update resulting from the loop body $(q' = q - y \wedge y' = y + 1)$. The corresponding set of executions contains, for instance, the points $\mathbf{x}_p = (4, 2, 2, 3)^T$, and $\mathbf{x}_n = (4, -2, 6, -1)^T$, where $\mathbf{x} = (q, y, q', y')^T$.

2.2   Ranking Functions

Termination of a loop program Ω can be proved by means of ranking functions. A ranking function for Ω is a function f from $\mathbb{R}^n$ to $\mathbb{R}_{\geq 0}$ such that there exists $\delta \in \mathbb{R}_{>0}$ such that for each $(\mathbf{x}, \mathbf{x}') \in \Omega$ it holds $f(\mathbf{x}) \geq f(\mathbf{x}') + \delta$ or, equivalently, $f(\mathbf{x}) - f(\mathbf{x}') \geq \delta$. In a way similar to [16, Lemma 3.5], it is possible to show that Ω is well founded if and only if there exists a ranking function for Ω.

Among other ranking functions, the authors of [3,16] introduce the concept of k-nested linear ranking function, where k linear functions are used in different phases instead of a single function. In fact, for an affine linear ranking function, its value over a program state is decreasing at each iteration of the loop, which is sometimes too restrictive. To relax this restriction, a k-nested ranking function consists of k phases that allow the value to increase in the first few phases. In other words, each phase has an affine linear ranking function, but this affine linear function cannot increase by more than the value of the previous phase's affine linear function. Thus once the previous phase is finished (the function becomes non-positive), its value starts decreasing.

With the following definition we generalize the original definition of k-nested ranking function given in [3,16] to the nonlinear setting.

Definition 2 (k-Nested Ranking Function). *Given a loop program Ω, let $k \in \mathbb{N}_{>0}$ and, for each $i \in \{1, \dots, k\}$, $f_i(\mathbf{x})$ be a polynomial or an algebraic fraction over the program variables $\mathbf{x}$. We call the k-tuple $\langle f_1, f_2, \dots, f_k \rangle$ a k-nested ranking function of Ω if the following condition holds for a set of parameters $\{ C_i \in \mathbb{R}_{>0} \mid 1 \leq i \leq k+1 \}$:*

$$\forall (\mathbf{x}, \mathbf{x}') \in \Omega : \begin{cases} f_1(\mathbf{x}) - f_1(\mathbf{x}') \geq C_1 \\ f_2(\mathbf{x}) - f_2(\mathbf{x}') + f_1(\mathbf{x}) \geq C_2 \\ \quad \vdots \\ f_k(\mathbf{x}) - f_k(\mathbf{x}') + f_{k-1}(\mathbf{x}) \geq C_k \\ f_k(\mathbf{x}) \geq C_{k+1} \end{cases} \tag{1}$$

Remark 1. The above definition is equivalent but slightly different from the original one given in [3,16]. The first, main difference is that we allow each component of a nested ranking function to be a nonlinear expression, instead of only an affine linear function. The second difference is that we require that

$f_i(\mathbf{x}) - f_i(\mathbf{x}') + f_{i-1}(\mathbf{x}) \geq C_i$ for $C_i \in \mathbb{R}_{>0}$ instead of $f_i(\mathbf{x}) - f_i(\mathbf{x}') + f_{i-1}(\mathbf{x}) > 0$, where for the latter the domain of the functions is a well-ordered set instead of the set of non-negative real numbers as the former.

Consider again the loop program in Fig. 1; this program does not have an affine linear ranking function of the form $f(q, y) = aq + by + c$ when $a > 0$, since the requirement $f(q, y) - f(q', y') \geq C > 0$ implies $y \geq (b + C)/a$, which is clearly not satisfied by some of the possible values of y. When $a < 0$, the proof is similar and f is clearly not a valid ranking function for the program when $a = 0$. However, as shown in [16], there exists a 2-nested ranking function showing program's termination: $f_1(q, y) = 1 - y$ and $f_2(q, y) = q + 1$ with $C_1 = C_2 = C_3 = \frac{1}{2}$. Intuitively, the first phase occurs when $y < 1$, for which the value of the function f_1 is positive and decreases with each iteration; once the first phase is completed, i.e., the value of f_1 is non-positive by $y \geq 1$, the value of f_2 starts to decrease until the loop condition $q > 0$ is violated. This proves the termination of the loop program.

2.3   Fixed Points

A sufficient condition for a program to be nonterminating is the presence of fixed points, i.e., points for which the loop does not change the variables' value.

Definition 3 (Fixed point). *Given a loop program specified by Ω, we say that $\mathbf{x} \in \mathbb{R}^n$ is a* fixed point *of the loop if $(\mathbf{x}, \mathbf{x}) \in \Omega$.*

Clearly, for any loop defined by Ω, if it has a fixed point $(\mathbf{x}, \mathbf{x}')$ with $\mathbf{x}' = \mathbf{x}$, then it can not have ranking functions: for any possible candidate ranking function f, we have $f(\mathbf{x}) - f(\mathbf{x}') = f(\mathbf{x}) - f(\mathbf{x}) = 0 \not\geq C$ for any $C > 0$.

Checking if a loop Ω has a fixed point is equivalent to check if the system

$$Sys \triangleq (\mathbf{x}, \mathbf{x}') \in \Omega \land \mathbf{x} = \mathbf{x}'$$

has a solution. This can be done by, e.g., SMT techniques.

2.4   Support-Vector Machine Learning

Support-Vector Machines (SVM), originally introduced in [11] as Support-Vector Networks, are supervised learning algorithms that can be used to classify data. The main task of SVM is to find a hyperplane separating the data in the provided training set so that it maximizes the margin between the points with two different labels $\{+1, -1\}$ in the training set.

Formally, given a training set $D = \{\, (\mathbf{v}_i, l_i) \in \mathbb{R}^n \times \{-1, +1\} \mid 1 \leq i \leq d \,\}$ of d points $\mathbf{v}_i \in \mathbb{R}^n$, each one labelled with $l_i \in \{-1, +1\}$, SVM aims to find a separating vector $\mathbf{w} \in \mathbb{R}^n$ and a constant $b \in \mathbb{R}$ such that

$$\begin{cases} \mathbf{w}^T \mathbf{v}_i + b \geq +1 & \text{if } l_i = +1, \\ \mathbf{w}^T \mathbf{v}_i + b \leq -1 & \text{if } l_i = -1. \end{cases}$$

In this paper, we reduce the problem of finding a nested ranking function of a given program to the problem of finding a hyperplane separating data with different labels.

Algorithm 1. The SVM-based algorithm for synthesizing k-nested ranking functions

---

Input: Program Ω, initial sample size n, functions template $U = \langle U_1, \ldots, U_k \rangle$
Output: The k-nested ranking coefficients $(\mathbf{a}_k^T, \ldots, \mathbf{a}_1^T)$ if Ω is well-founded;
            "nonterminating" if Ω contains fixed points; "unknown" otherwise

```
1  begin
2  |   if HASFIXEDPOINT(Ω) then
3  |   |   return (nonterminating, GETFIXEDPOINT(Ω));
4  |   D := {(O, -1)};
5  |   for i := 1 to n do
6  |   |   Sample (x, x') randomly from Ω;
7  |   |   D := D ∪ GETDATAPOINT(U, (x, x'));
8  |   while true do
9  |   |   svm := SVM(D);
10 |   |   if svm = (aₖᵀ, ..., a₁ᵀ) then
11 |   |   |   check := VERIFY(svm, U, Ω);
12 |   |   |   if check = true then
13 |   |   |   |   return (terminating, svm);
14 |   |   |   else // check is a counterexample of the form (x, x')
15 |   |   |   |   D := D ∪ GETDATAPOINT(U, check);
16 |   |   else // SVM failed to separate O from the points from G(Ω)
17 |   |   |   return unknown
```

---

3   SVM-Based Synthesis of Nested Ranking Functions

In this section we present our algorithm, shown in Algorithm 1, to synthesize a k-nested ranking function for an input program Ω based on a given template U, provided such a function exists. We first present in Sect. 3.1 an overview of the way Algorithm 1 works. Later in Sect. 3.2, we explain how to reduce the problem of finding a nested ranking function of a program to the problem of constructing a hyperplane separating data, which leads to a method to sample points from the given program that fits the SVM methods for finding separating hyperplanes. This gives us the main result of the paper in Theorem 1, namely the equivalence of the existence of a hyperplane separating the origin $\mathbf{O}$ from $G(\Omega)$ from the program Ω and the existence of a nested ranking function for Ω. Since Algorithm 1 relies on a given template of a nested ranking function we want to learn, we also present in Sect. 3.3 a method to construct a valid template which guarantees that $\mathbf{O}$ is not part of $G(\Omega)$ from the program Ω.

3.1   Overview of the SVM Synthesis Algorithm

Algorithm 1 works as follows: initially it checks, by means of the call to the procedure HASFIXEDPOINT(Ω), whether Ω contains a fixed point $(\mathbf{x}, \mathbf{x})$. If for some point $\mathbf{x}$ the body of the loop program does not modify the variables' value, then we can for sure return "nonterminating", as witnessed by $(\mathbf{x}, \mathbf{x})$ itself.

Note that we can easily extend Algorithm 1 to cover more nonterminating behaviors by using other nontermination analysis techniques, like geometric nontermination arguments [17]; here we focus on proving the termination programs by means of the SVM-based k-nested ranking function termination argument.

If no fixed point is found, the algorithm then tries to learn a hyperplane via SVM in order to construct a nested ranking function based on the given template U, which needs sampling points from the program. According to Theorem 1, a valid hyperplane has to separate the origin $\mathbf{O}$ from all other points corresponding to the executions of the program, in order to represent a k-nested ranking function. Therefore, the algorithm first samples randomly n points from the program Ω and adds their corresponding entries, labelled with $+1$, to the data set D, which already contains the origin $\mathbf{O}$ with label -1. The entries are generated by the procedure GETDATAPOINT, based on the construction we give below in Sect. 3.2.

Once the initial data points are obtained, the main loop of the algorithm calls SVM to separate the origin from the program points. SVM can return two answers: either the coefficients $(\mathbf{a}_k^T, \ldots, \mathbf{a}_1^T)$ for the k-nested ranking function defined according to the input template $U = \langle U_1, \ldots, U_k \rangle$, or a failure in separating the data points. In the latter case, the algorithm returns "unknown", since there are three motivations for such a failure: (1) the loop is simply nonterminating; (2) the dimension of the given template U is not enough to separate $\mathbf{O}$ from $G(\Omega)$, e.g., U is a template for a 3-nested ranking function but Ω requires a 5-nested ranking function; or (3) the shape of the given template U is not suitable to separate $\mathbf{O}$ from $G(\Omega)$, e.g., the current template U represents a k-nested affine linear ranking function but Ω needs a k-nested quadratic ranking function. In case SVM returned the coefficients $(\mathbf{a}_k^T, \ldots, \mathbf{a}_1^T)$, they are used by VERIFY to construct the k-nested ranking function $\langle \mathbf{a}_1^T \cdot U_1, \ldots, \mathbf{a}_k^T \cdot U_k \rangle$ which is checked against Condition (1) in Definition 2. If it is satisfied, then the algorithm returns "terminating" together with the coefficients for the ranking function; otherwise, VERIFY returns a point $(\mathbf{x}, \mathbf{x}') \in \Omega$ for which Condition (1) in Definition 2 does not hold. This point is used by the procedure GETDATAPOINT to extend D with new data points, before calling SVM in the next iteration of the algorithm.

3.2   SVM Data Points

We now show how to generate data points for SVM, given the values $(\mathbf{x}, \mathbf{x}')$ of the program variables and the template U for the k-nested ranking function. In the remainder of this section we may write $f(\mathbf{x})$ instead of just f when referring to f as a function, to remark the fact that f uses variables $\mathbf{x}$ in its definition.

Let $\langle f_1, \ldots, f_k \rangle$ be a k-tuple representing a k-nested ranking function; each function f_j can be written as $f_j(\mathbf{x}) = \mathbf{a}_j^T \cdot U_j(\mathbf{x})$ where $\mathbf{a}_j = (a_{j,1}, \ldots, a_{j,s_j})$ is a real vector of coefficients and $U_j(\mathbf{x}) = (U_{j,1}(\mathbf{x}), \ldots, U_{j,s_j}(\mathbf{x}))^T$ is an s_j-tuple with $U_{j,i}(\mathbf{x}) = \frac{q_{j,i}(\mathbf{x})}{p_{j,i}(\mathbf{x})}$, where $q_{j,i}(\mathbf{x}), p_{j,i}(\mathbf{x}) \in \mathbb{R}[\mathbf{x}]$, for $i \in \{1, \ldots, s_j\}$. Note that in case the polynomial $p_{j,i}(\mathbf{x})$ is the constant 1, then we have that $U_{j,i}(\mathbf{x}) = q_{j,i}(\mathbf{x})$ is exactly a polynomial in $\mathbf{x}$. As an example, consider the vector of variables $\mathbf{x} = (x, y)^T$ and the function $f_j(\mathbf{x}) = 3x^2 - 4xy + \frac{5y^3}{3x^3+2y+1} + 7$. It is easy to recognize that $f_j(\mathbf{x})$ can also be written as $f_j(\mathbf{x}) = \mathbf{a}_j^T \cdot U_j(\mathbf{x})$, where $\mathbf{a}_j^T = (3, -4, 5, 7)$ and $U_j(\mathbf{x}) = (x^2, xy, \frac{y^3}{3x^3+2y+1}, 1)^T$. When synthesizing the k-nested ranking function, the vector U_j comes from the given template U while the vector of coefficients $\mathbf{a}_j^T$ is computed for obtaining the separating hyperplane.

Formula (1) can thus be rewritten as

$$\forall (\mathbf{x}, \mathbf{x}') \in \varOmega : \begin{cases} \mathbf{a}_1^T \cdot (U_1(\mathbf{x}) - U_1(\mathbf{x}')) \geq C_1 \\ \mathbf{a}_2^T \cdot (U_2(\mathbf{x}) - U_2(\mathbf{x}')) + \mathbf{a}_1^T \cdot U_1(\mathbf{x}) \geq C_2 \\ \quad \vdots \\ \mathbf{a}_k^T \cdot (U_k(\mathbf{x}) - U_k(\mathbf{x}')) + \mathbf{a}_{k-1}^T \cdot U_{k-1}(\mathbf{x}) \geq C_k \\ \mathbf{a}_k^T \cdot U_k(\mathbf{x}) \geq C_{k+1} \end{cases} \tag{2}$$

which can be written in compact vector form by means of the following notation. For each $i \in \{1, \ldots, k+1\}$, let G_i be a function mapping $(\mathbf{x}, \mathbf{x}')$ to a column vector of size k defined as follows.

$$G_1(\mathbf{x}, \mathbf{x}') \mapsto \begin{pmatrix} 0 \\ \vdots \\ 0 \\ 0 \\ U_1(\mathbf{x}) - U_1(\mathbf{x}') \end{pmatrix}, \quad G_2(\mathbf{x}, \mathbf{x}') \mapsto \begin{pmatrix} 0 \\ \vdots \\ 0 \\ U_2(\mathbf{x}) - U_2(\mathbf{x}') \\ U_1(\mathbf{x}) \end{pmatrix}, \quad \cdots$$

$$\cdots, \quad G_k(\mathbf{x}, \mathbf{x}') \mapsto \begin{pmatrix} U_k(\mathbf{x}) - U_k(\mathbf{x}') \\ U_{k-1}(\mathbf{x}) \\ 0 \\ \vdots \\ 0 \end{pmatrix}, \quad G_{k+1}(\mathbf{x}, \mathbf{x}') \mapsto \begin{pmatrix} U_k(\mathbf{x}) \\ 0 \\ 0 \\ \vdots \\ 0 \end{pmatrix}. \tag{3}$$

It is easy to see that each $G_i(\mathbf{x}, \mathbf{x}')$ is a mapping from $\mathbb{R}^{2n}$ to $\mathbb{R}^{\sum_{j=1}^{k} |a_j|}$. Then Formula (2) becomes

$$\forall (\mathbf{x}, \mathbf{x}') \in \varOmega : \begin{cases} (\mathbf{a}_k^T, \cdots, \mathbf{a}_1^T) \cdot G_1(\mathbf{x}, \mathbf{x}') \geq C_1 \\ (\mathbf{a}_k^T, \cdots, \mathbf{a}_1^T) \cdot G_2(\mathbf{x}, \mathbf{x}') \geq C_2 \\ \quad \vdots \\ (\mathbf{a}_k^T, \cdots, \mathbf{a}_1^T) \cdot G_k(\mathbf{x}, \mathbf{x}') \geq C_k \\ (\mathbf{a}_k^T, \cdots, \mathbf{a}_1^T) \cdot G_{k+1}(\mathbf{x}, \mathbf{x}') \geq C_{k+1} \end{cases}.$$

Let $G_i(\varOmega)$ be the image of $G_i(\mathbf{x}, \mathbf{x}')$ over the set $\varOmega$ and $(\mathbf{a}_k^T, \cdots, \mathbf{a}_1^T) \cdot G_i(\varOmega) = \{ (\mathbf{a}_k^T, \cdots, \mathbf{a}_1^T) \cdot \mathbf{v} \mid \mathbf{v} \in G_i(\varOmega) \}$. Therefore, by Definition 2, we know that for a loop defined by $\varOmega$, a nested ranking function exists if and only if there exists a vector $\mathbf{w}^T = (\mathbf{a}_k^T, \cdots, \mathbf{a}_1^T)$ and strictly positive real numbers $C_1, \ldots, C_{k+1}$ such that

$$\begin{cases} (\mathbf{a}_k^T, \cdots, \mathbf{a}_1^T) \cdot G_1(\Omega) \geq C_1 \\ (\mathbf{a}_k^T, \cdots, \mathbf{a}_1^T) \cdot G_2(\Omega) \geq C_2 \\ \quad\vdots \\ (\mathbf{a}_k^T, \cdots, \mathbf{a}_1^T) \cdot G_k(\Omega) \geq C_k \\ (\mathbf{a}_k^T, \cdots, \mathbf{a}_1^T) \cdot G_{k+1}(\Omega) \geq C_{k+1} \end{cases} \tag{4}$$

This implies that, if there exist a vector $\mathbf{w}^T = (\mathbf{a}_k^T, \cdots, \mathbf{a}_1^T)$ and positive numbers $C_1, \ldots, C_{k+1}$ such that Formula (4) holds, then we can get the k-nested polynomial ranking function $\langle \mathbf{a}_1^T \cdot U_1(\mathbf{x}), \ldots, \mathbf{a}_k^T \cdot U_k(\mathbf{x}) \rangle$.

The following theorem equivalently reduces the existence of nested polynomial ranking functions to the existence of a separating hyperplane between a point and a set. Let $m = \sum_{i=1}^{k} |\mathbf{a}_i|$ and $G(\Omega) = \bigcup_{i=1}^{k+1} G_i(\Omega)$.

Theorem 1. *Given a loop specified by Ω, it has a nested polynomial ranking function as defined in Definition 2 if and only if there exists a hyperplane $L(\mathbf{v})$ strictly separating the origin $\mathbf{O} \in \mathbb{R}^m$ from $G(\Omega) \subseteq \mathbb{R}^m$.*

Proof. Suppose that Ω has a k-nested polynomial ranking function defined as in Definition 2. Then, by Formula (4), there must exist a vector $\mathbf{w} = (\mathbf{a}_k^T, \cdots, \mathbf{a}_1^T)^T$ and strictly positive real numbers $C_1, \ldots, C_{k+1}$ such that Formula (4) holds.

Let $L(\mathbf{v}) = \mathbf{w}^T \cdot \mathbf{v} - \frac{\min\{C_i\}_{i=1}^{k+1}}{2}$. We claim that the linear function L strictly separates the origin $\mathbf{O} \in \mathbb{R}^m$ from $G(\Omega) \subseteq \mathbb{R}^m$. First, we have $L(\mathbf{O}) = \mathbf{w}^T \cdot \mathbf{O} - \frac{\min\{C_i\}_{i=1}^{k+1}}{2} = -\frac{\min\{C_i\}_{i=1}^{k+1}}{2} < 0$, since $\mathbf{O} = (0, \ldots, 0)^T$ and $C_j > 0$ for $j \in \{1, \ldots, k+1\}$. By the fact that $\mathbf{w} = (\mathbf{a}_k^T, \cdots, \mathbf{a}_1^T)^T$ and strictly positive real numbers $C_1, \ldots, C_{k+1}$ satisfy Formula (4), it follows that for each $\mathbf{v} \in G(\Omega)$,

$$L(\mathbf{v}) \geq \min\{C_i\}_{i=1}^{k+1} - \frac{\min\{C_i\}_{i=1}^{k+1}}{2} = \frac{\min\{C_i\}_{i=1}^{k+1}}{2} > 0$$

according to Formula (4). Therefore, $L(\mathbf{v})$ strictly separates the origin $\mathbf{O} \in \mathbb{R}^m$ from $G(\Omega) \subseteq \mathbb{R}^m$, as required.

Conversely, assume that there exists a hyperplane $L(\mathbf{v}) = \mathbf{w}^T \cdot \mathbf{v} + b$ strictly separating $\mathbf{O} \in \mathbb{R}^m$ from $G(\Omega) \subseteq \mathbb{R}^m$, where $\mathbf{w} = (\mathbf{a}_k^T, \cdots, \mathbf{a}_1^T)^T$. Then, there are two cases to consider:

1. $L(\mathbf{O}) < 0$ and for each $\mathbf{v} \in G(\Omega)$, $L(\mathbf{v}) > 0$, or
2. $L(\mathbf{O}) > 0$ and for each $\mathbf{v} \in G(\Omega)$, $L(\mathbf{v}) < 0$.

We now show that in both cases, it is always possible to find a vector $\mathbf{w}^T$ and strictly positive real numbers $C_1, \ldots, C_{k+1}$ which satisfy Formula (4). We just need to consider the first case; a symmetric analysis can be applied to the second.

Let us consider the first case, i.e., $L(\mathbf{O}) < 0$ and for each $\mathbf{v} \in G(\Omega)$ it is the case that $L(\mathbf{v}) > 0$. If this happens, then this means that $L(\mathbf{O}) = \mathbf{w}^T \cdot \mathbf{O} + b < 0$. Hence $b < 0$. Since for each $\mathbf{v} \in G(\Omega)$, $L(\mathbf{v}) = \mathbf{w}^T \cdot \mathbf{v} + b > 0$, i.e, $\mathbf{w}^T \cdot \mathbf{v} > -b$, dividing both sides of the above inequality by $-b$, we have for each $\mathbf{v} \in G(\Omega)$

$$-\frac{\mathbf{w}^T}{b} \cdot \mathbf{v} > 1. \tag{5}$$

Set $\mathbf{w}' = -\frac{\mathbf{w}}{b}$ and set $C_1' = C_2' = \cdots = C_{k+1}' = 1$. Then by Formula (5), since $G(\Omega) = \bigcup_{j=1}^{k+1} G_j(\Omega)$, we have for each $j \in \{1, \ldots, k+1\}$, $\mathbf{w}'^T \cdot G_j(\Omega) \geq 1$. This immediately implies that, for $\mathbf{w} = (\mathbf{a}_k^T, \ldots, \mathbf{a}_1^T)^T$, the vector

$$\mathbf{w}' = \left(-\frac{\mathbf{a}_k^T}{b}, -\frac{\mathbf{a}_{k-1}^T}{b}, \cdots, -\frac{\mathbf{a}_1^T}{b} \right)^T$$

and strictly positive real numbers $C_1', \ldots, C_{k+1}'$ satisfy Formula (4). Then, the loop specified by Ω indeed has a nested ranking function as by Definition 2.   □

Remark 2. Theorem 1 relates the computation of nested polynomial ranking functions for the loop defined by Ω to the detection of a separating hyperplane between the origin $\mathbf{O} \in \mathbb{R}^m$ and $G(\Omega) \subseteq \mathbb{R}^m$. Since the latter can be regarded as a binary classification problem, SVM algorithms fit well the task of computing such a hyperplane strictly separating $\mathbf{O}$ from $G(\Omega)$. The hyperplane computed by an SVM algorithm (cf. Sect. 2.4) clearly works in Theorem 1; however, in case the SVM algorithm fails to separate $\mathbf{O}$ from $G(\Omega)$, this does not imply by Theorem 1 that Ω has no nested ranking function, since the requirement about the separating hyperplane in Sect. 2.4 is stricter than the one in Theorem 1.

To compute a strictly separating hyperplane between the origin $\mathbf{O} \in \mathbb{R}^m$ and $G(\Omega) \subseteq \mathbb{R}^m$ by SVM algorithms, a key point is to guarantee that $\mathbf{O} \notin G(\Omega)$. Otherwise, if $\mathbf{O} \in G(\Omega)$, then the vector $\mathbf{w} = (\mathbf{a}_k^T, \ldots, \mathbf{a}_1^T)^T$ satisfying Formula (4) simply can not exist. Since the definition of $G(\mathbf{x}, \mathbf{x}')$ depends on $U(\mathbf{x}) = (U_1(\mathbf{x}), \ldots, U_k(\mathbf{x}))^T$ (cf. Notation (3)), we now present a method for constructing $U(\mathbf{x})$ such that $\mathbf{O} \notin G(\Omega)$.

3.3   The Construction of $U(\mathbf{x})$ Ensuring $\mathbf{O} \notin G(\Omega)$

In this section, we present how to build a vector $U(\mathbf{x}) = (U_1(\mathbf{x}), \ldots, U_k(\mathbf{x}))^T$ that can be used as input template U in Algorithm 1 such that it is guaranteed that $\mathbf{O} \notin G(\Omega)$, provided Ω has no fixed point. Note, however, that it is still possible for the SVM algorithm to fail to separate $\mathbf{O}$ from $G(\Omega)$ even when $\mathbf{O} \notin G(\Omega)$: this can happen, for instance, when the program alternates between two different points, which indicates that the given program is nonterminating.

For a loop program Ω, suppose it has no fixed points (for Algorithm 1, this is guaranteed to hold at line 4); otherwise, for a fixed point $(\mathbf{x}, \mathbf{x}) \in \Omega$, we would have $G_1(\mathbf{x}, \mathbf{x}) = \mathbf{O}$ (cf. Notation (3)), which implies $\mathbf{O} \in \bigcup_{i=1}^{k+1} G_i(\Omega) = G(\Omega)$. So, assume that $\mathbf{x} \neq \mathbf{x}'$ for each $(\mathbf{x}, \mathbf{x}') \in \Omega$. For each $j \in \{1, \ldots, k-1\}$, we can construct the vector $U_j(\mathbf{x})$ as

$$U_j(\mathbf{x}) = \left(\underbrace{x_1, \ldots, x_n}_{\mathbf{x}}, \frac{q_{j,n+1}(\mathbf{x})}{p_{j,n+1}(\mathbf{x})}, \ldots, \frac{q_{j,s_j}(\mathbf{x})}{p_{j,s_j}(\mathbf{x})} \right)^T \tag{6}$$

where $q_{j,i}(\mathbf{x}), p_{j,i}(\mathbf{x}) \in \mathbb{R}[\mathbf{x}]$ for each $i \in \{n+1, \ldots, s_j\}$, which control the shape of the separating hyperplane. Intuitively, the first n components of $U_j(\mathbf{x})$

guarantee $\mathbf{O} \notin G_j(\Omega)$ while the last $s_j - n$ components increase the dimension of the image space so to increase the chance of the existence of a strictly separating hyperplane between $\mathbf{O}$ and $G_j(\Omega)$. This implies that $U_j(\mathbf{x}) - U_j(\mathbf{x}')$ is the vector

$$
\Bigg(\underbrace{x_1 - x_1', \dots, x_n - x_n'}_{\mathbf{x} - \mathbf{x}'}, \frac{q_{j,n+1}(\mathbf{x})}{p_{j,n+1}(\mathbf{x})} - \frac{q_{j,n+1}(\mathbf{x}')}{p_{j,n+1}(\mathbf{x}')}, \dots, \frac{q_{j,s_j}(\mathbf{x})}{p_{j,s_j}(\mathbf{x})} - \frac{q_{j,s_j}(\mathbf{x}')}{p_{j,s_j}(\mathbf{x}')} \Bigg)^T .
$$

Since we assume that the loop Ω has no fixed points, it is not difficult to see that $\mathbf{O} \notin G_j(\Omega)$ for each $j \in \{1, \dots, k-1\}$. Assume this is not the case, i.e., $\mathbf{O} \in G_j(\Omega)$: then there must exist $(\hat{\mathbf{x}}, \hat{\mathbf{x}}') \in \Omega$ such that $G_j(\hat{\mathbf{x}}, \hat{\mathbf{x}}') = (0, \dots, 0)^T$. This implies that $U_j(\hat{\mathbf{x}}) - U_j(\hat{\mathbf{x}}') = \mathbf{0}$ which forces to have $\hat{\mathbf{x}}' = \hat{\mathbf{x}}$ (cf. the first n components of the vector $U_j(\hat{\mathbf{x}}) - U_j(\hat{\mathbf{x}}')$ above), i.e., $\hat{\mathbf{x}}$ is a fixed point of the loop Ω. Having $\hat{\mathbf{x}}' = \hat{\mathbf{x}}$ clearly contradicts the assumption that Ω has no fixed points, thus when the loop Ω has no fixed points, we have $\mathbf{O} \notin G_j(\Omega)$.

Having shown how to construct the vector $U_j(\mathbf{x})$ for $j \in \{1, \dots, k-1\}$, it remains to construct $U_k(\mathbf{x})$ such that $\mathbf{O} \notin G_k(\Omega)$ and $\mathbf{O} \notin G_{k+1}(\Omega)$, which also depend on $U_k(\mathbf{x})$ according to Notation (3). We let $U_k(\mathbf{x})$ be the vector

$$
U_k(\mathbf{x}) = \Bigg(\underbrace{x_1, \dots, x_n}_{\mathbf{x}}, \frac{q_{k,n+1}(\mathbf{x})}{p_{k,n+1}(\mathbf{x})}, \dots, \frac{q_{k,s_k}(\mathbf{x})}{p_{k,s_k}(\mathbf{x})} \Bigg)^T
$$

like for the other U_j vectors (cf. Notation (6)) but we additionally require that there exists $\ell \in \{n+1, \dots, s_k\}$ such that $\frac{q_{k,\ell}(\mathbf{x})}{p_{k,\ell}(\mathbf{x})}$ is positive on Ω. In general, one can set $q_{k,\ell}(\mathbf{x}) = s(\mathbf{x}) + 1$ and $p_{k,\ell}(\mathbf{x}) = 1$, where $s(\mathbf{x})$ is a sum of squares of polynomials; for example, we can set $s(\mathbf{x}) = \sum_{i=1}^{n} x_i^2$. It is not difficult to see that when $U_k(\mathbf{x})$ is in the above form, we have $\mathbf{O} \notin G_k(\Omega)$ and $\mathbf{O} \notin G_{k+1}(\Omega)$. Assume for the sake of contradiction that $\mathbf{O} \in G_k(\Omega)$; then there exists $(\hat{\mathbf{x}}, \hat{\mathbf{x}}') \in \Omega$ such that $G_k(\hat{\mathbf{x}}, \hat{\mathbf{x}}') = (0, \dots, 0)^T$. By Notation (3), since $U_k(\mathbf{x}) - U_k(\mathbf{x}')$ is a subvector of $G_k(\mathbf{x}, \mathbf{x}')$, it follows that $U_k(\hat{\mathbf{x}}) - U_k(\hat{\mathbf{x}}') = \mathbf{0}$ which forces to have $\hat{\mathbf{x}}' = \hat{\mathbf{x}}$ (cf. the first n components of the vector $U_k(\hat{\mathbf{x}}) - U_k(\hat{\mathbf{x}}')$ above), i.e., $\hat{\mathbf{x}}$ is a fixed point of the loop Ω, contradicting the assumption that Ω has no fixed points.

Assume now for the sake of contradiction that $\mathbf{O} \in G_{k+1}(\Omega)$; then there exists $(\hat{\mathbf{x}}, \hat{\mathbf{x}}') \in \Omega$ such that $G_{k+1}(\hat{\mathbf{x}}, \hat{\mathbf{x}}') = (0, \dots, 0)^T$. By Notation (3), since $U_k(\mathbf{x})$ is a subvector of $G_{k+1}(\mathbf{x}, \mathbf{x}')$, it follows that $U_k(\hat{\mathbf{x}}) = \mathbf{0}$. This in particular implies that $\frac{q_{k,s_j}(\mathbf{x})}{p_{k,s_j}(\mathbf{x})} = 0$ for all $j \in \{n+1, \dots, s_k\}$, contradicting the requirement that there exists $\ell \in \{n+1, \dots, s_k\}$ such that $\frac{q_{k,\ell}(\mathbf{x})}{p_{k,\ell}(\mathbf{x})}$ is positive on Ω.

4 Experimental Evaluation

We have implemented Algorithm 1 in a prototype tool named SVMRANKER. We also used LASSORANKER, part of the open-source ULTIMATE AUTOMIZER

Table 1. Summary of the experiments

	Terminating	Non-terminating	Unknown	Timeout
SVMRANKER	40	34	0	60
LASSORANKER	24	37	73	0
Common cases	19	34	0	0

suite [15], as reference for the termination analysis, for the cases for which it provided a definitive answer. For our experiments, we used a laptop equipped with a 2.5 GHz Intel Core i5-7300HQ CPU and 8 GB 2400 MHz DDR3 RAM; we set the timeout to 300 s for each experiment. The programs we used as benchmarks include several Boogie files taken from the ULTIMATE AUTOMIZER repository as well as from the programs listed in [12, 26], which admit the Ω representation based on Definition 1.

4.1 Overview of the Experiments

Table 1 shows an overview of the outcome of the experiments. As we can see, SVMRANKER has been able to solve many more problems than LASSORANKER, giving always answers compatible with those from LASSORANKER.

It is worthwhile to observe that SVMRANKER and LASSORANKER behave similarly for nonterminating programs: they established nontermination for the same 34 experiments, with LASSORANKER successfully classifying 3 more cases by means of geometric nontermination arguments [17]. Regarding the terminating programs, the situation is different: while the number of programs marked as terminating is rather high (40 for SVMRANKER and 24 for LASSORANKER), they gave the same answer for just 19 cases; this means that SVMRANKER has been able to solve 21 cases not solved by LASSORANKER, which has solved instead 5 cases not managed by SVMRANKER. In particular, the latter cases involve for four programs the use of conditional ranking functions, i.e., ranking functions making use of "if-then-else" statements, which are not supported yet by our algorithm; for the remaining case, in one iteration Z3 made SVMRANKER go timeout during the VERIFY procedure; in general, for the cases where SVM-RANKER reached the timeout, a large part of the execution time has been used by Z3 for the verification of the candidate nested ranking function.

This means that the SVM-based technique we proposed in Sect. 3 complements rather well the large set of algorithms available in LASSORANKER for establishing the termination of loops. By combining the techniques in LASSO-RANKER and the SVM-based one we propose, we would have been able to classify 82 programs out of 134, instead of just 61 for LASSORANKER alone.

To prove termination of the 40 terminating programs, SVMRANKER used an 1-nested affine linear ranking function for 30 cases, a 3-nested affine linear ranking function for 7 cases, a 5-nested affine linear ranking function for 1 case, and an 1-nested nonlinear ranking function for the remaining 2 cases.

Regarding the running time, both SVMRANKER and LASSORANKER completed the majority of the experiments with a definitive answer within 1 second, where we consider only the time actually spent for the analysis. Of the remaining cases, usually LASSORANKER is much faster than SVMRANKER in giving an answer, but not always: in a couple of cases, it took longer for LASSORANKER to return "unknown" than for SVMRANKER to return "terminating".

4.2 Discussion

SVMRANKER implements and extends Algorithm 1 in several ways.

SVMRANKER is coded in Python; the procedure SVM is based on the Python SCIKIT-LEARN library while HASFIXEDPOINT and VERIFY delegate their functionalities to Z3 [19] by means of the Python bindings Z3 provides.

Algorithm 1 wants as input the template for the ranking function, just like many other algorithms implemented in LASSORANKER. However, the algorithms in LASSORANKER are only applicable to templates of linear functions and linear-constraint program loops. Given the difficulty of selecting a good template, SVMRANKER works as follows: it tries to use k-nested ranking functions, with k being an increasing odd number at most 7. The functions used in the nested ranking functions are either affine linear functions or nonlinear functions; the latter involve monomials obtained by randomly choosing for each program variable its exponent in the set $\{-3, -2, \ldots, 3\} \cup \{-\frac{1}{2}, \frac{1}{2}\}$. As a result of this random choice, it may happen that a program is classified as terminating by a k-nested ranking function with k larger than needed; in the experiments we have found some case where a 3-nested affine linear ranking function was used to prove termination, with the last function being a constant, i.e., it was actually a 2-nested affine linear ranking function. An interesting research topic would be the design of heuristics able to provide good candidate templates based on the input loop program, instead of using predefined templates or randomly generated ones.

It is worthwhile to stress that Algorithm 1 and SVMRANKER are able to work with any template U for the k-nested ranking function with no changes in the implementation. This means that it is extremely easy to extend both with new templates as well as with the candidate templates provided by the above heuristics, once designed. The running time of SVMRANKER is likely to be affected when using complex templates, since the VERIFY procedure (currently based on Z3) needs to verify whether the obtained k-nested function is a valid k-nested ranking function and this may require more time for complex functions.

SVMRANKER iterates the main loop of Algorithm 1 at most 25 times, since in very few cases SVMRANKER would be able to prove termination by using more iterations without reaching the timeout. By limiting the number of iterations, we also limit the growth of the set of sampled points and counterexamples: since the SVM algorithms' complexity is at least quadratic in the size of the training set [22], adding more and more counterexamples when the current template is not suitable for proving termination would just result in a general slow-down of SVM without reasonable possibility to get a useful answer from SVMRANKER.

Limiting the number of iterations with a fixed bound is important to avoid wasting too much time while working with templates that are not suitable for proving termination; with the limit in place, it is important to make VERIFY (or, Z3 in SVMRANKER) return "good" counterexamples, so to be able to discover quickly whether the current template is suitable for proving termination: "good" counterexamples, like the ones corresponding to points close to the origin, allow the algorithm to refine quickly the training set and rule out other possible "bad" counterexamples. As an example, consider the origin $\mathbf{O} = (0,0)$ and the two data points $(4,2)$ and $(1000,500)$. Assume that the training set contains only the origin $\mathbf{O}$ and one point: a separation hyperplane for the former is the diagonal line passing through $(2,1) = G(\mathbf{x}_g, \mathbf{x}'_g)$, while for the latter passes through $(500,250) = G(\mathbf{x}_b, \mathbf{x}'_b)$, for appropriate program variables $\mathbf{x}_g$ and $\mathbf{x}_b$ and their updates $\mathbf{x}'_g$ and $\mathbf{x}'_b$, respectively. The counterexample $(\mathbf{x}_g, \mathbf{x}'_g)$ is "better" than $(\mathbf{x}_b, \mathbf{x}'_b)$, since the separation hyperplane passing through $(2,1)$ is able to rule out all counterexamples $(\mathbf{x}, \mathbf{x}')$ inducing points $G(\mathbf{x}, \mathbf{x}')$ lying on the segment between $(2,1)$ and $(500,250)$, each of which may be returned by the VERIFY function as counterexample for the hyperplane passing through $(500,250)$. We think that finding a good measure for the "quality" of the counterexample and ways to optimize it is an interesting future work with practical improvements on program termination analysis in general.

5   Conclusion

In this paper, we considered the synthesis of k-nested ranking functions for proving termination of loop programs; we showed that the existence of a nested ranking function for a program Ω is equivalent to the existence of a hyperplane separating the origin $\mathbf{O}$ from $G(\Omega)$. This allowed us to use SVM techniques for the synthesis of k-nested linear and nonlinear ranking functions. We showed how to define the $G(\Omega)$ so that the separating hyperplane gives rise to a nested ranking function for the loop; we showed as well how to guarantee by construction that $\mathbf{O} \notin G(\Omega)$ by crafting an appropriate template U, as long as Ω has no fixed points. Experimental evaluation on our prototype SVMRANKER confirmed that our SVM-based synthesis algorithm is a valuable approach complementing the techniques used in LASSORANKER, the termination engine of the leading program analysis tool ULTIMATE AUTOMIZER: we have been able to prove termination for 21 programs (out of 45 shown to terminate by at least one of the tools) for which LASSORANKER returned "unknown".

As future work, we plan to investigate heuristics for generating good templates for SVMRANKER from the program to be analyzed, as well as heuristics to improve the quality of the counterexamples returned to the current candidate nested ranking function, so to speed up the analysis for terminating programs.

Acknowledgement. This work is supported by the National Natural Science Foundation of China (Grants Nos. 61532019, 61761136011, 61572024), the Natural Science Foundation of Chongqing (Grant No. cstc2019jcyj-msxmX0638) and the Guangdong Science and Technology Department (Grant No. 2018B010107004).

References

1. Bagnara, R., Mesnard, F.: Eventual linear ranking functions. In: PPDP, pp. 229–238 (2013)
2. Ben-Amram, A.M., Genaim, S.: Ranking functions for linear-constraint loops. J. ACM **61**(4), 26:1–26:55 (2014)
3. Ben-Amram, A.M., Genaim, S.: On multiphase-linear ranking functions. In: Majumdar, R., Kunčak, V. (eds.) CAV 2017. LNCS, vol. 10427, pp. 601–620. Springer, Cham (2017). https://doi.org/10.1007/978-3-319-63390-9_32
4. Beyer, D.: Automatic verification of C and Java programs: SV-COMP 2019. In: Beyer, D., Huisman, M., Kordon, F., Steffen, B. (eds.) TACAS 2019. LNCS, vol. 11429, pp. 133–155. Springer, Cham (2019). https://doi.org/10.1007/978-3-030-17502-3_9
5. Bradley, A.R., Manna, Z., Sipma, H.B.: Linear ranking with reachability. In: Etessami, K., Rajamani, S.K. (eds.) CAV 2005. LNCS, vol. 3576, pp. 491–504. Springer, Heidelberg (2005). https://doi.org/10.1007/11513988_48
6. Bradley, A.R., Manna, Z., Sipma, H.B.: The polyranking principle. In: Caires, L., Italiano, G.F., Monteiro, L., Palamidessi, C., Yung, M. (eds.) ICALP 2005. LNCS, vol. 3580, pp. 1349–1361. Springer, Heidelberg (2005). https://doi.org/10.1007/11523468_109
7. Chen, Y., Xia, B., Yang, L., Zhan, N., Zhou, C.: Discovering non-linear ranking functions by solving semi-algebraic systems. In: Jones, C.B., Liu, Z., Woodcock, J. (eds.) ICTAC 2007. LNCS, vol. 4711, pp. 34–49. Springer, Heidelberg (2007). https://doi.org/10.1007/978-3-540-75292-9_3
8. Colón, M.A., Sipma, H.B.: Synthesis of linear ranking functions. In: Margaria, T., Yi, W. (eds.) TACAS 2001. LNCS, vol. 2031, pp. 67–81. Springer, Heidelberg (2001). https://doi.org/10.1007/3-540-45319-9_6
9. Colón, M.A., Sipma, H.B.: Practical methods for proving program termination. In: Brinksma, E., Larsen, K.G. (eds.) CAV 2002. LNCS, vol. 2404, pp. 442–454. Springer, Heidelberg (2002). https://doi.org/10.1007/3-540-45657-0_36
10. Cook, B., Podelski, A., Rybalchenko, A.: Proving program termination. Commun. ACM **54**(5), 88–98 (2011)
11. Cortes, C., Vapnik, V.: Support-vector networks. Mach. Learn. **20**(3), 273–297 (1995)
12. Cousot, P.: Proving program invariance and termination by parametric abstraction, Lagrangian relaxation and semidefinite programming. In: Cousot, R. (ed.) VMCAI 2005. LNCS, vol. 3385, pp. 1–24. Springer, Heidelberg (2005). https://doi.org/10.1007/978-3-540-30579-8_1
13. Feautrier, P.: Some efficient solutions to the affine scheduling problem. I. One-dimensional time. IJPP **21**(5), 313–347 (1992)
14. Heizmann, M., Hoenicke, J., Leike, J., Podelski, A.: Linear ranking for linear lasso programs. In: Van Hung, D., Ogawa, M. (eds.) ATVA 2013. LNCS, vol. 8172, pp. 365–380. Springer, Cham (2013). https://doi.org/10.1007/978-3-319-02444-8_26
15. Heizmann, M., Hoenicke, J., Podelski, A.: Termination analysis by learning terminating programs. In: Biere, A., Bloem, R. (eds.) CAV 2014. LNCS, vol. 8559, pp. 797–813. Springer, Cham (2014). https://doi.org/10.1007/978-3-319-08867-9_53
16. Leike, J., Heizmann, M.: Ranking templates for linear loops. LMCS **11**(1) (2015)
17. Leike, J., Heizmann, M.: Geometric nontermination arguments. In: Beyer, D., Huisman, M. (eds.) TACAS 2018, Part II. LNCS, vol. 10806, pp. 266–283. Springer, Cham (2018). https://doi.org/10.1007/978-3-319-89963-3_16

18. Li, Y., Zhu, G., Feng, Y.: The L-depth eventual linear ranking functions for single-path linear constraint loops. In: TASE, pp. 30–37 (2016)
19. de Moura, L., Bjørner, N.: Z3: an efficient SMT solver. In: Ramakrishnan, C.R., Rehof, J. (eds.) TACAS 2008. LNCS, vol. 4963, pp. 337–340. Springer, Heidelberg (2008). https://doi.org/10.1007/978-3-540-78800-3_24
20. Podelski, A., Rybalchenko, A.: A complete method for the synthesis of linear ranking functions. In: Steffen, B., Levi, G. (eds.) VMCAI 2004. LNCS, vol. 2937, pp. 239–251. Springer, Heidelberg (2004). https://doi.org/10.1007/978-3-540-24622-0_20
21. Shen, L., Wu, M., Yang, Z., Zeng, Z.: Generating exact nonlinear ranking functions by symbolic-numeric hybrid method. J. Syst. Sci. Complex. **26**(2), 291–301 (2013)
22. Smola, A.J., Schölkopf, B.: A tutorial on support vector regression. Stat. Comput. **14**(3), 199–222 (2004)
23. Sohn, K., Gelder, A.V.: Termination detection in logic programs using argument sizes. In: PODS, pp. 216–226 (1991)
24. Turing, A.M.: On computable numbers, with an application to the Entscheidungsproblem. Proc. Lond. Math. Soc. **2**(42), 230–265 (1937)
25. Turing, A.M.: On computable numbers, with an application to the Entscheidungsproblem: a correction. Proc. Lond. Math. Soc. **2**(42), 544–546 (1937)
26. Yuan, Y., Li, Y.: Ranking function detection via SVM: a more general method. IEEE Access **7**, 9971–9979 (2019)

A First Step in the Translation of Alloy to Coq

Salwa Souaf[1,2(✉)] and Frédéric Loulergue[1(✉)]

[1] School of Informatics Computing and Cyber Systems,
Northern Arizona University, Flagstaff, USA
{salwa.souaf,frederic.loulergue}@nau.edu
[2] INSA Centre Val de Loire, LIFO EA 4022, Bourges, France
salwa.souaf@insa-cvl.fr

Abstract. Alloy is both a formal language and a tool for software modeling. The language is basically first order relational logic. The analyzer is based on instance finding: it tries to refute assertions and if it succeeds it reports a counterexample. It works by translating Alloy models and instance finding into SAT problems. If no instance is found it does not mean the assertion is satisfied. Alloy relies on the small scope hypothesis: examining all small cases is likely to produce interesting counterexamples. This is very valuable when developing a system. However, Alloy cannot show their absence. In this paper, we propose an approach where Alloy can be used as a first step, and then using a tool we develop, Alloy models can be translated to Coq code to be proved correct interactively.

Keywords: First order relational logic · Calculus of inductive construction · Translation

1 Introduction

There are many different formal methods, ranging from completely automated tools, for e.g. static analyzers and sanitizers [24], to interactive theorem proving that requires a lot of human work.

Often, the users of such tools need to provide a specification of the analyzed system. Analyzing this specification can then be automatic or interactive. Alloy and the Alloy analyzer [10] fall into the first category. Alloy was and is used in many different domains. For example software engineering [7], and security [20]. More specific applications of it, as presented by Torlak et al. in [28], are modeling and analysis of software systems, bounded program verification and test-case generation. Multiple systems have been studied using Alloy: the flash file system [12,13], the Mondex electronics purse [21], a proton therapy machine [22], an information system library [6], *etc.*

When it comes to bounded program verification two related works were presented in detail in [28]. The Jalloy tool [11] checks a Java method against a specification of its behavior. It starts by translating the method to Alloy then

© Springer Nature Switzerland AG 2019
Y. Ait-Ameur and S. Qin (Eds.): ICFEM 2019, LNCS 11852, pp. 455–469, 2019.
https://doi.org/10.1007/978-3-030-32409-4_28

invoking an early prototype of the Alloy Analyzer on the resulting constraints. The second work was built on the previous work and is called Forge [4]. It employed a new translation from procedural code to relational logic involving symbolic execution, using the KodKod API [27]. Alloy have also been exploited in many tools for test-case generation, to mention: TestEra [16] and Whispec [23]. While TestEra [16] employs Alloy in a specification-based black-box framework for testing of Java programs, Whispec [23] is an approach for specification-based white-box testing using Kodkod. KodKod [5], that is at the heart of Alloy's engine is also used in Niptick [2] a counter-example finder for the proof assistant Isabelle.

Alloy is a lightweight formal method as it relies on the small scope hypothesis: examining all small cases is likely to produce interesting counterexamples. However, the Alloy analyzer cannot show the absence of errors. Other formal tools such as the interactive theorem provers Coq [26] and Isabelle [18] have been used to provide very strong guarantees on verified software, including a C compiler [15] and the kernel of an operating system [14].

We think it is very valuable to use lightweight formal methods. In practice, if one is to use a tool such as Alloy as a first step, then wants to use a more heavyweight tools such as Coq as a second step, the formalization done first is lost. To support the transition from Alloy to Coq, we propose a translator from Alloy models to Coq code.

The paper is organized as follows. In Sect. 2 we briefly present Alloy and Coq. The principles of the tool we propose are described in Sect. 3, including examples of translation. We compare our approach to related work in Sect. 4, discuss the current limitations of our tool in Sect. 5, and conclude in Sect. 6.

2   An Overview of Alloy and Coq

2.1   Alloy and the Alloy Analyzer

Alloy [9] is both a language and an analyzer for writing and checking formal models. This section provides the details of the properties and main components of this language.

Alloy Properties. Alloy have been widely used for modeling systems in order to simulate them and verify their properties. It allows a simplified view of the systems by abstracting implementation details and focusing on their properties and constraints. The language has a simple syntax based on the Z language. It is a structural language: it allows to model complex structures with hierarchies and relations. Although it offers the possibility to define entities with properties and constraints to describe systems, it does not conduct treatments. Alloy is an analyzable language. The properties of an Alloy model can be checked and simulated using the Alloy Analyzer.

Atoms & Relations. In Alloy, atoms are the basic elementary entities. It is an abstract concept that is used to model aspects of the real world. Alloy data types are universally based on relations. They represent a concept that serves to define correlations between atoms. Relations and atoms cooperate to represent different aspects of a system. Relations can have an n arity and can be declared as $f : A_1 \rightarrow \ldots \rightarrow A_n$.

Signatures represent the entities of a system. A signature is the only element to represent the types and atoms in an Alloy model. Although it is a non-object-oriented language, Alloy allows inheritance between signatures. A signature can have attributes as explained below.

Facts in Alloy are used to describe different constraints about the system being modeled that remain always true. In Alloy, all facts are defined using the keyword *fact*.

Predicates are an abstraction of logical formulas for reuse purposes. A predicate can be defined with parameters used in the logical formula of its body. Predicates are often used in assertions that we want to verify on the model.

Functions return typed values for reuse and model clarity sake.

Assertions are used to specify properties about the model that we expect to hold or that we want to check if they hold. Once an assertion is stated we can check if it holds in a specific scope, using the keyword **check** and feeding the model to the Alloy Analyzer. The analyzer looks for a counterexample to the assertion within the specified scope.

The scope is the cardinality, specified by the user, of the top level signatures in a model. Although working within limited scopes ensures that the model-finding problem is decidable, it limits the generality of the results produced by the Alloy Analyzer. Jackson explains this design decision through the *small scope hypothesis*: most bugs can be found by testing programs for all test inputs within a small scope. For more details refer to [10, section 5].

We discuss more specific Alloy syntax and semantics on the example of Fig. 1 that is basically the example of [10, page 16]. We will use this example as running example throughout the paper. The interested reader can refer to [10] for a longer discussion of this example.

Name and Addr are two *signatures* in Alloy terminology. They are sets. Book is also a signature containing an attribute, addr. While addr is given type Name →Addr, the fact that it is an attribute of Book means it is actually a ternary relation between Book, Name and Addr. In lines 3 and 4 of Fig. 1 we can see the definition of the predicates add and del both defining two different states of book, the first by adding a new entry (i.e. addr) and the second by deleting an existing one. In this code, + means union, − set difference, and .. is the relational join of Alloy. One specificity of the join operation in Alloy is that in an expression r1.r2, the right-most column of relation r1 and the left-most column of relation r2 are not in the join result. The function lookup returns the Addr associated to the Name n in the book b, n and b given as arguments of the function.

We can see how assertions are defined for this example in lines 11–21. The assertion delUndoesAdd is stating that by adding an entry to a book then deleting it we go back to the initial state of the book (taking into consideration that these are the only two operations done on the book). In order to check if this assertion holds, we execute the **check** stated in line 22 using the Alloy Analyzer (the scope in this case is 5 atoms, if the scope is not specified it is set to 3).

```
1    sig Name, Addr { }
2    sig Book { addr: Name → Addr }
3    pred add [b, b': Book, n: Name, a: Addr] { b'.addr = b.addr + n→a }
4    pred del [b, b': Book, n: Name] { b'.addr = b.addr − n→Addr }
5    fun lookup [b: Book, n: Name] : set Addr { n.(b.addr) }
6    assert delUndoesAdd {
7      all b, b', b'': Book, n: Name, a: Addr |
8        no n.(b.addr) and add [b, b', n, a] and del [b', b'', n]
9        implies b.addr = b''.addr
10   }
11   assert addIdempotent {
12     all b, b', b'': Book, n: Name, a: Addr |
13       add [b, b', n, a] and add [b, b'', n, a]
14       implies b'.addr = b''.addr
15   }
16   assert addLocal {
17     all b, b': Book, n, n': Name, a: Addr |
18       add [b, b', n] and n != n'
19       implies
20       lookup [b, n'] = lookup [b', n']
21   }
22   check delUndoesAdd for 5
```

Fig. 1. Alloy example

2.2 The Coq Proof Assistant

The Coq proof assistant is based on the calculus of inductive constructions [19], a higher-order typed λ-calculus. Coq and the calculus of inductive constructions are based on the Curry-Howard correspondence: a type corresponds to the statement of a theorem, and a program to the proof of a theorem.

The core of Coq is very small. For example there is no pre-defined data type. All definitions are typed in Coq. Therefore a user-defined type has a type, named a sort. There are three sorts in Coq: **Set** is the sort of types that correspond to types found is usual programming language. It is the sort of the "computational" types. **Prop** is the sort of "logical" types. Both **Set** and **Prop** are typed: their type is **Type**. Most of the time when using Coq, the type of **Type** will be displayed as **Type**. Actually there is a countable infinity of sorts **Type**.

```
1   Definition id: ∀ (A:Type), A → A :=      11      | S n1 ⇒ S(add n1 n2)
2      fun A x ⇒ x.                           12      end.
3                                             13
4   Inductive nat : Set :=                    14   Lemma add_n_O: ∀ n,
5   | O : nat                                 15      add n O = n.
6   | S : nat → nat.                          16   Proof.
7                                             17      induction n as [ | n IH ].
8   Fixpoint add (n1 n2:nat) : nat :=         18      − trivial.
9      match n1 with                          19      − simpl. rewrite IH. trivial.
10     | O ⇒ n2                               20   Qed.
```

Fig. 2. Coq example

In Gallina, the language of Coq, a definition contains three components: a name, a type, and a term. For example the polymorphic identity function can be defined as shown in lines 1–2 of Fig. 2.

As the core does not contain predefined types (but the sorts **Set**, **Prop** and **Type**), Coq provides a mechanism to define new inductive types. This is done by giving a list of *constructors* for values of the defined type. For example, Peano natural numbers are defined in lines 4–6 of Fig. 2. There are two constructors for values of type nat: O and S the latter taking a nat as argument.

Functions are most often written using pattern matching as in lines 8–12 of Fig. 2. For each possible way of constructing a value of the type of the matched expression (in this case n1 of type nat), the pattern matching construct returns (after ⇒) a specific result. The patterns (on the left-hand side of ⇒) may contain variables: in case the matching succeeds, the free variables are bound to the matched values in the right-hand side of ⇒. Note that add is a recursive function (**Fixpoint** keyword). Only terminating functions are allowed in Coq: in this case the system checks the termination by checking that the recursive call is done on a strict syntactic subterm of n1.

Coq is a proof assistant: it is possible to define theorems and prove them. As mentioned at the beginning of this section, a Coq definition contains three elements: a name, a type and a term. In the case of a theorem (or lemma, proposition, *etc.*), the term (i.e. the proof) is usually not written as a program (even though the Curry-Howard correspondence states a program and a proof are the same thing): the proof script language of Coq is used instead. In the code of Fig. 2, add_n_O is the name of the lemma, ∀ n, add n O = n is its type, and the proof script between **Proof** and **Qed** builds a term that is the proof of the lemma.

One important feature of Coq is that computational terms can be embedded into types. For example the library **Vector** of Coq standard library contains the following inductive type definition:

```
1   Inductive t (A : Type) : nat → Type :=
2   | nil : t A 0    | cons : ∀ (h:A) (n:nat), t A n → t A (S n).
```

The size of a value of this type contains the length of the vector. For example, a value of type Vector.t nat 10 is a vector containing ten nat values. Vector.t is called a *dependent type*.

This feature can also be used to define predicates as inductive types. For example the < predicates on Peano natural numbers is defined in the Coq standard library as:

```
1  Inductive le (n : nat) : nat → Prop :=
2   | le_n : le n n   | le_S : ∀ m : nat, le n m → le n (S m).
```

More generally, Coq functions can take both computational values and types as arguments, and also return them as results. As values of some types (like add_n_O) are proofs, Coq functions can also take proofs as arguments and return proofs as results. We use these features in the Coq code generated from Alloy models.

It is also possible to *declare* values in Coq: in this case we have only a name and a type. In the case of a value that needs a proof, it means an axiom is introduced in Coq's logic. Note that when such declarations can be written inside a section, in such a way that at the closing of the section, all the elements that depend on these hypotheses are added additional arguments corresponding to these hypotheses.

3   The Transformation

3.1   Basic Principles

Logical Quantifiers and Connectors. Logical elements present in the Alloy language, are also present in Gallina, either as primitives (universal quantification) or defined in the standard library (existential quantification, negation, conjunction, disjunction). The design choices thus appear when translating the relational parts of Alloy.

Sets, Relations and Elements. In the Coq standard library, sets and binary relations are formalized using predicates. Given a type A, a subset of A is formalized as a predicate on A, i.e. a value of type A→**Prop**, and a binary relation on types A and B as a value of type A→B→**Prop**. We could use directly such a formalization, and consider higher arities: the simple example of Fig. 1 indeed contains a relation of arity 3. Some other translation tools from Alloy to provers (discussed in Sect. 4) have explicit different translations for sets, binary relations, ternary translations, *etc.* Some of them are limited to a given arity.

However, in addition to a "raw" translation from Alloy to Coq, we wanted our tool to provide some support to ease the proof in Coq of the assertions of an Alloy model. Such a support includes general lemmas about the properties of the set and relational operations of Alloy. While of course possible in Coq, we chose to avoid such a solution as it would mean we would have to generate as many versions of the operations as there are combination of the arities, and as many supporting lemmas as there are combinations of these operations. Also in Alloy, relational operations can be applied to elements that are seen as singleton sets.

Therefore we chose to generalize the approach present in the Coq standard library: considering a type U (the universe of Alloy), a relation of arity n (with $0 < n$) is formalized as a value of type U→...→U→**Prop** that contains n U.

To be able to define operations on arbitrary relations, we first need to express the arity of a relation. This is done by the following definition:

```
1  Fixpoint arity (n : nat): Type :=
2    match n with
3     | 0 ⇒ Prop
4     | S n' ⇒ U → arity n'
5    end.
```

Therefore arity 1 simplifies to U→**Prop**, arity 2 to U→U→**Prop**, *etc*. With this definition we are able to translate any Alloy signature into a set of declarations of Coq values whose types are declared using arity.

To model an element as a singleton set, we define a Singleton predicate:

```
1   Fixpoint Singleton n (R: arity (S n)) : Prop :=
2     match n with
3     | 0 ⇒ ∃! (x:U), R x
4     | S n' ⇒ ∃! (x:U), Singleton n' (R x)
5     end.
```

Basically what this predicate does is that for a relation R of arity n greater than 1, it indicates there exists a unique element x of U such that the partial application R x is also a singleton relation. For a relation of arity 1, it just states that there exists a unique x such that R x.

Unfortunately the code above is not accepted by Coq. The problem is that Coq cannot determine without additional information that R x can be considered as a value of type arity n. To help the system we need "cast" functions (Fig. 3). Note that both these functions are defined using the proof script language of Coq. However, these cast functions are not enough: we need to provide them a proof as their last argument. This proof is simple, that is actually a proof by reflexivity, and we can use what Chlipala calls the "convoy pattern" [3, page 172] to get these proofs in the right hand sides of the pattern matching construction.

```
1    Definition cast n1 (R1 : arity n1) (H: n1 = 0) : Prop.
2      subst. simpl in *. trivial.
3    Defined.
4    Definition cast' n1 n1' (R1 : arity n1) (H: n1 = S n1') : arity (S n1').
5      subst. simpl in *. trivial.
6    Defined.
7    Fixpoint Singleton n (R: arity (S n)) : Prop:=
8      match n as m return n = m → Prop with
9      | 0 ⇒ fun H ⇒ ∃! x, cast _ (R x) H
10     | S n' ⇒ fun H ⇒ ∃! y, Singleton n' (cast' _ _ (R y) H)
11     end eq_refl.
```

Fig. 3. Actual definition of singleton

This small example shows that while having generic arity relations is indeed very generic, it makes the formalization more technically challenging. However, by providing general theorems on the Coq formalization of Alloy operations, we think the user of our tool will not have to deal with such technicalities most of the time.

Operations. All the basic relational operations have the same shape as Singleton. For example the inclusion operator **in** of Alloy is translated as (the cast and convoy pattern are omitted):

```
1   Fixpoint IN n (R1: arity n)(R2: arity n): Prop :=
2     match n with
3     | 0 ⇒ R1 → R2
```

```
4     | S n' ⇒ ∀ (x:U), IN n' (R1 x) (R2 x)
5     end.
```

Basically it means that for all n-tuple t, if R1 t then R2 t. The Alloy equality is not translated as the default syntactic equality (up to reduction) of Coq, but as:

```
1   Definition EQUAL n (R1: arity n)(R2: arity n): Prop :=
2     (IN R1 R2) ∧ (IN R2 R1).
```

Note that all the first nat arguments of these definitions are made implicit. It is therefore not necessary to give them explicitly when using these definitions: Coq infers them. Also instead of writing EQUAL a b, we use Coq's notations a == b.

Slightly more challenging operations are the join and the product. Again omitting the casts and the convoy pattern, the Alloy join operation is defined as shown in Fig. 4.

```
1   Fixpoint JOIN_R n2 (R1: arity 1)(R2: arity (S n2)) : arity n2 :=
2     match n2 with
3     | 0 ⇒ ∃ x:U, (R1 x) ∧ (R2 x)
4     | S n2' ⇒ fun (y:U) ⇒ JOIN_R n2' R1 (fun (x:U) ⇒ R2 x y)
5     end.
6   Fixpoint JOIN n1 n2 (R1: arity (S n1)) (R2: arity(S n2)) : arity(n1+n2) :=
7     match n1 with
8     | 0 ⇒ JOIN_R n2 R1 R2
9     | S n1' ⇒ fun (y:U) ⇒ JOIN n1' n2 (R1 y) R2
10    end.
```

Fig. 4. Definition of join (details omitted)

Operation Properties. As mentioned before, in addition to translate the definitions, operations, formulas of Alloy, we also provide properties of Alloy operations. The first set of properties concerns the Alloy equality ==: we proved it is an equivalence relation and also that it is compatible with the Alloy operations, i.e. for an operation f, if for all a, b such that a == b, then f a == f b. This allows to use the rewriting tactics of Coq while writing proofs. These are very important as most of the other properties are stated as equalities using ==.

The second set of properties are mostly algebraic properties. For example we have:

```
1   Lemma UNION_idem: ∀ n (R: arity n), UNION R R == R.
```

We developed a tactic that is able to prove most of these properties, the proof script in this case is **Proof.** solve_alloy. **Qed.**

Other properties are more specific to Alloy operations. For example we provide a lemma that states that if the join of a binary relation with itself contains the relation, then this relation is transitive:

```
1   Lemma JOIN_IN_transitive : ∀ R: arity 2,
2     IN (JOIN R R) R ↔ (∀ x y z, R x y → R y z → R x z).
```

3.2   Alloy Models Translation

Now that we have translated the basic elements of the Alloy language, we use them to translate Alloy models. Here we present how each of the Alloy models components is translated into Coq syntax and the reasoning behind it. We continue using the example given in Fig. 1.

Signatures. As we presented so far, everything that is going to be in our Coq translation of the Alloy models should be of type arity n. In order to follow this reasoning and to be able to manipulate Alloy signatures, we have decided to represent them in the format of Coq Variables (declarations) by specifying first their arity. Top-level signatures like Name, Addr and Book are sets and thus unary (i.e. arity 1) relations. Signature attributes are declared as relations (arity greater than 1) then a Hypothesis is added to the Coq code for their types, lines 2 and 3 in the following Coq translation shows the example of attribute addr:

```
1   Variable Name Addr Book: arity 1.
2   Variable addr: arity 3.
3   Hypothesis addr_sig: IN addr (PRODUCT Book (PRODUCT Name Addr)).
```

Facts. A way to declaring facts about a system in Coq is by stating Hypothesis. Thus, Alloy model facts are translated in our tool to Hypothesis and the syntax is as follows:

```
1   Hypothesis Model_fact: translated_fact_formula.
```

Functions and Predicates. Both are transformed in the same way to Coq syntax. For reasons of re-usability and ease of application we have decided to transform them into Coq inductive type definitions. The following examples are transformation of the del predicate and lookup function presented in Fig. 1. When writing the constructor for the inductive type, we start by modeling the "types" of the arguments as inclusions, possibly with additional expressions for modeling the cardinality. In the example of del, the argument b has type Book thus In b Book, but also b is an element, thus ONE b. We formalize functions as predicates, but with an additional argument that models the result returned by the function. In the case of lookup, the result is the value r_lookup:

```
1    Inductive del: arity 1 → arity 1 → arity 1 →  Prop:=
2    | del_def: ∀ (b: arity  1) (b': arity  1)  (n: arity  1),
3       IN b Book ∧  (ONE b)  →
4       IN b' Book ∧  (ONE b')  →
5       IN n Name ∧  (ONE n)  →
6       JOIN b' addr == DIFFERENCE (JOIN b addr) (PRODUCT n Addr)  →
7       del b b' n.
8
9    Inductive lookup: arity 1 → arity 1 → arity 1 →  Prop:=
10   | lookup_def: ∀ (r_lookup: arity 1) (b: arity  1)  (n: arity  1),
11      IN r_lookup Addr →
12      IN b Book ∧  (ONE b)  →
13      IN n Name ∧  (ONE n)  →
14      r_lookup == JOIN n (JOIN b addr)  →
15      lookup b n  r_lookup .
```

Assertions are defined in Coq syntax and then stated as Lemmas when called in an Alloy **check** block. Thus, the assertion delUndoesAdd is transformed as follows:

```
1   Definition delUndoesAdd:=
2      ∀ (b: arity  1) (b': arity  1) (b'': arity  1) (n: arity  1)(a: arity  1),
```

```
3   ( NO (JOIN n (JOIN b addr)) ∧ add b b' n a ∧ del b' b'' n ) →
4   JOIN b addr == JOIN b'' addr.
5
6   Lemma delUndoesAdd_Lemma: delUndoesAdd.
```

3.3   The Address Book Example

In the previous subsections, we presented most of the translation of the Alloy example of Fig. 1. Figures 5, 6 and 7 present the automatic translation using our tool of the two other assertions addIdempotent and addLocal, as well as the proof scripts we wrote to prove two of the corresponding lemmas.

```
1   Definition addIdempotent:=          7   Definition addLocal:=
2   ∀ (b b' b'' a n: arity 1),          8   ∀ (b b b' a n n': arity 1) r_1 r_2,
3   (add_ b b' n a ∧ add_ b' b'' n a ) →  9   lookup b n' r_1 →
4   JOIN b' addr == JOIN b'' addr.      10   lookup b' n' r_2 →
5                                       11   (add_ b b' n a ∧ not(n == n')) →
6                                       12   r_1 == r_2 .
```

Fig. 5. Translation of the assertions addIdempotent and addLocal

A recommended style in Coq, is to avoid using explicitly automatically generated names by tactics. Our destruct_and tactics, that basically systematically replaces hypotheses of the form A∧ B by two hypotheses A and B, automatically generates names for these new hypotheses. The inversion tactic also automatically generates names. To explicitly give names to the hypotheses we want to manipulate explicitly, we use the assert tactic of Coq that is used to prove an intermediate result. In our case, we just state and give an explicit name for already existing hypotheses, hence the use of the trivial tactic to prove the assertion (for e.g. lines 10–11 of Fig. 6). To get the formulas corresponding to the definition of an Alloy predicate, or an Alloy function, the inversion tactic of Coq is needed (e.g. line 7 of Fig. 6 and line 7 of Fig. 7). Using the assert tactic, we give explicit names to the hypotheses generated by inversion (for e.g., lines 8–9 of Fig. 7).

The two other main characteristics of these proof scripts are:

- The use of the rewrite tactic, that relies on the proofs of == is an equivalence relation, and the Alloy operations are compatible with this equivalence relation (e.g. line 13 of Fig. 6 and line 10 of Fig. 7).
- The systematic use of properties proved on Alloy operations: for example the distributivity of the union over the difference (line 15 of Fig. 6) and the associativity and idempotence of the union (line 11 of Fig. 7).

Most of the proof scripts are based on the element described above. The exception are lines 20–23 of Fig. 6. The proof of the condition of the lemma DIFFERENCE_NO_INTERSECT is in a way more "low-level" than the other parts of the proof scripts as it directly makes use of the definitions of some Alloy operations. One non standard Coq tactic is castsimpl: it is a tactic we provide, and that simplifies the application of the Alloy operations and also removes all the casts in the hypotheses and the goal. In the example the goal before calling castsimpl is:

```
1    Lemma delUndoesAdd_Lemma : delUndoesAdd.
2    Proof.
3      unfold delUndoesAdd.
4      intros b b' b'' n a H. destruct_and.
5      assert(Hadd: add_ b b' n a) by trivial.
6      assert(Hdel: del b' b'' n) by trivial.
7      inversion Hadd; inversion Hdel; subst.
8      destruct_and.
9      (* We are ready to prove: JOIN b addr == JOIN b'' addr *)
10     assert(Hr1: JOIN b'' addr ==  DIFFERENCE (JOIN b' addr) (PRODUCT n Addr)) by trivial.
11     assert(Hr2: JOIN b' addr == UNION (JOIN b addr) (PRODUCT n a)) by trivial.
12     rewrite Hr1, Hr2.
13     rewrite UNION_DIFFERENCE_distr_l with (R1:=JOIN b addr).
14     rewrite UNION_NO_l by
15        (apply DIFFERENCE_IN_NO;
16        apply PRODUCT_IN_compat with (R1:=n);
17        auto using IN_refl).
18     rewrite DIFFERENCE_NO_INTERSECT by
19        (assert(HH: NO (JOIN n (JOIN b addr))) by trivial;
20        castsimpl; intros;
21        specialize(HH x);
22        contradict HH;
23        intuition eauto).
24     reflexivity.
25   Qed.
```

Fig. 6. Proof of Lemma delUndoesAdd

```
1    Lemma addIdempotent_Lemma: addIdempotent.
2    Proof.
3      unfold addIdempotent.
4      intros b b' b'' n a H. destruct_and.
5      assert(Hadd1: add_ b b' n a) by trivial.
6      assert(Hadd2: add_ b' b'' n a) by trivial.
7      inversion Hadd1; inversion Hadd2; subst.
8      assert(Hr1: JOIN b'' addr == UNION (JOIN b' addr)(PRODUCT n a)) by trivial.
9      assert(Hr2: JOIN b' addr == UNION (JOIN b addr)(PRODUCT n a)) by trivial.
10     rewrite Hr1, Hr2.
11     rewrite ← UNION_assoc, UNION_idem.
12     reflexivity.
13   Qed.
```

Fig. 7. Proof of Lemma addIdempotent

```
1    NO (INTERSECT (JOIN b addr) (PRODUCT n Addr))
```

meaning we have to prove that the intersection of JOIN b addr and PRODUCT n Addr
is empty, while after it is:

```
1    ∀ y x : U, ~ ((∃ x0 : U, b x0 ∧  addr x0 y x) ∧  n y ∧  Addr x)
```

As castsimpl simplifies the hypothesis HH in a similar way, it is quite easy to finish the
proof.

These two proof scripts show that while most of the time the user can rely on proofs by rewrite and application of operation properties, when it is not possible, the proof writing remains accessible. With these two proofs, we guarantee that the Alloy assertions hold for arbitrary sets and relations Book, Name, Addr and addr.

The Tool. The tool is written in Java and relies on ANTLR for parsing. There are about 2 KLoC of non-generated Java code, and the Coq supporting library Alloy is about 600 LoC. The tool and the complete examples are available at: https://alloy2coq. github.io.

4 Related Work

Although theorem provers have proved their effectiveness in proving detailed properties of multiple complex system specifications, they are still considered to be too expensive to use frequently during software development. Lightweight formal methods, on the other hand, are frequently used for checking software during design and implementation stages. Alloy, is a popular language and tool used for checking software systems against their requirements. On one hand, one of Alloy's strong suits is the counterexample returned in case of unfulfilled requirements. On the other hand, lack of counterexample, generally, does not give a correctness proof. Thus, for critical systems, a second round of analysis might be crucial. Several previous works have addressed the verification of Alloy specifications.

In [1], Arkoudas et al. present a tool, Prioni, that integrates model checking and theorem proving for relational reasoning. Prioni takes as input formulas written in Alloy. It first uses the Alloy Analyzer to check their validity for a given scope. Once no counterexample is found, Prioni translates these Alloy formulas into Athena, a denotational proof language, proof obligations and uses the Athena tool for proof discovery and checking. Unlike Prioni, that only analyzes finite domains due to the fact that Athena cannot handle infinite sets, our proposed solution handles infinite domains. Another solution that works on infinite domains is presented in [29]. Kelloy [29] is a tool for verifying Alloy specifications with respect to potentially infinite domains.

Kelloy is an engine for verifying Alloy specifications aiming to bridge the gap between lightweight formal methods and theorem provers. It provides: a fully automatic translation of Alloy language to KFOL (the first-order logic of KeY, the deductive theorem prover used in Kelloy), an Alloy-specific extension to KeY's calculus and a reasoning strategy that improves KeY's capability in finding proofs and generates intermediate proof obligations that are easy to understand.

Unlike Prioni and the transformation tool we are presenting, Kelloy was developed in a way that only takes into consideration translation of Alloy relations up to ternary relations (i.e. arity 3). Such an approach requires to define the Alloy operations for all the different combinations of the arities in KFOL.

Mariano et al. [17] followed an approach closer to ours. They present an extension of PVS (Prototype Verification System), called Dynamite, that embeds Alloy calculus. It automatically adds and analyzes new hypotheses with the aid of the Alloy Analyzer. The generated PVS sequents get cluttered with some unnecessary formulas, thus, Alloy unsat-core extraction feature is used in order to refine proof sequents. Although both our work and that presented in [17] relies on users conducting proof manually, we provide a library with predefined lemmas to provide assistance in the proof process.

5   Discussion

The tool presented in this article shows the potential of translating and proving the correctness of critical Alloy models, but it still has some limitations in its current state.

The first limitation is the subset of the Alloy language that is supported. There is one aspect that the current translation does not handle: the cardinality of sets and relations. The design choice we made is not incompatible with dealing with cardinalities. It however requires additional hypotheses. First the universe U should be countable: this is actually in line with what is considered in Alloy, but it is not set as an hypothesis in our current Coq modeling. Then to compute the cardinality (the # operator in Alloy), the argument should be a finite relation: we also plan to add this hypothesis each time the operator is used. Other Alloy features that we have yet to integrate into our tool are: integer support, Coq can handle integer definition and thus, adding this to our solution will only require some formalization efforts. The other feature that we need to improve farther is the arrow operation. For now, our arrow operation is by default a many to many arrow operation, while Alloy's arrow operation handles different multiplicities.

The second limitation is not related to the translation itself, but rather to the support provided to the user in the translated Coq code. Although we do provide a few Coq tactics to ease the work to prove what are assertions in Alloy, currently the proofs are written mostly manually by the users. We plan to enrich the Coq Alloy library with more powerful tactics.

In translating one formal language to another one, the question of the correctness of the translation arises. One possibility would be to have a Coq representation of Alloy's abstract syntax, and then give a Coq semantics to this syntax: this would be a formalization of Alloy in Coq. Then we could implement in Coq what is currently the back-end of our translation in Java: the generation of Coq code from Alloy's syntax. Proving the correctness of the translation would then mean check that the semantics and the translation are equivalent. However, it is very likely that the semantics could be given using the same basic constructs we use for our translation: they would be essentially no difference between the Coq *semantics* of Alloy, and the Coq *translation* of Alloy. Another possibility would be to have a deep embedding of both Alloy and Coq in Coq, and check that the translation (from syntax to syntax) preserves the semantics. However, our current formalization of Alloy in Coq uses features that formalizations of Coq in Coq (for e.g. [8]) do not currently handle.

6   Conclusion and Future Work

In this paper we presented a tool for translating Alloy models into Coq code. Alloy main objects are relations: sets are unary relations, elements are considered as singleton sets. We chose to keep this view in Coq and to consider, as in the module Relation_Definitions of Coq's standard library, that a relation is a function to **Prop**. This module however, only considers binary relations, therefore they have type U→U→**Prop** where U is the type of the universe.

We decided to generalize this approach. This choice required us to use dependent types everywhere in the Coq library that provides the primitive relational operations of Alloy and supports the translation. We use our tool on examples and prove with Coq the lemmas generated by the translation: this choice of Coq formalization seems appropriate.

One of the motivations for this tool is our project around a broker for the Cloud that takes into account user security requirements that can be expressed as first order relational logic formulas and that we checked using Alloy/Kodkod [25]. In order to increase the trust in this broker, we aim at formalizing all the hypothesis made on the system, and make sure that if the formal requirement given by the user contains no error and are added to the system, then conclusions about the security of the new state of the system can be drawn. This case study will require a significantly larger translation and Coq proofs than the examples we considered so far.

References

1. Arkoudas, K., Khurshid, S., Marinov, D., Rinard, M.: Integrating model checking and theorem proving for relational reasoning. In: Berghammer, R., Möller, B., Struth, G. (eds.) RelMiCS 2003. LNCS, vol. 3051, pp. 21–33. Springer, Heidelberg (2004). https://doi.org/10.1007/978-3-540-24771-5_3

2. Blanchette, J.C., Nipkow, T.: Nitpick: a counterexample generator for higher-order logic based on a relational model finder. In: Kaufmann, M., Paulson, L.C. (eds.) ITP 2010. LNCS, vol. 6172, pp. 131–146. Springer, Heidelberg (2010). https://doi.org/10.1007/978-3-642-14052-5_11

3. Chlipala, A.: Certified Programming with Dependent Types. MIT Press, Cambridge (2014)

4. Dennis, G.D.: A relational framework for bounded program verification. Ph.D. thesis, Massachusetts Institute of Technology (2009)

5. Torlak, E., Jackson, D.: Kodkod: a relational model finder. In: Grumberg, O., Huth, M. (eds.) TACAS 2007. LNCS, vol. 4424, pp. 632–647. Springer, Heidelberg (2007). https://doi.org/10.1007/978-3-540-71209-1_49

6. Frappier, M., Fraikin, B., Chossart, R., Chane-Yack-Fa, R., Ouenzar, M.: Comparison of model checking tools for information systems. In: Dong, J.S., Zhu, H. (eds.) ICFEM 2010. LNCS, vol. 6447, pp. 581–596. Springer, Heidelberg (2010). https://doi.org/10.1007/978-3-642-16901-4_38

7. Geri, G., Indrakshi, R., Kyriakos, A., Behzad, B., Manachai, T., Siv, H.H.: An aspect-oriented methodology for designing secure applications. Inf. Softw. Technol. **51**(5), 846–864 (2009)

8. Glondu, S.: Towards certification of the extraction of Coq. Theses, Université Paris Diderot, June 2012

9. Jackson, D.: Automating first-order relational logic. In: ACM SIGSOFT International Symposium on Foundations of Software Engineering (FSE), pp. 130–139. ACM, New York (2000)

10. Jackson, D.: Software Abstractions, revised edn. MIT Press, Cambridge (2012)

11. Jackson, D., Vaziri, M.: Finding bugs with a constraint solver. In: Proceedings of the 2000 ACM SIGSOFT International Symposium on Software Testing and Analysis, ISSTA 2000, pp. 14–25. ACM, New York (2000)

12. Kang, E., Jackson, D.: Formal modeling and analysis of a flash filesystem in Alloy. In: Börger, E., Butler, M., Bowen, J.P., Boca, P. (eds.) ABZ 2008. LNCS, vol. 5238, pp. 294–308. Springer, Heidelberg (2008). https://doi.org/10.1007/978-3-540-87603-8_23

13. Kang, E., Jackson, D.O.: Designing and analyzing a flash file system with Alloy. Int. J. Softw. Inform. **3**, 129–148 (2009)

14. Klein, G., et al.: seL4: formal verification of an operating-system kernel. Commun. ACM **53**(6), 107–115 (2010)

15. Leroy, X.: Formal verification of a realistic compiler. Commun. ACM **52**(7), 107–115 (2009)
16. Marinov, D., Khurshid, S.: TesTera: a novel framework for automated testing of java programs. In: Proceedings 16th Annual International Conference on Automated Software Engineering (ASE 2001), pp. 22–31, November 2001
17. Moscato, M.M., Pombo, C.L., Frias, M.F.: Dynamite: a tool for the verification of Alloy models based on PVS. ACM Trans. Softw. Eng. Methodol. **23**, 20:1–20:37 (2014)
18. Nipkow, T., Paulson, L.C., Wenzel, M.: Isabelle/HOL — A Proof Assistant for Higher-Order Logic. LNCS, vol. 2283. Springer, Heidelberg (2002). https://doi.org/10.1007/3-540-45949-9
19. Paulin-Mohring, C.: Introduction to the calculus of inductive constructions. In: Woltzenlogel Paleo, B., Delahaye, D. (eds.) All about Proofs, Proofs for All. Studies in Logic (Mathematical logic and foundations), vol. 55. College Publications (2015)
20. Power, D., Slaymaker, M., Simpson, A.: Automatic conformance checking of role-based access control policies via Alloy. In: Erlingsson, Ú., Wieringa, R., Zannone, N. (eds.) ESSoS 2011. LNCS, vol. 6542, pp. 15–28. Springer, Heidelberg (2011). https://doi.org/10.1007/978-3-642-19125-1_2
21. Ramananandro, T.: Mondex, an electronic purse: specification and refinement checks with the Alloy model-finding method. Form. Asp. Comput. **20**(1), 21–39 (2008)
22. Seater, R., Jackson, D., Gheyi, R.: Requirement progression in problem frames: deriving specifications from requirements. Requir. Eng. **12**(2), 77–102 (2007)
23. Shao, D., Khurshid, S., Perry, D.E.: Whispec: white-box testing of libraries using declarative specifications. In: Proceedings of the 2007 Symposium on Library-Centric Software Design, LCSD 2007, pp. 11–20. ACM, New York (2007)
24. Song, D., et al.: Sok: Sanitizing for security. CoRR abs/1806.04355 (2018). http://arxiv.org/abs/1806.04355
25. Souaf, S., Berthomé, P., Loulergue, F.: A cloud brokerage solution: formal methods meet security in cloud federations. In: International Conference on High Performance Computing Simulation (HPCS). IEEE (2018)
26. The Coq Development Team: The Coq Proof Assistant. http://coq.inria.fr
27. Torlak, E.: A constraint solver for software engineering : finding models and cores of large relational specifications. Ph.D. thesis, Massachusetts Institute of Technology (2009)
28. Torlak, E., Taghdiri, M., Dennis, G., Near, J.: Applications and extensions of Alloy: past, present, and future. Math. Struct. Comput. Sci. **23**, 915–933 (2013)
29. Ulbrich, M., Geilmann, U., El Ghazi, A.A., Taghdiri, M.: A proof assistant for Alloy specifications. In: Flanagan, C., König, B. (eds.) TACAS 2012. LNCS, vol. 7214, pp. 422–436. Springer, Heidelberg (2012). https://doi.org/10.1007/978-3-642-28756-5_29

Assessment of a Formal Requirements Modeling Approach on a Transportation System

Steve Jeffrey Tueno Fotso[1,2(✉)], Régine Laleau[1], Marc Frappier[2],
Amel Mammar[3], Francois Thibodeau[4], and Mama Nsangou Mouchili[4]

[1] LACL, Université Paris-Est Créteil, Créteil, France
{steve.tueno-fotso,laleau}@u-pec.fr
[2] GRIL, Université de Sherbrooke, Québec, Canada
Marc.Frappier@USherbrooke.ca
[3] SAMOVAR, CNRS, Télécom-SudParis,
Institut Polytechnique de Paris, Évry, France
amel.mammar@telecom-sudparis.eu
[4] Ville de Montréal, Québec, Canada
francoisthibodeau@ville.montreal.qc.ca, Mama.NsangouMouchili@stantec.com

Abstract. This paper describes a case study of the SysML/KAOS method for a road transportation system for the City of Montreal (VdM), the second-largest city in Canada. The transportation system was developed from unstructured requirements represented in textual and schematic documents. Therefore, the VdM wanted to investigate new ways of organising and analysing the requirements of traffic projects, in order to increase the level of confidence in their safety, usability and reusability. This paper describes the formal specification, verification and validation of system requirements and provides an appraisal of the SysML/KAOS requirements engineering method on an industrial-scale case study. SysML/KAOS is designed within the *ANR FORMOSE* project to bridge the gap between stakeholder needs and the formal specification of system functionalities and domain constraints. The method has proven useful to deal with the seven refinement levels, twelve components (human, hardware, software and cyber-physical) and a hundred functional and non-functional goals that constitute the specification of the road transportation system, mainly focused on the safe movement of vehicles on road. It especially facilitated their validation with VdM stakeholders who had never dealt with formal methods and requirements engineering. Animation tools (*ProB* and *B-Motion Studio*) were also used to validate the formal specification with VdM stakeholders. This paper also reports improvements identified to enhance the expressiveness of SysML/KAOS goal modeling languages during validation sessions with VdM stakeholders. This includes the introduction of a non-functional goal refinement strategy based on logical formulas and of an obstacle modeling language.

French National Research Agency (ANR).
Natural Sciences and Engineering Research Council of Canada (NSERC).

Y. Ait-Ameur and S. Qin (Eds.): ICFEM 2019, LNCS 11852, pp. 470–486, 2019.
https://doi.org/10.1007/978-3-030-32409-4_29

Keywords: Road transportation system · Requirements engineering · Formal models · Domain modeling · *SysML/KAOS* · *B System* · *Event-B*

1   Introduction

SysML/KAOS is a requirements engineering method which aims to emphasize the impact of formal specification and verification activities on the quality of requirements, while taking into account the domain constraints and improving validation with stakeholders. The main interest is on critical and complex areas such as railway, aeronautics or road transportation. The method involves a functional [16] and a non-functional [12,13] goal modeling languages to represent system requirements extracted from artifacts that describe stakeholder needs. The functional goal model represents system functionalities while the non-functional one represents constraints on their satisfaction. In addition, a domain modeling language [11,28] is used to represent application domain entities and their properties. The system complexity is mastered in SysML/KAOS thanks to refinements and decompositions. In [22], Matoussi *et al.* have defined translation rules to automatically produce a *B System* specification [7] from *SysML/KAOS* functional goal models. They provide the *behavioral part* (events) of the specification. Regarding domain models, rules have been defined and formally verified [11,29] to automatically generate the *structural part* (sets, constant and their properties, variables and their invariant) of the specification and the initialisation of state variables. Once the event bodies manually specified, the *B System* specification can be formally verified and validated to assess the requirements. This can be done using the full range of tools that support the *B* method [3], positively assessed on a number of industrial projects for more than 25 years [18].

In 2014, *La Ville de Montréal* (VdM) proceeded to replace the *Bonaventure highway (A-10)* with an urban boulevard [1]. As part of this reconfiguration, the *Québec Ministry of Transport (MTQ)* emphasized some requirements such as ensuring that the interventions carried out do not reduce the safety of road users. To allow the identified requirements to be taken into account, a number of additional options have been developed including (1) the addition of signaling equipments and (2) the setting up of an intelligent transportation system. The transportation system was developed based on textual and schematic documents [1]. Not only does this documentation not allow a clear identification of requirements, but it rarely shows the justification and validity of the choices made. Therefore, the VdM wanted to investigate a way of organising and analysing the requirements of traffic projects, in order to increase the level of confidence in their safety, usability, reusability and efficiency. This paper describes the formal specification, verification and validation of requirements of the transportation system and of the supervisor in charge of ensuring optimal operation of the involved components. SysML/KAOS was chosen because it includes an expressive and intuitive goal modeling language to represent system requirements, and a domain modeling language to represent application domain entities and their properties using ontologies. Furthermore, the rules required to automatically generate a *B System* specification from goal and domain models are defined and the most relevant ones have been formally verified [11]. For space limitations, we will not describe the modeling of non-functional goals. Interested readers are invited to refer to [1] for a complete overview of modeling deliverables.

The remainder of this paper is structured as follows: Sect. 2 briefly describes the *B System* formal method, the SysML/KAOS requirements engineering method and its goal and domain modeling languages, and the *B System* formalisation of SysML/KAOS models. Follows a presentation, in Sect. 3, of the work done on the case study. Section 4 discusses validation and verification of the formal specification and describes the relevant lessons learned from this case study. Finally, Sect. 5 reports our conclusion and future work.

2   Context

2.1   B System

Event-B [2] is an industrial-strength formal method for *system modeling*. It allows the incremental construction of system specifications, using stepwise refinement, and the proof of useful properties. *B System* is an *Event-B* syntactic variant proposed by *ClearSy*, an industrial partner in the *FORMOSE* project [4], and supported by *Atelier B* [7]. It shares the same semantics with *Event-B*.

A *B System* specification consists of components. Each component can be either a system or a refinement and it may define static or dynamic elements. A refinement is a component which refines another one in order to concretise the system construction: addition of functionalities or specification of the achievement of some purposes. Constants, abstract and enumerated sets (user-defined types), and their properties, constitute the static part. The dynamic part includes the representation of system state using variables constrained through an invariant Inv (first-order predicates that constrain the possible values that the variables may hold) and updated through events. Each event has a **guard** G and an **action** Act. An event is said to be enabled when its guard G holds. A system transition consists in the triggering of a single event, among all enabled ones. Action Act of an event describes the updates made to state variables.

The triggering of an event should maintain the invariant Inv. To this aim, a proof obligation is generated for each event: $\forall T, C, X.\ (A \land G \land Inv \Rightarrow [Act]Inv)$. Other proof obligations include *event feasibility* (existence, for each event, of a state where it can be triggered) and *system refinement* (the specification of a refinement conforms to that of the refined component) [2].

2.2   SysML/KAOS

SysML/KAOS is a requirements engineering method which defines a functional and non-functional goal modeling and a domain modeling languages. An overview of its specification process is provided in [9]. The first step is to use SysML/KAOS languages to build models of the system and of its application domain. The second step is to automatically translate the goal model into a *B System* specification, following the rules provided in [22], and to complete the specification with the result of the translation of domain models, following the formally verified rules provided in [11,27]. Goal models provide the **behavioral part** (events) of the specification while domain models provide its **structural part** (sets, constant and their properties, variables and their invariant) and the initialisation of state variables. It remains to manually specify the body of events and to formally verify and validate the specification with *B System* tools. When updates are performed within the *B System* specification, back propagation rules such as those described in [9] are used to update SysML/KAOS models accordingly.

SysML/KAOS is supported by integrated development environments *Openflexo* [23] and *Atelier B* [7]. Openflexo supports goal and domain modeling and the automatic generation of the corresponding *B System* specification, while Atelier B supports the specification, verification and validation of *B System* models. These last activities can also be carried out under Rodin [5] since Event-B and *B System* share the same semantics.

SysML/KAOS Functional Goal Modeling. The SysML/KAOS functional goal modeling language [16] combines the traceability provided by *SysML* [14] with goal expressiveness provided by KAOS [17]. It allows the representation of functional requirements to be satisfied by a system and of functional expectations with regards to the environment through a hierarchy of goals. A functional goal in SysML/KAOS describes the expected behaviour of the system once a certain condition holds. The functional goal hierarchy is built through a succession of refinements using two main operators: **AND** and **OR**. An **AND refinement** decomposes a goal into subgoals, and all of them must be achieved to realise the parent goal. An **OR refinement** decomposes a goal into subgoals such that the achievement of only one of them is sufficient for the achievement of the parent goal. The refinement process ends when it is possible to assign the leaf goals to a subsystem or to an agent (environment agent or software agent). Subsequently, if needed, further goal diagrams can be defined for the different subsystems.

SysML/KAOS Domain Modeling. Domain models in SysML/KAOS are represented using ontologies. These ontologies are expressed using the SysML/KAOS domain modeling language [27,28], based on *OWL* [26] and *PLIB* [25], two well-known and complementary ontology modeling formalisms. Each domain model corresponds to a refinement level in the functional goal model. Domain models can be linked together to form a hierarchy. A domain model can define multiple elements. *Concepts* designate collections of *individuals* with common properties. A concept can be declared *variable* when the set of its individuals can be updated by adding or deleting individuals. Otherwise, it is considered to be *constant*. In addition, a concept can be an enumeration if all its individuals are defined within the domain model. An individual can be *variable* if it is introduced to represent a system state variable: it can represent different individuals at different system states. Otherwise, it is *constant*. *Associations* are concepts used to capture links between concepts. *Logical formulas* are used to represent constraints between different elements of the domain model in the form of *Horn clauses*.

2.3   B System Formalisation of SysML/KAOS Models

The formalisation of SysML/KAOS functional goal models is detailed in [22]. The proposed rules allow the generation of a formal model whose structure reflects the hierarchy of the functional goal model: one component is associated with each level of the goal hierarchy; this component defines one event for each goal. As the semantics of the refinement between goals is different from that of the refinement between *B System* components, new proof obligations for goal refinement are defined in [22]. They depend on the goal refinement operator used and complete the *B System* proof obligations for invariant preservation and for event feasibility.

Nevertheless, the generated *B System* specification does not contain the system structure, that are variables with their associated invariant and constants with their associated properties. This structure is provided by the translation of SysML/KAOS domain models. The corresponding translation rules are fully described in [27] and their formal verification is described in [11]. In short, domain models identify *B System* components. Concepts give *B System* types while individuals give set items. Logical formulas give *B System* properties and invariants. The rules also allow the extraction of the initialisation of state variables.

3   Specification of the Road Transportation System

3.1   Main Characteristics of the System

The VdM needs to proceed with the replacement of the Bonaventure highway (A-10) with an urban boulevard while ensuring that the interventions carried out do not reduce the safety of road users (MTQ) and that the municipal road traffic is at least maintained (VdM) (see reference documents [1]). Regarding the *Nazareth* street and especially the exit of the *Ville-Marie* highway to Nazareth street, it was difficult to respond to both the issues identified by the VdM and the safety issue formulated by the MTQ, especially because of the curvature of the highway exit. Indeed, the accumulation of vehicles at the highway exit is likely to cause accidents because the curvature limits the line of sight of drivers that engage on the exit when they are at the upstream of the curvature. It is thus necessary (i) to determine the level of traffic at every moment, (ii) to regulate the traffic level in order to limit the exit congestion in reasonable proportions, and (iii) to notify drivers, especially those located at the upstream of the curvature, as to the level of the traffic and the expected behavior. The VdM has therefore decided the addition of: (1) two travel lanes for the Ville-Marie highway exit to Nazareth street to the three lanes of Nazareth street and (2) sensors such as thermal imaging cameras and traffic control radars to ensure the determination of the level of traffic. Traffic regulation consists in defining the most appropriate traffic signal program, taking into account the level of traffic. It is performed by an automaton connected to VdM sensors. An urban mobility management center (CGMU) has been set up by the VdM to ensure that the level of traffic is properly regulated (traffic level supervision) and notify drivers (level of traffic and expected behavior). To ensure the satisfaction of its safety requirement, the MTQ has also set up a mobility management center (CIGC) and an intelligent transportation system that includes an automated incident detection system (AID). The AID is connected to the CGMU and provides a more accurate measurement of the level of traffic that helps to validate the inputs from VdM sensors. It uses thermal cameras and a software to analyse the traffic in real-time and detect road incidents. As the CGMU, the CIGC is responsible for sending some notifications to drivers through variable message signs (PMVs) or through GPS navigation softwares such as *Waze* or *Google Maps*.

The SysML/KAOS method is used to provide a framework for the formal specification, verification and validation of requirements of the integrated components and of the supervisor responsible for ensuring the optimal operation of these components. It should be noted that for space limitations, we will not describe the modeling of non-functional goals. Interested readers are invited to refer to [1] for a complete overview of modeling deliverables.

3.2   Functional Goal and Obstacle Modeling

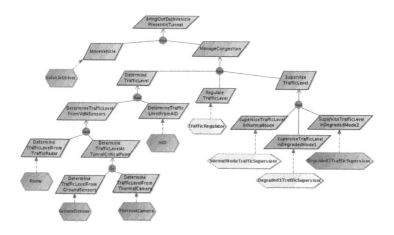

Fig. 1. High-level system functional goal diagram

Functional Goal Modeling. Figure 1 provides an overview of the goal diagram that represents the functionalities of the high-level system. The main identified purpose is *to allow each vehicle on the Ville-Marie highway exit that connects to Nazareth street to exit.* The purpose gives the most abstract goal *BringOutEachVehiclePresentInTunnel* of the goal diagram which is refined using the **AND** operator into two subgoals: drive vehicle according to road signing (goal *MoveVehicle*) and manage congestion (goal *ManageCongestion*). The leaf goal *MoveVehicle* is assigned to *environment agent VehicleDriver* (the vehicle driver) to state the assumption that the driver has the responsibility to drive its vehicle according to road signs. The assumptions are expressed in domain models as domain constraints. For instance, the previous assumption entails that *"each vehicle speed does not exceed the speed limit"*. For congestion management, it is necessary to be able to: (1) determine the traffic level from sensors (goal *DetermineTrafficLevel*), (2) regulate the traffic (goal *RegulateTrafficLevel*), and (3) supervise traffic regulation and, if necessary, adjust the traffic signal program defined by the traffic signal controller (goal *SuperviseTrafficLevel*). The goal *RegulateTrafficLevel* is assigned to the *TrafficRegulator subsystem* for which the functionalities are represented by the goal diagram of Fig. 2(a) [1]: determine the level of traffic from measurements of VdM sensors (goal *CommunicateTrafficLeveltoTrafficSignalController*) and define the most appropriate traffic signal program (goal *ApplyAppropriateTrafficSignalProgram*).

Since the level of traffic is determined using VdM sensors and the MTQ's AID, goal *DetermineTrafficLevel* is AND-refined into subgoals *DetermineTrafficLevelFromVdMSensors*, for VdM sensors, and *DetermineTrafficLevelFromAID*, for the MTQ's AID. The VdM sensors include a traffic control radar and a redundant sensor. Indeed, the highway exit is splitted into four zones, until the point where the last vehicle should be in case of maximum congestion lengthening (*Xmax*). The radar covers the four zones. However, a redundant sensor (ground sensor or thermal camera) is needed for the fourth zone (the one that ends at *Xmax*) to ensure that the maximum congestion lengthening will be detected even in case of a radar failure.

Knowing that the communication links from CGMU to VdM sensors and from CIGC to CGMU are subject to failure, an obstacle analysis was carried out based on the obstacle modeling language of KAOS [30].

Obstacle Modeling. An obstacle is an obstruction to the satisfaction of a functional goal. Obstacle modeling allows analysis of expected system behaviors when obstacles prevent the satisfaction of one or more functional goals [30].

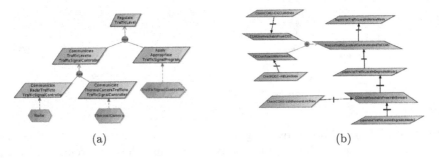

(a)   (b)

Fig. 2. (a) Functional goal diagram of the *TrafficRegulator* subsystem; (b) Obstacle model related to the unreliability of links to CGMU

Obstacles can be refined to specify their causes: an obstacle can be caused by a conjunction or disjunction of more specific ones. New functional goals or countermeasures can therefore be defined to prevent, detect or mitigate obstacles, thus ensuring adequate behavior of the system. Figure 2(b) illustrates the obstacle modeling, related to the unreliability of CGMU to VdM sensors and CIGC to CGMU links, that entailed the definition of the three supervision modes of Fig. 1 (goals *SuperviseTrafficLevelinNormalMode*, *SuperviseTrafficLevelinDegradedMode1* and *SuperviseTrafficLevelinDegradedMode2*). Each black arrow goes from an introduced element (functional goal or obstacle) to the element that entails it. When all is well, the supervision is performed in *normal mode* (goal *SuperviseTrafficLevelinNormalMode* refined in another goal diagram [1]: each management center (CGMU and CIGC) receives traffic data from its sensors and notifies the other as to its traffic knowledge. Since AID measurements are more accurate, in normal mode, they will be systematically used by CIGC and CGMU to undertake supervision actions: ensure the appropriateness of the traffic signal program and ensure the appropriateness of user notifications.

The normal mode traffic supervision may be obstructed by the impossibility for AID to send a precise traffic measurement to CGMU (obstacle *PreciseTrafficLevelNotCommunicatedToCGMU* of Fig. 2(b)). This can be due to the unavailability of the communication channel between the CGMU and the CIGC (obstacle *CGMUnotReachableFromCIGC*) or by that of the one between AID and CIGC (obstacle *CIGCnotReachableFromAID*). A countermeasure to detect the occurrence of obstacle *CGMUnotReachableFromCIGC* is to regularly check the state of the communication channel between the CGMU and the CIGC (goal *CheckCGMU-CIGCLinkState*). Similarly, goal *CheckCIGC-AIDLinkState* is proposed as countermeasure to obstacle *CIGCnotReachableFromAID*. The functional goal *SuperviseTrafficLevelinDegradedMode1* (Figs. 1 and 2(b)) allows the supervision to be performed properly despite an occurrence of obstacle *PreciseTrafficLevelNotCommunicatedToCGMU*, by defining an alternative that allows the CGMU to perform the supervision without the need of the CIGC: only VdM sensors are considered to determine the level of traffic. However, an obstacle to the satisfaction of goal *SuperviseTrafficLevelinDegradedMode1* is *CGMUnotReachableFromVdMSensors*, related to the impossibility for CGMU to obtain measurements from VdM sensors. A detection countermeasure therefore consists in regularly probing the state of the communication channel between CGMU and VdM sensors (goal *CheckCGMU-VdMSensorsLinkState*). An additional goal *SuperviseTrafficLevelinDegradedMode2* (Figs. 1 and 2(b)) is defined as a mitigation countermeasure and consists in sending a human agent for local traffic supervision.

A non-functional goal model was built specifically for security and safety requirements. It is not presented in this paper for space limitations.

3.3 Domain Modeling

Six domain models were constructed for the six refinement levels of the functional goal model [1]. For space limitations, we will focus only on the first one.

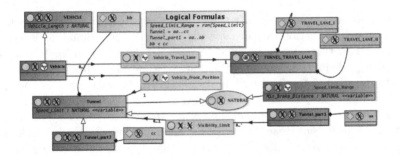

Fig. 3. Ontology associated with the root level of Fig. 1

Root Level. Figure 3 represents the domain model associated with the root goal *BringOutEachVehiclePresentInTunnel* of the diagram of Fig. 1. The domain model introduces the entities required to represent the exit of the Ville-Marie highway to Nazareth street and to localise vehicles. Its aim is to enable the specification of vehicle exits. Therefore, a concept VEHICLE is defined to represent all vehicles likely to engage on the highway exit. Association Vehicle_Length captures the length of each vehicle as a natural number. A variable concept named Vehicle is defined as a subconcept of VEHICLE to represent the vehicles currently engaged on the highway exit. Its cardinality is used to quantify the level of traffic. Each vehicle engaged on the highway exit is localised by the position of its front (variable association Vehicle_Front_Position) and by its travel lane (variable association Vehicle_Travel_Lane). Indeed, the highway exit has two travel lanes (see [1]): a main one represented by individual TRAVEL_LANE_I and a secondary one, represented by TRAVEL_LANE_II, which appears when the vehicle gets closer to the Nazareth street.

Logical formulas are defined to represent properties that need to be guaranteed in all system states. For instance, the logical formula below ensures that the locations occupied by two distinct vehicles are always distinct (absence of collisions [20]):

$\forall xx1, xx2 \cdot ((xx1 \in Vehicle \wedge xx2 \in Vehicle \wedge xx1 \neq xx2$
$\wedge Vehicle\_Travel\_Lane(xx1) = Vehicle\_Travel\_Lane(xx2))$
$\Rightarrow ((Vehicle\_Front\_Position(xx1) - Vehicle\_Length(xx1)) .. Vehicle\_Front\_Position(xx1)$
$\cap (Vehicle\_Front\_Position(xx2) - Vehicle\_Length(xx2)) .. Vehicle\_Front\_Position(xx2) = \emptyset))$

The highway exit is represented by a concept Tunnel defined as a range of integers (Tunnel = aa .. cc). Association Speed_Limit captures the speed limit (in *KM/H*) defined at each position of the highway exit. It is variable because the speed limit is likely to be updated depending on traffic level. Concept Tunnel_part1 is the subpart of the highway exit that contains the curvature which limits the visibility of upstream vehicles. Therefore, an association named Visibility_Limit is used to associate a visibility limit to parts of Tunnel_part1: each user whose vehicle A has its front located at $xx \in$ Tunnel is supposed to be able to see vehicle B in front of him (and consequently to act in a way to avoid a collision) unless $xx \in dom(\texttt{Visibility\_Limit})$ and the rear of vehicle B is located beyond $\texttt{Visibility\_Limit}(xx)$. Finally, association $Min\_Brake\_Distance$ sets a minimum braking distance for each speed defined as speed limit. Therefore, it is necessary to ensure that for each speed limit defined for a location xx, if a visibility limit is applicable at xx ($xx \in dom(\texttt{Visibility\_Limit})$), the speed limit is defined such that the minimum braking distance is less than the distance between xx and $\texttt{Visibility\_Limit}(xx)$:

$$\forall xx \cdot (xx \in dom(Visibility\_Limit) \Rightarrow Visibility\_Limit(xx) > xx)$$

Following Refinement Levels. The domain model associated with the first refinement level of the goal diagram of Fig. 1 refines the one associated with the root level (Fig. 3) and introduces the entities required to represent the traffic level which depends on vehicle speeds and locations. For instance, a natural number (individual $\texttt{MAXIMAL\_TUNNEL\_OCCUPATION}$) is defined to represent the maximum number of vehicles allowed at the highway exit and a variable association $\texttt{Vehicle\_Speed}$ is defined to represent speeds of vehicles. We assume that the vehicles are driven according to road signing. The assumption is represented by a logical formula stating that the speed of any vehicle must always be lower than the speed limit associated with its location:

$$\forall xx \cdot (xx \in Vehicle \Rightarrow Vehicle\_Speed(xx) \leq Speed\_Limit(Vehicle\_Front\_Position(xx)))$$

Four traffic levels are considered: *normal, dense, slowed* and *congestion* [1]. A variable individual $\texttt{traffic\_level}$ is defined to represent the current known traffic level. Each traffic level is defined by an individual and a logical formula that specifies its requirements. For instance, the traffic level is normal when the highway exit is occupied at 40% or less and vehicle speeds are higher than 40 KM/H [1]:

$$(traffic\_level = NORMAL \Rightarrow (((card(Vehicle) * 100)/MAXIMAL\_TUNNEL\_$$
$$OCCUPATION) < 40 \wedge (\forall xx \cdot (xx \in Vehicle \Rightarrow Vehicle\_Speed(xx) \geq 40))))$$

The domain model associated with the second refinement level of the goal model introduces the entities required to distinguish between environment variables, which represent the actual state of the real environment and controller variables, which represent the measured value of the environment, as seen by the controller (measured vehicle front positions, measured vehicle speeds, etc.). This distinction is necessary to handle measurement errors and control delays [24]. The next domain model introduces the traffic level sensors and supervision modes (normal and degraded). It also introduces traffic lights and signaling programs to allow the specification of traffic regulation. Finally, the fifth and sixth domain models introduces the communication channels, from sensors to management centers (CGMU and CIGC) and between management centers, to allow the specification of traffic supervisions.

3.4   The B System Specification

The full specification, verified using the *Rodin* platform [5], can be found in [1]. Each refinement level is the result of the automatic translation of goal and domain models, except the body of events that are provided manually. For instance, the root level of the goal diagram of Fig. 1 gives the *B System* event *BringOutEachVehiclePresentInTunnel* specified in the root machine as:

BringOutEachVehiclePresentInTunnel $\cong$
SELECT Vehicle_Out, Vehicle_In, newVehicleFronts, newTravelLanes
WHERE
    grd0: $Vehicle \neq \emptyset$
    grd1: $partition(Vehicle, Vehicle\_Out, Vehicle\_In)$
    grd2: $newVehicleFronts \in Vehicle\_In \to Tunnel$
    grd3: $newTravelLanes \in Vehicle\_In \to TUNNEL\_TRAVEL\_LANE$
    grd4: $\forall xx \cdot ((xx \in Vehicle\_In \wedge newVehicleFronts(xx) \in Tunnel\_part1)$
        $\Rightarrow newTravelLanes(xx) = TRAVEL\_LANE\_I)$
    grd5: $\forall xx1, xx2 \cdot ((xx1 \in Vehicle\_In \wedge xx2 \in Vehicle\_In \wedge xx1 \neq xx2)$
        $\Rightarrow ((newVehicleFronts(xx1) - Vehicle\_Length(xx1)) \,..\, newVehicleFronts(xx1)$
        $\cap (newVehicleFronts(xx2) - Vehicle\_Length(xx2)) \,..\, newVehicleFronts(xx2) = \emptyset$
        $\vee newTravelLanes(xx1) \neq newTravelLanes(xx2)))$
THEN
    act0: $Vehicle := Vehicle \setminus Vehicle\_Out$
    act1: $Vehicle\_Front\_Position := newVehicleFronts$
    act2: $Vehicle\_Travel\_Lane := newTravelLanes$

This event states that when vehicles are present on the highway exit (**grd0**), we observe some exiting (**act0**) and others moving, by nondeterministically changing their traffic lanes (**grd3** and **act2**) and front positions (**grd2** and **act1**), while ensuring the preservation of safety invariants (**grd4** and **grd5**). Guard **grd1** ensures that each vehicle ($x \in Vehicle$) either exits ($x \in Vehicle\_Out$) or moves ($x \in Vehicle\_In$).

In the first refinement level of the *B System* specification, event *BringOutEachVehiclePresentInTunnel* is refined by events *ManageCongestion* and *MoveVehicle*, the last being specified as[1]:

---

[1] Event specification restricted to show only the most relevant part with respect to the one of event *BringOutEachVehiclePresentInTunnel*. The full version can be found in [1].

MoveVehicle $\cong$

SELECT newTravelLanes, updatedVehicleFronts, newVehicleSpeeds, Vehicle_Out, Vehicle_In, trafficLevel, newVehicleFronts

WHERE

    grd0: $delay \in \mathbb{N}_1$

    grd1: $Vehicle \neq \emptyset$

    grd2: $updatedVehicleFronts = (\lambda xx \cdot xx \in Vehicle | Vehicle\_Front\_Position(xx)$
        $+ Vehicle\_Speed(xx) * delay)$

    grd3: $Vehicle\_In = updatedVehicleFronts^{-1}[Tunnel]$

    grd4: $Vehicle\_Out = Vehicle \setminus Vehicle\_In$

    grd5: $newVehicleSpeeds \in Vehicle\_In \rightarrow \mathbb{N}$

    grd6: $\forall xx \cdot (xx \in Vehicle\_In$
        $\Rightarrow newVehicleSpeeds(xx) \in 0 \mathbin{..} Speed\_Limit(updatedVehicleFronts(xx)))$

    grd7: $newTravelLanes \in Vehicle\_In \rightarrow TUNNEL\_TRAVEL\_LANE$

    grd8: $newVehicleFronts = Vehicle\_Out \mathbin{\lhd\mkern-14mu-} updatedVehicleFronts$

    grd9: $trafficLevel \in TRAFFIC\_LEVEL$

    grd10: $(trafficLevel = NORMAL \Rightarrow (((card(Vehicle\_In) * 100)$
        $/MAXIMAL\_TUNNEL\_OCCUPATION) < 40$
        $\wedge (\forall xx \cdot (xx \in Vehicle\_In \Rightarrow newVehicleSpeeds(xx) \geq 40))))$

••• THEN •••

    act3: $traffic\_level := trafficLevel$

    act4: $Vehicle\_Speed := newVehicleSpeeds$

It states that after a certain delay *delay* (**grd0**), all vehicles present on the highway exit move a distance corresponding to the product of their speed by *delay* (**grd2**). Exiting vehicles (*Vehicle_Out*) are those that are driven out of the highway by their displacement (**grd4**). The others (*Vehicle_In*: vehicles that remain in the highway after their displacement (**grd3**)) nondeterministically change their speed (**grd5**, **grd6** and **act4**) and lane (**grd7**) while ensuring the preservation of safety invariants. Finally, the traffic level is updated (**act3**) to reflect the new system state (**grd9**, **grd10**, ...).

4 Discussion

4.1 Validation and Verification

The SysML/KAOS method not only makes it possible to verify the consistency of requirements and their refinement logic, but also to better present and validate the requirements with the various stakeholders. Indeed, SysML/KAOS includes semi-formal languages for a high-level representation of system goals and application domain properties. This ensures a better reusability and readability of models. Improved readability is confirmed by VdM stakeholders who were involved to assess each modeling deliverable during scheduled validation sessions: four validation sessions were organised and allowed to introduce SysML/KAOS to VdM stakeholders and to obtain their feedbacks related to the constructed SysML/KAOS models. The improved readability was also confirmed after an evaluation was conducted among members of the FORMOSE project, within the framework of another case study [10]. Of the fifteen or so surveyed members representing various academic[2] and industrial[3] partners, all found the readability of SysML/KAOS models much better than that of a *B System* specification.

The method also includes rules for obtaining a *B System* specification and the proof obligations required to guarantee consistency of goal refinements and accuracy of requirements with respect to environment constraints. For instance, proof obligations related to SysML/KAOS refinements allowed us to identify a missing goal in goal diagrams. Indeed, the first version of the goal diagram of Fig. 1 was not defining a goal to ensure that vehicles are driven according to road signs. Therefore, it was impossible to ensure that a vehicle in the tunnel would be driven out. Thus, trying to formally ensure root goal satisfaction allowed us to introduce the *MoveVehicle* goal assigned to agent *VehicleDriver*.

SysML/KAOS bridges the gap between the system textual description and its *B System* specification. Table 1 summarises the key characteristics related to the formal specification of the first four refinement levels. The proof obligations, generated to ensure correctness of the *B System* specification, have been discharged using the Rodin tool extended with *SMT solvers* and *Atelier B provers* [8]. The interactive proof was more required for level **L3** because of the introduction of a distinction between the real and measured (by traffic sensors) views of traffic level. Indeed, this introduction required several adaptations and additions, of invariants and events, related for example to order in measurement acquisitions (enforced using controlled variables), sensor coverages and measurement defects (handled with degraded modes).

Table 1. Key characteristics related to the formal specification

Refinement level	L0	L1	L2	L3
Invariants	8	8	14	26
Proof Obligations (PO)	21	52	36	85
Automatically discharged POs	19	51	36	66
Interactively discharged POs	2	1	0	19

Mashkoor *et al.* [20,21] advocate the use of animation, supported by tools, to assist validation of a formal specification with non-expert stakeholders. *ProB* [19] and *B-Motion Studio* [15] are industrial-strength tools used to animate and validate a *B System* specification. They provide a way to define a high-level graphical representation of the states of the system. We used them to validate the formal specification with VdM stakeholders, in addition to graphical models constructed using the SysML/KAOS goal and domain modeling languages.

The validation by animation was performed following the *VTA (Verify-Transform-Animate)* framework [21]. The SysML/KAOS functional goal model

---

[2] *University Paris Est Créteil; University of Sherbrooke; IMT Brest, France; etc.*

[3] *THALES, France; ClearSy Systems Engineering, France; Openflexo, France.*

provides the way to group requirements into observation levels (each observation level corresponds to a refinement level) as required by the VTA. The specification obtained from SysML/KAOS models, once completed with event bodies, has been verified with Rodin provers, transformed and animated. The formal model transformation has for instance consisted in (1) transforming abstract sets into concrete ones such as $VEHICLE$ in $\{V1, V2, V3, V4, V5\}$ and $Tunnel$ in $0..30$, and (2) introducing events to specify changes in environment structure such as $ctrl\_ChangeSpeed$ used to change a vehicle speed during animation. In addition, units were converted (KM to M for distances, hours (H) to seconds (S) for times, KM/H to M/S for speeds) to precisely observe the system behavior. The transformed model can be found in [1].

For example, the Figure below is an overview of a validation session with VdM stakeholders performed using ProB and B-Motion Studio. The top view presents an illustration of the traffic state on the highway exit while the bottom view presents a history of events triggered to reach this state. The maximum number of vehicles allowed is set to 4 and vehicles are not moving (speeds are set to 0). Therefore, the traffic level is congestion (highway exit occupied at 40% or more and vehicle speeds less than 15 KM/H [1]). The formal validation allowed us to detect inconsistencies in textual documents that describe the road transportation system. For instance, we have detected that the four defined traffic levels were not sufficient [1]: *normal*, *dense*, *slowed* and *congestion*. Indeed, the ProB model checker has determined traffic states that do not correspond to any of the defined traffic levels. This is for instance the case when occupancy is exactly 40% or when the speeds are between 15 and 24 KM/H. The observations, validated with VdM stakeholders, were reported to document authors from VdM and MTQ.

4.2   Lessons Learned, Improvements and Related Work

The development team is composed of six members (the authors of this paper). Four are academia stakeholders with good expertise in the formal specification of complex systems while the others are VdM stakeholders with expertise neither in requirements engineering nor in formal methods. Other members of the FORMOSE project have been involved in providing feedbacks related to the use of the SysML/KAOS method. It took three months (September-December, 2018: 16 h per week) to formally specify, verify and validate the requirements. Indeed, the specification of the body of formal events and logical formulas and the formal assessment (verification and validation) of the specification can only be manual and therefore required time, in addition to experts in formal methods. But this is the price to pay to achieve a formal verification and validation of requirements.

From the textual description of the road transportation system (see reference documents [1]) and of the AID, seven goal model refinement levels with a hundred functional and non-functional goals were defined. This allowed us to specify and ensure consistency of the high level requirements of twelve components: humans, hardwares (like radar or thermal camera), softwares (like the traffic supervisor) and cyber-physical systems (like CGMU or AID). Furthermore, six domain models were constructed to formally specify the entities and constraints of the application domain required to ensure satisfaction of functional requirements. At each deliverable release, a plenary meeting was held with VdM stakeholders to validate the work done, through semi-structured interviews, and assess the method contributions and progress. We noted the need of (cf. [1] for the full list):

- A non-functional goal refinement strategy based on logical formulas that allows to refine a non-functional goal NFG into (NFG, P_1), ..., (NFG, P_n) where P_1, ..., P_n are logical formulas: the satisfaction of NFG depends on the satisfaction of NFG when P_1 is true, ..., and of NFG when P_n is true. For example, the satisfaction of a non-functional goal *Cost [Actuator]* (ensure an efficient cost for actuators) depends on the satisfaction of *Cost [Actuator]* when the user has a smart device and when the user doesn't. Indeed, it is better to send notifications through GPS platforms only when users have smart devices. When a smart device is not available, the only viable option is to use variable message signs.
- An obstacle modeling language like that of [30] that distinguishes countermeasures used to detect the occurrence of an obstacle from those used to circumvent it.
- A tool support of the propagation of errors and inconsistencies detected when discharging proof obligations to the corresponding SysML/KAOS models.

This work is closely related with the one of Mashkoor *et al.* [20]. While in [20], the transportation system is directly specified in *Event-B*, the SysML/KAOS method uses goal models to represent system requirements and ontologies to represent domain entities and constraints. Ontologies give the structural part of the *B System* model while goal models provide the behavioral part. The use of SysML/KAOS modeling languages has several advantages, such as a better reusability, maintainability and readability of models. They also facilitate validations with stakeholders while providing and enforcing the refinement logic.

5 Conclusion and Future Work

This paper focusses on the use and assessment of the SysML/KAOS method for the high level modeling of requirements, domain and safety invariants related to a road transportation system for the City of Montreal (VdM) [1]. Translation rules, supported by tools, were used to obtain a formal specification containing the system structure and the skeleton of events. The Rodin platform [5] was used to verify the specification and *ProB* [19] and *B-Motion Studio* [15] to animate and validate it. Compared to other requirements engineering methods such as *KAOS* [30] or *i** [31], SysML/KAOS fills the gap between the goal and domain models on one hand and *B System* (and Event-B) models on the other hand, while being fully tooled.

VdM stakeholders were involved to assess the modeling deliverables and process and expressed the wish to see the method used in other VdM transportation projects. SysML/KAOS has proven its usefulness and the proposed improvements will be taken into account in next releases of supporting tools.

References

1. Road transportation system: SysML/KAOS requirements modeling (2018). https://github.com/stuenofotso/SysML_KAOS_Domain_Model_Parser/tree/master/Bonaventure_project
2. Abrial, J.: Modeling in Event-B - System and Software Engineering. Cambridge University Press, New York (2010)
3. Abrial, J.R., Abrial, J.R.: The B-Book: Assigning Programs to Meanings. Cambridge University Press, New York (2005)
4. ANR-14-CE28-0009: Formose ANR project (2017)
5. Butler, M.J., Jones, C.B., Romanovsky, A., Troubitsyna, E. (eds.): Rigorous Development of Complex Fault-Tolerant Systems. LNCS, vol. 4157. Springer, Heidelberg (2006). https://doi.org/10.1007/11916246
6. Butler, M., Raschke, A., Hoang, T.S., Reichl, K. (eds.): ABZ 2018. LNCS, vol. 10817. Springer, Cham (2018). https://doi.org/10.1007/978-3-319-91271-4
7. ClearSy: Atelier B: B System (2014). http://clearsy.com/
8. Deploy Project: Rodin Atelier B Provers Plug-in (2017). https://www3.hhu.de
9. Fotso, S.J.T., Frappier, M., Laleau, R., Mammar, A.: Back propagating B system updates on SysML/KAOS domain models. In: ICECCS, pp. 160–169. IEEE (2018)
10. Fotso, S.J.T., Frappier, M., Laleau, R., Mammar, A.: Modeling the hybrid ERTMS/ETCS level 3 standard using a formal requirements engineering approach. In: Butler et al. [6], pp. 262–276
11. Fotso, S.J.T., Mammar, A., Laleau, R., Frappier, M.: Event-B expression and verification of translation rules between SysML/KAOS domain models and B system specifications. In: Butler et al. [6], pp. 55–70
12. Gnaho, C., Laleau, R., Semmak, F., Bruel, J.M.: bCMS requirements modelling using SysML/KAOS
13. Gnaho, C., Semmak, F., Laleau, R.: An overview of a SysML extension for goal-oriented NFR modelling. In: RCIS 2013, Paris, France, 29–31 May 2013, pp. 1–2. IEEE (2013)
14. Hause, M., et al.: The SysML modelling language. In: Fifteenth European Systems Engineering Conference, vol. 9. Citeseer (2006)
15. Ladenberger, L., Bendisposto, J., Leuschel, M.: Visualising event-B models with B-motion studio. In: Alpuente, M., Cook, B., Joubert, C. (eds.) FMICS 2009. LNCS, vol. 5825, pp. 202–204. Springer, Heidelberg (2009). https://doi.org/10.1007/978-3-642-04570-7_17
16. Laleau, R., Semmak, F., Matoussi, A., Petit, D., Hammad, A., Tatibouet, B.: A first attempt to combine SysML requirements diagrams and B. Innov. Syst. Softw. Eng. **6**(1–2), 47–54 (2010)
17. van Lamsweerde, A.: Requirements Engineering - From System Goals to UML Models to Software Specifications. Wiley, Chichester (2009)

18. Lecomte, T., Deharbe, D., Prun, E., Mottin, E.: Applying a formal method in industry: a 25-year trajectory. In: Cavalheiro, S., Fiadeiro, J. (eds.) SBMF 2017. LNCS, vol. 10623, pp. 70–87. Springer, Cham (2017). https://doi.org/10.1007/978-3-319-70848-5_6

19. Leuschel, M., Butler, M.: ProB: a model checker for B. In: Araki, K., Gnesi, S., Mandrioli, D. (eds.) FME 2003. LNCS, vol. 2805, pp. 855–874. Springer, Heidelberg (2003). https://doi.org/10.1007/978-3-540-45236-2_46

20. Mashkoor, A., Jacquot, J.: Utilizing Event-B for domain engineering: a critical analysis. Requir. Eng. **16**(3), 191–207 (2011)

21. Mashkoor, A., Jacquot, J.: Validation of formal specifications through transformation and animation. Requir. Eng. **22**(4), 433–451 (2017)

22. Matoussi, A., Gervais, F., Laleau, R.: A goal-based approach to guide the design of an abstract Event-B specification. In: ICECCS 2011, pp. 139–148 (2011)

23. Openflexo: Openflexo project (2019). http://www.openflexo.org

24. Parnas, D.L., Madey, J.: Functional documents for computer systems. Sci. Comput. Program. **25**(1), 41–61 (1995)

25. Pierra, G.: The PLIB ontology-based approach to data integration. In: Jacquart, R. (ed.) Building the Information Society. IIFIP, vol. 156, pp. 13–18. Springer, Boston (2004). https://doi.org/10.1007/978-1-4020-8157-6_2

26. Sengupta, K., Hitzler, P.: Web ontology language (OWL). In: Staab, S., Studer, R. (eds.) Encyclopedia of Social Network Analysis and Mining, pp. 2374–2378. Springer, Heidelberg (2014). https://doi.org/10.1007/978-3-540-24750-0_4

27. Tueno, S., Frappier, M., Laleau, R., Mammar, A., Barradas, H.R.: The Generic SysML/KAOS Domain Metamodel. ArXiv e-prints, cs.SE, 1811.04732, November 2018

28. Tueno, S., Laleau, R., Mammar, A., Frappier, M.: Towards using ontologies for domain modeling within the SysML/KAOS approach. In: IEEE Proceedings of MoDRE Workshop, 25th IEEE International Requirements Engineering Conference

29. Tueno, S., Laleau, R., Mammar, A., Frappier, M.: Formal representation of SysML/KAOS domain models. ArXiv e-prints, cs.SE, 1712.07406, December 2017

30. Van Lamsweerde, A.: Requirements Engineering: From System Goals to UML Models to Software, vol. 10. Wiley, Chichester (2009)

31. Yu, E.S.K.: Towards modeling and reasoning support for early-phase requirements engineering. In: RE, pp. 226–235. IEEE Computer Society (1997)

Doctoral Symposium Papers

Design Model Repair with Formal Verification

Cheng-Hao Cai(✉) [iD], Jing Sun [iD], and Gillian Dobbie [iD]

School of Computer Science, University of Auckland, Auckland, New Zealand
{chenghao.cai,jing.sun,g.dobbie}@auckland.ac.nz

Abstract. The main research content of this topic is model repair in formal methods. Formal verification can verify the correctness of a model using rigorous mathematical methods. However, the repair of incorrect models is usually done by humans. In order to automate the model repair, we combine the B method, formal verification, probabilistic methods, satisfiability modulo theories and program synthesis, and we study various automatic model repair algorithms, which are used to fix reachability and eliminate invariant violations and deadlock states in incorrect models.

Keywords: Model repair · B method · Model checking · Refinement

1 Introduction

This work targets to an automatic model repair problem based on formal verification. Given a model described by a logical language and a set of properties that are needed to be satisfied, formal verification tools can verify whether the model satisfies these properties. If any properties are not satisfied, then the model may be incorrect. The question is: can a computer automatically fix the model?

The B method [2] is a correct-by-construction software development technique. Its core idea is to start with a highly abstract model, gradually refine the model and finally convert the refined model to complete software. During the design and refinement process, the correctness of the model is verified using formal logics several times, so that the final software is highly reliable. At present, there are efficient B model checkers such as ProB [8] and Rodin [3]. Although model checking is automated, subsequent model repair processes still require the involvement of humans. Humans need to analyse the results of the model checking, find out the errors in the model, propose possible repair solutions and manually repair the model, but this process is often inefficient. In order to improve the efficiency of model design, we have proposed a number of automatic model repair algorithms.

This work is supported by the State Scholarship Fund sponsored by the China Scholarship Council [Grant Number: 201708060334].

© Springer Nature Switzerland AG 2019
Y. Ait-Ameur and S. Qin (Eds.): ICFEM 2019, LNCS 11852, pp. 489–492, 2019.
https://doi.org/10.1007/978-3-030-32409-4_30

Currently, we have developed algorithms that can automatically eliminate deadlock states, invariant violations and assertion violations in B models [6]. The algorithms use model checking techniques to calculate the finite state space of a model, find error states in the state space, calculate candidate repairs with satisfiability modulo theories (SMT) and use probabilistic methods to select repairs. Moreover, we have developed an algorithm that can be used for reachability repair. It complements missing parts of a model using probabilistic methods, so that the model can reach a set of previously unreachable states. Further, we have confirmed the effectiveness of the algorithms via experiments.

2   Related Work

B model repair is currently an emerging research direction. It has been proposed in [11] and further improved in [12], where inductive programming is used to generate repairs for given I/O examples. For example, to generate a new operation, a number of instances of pre- and post-states must be given. Then a precondition that covers the pre-states and a post-condition (i.e., substitution) that transitions the pre-states to the post-states are synthesised using inductive programming, and the two conditions constitute a new operation. Additionally, a model repair approach based on refinement checking has been proposed in [4], which replaces model components that violate refinement conditions with other components that satisfy the conditions.

Recently, a number of techniques for automatic software repair have been developed, including those of imperative programming languages [7]. These techniques mainly include two parts: fault localisation and repair generation. At present, one of the most commonly used fault localisation methods is spectrum-based fault localisation [1]. Its central idea is to obtain execution paths of a program using test suites and estimate possible locations of errors by observing overlapping parts of these paths. Methods for repair synthesis include template-based repair, mutation repair, genetic programming, etc [7]. Similar to B model repair, the above automatic software repair techniques aim to improve the efficiency of finding and eliminating bugs in software development processes. According to [9], one of the key problems of automatic software (or model) repair is that the number of candidate fixes is generally huge, which results in a combinatorial explosion. To solve this problem, repair algorithms usually include evaluation functions for filtering high-quality fixes from candidate fixes.

3   Proposed Solutions

In order to achieve automatic model repair, we have proposed a semantic learning algorithm for constructing the evaluation function of filtering high-quality repairs. The core idea of semantic learning is to obtain the design intent of a model from the state space of the model using classification techniques. The model's state space is a collection of valid state transitions. Using a binary classifier, the state space can be probabilistically modelled to produce a semantic model that predicts whether any state transition is valid. The semantic model is used to calculate scores of repair. For details on how to vectorise state spaces, train classifiers and score repairs, please refer to our GitHub repository [1].

Additionally, we proposed three general-purpose repair operators: insertion, modification and deletion. Insertion is a reachability repair operator. Given a model M and a desired state s, if s is unreachable, then inserting an additional state transition into the state space of M can make s reachable. In this process, the semantic model is used to rank candidate insertions. Modification is used to fix existing state transitions that violate given properties. Given a property P that a model M needs to satisfy, if any state transitions produced by M do not satisfy P, then a SMT solver is used to search for candidate edits to make these transitions satisfy P, and the semantic model is used to score and rank the edits. In order to apply modifications, scores of the edits need to achieve a certain level. If not, then deletion is used to remove the faulty state transitions.

The significance of the above methods is that they provide a general-purpose model repair strategy, and probabilistic machine learning techniques, especially classification algorithms, can assist in the model design process. As semantic learning and the three repair operators are based on the model's state space, they can be used not only for the B method, but also for other formal design methods based on the checking of state space. The classification algorithms allow the intent of model design to be modelled as evaluation functions, leading to more efficient repairs. At present, there are many studies related to classification algorithms, and these algorithms can be directly used for semantic learning. If we try more classification algorithms in the future, the predictive performance of the semantic model may be further improved.

4   Current Results and Future Work

We are currently developing a tool named B-repair that implements the B model repair algorithms described in Sect. 3. B-repair uses scikit-learn [10] and Silas [5] as semantic learners to support binary classifiers such as logistic regression models, support vector machines, random forests and artificial neural networks. Moreover, B-repair uses ProB [8] as a model checker and a SMT solver. Currently, B-repair can automatically eliminate invariant violations, assertion violations and deadlock states in B models using modifications and deletions, and it can use insertions to achieve simple reachability repair. Additionally, it supports batch repairs, which can fix multiple errors in a model at the same epoch. In order to improve B-repair, we are developing more complex repair functions, optimising the classifiers and extending the model repair algorithms to refinement.

We tested B-repair using a collection of representative models in the ProB Public Examples Repository. The results revealed that the semantic learning method led to 98.3% of average prediction accuracy. Moreover, we seeded faults into the models and individually used the three repair operators to repair the models. Results revealed that the deletion operator was able to eliminate all

---

[1] Our repository is on https://github.com/cchrewrite/B-Model-Repair.

invariant violations in the models, and average repair accuracies of insertion and modification reached 86.7% and 89.8%, respectively.

In the future, our work will include the following aspects. First, we will collect model quality criteria from past studies and use them to evaluate results of model repair. Second, we will make a benchmark dataset of B model repair and perform a comprehensive performance test on B-repair. Finally, we will combine model repair with refinement checking to achieve a complete software development process.

References

1. Abreu, R., Zoeteweij, P., Golsteijn, R., van Gemund, A.J.C.: A practical evaluation of spectrum-based fault localization. J. Syst. Softw. **82**(11), 1780–1792 (2009)
2. Abrial, J.: The B-Book - Assigning Programs to Meanings. Cambridge University Press, Cambridge (2005)
3. Abrial, J., Butler, M.J., Hallerstede, S., Hoang, T.S., Mehta, F., Voisin, L.: Rodin: an open toolset for modelling and reasoning in Event-B. Int. J. Softw. Tools Technol. Transf. **12**(6), 447–466 (2010)
4. Babin, G., Ameur, Y.A., Singh, N.K., Pantel, M.: A system substitution mechanism for hybrid systems in Event-B. In: Proceedings of Formal Methods and Software Engineering - 18th International Conference on Formal Engineering Methods, ICFEM 2016, Tokyo, Japan, 14–18 November 2016, pp. 106–121 (2016)
5. Bride, H., Dong, J., Dong, J.S., Hóu, Z.: Towards dependable and explainable machine learning using automated reasoning. In: Proceedings of Formal Methods and Software Engineering - 20th International Conference on Formal Engineering Methods, ICFEM 2018, Gold Coast, QLD, Australia, 12–16 November 2018, pp. 412–416 (2018)
6. Cai, C., Sun, J., Dobbie, G.: B-repair: repairing B-models using machine learning. In: 23rd International Conference on Engineering of Complex Computer Systems, ICECCS 2018, Melbourne, Australia, 12–14 December 2018, pp. 31–40 (2018)
7. Gazzola, L., Micucci, D., Mariani, L.: Automatic software repair: a survey. IEEE Trans. Softw. Eng. **45**(1), 34–67 (2019)
8. Leuschel, M., Butler, M.J.: ProB: an automated analysis toolset for the B method. STTT **10**(2), 185–203 (2008)
9. Mechtaev, S., Gao, X., Tan, S.H., Roychoudhury, A.: Test-equivalence analysis for automatic patch generation. ACM Trans. Softw. Eng. Methodol. **27**(4), 15:1–15:37 (2018)
10. Pedregosa, F., et al.: Scikit-learn: machine learning in Python. J. Mach. Learn. Res. **12**, 2825–2830 (2011)
11. Schmidt, J., Krings, S., Leuschel, M.: Interactive model repair by synthesis. In: Proceedings of Abstract State Machines, Alloy, B, TLA, VDM, and Z - 5th International Conference, ABZ 2016, Linz, Austria, 23–27 May 2016, pp. 303–307 (2016)
12. Schmidt, J., Krings, S., Leuschel, M.: Repair and generation of formal models using synthesis. In: Integrated Formal Methods - 14th International Conference, IFM 2018, Maynooth, Ireland, 5–7 September 2018, pp. 346–366 (2018)

A Performance-Sensitive Malware Detection System on Mobile Platform

Ruitao Feng, Yang Liu[(✉)], and Shangwei Lin

Nanyang Technological University, Singapore, Singapore
yangliu@ntu.edu.sg

Abstract. Apart from the Android apps provided by the official market, apps from unofficial markets and third-party resources are always causing a serious security threat to end-users. Because of the overhead of the network, uploading the app to the server for detection is a time-consuming task. In addition, the uploading process also suffers from the threat of attackers. Consequently, a last line of defense on Android devices is necessary and much-needed. To address these problems, we propose an effective Android malware detection system, leveraging deep learning to provide a real-time secure and fast response environment on Android devices.

Keywords: Android malware · Malware detection · Deep neural network · Mobile platform

1 Introduction and Background

With the currently increasing number of Android devices and apps, more and more Android users store personal data such as online banking and shopping in their Android devices. Consequently, Android malware is one of the most security threats in this security field. It is not surprising that the demands of Android malware detection approaches have been proposed such as signature-based approach [1,2], behavior-based approach [3,4], information-flow analysis-based approach [5–7]. We note that learning-based approach [8–11] is one of the most promising techniques in detecting Android malware. With the available big data and hardware evolution over the past decade, deep learning has achieved tremendous success in many cutting-edge domains, including Android malware detection. Actually, all of the above solutions are under server side for Android markets. However, when a new Android malware family is reported, not all the Android markets are able to respond in a reasonable time. Since the number of the real-world Android apps is extremely large, it is a time-consuming task to perform the complete detection with that large number of apps. Moreover, end-users consider their app sources are all trust and secure enough. But the app from unofficial markets and third-party resources like XDA[1] are more vulnerable

---

[1] https://forum.xda-developers.com/.

© Springer Nature Switzerland AG 2019
Y. Ait-Ameur and S. Qin (Eds.): ICFEM 2019, LNCS 11852, pp. 493–497, 2019.
https://doi.org/10.1007/978-3-030-32409-4_31

in the wild. The security of these kinds of apps is indeed unpredictable and uncontrollable. The traditional cloud based malware detection is challenging to detect such applications: (1) it is a time-consuming task to upload the app to server before the installation, especially for larger apps; (2) the uploading process on the Internet is not secure. Hence, a last line of defense on Android devices is necessary and much-needed. To address the severe problem, we intend to conduct Android malware detection on Android devices.

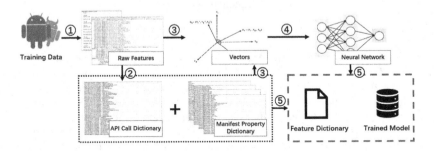

Fig. 1. The processes of feature preparation and deep learning model training

Fig. 2. The overview and workflow of MobiDroid

2   Current Research and Preliminary Results

2.1   Approach

As shown in Fig. 1, the first part of our system contains *feature preparation* and *DL model training*. We select 3 kinds of feature based on the investigation of existing studies, which are `manifest properties, API calls, opcode` sequences, as the input of our deep neural network. The first part allows to generate a *trained DL model* and a *vector dictionary* for the second part. To make the model adaptive to Android devices, we then migrate the pre-build DL model from the first part to a TENSORFLOW LITE model. Also, a quantization phase is presented as a performance optimization for the mobile platforms. As shown in Fig. 2, when an application is downloaded, a feature vector is able to be extracted from it and delivered to our detection system. Hence, after predicting with the loaded model, we obtain a certain level of confidence based on predictive output to know whether the downloaded Android app is a malware.

2.2 Experiment and Result

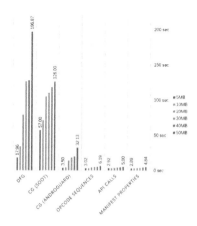

Fig. 3. Processing time of different feature types

Performance Comparison of Feature Types. We analyze the processing and analyzing time for each of the potential input features on both server-side and mobile device to decide the feature type selection. The result in Fig. 3 shows the time consuming of most full-scale information graphs are too large for our performance-sensitive approach on mobile device. Other features' processing and analyzing time costs, like opcode sequences, API calls, and manifest properties, are much more acceptable. Therefore, we decide to accept these 3 kinds of features as our model inputs.

Accuracy and Time Cost on Mobile Device. To evaluate the response time of our mobile detection system, we measure both feature preprocessing and prediction time for both quantized and non-quantized DL models on our Android devices. The preprocessing time consists of raw data processing and features analyzing time for each feature. The predicting time is the time measured from loading inputs to get the result. In Table 1, by comparing quantized and non-quantized models, the result of prediction time shows that quantization reduces a lot of time cost. Meanwhile, the accuracy of our test remains unchanged.

Table 1. Performances of MobiDroid

Devices	Quantization	Accuracy	Preparation Time (s)	Prediction Time (s)
Nexus 6	No	97.35%	16.60	9.35
	Yes	97.35%		7.23
Nexus 6P	No	97.35%	13.56	6.54
	Yes	97.35%		4.20

3 Future Work

In the future, we will extend our current work to improve the run-time performance of mobile detection system. Currently, we are trying to use some more efficient features, like binary code etc., in our work to bring the user a better experience. We will also consider extending our feature selection method to provide more application information and increase feature semantics.

References

1. Schlegel, R., Zhang, K., Zhou, X.Y., Intwala, M., Kapadia, A., Wang, X.: Soundcomber: a stealthy and context-aware sound trojan for smartphones. In: NDSS, vol. 11, pp. 17–33, February 2011
2. Zhou, Y., Wang, Z., Zhou, W., Jiang, X.: Hey, you, get off of my market: detecting malicious apps in official and alternative android markets. In: NDSS, vol. 25, No. 4, pp. 50–52, February 2012
3. Yan, L.K., Yin, H.: DroidScope: seamlessly reconstructing the OS and dalvik semantic views for dynamic android malware analysis. In: Presented as part of the 21st USENIX Security Symposium (USENIX Security 12), pp. 569–584 (2012)
4. Wu, C., Zhou, Y., Patel, K., Liang, Z., Jiang, X. AirBag: Boosting smartphone resistance to malware infection, In: NDSS, February 2014
5. Arzt, S., Rasthofer, S., Fritz, C., Bodden, E., Bartel, A., Klein, J., McDaniel, P.: FlowDroid: Precise context, flow, field, object-sensitive and lifecycle-aware taint analysis for android apps. ACM SIGPLAN Not. **49**(6), 259–269 (2014)
6. Li, L., et al.: IccTa: Detecting inter-component privacy leaks in android apps. In: Proceedings of the 37th International Conference on Software Engineering-Volume 1, pp. 280–291. IEEE Press, May 2015
7. Wong, M.Y., Lie, D.: IntelliDroid: a targeted input generator for the dynamic analysis of android malware. In: NDSS, vol. 16, pp. 21–24, February 2016
8. Arp, D., Spreitzenbarth, M., Hubner, M., Gascon, H., Rieck, K.: DREBIN: effective and explainable detection of Android malware in your pocket. In: NDSS (2014)
9. Yang, C., Xu, Z., Gu, G., Yegneswaran, V., Porras, P.: DroidMiner: automated mining and characterization of fine-grained malicious behaviors in android applications. In: Kutyłowski, M., Vaidya, J. (eds.) ESORICS 2014. LNCS, vol. 8712, pp. 163–182. Springer, Cham (2014). https://doi.org/10.1007/978-3-319-11203-9_10

10. Chen, S., Xue, M., Tang, Z., Xu, L., Zhu, H.: Stormdroid: A streaminglized machine learning-based system for detecting android malware. In Proceedings of the 11th ACM on Asia Conference on Computer and Communications Security, pp. 377–388. ACM, May 2016
11. Chen, S., Xue, M., Fan, L., Hao, S., Xu, L., Zhu, H., and Li, B. (2018). Automated poisoning attacks and defenses in malware detection systems: An adversarial machine learning approach. computers & security, 73, 326–344

Certifying Hardware Model Checking Results

Zhengqi Yu[1]([✉]), Armin Biere[1], and Keijo Heljanko[2]

[1] Johannes Kepler University Linz, Linz, Austria
zhengqi.yu@jku.at
[2] University of Helsinki, Helsinki, Finland

Abstract. Model checking is used widely as a formal verification technique for safety-critical systems. Certifying the correctness of model checking results helps increasing confidence in the verification procedure. This can be achieved by additional book-keeping inside existing model checkers. Based on this, we extended an existing BDD-based model checker as well as an IC3-based incremental inductive model checker, to generate certificates during the model checking procedure. We also introduce a proof checker which provides a standardised way to validate certificates generated from model checkers in conjunction with a SAT solver. The main goal is to establish a certification process for the hardware model checking competition.

1 Introduction

The verification of software and hardware systems has become increasingly important in modern world with the increase in complexity of system design and analysis, especially for safety-critical systems. Model checking [1–3] is a formal method widely adopted for automatic system verification, such as model checking of safety critical software in the nuclear engineering domain [4]. A model checker typically takes the model of a system and some properties corresponding to certain specification as inputs, and verifies if the properties are satisfied in the given model. As model checkers themselves are complicated programs, any programming errors can potentially lead to incorrect verification results, which can directly affect the analysis of system designs. It is therefore crucial to ensure the correctness in the process of system verification. Certifying model checkers increases confidence in model checking results, since the certificates can be validated by proof checkers or SAT solvers which are much simpler pieces of software with less complexity.

Various work has been done in this area. In SAT, certifying proofs is an established technology [5] and for instance mandatory in the SAT competition since 2013. In [6], the authors present an approach for certifying liveness properties using the k-liveness [7,8] approach to map the problem into a safety property and then proving an inductive invariant. The paper uses an IC3-based model checker

Funded by FWF project W1255-N23 and Academy of Finland project 325300.

ⓒ Springer Nature Switzerland AG 2019
Y. Ait-Ameur and S. Qin (Eds.): ICFEM 2019, LNCS 11852, pp. 498–502, 2019.
https://doi.org/10.1007/978-3-030-32409-4_32

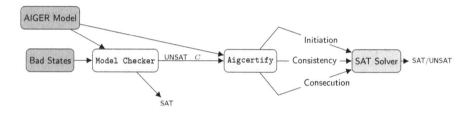

Fig. 1. Certifying procedure

and suggests validating the invariants provided by IC3 using a SAT solver but provides no experimental data on the invariant validation. In [9], the authors discussed certifying LTL model checking and their experimental results are also obtained from an IC3-based model checker.

In this paper, we present an automatic proof checker AIGCERTIFY which provides a *standardised* way to certify different types of model checkers with AIGER format. We experimented our tool with AIGTRAV, a BDD-based model checker developed at JKU Linz, and IIMC[10], which is an IC3-based model checker. Our ongoing work involves certifying k-induction-based model checkers.

2   Approach

Figure 1 shows the data flow of the certifying procedure, and here we are only dealing with examples with positive model checking results, as the results of counter-examples can be checked using counter-example validation.

The main idea is to use an inductive invariant as certificate, which is stored as an AIGER file. This certificate has to imply the given safety property (the negation of the bad state predicate). Here we use I to denote Boolean formula encoding of the initial states, C is the certificate given by the model checker and C' represents the certificate after a transition, B is the predicate representing the bad states, and T is the transition relation. There are three conditions that the inductive invariant must satisfy:

Condition	Formula	The inductive invariant ...
Initiation	$I \implies C$	... must hold at all initial states.
Consistency	$C \implies \neg B$	... must hold at states that are not bad states.
Consecution	$C \wedge T \implies C'$	... is preserved during the transition

For instance in BDD-based model checking the Boolean formula encoding the set of reachable states is such an inductive invariant C.

We have implemented AIGCERTIFY as a proof checker, which accepts a certificate as an AIGER file, either in binary or ASCII format, which will generate CNF proof obligations in DIMACS format. As an automatic proof checker, it is designed to work with different types of model checkers. We therefore define the format of a certificate that AIGCERIFY accepts, which can be obtained during the verification procedure inside a model checker. An AIGER model consists of M (maximum variables), I (inputs), L (latches), O (outputs), A (AND gates) which are represented as literals indicated as numbers. Due to the space limit, we cannot include a full description of the AIGER format here, but more information can be found in [11]. The format of a certificate is defined as follows:

Definition 1 (Format). *Given a model M with $(M_M, I_M, L_M, O_M, A_M)$, a certificate C with $(M_C, I_C, L_C, O_C, A_C)$, the format of a certificate in AIGER must satisfy the following:*

- $I_C = L_M$
- $L_C = 0$
- *Let $m_0, ..., m_{L_M-1} \in \mathbb{N}$ be the set of latches of M, and $c_0, ..., c_{I_C-1} \in \mathbb{N}$ be the set of inputs of C, for an arbitrary c_i with $0 \le i < I_C$, $c_i = m_i - I_M$.*

We extended AIGTRAV, to generate the inductive invariant in AIGER format after it finishes model checking. Our implementation also includes a conversion from the BDD structure to AIGER format. The resulting invariant can then be verified by the proof checker AIGCERTIFY.

In addition, we experimented with IIMC [10], which already provides an internal proof certificate as one of the features of the IC3 model checking algorithm. The proof certificate of IC3-based model checking can be obtained directly from the one-step inductive strengthening. We extended the source code to provide the inductive invariant in AIGER format which can then be used by AIGCERTIFY.

3   Implementation and Experiments

We have implemented AIGCERTIFY as a proof checker in order to verify the correctness of certificates generated from model checkers to increase confidence in verification. It accepts a model and a certificate both in AIGER format as inputs, as defined in Definition 1, and generates three conditions (explained in Sect. 2) as separate AIGER files, which are then checked by an existing SAT solver (like PicoSAT [12]). For additional validation the SAT solver can also generate proofs that can be further checked by a SAT proof checker (such as DRAT-TRIM [5]), resulting in a two stage proof validation.

The variable ordering of the AIGER model is assumed to be the same as that of the certificate, which ensures they are referring to the same set of latches. We utilise the AIGER library `simpaig.c` which provides a simple AIG data structure that allows operations on variables and AND gates.

The preservation condition requires the certificate to hold after each transition. Typically, a transition relation is the conjunction of the values of current inputs and states, and the values of next states. In AIGER format, the next states are represented by the next values defined for the latches.

The three output AIGER files are converted to CNF files by the AIGER library `aigtocnf.c` using Tseitin encoding, and in our experimental results they are then validated by the existing SAT solver, PicoSAT [12]. These three conditions form the proof for the model checking procedure, and if all three CNFs are verified to hold, the certificate is proved successfully. It is further possible to certify SAT solving by generating and checking propositional DRAT proofs [13]. We are currently applying our approach to benchmarks from HWMCC'17 [14].

4 Discussion and Conclusion

We introduced our tool AIGCERTIFY which is designed to be a uniform proof checker for different types of model checkers, including BDD-based and SAT-based. We experimented with existing model checking tools to work in conjunction with it. The ongoing work of our project includes generating certificates from k-induction-based model checkers which can then be verified by AIGCERTIFY, which also involves formally defining the inductive invariant of k-induction-based model checking. This might also draw inspiration from [15,16]. Even though our focus is currently on providing certificates for the hardware model checking competition, similar ideas might be applicable to software model checking too.

References

1. Clarke, E.M., Henzinger, T.A., Veith, H., Bloem, R. (eds.): Handbook of Model Checking. Springer, Cham (2018). https://doi.org/10.1007/978-3-319-10575-8
2. Clarke, E.M., Grumberg, O., Kroening, D., Peled, D., Veith, H.: Model Checking. MIT Press, Cambridge (2018)
3. Baier, C., Katoen, J.: Principles of Model Checking. MIT Press, Cambridge (2008)
4. Lahtinen, J., Valkonen, J., Björkman, K., Frits, J., Niemelä, I., Heljanko, K.: Model checking of safety-critical software in the nuclear engineering domain. Reliab. Eng. Syst. Saf. **105**, 104–113 (2012)
5. Heule, M., Hunt, W., Wetzler, N.: Trimming while checking clausal proofs. In: FMCAD 2013, pp. 181–188 (2013)
6. Kuismin, T., Heljanko, K.: Increasing confidence in liveness model checking results with proofs. In: Bertacco, V., Legay, A. (eds.) HVC 2013. LNCS, vol. 8244, pp. 32–43. Springer, Cham (2013). https://doi.org/10.1007/978-3-319-03077-7_3
7. Claessen, K., Sörensson, N.: A liveness checking algorithm that counts. In: FMCAD 2012, Cambridge, UK, pp. 52–59. IEEE (2012)
8. Gan, X., Dubrovin, J., Heljanko, K.: A symbolic model checking approach to verifying satellite onboard software. Sci. Comput. Program. **82**, 44–55 (2014)
9. Griggio, A., Roveri, M., Tonetta, S.: Certifying proofs for LTL model checking. In: Bjørner, N., Gurfinkel, A. (eds.) FMCAD 2018, pp. 1–9. IEEE (2018)
10. Bradley, A., Somenzi, F., Hassan, Z.: IIMC: incremental inductive model checker. http://www.github.com/mgudemann/iimc
11. Biere, A., Heljanko, K., Wieringa, S.: AIGER 1.9 and beyond. FMV Reports Series, Institute for Formal Models and Verification, Johannes Kepler University Linz, Austria, Technical report (2011)

12. Biere, A.: Lingeling, Plingeling, PicoSAT and PrecoSAT at SAT race 2010. FMV Reports Series, Institute for Formal Models and Verification, Johannes Kepler University Linz, Austria, Technical report (2010)

13. Wetzler, N., Heule, M.J.H., Hunt, W.A.: DRAT-trim: efficient checking and trimming using expressive clausal proofs. In: Sinz, C., Egly, U. (eds.) SAT 2014. LNCS, vol. 8561, pp. 422–429. Springer, Cham (2014). https://doi.org/10.1007/978-3-319-09284-3_31

14. Biere, A., van Dijk, T., Heljanko, K.: Hardware model checking competition 2017. In: Stewart, D., Weissenbacher, G. (eds.) FMCAD, p. 9. IEEE (2017)

15. Vediramana Krishnan, H.G., Vizel, Y., Ganesh, V., Gurfinkel, A.: Interpolating strong induction. In: Dillig, I., Tasiran, S. (eds.) CAV 2019, Part II. LNCS, vol. 11562, pp. 367–385. Springer, Cham (2019). https://doi.org/10.1007/978-3-030-25543-5_21

16. Bjørner, N., Gurfinkel, A., McMillan, K., Rybalchenko, A.: Horn clause solvers for program verification. In: Beklemishev, L.D., Blass, A., Dershowitz, N., Finkbeiner, B., Schulte, W. (eds.) Fields of Logic and Computation II. LNCS, vol. 9300, pp. 24–51. Springer, Cham (2015). https://doi.org/10.1007/978-3-319-23534-9_2

A Note on Failure Mode Reasoning

Hamid Jahanian[✉]

Macquarie University, Sydney, Australia
hamid.jahanian@hdr.mq.edu.au

Abstract. Safety Instrumented Systems (SIS) protect major hazard facilities against catastrophic accidents. A SIS consists of hardware components and a software part, the program. Failure Mode Reasoning (FMR) is a novel abstraction technique for identifying and quantifying failure modes of SIS hardware components based on an analysis of the SIS program. In FMR, the program is divided into smaller segments, for each of which the input failure modes are identified based on the function of the segment and the given failure mode at its output. The results of segment analyses are then combined and simplified in order to derive a short list of failure modes. The list can also be used to calculate the aggregated probability of failure. This note outlines the underlying concepts of FMR.

1 Introduction

In the process industry, Safety Instrumented Systems (SIS) are protection mechanisms against major plant accidents. Plant accidents can have catastrophic consequences. A recent explosion at a chemical plant in eastern China killed over 70 people and injured more than 600. SIS' play a critical role in preventing accidents and protecting people. However, failure of SIS components can result in the SIS being unavailable to respond to hazardous situations, which can in turn lead to devastating consequences. It is therefore crucial to correctly identify and quantify SIS failure modes early in the design and realization stage. This paper concerns a new method for achieving this objective.

Well established methods, such as Failure Mode and Effect Analysis (FMEA) [1] and Fault Tree Analysis (FTA) [2] already exist in the industry for analyzing and quantifying SIS failure modes. Such methods rely on the analyst's prior knowledge of the system behavior, which is determined by hardware components as well as the program. Not only are such analyses inherently subject to human-error, they also require expertise, time and effort. This is particularly challenging when it comes to the program, as the interlocks in a program are far more complicated. Consequently, the impact of program is often undermined and, as a result, the validity and accuracy of the analysis is compromised.

We are introducing a new method, Failure Mode Reasoning (FMR), that circumvents the need for by-hand analysis of parts of SIS. Using a special calculus built on failure modes, FMR analyzes the SIS program to identify those hardware faults at SIS inputs that can result in a given failure at its output. The main

© Springer Nature Switzerland AG 2019
Y. Ait-Ameur and S. Qin (Eds.): ICFEM 2019, LNCS 11852, pp. 503–506, 2019.
https://doi.org/10.1007/978-3-030-32409-4_33

outcome of FMR is a short list of failure modes, which can be used to calculate the probability of failure.

2   The Problem and the Solution

A typical SIS consists of three main subsystems: sensors that measure the process conditions (e.g. pressure and temperature), logic solver (e.g. a CPU) that processes the program, and final elements (e.g. valves) that isolate the plant from hazard when needed. Figure 1b shows a simple SIS consisting of two sensors, one logic solver and one final element. This SIS is to protect the downstream process against high pressure in the upstream gas pipe. The sensors measure the gas pressure and the logic solver initiates a command to close the valve if the gas pressure exceeds a threshold limit. Figure 1a shows a fault tree that is meant to model the failure of this SIS: the SIS fails if both sensors fail, or if the logic solver fails, or if the final element fails.

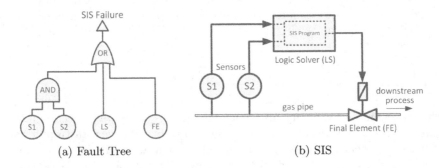

(a) Fault Tree   (b) SIS

Fig. 1. An example SIS and a proposed fault tree

The fault tree in Fig. 1a is based on the assumption that the two sensors are redundant; i.e., having one sensor in a healthy state is sufficient to detect potential hazards. The validity of this assumption, and thus the validity of the fault tree, directly depends on the details of SIS program: if the readings of sensors are averaged first and then compared to the high pressure limit, the proposed fault tree is incorrect; because failure of one sensor will affect the average of the two. But if each sensor reading is separately compared to the threshold limit first, the sensors can be considered redundant and the fault tree will be correct. The soundness of a fault tree highly depends on the analyst's knowledge, and as can be seen in this example, this knowledge cannot be complete without including the impact of the program. Despite its critical role, SIS program is often ignored or underestimated in real scenario safety analyses. It is not unusual for a SIS program to have hundreds of inputs and thousands of Function Blocks (FB) that process those inputs. Conducting a detailed analysis of program at such a scale is a real challenge for a human analyst.

FMR concerns a new automated method that addresses this problem. Using its own calculus, FMR analyzes the SIS program from the perspective of failure. The program is divided into smaller segments and for each segment the failure modes of inputs are reasoned based on the failure modes of the output and the intended function of the segment. The findings of the segments are then combined and simplified to produce the short list of failure modes of SIS sensors, which can also be used to calculate the aggregated probability of failure.

3   Failure Mode Reasoning

Consider the state space pair $(\tilde{S}, S)$ where $\tilde{S}$ represents the state of system reported in the SIS program variables and S represents the intended (real) state of the variables. Ideally, $\tilde{S}$ should be the same as S. This takes place when there is no faults in the system; i.e. the sensors correctly sense the real state of the plant. When $\tilde{S} \neq S$, the SIS may produce an undesired output; e.g. not initiate a safety command when it should. The failure of SIS output depends on the manner in which $\tilde{S}$ deviates from S. Such deviations are categorized as failure modes. A failure mode is a manner in which the reported value at a state variable differs from its intended value. In FMR, the basic failure modes are expressed by $\dot{h}, \dot{l}, \dot{t},$ and $\dot{f}$, which represent *High, Low, True* and *False* by *fault* respectively.

The purpose of FMR is to predict the failure modes at SIS inputs which can lead to a particular failure mode at SIS output. Failure modes can be analyzed at two levels: at the FB level and at the SIS program level. At the FB level, we study one FB in isolation and we define how different failure modes at the FB input can lead to failure modes at its output. Once the FB failure model is *proposed* and proven, it can be used wherever an instance of the corresponding FB is used in the SIS program.

The failure model of the SIS program, on the other hand, is *composed* by combining (parts of) the failure models of individual FBs. The question we are trying to answer here is: given the specific SIS program and a specific failure mode at its output, what are the combinations of failure modes at the inputs of program that can lead to the given output failure mode? In answering this question, we start at the final SIS output and scan through the program in reverse direction, towards its inputs. At each stage of analysis the failure model of an individual FB is employed to reason about the local failure behaviors. Once the local analyses are concluded, the results are logically combined and simplified to derive the short list of global failure modes, i.e. the failure modes of SIS sensors. In the final stage, the short list will be used to calculate the aggregated probability of SIS failure based on the failure rates of its sensors.

A major innovation in this research is to show that the analysis can be done directly on failure modes, allowing for a more efficient analysis, whilst ensuring that all possible failure modes are computed.

4   Discussion and Related Works

What FMR does is very similar to FTA. In both methods a deductive analysis is employed to calculate the set of root causes that can lead to an undesired top event. In a FTA the top event can be the failure state of any type of system, e.g. failure of a physical brake system in an airplane. In FMR the top event is always a failure at the output of a SIS program. In FTA, the root causes are often referred to as cut-sets, or failure sets. In FMR, the root causes are combinations of faults at the SIS inputs. One could even consider FMR as a fault tree model of SIS program; except that FMR does not actually create a fault tree, but instead, the method directly uses the SIS program to conduct its analysis. For the same reason, the application of FMR is limited to the information that can be extracted from that program.

Automatic synthesis of FTA has been presented by other researches in recent years, such as Hierarchically Performed Hazard Origin and Propagation Studies (HiP-HOPS) [3]. The common concept in these methods is that if we have the typical definition of fault tree for individual components, then we can synthesize the system level fault tree by interconnecting the components fault tree. At a conceptual level, this idea is utilized by FMR too; however, the *components* in FMR are the FBs, as opposed to the other methods that analyze general systems and components. Also, while the other methods rely on separate system models or specifications to generate fault trees, FMR uses the actual running program in SIS; which is by far the most accurate, detailed, and specific source of information if one wishes to study the behavior of a system.

5   Current Experiments and Future Works

The scale and complexity of real-life SIS programs makes their by-hand analysis a challenge. A software tool is required to automatically read and analyze the program with minimum chance of error. The author has already developed a prototype tool that parses an offline copy of a SIS program in XML format, analyzes it based on FMR, generates the short list of failure modes, and calculates the probability of failure. The tool has been tested in a power plant project where a SIS with over 200 inputs was installed as a protection system for an industrial boiler. The preliminary results show that the analysis time can be reduced to less than 10%, assuming that the analyst would include the program in his analysis in the first place, and that he has the skills to conduct such analysis.

In addition to empowering the FMR tool and testing it in different project environments, we are also working towards extending the mathematical concepts of FMR to deal with more complex dynamics in SIS programs, including the situations where feedback loops and time delays affect the transition of faults from inputs to outputs.

References

1. IEC 60812 Ed. 2.0: Analysis techniques for system reliability - Procedure for failure mode and effects analysis (FMEA). IEC (2006)
2. Vesely, W., Stamatelatos, M., Dugan, J., Fragola, J., Minarick III, J., Railsback, J.: Fault Tree Handbook with Aerospace Applications. Technical report, NASA (2002)
3. Sharvia, S., Papadopoulos, Y.: Integrating model checking with HiP-HOPS in model-based safety analysis. Reliab. Eng. Syst. Saf. **135**, 64–80 (2015)

Robustness of Piece-Wise Linear Neural Network with Feasible Region Approaches

Jay Hoon Jung[1(✉)] and YoungMin Kwon[2]

[1] Department of Computer Science, Stony Brook University,
Stony Brook, NY 11794, USA
jay.jung@stonybrook.edu
[2] Department of Computer Science, The State University of New York at Korea,
Incheon, Korea
youngmin.kwon@sunykorea.ac.kr

Abstract. A *Piece-wise Linear Neural Network* (PLNN) is a deep neural network composed of only *Rectified Linear Units* (ReLU) activation function. Interestingly, even though PLNNs are a nonlinear system in general, we show that PLNNs can be expressed in terms of linear constraints because ReLU function is a piece-wise linear function. We suggested that the robustness of *Neural Networks* (NNs) can be verified by investigating the feasible region of these constraints. Intuitively, suggested robustness represents the minimum Euclidean distance from the input needed to change its predicted class. Moreover, the run-time of calculating robustness is as fast as a feed forward neural network.

Keywords: Robustness · Deep neural network · Piece-wise Linear Neural Network

1   Introduction

The *Deep Neural Networks* (DNNs) have been successfully performing complex tasks. Despite their success, even more accurate than human experts in some areas, adversarial attacks can fool NNs far too easily [1]. Subsequently, several methods have been suggested to enhance the robustness of NNs [1,2]. It is however not clear how robust these methods actually are. Therefore, transforming the input-to-output mapping of NNs into a system of inequalities, we suggest a method to measure the robustness of NNs when an input is given.

2   Framework

In this section, we will define a *trained* neural network model mathematically. The basic assumption of this work is that there are only fully-connected layers in

This work was supported by MSIP, Korea under the ITCCP program (IITP-2019-2011-1-00783) and by KEIT under the GATC program (10077300).

Y. Ait-Ameur and S. Qin (Eds.): ICFEM 2019, LNCS 11852, pp. 507–511, 2019.
https://doi.org/10.1007/978-3-030-32409-4_34

a NN and that the activation functions for NN models are rectified linear units
(ReLU) functions. $ReLU(x)$ is a linear function of x if $x \geq 0$, but is equal to 0
if $x < 0$. In other words, $ReLU(x)$ is a piece-wise linear function. We will prove
that an output layer of a NN model is also a piece-wise linear function.

For a given neural network model M with $(n_l + 1)$ layers, $w_{i,j}^l$ denotes the
weight from the ith node in the lth layer to the jth node in the $(l+1)^{st}$ layer,
and L_i^l and b_i^l denote the ith node (or its value) and the ith bias in the lth layer
respectively. Especially, let L^0 and L^{n_l} be the input layer and the output layer
with dimensions of n_{in} and n_{out} respectively. All indices such as l, i, j, n_{in}, n_{out},
and n_l are integers.

If rectified linear units function, $ReLU(x)$, is the activation function for a NN
model M, then the value of a node L_j^{l+1} is $L_j^{l+1} = ReLU\left(\sum_i(w_{i,j}^l \cdot L_i^l) + b_j^{l+1}\right)$
by the definition of artificial neurons. Observe that even though the weights $w_{i,j}^l$
are constants for a trained model M, L_i^l is a variable and dependent on an input
I. When $L_j^{n_l+1} = O_j$ where O_j denotes the jth node in the output layer where
$0 \leq j \leq n_{out}$, there is no activation functions, i.e., $O_j = \sum_i(w_{i,j}^{n_l} \cdot L_i^{n_l}) + b_j^{n_l+1}$.
In addition, the first layer is the input layer, i.e., $L_i^0 = I_i$ for $i = 0, \ldots, n_{in}$.

Definition 1. *A trained model M can be represented by a tuple $\mathcal{M} = (\mathcal{W}, \mathcal{B})$,
where $\mathcal{W} = \{w_{0,0}^0, w_{0,1}^0, w_{0,2}^0, \ldots, w_{i',n_{out}}^{n_l}\}$ is the set of weights, $\mathcal{B} = \{b_0^1, b_1^1, b_2^1,
\ldots, b_{n_{out}}^{n_l}\}$ is the set of biases, and i' is the dimension of the $(n_l - 1)^{th}$ layer.*

Interestingly, the indices of each element of $\mathcal{M}$ reveals the structure of its NN
model M. For example, the last superscript index plus one, (n_l+1), indicates the
number of layers in the NN model and the subscript indices suggest the number
of nodes in each layer.

Definition 2. *When an input I is fed into a trained model M, its snapshot of
states can be represented by a triple $\mathcal{M}_I = (\mathcal{W}, \mathcal{B}, \pounds, \mathcal{O})$, where $\mathcal{W} = \{w_{0,0}^0, w_{0,1}^0,
w_{0,2}^0, \ldots, w_{i',n_{out}}^{n_l}\}$, and $\mathcal{B} = \{b_0^1, b_1^1, b_2^1, \ldots, b_{n_{out}}^{n_l}\}$ are the set of weights and
the set of biases of $\mathcal{M}$ respectively; $\pounds = \{L_0^0, L_1^0, L_2^0, \ldots, L_{n_{out}-1}^{n_l}\}$, and $\mathcal{O} =
\{L_0^{n_l+1}, L_1^{n_l+1}, \ldots, L_{n_{out}}^{n_l+1}\}$ are the set of node values and output node values
respectively.*

The difference between $\mathcal{M}$ and $\mathcal{M}_I$ is that while $\mathcal{M}$ is a structure, $\mathcal{M}_I$ is a
snapshot of $\mathcal{M}$ with the nodes of L_j^l loaded with their values from the input I.

Theorem 1. *For any NN models M_I and any l*

$$L_j^l = \sum_i (\alpha_{i,j} \cdot I_i) + c_j^l \tag{1}$$

where $\alpha_{i,j}$, and c_j^l are a constant within a polytope.

A proof of this theorem is omitted due to the page limit, but it can be
proved using the induction. When $l + 1 = n_l$, that is, $O_j = L_j$, the output
layer of a NN is a piece-wise linear function of the input layer. Specifically, each

parameter to ReLU function defines a half-space in the input space I such that $\{I_i : \sum_i(\alpha_{i,j} \cdot I_i) + c_j \geq 0\}$ and their intersections define a polytope n, in the input space. Because $\alpha_{i,j}$ and c_j are constants within each polytope, the output layer of a NN is a piece-wise linear function of the input layer.

Definition 3. *A neural network constraint set is a system of linear inequalities defined by ReLU functions for each node L_j^{l+1} in terms of the input I_i.*

Naturally, the number of neural network constraints is equal to that of nodes in hidden layer since input and output layers do not have any activation functions. At the same time, a neural network constraint set can be expressed in a matrix form such as $\beta \cdot I \leq D$, where β and D are a coefficient matrix and a constant matrix respectively.

Definition 4 (A Canonical Form). *For any NN model M_I, NN can be expressed in a canonical form as*

$$O = A \cdot I + C \text{ if } \beta \cdot I \leq D \tag{2}$$

where O, I, A, and C are the output, input, coefficient, and constant matrices in Eq. (1). β and D are the coefficient and constant matrices for a neural network constraints set.

Interestingly, O, A, C, β and D are determined by an input I. The input decides whether each node activates or not so that the output is calculated based on these activations. In other words, there is a set of inputs which share the same inequality, $\beta \cdot I \leq D$. Each row of the inequality defines a half-space in the input space and their conjunction defines a polytope . In the interior of the feasible region, these inputs have same A and C. We can compute how much perturbation is needed for an input to be classified differently if we know how far the input is located from the boundaries of the feasible region.

The output, O, is however not identical for all inputs within the same feasible region. In the classification problem, the maximum value among the components of the output decides which class the input belongs. Hence, to obtain a region with a homogeneous output and to measure the robustness of an input, we need to add more inequalities after the output layer.

Definition 5 (Expanded Neural Network). *For any M_I, let k be an index of the currently predicted class. An expanded NN for M_I can be represented by a tuple $\mathcal{E}_I^k = (\mathcal{W}', \mathcal{B}', \mathcal{L}', \mathcal{O}')$, where $\mathcal{W}' = \mathcal{W} \cup \{w_{0,0}^{n_l+1}, w_{0,1}^{n_l+1}, w_{0,2}^{n_l+1}, \ldots, w_{n_{out},n_{out}}^{n_l+1}\}$, $\mathcal{B}' = \mathcal{B}$, $\mathcal{L}' = \mathcal{L} \cup \{L_0^{n_l+1}, L_1^{n_l+1}, L_2^{n_l+1}, \ldots, L_{n_{out}-1}^{n_l+1}\}$ and $\mathcal{O}' = \mathcal{O}$, when*

$$L_j^{n+1} = \sum_i^{n_l+1} w_{i,j}^{n_l+1} \cdot \mathcal{O}_j \text{ where } w_{i,j}^{n_l+1} = \begin{cases} 1 & \text{if } j = k \\ -1 & \text{if } j = i \\ 0 & \text{otherwise} \end{cases} \tag{3}$$

The expanded NN, $\mathcal{E}_I^k$, is a NN that has a layer added after the output layer. There are n_{out} nodes in the newly added layer. Each node in the last layer represents the difference between the currently predicted class and the other. By Definition 3, n_{out} inequalities are added to the neural network constraint set. Furthermore, the newly added constraints ensure that any inputs in a feasible region are classified as a same class.

3   Robustness

Definition 6 (Robustness). *Robustness,* **R,** *of an expanded NN* $\mathcal{E}_I^k$ *is defined as*

$$\mathbf{R} = \min_i \frac{|\beta_i \cdot \mathbf{I} - \mathbf{D}|}{||\beta_i||} \tag{4}$$

where β_i *is the* i^{th} *row of* β*, and* **I** *and* **D** *are defined in Definition 4.*

Note that a constraint set of a NN is different from that of an *expanded* NN in which the feasible region is homogeneous. Robustness of an input is defined as the smallest Euclidean distance between an input and hyperplanes given by a neural net constraint set of an expanded NN $\mathcal{E}_I^k$. Intuitively, the robustness is the minimum perturbation needed to change a predicted class.

The execution time for calculating the robustness is spractical since we convert NNs into linear forms as in Definition 4 despite NNs' complex structure. The time complexity for calculating the robustness, when β is given, is $O((h + n_{out}) \times n_{in})$ since the dimensions of β is $(h + n_{out}) \times n_{in}$, where h is the number of all nodes in any hidden layers. The number of operations to calculate β is dependent on the structure of NNs. Suppose n_i is the number of nodes in L^i. A matrix that describes the connection between L^i and L^{i+1} has the dimension of $(n_i \times n_{i+1})$. Feed-forward calculation is simply the multiplication of these matrices in which complexity is $O(\sum_{i=0}^{n_l}(n_0 \cdot n_{i+1} \cdot n_{i+2}))$. Hence, the total run-time becomes $O(n_l \cdot h^2)$ since $n_i \leq h$ for any i.

4   Conclusion and Future Works

We presented that a PLNN can be expressed in a canonical form as described in Definition 4. Adding a carefully designed extra layer, we can obtain the exact feasible region whose interior points in terms of the input space are classified as the same class. Therefore, we can define robustness of a classification by the shortest distance to the boundaries of the region in the expanded NN. For future work, we are working on computing the robustness with popular data sets such as MNIST, and ImageNet.

References

1. Goodfellow, I., Shlens, J., Szegedy, C.: Explaining and harnessing adversarial examples. In: International Conference on Learning Representations (2015). http://arxiv.org/abs/1412.6572
2. Gu, S., Rigazio, L.: Towards deep neural network architectures robust to adversarial examples. In: 3rd International Conference on Learning Representations, ICLR 2015, San Diego, CA, USA, 7–9 May 2015. Workshop Track Proceedings (2015)

Formal Specification and Verification
of Smart Contracts

Jiao Jiao[✉]

School of Computer Science and Engineering,
Nanyang Technological University, Singapore, Singapore
jiao0023@ntu.edu.sg

Abstract. Smart contracts can be regarded as one of the most popular blockchain-based applications. The decentralized nature of blockchain introduces vulnerabilities absent in non-distributed programs. Furthermore, it is very difficult, if not impossible, to patch a smart contract after it is deployed. Therefore, smart contracts must be formally verified before they are deployed on the blockchain. In this work, we study the formal specification and verification of smart contracts.

1 Introduction

A smart contract is a computer program written in certain high-level programming languages, such as Solidity, Bamboo, Vyper, etc, to achieve its functionality. Smart contracts must be verified for multiple reasons. Firstly, due to the decentralized nature of blockchain, smart contracts are different from programs written in other programming languages (e.g., C/Java), making programming smart contracts error-prone without a proper understanding of the underlying semantic model. Secondly, a smart contract can be deployed on the blockchain by any user in the network. Verifying smart contracts against vulnerabilities in deployed contracts is crucial for protecting digital assets. Thirdly, it is very difficult, if not impossible, to patch a smart contract once it is deployed.

There has been a surge of interest in developing analysis and verification techniques for smart contracts. Some of the existing works focus on EVM (Ethereum Virtual Machine). For instance, Oyente [6] is a symbolic execution engine for analyzing Solidity smart contracts by translating them into EVM bytecode. Furthermore, a complete formal executable semantics of EVM [3] is developed in the K-framework to facilitate the formal verification of smart contracts at the bytecode level. In other works, Solidity contracts are translated into programs in intermediate languages for analysis and verification. Specifically speaking, Solidity programs are formalized with an abstract language and then translated into LLVM bitcode in Zeus [5]. In addition, the formalization in F* [1] is an intermediate-level language for the equivalence checking of Solidity programs and EVM bytecode. To conclude, most of the existing approaches either focus on EVM bytecode, or translate Solidity smart contracts into programs in intermediate languages that are suitable for verifying smart contracts or detecting

© Springer Nature Switzerland AG 2019
Y. Ait-Ameur and S. Qin (Eds.): ICFEM 2019, LNCS 11852, pp. 512–516, 2019.
https://doi.org/10.1007/978-3-030-32409-4_35

potential issues in associated verifiers or checkers. Furthermore, none of the existing works can directly handle smart contracts written in different high-level programming languages without translating them into EVM bytecode or intermediate languages, and the verification is limited to certain vulnerabilities.

A direct executable formal semantics of the high-level smart contract programming language is a must for both understanding and verifying smart contracts. The first reason is that programmers write and reason about smart contracts at the level of source code without the semantics of which they are required to understand how source programs are compiled into bytecode in order to understand them, which is far from trivial. Furthermore, both high-level [4] and low-level [2,3] semantics definitions are necessary to conduct equivalence checking to guarantee that security properties are preserved at both levels and reason about compiler bugs. Secondly, even though smart contracts can be transformed into programs in intermediate languages to be analyzed and verified in existing model checkers and verifiers, the equivalence checking of the high-level programming language of smart contracts and the intermediate language considered is crucial to the validity of the verification.

2   Formal Specification and Verification of Smart Contracts

Generally speaking, we construct a general semantic model for smart contracts based on the commonly shared semantic features. The direct semantics of any high-level smart contract programming language can be developed by rewriting its syntax to the corresponding logical parts in the general semantic model. Based on this specification, security properties can be formalized and then verified.

2.1   A General Semantic Model

Different kinds of high-level smart contract programming languages vary in syntax but share a lot in common in semantics in order to achieve the equivalent functionality. Considering this fact, we construct a general semantic model for all kinds of high-level smart contract programming languages. The semantics of a high-level smart contract programming language can be summarized into three aspects in terms of its functionality, namely memory operations, new contract instance creations and function calls. Particularly, new contract instance creations and function calls are two kinds of transactions on the blockchain.

2.2   Direct Semantics Generation

The direct semantics of a high-level smart contract programming language can be developed based on the general semantic model. From the perspective of rewriting logic, a language semantics definition is a set of rewriting steps from the language syntax to its evaluations. Each of these rewriting steps implements a function to move the language a step further to its final evaluation. The general semantic model which consists of a set of internal rewriting steps can be regarded as a logical intermediate language to construct the semantics. In this way, we take the benefits of intermediate languages but also exclude the equivalence checking issues since there is no semantic-level gap. Considering the fact that different smart contract languages mainly differ in syntax and share a lot in common in semantics, the direct semantics of a particular smart contract language can be constructed by rewriting its syntax to the general semantic model with several functional steps. For unique features which are absent in the general semantic model, semantics rules are constructed from scratch.

2.3   Formal Verification of Smart Contracts

Based on the formal specification of smart contracts, security properties can be formally defined from the perspectives of programming correctness and user-defined correctness to prevent attacks. Based on the formal definitions, verification algorithms for these properties can be developed with the direct executable formal semantics of the high-level smart contract programming language. This direct semantics makes the verification of security properties straightforward. This is because vulnerabilities in smart contracts are introduced by logical errors in the program execution which can be fully captured by the semantics.

3   Current Results

We propose a general formal semantic framework for smart contracts based on a general semantic model of high-level smart contract programming languages. Different from previous works which either analyze and verify smart contracts on EVM semantics or interpret Solidity semantics with the semantics of intermediate languages, the proposed framework aims to generate a direct executable formal semantics of any high-level smart contract programming language to facilitate the high-level verification of contracts.

We evaluate the proposed general formal semantic framework for smart contracts by showing that the generated semantics is complete and correct with respect to the compiler test set. We take Solidity as an object for the evaluation since there are sufficient Solidity smart contracts available for testing the generated Solidity semantics. The generated Solidity semantics is evaluated from two perspectives: the first one is its coverage (i.e., completeness), and the second is its correctness (i.e., consistency with Solidity compilers). Evaluation results (cf. Table 1) show that the Solidity semantics developed with the proposed framework completely covers the supported high-level core language features specified by the official documentation and is consistent with the official Solidity compiler.

4   Future Work

- Defining High-level Security Properties: We plan to define some security properties to prevent both existing and potential attacks, and develop verification

Table 1. Coverage of the generated solidity semantics

Features	Coverage	Features	Coverage
Types(Core)		**Statements(Core)**	
Elementary Types		If Statement	FC
address	FC	While Statement	FC
bool	FC	For Statement	FC
string	FC	Block	FC
Int	FC	Inline Assembly	N
Uint	FC	Statement	
Byte	FC	Do While Statement	FC
Fixed	N	Place Holder Statement	FC
Ufixed	N	Continue	FC
User-defined Types	FC	Break	FC
Mappings	FC	Return	FC
Array Types	FC	Throw,Revert,Assert,Require	FC
Function Types	FC	Simple Statement	FC
address payable	FC	Emit Statement	FC
Functions(Core)		**Expressions(Core)**	
Function Definitions		Bitwise Operations	FC
Constructors	FC	Arithmetic Operations	FC
Normal Functions	FC	Logical Operations	FC
Fallback Functions	FC	Comparison Operations	FC
Modifiers	FC	Assignment	FC
Function Calls		Look Up	FC
Internal Function Calls	FC	New Expression	FC
External Function Calls	FC	Other Expressions	FC
Using For	FC	**Inheritance**	FC
Event	FC		

FC: Fully Covered and Consistent with Solidity IDE   N: Not Covered

algorithms for these properties with the high-level semantics developed with the proposed general formal semantic framework.

- Automatic Verification: We will develop a practical tool to formally verify smart contracts written in different high-level programming languages.
- Equivalence Checking on High-level Programs and Low-level Bytecode: We will conduct equivalence checking on high-level programs and low-level bytecode to guarantee that security properties are preserved at both levels and reason about compiler bugs.

References

1. Bhargavan, K., et al.: Formal verification of smart contracts. In: CCS 2016, pp. 91–96. ACM (2016)
2. Grishchenko, I., Maffei, M., Schneidewind, C.: A semantic framework for the security analysis of Ethereum smart contracts. In: Bauer, L., Küsters, R. (eds.) POST 2018. LNCS, vol. 10804, pp. 243–269. Springer, Cham (2018). https://doi.org/10.1007/978-3-319-89722-6_10
3. Hildenbrandt, E., et al.: KEVM: a complete semantics of the Ethereum virtual machine, August 2017
4. Jiao, J., Kan, S., Lin, S., Sanán, D., Liu, Y., Sun, J.: Executable operational semantics of solidity. CoRR, abs/1804.01295 (2018)

5. Kalra, S., Goel, S., Dhawan, M., Sharma, S.: ZEUS: analyzing safety of smart contracts. In: NDSS 2018. The Internet Society (2018)
6. Luu, L., Chu, D., Olickel, H., Saxena, P., Hobor, A.: Making smart contracts smarter. In: CCS 2016, pp. 254–269. ACM (2016)

Spatio-Temporal Specification Language for Cyber-Physical Systems

Tengfei Li[(✉)] [iD]

Shanghai Key Laboratory of Trustworthy Computing, East China Normal University,
Shanghai 200062, China
tengfeili2015@gmail.com

Abstract. Specifying spatio-temporal aspects with changes of spatial entities in dense time is one of the important areas in cyber-physical systems. The major problem is the complexity and verifiability of dense time and real-valued variables of the spatio-temporal properties of cyber-physical systems. We propose a spatio-temporal specification language, named STSL, which integrates Signal Temporal Logic (STL) with a spatial logic $S4_u$ to deal with the changes of real values spatial entities in dense time. We present a Hilbert-style axiomatization for the proposed STSL and provide the soundness and completeness result. Further, we provide the satisfiable relation of spatio-temporal formulas and the corresponding complexity and a decision procedure is present to check the satisfiability problem of the decidable fragment of STSL. Besides, spatio-temporal model is monitored at runtime for the changes of spatial signals over time using MATLAB.

Keywords: Signal Temporal Logic (STL) · $S4_u$ · Spatio-Temporal Specification Language (STSL) · Axiomatization system · Decidability · Runtime monitoring

1 Problem Statement

It is a challenging work to model cyber-physical systems, not only because cyber-physical systems integrate cyber systems, physical environment and the interactive part of them, but also because cyber-physical systems combine temporal and spatial aspects, discrete and continuous behavior, and uncertainty. Describing spatio-temporal aspects is one of the important areas in cyber-physical systems. The major problem isn't only the expressivness of dense time and real-valued variables of the spatio-temporal properties, but also multidimensional complexity and verifiability for modeling and analysis of the spatio-temporal behaviors of cyber-physical systems.

The work is supervised by Prof. Jing Liu, and partially supported by funding under National Key Research and Development Project 2017YFB1001800, NSFC 61572195 and Shanghai SHEITC Project 2017-GYHLW-01036.

ⓒ Springer Nature Switzerland AG 2019
Y. Ait-Ameur and S. Qin (Eds.): ICFEM 2019, LNCS 11852, pp. 517–521, 2019.
https://doi.org/10.1007/978-3-030-32409-4_36

Logic-based approaches [8] play a significant role in cyber-physical systems since Pnueli introduces temporal logics to computer science. Spatio-temporal logics extend temporal logics to express spatial evolution. Although there are other temporal languages like metric temporal logic (MTL), signal temporal logic (STL) that can be used to express dense time, their extensions can only describe discrete space.

Existing methods are insufficient for dense time and real-valued signals of the spatio-temporal properties. Meanwhile, the corresponding theory, solid tools and applications aren't well-developed yet.

2   Related Work

Generally, there are two kinds of logic-based approaches to specify spatio-temporal properties: the extension of temporal logic with spatial modality and the combinations of spatial logic and temporal logic.

Some spatio-temporal logics are extensions of temporal logic with spatial modality. Bartocci et al. [2] extend temporal modalities with spatial directions to reason reaction diffusion systems. Nenzi et al. [8] present SSTL to combine the until temporal modality with two spatial modalities, so that one can express that something is true somewhere nearby and being surrounded by a region that satisfies a given spatio-temporal property. Balbiani [1] explores the bidimensional space in multi-agent systems through extending dynamic logic with formulas representing the agents' positions and programs moving from one position to another position. Andreas [9] et al. present Shape Calculus based on Duration Calculus extended bounded polyhedra for the n-dimensional space for the specification and verification of mobile real-time systems.

The combinations of temporal logic and spatial logic inherit the expressiveness of the two logics. Haghighi et al. [6] present a combination of signal temporal logic (STL) and tree spatial superposition logic (TSSL) and apply SpaTeL to networked systems. Ciancia et.al [5] present STLCS enhances SLCS with temporal operators and features the CTL path quantifiers $\forall$ ("for all paths") and $\exists$ ("there exists a path"). Bennett [3] et al. construct a multi-dimensional modal logic named PSTL through the Cartesian product of the temporal logic PTL and the modal logic $S4_u$. Sun [10] et al. present a combination of MTL and $S4_u$ to specify safety properties of cyber-Physical systems.

3   Proposed Approaches

STL is present to express properties with continuous behaviors. In order to specify continuous change of spatial entities, we extend the real-value interval into spatio-temporal domain through combining of STL and $S4_u$, named STSL. Formally, the spatial temporal interval I is defined as $[(t, l), (t', l')]$, $\forall t, t' \in \mathbb{T}$, $\forall l, l' \in \mathbb{L}$ and $t < t'$. We present two interpretations: $STSL_{PC}$ and $STSL_{OC}$.

STSL_{PC} expresses changes over time of the truth-values of purely spatial propositions. While STSL_{OC} expresses changes or evolution of spatial objects over time.

STSL_{PC} expresses the change of truth-value of proposition and it is the elementary requirement for a combined spatio-temporal logic. Specifically, STSL_{PC} is defined on spatio-temporal terms τ over the spatio-temporal interval I, which is the fusion of temporal logic STL and modal spatial logic $\mathcal{S}4_u$ so that the language can express the changes over time of the truth-values of purely spatial propositions. The syntax of STSL_{PC} is given by:

$$\tau ::= p \mid \overline{\tau} \mid \tau_1 \sqcap \tau_2 \mid \mathbb{I}\tau$$
$$\varphi ::= \boxtimes \tau \mid x_i \geq 0 \mid \neg\varphi \mid \varphi_1 \wedge \varphi_2 \mid \varphi_1 \mathcal{U}_I \varphi_2$$

where, τ is a spatio-temporal term, p is a spatio-temporal variable, $\overline{\tau}$ is the complementary of τ, $\tau_1 \sqcap \tau_2$ is the intersection of τ_1 and τ_2, $\mathbb{I}$ is the *interior* operator under the topological space interpretation. Moreover, the dual operator of $\mathbb{I}$ is the *closure* operator $\mathbb{C}$, which means possible or consistent. $x_i \geq 0$ is an atomic predicate, $\neg$, $\vee$ and $\wedge$ are the Boolean operators, $\mathcal{U}_I$ is the *until* operator.

The semantics of STSL_{PC} is divided into Boolean semantics and quantitative semantics, which returns purely spatial propositions and real-valued spatial objects. The quantitative semantics can be transformed to Boolean semantics by a predicate μ_i. A spatio-temporal model is defined on topological space and temporal model. Formally, a spatio-temporal model $\mathfrak{M} = (\mathfrak{T}, \mathfrak{L}, \mathfrak{V})$, where

- $\mathfrak{T}$ is a pair $(\mathbb{T}, <)$, where $\mathbb{T}$ is a set of time point and $<$ an irreflexive, transitive and asymmetric relation on $\mathbb{T}$ with a linear strict time flow,
- $\mathfrak{L}$ is a topological space domain with the definition of $(\mathrm{U}, \mathbb{I})$ in which U is a nonempty set, the universe of the space, and $\mathbb{I}$ is the interior operator on U satisfying the standard Kuratowski axioms: $\forall X, Y \subseteq \mathrm{U}, \mathbb{I}(X \cap Y) = \mathbb{I}X \cap \mathbb{I}Y, \mathbb{I}X \subseteq \mathbb{I}\mathbb{I}X$ and $\mathbb{I}(\mathrm{U}) = \mathrm{U}$,
- $\mathfrak{V}$ is a valuation on the time point set $\mathfrak{T}$ and the spatial variable set $\mathbb{P}$, i.e., $\forall p \in \mathbb{P}$, and $t \in \mathbb{T}$. Formally, $\mathfrak{V}(p, t) = \{\mu_i \mid \forall i \in \mathbb{N}, x_i \geq 0\}$ means the space occupied by p at time point t.

The Boolean satisfaction relation for an STSL_{OC} formula φ over a spatio-temporal model $\mathfrak{M}$ is given by:

- $(\mathfrak{M}, t) \models \boxtimes \tau \Leftrightarrow \mathfrak{V}(\tau, t) = true$
- $(\mathfrak{M}, t) \models x_i \geq 0 \Leftrightarrow x_i \geq 0$
- $(\mathfrak{M}, t) \models \neg\varphi \Leftrightarrow (\mathfrak{M}, t) \not\models \varphi$
- $(\mathfrak{M}, t) \models \varphi_1 \wedge \varphi_2 \Leftrightarrow (\mathfrak{M}, t) \models \varphi_1$ and $(\mathfrak{M}, t) \models \varphi_2$
- $(\mathfrak{M}, t) \models \varphi_1 \mathcal{U}_I \varphi_2 \Leftrightarrow \exists t' \in t + I$ s.t. $(\mathfrak{M}, t') \models \varphi_2$ and $\forall t'' \in [t, t']$, $(\mathfrak{M}, t'') \models \varphi_1$

A model $\mathfrak{M}$ satisfies φ in t, denoted by $(\mathfrak{M}, t) \models \varphi$. The Boolean and quantitative semantics for interpreting the expressiveness of STSL_{PC} and STSL_{OC} are present according to the satisfiable relations that a spatio-temporal model holds the spatio-temporal specification.

4   Current Results and Future Work

The proposed approach contains axiomatization, decidability and runtime monitoring. The axiomatization presents a Hilbert-style axiom system and the soundness and completeness results are proved from the perspective of mathematics. Decidability presents the undecidable and decidable fragment, an SMT-based approach is present to verify the spatio-temporal properties. Bases, we present a runtime monitoring for the language in MATLAB.

Currently, the work of axiomatization presents the incompleteness of $STSL_{OC}$, while $STSL_{PC}$ is sound and weakly complete based on the spatio-temporal extensions of maximum consistency set and canonical model [7]. The decidability of STSL present that the satisfiability problem of $STSL_{OC}$ is undecidable, even the quantitive interpretation of $STSL_{PC}$ is still undecidable. But the Boolean interpretation of $STSL_{PC}$ is decidable and the complexity is EXPSPACE-complete, and the formal verification is based on the SMT approach to satisfiability of MITL [4].

Runtime monitoring of STSL is work in process. We build the spatio-temporal model to monitor the changes of spatial signals over time, where the spatio-temporal model is built within MATLAB and formulas are specified with the proposed STSL.

References

1. Balbiani, P., Fernández-Duque, D., Lorini, E.: Exploring the bidimensional space: a dynamic logic point of view. In: The 16th Conference on Autonomous Agents and MultiAgent Systems, pp. 132–140. Springer (2017)
2. Bartocci, E., Gol, E.A., Haghighi, I., Belta, C.: A formal methods approach to pattern recognition and synthesis in reaction diffusion networks. IEEE Trans. Control of Network Syst. 5(1), 308–320 (2018)
3. Bennett, B., Cohn, A.G., Wolter, F., Zakharyaschev, M.: Multi-dimensional modal logic as a framework for spatio-temporal reasoning. Applied Intell. 17(3), 239–251 (2002)
4. Bersani, M.M., Rossi, M., San Pietro, P.: An SMT-based approach to satisfiability checking of MITL. Inf. Comput. 245, 72–97 (2015)
5. Ciancia, V., Gilmore, S., Grilletti, G., Latella, D., Loreti, M., Massink, M.: Spatio-temporal model checking of vehicular movement in public transport systems. Int. J. Software Tools Technol. Transf. pp. 1–23 (2018)
6. Haghighi, I., Jones, A., Kong, Z., Bartocci, E., Gros, R., Belta, C.: Spatel: a novel spatial-temporal logic and its applications to networked systems. In: Proceedings of the 18th International Conference on Hybrid Systems: Computation and Control, pp. 189–198. ACM (2015)
7. Li, T., Jing, L., Dongdong, A., Haiying, S.: A sound and complete axiomatisation for spatio-temporal specification language. In: The 31st International Conference on Software Engineering & Knowledge Engineering, pp. 153–204. KSI (2019)
8. Nenzi, L., Bortolussi, L., Ciancia, V., Loreti, M., Massink, M.: Qualitative and quantitative monitoring of spatio-temporal properties with SSTL. Logical Meth. Comput. Sci. 14(4) (2017)

9. Schäfer, A.: A calculus for shapes in time and space. In: Liu, Z., Araki, K. (eds.) ICTAC 2004. LNCS, vol. 3407, pp. 463–477. Springer, Heidelberg (2005). https://doi.org/10.1007/978-3-540-31862-0_33

10. Sun, H., Liu, J., Chen, X., Du, D.: Specifying cyber physical system safety properties with metric temporal spatial logic. In: 2015 Asia-Pacific Software Engineering Conference (APSEC), pp. 254–260. IEEE (2015)

A Modeling Framework of Cyber-Physical-Social Systems with Human Behavior Classification Based on Machine Learning

Dongdong An[1(✉)], Jing Liu[1(✉)], Xiaohong Chen[1(✉)], Tengfei Li[1(✉)], and Ling Yin[2]

[1] School of Computer Science and Software Engineering,
East China Normal University, Shanghai 200062, China
anndongdong@gmail.com, {jliu,xhchen}@sei.ecnu.edu.cn,
tengfeili2015@gmail.com
[2] Shanghai University of Engineering Science, Shanghai, China
yinling_86@163.com

Abstract. Cyber-Physical-Social Systems (CPSS) is an emerging complicated topic in recent years which focuses on the researches of a combination of cyberspace, physical space and social space. Different from traditional Cyber-Physical-Systems, CPSS contain human who interacts with the cyber and physical part more frequently. So how to capture and analyse human behaviors play a vital role in CPSS performance evaluation. To improve the analysis accuracy of CPSS, the paper proposes a new modelling framework – stohMCharts (stochastic hybrid MARTE statecharts) which is an extension of MARTE statecharts for stochastic hybrid system modelling and analysis. Compared to MARTE statechart, in stohMCharts, we can model the CPSS in a unified way. Also, we associate stohMCharts to NSHA (Networks Stochastic Hybrid Automata) and use statistical model checker UPPAAL-SMC to verify the stohMCharts. We apply an autonomous car as an example to explain the efficiency of our proposed approaches.

Keywords: Statistical model checking · Cyber-Physical-Social Systems · Stochastic hybrid MARTE statecharts · Stochastic Hybrid Automata

1 Problem Statement

Our society is rapidly developing towards Cyber-Physical-Social Systems that interact and collaborate with humans. For example: autonomous vehicles interacting with pedestrians and human-drive vehicles, medical robots collaborate with doctors. Human play a central role in CPSS. The continuing interactions

The paper is partially supported by funding under the National Key Research and Development Project 2017YFB1001800, NSFC 61572195 and NFSC61802251.

© Springer Nature Switzerland AG 2019
Y. Ait-Ameur and S. Qin (Eds.): ICFEM 2019, LNCS 11852, pp. 522–525, 2019.
https://doi.org/10.1007/978-3-030-32409-4_37

of human lead to many safety concerns. The system reactions have direct consequence on the environment the human live in. Furthermore, these actions highly
depend on learned models of the environment or the human they interact with.
The safety-critical nature of the CPSS demands providing correct guarantees
about their actions, models and performance. This brings us to a series of cardi-
nal problems we need to research in CPSS. How do we model human behaviours?
How do we model the interactions between the human and the systems? What
models are suitable for formal analysis and verification of CPSS? How do we
address safety in reactive, stochastic environments?

2   Proposed Approaches

The technology paradigm provides relevant information services. For example, to
discover neighborhoods and communities that consider human and social dynamics as an integral part of CPS is termed CPSS. As depicted in Fig. 1, in social
space, we classify the human behaviors based on machine learning algorithms,
the most used methods are naive bayes [4], support vector machine [6], k-nearest
neighbor [5], decision tree [1] and random forest [3] etc. When the human behaviors indicate the driving behaviors, we can predicate the new driver driving style
based on the classification rule, so we can get the probability distribution of the
driving style. The parameters of StohMChart in cyber space are the analysis
results of social space.

It shows the workflow of our approach and the overview of our framework
in Fig. 2. we first model the CPSS with stohMChart which extended hMChart
with uncertainty information (e.g., measuring human variations, action execution time). We then actively update the human models by online information
gathering. We also efficiently learn human's preferences by actively synthesizing
comparison queries, and then analyze the accuracy of our human models for
the purpose of verification. We transformed the stohMChart model to NSHA
(Network of Stochastic Hybrid Automata) based on mapping rules. To allow the
quantitative analysis of stohMChart model via performance queries, we translate the design specification into the properties in the form of PCTL (Probabilistic Computation Temporal Logic). After both NSHA models and performance
query-based properties are ready, the framework employs the statistical model
checker UPPAAL-SMC to conduct the quantitative analysis of CPSS stochastic
behaviors. In the following subsections, we will introduce the definition of stohM-
Chart syntax and semantics as well as the major components of our framework.

The syntax of stohMChart

A stohMChart is a tuple $stohMChart = \{L, l_0, \mathfrak{T}, Cmds, A, \mathfrak{C}, Inv, \mathfrak{D}\}$ where

1. $L = \{l_0, l_1, ..., l_m\}$ is a set of locations. $l_0 \in L$ is the initial location.
2. $\mathfrak{T} \subseteq L \times Cmds \times \Sigma \times 2^{\mathfrak{X} \cup V} \times L$ is a set of transitions.
3. $Cmds = \{g_0, g_1, ..., g_p\}$ is a set of probabilistic guard commands of the form
   $g \rightarrow p_1 : u_1 + ... + p_m : u_m$ where
   - $g \subseteq L \times R^k$ is a guard, $k \in N^+$ is the dimension of the stohMChart, i.e.
     there are k variables (including clock variables) in the model.

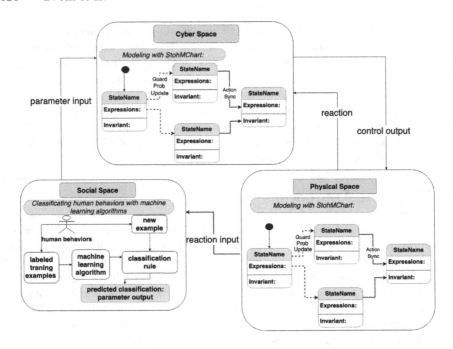

Fig. 1. The three parts of cyber-physical-social systems

- For all $1 \leq i \leq m$, we get $p_i \geq 0$ and $\Sigma_{i=1}^{m} p_i = 1$.
- The update function is defined as $\Lambda : (L \times R^k) \rightarrow 2^{L \times R^k}$ for $1 \leq i \leq m$.
4. $A = \{act_0, act_1, act_2, ..., act_n\}$ is a set of actions. We define a single action τ representing the passing of time.

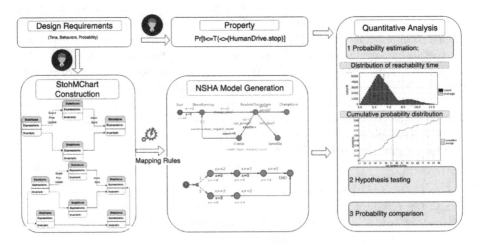

Fig. 2. The overview of our framework

5. $\mathfrak{C}$ is a finite set of clocks constraints, $\{c_1, c_2...\}$ are clocks.
6. $Inv = \{i_0, i_1, ..., i_n\}$ is a set of invariants. $Inv : L \rightarrow Exp$ assigns a set of invariants L to each location.
7. $\mathfrak{D}$ is the delay function. $\mathfrak{D} : (l, v, e) \rightarrow \text{Normal}(\mu, \delta)/\text{Exp(rate)}/\text{Uniform(a,b)}$.

3   Conclusion and Future Work

– We integrate human behavior classification based on machine learning with statistical model checking to analysis cyber-physical-social systems.
– We present a new formal visual language, *stohMCharts* (Stochastic Hybrid MARTE Statecharts) by extending the syntax and semantics of *hMChart* and importing the modeling & analysis of the stochastic behaviors of an uncertain environment and in particular human behaviors.
– To automate the quantitative analysis of CPSS designs, we rely on *NSHA (Network of Stochastic Hybrid Automata)* [2] as the model of computation in our approach. We propose a set of mapping rules and construction algorithm that can automatically transform stohMChart in CPSS design into NSHA.
– We integrate our formal framework which supports the quantitative performance analysis of *stohMChart* with the statistical model checker UPPAAL-SMC.

Future Work. Considerably more work will need to be done to determine which machine learning algorithm should be choose depend on different human behavior. Further research could usefully explore how to automatically transfer the parameter to the StohMChart from classification results. Another work is to develop an algorithm and a tool to automatic generate UPPAAL-SMC model from stohMCharts. This research has thrown up many questions in need of further investigation.

References

1. Chen, W., et al.: A novel ensemble approach of bivariate statistical-based logistic model tree classifier for landslide susceptibility assessment. Geocarto Int. **33**(12), 1398–1420 (2018)
2. David, A., Larsen, K.G., Legay, A., Poulsen, D.B.: Statistical model checking of dynamic networks of stochastic hybrid automata. Electr. Commun. EASST **66** (2014)
3. Dogru, N., Subasi, A.: Traffic accident detection using random forest classifier. In: 2018 15th Learning and Technology Conference (L&T), pp. 40–45. IEEE (2018)
4. Li, T., Li, J., Liu, Z., Li, P., Jia, C.: Differentially private Naive Bayes learning over multiple data sources. Inf. Sci. **444**, 89–104 (2018)
5. Noi, P.T., Kappas, M.: Comparison of random forest, k-nearest neighbor, and support vector machine classifiers for land cover classification using sentinel-2 imagery. Sensors **18**(1), 18 (2018)
6. Xu, J., Xu, C., Zou, B., Tang, Y.Y., Peng, J., You, X.: New incremental learning algorithm with support vector machines. IEEE Trans. Syst. Man Cybern. Syst. (2018)

Author Index

Printed in the United States
By Bookmasters